3 Bände DM 250,-

THE ENCYCLOPEDIA OF TAROT

Balbi Tarot Card A stylized rendition by Domenico Balbi of Stuart R. Kaplan as card no. IV, The Emperor, in the Balbi tarot pack.

THE ENCYCLOPEDIA OF TAROT

Stuart R. Kaplan

U. S. GAMES SYSTEMS, INC.
Publishers   New York 10016

OTHER WORKS BY THE SAME AUTHOR

TAROT

Commentary on the Oswald Wirth Tarot Deck
The Devil's Tarot Deck Instructions
James Bond 007 Tarot Book
Official Rules of the Tarotrump Card Game
The Rider Tarot Deck Instructions
Royal Fez Moroccan Tarot Deck Instructions
Spanish Tarot Deck Instructions
Tarot Cards for Fun and Fortune-Telling
Tarot Classic
Tarot of the Witches Instructions
The Visconti-Sforza Tarocchi Deck Instructions

HISTORY AND CURRENT EVENTS

The American Historical Playing Card Deck: Portraits in American History
Political Satire Playing Card Deck Instructions

MINING

Mining, Minerals and Geosciences: A Guide to Information Sources

FIRST EDITION
First printing 1978

PRINTED IN THE UNITED STATES OF AMERICA
by Noble Offset Printers, Inc., New York 10003

Library of Congress catalog card number: 77-94173
ISBN 0-913866-11-3

Copyright © 1978 by Stuart R. Kaplan

All rights reserved. No part of this book may be reproduced in any form without permission in writing from the author or publisher, except by a reviewer who wishes to quote brief passages in connection with a review written for inclusion in a magazine or newspaper.

DEDICATION

To my wife
Marilyn
who helped make it possible,
and to our children
Mark, Peter,
Michael, Christopher
and Jennifer,
who make it worthwhile.

ACKNOWLEDGEMENTS

Grateful appreciation is acknowledged to the following persons whose valuable comments, suggestions and criticisms greatly assisted in the preparation and editing of this book: Jan Bauwens, George Bennett, Janet Bennett, Ronald and Charlotte Decker, Albert Field, Detlef Hoffmann, William B. Keller, Sylvia Mann, Gertrude Moakley, Edwin Nigg, Jane Raymond, William Voelkle, Virginia and Harold Wayland, and Donald Weiser.

The author wishes to also thank the following persons whose various contributions helped make this book possible:

Hector Alfonso (USA), Frank Andrews (USA), Vito Arienti (Italy), Domenico Balbi (Italy), Fritz Becker (East Germany), Flora Beresford (India), Alain Bourveau (France), Franz Braun (West Germany), Earl Brown (USA), Don L. Busby (England), Eddie Cass (England), Richard Cavendish (England), Maurice and Lorna Collett (England), Frederic Davies (England), David Diaz (USA), Nik Douglas (England), Martin Drayson (USA), Michael Dummett (England), Elmar Faber (East Germany), Felix Alfaro Fournier (Spain), Ramon Alfaro Fournier (Spain), Carole Freddo (USA), Alexandra Gabrielli (Netherlands), James Gaynor (USA), Robert A. Gilbert (England), Eden Gray (USA), Kay Gregory (USA), Fergus Hall (Scotland), Norman R. Handelsman (USA), Peter Huckersby (England), Paul Janssens (Belgium), Pierrette Jean-Richard (France), K. Frank Jensen (Denmark), Guy deLagerburg (USA), Latham Lambert (USA), Susan Lambert (England), Jean-Marie Lhote (France), Marie Elena Longo (USA), Mario Lucchetti (Italy), Boris Mandrovsky (USA), Christopher McIntosh (England), Emanuel S. Newman (USA), Dorothy Powills (USA), Ernst R. Ragg (Austria), John Robinson (England), Ruth Robinson (USA), Agnes and Allan Ryan (USA), Alberto Sz. de San Pedro (Spain), Dorothy Sigler (USA), Jean-Marie Simon (France), Penny Slinger (England), Kristen L. Spangenberg (USA), William Stroup (USA), Connie Taylor (USA), Fred G. Taylor (USA), Walter Volz (West Germany), David Westnedge (England), Albert F. Widmark (USA), and Martha Wolff (USA).

CONTENTS

LIST OF ILLUSTRATIONS ix
PREFACE xii
ODE TO ANCIENT TAROT CARDS xv

I AN INTRODUCTION TO TAROT CARDS 1

Terminology • trionfi • tarocchi • tarocco • tarot • anagrams • trumps • triumphi • arcana • atouts • atutti • tarotee • tarotiers • ros • ro • rog • royal road • sano tarot.

The Major Arcana Cards • fifteenth-century manuscript • titles of the twenty-two Major Arcana cards • Major Arcana related to suit signs and astrological correspondences • sequential description of life.

The Minor Arcana Cards • suit derivations • listing of suit titles and theories of origin • listing of court cards and theories of origin • historical figures • pip cards • tarot back designs • tarot card size variations • standard fifty-two-card packs • listing of suit titles • derivation • numerical comparisons • soldier's almanack, Bible and prayer book.

II ORIGINS OF TAROCCHI CARDS 12

Prehistoric man and oral cultures • Thoth and Egyptian hieroglyphic books • Egyptian hieroglyphic paintings • the Bembine tablet • God, man and universe • the mystical number seven • the Torah • Hebrew alphabet • the Kabbalah and Tree of Life • Tetragrammaton and Jehovah • the Table of Cebes • Vishnu • Ardhanari • chaturanga and chess • chahar-taj • Hindustans and Saracens • pre-Columbian symbolism • dice • Chinese dominoes • Korean arrow • naibi • mat and pagad • Seun-ho • Chad • Fez, Morocco • Giotto • Guelphs and Ghibellines • Waldenses • Petrarch's Triumphi • Gypsies, Bohemians, Zingari • Jacquemin Gringonneur • fleur-de-lis • fourteenth-century designs • formschneiders and briefmahlers, briefes and karten • Tarot River and Taro village • carnival and processionals • Rosicrucians, Templars and Freemasons • occult revival: Gebelin, Levi, Papus, Mathers, Waite, etc.

III EARLIEST REFERENCES TO PLAYING CARDS 24

Published References • Bern, 1367 • Naibbe, 1376 • Johannes, 1377 • Wenceslas and Jeanne, 1379 • Archives of Marseilles, 1381 • Ordinance of Lille, 1382 • Poupart, Charles VI and Gringonneur, 1392 • Morelli, 1393 • Charles V, 1369, and Prevot of Paris, 1397 • Ulm, 1397 • Synod of Langres, 1404 • St. Bernardin, 1423 • Decembrio, 1440 • Magistracy of Venice, 1441 • Isabelle of Lorraine, 1449 • Treatise of Theology, 1457 • Parliament Rolls, 1464, and Statute, 1496 • Biblioteca Vaticana, Codices, Lazzarelli, 1471 • Ulm, 1474 • Platina, 1475 • Martius, 1488 • Boiardo's *Tutte Le Opera* • Sermones de Ludo Cumalis, 1500 • Berni, 1526 • Marcolini's *Le Sorti*, 1540 • Aretino's *Les Cartes Parlantes*, 1540 • Vives' *Ludus Chartarum*, 1545 • Lollio, 1550 • Bertoni, 1550 • Ringhieri, 1551 • Grazzini, 1559 • Susio, 1570 • Bargagli, 1572 • Garzoni, 1587 • Bynneman.

Interpolations and Translation Errors • Pipozzo di Sandro's *Trattato del governo* • Das Guldin Spil • Synod of Wurzburg • William de Guilleville's *Le Pelerinaige de l'Homme* • Renard le Contrefait • Alphonse XI, King of Castille, and Guevara's *Familiar Epistles* • Le Roman du Moi Meliadus de Leonnoys • *Historique et Chronique de Provence* • "Magasin Pittoresque" • Jehan de Saintre • Bussi, Covelluzzo and Viterbo • Nuremberg Ordinance • *Laws of the Kingdom of Spain* • Tarocchini of Bologna and Prince Fibbia • Chronicles of Cremona • Maffei's *Commentariorum Urbanorum*.

Omissions • Ovid's *De Arte Amatoria* • Christian Church • Sanskrit manuscripts • John of Salisbury • Council of Worcester • Town book of Augsburg • Wardrobe rolls of Edward I • Eleventh- to fourteenth-century romances • Machau's *Confort d'Amy* • Petrarch, Boccaccio, Chaucer and *The Arabian Nights*.

IV EARLY TYPES OF TAROCCHI AND SIMILAR PLAYING CARDS 35

Tarocchi and Related Packs • Visconti and Visconti-Sforza tarocchi • Tarocchi of Mantegna • Piedmontese or Tarocchi of Venice • Tarocchini di Bologna • Minchiate of Florence • Tarocchini of Mitelli • Tarocco Siciliano • Other Similar Packs • Mamluk • Trappola • Ambras Hofjagdspiel hunting pack.

V THE VISCONTI AND SFORZA FAMILIES AND THEIR HERALDIC DEVICES 60

The Visconti family • Bernabo • Beatrice • Galeazzo • Giangaleazzo • Isabelle • Giovanni • Filippo • Beatrice di Guglielmo Ventimiglia Lascaris • Maria di Savoy • Bianca Maria • The Sforza family • Alberico da Barbiano • Muzio Attendolo • Francesco • Cardinal Ascanio Maria • Galeazzo Maria • Bona of Savoy • Gian Galeazzo • Ludovico • Beatrice d'Este.

Heraldic devices • Visconti family • a bird • ducal crown • sun with rays • black imperial eagle • *A bon droit* • Sforza family • a lion • three interlocking rings • a fountain.

VI LOCATING THE VISCONTI AND VISCONTI-SFORZA TAROCCHI DECKS 63

Pierpont Morgan–Bergamo • Cary-Yale • Brera-Brambilla • Rosenthal • Von Bartsch (Montreal Museum of Fine Arts, Cleveland Stewart-Patterson and P. Tozzi) • Museo Fournier • Victoria & Albert Museum • Guildhall • Andrioletti • Marzoli • Biedak.

VII THE PIERPONT MORGAN-BERGAMO VISCONTI-SFORZA TAROCCHI DECK 65

The twenty-two Major Arcana cards • The Fool • The Magician • The Popess • The Empress • The Emperor • The Pope • The Lovers • The Chariot • Justice • The Hermit • The Wheel of Fortune • Strength • The Hanged Man • Death • Temperance •

vii

The Devil • The Falling Tower • The Star • The Moon • The Sun • Judgment • The World.

The fifty-six Minor Arcana cards • Suit of swords • Suit of staves • Suit of cups • Suit of coins.

VIII THE OTHER VISCONTI-SFORZA TAROCCHI DECKS 87

Extant cards • Cary-Yale • Brera-Brambilla • Rosenthal • Von Bartsch (Montreal Museum of Fine Arts, Cleveland Stewart-Patterson and P. Tozzi) • Museo Fournier • Victoria & Albert Museum • Guildhall • Andrioletti • Marzoli • Biedak.

The Artists • Antonio Cicognara • Bonifacio Bembo • Dating the decks.

IX OTHER EARLY HAND-PAINTED CARDS 108

Kestner Museum • National Museum, Warsaw • Castello Ursino • Goldschmidt • Guildhall • Gringonneur • D'Este • Biblioteca Nazionale Universitaria, Torino • Edmond de Rothschild • Museo Civico Biblioteca e Archivio di Bassano del Grappa • Museo Correr, Venice.

X EARLY PRINTED TAROT CARDS 124

Metropolitan Museum of Art • Sola Busca • Bibliotheque de l'Ecole Nationale Superieure des Beaux-Arts • Edmond de Rothschild, Louvre • Rosenwald Collection, National Gallery of Art • Catelin Geofroy, Museum fur Kunsthandwerk • Municipal Library of Rouen • Colonna, British Museum • Paris card maker • Joannes Pelagius Mayer.

XI EIGHTEENTH- AND NINETEENTH-CENTURY TAROT DECKS 137

Tarot of Marseilles • Court de Gebelin • Etteilla • Vandenborre tarot • French tarot, 1720 • Geografia tarocchi • Jean Payen • N Conver • Lando tarot • French tarot • Jean Galler • Rochias Fils • Milanese tarot, F. Gumppenberg • French Revolutionary tarot, L. Carey • Italian Major Arcana cards • French Cartomancy pack • Fanciful tarot, Avondo Brothers • J. Gaudais • Edoardo Dotti • Piedmontese tarot, Versino • Doubleday tarot cards/Five oversize tarot cards/Egyptian Major Arcana cards • Gassmann • Milanese tarot • F. Strambo tarocchi • Vacchetta tarocchi • Indian "tarot."

XII TWENTIETH-CENTURY TAROT DECKS AND DESIGNS NOT READILY AVAILABLE 168

Acea Gypsy tarot • Adams / Cleveland / Hersh / MacPherson / Weiss • Alitalia tarot • Apocalypse / Bompiani / Cilento / Dykstra / Farcas / Izod / Kersaint / Williamson • Arcanes du Destin • Atkins / Heitmann / Klumper / Lucas / May / Picini / Balbi / Bennett / Brother Placid / Decker / Greenwich Library / Yves Jobert / Rivers / Sigler • Beaulieu / Laliberte / Le-Tan / Sigler • Benavides / Carter / Dorflinger / Fodera / Kloster / Nessim / Rota / Schlossman • Berthole tarot • British tarot • Chaboseau / Loring tarot • Cooper tarot • Dali / Gill / Iamblichus / Kaye / Littel / Metcalfe / Sherman / Tavaglione • Doctors van Leeuwen Porcelain tarot • Fatidic Egyptian tarot • Frownstrong / Gemrod / Hoffman / Holbein / Pry / Saba-Telli / Scott / Skell • Glass tarot • H. J. Heinz tarot • Peter Huckerby tarot • Insight Institute tarot • Knapp tarot • De Laurence tarot • Linweave tarot • Lover's tarot • M. Lubow / N. Lubow / Sharp / Waldner/Weil • Masenghini Tarocchino Milanese • Menegazzi Seashell tarocco • Sergio Minero tarot • Odell tarot • Ollgaard tarot • Ortega tarot • Papus tarot • Pastor tarot • Pop/Rock tarot • Rakoczi tarot • Ravenswood Eastern tarot • Le Taro Sacerdotal • Sacred Egyptian tarot • Schikowski tarot • Scott Major Arcana • Tellurian tarot • Connie Taylor tarot • Transitional tarot • Wollenhaupt-Brenner tarot.

XIII POPULAR TWENTIETH-CENTURY TAROT PACKS AND REPRINTS CURRENTLY AVAILABLE 227

Tarot de Acuario • Aquarian tarot • Tarot Arista • Astral tarot • Astro tarot • Balbi tarot • Baraja Egipcia • Grand Tarot Belline • Guido Bolzani tarocchi • Builders of the Adytum tarot • Church of Light tarot • Tarot Classic • Aleister Crowley "Thoth" tarot • D'Epinal tarot • Il Destino Svelato Dal Tarocco • Dynamic Games tarot • Egipcios tarot • Esoteric tarot • Etteilla tarot • Fergus Hall tarot • Gentilini tarocchi • Golden Dawn tarot • Golden Egyptian tarot/Morgan's tarot/Praktische tarot • Hoi Polloi tarot • Tarot of Oscar Ichazo • Tarot of Marseilles • Masenghini Tarocchi Piedmontese • Mountain Dream tarot • Muchery Astrological tarot • The New Tarot Deck • The New Tarot for the Aquarian Age • Nordic tarot • 1JJ Swiss tarot • Piatnik/Pointer tarot • Rider-Waite tarot • Royal Fez Moroccan tarot • Sheridan/Douglas tarot • Spanish tarot • Starter tarot • Tantric tarot • Taro Adivinhatorio • 20th Century tarot • Vandenborre tarot • Visconti-Sforza tarocchi • Oswald Wirth tarot • Xultun tarot • Yeager tarot of Meditation • Zigeuner tarot • Zolar's New Astrological tarot.

XIV TAROCK PACKS 295

Tarock game rules • Tarock packs • Gobl tarock • Napoleon tarock • Allegorical tarock • Turkish Costume tarock • Pfluger Scenic tarock • Historical tarock • Animal tarock (Bohemia) • Animal tarock (Germany) • Military tarock (Glanz, 1854) • Opera and Operetta tarock • Chinese tarock • Fool's tarock • Dance tarock • Theatrical tarock • Proverb tarock • Dondorf tarock No. 246 • Military tarock (Piatnik, 1882) • Nejedly tarock • Habsburger tarock No. 146 • Exotic tarock • Ditha Moser tarock • Soldaten tarock No. 217 • Piatnik genre tarock • Willer tarock • Paris Scenic tarock • Ladies tarock No. 162 • Tarotrump and tarock No. 4 • Coffee House tarock No. 9a • Piatnik tarock No. 36a • Cego pack.

XV INTERPRETING TAROT CARDS 327

The twenty-two Major Arcana Cards • The Fool • I The Magician • II The Popess • III The Empress • IIII The Emperor • V The Pope • VI The Lovers • VII The Chariot • VIII Justice • VIIII The Hermit • X The Wheel of Fortune • XI Strength • XII The Hanged Man • XIII Death • XIIII Temperance • XV The Devil • XVI The Tower • XVII The Star • XVIII The Moon • XVIIII The Sun • XX Judgment • XXI The World.

The fifty-six Minor Arcana Cards • Suit of swords • Suit of staves • Suit of cups • Suit of coins.

XVI SPREADING THE TAROT DECK 337

Ten-card spread with twenty-two Major Arcana cards • Sequence and meanings • Interpretations • Ten-card spread with forty-two cards • The name spread • The horseshoe spread • The royal spread • The seventh-card spread • The gypsy spread • Sample tarot card reading.

XVII CONCLUSIONS 345

BIBLIOGRAPHY 347

INDEX 377

LIST OF ILLUSTRATIONS

FRONTISPIECE
The Emperor by Balbi ii

CHAPTER I
Sermones De Luco Cumalis xvi
Tarot suit signs 6
Seven of staves 8
Tarot back designs 8
Tarot card size variations 9
Standard suit signs 10

CHAPTER II
Antoine Court de Gebelin 13
Monde Primitif and Du Jeu des Tarots 13
God, Man and the Universe 14
Early alphabets with the applicable Major Arcana .. 15
The Tree of Life 17
Ardhanari 19
Cupid from Petrarch 21
Eliphas Levi 22
Arthur Edward Waite 23

CHAPTER III
Prohibition against cards 25
Ludus cartarum 25
Euterpe 26
Codice at the Vatican 27
Capitolo del Gioco della Primiera 29
Charles VI 34

CHAPTER IV
Visconti and Visconti-Sforza tarocchi cards 36
Tarocchi of Mantegna cards
    S-series, I, XXV, XXVIIII and XXXXIIII 37
    E-series, I to XXXVI 38
    Twelve cards 40
    E-series, XXV and XXXXX 43
    E- and S-series, XVII, Poesia 43
    E- and S-series, XXXXVI, Jupiter 45
    E- and S-series, XXXXVII, Saturna 46
Albrecht Durer tarocchi cards 47
Piedmontese or Tarocchi of Venice cards 48
Tarocchini di Bologna cards 50
Minchiate cards, seventeenth century 51
Minchiate cards, eighteenth century 52
Tarocchini of Mitelli cards 54
Tarocco Siciliano cards 55
Mamluk cards 56
Trappola pack 57
The Pack of Princely Hunting cards of Ambras 58

CHAPTER V
Visconti heraldic devices 61
Sforza heraldic devices 62

CHAPTER VII
The Major Arcana cards of the Pierpont Morgan-Bergamo deck
    The Fool 65
    The Magician 66
    The Popess 66
    The Empress 67

    The Emperor 67
    The Pope 67
    The Lovers 68
    The Chariot 68
    Justice 68
    The Hermit 68
    The Wheel of Fortune 69
    Strength 70
    The Hanged Man 70
    Death 71
    Temperance 71
    The Devil 71
    The Falling Tower 72
    The Star 72
    The Moon 73
    The Sun 73
    Judgment 73
    The World 73
The Minor Arcana cards of the Pierpont Morgan-Bergamo pack
    King of swords 74
    Queen of swords 75
    Knight of swords 75
    Page of swords 75
    Ten and ace of swords 76
    King of staves 76
    Nine through two of swords 77
    Queen of staves 78
    Knight of staves 78
    Page of staves 78
    Ten and ace of staves 79
    King of cups 79
    Nine through two of staves 80
    Queen of cups 81
    Knight of cups 81
    Page of cups 81
    Ten and ace of cups 82
    King of coins 82
    Nine through two of cups 83
    Queen of coins 84
    Knight of coins 84
    Page of coins 85
    Ten and ace of coins 85
    Nine through two of coins 86

CHAPTER VIII
Cary-Yale Visconti-Sforza tarocchi cards
    The Emperor 88
    The Lovers 89
    Death and Judgment 90
    Hope and Charity 91
    The World and king of swords 92
    Eight of swords and female knight of staves ... 93
    Male page of cups and ace of cups 94
    Six of swords, six of arrows, male and female pages of
        cups, female knight of coins and two of coins 95
Brera-Brambilla Visconti-Sforza tarocchi cards
    The Emperor and The Wheel of Fortune 96
    Queen and knight of staves 97
    Knight and page of coins 97
    Ten of swords, ace of staves, the knight, page and five
        of cups and two of coins 98
Rosenthal Visconti-Sforza tarocchi cards 99
Von Bartsch Visconti-Sforza tarocchi cards
    The Wheel of Fortune and king of swords 100
    Nine Von Bartsch cards 101
    Temperance and page of cups 102
Fournier Visconti-Sforza tarocchi cards 103

Victoria & Albert Museum Visconti-Sforza tarocchi cards 104
The World, Guildhall Visconti-Sforza tarocchi card.........104
Page of coins, Andrioletti Visconti-Sforza tarocchi card 105
Page of staves, Marzoli Visconti-Sforza tarocchi card 105
King of cups, Biedak Visconti-Sforza tarocchi card 105

CHAPTER IX

Pages of swords and coins, Kestner Museum 108
Queen of cups and knight of coins, National Museum, Warsaw 109
The Chariot and The World, Museo Civico, Catania 109
Goldschmidt cards, Deutsches Spielkarten Museum..........110
Guildhall cards...111
Gringonneur cards, Bibliotheque Nationale
   The Fool and The Emperor............................112
   The Pope and The Lovers.............................113
   The Chariot and Justice..............................113
   The Hermit and Strength.............................114
   The Hanged Man and Death..........................114
   Temperance and The House of God 115
   The Moon and The Sun..............................115
   Judgment and The World.............................116
   Valet or page of swords..............................116
D'Este cards, Cary Collection..............................117
D'Este cards from D'Allemagne............................118
Biblioteca Nazionale Universitaria tarocchi cards 119
Knight of swords, Museum of Bassano del Grappa............120
Rothschild cards
   The Emperor and The Pope..........................121
   King and queen of staves.............................121
   Knight and page of staves 122
   Queen of swords and king of coins 122
Museo Correr cards......................................123

CHAPTER X

Italian tarocchi cards.....................................125
Sola-Busca tarocchi, twelve cards 126
Sola-Busca tarocchi, eleven cards..........................127
Tarot or minchiate cards 128
Rothschild tarot or minchiate cards 129
Rosenwald tarot, twelve cards.............................130
Rosenwald tarot, twelve cards.............................131
Catelin Geofroy tarot cards 132
Classical tarot cards 133
Colonna cards 134
Parisian tarot cards 135
Tarot cards from a Swiss pack 136

CHAPTER XI

Tarot of Marseilles 138
Court de Gebelin tarots 139
Etteilla tarot cards.......................................141
Etteilla tarot cards.......................................142
Etteilla tarot cards.......................................143
Etteilla tarot cards.......................................144
Vandenborre tarot.......................................145
Tarot cards from a French pack 146
Geografia tarocchi.......................................147
Tarot deck by Jean Payen 148
N. Conver tarot...149
Lando tarot...150
French tarot cards from three packs 151
Tarot pack by Jean Galler 152
Rochias Fils tarot..153
Milanese tarot by F. Gumppenberg 154
French Revolutionary tarot by L. Cary 155
Italian Major Arcana cards 156
Tarot designs from a French cartomancy pack 157
Fanciful tarot pack by Avondo Brothers 158
Tarot pack by J. Gaudais 159
Tarot pack by Edoardo Dotti 160
Piedmontese tarot pack by Giuseppe Versino 161
Doubleday tarot/Five oversize tarot cards/Egyptian Major
   Arcana cards......................................162
Tarot pack by Gassmann 163
Milanese tarot by G. Sironi 164
F. Strambo tarocchi.....................................165
Vacchetta tarocchi 166
Indian tarot cards 167

CHAPTER XII

Acea Gypsy tarot 169
Adams/Cleveland/Hersh/MacPherson/Weiss................171
Alitalia tarot..172
Apocalypse/Bompiani/Cilento/Dykstra/Farcas/Izod/Kersaint/
   Williamson..173
Arcanes du Destin.......................................175
Atkins/Heitmann/Klumper/Lucas/May/Picini 177
Balbi/Bennett/Brother Placid/Decker/Greenwich Library/
   Yves Jobert/Rivers/Sigler............................178
Beaulieu/Laliberte/Le-Tan/Sigler...........................179
Benavides/Carter/Dorflinger/Fodera/Kloster/Nessim/Rota/
   Schlossman..181
Berthole tarot...182
British tarot...183
Chaboseau/Loring tarot 184
Cooper tarot..185
Dali/Gill/Iamblichus/Kaye/Littel/Metcalfe/Sherman/
   Tavaglione 187
Doctors van Leeuwen Porcelain tarot 188
Fatidic Egyptian tarot....................................190
Frownstrong/Gemrod/Hoffman/Holbein/Pry/Saba-Telli/Scott/
   Skell..193
Glass tarot 194
H. J. Heinz tarot..195
Peter Huckerby tarot....................................196
Insight Institute tarot....................................197
Knapp tarot 198
De Laurence tarot.......................................199
Linweave tarot..200
Lover's tarot 201
M. Lubow/N. Lubow/Sharp/Waldner/Weil 202
Masenghini Tarocchino Milanese 203
Menegazzi Seashell tarocco 204
Sergio Minero tarot 205
Odell tarot..207
Ollgaard tarot...209
Ortega tarot 210
Papus tarot 211
Pastor tarot...212
Pop/Rock tarot calendar 213
Rakoczi tarot 214
Ravenswood Eastern tarot 216
Le Taro Sacerdotal......................................218
Sacred Egyptian tarot....................................219
Schikowski tarot...220
Scott Major Arcana cards 221
Connie Taylor tarot.....................................222
Tellurian tarot 223
Transitional tarot 225
Wollenhaupt-Brenner tarot 226

CHAPTER XIII

Tarot de Acuario 228
Aquarian tarot..229
Tarot Arista...231
Astral tarot 232
Astro tarot..233
Balbi tarot...235
Baraja Egipcia 236
Grand Tarot Belline.....................................237
Guido Bolzani tarocchi 238
Builders of the Adytum tarot 239
Church of Light tarot 241
Tarot Classic..242
Aleister Crowley "Thoth" tarot 243
D'Epinal tarot 245
Il Destino Svelato Dal Tarocco 246
Dynamic Games tarot...................................247
Egipcios tarot 249
Esoteric tarot 251
Etteilla tarot...252
Fergus Hall tarot..253
Gentilini tarocchi..255
Golden Dawn tarot 256
Golden Egyptian tarot/Morgan's tarot/Praktische tarot......257
Hoi Polloi tarot 259
Tarot of Oscar Ichazo 261
Tarot of Marseilles 262
Masenghini Tarocchi Piedmontese 263
Mountain Dream tarot 265

Muchery Astrological tarot	266
The New Tarot Deck	267
The New Tarot for the Aquarian Age	268
Nordic tarot	269
1JJ Swiss tarot	270
Piatnik/Pointner tarot	271
Rider-Waite tarot	273
Royal Fez Moroccan tarot, suit of swords	274
Royal Fez Moroccan tarot	275
Sheridan/Douglas tarot	276
Spanish tarot	277
Starter tarot	278
Tantric tarot	280
Taro Adivinhatorio	282
20th Century tarot	283
Vandenborre tarot	284
Visconti-Sforza tarocchi	285
Oswald Wirth tarot	286
Xultun tarot	288
Yeager tarot of Meditation	291
Zigeuner tarot	293
Zolar's New Astrological tarot	294

CHAPTER XIV

Gobl tarock	297
Napoleon tarock	298
Allegorical tarock	299
Turkish Costume tarock	300
Pfluger Scenic tarock	301
Historical tarock	302
Animal tarock (Bohemia)	303
Animal tarock (Germany)	304
Military tarock (circa 1854)	305
Opera and Operetta tarock	306
Chinese tarock	307
Fool's tarock	308
Dance tarock	309
Theatrical tarock	310
Proverb tarock	311
Dondorf tarock no. 246	312
Military tarock (circa 1882)	313
Nejedly tarock	314
Habsburger tarock no. 146	315
Exotic tarock	316
Ditha Moser tarock	317
Soldaten tarock	318
Piatnik genre tarock	319
Willer tarock	320
Paris Scenic tarock	321
Ladies tarock no. 162	322
Tarotrump and tarock no. 4	323
Coffee House tarock no. 9a	324
Tarock no. 36a by Piatnik	325
Cego pack	326

CHAPTER XVI

Ten-card spread with twenty-two Major Arcana	337
Ten-card spread with forty-two cards	339
The name spread	339
The horseshoe spread	349
The royal spread	341
The seventh-card spread	341
The gypsy spread	342
Sample tarot card reading	343

COLOR PLATES

1. The Fool by Johanna Sherman
2. The Lovers, Gringonneur
3. XIII Death, seventeenth-century minchiate pack
4. The Magician, Pierpont Morgan-Bergamo tarocchi deck
5. The Fool, Etteilla pack
6. Temperance, miniature Rider-Waite deck
7. The Fool, Fergus Hall tarot pack
8. IIII The Grandfather, French Revolutionary tarot by L. Cary
9. Male knight of cups, Cary-Yale Visconti-Sforza tarocchi deck
10. II The Popess, Gassmann tarot deck
11. XV The Devil, J. Galler tarot deck
12. 15 The Devil, oversize tarot
13. VI The Lovers, Jacques Rochias fils tarot
14. VII Animal tarock by W. Sewera
15. Knight of disks, Aleister Crowley Thoth tarot
16. Queen of spades, Polish animal tarock by J. DuPont
17. The Pope, J. A. Knapp tarot
18. II Junon, J. Jerger tarot
19. Queen of batons, Zigeuner tarot by Walter Wegmuller
20. II The Popess, Oswald Wirth tarot
21. XVI The Tower by Edoardo Dotti
22. IX Historical tarock by Gumppenberg
23. XVI Ditha Moser tarock
24. 17 Crowning of Empress Josephine, Napoleon tarock
25. VIII Chinese tarock by Ferd Piatnik
26. XIII Military tarock by Jos Glanz
27. XXI Notre Dame, Paris scenic tarock by Jos Glanz
28. XVI Rural scene from Ladies tarock No. 162 by Ferd Piatnik
29. XII Exotic tarock by Modiano
30. XX World War I Soldaten tarock No. 217 by Ferd Piatnik
31. XVII Dance tarock by E. Knepper
32. X Revolution of 1848 tarock by Anton Elfinger
33. X Opera tarock by C. Titze and Schinkay
34. XIX Allegorical tarock by Joseph Estel
35. III Fool's tarock by Josef Surch

PREFACE

A collector of tarot cards generally remembers the circumstances surrounding the time he or she first saw a tarot deck. In mid-February, 1968, I visited the annual Nuremberg Toy Fair in West Germany. On the last day of the fair I wandered into a small booth displaying playing cards published by AGMuller & Cie, Neuhausen am Rheinfall, Switzerland.

Edwin Nigg, export manager for AGMuller & Cie, showed me an intriguing set of seventy-eight colorful cards called the IJJ Swiss Tarot deck. This was the first time I had seen a tarot pack and I found the imagery on the cards both compelling and puzzling. Such card titles on the trump cards as the Empress, The Emperor and The Lovers were self-explanatory; other titles were obscure. Only much later did I learn that the two "J's" in lJJ stood for Junon and Jupiter, alternate titles for The Popess and The Pope popularized by card makers in eighteenth-century southern France as a conciliatory gesture toward the Church. An earlier Swiss deck with cards titled Juno and Jupiter was produced in 1680 by Joannes Pelagius Mayer of Constance.

At the close of the Nuremberg Toy Fair I returned to New York and the following week I showed the lJJ Swiss Tarot deck to Henry Levy. Levy was then a buyer at Brentano's and placed a small trial order for tarot decks with the admonishment to be certain to include with each deck a booklet of instructions about the origin and use of the cards. Thus began my initial research into tarot; during the past nine years I have authored several books and booklets about the history and development of tarot cards and methods of divination.

Tarot symbolism has had a remarkably consistent development during the past several centuries. Nevertheless, important variations have been added by each new artist who has interpreted the symbolism of the twenty-two Major Arcana cards according to his own personal viewpoint. In this new work I have sought to bring together a large number of photographs and descriptive information about several hundred different tarot decks, starting with the several extant hand-painted, fifteenth-century Visconti-Sforza *tarocchi* decks.

The chapter entitled "Introduction to Tarot Cards" defines terminology associated with tarot during the past five hundred years. This chapter also includes early listings and descriptions of the Major Arcana and Minor Arcana cards and theories as to the origin of the four suits and court cards.

In "Origins of *Tarocchi* Cards," I have presented more than thirty-five theories often associated with the early origins of tarot, from oral culture to occult interpretations of the Tree of Life and the Tetragrammaton. In "Earliest References to Playing Cards," published references about playing cards during the fourteenth to sixteenth centuries are discussed. Included are several interpolations and translation errors that have confused past researchers, often causing incorrect assumptions about the history of playing cards and tarot. The section on omissions cites the failure of several important writers of antiquity and the Middle Ages to mention playing cards and tarot, which suggests that cards were not known in their time.

Chapter IV, "Early Types of *Tarocchi* and Similar Playing Cards," describes some of the first known tarot decks and several related decks that may share a common origin, including the Tarocchi of Mantegna, Tarocchini of Bologna and minchiate packs. The next four chapters describe the Visconti and Sforza families, their heraldic devices and detailed information about all the extant Visconti-Sforza cards, 239 in total and which may descend from eleven distinct groups of cards.

Chapter IX, "Other Early Hand-Painted Cards," describes several sets of hand-painted cards including the famous incomplete set of Gringonneur cards. There also exist today many early printed cards, and Chapter X, "Early Printed Tarot Cards," includes a description of, among others, the Sola Busca pack and the Catelin Geofroy pack dated 1557.

Chapter XI, "Eighteenth-and Nineteenth-Century Tarot Decks," discusses the Court de Gebelin cards, the Tarot of Marseilles pack and over thirty additional decks with traditional and historical designs.

I have thought it best to divide the large number of tarot decks of the twentieth century into two distinct chapters. "Twentieth-Century Tarot Decks and Designs Not Readily Available" includes the designs of over ninety-five artists; "Popular Twentieth-Century Tarot Packs and Reprints Currently Available" describes nearly fifty tarot packs generally available to collectors.

This encyclopedia would not be complete without detailed information about the game of tarot, known in Europe as tarock. Chapter XIV contains photographs and descriptions of some thirty decks used for playing the game of tarock rather than for fortune-telling.

The popularity of tarot cards for fortune-telling is well known. In Chapter XV, "Interpreting Tarot Cards," I have sought to present a composite interpretation of each tarot card based upon much traditional material written during the past two centuries. In Chapter XVI, "Spreading the Tarot Deck," readers are shown several popular card spreads.

The bibliography in this book contains over one thousand seven hundred entries dealing with tarot and the history of playing cards. The surprisingly large number of works attests to the substantial interest in the subject matter.

Few books, if any, have been written with both the art historian *and* the occultist in mind. One of the objectives of this work is to bridge the gap between these groups so that the serious card collector and art historian may learn about fortune-telling with tarot cards, which for centuries has fascinated millions of people from all walks of life, and the occultist may learn about the historical and artistic background of early *tarocchi* cards.

Some authors have felt obliged to apologize for doing scholarly research on such a lightly viewed topic as the history of playing cards. However, virtually every American and European family owns or knows of playing cards, and probably no other game of amusement enjoys such popularity, as evidenced by the existence throughout the world of an estimated several billions of packs of cards, including many millions of tarot decks.

The diverse imagery on cards from different packs has led to scholarly investigations from the standpoints of art, iconography, symbolism, fortune-telling and gambling. As a collector of rare books on the history of playing cards, especially tarot books, as well of the original packs of cards themselves, I have at my disposal an extensive private library that has proved invaluable during my research. Access to many important books and decks has allowed me to draw upon the diverse viewpoints (often conflicting) of earlier researchers. I have enjoyed many evenings with friends from the past: Rive, Singer, Cicognara, Chatto, Duchesne, Lévi, Taylor, Willshire, Merlin, Papus, O'Donoghue, Steele and D'Allemagne, to name a few.

Each of us usually discovers a card from the tarot pack that holds a special personal attraction. I have always been fascinated by The Fool. Perhaps my preference was predestined since I was born on April 1st—April Fool's Day. In The Fool card the world beckons beyond the young man as he eagerly ventures forth to savor of life. He is the eternal optimist who is anxious to learn—and he is willing to share his knowledge with other persons who seek to satisfy their own curiosity.

It is my present thinking to publish a companion volume to this work that will include photographs of cards from some additional 150 to 200 tarot packs and other early decks with accompanying commentary. Whether I commit myself to this new task will depend on the reception of this initial volume.

The disclosure of the existence of eleven different groups of Visconti and Visconti-Sforza cards may lead to the discovery of other hitherto unknown early cards. Should this volume kindle a spark in the reader that makes him venture forth to areas yet untouched, I shall feel the results have justified my effort.

Stuart R. Kaplan

ODE

In this ode to ancient tarot cards

I touch with care new friendships painted
on pasteboard faces drawn
during man's obscure dawn.

The single-ended carnival figures
clad in full-length costumes conceal
the profound knowledge of antiquity.

Each gamester skillfully plays
with the arcane figures at his command.
The fanciful trickster separates
the fool from his money while
the wicked fortune-teller
with astonishing accuracy lays bare
the great prophecies of life.

As one card falls another
dares to take its place
much like the evolution of life itself.

The relentless processional
out of the past
unmasks each symbol of the present
and portends the limits which exist in
    the future.

Despite the sly tricksters,
the gamesters,
the crafty gamblers,
the fortune-tellers,
none can answer the simplest of arcane
    questions,
whether the Major and Minor Arcana
    were created together,
or took form each born of separate genius.

One yearns to discover
the ingenious mind that started it all.

What chance to find
face to face the wit who wrote
life is but a game of cards.

Instead we resign ourselves to accept
the allegorical pictures which we do not
fully understand.

Beautiful cardboard face
I love you as an old friend
despite your unyielding guard
of the symbols shrouded
in the mysterious tarot pack
that beguile and defy us all.

                              Stuart R. Kaplan

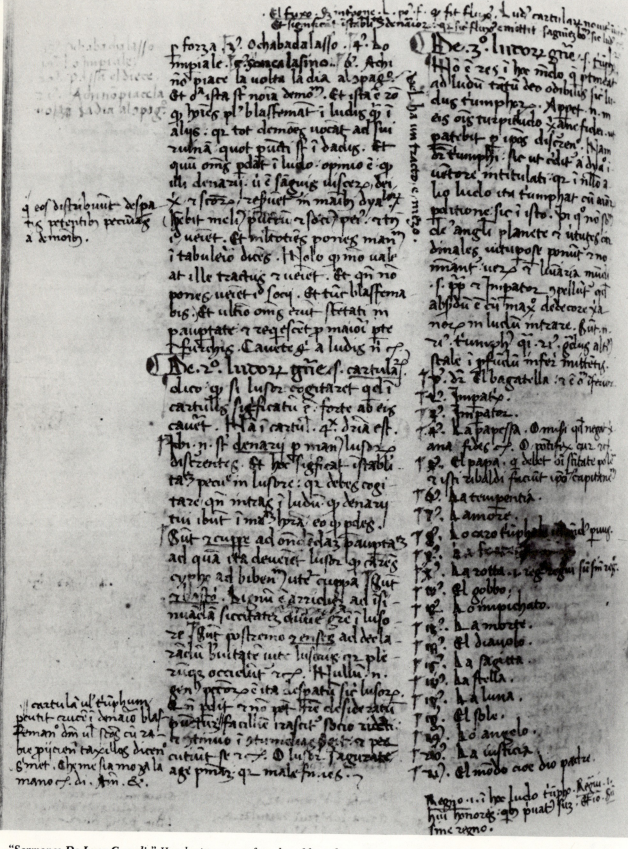

"Sermones De Luco Cumalis" Handwritten page from late-fifteenth-century manuscript. *The lower half of the right column contains the earliest list of* atouts.

I
AN INTRODUCTION TO TAROT CARDS

THERE EXIST TODAY several fifteenth-century Visconti-Sforza *tarocchi* decks which comprise the earliest known tarot cards. The reproduction in 1975 of the most complete of these packs—the Pierpont Morgan–Bergamo *tarocchi* deck whose original cards are divided between the Pierpont Morgan Library, New York, and the Accademia Carrara and Colleoni family, Bergamo, Italy—is an important event for tarot collectors and researchers of art history.

Italy holds the honor of having produced several of the earliest known *tarocchi* packs that contain the mystical and allegorical trump cards. Throughout five centuries the provocative symbolism of the twenty-two Major Arcana cards has continued to intrigue art historians, artists and occultists. For over five hundred years card designers and artists have faithfully preserved the same dominant symbolism of the Major Arcana cards while often adding their personal interpretations in the form of slight modifications to the designs based upon the fashions, events and important topics of the day. There exist in leading museums, libraries and private collections many hundreds of such modified tarot designs, the work of such artists as the fifteenth-century genius Bonifacio Bembo, modern painters such as Salvador Dali and Larry Rivers, and many lesser known but talented artists such as Pamela Colman Smith (Rider-Waite pack), Lady Frieda Harris (Crowley "Thoth" cards), Fergus Hall (James Bond 007 tarot cards), David Palladini (Aquarian tarot) and Domenico Balbi (Balbi pack).

The development of tarot symbolism during the last five centuries, beginning with the earliest known Italian *tarocchi* cards, is an intriguing story.

TERMINOLOGY

The term *trionfi* was used in Italy in the fifteenth century to describe the twenty-two Major Arcana cards. The term *tarocchi* subsequently came into usage in Italy in the early sixteenth century, first referring to the twenty-two Major Arcana cards, and thereafter to the complete seventy-eight-card deck, consisting of the twenty-two Major Arcana and fifty-six Minor Arcana or suit cards. The words *tarocchi* and *tarocco* are often used interchangeably, although *tarocchi* is actually the plural of *tarocco*. Tarot, the French derivative of *tarocchi*, has come into widespread usage in the English language. In pronouncing the word *tarot*, the final *t* is silent.

MacGregor Mathers, writing in 1888, describes several anagrams derived from the word *taro*:

Tora—law (Hebrew)
Troa—gate (Hebrew)
Rota—wheel (Latin)
Orat—it speaks, argues or entreats (Latin)
Taor or Taur—Egyptian goddess of darkness
Ator or Athor—Egyptian Hathor, goddess of joy

The term *trumps* is derived from the Latin *triumphi*. The twenty-two trump cards, also known as the Major Arcana or Greater Arcana cards, each contain a symbolic or allegorical picture. *Arcana* is a Latin word meaning mysterious or secret; the Italian word *arcana*, derived from the Latin, has the same meaning. The trumps are also known as *atouts* in French and *atutti* in Italian. *Atouts* denote cards of higher value than the rest, that is, *a tous* or *a tutti*, superior to all others.

Some researchers believe the word *tarot* derives from the term *tarotée*, the name applied to the design on the back of early cards—a multiple series of crisscrossing solid or dotted lines in varying widths. However, it is likely that the word *tarotée* itself was derived from *tarocchi* since the use of the word *tarocchi* predates that of the word *tarotée*. In the statutes of the guild of card makers of Paris in the year 1594 the cartiers called themselves *tarotiers*, another form of the word *tarot*.

Antoine Court de Gebelin wrote in the late eighteenth century an exhaustive treatise entitled *Monde Primitif* which dealt with all aspects of ancient civilization. He proposed that the word *tarot* was composed of the Egyptian words *tar*, signifying way or road, and *ro*, *ros* and *rog*, implying king or royal.

Nancy Fullwood, writing in 1929, described tarot as meaning the *royal road*. Fullwood maintained that there exist seven royal roads that are both realms of being and the great primal forces that govern life. *Pano tarot* vibrates through the universe as pure Spiritual Mind. *Fano tarot* vibrations make the Force of Heart in the universe. *Tano tarot* vibrates through the universe as the Force of Material Wealth. The vibrations of *Sano tarot* make the Force of Inspiration, those of *Rano tarot* the Force of Faith and those of *Gano tarot* the Force of Universal Love. *Ono tarot* vibrates the Force of Hope in the universe. In sum, it is these seven tarots through which the gods lead the seeker of truth.

Through the centuries playing cards alternately have been called the Devil's Picture Book, the Devil's Bible, painted pasteboards and pagan idols. Whatever their name, the symbolic and allegorical cards have captured the imaginations of the high and mighty, the impoverished and destitute. Indeed, tarot has intrigued persons from all walks of life, economic circumstances and fields of endeavor.

THE MAJOR ARCANA CARDS

The twenty-two symbolic and allegorical Major Arcana cards depict and create the continuous and ever-changing physical and spiritual forces affecting humanity. To some persons, the trump cards are a pictorial processional of life's fateful events.

What appears to be the oldest list of standard trumps is contained in a late-fifteenth-century manuscript of a sermon against gambling. The author, a priest, describes and condemns the use of dice and ordinary cards in the four suits of cups, coins, swords and staves. He then lists the names of the *triumphi* in the following manner:

1. *Primus dicitur El bagatella (et est omnium inferior)* (The Magician or The Juggler)
2. *Imperatrix* (The Empress)
3. *Imperator* (The Emperor)
4. *La papessa (O miseri quod negat Christiana fides)* (The Popess or The High Priestess)

TITLES OF THE 22 MAJOR ARCANA CARDS IN ENGLISH, FRENCH, ITALIAN AND GERMAN

Number	English	French	Italian	German
	The Fool, The Foolish Man, The Vagabond	*Le Mat, Le Fou, Le Fol*	*Il Matto, Il Folle, Il Pazzo*	*Der Narr*
I	The Magician, The Juggler, The Wizard, The Thimble-rigger, The Minstrel, Quarterpenny, The Cups Player, The Mountebank, The Magus, The Pagad, The Pagat, The Paghead	*Le Bateleur, Le Joueur de Gobelets*	*Il Bagatino, Il Bagatto, Il Bagattel, Il Bagat, Il Bagotti, Il Bigatto*	*Der Magier, Der Gaukler*
II	The Popess, The High Priestess, The Female Pope, Pope Joan, Junon, Wise Woman, Bacchus	*La Papesse*	*La Papessa*	*Die Papstin, Die Höhepriesterin*
III	The Empress, Isis, The Queen	*L'Impératrice*	*L'Imperatrice*	*Die Herrscherin, Die Kaiserin, Die Königin*
IIII	The Emperor, Osiris, The King	*L'Empereur*	*L'Imperadore, L'Imperatore*	*Der Herrscher, Der Kaiser, Die König*
V	The Pope, The Hierophant, The Head Priest, Grand Master, Jupiter, Spanish Captain	*Le Pape*	*Il Papa*	*Der Papst, Der Höhepriester*
VI	The Lovers, Marriage, Eros, Hermes	*L'Amoureux*	*L'Amore, Gli Amanti, Gli Innamorati*	*Die Liebenden, Der Scheideweg, Die Entscheidung*
VII	The Chariot, Triumphal Car, Wagon	*Le Chariot*	*Il Carro*	*Der Triumphwagen, Der Wagen*
VIII	Justice, The Scales	*La Justice*	*La Giustizia*	*Gerechtigkeit*
VIIII	The Hermit, Father Time, The Hunchback, The Aged Man, The Sage	*L'Ermite, Le Vieillard, Capuchin, Le Prêtre*	*L'Ermita, Il Gobbo, Il Vecchio, L'Eremita*	*Der Einsiedler, Der Eremit, Der Weise*

5. *El papa (O pontifex cur, &c. qui debet omni sanctitate polere, et isti ribaldi faciunt ipsorum capitaneum)* (The Pope or Hierophant)
6. *La temperentia* (Temperance)
7. *L'amore* (The Lovers or Love)
8. *Lo caro triumphale (vel mundus parvus)* (The Chariot or The Car)
9. *La forteza* (Strength)
10. *La rotta (id est regno, regnavi, sum sine regno)* (The Wheel or Wheel of Fortune)
11. *El gobbo* (The Hermit or Father Time)
12. *Lo impichato* (The Hanged Man)
13. *La morte* (Death)
14. *El diavolo* (The Devil)
15. *La sagitta* (The Arrow)
16. *La stella* (The Star)
17. *La luna* (The Moon)
18. *El sole* (The Sun)
19. *Lo angelo* (The Angel)
20. *La iusticia* (Justice)
21. *El mondo (cioe Dio Padre)* (The World)
22. *El matto sine nulla (nisi velint)* (The Fool)

It is interesting to note that the sequence given for the Major Arcana cards and several titles vary from the popular versions today. The Empress is in second place and The Popess is moved to fourth place. The Tower is called The Arrow, reflecting the arrow ray that strikes the crown of the tower. Judgment is replaced by The Angel.

The manuscript clearly distinguishes between cards and trumps, evidencing that they did not form one game but were separate entities. According to the manuscript, there is nothing in the world so hateful to God as the game

Number	English	French	Italian	German
X	The Wheel of Fortune, Fate, Chance, Rota	La Roue de Fortune	La Ruota, Rota di Fortuna, Ruota della Fortuna, La Fortuna	Das Rad des Lebens, Schicksasrad, Das Glücksrad
XI	Strength, Force, Fortitude	La Force	La Fortezza, La Forza	Die Kraft
XII	The Hanged Man, The Hanging Man, The Traitor, The Thief, Tau Cross, Judas	Le Pendu	Il Penduto, L'Appeso, Il Traditore, L'Impiccato	Der Erhängte, Der Aufgehangte, Die Prüfung
XIII	Death, The Skeleton	La Mort	Il Morte, Lo Specchio, La Morte	Der Tod
XIIII	Temperance	La Tempérance	La Temperanza	Der Ausgleich, Die Ausgewogenheit, Die Mässigkeit
XV	The Devil, Typhon, Satan, Lucifer	Le Diable	Il Diavolo	Der Teufel
XVI	The Tower, The Lightning Struck Tower, The House of God, The Hospital, The Tower of Babel, Fire of Heaven, The Devil's House, The Castle of Plutus	La Maison de Dieu, Le Foudre	La Casa del Diavolo, La Torre, Il Fuoco, La Saetta	Der Turm, Der Vom Blitz Getroffene Turm, Die Zerstörung
XVII	The Star, Dog Star	L'Étoile	La Stella, Le Stelle	Der Stern
XVIII	The Moon	La Lune	La Luna	Der Mond
XVIIII	The Sun	Le Soleil	Il Sole	Die Sonne
XX	Judgment, The Last Judgment, The Angel	Le Jugement, L'Ange	L'Angelo, Il Giudizio, La Trompete	Das Gericht
XXI	The World, The Universe	Le Monde	Il Mondo	Die Welt

THE MAJOR ARCANA CARDS RELATED TO SUIT SIGNS

Swords		Batons		Cups		Coins	
VII	The Chariot		The Fool	VI	The Lovers	II	The High Priestess
VIII	Justice	III	The Empress	XIIII	Temperance	V	The Hierophant
XI	Strength	IIII	The Emperor	XVII	The Star	X	The Wheel of Fortune
XIII	Death	VIIII	The Hermit	XVIII	The Moon	XV	The Devil
XX	Judgment	XII	The Hanged Man	XVIIII	The Sun	XVI	The Tower

of trumps, which ridicules the Christian faith by depicting angels, the cardinal virtues, the Pope and the Emperor on cards.

The Roman numerals which appear on the Major Arcana cards often vary between standard Roman letters and the sequence used in the subtractive principle. Thus, card number four may be written IIII or, under the subtractive principle, IV, which became popular during the Middle Ages and is the standard form used today.

The twenty-two Major Arcana cards in most tarot decks published in America and Europe contain card titles in English, French, Italian or German.

A study of the twenty-two Major Arcana cards reveals several distinct groups. Emile Grillot de Givry, writing in 1929, notes that there are six titled personages belonging to human society: The Empress and The Emperor, The High Priestess and The Pope, and The Juggler and The Hermit. There are two allegorical personages: The Devil and Death. If we assume The Hanged Man represents Prudence, then there are four cardinal virtues: Justice, Strength, Temperance and Prudence. Three astronomical elements are The Sun, The Moon and The Star. Two cards relating to chance in human life are The Lovers and The Wheel of Fortune. Finally, the four elements of cosmic fatality are The Chariot, The House of God, Judgment and The World.

Another division of the twenty-two Major Arcana cards is possible by assigning the cards to one of four groups associated with the suit signs: swords, batons, cups and coins.

The first and last numbered Major Arcana cards—The Magician and The World—can stand by themselves, or they can readily be fitted into the baton group. The Magi-

ASTROLOGICAL CORRESPONDENCES TO THE TWENTY-TWO MAJOR ARCANA CARDS BASED UPON SEVEN AUTHORS

	Major Arcana	Etteilla	Sepher Yetzirah	T. Basilide
I	The Magician	—	—	—
II	The High Priestess	Moon	Saturn	Taurus
III	The Empress	Venus	Jupiter	Venus
IIII	The Emperor	Jupiter	Mars	Jupiter
V	The Hierophant	Aries	Aries	Aries
VI	The Lovers	Taurus	Taurus	Sagittarius
VII	The Chariot	Gemini	Gemini	Mars
VIII	Justice	Cancer	Cancer	Libra
VIIII	The Hermit	Leo	Leo	Virgo
X	The Wheel of Fortune	Virgo	Virgo	Mercury
XI	Strength	Mars	Sun	—
XII	The Hanged Man	Libra	Libra	Saturn
XIII	Death	—	—	Capricorn
XIIII	Temperance	Scorpio	Scorpio	Moon
XV	The Devil	Sagittarius	Sagittarius	Gemini
XVI	The House of God	Capricorn	Capricorn	Scorpio
XVII	The Stars	Mercury	Venus	Aquarius
XVIII	The Moon	Aquarius	Aquarius	Cancer
XVIIII	The Sun	Cancer	Pisces	Leo
XX	Judgment	Saturn	Mercury	Pisces
XXI	The World	—	—	—
XXII	The Fool	Sun	Moon	Sun

cian card, with its symbols of all four suits on the table, is apparently assignable to any of the four groups.

Numerous attempts have been made by writers to assign astrological correspondences to the twenty-two Major Arcana cards. Oswald Wirth, writing in 1927, summarized a few such attempts beginning with Etteilla in the late eighteenth century; the divergent viewpoints are obvious.

The entire sequence of twenty-two Major Arcana cards has been viewed by some researchers as embodying the synthesis of all knowledge and a description of all the events in an individual's life span. MacGregor Mathers described a series of connected thoughts based upon the Major Arcana cards that runs somewhat as follows:

The human *will* (I The Magician), enlightened by *science* (II The High Priestess) and manifested by *action* (III The Empress), should find its *realization* (IIII The Emperor) in deeds of *mercy* and *beneficence* (V The Hierophant). *Wise disposition* (VI The Lovers) will bring *victory* (VII The Chariot) through *equilibrium* (VIII Justice) and *prudence* (VIIII The Hermit) over the fluctuations of *fortune* (X The Wheel of Fortune). *Fortitude* (XI Strength), sanctified by *sacrifice* of one's self (XII The Hanged Man), will triumph over *disaster* (XIII Death), and thus a wise *combination* (XIIII Temperance) will enable one to defy *fate* (XV The Devil). In each *misfortune* (XVI The Tower) there is always the star of *hope* (XVII The Star) shining through the twilight of *deception* (XVIII The Moon) to ultimate *happiness* (XVIIII The Sun) in the *final result* (XX Judgment). On the other hand, *folly* (The Fool) will bring about an evil *reward* (XXI The World).

THE MINOR ARCANA CARDS

The fifty-six suit cards, called the Minor Arcana or Lesser Arcana, are divided into four suits. Each suit contains fourteen cards. The four court cards, also called coate, costume or figure cards, are king, queen, knight and page. The ten pip or numeral cards run in sequence from ten to ace, and the symbol of the suit—sword, stave, cup or coin—is repeated in the same number as is necessary to identify the card; thus seven swords represent the seven of swords.

Suit Derivations Card makers from the earliest times to the present have sought to introduce a variety of suit signs including stars, arrows, birds, dogs, falcons, mirrors, columns, moons and anchors, but none of the innovations struck the popular fancy. The suit signs prevalent today in tarot packs of the United States, United Kingdom, France, Italy and certain other European countries are:

English	French	Italian	Corresponding to
Swords	Épées	Spade	Spades
Staves, wands, scepters, batons, clubs	Batons	Bastoni	Clubs
Cups, chalices, goblets	Coupes	Coppe	Hearts
Coins, money, pentacles, circles	Deniers	Denari	Diamonds

Richard Ettinghausen, writing in 1974 in "Further Comments on Mamluk Playing Cards," includes a repro-

Ely Star		Georges Muchery		Aleister Crowley	Oswald Wirth
Planet	Zodiac Sign	Planet	Zodiac Sign	Planet, Element or Sign	
—	—	Sun	Leo	Mercury	Taurus
Moon	—	Moon	Cancer	Moon	—
—	—	Mercury	Gemini	Venus	—
Jupiter	—	Venus	Taurus	Aries	Virgo
—	Aries	Jupiter	Sagittarius	Taurus	Aries
Moon	Taurus	Mercury	Virgo	Gemini	Sagittarius
Sun	Gemini	Venus	Libra	Cancer	—
Venus	Cancer	Mars	Scorpio	Libra	Libra
Jupiter	Leo	Jupiter	Sagittarius	Virgo	—
Mercury	Virgo	Mars	Scorpio	Jupiter	Capricorn
Mars	—	Mars	Aries	Leo	Leo
Moon	Libra	Jupiter	Pisces	Water	—
—	—	Saturn	Aquarius	Scorpio	—
Sun	Scorpio	Saturn	Capricorn	Sagittarius	Aquarius
Saturn	Sagittarius	Venus	Libra	Capricorn	—
Jupiter	Capricorn	Venus	Taurus	Mars	Scorpio
Mercury	—	Mercury	Gemini	Aquarius	Pisces
Venus	Aquarius	Moon	Cancer	Pisces	Cancer
Jupiter	Pisces	Sun	Leo	Sun	Gemini
Saturn	—	Mercury	Virgo	Fire	—
Sun	—	Sun	Leo	Saturn	—
—	—	Moon	Cancer	Air	—

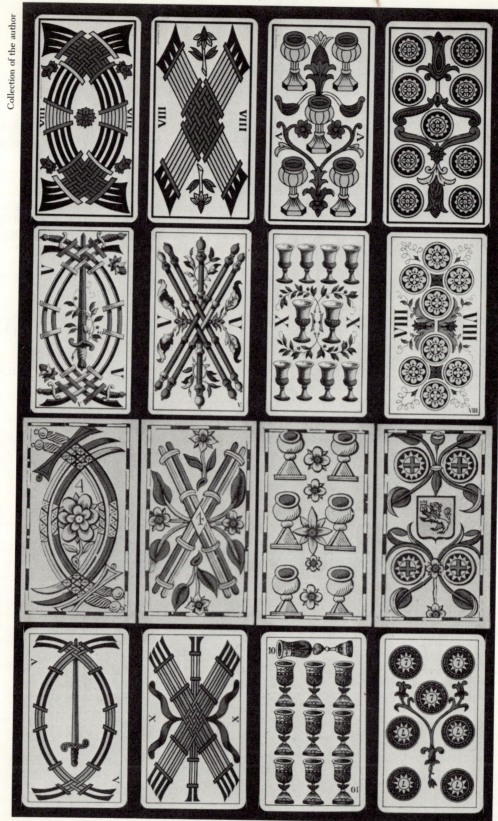

Tarot suit signs   Italian suit signs are depicted in most tarot packs produced in Italy, France and other countries. Left to right: Swords, staves (batons), cups and coins. In most tarot packs the suited swords are curved and interlace at top and bottom, while the staves or batons are straight and interlace at the center. This is one easy method of distinguishing between the otherwise similar, and sometimes confusing, suits of swords and staves. Cards illustrated (top to bottom row) are from the Tarot of Marseilles, 1JJ Swiss tarot, Vandenborre tarot and Tarocchi Piedmontese decks.

duction of a paper fragment from the Museum of Islamic Art, Cairo, which may represent an early Egyptian court card showing a king(?) and a large bird. If this is a fragment of a court card rather than simply of a court scene, it would place one of the earliest existing cards in Egypt, thus supporting the theory that the early cards developed from an Egyptian source. One widely held belief is that the card suits represent the four castes along the Nile River in ancient times.

Another popular theory supposes that the suits represent the four divisions of the populace in medieval Europe: swords (spades) for knights, nobility and aristocracy; staves (clubs) for peasants and the lower classes; cups (hearts) for the clergy and other ecclesiastical groups; and coins (diamonds) for the commercial class. Other writers associate the four suits with the objects held in the four arms of the Indian deity Vishnu and the composite deity Ardhanari.

Galcottus Martius, writing about 1488 to 1490, refers to the four suits of the game of cards as swords, spears, cups and country loaves of bread. Pietro Aretino, writing in the mid-sixteenth century in "*Les Cartes Parlantes*" (the talking cards), refers to cards as a hazardous game and interprets the suits. Thus, swords recall the death of those who despair and become mad over gaming; staves or batons, the punishment of those who cheat; cups, the wine in which the disputes of gamesters are settled; and coins, the sustenance and food of play.

Early French writers associate the four suits with warfare. Spades designate the cache or stores of arms necessary for battle. Clubs (trefoils) represent the common meadow plant and signify that a general should never encamp his troops in places lacking forage for horses or where it would be difficult to transport it. Hearts represent the courage and leadership of officers, and diamonds the type of strong and heavy arrows shot from a harquebus.

Covarrubias, writing in the early seventeenth century, suggests that the four suits in playing cards are meant to represent the most hurtful and mortal dangers to mankind. The first suit, swords, serves to draw men into combat. Clubs, less effective warlike weaponry, succeeded fists and eventually were superseded in combat by the superior sword. Cups, which seem to have been invented to sustain life, have proved to be the source of innumerable brawls and quarrels. Lastly, no less dangerous than iron swords and wooden clubs are gold coins—the wealth that incites men to robbery and murder. Thus, swords and clubs are symbols of violence, cups of drunkenness and disorder, and coins of greed and crime.

By contrast, some view the suit signs as emblems of four virtues; namely, justice (the sword), fortitude (the club), faith (the cup) and charity (the coin).

The four suits have also been viewed as geographical and political representations. In this theory the swords represent the Orient, the staves South America, the cups North America and the coins Europe. The kings represent government, queens religious belief, knights history and nationalistic viewpoints, and pages the arts and sciences. The ten pip cards of each suit represent the different nations comprising the larger geographical divisions.

Other theories suggest that the four suits were meant to signify the four seasons of the year—spring, summer, fall, winter—or the four elements—earth, fire, water and air—or even the four Hebrew letters of Yod-He-Vau-He, transliterated as JHVH and representing Jehovah or God.

According to many occultists, the four suits of the tarot pack are assigned to the four worlds of the kabbalists and the four elements of the alchemists. Thus, the suit of staves is assigned to Atziluth and fire; the suit of cups to Briah and water; the suit of swords to Yetzirah and air; and the suit of pentacles or coins to Assiah and earth.

Court Cards Originally called *coate* cards, by reason of the flowing robes worn by the figures, the cards depicting full-length figures eventually became known as *court* or *picture* cards.

Standard playing card packs contain three court cards, while tarot packs contain four court cards by the addition of a knight. The court cards in the tarot pack are called:

English	French	Italian
King	*Roi*	*Re*
Queen	*Reine*	*Dama*
Knight, Horseman	*Cavalier*	*Cavallo*
Page, Knave	*Valet*	*Fante*

According to one explanation of the costumed figures in standard packs, the queen of spades, which on French cards is named *Pallas*, was meant to represent Joan of Arc, the Maid of Orleans. If such is the case, and if the adoption was intended as a tribute to her memory, it must have occurred after the year 1421 when she rendered the French people such important service, and probably before the close of the reign of Charles VII, who died in 1461. The names associated with all the court cards are:

	Spades (Piques)	*Clubs* (Trèfles)	*Hearts* (Coeurs)	*Diamonds* (Carreaux)
King	David	Alexander	Charlemagne	Caesar
Queen	Pallas	Argine	Judith	Rachel
Knave	Hogier	Lancelot	la Hire	Hector

Père Gabriel Daniel, in *Memoire sur l'origine du jeu de piquet trouvé dans l'histoire sous le règne de Charles VII*, conjectures that the four queens are intended to represent four principal female characters in the reign of Charles VII. The queen of spades, Pallas, the virgin goddess of war and wisdom, is strikingly similar to Joan of Arc, in whom the attributes of the goddess—martial character, wisdom and chastity—are found united. Thus, concludes Daniel, probably out of gratitude for her services, Charles VII gave the Maid of Orleans a place in this military game. The queen of clubs is called Argine, which is an anagram of *Regina* and therefore meant to represent Mary of Anjou, wife of Charles VII. Rachel, the queen of diamonds, was celebrated in the Scriptures for her beauty and was therefore chosen to represent Charles's mistress, Agnès Sorel, who was called the Lady of Beauty. Judith, the queen of hearts, was intended to represent Isabel of Bavaria, the mother of Charles VII.

Hogier was a knight under Charlemagne, even though he is included in the suit of spades rather than hearts. Lancelot was a knight at the Court of King Arthur. La Hire is believed to have been a hireling of Charles VII, and it is possible that he represents a fifteenth-century knight, Stephen de Vignoles, who is frequently credited with designing the French court cards and suit signs as we know them today. Hector was a Trojan warrior. Numerous variations of these figures have appeared during the past several centuries, especially by local French card makers.

The Encyclopedia of Tarot

Seven of Staves Top row, left to right: Geometric designs in *1JJ Swiss tarot, Spanish tarot, Tarot Classic.* Bottom row: Illustrative scenes in *Aquarian tarot, Rider-Waite tarot, Royal Fez Moroccan tarot.*

Pip Cards Pip cards are the ten through ace in each suit of the Minor Arcana. Traditionally, the pip cards in tarot packs contain repetitive suit symbols displayed in a geometric pattern such as six swords, five cups and four coins. Since 1910, when the Rider-Waite tarot deck was created, numerous tarot packs have featured illustrative scenes on the pip cards in place of the traditional geometric suit signs. The suit signs are usually interwoven into each overall card design, and the resulting illustrated pip cards are easier to interpret during card readings. Tarot decks with illustrative scenes on the pip cards include Acuario tarot, Aquarian tarot, British tarot, De Laurence tarot, Dynamic Games tarot, Egipcios tarot, Etteilla tarot, Hoi Polloi tarot, Il Destino Svelato Dal Tarocco, Mountain Dream tarot, The New tarot, Odell tarot, Ravenswood Eastern tarot, Rider-Waite tarot, Royal Fez Moroccan tarot, Sheridan/Douglas tarot, Tantric tarot, Taro Adivinhatorio and Xultun tarot.

TAROT DECK BACK DESIGNS

Recognition of back designs can aid in the identification of tarot decks. When studying antique cards, the same back design on all seventy-eight cards assures that the cards are from the same deck and not commingled with cards from some other deck.

Some of the different back designs found in Italian tarot decks are patterns of red or blue stars, lozenges with stars, wavy lines with dots, repeating ermine spots and diagonal patterns. Sometimes the back designs are inscribed with such words as *"al Mondo,"* "Milano" and "Ferrara."

French tarot packs contain a variety of back designs including patterns of hexagons enclosing suns, mottled colors including green, brown and red, lozenges enclosing crosses or suns, ermine spots, repeating stars and a *tarotée* design of crisscrossing lines.

STANDARD FIFTY-TWO-CARD PACKS

Most Western countries use the so-called French suit marks of spades, clubs, hearts and diamonds in standard packs of playing cards. However, some countries retain their traditional suit marks, as shown in the illustration comparing standard suit signs in the United States and Europe.

Some scholars believe the standard fifty-two-card playing card deck derives from the early *tarocchi* packs—the knight and page were combined to form the jack and the twenty-two trump cards were dropped (with the exception

---

Tarot Back Designs (left to right): *Mottled green from J. Jerger tarot deck (page 151), repeating hexagons enclosing suns from Galler tarot deck (page 152), alternating dot with plus sign and rays from L. Carey tarot deck (page 155), wavy diagonal lines with alternating stars and short dashes from Gassmann tarot deck (page 163),* tarotée *design of crisscrossing lines from 1JJ Swiss tarot deck (page 268).*

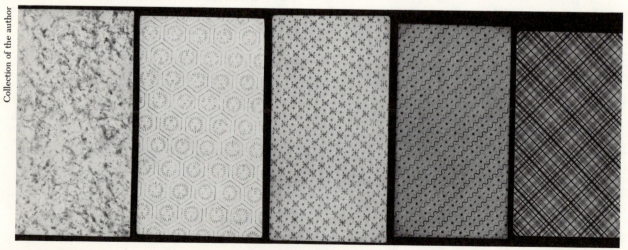

TAROT CARD SIZE VARIATIONS

Size Variations of Tarot Cards. 1 Pierpont Morgan-Bergamo Visconti-Sforza tarocchi, 2 Grand Tarot Belline, 3 Zigeuner tarot, 4 Aleister Crowley "Thoth" tarot, 5 Xultun tarot, 6 Oswald Wirth tarot, 7 Tarot of Marseilles, 8 Rider-Waite tarot, 9 Aquarian tarot, 10 Mountain Dream tarot, 11 Tarot Classic and 1JJ Tarot, 12 The Church of Light tarot, 13 The New Tarot Deck, 14 Miniature Rider-Waite tarot, 15 The World's Tiniest Rider-Waite tarot.

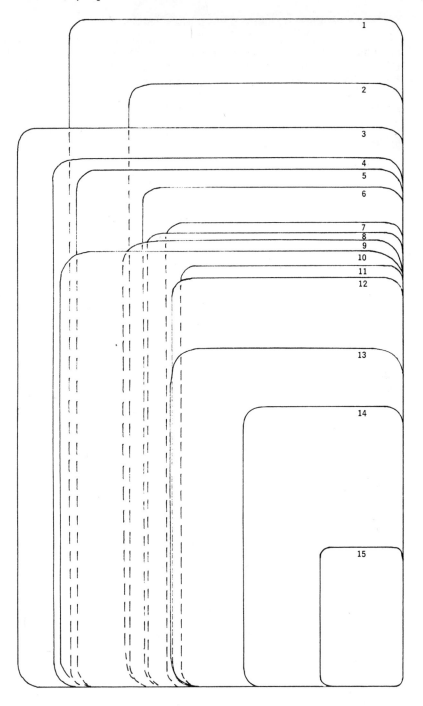

of The Fool, which survives as the joker). There is reason to believe that in standard decks the Italians and the French simply dropped the knight. The queen was dropped in Spanish tradition and Spanish packs have the *Rey* (king), *Caballo* (cavalier on horseback) and *La Sota* (a helper). In German tradition, in addition to the *König* (king), a new convention of the *Ober* and *Unter* was adopted.

The Fool is absent from traditional fifty-two-, fifty-eight-, forty- and thirty-two-card packs until the middle of the nineteenth century. At this time, the joker, occasionally pictured as a fool, begins to appear in fifty-two-card American packs. Thus, it is difficult to substantiate any direct link between The Fool and the joker, beyond the obvious humorous connotation.

No one knows with certainty that the twenty-two Major Arcana and the fifty-six Minor Arcana were originally devised as a complete seventy-eight-card deck. It is theorized that the court and pip cards of the Minor Arcana developed independently of the trumps and at a later date the trumps were added to form the complete *tarocchi* pack.

Popular writers of the last century often made numerical comparisons between the fifty-two-card pack and the calendar.

Fifty-two cards in a pack suggest the fifty-two weeks of the year.

Thirteen cards in each suit suggest the thirteen lunar

months of the year and the thirteen weeks in each quarter.

Four suits in the pack suggest the four seasons of the year.

Twelve court or picture cards in the pack suggest the twelve months of the year and the twelve signs of the zodiac.

Furthermore, if we add together:

The pips on the plain cards of the four suits	= 220
The pips on the twelve picture cards	= 12
Twelve picture cards counted as 10 each	= 120
The number of cards in each suit	= 13
We shall obtain the number of days in the year	365

Finally, adding all the letters in ace, two, three, etc., through king, the total is fifty-two. The same is true in French and German.

A comparison of the twelve court cards in American packs reveals that generally eight of the courts face to the left and four face to the right. The kings and jacks all have swords or rods at their left. The queens all have flowers. The king of diamonds and the jacks of hearts and spades have only one eye. The king of diamonds has a battle-ax; the king of clubs carries a sword and wears a flower at his belt. The king of hearts is the only court figure with four arms. Most kings and jacks are depicted with moustaches.

In the sixteenth century a book written by Jacob Cammerlander described each pip card with its moral and spiritual associations. For example, in the suit of hearts the five stands for the five books of Moses, four hearts suggests

STANDARD SUIT SIGNS IN UNITED STATES AND EUROPE

U.S./BRITAIN:	Spades	Clubs	Hearts	Diamonds
FRANCE:	Piques	Trèfles	Coeurs	Carreaux
GERMANY:	Laube or Grüne	Eicheln	Herzen	Schellen
HOLLAND:	Schoppen	Klaveren	Harten	Ruiten
ITALY:	Spade	Bastoni	Coppe	Denari
SPAIN:	Espadas	Bastos	Copas	Oros
SWITZERLAND:	Schilten	Eicheln	Rosen	Schellen

the four evangelists, three hearts the Trinity, and two hearts the tablets of the Ten Commandments.

By the eighteenth century a popular story was often repeated about a soldier observed in church with a deck of playing cards. Different versions of this quaint story have appeared through the years, including the following modified version:

Soldier's Almanack, Bible and Prayer Book

Richard Middleton (or Midaleton), a soldier, attending divine service with the rest of his regiment at a church, instead of pulling out a missal to follow the priest's text, spread a pack of cards before him. This singular behavior did not long pass unnoticed, either by the priest or the sergeant of the company; the latter in particular requested him to put up the cards, and after his refusal conducted him before the Mayor, to whom he preferred a formal complaint about Richard's sacrilegious behavior.

"Well, soldier!" said the Mayor. "What excuse have you for such strange behavior? If you can make any apology, it's well; if you cannot, I will cause you to be severely punished for it."

"Since your honor is so good," replied Richard, "I will inform you. I am a poor soldier without much money and I cannot afford to buy a missal. But for me it doesn't matter whether I read the mass in a missal or a group of cards because the cards are reminders of the importance of God."

On saying this, Richard drew out his pack of cards, and presenting one of the aces to the Mayor, continued his address as follows:

"When I see an ace it reminds me that there is only one God; and on the first day God created Earth. One is the common measure of all things; it is indivisible, not to be multiplied. There is only one superior intelligence in the intellectual world, man.

"Two reminds me of the second day of creation when God said, 'Let there be light'; the two also represents the Old and the New Testaments and the sacred ritual of marriage. When the beasts of the field took refuge in Noah's Ark they entered by twos.

"Three puts me in mind of the Holy Trinity—the Father, the Son and the Holy Spirit; and on the third day God separated the water and earth. Three also has a mysterious value, as shown in Time's trinity of the Past, Present and Future. In man there is the brain, the intellectual; the heart, the celestial; and the body, the elemental. In space there is length, breadth and thickness.

"Four calls to remembrance the four evangelists—Matthew, Mark, Luke and John—and on the fourth day God made the sun, moon and stars, which regulate the years, months and days. Four also signifies solidity and foundation; there are four elements, four cardinal points and four seasons.

"Five reminds me of the five great prophets chosen by God to instruct the ancient Jewish people, and the five Wise Virgins who were ordered to trim their lamps; and on the fifth day God created the fish and birds. There are five senses and the Pentagram is composed of five letters; five, as it divides ten, the sum of all numbers, is also the number of justice.

"In considering card number six, I remember that God created the world in six days, and on the sixth day He created the animals that live on dry land, including man according to his own likeness. Six is also the perfect number because it alone, by addition of its half, its third and its sixth, re-forms itself. It also represents servitude by reason of the divine injunction, 'Six days shalt thou labor, and on the seventh day thou shalt rest.'

"On the seventh day God rested, and seven also reminds me of the Seven Wonders of the World. Seven represents life because it contains body, consisting of the four elements of spirit, flesh, bone and humor, and soul, made up of three elements, passion, desire and reason.

"Eight recalls to mind the eight righteous persons preserved from the Great Deluge—Noah, his wife, their eldest son, Shem, second son, Ham, third son, Japheth, and their son's wives. Eight also represents justice and fullness. Divided, its halves are equal; twice divided, it is still even.

"Nine is the number of muses who presided over the arts and sciences, and there were nine lepers who cleansed Our Savior.

"Ten suggests the Ten Commandments that God gave Moses on Mount Sinai on the tablets of stone. Ten also represents completeness because one cannot count beyond it except by combinations formed with other numbers."

The soldier set aside the knave (page) and then continued. "When I see the queen it puts me in mind of Eve and the Queen of Sheba, and also the humble Virgin who brought Jesus Christ into the world. The queen or number twelve also suggests the twelve signs of the zodiac, the Twelve Apostles, the Twelve Tribes of Israel and the twelve gates to Jerusalem.

"The king, it brings to mind the Great King of Heaven and Earth, which is God Almighty, and likewise Adam, and Solomon, son of David and Bathsheba."

The soldier paused, but seeing his interrogators avidly listening to his story, he quickly continued. "When I consider the number of cards in my deck, I find there are fifty-two, representing the fifty-two weeks of the year, and among them are twelve figure cards representing the twelve months of the year and the twelve signs of the zodiac. And the forty pip cards remind me of the forty days and forty nights that Moses spent on Mount Sinai to receive from God the sacred laws and commandments for the people of Israel."

"Well," said the Mayor, "you have given a good description of all the cards except one, which is lacking."

"Which is that?" asked the soldier.

"The knave [page]," replied the Mayor.

"If your honor will not be angry with me," said Richard, "I have saved that card for last."

"And why is that?" asked the Mayor.

"Because the greatest knave I know," replied the young soldier, "is the sergeant who brought me here before you."

At that the Mayor smiled and replied, "Whether he be the greatest knave I do not know, but I am sure he is the greatest fool." Whereupon the Mayor called his servants, ordered them to entertain the soldier well, gave him a piece of money and said he was the cleverest fellow he had ever heard in his life.

II

ORIGINS OF TAROCCHI CARDS

THE ORIGINS OF PLAYING CARDS—both the twenty-two Major Arcana and the fifty-six suited cards—remain obscure. An early pack of suited cards—perhaps the earliest extant deck—is the hand-painted German "Hunting" pack of Stuttgart, which dates from about 1420–1430 and contains no trumps. These cards depict a hunting series with dogs, stags, ducks and falcons for suit signs. The earliest Visconti-Sforza *tarocchi* cards also date from this period. The following are some of the popular theories advanced during the past several centuries regarding the possible origin of *tarocchi* cards.

PREHISTORIC MAN AND ORAL CULTURES

Prior to recorded history, prehistoric man developed various systems of oral culture and tradition based upon a subtle knowledge of astronomy and calendric counters. It is generally believed that early man carefully observed the sidereal phases of the day, month and year, and the changing positions of the planets. These were astronomical events he could easily study and he recorded these events by calendric counters such as markings on a stretched piece of animal hide, engravings or scratchings on a bone, and notches on a tree branch. Important cultural events were eventually expressed in metaphorical and allegorical forms as myths, legends and fables, which were verbally transmitted from generation to generation over periods of time extending many thousands and even tens of thousands of years.

Some fragments of these early oral traditions survived into recorded time in the form of popular myths and beliefs. For example, the devil is an antlered figure associated with sorcery and evil, and the hermit is a hooded figure holding a candle and representing the winter solstice. Both these figures are found in the Major Arcana of the tarot pack. Many of the pictorial images on the Major Arcana cards have been distorted by time and the ignorance of their interpreters. Thus, most tarot pictures as popularized during the past five hundred years are unrecognizable in terms of early myths and oral culture. Literal interpretations of many early myths are the basis of numerous superstitions and ceremonies practiced today by religious groups, fraternal orders, secret societies and followers of the occult.

Some scholars including Arthur Corwin, who has been researching the subject since the 1960s, view the allegorical symbolism of tarot cards as pictorial metaphors that express the preoccupation of early man with the task of timekeeping. The calendar was an important point of reference to early man. He kept accurate records of the celestial changes that occurred on a daily, monthly and annual basis. He observed the precession of the equinox, the astronomical motions of the stars and planets, and other repetitive events. The calendar was used as a means of survival, including planning for winter food storage, preparing necessary shelter, communicating on a daily basis with other human beings and recording the length of time required for birth.

THOTH AND EGYPTIAN HIEROGLYPHIC BOOKS

In 1781, writing in *Monde Primitif*, Court de Gebelin advanced the theory that the Major Arcana cards constituted the Egyptian hieroglyphic Book of Thoth, saved from the ruins of burning Egyptian temples thousands of years ago. The Book of Thoth, also known as the Book of Tarot and the Book of the Leaves of Gold, allegedly contained the synthesis of all human knowledge and profound mysticism. Thoth was the Egyptian god of wisdom, occult arts and sciences; he was also scribe and secretary to the other gods in the Egyptian pantheon and his seat was at Hermopolis. Thoth's duties were to measure time and foretell the future. He was also credited with the invention of both numbers and sacred writing and in ancient reliefs he was often represented with a man's body and the head and neck of an ibis, a sacred bird similar to a heron or crane, whose stride, according to popular belief, measured exactly a cubit, the unit of measurement employed in building temples. Consistent with mythological belief, Thoth was often portrayed carrying a pen, tablet and palm branch.

Thoth was given the name Hermes Trismegistus by the Greeks and his sacred works were called "Hermetic." The Greek deity Hermes was the god of commerce, invention, cunning and theft; he was also the messenger of the gods and guide of souls to their final resting place. The name Hermes Trismegistus means *three times master* or *the thrice great Hermes,* and refers to his supposed authorship of works on alchemy, astrology and magic.

Court de Gebelin wrote in *Monde Primitif*:

Imagine the surprise which the discovery of an Egyptian book would cause if we learned that a work of the ancient Egyptians still existed in our time—one of the books saved from the flames which consumed their superb libraries—and which contained their purest beliefs regarding interesting things. Everyone would, no doubt, be eager to know about such a precious and extraordinary book which is already in very general use in a large part of Europe and has been in the hands of everyone for a number of centuries. Wouldn't it be the greatest surprise, if we vouched that we never suspected the book was Egyptian, and that we own it without really owning it, because we have never tried to decipher one page of it, or to look upon the fruit of its exquisite wisdom.

This Egyptian book does exist. This Egyptian book is all that remains in our time of their superb libraries. It is even so common that not one scholar has condescended to bother with it since no one before us has ever suspected its illustrious origin. This book is composed of seventy-seven, even seventy-eight sheets or pictures, divided into five classes, each showing things which are as varied as they are amusing and instructive. In a word, this book is the game of tarot, a game unknown in Paris, it is true, but very well known in Italy, Germany and even in Provence. This game is bizarre because of the kinds of figures appearing on its cards as well as their great number.

Antoine Court de Gebelin

Title page from Monde Primitif and first page from "Du Jeu Des Tarots"

Court de Gébelin died in Paris on May 10, 1784. The Rosetta Stone was discovered in 1799 during Napoleon's campaign in Egypt and it provided the key to the language of ancient Egypt. With the stone, the French scholar Jean François Champollion solved the problem in 1822 of how to read hieroglyphic writing.

EGYPTIAN HIEROGLYPHIC PAINTINGS

Paul Christian, writing in the late nineteenth century, interpreted the twenty-two Major Arcana cards as hieroglyphic paintings. These paintings were originally displayed on columns in an ancient Egyptian gallery that the neophyte was obliged to enter during initiation. Eleven symbolic pictures were placed on each side, arranged in pairs, so that the last picture was opposite the first, the next to last picture opposite the second and so on, in the following order:

```
0  21  20  19  18  17  16  15  14  13  12
1   2   3   4   5   6   7   8   9  10  11
```

These pictures were carefully explained to the initiate so that he might learn and understand the rules and principles of wisdom.

THE BEMBINE TABLET

Athanasius Kircher, writing in *Oedipus Aegyptiacus*, which was published in Rome in 1652–1654, described the *Mensa Isiaca*, also known as the Tablet of Isis and the Bembine Tablet, so-called because its discovery was connected with the name of Cardinal Bembo, historian of the Republic of Venice and librarian at St. Mark's prior to his death in 1547. A folding plate was included in the Kircher work, and a more elaborate plate appeared in 1669 in *Mensa Isiaca* by Laurentius Pignorius. The original bronze tablet, which is lost, was divided into three equal horizontal compartments. The upper portion contained the twelve houses of heaven divided by the four seasons of the year, the signs of the zodiac, the governors of the world; to these Eliphas Lévi, in *Le Dogme et Rituel de la Haute Magie*, added the four-lettered sacred name of the Tetragrammaton. The lower portion of the tablet showed the distributions of labor or work periods throughout the year. The center section was divided into seven parts and, reputedly, contained the twenty-one sacred signs of the alphabet of Thoth which formed the original symbolism of the tarot. In the midst of the table was a great covered throne with a seated female figure representing Isis. The ornamented border enclosing the three main panels of the Bembine Tablet contained different symbols including human beings, birds, reptiles, animals, snakes, composite forms, flowers, cups and scepters. The Tablet of Isis may have been a table or altar and its emblems part of the mysteries hidden in the great Egyptian temples and revealed by priests to the neophytes who came to be instructed in the secrets of the sacerdotal caste. Numerous interpretations of the Bembine Tablet have been put forth by writers including Eliphas Lévi, W. Wynn Westcott, and Manley P. Hall who makes important contributions to the knowledge of this subject.

GOD, MAN AND THE UNIVERSE

P. D. Ouspensky, writing in 1913 in St. Petersburg, Russia, structured the tarot deck as a representation of God, man and the universe. Ouspensky placed the twenty-one numbered Major Arcana cards in the shape of a triangle, seven cards on each side, and used a point in the center of the triangle to represent the zero card. Around the triangle he then formed a square with the fifty-six Minor Arcana cards, fourteen cards on each side.

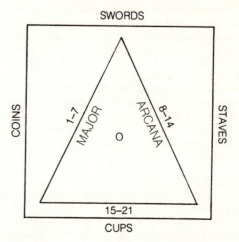

God, Man and the Universe as Synthesized by P. D. Ouspensky.

The Ouspensky theory of the tarot pack was expressed in a diagram of a center dot, triangle and square. Thus, the multifaceted tarot was shown to synthesize the relationship among the world of ideas, the consciousness of man and the physical world. The triangle represented God (and the Trinity) in the world of ideas, the center point was man's soul, and the four-sided square was the visible physical or phenomenal world. Such an idea presumably could not have originated with ignorant people, and the tarot, Ouspensky therefore concluded, has an ancient origin and deep meaning.

THE MYSTICAL NUMBER 7

Antonio Dragoni suggested in 1814 that the twenty-one Major Arcana cards (omitting The Fool) represented the Egyptian doctrine, allegedly revered by Pythagoras, of the perfect number 3 and the mystical number 7. Setting aside The Fool, there remain in the tarot pack seventy-seven cards, or 11 times 7. These seventy-seven cards are further divided into two classes, the twenty-one emblematic cards (3 times 7) and the fifty-six Minor Arcana cards (8 times 7). It is probable that the number 7 assumed great importance when the science of astrology began to take form, and was associated by the ancients with the seven known planets—Mercury, Venus, Mars, Jupiter, Saturn and the Sun and Moon. Furthermore, the tarot represents three classes of images that symbolize the first three ages of the world—the Golden, the Silver and the Bronze.

THE TORAH

Some scholars are attracted to the similarity between the Hebrew word "Torah" (pronounced *tora*) and the word "tarot"; when read in the Hebrew fashion from right to left, tarot (pronounced *taro*) becomes *tora*. Indeed, the Major Arcana cards are viewed by many persons as the synthesized totality of all knowledge and experience, as is the Torah.

HEBREW ALPHABET

One cannot dismiss the congruence between the twenty-two letters of the Hebrew alphabet and the twenty-two Major Arcana cards. Many scholars of the occult (Eliphas Lévi, Papus, Oswald Wirth and Arthur Edward Waite, for example) assign a Hebrew letter to each Major Arcana card. Aleph generally denotes The Fool, or The Magician, depending upon which card the interpreter considers as the first card in the Major Arcana sequence.

It is interesting to speculate on the possible development of the twenty-two Major Arcana cards from early alphabets, as illustrated in the chart below.

THE KABBALAH AND THE TREE OF LIFE

The twenty-two paths connecting the ten *sephiroth* in the Tree of Life of the Kabbalah are often associated with the twenty-two Major Arcana cards. The Kabbalah is a Jewish system of theosophy that deals with the mystical apprehensions of God and teaches that creation was accomplished through emanation and thaumaturgy. One version holds that the Kabbalah was first taught by God himself to a select company of angels who formed a theosophic school in Paradise. Another version contends that the Kabbalah was given directly by God to Moses during his forty-day stay on Mount Sinai. Moses allegedly ini-

Modern Characters	Ancient Phoenician	Ancient Hebrew	Ancient Greek	Samaritan	Oscan & Sammite	Early Roman	Modern Hebrew	Greek Names	Major Arcana
A							Aleph	Alpha	I The Magician
B							Beth	Beta	II The High Priestess
G							Gimel	Gamma	III The Empress
D							Daleth	Delta	IIII The Emperor
E							He	Epsilon	V The Hierophant
F							Vau	Digamma	VI The Lovers
Z							Zain	Zeta	VII The Chariot
HE							Cheth	Eta	VIII Justice
TH							Teth	Theta	VIIII The Hermit
I							Yod	Iota	X The Wheel of Fortune
K							Caph	Kappa	XI Strength
L							Lamed	Lambda	XII The Hanged Man
M							Mem	Mem	XIII Death
N							Nun	Nun	XIIII Temperance
S							Samech	Xsi	XV The Devil
O							Ain	Omicron	XVI The Tower
P							Pe	Pi	XVII The Star
TZ							Tsade		XVIII The Moon
KO							Koph	Koph	XVIIII The Sun
R							Resch	Resch	XX Judgment
SH							Shin	Sigma	O The Fool
T							Tau	Tau	XXI The World

Reprinted with additions from *The Origin and Progress of the Art of Writing* by Henry Noel Humphreys

Early Alphabets from Ancient Phoenician to Modern Hebrew with the Applicable Major Arcana.

HEBREW	LEVI, PAPUS AND WIRTH	WAITE
Aleph א	I The Magician or Juggler	0 The Fool
Beth ב	II The Female Pope	I The Magician
Gimel ג	III The Empress	II The High Priestess
Daleth ד	IIII The Emperor	III The Empress
Heh ה	V The Pope	IIII The Emperor
Vau ו	VI Vice & Virtue or The Lovers	V The Hierophant
Zain ז	VII The Chariot	VI The Lovers
Cheth ח	VIII Justice	VII The Chariot
Teth ט	VIIII The Hermit	VIII Fortitude or Strength
Yod י	X The Wheel of Fortune	VIIII The Hermit
Caph כ	XI Strength	X The Wheel of Fortune
Lamed ל	XII The Hanged Man	XI Justice
Mem מ	XIII Death	XII The Hanged Man
Nun נ	XIIII Temperance	XIII Death
Samech ס	XV The Devil	XIIII Temperance
Ayin ע	XVI The Tower	XV The Devil
Peh פ	XVII The Star	XVI The Tower
Tzaddi צ	XVIII The Moon	XVII The Star
Qoph ק	XVIIII The Sun	XVIII The Moon
Resh ר	XX Judgment	XVIIII The Sun
Shin ש	0 The Fool	XX Judgment
Tau ת	XXI The Universe or The World	XXI The Universe or The World

Hebrew Attributions to the Major Arcana *Letters of the Hebrew alphabet are shown with their attributions according to Levi, Papus and Wirth as compared to Waite.*

tiated the Seventy Elders into the secrets of the doctrine, and they transmitted them orally from generation to generation. It is believed that David and Solomon were deeply initiated into the Kabbalah and the secret Kabbalah was never written down until Rabbi Simon Ben Jochai's treatises were collated into the *Zohar* or Book of Splendors.

The word "Kabbalah" means "doctrines received from tradition." In ancient Hebrew literature "Kabbalah" denotes the entire body of religious writings, the Pentateuch excepted.

The main sources used for making the Kabbalah are the *Sepher Yezirah* or Book of Creation, which is a compendium of medieval mysticism and science that came to be known as Kabbalism during the early Middle Ages. The Kabbalah deals with the nature of God and his divine emanations. God, in the Kabbalah, is known as En Soph, and he fills and contains the universe. To justify his existence the Deity had to become active and creative, and this he achieved through the medium of the ten *sephiroth* or intelligences that emanate from him like rays proceeding from a luminary. The first *sephirah* or emanation is the wish to become manifest, and this contains nine other *sephiroth*, which emanate one from the other—the second from the first, the third from the second and so forth—and are known as (1) Crown or Primum Mobil; (2) Wisdom; (3) Intelligence and Understanding; (4) Kindness, Love and Mercy; (5) Strength, Severity and Justice; (6) Beauty; (7) Force, Firmness or Victory; (8) Splendor; (9) Foundation; and (10) Kingdom. From the junction of pairs of *sephiroth*, other emanations are formed: from Wisdom and Intelligence proceeds Kindness; from Kindness and Strength comes Beauty. The fundamental ten *sephiroth* show the gradual development of the world out of nothing into ten successive emanations, each lower *sephirah* developing from the preceding *sephirah* and the higher *sephirah* having all the powers of the *sephiroth* beneath it. The *sephiroth* are also symbolic of primordial man and heavenly man, of whom earthly man is but the shadow. They form three triads that, respectively, represent intellectual, moral and physical qualities: the first, Wisdom, Intelligence and Crown; the second, Kindness and Love, Strength and Justice and Beauty; the third, Force (or Firmness), Splendor and Foundation. The whole is encircled or bound by Kingdom, the tenth *sephirah*. Each of these triads symbolizes a portion of the human frame: the first the head, the second the arms, the third the legs. Although these *sephiroth* are distinct emanations of God, they simply represent different aspects of the One Being.

Thus, the thirty-two ways of secret wisdom of the Kabbalah are divided into two groups: the "fundamental ten" and the twenty-two paths. The twenty-two *true* paths, which connect the ten *sephiroth*, allegedly coincide with the twenty-two Major Arcana cards of the tarot pack.

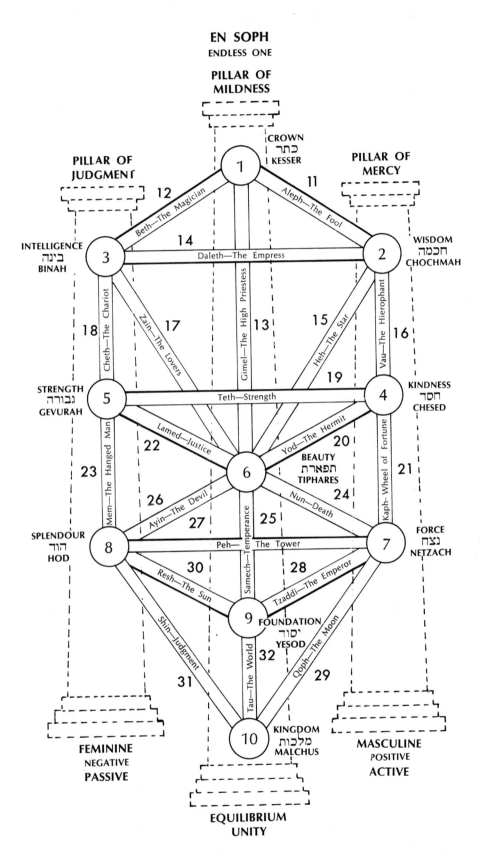

The Tree of Life The ten sephiroth are connected by the twenty-two paths as represented by the twenty-two Major Arcana cards.

TETRAGRAMMATON AND JEHOVAH

Papus, writing in 1889, believed that the tarot pack developed from the theosophic doctrine based upon Tetragrammaton, the four Hebrew letters of Yod-He-Vau-He. The letters are frequently transliterated as YHWH, JHVH or IHVH and are pronounced *Yahweh* or *Jehovah*, the ineffable name of God. Some occultists believe that the four letters of Tetragrammaton govern the four suits (Yod); the four court cards (He); the forty pip cards, divided into ten sets of four cards each (Vau); and the twenty-two Major Arcana cards, divided into three septenaries plus The Fool (He). Aleister Crowley, in the Thoth tarot deck, arranged and symbolized the court cards so that the king indicated the swift action of Yod, the queen the steadfast forces of He, the prince (replaces knight) Vau, and the princess (page) the final He of the sacred name.

THE TABLE OF CEBES

Manley P. Hall, writing in *An Encyclopedic Outline of Masonic, Hermetic, Qabbolistic and Rosicrucian Symbolical Philosophy*, suggested that one possible origin of tarot cards might be the mysterious Table of Cebes, based upon the ancient Greek philosopher who, it is said, designed a hieroglyphic picture setting forth the entire progress of human life. Myriads of human creatures are shown climbing a great mountain in search of the goal of human attainment—true happiness.

VISHNU

Some writers believe the earliest cards are derived from images of the Indian deity Vishnu, the preserver of the world and one of the three great names for God, the other two names being Brahma, creator of the world, and Siva, its destroyer. Vishnu is depicted in Indian art with four hands holding four objects—a lotus, mace, conch and discus—that are sometimes associated with the four suits. Additionally, Vishnu has ten traditional avatars, nine past and one, Kalki, the White Horse, yet to come, and these ten avatars correspond numerically to the ten *sephiroth* in the Tree of Life as well as to the ten pip cards in each suit. Early Indian playing cards contain either eight or ten suits to a set and each suit comprises twelve cards, consisting of numerals 1 to 10 plus two court cards. The suit signs of the ten-suited pack are similar to the ten incarnations or avatars of Vishnu.

Michel Constant Leber, writing around 1842, believed that some of the Major Arcana cards were derived from early Eastern idols and symbols that subsequently changed under the influence of Christian dogma. Thus, Vishnu, the Indian deity, became *Le Pape*, the head of the Catholic Church; *La Maison de Dieu* replaced an oriental pagoda; and the cloaked *L'ermite* was derived from a Muslim dervish.

ARDHANARI

One of the androgynous Hindu deities is known as Ardhanari; one-half of the god is Siva and the other half is his wife of many names. This composite god has four arms: Siva holds in his hands a cup or drum *(damaru)* and a wand or trident, while behind him sits a bull; his wife holds a sword and circular ring or shield, and crouched behind her is a tiger. Thus, the four objects held by Ardhanari are similar to the four suits in playing cards. In Hindu mythology the wife or *sakti* of Siva was also known as Bhairavi, the redoubtable; Ambika, the progenitor; Sati, the perfect wife; Gauri, the brilliant; and Durga, the inaccessible who had ten arms.

CHATURANGA AND CHESS

The Indian game of Chaturanga or Four Kings (circa fifth or sixth century A.D.) is an ancient version of chess. The original Indian game had a vizier and elephant instead of today's queen and bishop. Some researchers have suggested that playing cards are a simplified version of chessmen, possibly the device of players who lacked ornate chess figures and instead chose to portray the different figures in simple fashion on small flat surfaces. That playing cards bear a striking resemblance to certain chess pieces is undeniable. The court cards bearing the same names are similar to the king and the knights; the pip cards resemble chess pawns. However, just as there are similarities between chess and cards, there are numerous differences: a chess player controls eight pieces representative of the royal court and eight pawns; a card suit contains only three or four court figures and ten numerals. During play the chess pieces are fully exposed and the game consists mainly of strategy; during play with cards much depends upon chance and the cards held by a player are kept secret.

The symbolism of chess, described in 1928 by Manley P. Hall, is as follows: The white king is Ormuzd and his side or suit represents the True Self. The black king is Ahriman and his retinue symbolizes the Not-Self and False Ego. Of the philosophical constitution of man, the kings represent the spirit, the queens the mind, the bishops the emotions, the knights the vitality, and the castles or rooks the physical body. Pawns are the sensory impulses and perceptive faculties. The king, being the spirit, cannot be captured, but loses the battle when so surrounded that he cannot escape. Thus, some or all of the ancient symbolism of chess pieces may have found its way into the tarot pack.

CHAHAR-TAJ

William Andrew Chatto, writing in 1848, pointed out that the word *chahar* or *chatur* in the Hindustani language, or *chartah* as written in English, signifies four, and apparently enters into the composition of the Hindustani word for chess, *Chaturanga*. Chatto believed both chess and cards were probably invented in Hindustan, and therefore the words *chahar* or *chatur* may have formed a portion of the original word for cards. The common term for cards in Hindustani is *taj* or *tas*, suggesting a leaf, *folium*. In its figurative sense *taj* or *tas* might signify a diadem or crown,

INCARNATIONS OF VISHNU ASSOCIATED WITH SUIT SIGNS

Incarnation	Name	Suit Sign
First	Matsya	Fish
Second	Kurma	Tortoises
Third	Varah	Boars
Fourth	Nara-simha	Lions
Fifth	Vamana	Dwarfs or Water Jars
Sixth	Paracu-rama	Axes
Seventh	Rama-chandra	Arrows
Eighth	Krishna	Cows
Ninth	Buddha	Shells
Tenth	Kalki	Swords or Horses

Ardhanari   *The Hindu androgyne holds in its four arms the suit signs associated with playing cards.*

suggesting regal authority. Thus, the compound term for cards might read *chahar-taj* or *chahar-tas*, suggestive of "Four Kings," the early name for chess, and almost identical in sound with the Latin *chartae* or *chartas*. It was Chatto who theorized that the name for cards was altered when passing from Hindustan, through other countries, into Europe, just as we find *Chaturanga*, the Sanscrit name for chess, transformed into the Persian *chatrang*, the Arabic *shatranj*, the Greek *zatrikion*, the Spanish *ajedrez*, the Italian *scacchi*, the French *échecs*, and the English *chess*.

HINDUSTANS AND SARACENS

Samuel Weller Singer, writing in 1816, proposed to show that cards were invented by the Hindustanis, probably as an extension or alteration of the game of chess, and that in time the Saracens introduced playing cards into Europe. According to Singer, the Saracens, having spread with rapidity over Asia and Africa, attempted to cross the sea as early as the seventh century. In the year 652 they invaded Sicily, which they completely conquered by 832. They were in Spain in the year 710, and about 731 they penetrated through Languedoc into France as far as Arles. The Saracens proceeded from Sicily to Calabria, and a few years afterward to Rome and Tuscany. They maintained themselves in different parts of Italy until the tenth century, and their power was such that the Pope and other Italian princes made use of their assistance in their wars with each other. In the beginning of the tenth century a party of Saracens settled on the borders of Piedmont and penetrated as far as the Alps in the Valais. Safety from their inroads was purchased by ceding to them a tract of country among the mountains in about the middle of that century.

The long continuance of the Saracens in the immediate vicinity of the Italian, Spanish and French afforded these peoples opportunities for becoming acquainted with Saracen literature, arts, customs and amusements. Singer concluded that the European nations might have obtained playing cards from these oriental invaders, who at the time were an enlightened people compared to the inhabitants of Europe.

PRE-COLUMBIAN SYMBOLISM

There exist today many codices prepared by Mexican and Central American Indians in the centuries prior to the Spanish conquest. Some scholars believe the hand-painted images in these codices bear certain affinities to the Major Arcana and Minor Arcana tarot cards. The *Tonalamatl* or Book of the Days was called by Torquemada "the book of luck or chance" and also "the book of the bad days and the good days," and it was used by the Aztec priests to reveal events of a prophetic nature. The corresponding Mayan books were called *Tzolkin* and served the same purposes of future prediction. The oriental influence so prevalent in pre-Columbian art suggests an early link with the East. A recent tarot deck featuring pre-Columbian symbolism taken from lintels and glyphs at Tikal was designed by Peter Balin in 1972.

DICE

One of several popular gambling devices in Europe at the end of the fourteenth century was dice. The numerical possibilities, from *one* on a single die to *twelve*, or two sixes, on a pair of dice, suggest that the numeral or pip cards numbered from one to ten, and at least two of the court cards—a total of twelve cards in all—may derive from dice and were further developed at a later date into several sets or suits in addition to a third court card.

CHINESE DOMINOES

Marked in the same manner as the dice from which they apparently derived, Chinese dominoes are thought to have been originally used for divination. There are twenty-one distinct pieces, representing the permutations of two dice. Eleven of these pieces are doubled, making a total of thirty-two in the set. It is believed by some researchers that playing cards evolved from dice through the Chinese wooden domino.

KOREAN ARROW

The eight-suited Korean decks, known as Htou-Tjyen, comprise eighty cards. These cards are generally strips of oiled paper eight inches long by one-quarter inch wide. The backs are uniformly marked with the image of an arrow feather. The card faces appear to be highly conventionalized shaftments of arrows, retaining in their suit markings the same symbolism as that of the Korean quiver or arrow from which they are derived. Thus, there is some justification for the belief that cards developed from Korean divinatory arrows.

NAIBI

The root word *naibi,* possibly an early Arabic or Hindustani name for playing cards, is similar to the word *naipes,* the present Spanish word applied to cards. Several early writers have suggested that both these words seem analogous to the Hebrew and Arabic words *nabi, naba* and *nabaa,* which convey the idea of prophecy, thus suggesting an early Eastern derivative for the Spanish name for cards. Jan Bauwens suggests that the word *naipes* may derive from the Arabic word *na'ib* for lieutenant, thus raising the possibility that the Spanish name for cards is derived from the title found on one of the early Mamluk cards. However, no known Arabic manuscript purports to give the word *na'ib* any signification for playing cards, and it is well known that cards and gambling are forbidden by the Koran. It is probably well to note here, however unlikely the derivation, that in the Royal Spanish Academy's Dictionary of 1734 the word *naipes* is given as derived from the initials N.P., standing for Nicolas Pepin, the supposed inventor of playing cards.

MAT AND PAGAD

According to Court de Gebelin, the French word *mat* (in Italian, *matto*) is derived from the oriental word *mat,* and is generally used to designate the Fool (*Le Mat*), the first and unnumbered Major Arcana card. *Pagad,* the conjurer of Eastern origin, derives from *pag* (chief, master or lord) and *gad* (fortune). The use of these oriental words has suggested to Gebelin and other researchers the possible oriental origin of tarot cards.

SEUN-HO

William Andrew Chatto points out that in the Chinese dictionary entitled *Ching-tsze-tung,* compiled by Eul-koung and first published in 1678 A.D., it is said that cards were invented in China during the reign of Seun-ho in 1120 to amuse his numerous concubines. Thereafter, goes the story, playing cards became common during the reign of Kaou-tsung, who ascended the throne in 1131.

CHAD

Rudolf von Leyden makes reference to an early Indian card game called Chad, which is described in detail in the *Shree Tatva Nidhi.* There were thirteen varieties of the game, each variety called by a religious or mythological name such as *Chamundeswari, Panch Pandava* and *Nawa Graha.* The number of suits varied from four to eighteen and the number of cards in each suit from nine to eighteen. In addition, a number of loose cards in the various games brought the total number of cards in one pack to 320, and Von Leyden suggests that the loose cards may correspond to the Major Arcana cards. But it is probable that the Chad games of Mysore were invented about 1800 and thus follow by several centuries the earliest known tarot cards.

FEZ, MOROCCO

In the 1920s Paul Foster Case advanced the theory that the tarot pack was invented around the year 1200 when a group of scholars from many nations met at Fez, Morocco. Seeking a means of communication, they devised a universal language of pictorial symbols.

GIOTTO (1266?–1337)

The great artist of the early Italian Renaissance, Giotto di Bondone, is best known for his frescoes. Ronald Decker, an American art historian specializing in the Italian Renaissance, suggests that the Giotto frescoes in the Arena Chapel in Padua, which contain virtues, vices and other scenes, are suggestive of many of the Major Arcana cards.

GUELPHS AND GHIBELLINES

During the thirteenth and early fourteenth centuries there was considerable civil dissension in Italy between two warring groups. The Guelphs supported the Pope and opposed the authority of the German Emperor; the Ghibellines favored the imperial cause. Some Italian writers have placed the invention of the game of *tarocchi* during the period of struggle between the Guelphs and Ghibellines, even suggesting that the figures on the tarot pack relate to events and persons prominent in Italy during the civil dissension.

WALDENSES

Some authors suggest that the Waldenses, a medieval Christian sect of dissenters, may have been the originators of the trumps and the amalgamators of the two types of cards—the Major Arcana and the Minor Arcana—that form the basis of the game of *tarocchi.* The sect was named after Peter Waldo, a rich merchant of Lyon who helped the poor in 1170. The Waldensian ministers, commonly known as *barbe,* traveled throughout Italy in search of converts and used allegorical illustrations in their instruction.

PETRARCH'S *TRIUMPHI*

Gertrude Moakley, writing in 1966 in *The Tarot Cards Painted by Bonifacio Bembo for the Visconti-Sforza Family,* believes that early Italian *tarocchi* and *minchiate* packs were inspired by Petrarch's famous fourteenth century poem, *Triumphi.* The poem describes six triumphs. The first is Cupid, who triumphs over god and men. He is often illustrated aiming darts or arrows at his unhappy captives while

Cupid from Petrarch's famous poem, Triumphi.

riding on a great car drawn by white horses. Chastity, who celebrates Laura's refusal of Petrarch's love, is shown as a silver-clad figure with ermine banner who rides on a car drawn by unicorns. The third triumph is Death in the form of a skeleton riding on a car drawn by black oxen. Fame is shown on a car drawn by elephants, blowing her many-mouthed trumpet. Time is depicted as an aged man leaning on crutches and holding an hourglass; his car is drawn by stags. The final triumph, Eternity, which reunites Petrarch and Laura in everlasting bliss, is shown as an image of the Holy Trinity mounted on a car drawn by four living creatures which are the symbols of the first four gospels of the New Testament: a man, an eagle, a lion and an ox. These same symbols appear in the four corners of The World card of standard Major Arcana.

GYPSIES, BOHEMIANS, ZINGARI

The name *gypsy* is an abbreviation of "Egyptian" and refers to the area of "Little Egypt" or "Egypt Minor," a region of Near Eastern Asia. Gypsies speak of themselves as Romany. Small wandering bands of gypsies, Bohemians or *zingari* may have brought playing cards to Europe at the end of the fourteenth century, or at the beginning of the fifteenth century, when large groups were driven from India by Timur Lenk, the Islamic ruler who conquered much of central Asia. However, the arrival of cards in Europe seems to predate the immigration of the gypsies, who may have popularized cards as a means of divination.

JACQUEMIN GRINGONNEUR

In the accounts book of Charles Poupart, treasurer to Charles VI of France, there exists a passage stating that in 1392 Jacquemin Gringonneur was paid fifty-six sols of Paris to paint three packs of cards in gilt to amuse the king. Seventeen of the so-called Gringonneur tarot cards, without inscriptions, letters or numbers, are today in the archives of the Bibliothèque Nationale in Paris. It is thought, however, that these cards may be of fifteenth-century Venetian origin and the three packs in gilt have been lost.

FLEUR-DE-LIS

The fact that the fleur-de-lis is found on certain court cards suggests to some people that cards were invented in France. However, this assumption appears unfounded since the same heraldic symbol of a stylized three-petaled iris is found among the ornaments of the Romans at an early period, on the scepters and crowns of the emperors of the West during the Middle Ages, and on those of the kings of Castile and England before the Norman Conquest.

FOURTEENTH-CENTURY DESIGNS

The Major Arcana cards contain evidence, according to Roger Tilley, that indicates the trumps could not have been designed in Europe before the fourteenth century. In this regard, Tilley cites the coal-shaped headdress of The Emperor; the young man in The Lovers' card, who is clad in doublet and hose, which only became prevalent about 1335; the crown of The Pope with its third coronet, which was first added in 1315 or 1316; and the charioteer, wearing a metal breastplate ornamented with pauldrons, which came into fashion in the fifteenth century as a decorative design, pauldrons having proved impractical in battle because the enemy's sword caught on the surface rather than glanced off.

FORMSCHNEIDERS AND *BRIEFMAHLERS*, *BRIEFES* AND *KARTEN*

Baron Heineken, writing in 1771, advanced the German claim to originating the first *printed* cards from wood blocks on the premise that the first wood engravers in Europe were German card makers. Those who carved the wood blocks were called *Formschneiders* or block cutters; the artists who illuminated the impressions were called *Briefmahlers* or card painters. The production of the so-called printed cards, according to Heineken, eventually led to widespread wood-block printing of scriptural and religious pieces. However, it seems more likely that wood-block printing was used first for religious pictures and later for playing cards. Early playing cards at Ulm were called *Briefes* or papers; subsequently they became known as *Karten*, perhaps after they began to be manufactured for export to Italy.

TARO RIVER AND TARO VILLAGE

Sylvia Mann, writing in *Collecting Playing Cards*, theorizes that tarot cards were either invented or popularized in the valley of the Taro River, tributary of the

Po River in north-central Italy, which runs close to the locality where some of the earliest Italian *tarocchi* cards are known to have existed. Alternatively, proponents of the oriental origin of cards cite the village of Taro, located in the Naga Hills district of Upper Burma, and Lake Tarok Tso in southwest Tibet.

CARNIVAL AND PROCESSIONALS

Gertrude Moakley, writing in 1966 in *The Tarot Cards Painted by Bonifacio Bembo*, advances the theory that the Visconti-Sforza *tarocchi* packs from mid-fifteenth-century Milan were pictorial representations of the popular triumphs—led by Bagatino, the Carnival King, and which ended with the Fool. These processionals signaled the end of the Carnival festivities and preceded the season of Lent.

ROSICRUCIANS, TEMPLARS AND FREEMASONS

The name "Rosicrucian" derives either from an appellation of the supposed founder, Christian Rosenkreuz, or from *rosa*, a rose, and *crux*, a cross. The emblem of the order is a cross with a red rose in the center. Tarot cards are believed by some to contain the total knowledge of the entire world, as preserved in the sacred and supreme symbolic book of the Rosicrucian movement and other secret societies such as the Knights Templars and Freemasons. The Rosicrucians, also known as the Ancient Mystic Order Rosae Crucis, study the mysteries and scientific laws of the world and the application of esoteric religious doctrine to modern life. The order, which arose in the late sixteenth century, allegedly traces its origin to Egypt in 1500 B.C., when the Pharaohs formed a society of thinkers and scientists. The tarot trumps are believed to have been used around the turn of the last century in the ceremonies of the Rosicrucian organization known as The Order of the Golden Dawn.

The Knights Templars of the Temple of Solomon originally were a military order, founded by a Burgundian, Hugues de Payns, and a French knight, Godeffroi de St. Omer, in 1119 for the purpose of protecting pilgrims journeying into the Holy Land. In time the organization incurred the ire of both the Church and the ruling nobility, which resulted in denunciation of the Templars and their dispersion into secret sects.

The Freemasons were members of a medieval guild of skilled masons that preserved ancient practices and rituals.

OCCULT REVIVAL

Any summary of the origins and development of tarot cards would be incomplete without mention of the French occult revival that spread throughout the West in the nineteenth century. Not only did it give an important place to tarot as a magical system, but by the end of the nineteenth century its teachings had spread to England where it had a profound influence on the development of twentieth-century tarot.

Court de Gebelin in 1781 in Paris proposed his theory that tarot was an occult device of Egyptian origin. After his death in 1787, his theories were expounded to a receptive and occult-minded public by Alliette, the French wigmaker who preferred to spell his name backwards, as Etteilla.

The tarot revival flourished in France at a time when the power of the monarchy was waning. In a climate of revolution and change, secret societies came into favor. In 1813 a form of Hebraic occultism was ambitiously propagated by Antoine Fabre d'Olivet in *Les vers dorés de Pythagore expliqués*, which was followed in 1816 by *La langue hebraique restituée*. In 1823 an author using the penname Lenain published *La Science kabbalistique ou l'art de connaitre les bons genies*, which contains an explanation of the Tetragrammaton, the four letters that form the sacred name of God. A two-volume historical analysis of magic, initiation and related subjects entitled *Des sciences occultes ou essai sur la magie, les prodigues et les miracles* was published in 1829 by Eusèbe Salverte. These volumes and many others helped to feed the rising interest in the occult.

In 1856 Eliphas Lévi published *Le Dogme et Rituel de la Haute Magie*. Lévi, whose real name was Alphonse Louis Constant, was the first writer to link the twenty-two Major Arcana with the twenty-two letters of the Hebrew alphabet. He also linked the four suits in the card pack with the Tetragrammaton, the four Hebrew letters of Yod-He-Vau-He, usually transliterated as YHWH or JHVH (Yahweh or Jehovah) and used as a substitute for the ineffable name of God.

Eliphas Levi

Christopher McIntosh, writing in 1972 in *Eliphas Lévi and the French Occult Revival*, describes a meeting in Paris in 1861 between Lévi and an Englishman named Kenneth Mackenzie, a member of the Societas Rosicruciana in Anglia. Lévi purportedly showed Mackenzie a small volume containing drawings of the twenty-two Major Arcana that Lévi had made himself by hand. Although he intended to publish his own pack eventually, the drawings as a complete set were never issued. When Lévi died at age sixty-five in 1875, his many followers enthusiastically continued his theories about magic and the association between tarot and the Kabbalah.

Paul Christian, whose real name was Jean Baptiste Pitois, was a disciple of Lévi. He held a post at the library of the Ministry of Public Instruction in Paris, which put him in contact with many strange books and manuscripts on magic and the occult. Christian devised a system of the tarot based upon Egyptian origins and involved with kabbalistic astrology. His best known works are *L'Homme rouge des Tuileries*, published in 1863, and *Histoire de la Magie*, issued in 1870.

Pictures of the Court de Gebelin cards were reproduced in 1888 by Ely Star in *Les Mystères de l'Horoscope*. In 1889 Oswald Wirth, the Swiss occultist and disciple of the Marquis Stanislas de Guaita, published his tarot designs in a limited edition of one hundred hand-painted copies of *Le livre de Thot. Les 22 arcanes du Tarot dessinés à l'usage des initiés sur les indications de Stanislas de Guaita*. Wirth was a Mason and a member of the Theosophical Society founded by Madame Blavatsky in New York in 1875. Guaita co-founded (with Josephin Peladan) the Kabbalistic Order of the Rose-Cross in 1888.

In 1889 there appeared *Le Tarot des Bohémiens* by Papus, whose real name was Gerard Encausse. *The Tarot of the Bohemians* is an erudite work that deals with tarot in terms of numerology, the Tree of Life and the sacred Tetragrammaton. Papus was a member of the Theosophical Society and eventually took over leadership of one of the obscure Martinist groups. He also founded the occult journal, *Le Voile d'Isis*. Eventually he became involved with the Kabbalistic Order of the Rose-Cross.

In England MacGregor Mathers, whose real name was Samuel Liddell Mathers, published in 1888 a small book on tarot fortune-telling, *The Tarot, Its Occult Signification, Use in Fortune-Telling, and Method of Play*. Mathers was connected with the Societas Rosicruciana in Anglia, known as *Soc. Ros.*, and in 1888 he helped to found the Hermetic Order of the Golden Dawn, which counted among its members Aleister Crowley, Arthur Edward Waite and the poet William Butler Yeats. Working with Pamela Colman Smith in 1910, Waite created a "rectified" tarot pack known as the Rider-Waite deck, which was first published by Rider and Company. Waite also published *The Pictorial Key to the Tarot*, subtitled *Being Fragments of a Secret Tradition under the Veil of Divination*.

Crowley also authored a guide to tarot, *The Book of Thoth*, based upon designs with erotic symbolism produced for him by Lady Frieda Harris. Crowley, who died in 1947, was heavily involved with the Order of the Temple of the Orient or O.T.O., a German occult organization preoccupied with sex magic.

In England the Insight Institute published a tarot deck utilizing designs drawn from the Tarot of Marseilles and Rider-Waite decks.

In the United States Paul Foster Case, an American occultist born in 1884 and influenced by The Order of the Golden Dawn, formed the Builders of the Adytum. He

Arthur Edward Waite

published *The Tarot: A Key to the Wisdom of the Ages* and issued a black and white set of tarot cards drawn by Jessie Burns Parke and modeled after the Rider-Waite pack.

The Church of Light issued a tarot pack based upon Egyptian symbolism as described by Elbert Benjamine, who wrote under the pseudonym C. C. Zain.

The J. A. Knapp tarot deck was produced under the auspices of Manley Palmer Hall, founder of the Philosophical Society. The Knapp cards contain one Hebrew letter at the bottom of each Major Arcana.

No one knows whether the original concept of tarot developed in the East or in Europe. Nevertheless, the development of the allegorical playing cards received strong impetus in Italy during the mid-fifteenth century and spread to France about the beginning of the sixteenth century. From France the game, utilizing Italian suit signs, was disseminated throughout Europe. In the nineteenth century the French occult revival did more than anything else to create widespread interest in the magical tarot, its profound symbolism and arcane meanings.

III
EARLIEST REFERENCES TO PLAYING CARDS

SOME OF THE EARLIEST published references to playing cards in Europe, either standard decks or *tarocchi* packs, are decrees, prohibitions, treatises and poems.

Bern, 1367 In a list of legal documents dating from about the end of the fourteenth century for the canton of Bern, there is reference to a prohibition against playing cards in the year 1367. The prohibition, believed to have been written by Konrad Justinger, is presently housed at the Österreichische Nationalbibliothek, Vienna.

Naibbe, 1376 A game called *naibbe* (cards) was forbidden in a decree by the city of Florence in 1376.

Johannes, 1377 Brother Johannes von Rheinfelden, a German monk, wrote in 1377 in Switzerland in his *Tractatus de moribus et disciplina humanae conversationis* about a game called *ludus cartarum*. The game reputedly described the state of the world as it then existed. The treatise refers to four kings—each holding the sign of his suit—followed by two "*marschalli*"—the first holding the sign upward in his hand in the same manner as the king, and the other holding the sign downward. These are followed by ten pip cards bearing the same suit signs, which indicates a pack of fifty-two cards. At the end of the manuscript is a note that implies it was copied in 1472; thus, the date 1377 is suspect.

Wencesles and Jeanne, 1379 Alexandre Pinchart, writing in 1870, cites an account book of Wencesles and Jeanne, who reigned in the old duchy of Brabant from the year 1355, that describes a fete held at Brussels in 1379 at which cards were played. On the 14th of May, 1379, the receiver general of Brabant gave to Monsieur and Madame four peters and two florins, valued at eight and a half moutons, to purchase a pack of cards, *quartespel mette copen*.

Archives of Marseilles, 1381 According to Henry René D'Allemagne, in the notarial archives of Marseilles, recorded by Laurent Aycardi, there is reference to an interdiction against the game of *nahipi* on August 30, 1381. The archives relate that Jacques Jean, son of a merchant in the city of Marseilles, at the moment of embarking on a trip to Alexandria, promised to abstain from engaging in any gambling including playing at cards.

Ordinance of Lille, 1382 D'Allemagne also cites an ordinance of the city of Lille, dated 1382, when Lille belonged to France, which forbid various games including dice and *quartes*, an early word for cards.

Poupart, Charles VI and Gringonneur, 1392 In the year 1392, or in the following year, there appears an entry in the account books of Charles Poupart, treasurer to Charles VI of France who lost his sanity. The entry reads:

> Given to Jacquemin Gringonneur, painter, for three packs of cards, gilt and colored, and variously ornamented, for the amusement of the king, fifty-six sols of Paris.

Morelli, 1393 The *Chronicle di Giovani Morelli* of the year 1393 printed for the first time in Florence in 1728 in *Historica Antica di Ricordano Morelli* by Manni, contains a warning against the use of dice by children. Morelli describes *naibi* as a kind of game, and from the context it appears it was one at which only children played, possibly for instructive purposes.

Charles V, 1369, and Prévôt of Paris, 1397 In a decree against gambling issued by Charles V of France in 1369, playing cards are not mentioned, even though other games of hazard are enumerated, including trictrac, tennis, ninepins, quoits, pall-mall and billiards. Twenty-eight years later the Prévôt de Paris, in an ordinance dated January 22, 1397, forbade "working people from playing tennis, ball, *cards*, or ninepins, excepting only on holidays." Thus, the introduction of playing cards into France occurred sometime between 1369 and 1397, probably closer to the latter date.

Ulm, 1397 According to Neubronner, an administrator at Ulm, Germany, about the year 1806, there was in the archives of that city an ancient parchment volume, called the Red Book on account of its red initial letters, which contained a prohibition against card playing dated 1397.

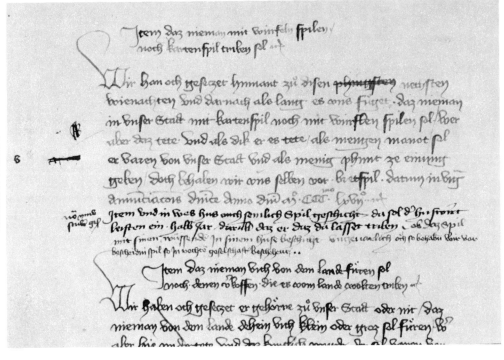

Fourteenth-Century Prohibition Against Cards Believed to have been written by the Bern chronicler, Konrad Justinger, this prohibition against different games includes playing cards (kartenspil) in the fifth line from the top; the date MCCCLXVII (1367) appears on line nine.

Ludus cartarum Brother Johannes, a German monk, wrote in 1377 in Switzerland about a game called ludus cartarum, and described fifty-two cards, but made no mention of tarot cards or any Major Arcana. Town authorities and bishops sought to prevent the use of playing cards in games of gambling; Johannes commented in his treatise on the value of playing cards for the furtherance of morals and education.

Euterpe The eighteenth card in the Tarocchi of Mantegna series, Euterpe, is depicted in an early codex from the library of the Duke of Urbino that is presently housed at the Biblioteca Vaticana. This and other prints of the Tarocchi of Mantegna series are contained in a poem by Ludovico Lazzarelli entitled "De Imaginibus gentilium Deorum" ("Of the Images of the Gods of the Pagans").

Synod of Langres, 1404 Laurentii Bochelli, writing in 1609 in *Decreta ecclesiae Gallicanae*, relates that at the Synod of Langres in 1404 Cardinal Louis de Bar, Bishop of Langres, forbade the clergy from indulging in various games including cards.

St. Bernardin, 1423 St. Bernardin of Siena preached in 1423 at the Church of San Petronio, Bologna, against the vices of gaming in general and playing cards in particular. He spoke of a pack of fifty-six cards, including queens, without mentioning *atutti*, which suggests that either the emblematic *atutti* were not known at the time or were in use as an acceptable children's game.

Decembrio, 1440 Around 1440 Decembrio, the official biographer of Filippo Maria Visconti, third Duke of Milan, wrote that the duke enjoyed playing at a game that used painted figures. According to Robert Steele, writing in 1900 in "A Notice of the *Ludus Triumphorum*," Decembrio also relates that Duke Filippo paid fifteen hundred gold pieces to Marziano da Tortona for a pack of cards decorated with images of gods, emblematic animals and figures of birds.

Magistracy of Venice, 1441 The magistracy of Venice issued an order in 1441 forbidding the introduction of foreign manufactured and printed colored figures into the city under the penalty of forfeiting such articles and being fined. This order appears to have been aimed at German card makers as a result of a petition from the fellowship of painters at Venice, who claimed that card making had fallen into total decay in Venice because great quantities of playing cards and colored printed figures were being imported.

Isabelle of Lorraine, 1449 According to P. Durrieu, writing in 1911 in *Michelino de Besozzo et les relations entre l'art italien et l'art français*, a series of sixteen cards is described in a letter dated 1449 from Jacobo Antonio Marcello, a servant of King René of Anjou, to Isabelle of Lorraine, first wife of King René.

Treatise of Theology, 1457 The *Treatise of Theology* written in 1457 by Saint Anthony, Bishop of Florence, refers to playing cards and tarot, thus suggesting that the trumps or trionfi were considered a separate game from playing cards, which comprised court cards and numeral or pip cards.

Parliament Rolls, 1464, and Statute, 1496 In the Parliament Rolls for the year 1464 playing cards are mentioned among other articles that are not to be imported into England. The prohibition suggests that cards were then manufactured in England. The records for King Henry VII include private expense money for losses at cards. Margaret, daughter of the monarch, played at cards soon after her arrival at Edinburgh, where she married James IV of Scotland. Cards are also mentioned in a statute in the eleventh year of the reign of Henry VII in 1496. It is not known whether cards were first brought to England by Eastern travelers or were introduced by the Spaniards, Italians or French.

Biblioteca Vaticana, Codices, Lazzarelli, 1471 Two codices at the Biblioteca Vaticana are illustrated with early *tarocchi* figures from the Tarocchi of Mantegna series. One of the manuscripts includes a poem by Ludovico Lazzarelli, entitled "*De Imaginibus gentilium Deorum*," presumed from the dedication to Duke Borso d'Este of Ferrara to date from 1471, the year in which he became duke and died. The poem describes classical gods based upon *tarocchi* figures. Allegedly, Lazzarelli came across the *tarocchi* prints in a Venetian bookstore and the figures of antique gods and liberal arts inspired him to compose his poem. Four figures—Juno, Neptune, Pluto and Victoria—are included in the codices but are not part of the Tarocchi of Mantegna series; probably they are the invention of Lazzarelli.

Ulm, 1474 An old manuscript chronicle, finished in 1474 and located in the library of the Stadthaus at Ulm, contains the notation that "playing cards were sent in large bales into Italy, Sicily, and other parts by sea, receiving in exchange spices and other merchandise."

Platina, 1475 Baptista Platina, writing in 1475 in his treatise *De Honesta Voluptate*, instructs his readers on the enjoyment of life. He mentions cards as a game gentlemen may play after dinner or supper to divert their minds, since "deep thinking after a hearty meal impedes digestion."

Collection of Biblioteca Vaticana

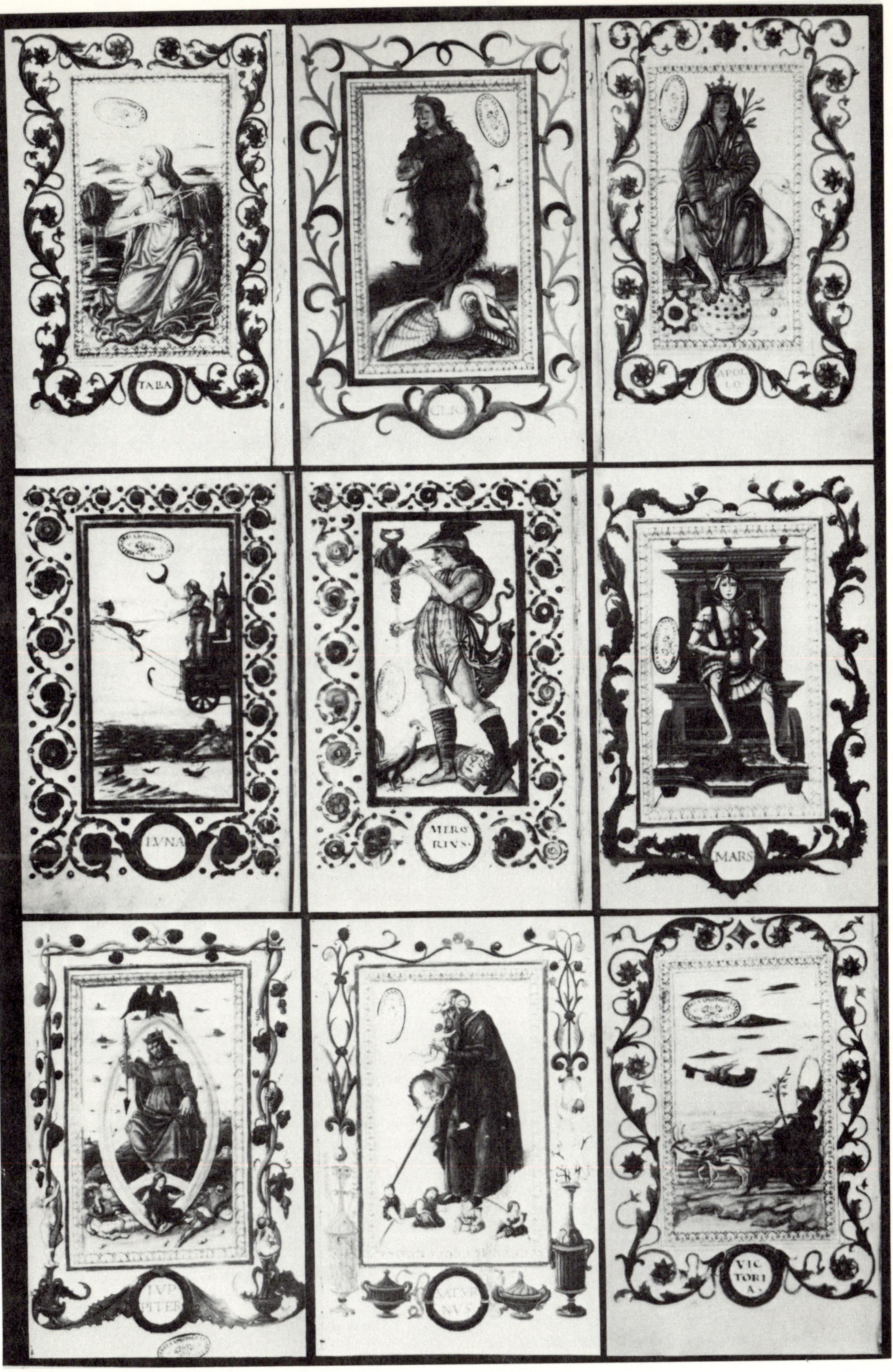

Codex at the Vatican *Nine of the twenty-two* tarocchi *illustrations contained in the fifteenth-century codex that includes Ludovico Lazzarelli's poem,* "De Imaginibus gentilium Deorum." *The titles of the tarocchi illustrations shown above, and their corresponding numbers in the Tarocchi of Mantegna prints, are Talia (XVI), Clio (XVIIII), Apollo (Apollon XX), Luna (XXXXI),* **Mercurius** *(Mercurio XXXXII), Mars (Marte XXXXV), Jupites (Jupiter XXXXVI), Saturnus (Saturna XXXXVII) and Victoria, one of four figures not found in the Tarocchi of Mantegna series and presumably the invention of Lazzarelli.*

"However," cautions Platina, "there is to be no cheating nor desire of gain, and any stakes are to be merely nominal, lest bad passions become excited and the process of healthy concoction be disturbed."

Martius, 1488 Galcottus Martius, a contemporary of Platina, is perhaps the earliest writer who speculated on the allegorical meanings of the four suits. Writing about 1488–1490 in his treatise *De Doctrina Promiscua*, Martius observes that the inventor of the game of cards must have been a man of shrewd wit when one considers the significance of swords, spears, cups and country loaves. When there is need of strength, as indicated by swords and spears, Martius suggests that many are better than just a few; in matters of meat and drink, however, as indicated by the loaves and cups, a little is better than a great or excessive amount, for it is certain that abstemious persons are of more lively wit than gluttons and drunkards, and much superior in the management of business. The cups are goblets for wine; what Martius calls country loaves, judging from their form and color (thin pieces of bread of a yellow color), are the marks that are ignorantly supposed to signify pieces of money.

Boiardo's Tutte le Opera In the late fifteenth century Count Matteo Maria Boiardo (1441–1494) described the *trionfi* or Major Arcana cards in a set of verses—two sonnets and seventy-eight *terzine*, one for each of the *tarocchi* cards. The first trump is The Fool, followed by cards titled with various personal emotions and experiences—Idleness, Labor, Desire, Reason, Secrecy, Grace, Disdain, Patience, Error, Perseverance, Doubt, Faith, Deception, Wisdom, Chance, Modesty, Peril, Experience, Time, Oblivion and Strength. The four suits are darts or arrows (for love), vases (for hope), eyes (for jealousy) and whips (for fear). Each of the sixteen court cards was represented by an important person from ancient times, or a mythological figure such as Venus for the queen of arrows, Judith for the queen of vases and Ptolemy for the cavalier of whips.

Sermones de Ludo Cumalis, 1500 A Latin manuscript, *Sermones de Ludo Cumalis*, dating from about 1500, contains the earliest known written list of the atouts or Major Arcana of the tarot series as we know them today. A page from the manuscript and the listing of titles is described in Chapter I (opposite page 1 and on page 2).

Berni, 1526 Francesco Berni, writing in *Capitolo del Gioco della Primiera*, makes what appears to be the earliest printed reference to *tarocchi*. The author styles himself "Messer Pietropaulo da San Chirico" and in the course of his mock commentary he describes the game of *primiera*, its laws and mode of playing. The commentary about *tarocchi* states:

> Another as more pleasing, prolonging the entertainment, and giving pleasure to the company in looking at the paintings, has found that the *Tarocchi* are an excellent game, and he seems to be in his glory, when he has in hand to the number of two hundred cards, which he can scarcely hold, and which, not to be overlooked, he shuffles as well as he can under the table. Let him look to it, who is pleased with the game of *Tarocco*, that the only signification of this word *Tarocco*, is stupid, foolish, simple, fit only to be used by bakers, cobblers, and the vulgar, to play at most for the fourth part of a *Carlino*, at *Tarocchi*, or at *Trionfi*, or any *Sminchiate* [sic] whatever: which in every way signifies only foolery and idleness, feasting the eye with the sun, and the moon, and the twelve (*signs*) as children do.

Marcolino's Le Sorti, 1540 The earliest printed work that expressly treats the subject of fortune-telling and divination with cards appears to be *Le Sorti di Francesco Marcolino da Forli, intitolate Giardino di Pensieri allo Illustrissimo Signore Hercole Estense, Duca di Ferrara*, published in Venice in 1540. This book was reissued in a second edition in 1550 under the title, *Le Ingeniose Sorti composte per Francesco Marcolini da Forli. Intitulate Giardino di Pensieri, Novamente Ristampate, e Novo et Bellissimo Ordine Riformate*. The author utilizes only nine cards from the suit of coins—king, knight, page, ten, nine, eight, seven, two and ace. Although the work does not depict tarot-type cards, it unquestionably proves that cards were used in divination in Italy in the early sixteenth century. The book resolves fifty questions, thirteen of which relate to men, thirteen to women, and the remaining twenty-four to both sexes. Questions are answered by a kind of oracular triplet, to which the reader is directed by drawing one or two cards. Besides the elaborate frontispiece and the numerous small cuts of cards, there are ninety-nine woodcuts throughout the volume that are emblematic of virtues and follies, and also depict a different celebrated philosopher or moralist from antiquity who presides over each group of forty-five possible answers to each question. The woodcuts in the Marcolino volume were designed by Giuseppe Porta and Salviati. Samuel Weller Singer, writing in 1816, suggested that Marcolino may have taken the idea for his book of fate from *Trionpho della Fortuna*, published in the year 1526 by Sigismondo Fanti of Ferrara, and also printed at Venice. Fanti's book resolves various questions through the use of the signs of the zodiac, the constellations, the sybils and various astrological personages. Instead of a three-line oracle, four-line stanzas are used to resolve the questions. Instead of cards, Fanti uses a pair of dice or the chance number on a dial that contains twenty-one figures.

Aretino's Les Cartes Parlantes, 1540 Pietro Aretino, writing about 1540 in *La Terza, et ultima parte de' Ragionamenti del divino Pietro Aretino*, describes cards as a hazardous game at which both money and credit may be lost. Each card is described with a more or less ingenious interpretation or allusion. Thus, The Pope represents fidelity and faithfulness in the game and sincerity in the player. The Emperor suggests the laws that govern people. The valet or knave represents the servitude of some to the game. Swords symbolize the death of those who despair while playing, batons the punishment for cheating. The cups recall the practice of drinking to settle disputes and the coins are the currency with which the game is played. The supplement dealing with cards—*Les Cartes Parlantes*—was not actually published until 1589.

Vives' Ludus Chartarum, 1545 Ludovico Vives, writing in 1545 in *Ludus Chartarum, Dialogus*, describes the method of playing the game of *tarocchi*. The trumps apparently were dealt counterclockwise, from right to left. It seems to have been a game like whist, with a permanent set of trumps and a complicated counting of values. In the two red suits, cups and coins, the numeral cards reverse their values and the six captures the seven, the seven captures the eight, etc.

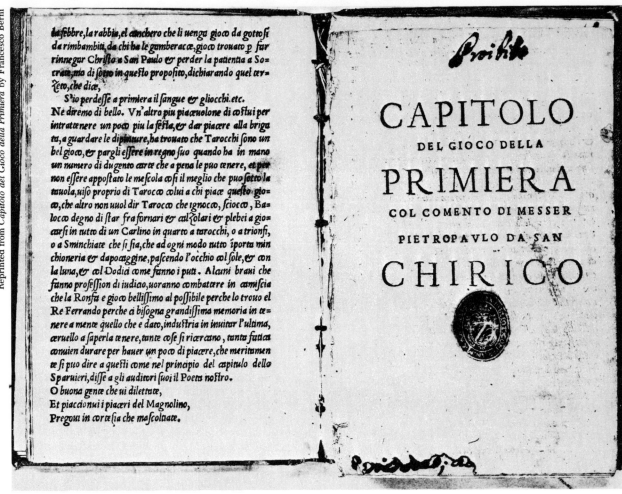

Capitolo del Gioco della Primiera   Title page (right) *and paragraph dealing with the game of* tarocchi (left).

Lollio, 1550   Flavio Alberti Lollio published in Venice in 1550 a general invective against gaming, and specified the game of *tarocco*, in a poem entitled "*Invettiva contra Il Giuoco del Tarocco*." Freely translated, the sixteenth-century work condemns *tarocco* as follows:

I have always been of the opinion that the most pleasant game one could play with cards was that of Tarocco: and now and then for amusement, and to lift the weary and afflicted spirit, I used to entertain myself with it; whiling away those hours least conducive to study; reminding myself that illustrious men had by a game lightened the burden of their weighty affairs, and relieved lofty thoughts and tedious cares.

In this fashion Palamede amused himself (if one may make a comparison) to lighten the worries and boredom which weighed upon his heart during the long siege of Troy, when he rediscovered dice. So, too, played the great Domitian: as well as Galba, the good Trojan, Nerva and many others, that for the sake of brevity I will forbear to mention.

But now I realize how deep in error I was; and I regret it: because this is a treacherous game, deceitful and inconsistent more than any other; full of torment, anguish, and trouble, which very seldom ever consoles anyone.

Evil game, perfidious and false, game that squanders your money, game that would impoverish Attalo and Midas, since it is the cousin of the Bassetta: And while man hopes to derive pleasure from it, it always keeps him in pain and fear.

Now the cards are being dealt: the first hand appears good, so you accept the invitation and you play again: the ones that follow show a new face, but they no longer care about your affairs: and thus you are left rather suspended: the other player believing himself to be favored by the cards will raise the stakes: then, pierced with shame, grief, envy and anger, you throw in your hand, and with lowered head come to naught.

Such a man does not feel any lesser sorrow than a captain who, believing he has won the battle, cries out Victory, Victory; but sees by a counterattack that his men are defeated and dispersed.

Thereupon two new hands follow, now good, now poor, and when you are waiting for the last one which might aid you, having already invited it, you see coming to you (alas, great pain) such raffish cards as may kill you, the complete opposite of your needs. So you are inflamed with pique, and while wrought with spite, you grudgingly pick up the remaining cards, which are twenty. These fill your hands and for a long while they give you toil and trouble in arranging Money, Clubs, Cups, and Swords and Triumphs. They must be put in order one by one, as a good shepherd who, having many sheep, gathers them into separate flocks. Thereupon, if you have four or five cards of *Ronfa*, you fear lest the King perish with the other court cards; whereupon the heart is consumed and the brain is tortured, suspended between hope and apprehension. Such is the exhaustion and the heartbreak that you are forced to hold up as a mirror such terrible cards that make you languish; as if you were a urinal, you are bound to serve your two other companions, answering to each move, and if by ignorance or by error you throw down an inappropriate card, you hear their voices rise up to heaven; and do not think that now your pains are at an end: one must reckon with any trivial card one plays, or else all ends in ruin. And if you sometimes chance on a good game, it will be played so badly that you lose a dozen or two, at times all of them.

How many times are you unable to cover The Fool?

Where did I leave off that tedious counting of each Triumph that comes out?

What else do they mean, The Magician and The Fool, other than that they be swindler and trickster?

What other meaning have The Popess, The Chariot, The Traitor, The Wheel, The Hunchback, Strength, The Star, The Sun, The Moon, Death and Hell, and all the rest of this motley crew? And that fantastic and bizarre name of *Tarocco*, is it without etymology?

Meanwhile, I fondly pray, with offerings and vows to the gods in heaven, that they cause all ink to vanish at once: the yellow, the green, the white, the red, and all other colors by which cards and Tarocco are made; that they make all paper go up in smoke; and that no one ever be found who dares to carve designs in wood by which the cards are made; so that this art so damaging and evil shall be at once wiped from people's hearts; and that posterity shall find no trace of it, and forever its memory will be obliterated.

It is interesting to note that *tarocco* was apparently played by three persons and that *cards* and *tarocco* were considered separate games.

Bertoni, 1550 G. Bertoni describes a poem, *Poesie leggende costumanze del medio evo*, dated about 1550, which associates the *tarocchi* trumps with the ladies of the court of Isabella D'Este of Ferrara. For example, The Angel or Judgment is for Diana Trotta, who through her beauty becomes divine; The Sun is for Virginia Trotta, who blinds with splendor all who look upon her; The Chariot is for Isabella Estense, who triumphs as a woman by her greatness; and The Fool is for Mamma Riminaldi, whose beauty includes her craziness. The sequence and title of each of the *tarocchi* trumps cited in the poem runs as follows: *Il Mondo* (The World), *La Justicia* (Justice), *L'Agnolo* (The Angel), *Il Sole* (The Sun), *La Luna* (The Moon), *La Stella* (The Star), *La Casa del Diavolo* (The House of the Devil), *Il Diavolo* (The Devil), *La Morte* (Death), *Il Traditore* (The Traitor), *Il Gobbo* (The Hunchback), *La Ruota* (The Wheel), *La Fortezza* (Strength), *L'Amore* (The Lovers), *Il Carro* (The Chariot), *La Temperanza* (Temperance), *Il Papa* (The Pope), *La Papessa* (The Popess), *L'Imperadore* (The Emperor), *L'Imperatrice* (The Empress), *Il Bagatino* (The Magician), *Il Matto* (The Fool).

Ringhieri, 1551 Innocentio Ringhieri wrote in Bologna, 1551, in *Cento Giuochi liberali et d'ingegno*, about the magnificent "Game of the King" which had suit signs representing moral virtues: cups (temperance), columns (strength), swords (justice) and mirrors (prudence).

Grazzini, 1559 In 1559 Antonio Francesco Grazzini wrote in *Tutti i trionfi, carri, mascherate o canti carnascialeschi andati per Firenze dal tempo del magnifico Lorenzo de' Medici fino all' anno* about the *tarocchi* trumps.

Susio, 1570 Giambattista Susio wrote around 1570 a poem that associated the ladies at the court of Mantua with the *tarocchi* trumps.

Bargagli, 1572 Girolamo Bargagli wrote in 1572 in *Dialogo da Giuochi* a brief passage stating that he saw the game of *tarocchi* played: "And furthermore (added *Mansueto*, the meek one), I saw the game of tarocchi played, and each participant was given the name from a card, and then the reasons were stated aloud why each participant had been attributed to such a tarocchi card."

Garzoni, 1587 Thomaso Garzoni, whose *La Piazza universale di tutte le Professioni del Mondo, e nobili ed ignobili* was first published in Venice in 1589, cites the game of tarot among the tavern games of the day. In the chapter entitled "*De' Giocatori in universale, ed in particolare*," Garzoni describes various personages in association with each of the *tarocchi* trumps. The passage listing the suits, pip cards, courts and trumps contains the following titles for the trump cards:

Il Mondo, la Giustitia, l'Angelo, il Sole, la Luna, la Stella, il Fuoco, il Diavolo, la Morte, l'Impiccato, il Vecchio, la Ruota, la Fortezza, l'Amore, il Carro, la Temperanza, il Papa, la Papessa, l'Imperadore, l'Imperatrice, il Bagatello and il Matto.

Bynneman H. Bynneman, a writer of the sixteenth century, makes mention of the pagan imagery of early cards:

The Playe of Cards is an invention of the Devill, which he found out, that he might the easilier bring in ydolatrie amongst men. For the Kings and Coate Cards that we use nowe, were in olde time the images of idols and false gods: which since they that would seeme christians, have chaunged into Charlemaigne, Launcelot, Hector, and such like names, because they would not seeme to imitate their idolatrie therein, and yet maintaine the playe itself.—*A Treatise wherein Dicing, Dauncing, Vaine Playes, and Enterludes, with other idle Pastimes, commonly used on the Sabbath day, are reproved by the Authoritie of the Word of God and Auntient Writers. Made Dialogue-wise, by John Northbrooke.*

Undoubtedly there exist additional early references to both standard and *tarocchi* playing cards, but the foregoing provides a representative sampling.

INTERPOLATIONS AND TRANSLATION ERRORS

It is important to note that some transcripts and translations of important early works contain interpolations. Additionally, some manuscripts attempt to assign an early date to the origin of cards while the facts support a more recent origin.

***Pipozzo di Sandro*'s Trattato del governo** In an Italian manuscript entitled *Trattato del governo della famiglia, or Treatise on the Government of the Family*, allegedly composed in 1299 by Pipozzo di Sandro, the author refers to playing cards: "*Se guichera di danari o cosi o alle carte, gli apparachierai la via.*" That is, "If he plays for money in this manner, or at cards, you must facilitate the means of his doing so." However, the transcript of Pipozzo's manuscript is probably from the fifteenth century and cannot be relied upon regarding the origin of cards.

Das Guldin Spil Ingold describes in *Das Guldin Spil* (*The Golden Game*) the principal games in Germany and he says of playing cards, "The game is right deceitful; and, as I have read, was first brought into Germany in the year 1300." However, *Das Guldin Spil* was written and published at Augsburg in 1472 and the author's comments on an event supposed to have taken place 172 years earlier are nothing more than hearsay.

Synod of Würzburg According to Wilhelm Schreiber, writing in 1937, the earliest reference to playing cards is in the *Synod of Würzburg* of 1329, when certain games, including cards, were forbidden by the government and the church. "*Ludos alearum, cartarum, schacorum, taxillorum, annulorum et globorum monachis et monialibus prohibemus districte.*" Schreiber further believes that the Würzburger prohibition was taken from an earlier edict dating from 1316 in Mainz. However, there is nothing to substantiate the date of this claim.

William de Guilleville's "Le Pelerinaige de l'Homme" In Verard's 1511 edition of William de Guilleville's allegorical poem entitled "*Le Pelerinaige de l'Homme*," originally completed about 1330, two verses allegedly refer to cards. In folio XLV Oysivete tempts the pilgrim to forego the "right way" by recounting to him the pleasures enjoyed by those who place themselves under her guidance:

> *. . . Je meyne gens au bois,*
> *Et la leur fais-je veoir danseurs,*
> *Jeux de basteaulx et de jougleurs,*
> *Jeux de tables et deschiquiers,*
> *De boulles et mereilliers.*
> *De cartes, jeux de tricherie,*
> *Et de mainte autre muserie.*

In folio LXXII *quartes*, as the word is spelled, is included as one of the games prohibited:

> *Mains ieux qui sont denyez,*
> *Aux merelles, quartes, et dez . . .*

However, an earlier manuscript copy of Guilleville's poem at the Bibliothèque Nationale does not contain the word *cartes* or *quartes*:

> *Ja leur fais je ceoir baleurs,*
> *Gieux de bastizux et de jugleurs,*
> *De tables et de eschequiers,*
> *De boules et de mereliers,*
> *De dez et d'entregsterie,*
> *Et de mainte autre muserie.*
>
> *Tant l'aime que je en suis sote,*
> *Et que en pers souvent ma cote,*
> *A mains jeux qui sont devees,*
> *Aux merelles, tables, et dez.*

Thus, we are forced to conclude that *cartes* and *quartes* are later interpolations and were not cited in the original fourteenth-century poem.

Renard le Contrefait The following four lines from the romance *Renard le Contrefait* have been put forth as evidence that cards were known in France at least as early as 1341, the year in which the romance was finished:

> *Si comme fols et folles sont,*
> *Oui pour gagner, au bordel vont;*
> *Jouent aux dez, aux cartes, aux tables,*
> *Oui a Dieu ne sont delectables.*

That is,

> If like fools, and fools they are,
> In order to win to the bordello go;
> Playing dice, cards and trictrac,
> Which to God are not delightful.

However, another manuscript of the same romance, apparently about a hundred years older, contains the same verse except that the word *cartes* is omitted:

> *Jouent a geux de dez ou de tables.*

That is,

> Playing at games of dice and trictrac.

Therefore, the word *cartes* appears to be a later interpolation.

Alphonse XI and Guevara's *Familiar Epistles* It has been claimed that the statutes of 1342 of Alphonse XI, King of Castile, forbade playing cards to the knights of the Order of the Band, indicating that cards were known in Spain at the beginning of the fourteenth century. However, this assertion appears to occur only in the French edition of Anthony Guevara's *Familiar Epistles*, translated by Dr. Guterrey, and is not found in the original Spanish edition or the translated English edition. Thus, this seems to be another instance of interpolation.

Le Roman du Roi Meliadus de Leonnoys Samuel Weller Singer describes a miniature contained in *The Romance of King Meliadus* that shows a king and three noblemen at play with cards while three others observe the game. The cards shown in the print are the five and two of coins and two of staves. It is believed that *Le Roman du Roi*

Meliadus de Leonnoys by Helie de Borron was written sometime in the latter half of the fourteenth century, but we do not know if the illustration postdates the writing of the manuscript. No mention of playing cards appears in the manuscript, but it is not unusual for early graphic illustrations to have no reference to the text they accompany.

Historique et Chronique de Provence Casar Nostradamus, writing in 1614 in *Historique et Chronique de Provence*, suggests that cards made their appearance about the year 1361 in Provence, the southeastern region of France bordering on the Mediterranean, and that the knave (*valet*) was then called *Tuchim*, the name given to a formidable band of robbers who were ravaging the region. But there is no evidence to substantiate this claim.

Magasin Pittoresque An article on cards in *Magasin Pittoresque* for April, 1836, contains an illustration represented by the author as being copied from a miniature in a manuscript of the *Cité de Dieu*, translated from St. Augustine by Raoul de Presle, who began the translation in 1371 and finished it in 1375. The author contends the miniature is of the same date as the translation and therefore seeks to validate the existence of playing cards in the early 1370s. However, it is not uncommon for later transcripts to include illustrations unknown at the time of the original edition. Additionally, the costumes of the persons in the miniature are suggestive of the reign of Charles VI in 1422 rather than the reign of Charles V, 1364–1380. Therefore, it is safe to conclude the miniature does not prove the existence of cards in the early 1370s.

Jehan de Saintre Writing in 1757, Jean Baptiste Bullet attempts to arrive at a precise date for the origin of cards by citing the *Chronique du Petit Jehan de Saintre*, one of the pages of Charles V, in which the pages are mentioned as playing at dice and, allegedly, cards. Since Charles V ascended to the throne in 1364 and died in 1380, if the chronicle is valid, this would serve to confine the possible date of the origin of cards to an interval of sixteen years. However, the chronicle is believed to have been written by Antoine de Lassale in 1459 and, therefore, the word "cards" is probably an interpolation of the author.

Bussi, Covelluzzo and Viterbo Feliciano Bussi relates in 1742 in his *History of Viterbo* that in 1379, during the schism caused by the opposition of the anti-Pope Clement to Urban VI, the mercenary troops of each party committed all manner of annoyances and spoliations in the Roman states, including the seizure of cattle. "And yet," adds the historian, "who could believe it! In this same year of so much distress there was introduced into Viterbo the game of cards, or, as I would say, playing cards, which previously were not in the least known in that city." The words of Covelluzzo, a fifteenth-century Italian chronicler, are repeated by Bussi in folio 28: "In the year 1379, was brought into Viterbo the game of cards, which comes from the country of the Saracens, and is with them called *naib*." If the passage in Covelluzzo is genuine, then cards would have been known to the Italian *condottieri* in 1379. However, since Covelluzzo did not live during the era of the schism but wrote about these some one hundred years later, we cannot accept his statements as proof of the existence of cards in the year 1379.

Nuremberg Ordinance G. G. von Murr, writing in 1776, contends that cards were known in the city of Nuremberg by the years 1380–1384 because the word *carten* is mentioned in a city ordinance with reference to game penalties. However, the ordinance with the word *carten* appears in folio 16, while the date 1384 appears in the fourth folio, and there is no proof that both were written in the same year; in fact, both might have been copied into the book at a later date.

Laws of the Kingdom of Spain *The Collection of the Laws of the Kingdom of Spain*, printed in 1640, contains a regulation issued by John I, King of Castile, in 1387, and another by John II, issued in Toledo in 1486, which prohibited the playing of cards, which the Spanish termed *naypes*. John I's edict has been used a good deal to uphold the theory that cards existed in 1387. But the word *naypes* is an apparent interpolation since it does not appear in *The Collection of the Regulations of Castile* printed at Medina del Campo in 1541. There the text of the regulation contains only a prohibition against playing dice and trictrac for money. This text conforms completely to an earlier edition of *The Regulations of Castile* printed in 1508.

Tarrochini of Bologna and Prince Fibbia Count Leopoldo Cicognara, writing in 1831 in *Memorie Spettanti alla Storia della Calcografia del Commend*, credits the invention of the Tarocchini of Bologna to Francesco Antelminelli Castracani Fibbia, Prince of Pisa, who died in 1419 while in exile in the city of Pisa. To support his contention, Cicognara cites a portrait of Fibbia that contains the inscription:

> Francesco Antelminelli Castracani Fibbia, Prince of Pisa, Montegiori, and Pietra Santa, and lord of Fusecchio, son of Giovanni, a native of Castruccio, Duke of Lucca, Pistoia, Pisa, having fled to Bologna and presented himself to Bentivogli, was made Generalissimo of the Bolognese armies, and was the first of this family, which was called in Bologna "dalle Fibbie." He married Francesca, daughter of Giovanni Bentivogli. Inventor of the game of Tarocchino in Bologna, he had from the XIV Reformatories of the city the privilege of placing the Fibbia arms on the Queen of Batons and those of his wife on the Queen of Coins. Born in the year 1360, he died in the year 1419.

Allegedly, the authorities of Bologna were so pleased with Fibbia's alteration of the Venetian *tarocchi* pack from seventy-eight to sixty-two cards that they granted him the privilege of placing his own shield of arms on the queen of *bastoni*, and that of his wife, who was of the Bentivogli family, on the queen of *denari*. If the story about Prince Fibbia is true, it would mean that the shortened sixty-two-card Tarocchini of Bologna pack dates no later than 1419, and that the full seventy-eight-card *tarocchi* decks, if they were parent decks, would date earlier, possibly the late fourteenth century. However, no examples of fourteenth-century *tarocchi* or *trionfi* exist today to support such a theory. Moreover, since the shortened sixty-two-card Tarocchini of Bologna deck undoubtedly evolves from the seventy-eight-card *tarocchi*, and since the earliest extant *tarocchi* decks—the Visconti-Sforza *tarocchi*—are reliably dated the mid-fifteenth century, it follows that Fibbia, who died in 1419, could not have invented the game.

Robert Steele, writing in 1901 in the *Journal of the Royal Society of Arts* in an article entitled "Early Playing Cards, Their Design and Decoration," reveals the discovery of the Fibbia portrait in the Palazzo Pallavicini in Bologna. Steele concludes that the portrait and the inscription alike must have been painted long after the death of the prince. Michael Dummett, writing in 1976 in *The Journal of The Playing Card Society*, describes the "rediscovery" by Signor Marco Santambrogio, a lecturer at the University of Bologna, of the Fibbia portrait housed at the Palazzo Fibbia in Bologna. Dummett concludes that the portrait dates from the latter half of the seventeenth century.

Chronicles of Cremona According to the *Chronicles of Cremona*, written by Domenico Bordigallo in the year 1484, Antonio Cicognara, an excellent painter and miniaturist, designed and illuminated a magnificent set of cards called *tarocchi* which were presented to Monsignore Ascanio Maria Sforza, Cardinal of the Holy Church, Bishop of Pavia, and the son of Francesco Sforza and Madonna Bianca Visconti. Count Cigognara relates in 1831 that Bordigallo's chronicle was brought to his attention by Antonio Dragoni, who, in turn, based his information on the notes of Giacomo Torresino, an eighteenth-century Cremonese antiquary. Dragoni was subsequently accused of forgery and his writings became suspect. Count Cicognara cited the Bordigallo manuscript in support of his contention that the early Visconti-Sforza *tarocchi* deck was painted by one of his ancestors, Antonio Cicognara. However, the passage referring to *tarocchi* cards does not appear in the original Latin version of Bordigallo's *Chronicles*, presently housed at the Biblioteca Treccani in Milan, and therefore Cicognara's contention appears to be without validity.

Maffei's **Commentariorum Urbanorum** Writing around the year 1480 in *Commentariorum Urbanorum*, Raphaelus Maffei (1451–1522), also known as Raphaelis Volaterrani, Il Volterrano and Volaterranus, allegedly described tarot cards and the Major Arcana series. This work was first published in 1506; later editions appeared in 1511, 1515, 1526, 1530, 1544 and 1552. It is said that this work describes the four suits as *spade, bastoni, choppe and denari*, each suit comprising ten numeral cards from ten to ace and four court cards, *il Re, la Reina, il Cavallo, il Fante* (king, queen, cavalier and knave) and the *atouts*:

il Mondo (the World)	*la Fortezza* (Courage)
la Giustitia (Justice)	*l'Amore* (Love)
l'Angelo (Angel)	*il Carro* (Chariot)
il Sole (Sun)	*la Temperanza* (Temperance)
la Luna (Moon)	
la Stella (Star)	*il Papa* (Pope)
il Fuoco (Fire)	*la Papessa* (Pope Joan)
il Diavolo (Devil)	*l'Imperadore* (Emperor)
la Morte (Death)	*l'Imperatrice* (Empress)
l'Impiccato (Hanged Man)	*il Bagatello* (Juggler)
il Vecchio (Old Man)	*il Matto* (Fool)
la Ruota (Wheel)	

Investigations of the 1511 and 1530 editions have failed to uncover any references to tarot cards and the Major Arcana series. Therefore, it is likely that the description allegedly reported by Maffei should be credited instead to Thomaso Garzoni who wrote about them in 1587.

The only reference to playing cards in *Commentariorum* appears in Tome III, Philologia, Libre XXIX, page 347 of the 1530 edition, in the section entitled *"De ludo diverso quo summi viri quandoque occupati fuerunt,"* which reads as follows:

Chartarum vero & sortium divinationis ludi priscis additi sunt, ab avaris ac perditis inventi, non sunt nostro dogmati, sed publicis veterum moribus una cum alea reiecti, caeteris cessationis gratia viros vel summos quandoque occupatos habuere.

The foregoing examples indicate that, as a rule, it is best to study early manuscripts in their original languages rather than rely on later translations, and that later writers, perhaps unintentionally, have credited rare early works with references that, in fact, they do not contain.

OMISSIONS

Omissions from early writings support the theory that playing cards were not known at the times cited for other games.

Ovid's **Ars Amatoria** Among all the games mentioned by ancient Greek and Roman writers, there is not one that can be supposed to refer to cards. Ovid (43 B.C.–17 A.D.), writing in *Ars Amatoria*, enumerates several games considered proper for young persons in society, but among them there is no mention of cards.

Christian Church From the beginnings of the Christian Church, the Church councils by their decrees and the Fathers by their censures denounced games of chance and gambling, expressly mentioning dice, osselets and trictrac. Cards, however, were not included before the fifteenth century.

Sanskrit Manuscripts Some ancient Sanskrit texts mention dicing and other early games such as chess and *pachis*, and sometimes the games are even illustrated in ancient paintings, but there is no early Sanskrit reference to playing cards.

John of Salisbury John of Salisbury, who was born in England about 1110, does not refer to playing cards in his work *De Nugis Curialium et Vestigiis Philosophorum, libri octo*, even though one chapter deals specifically with the use and abuse of gaming as a common pastime of the courtiers of his age.

Council of Worcester The thirty-eighth canon of the Council of Worcester, held in 1240, forbids clergymen to join in disreputable games or dancings, or to play at dice; neither shall they allow games of King and Queen to be acted, nor permit ram-raisings, nor public wrestlings. However, there is no reason to believe that the games *de Rege et Regina* refer to playing cards. The games—not game—of King and Queen were apparently a kind of mumming exhibition that the clergy enjoyed as spectators, not as performers.

Town Book of Augsburg The Town Book of Augsburg, 1275, mentions games but does not mention cards.

Wardrobe Rolls of Edward I The Wardrobe Rolls in 1278, the sixth year of the reign of Edward I, refer to the game of Four Kings. Subsequent translations have suggested that this was a card game. However, it seems safe to assume that cards were not known or in use at the time of Edward I because (a) chess, not playing cards, was known in the East by the term signifying Four Kings, (b) chess was a favorite amusement of the higher classes in Europe during the reign of Edward I, and (c) contemporary writers for about a century after the reign of Edward I are silent with respect to playing cards.

Code of Nuremberg The ancient Code of Nuremberg (1286–1299) prohibits gambling but fails to include cards.

Eleventh- to Fourteenth-Century Romances The romances written in the eleventh, twelfth, thirteenth and fourteenth centuries often contain a faithful picture of the times, including the habits and customs of the people, and even particulars of private life and amusements, yet cards are never mentioned among the games in use.

Machau's *Confort d'Amy* Guillaume de Machau, in a poem entitled *Confort d'Amy*, addressed to Charles V of France in 1364, the year he ascended the throne, inveighs against dice. However, he does not mention cards, but probably would have, if they had been known to him, since the reasons for interdicting dice would apply equally to cards.

Petrarch, Boccaccio, Chaucer and *The Arabian Nights* Francesco Petrarch (1304–1374) wrote a treatise about gaming without reference to playing cards. Giovanni Boccaccio (1313–1375) and Geoffrey Chaucer (1340–1400) both cited other forms of gaming in their works, but never playing cards. There is no reference to playing cards in *The Arabian Nights*, a fifteenth-century compilation.

Charles VI on his throne from a miniature in the manuscript of the Kings of France

IV
EARLY TYPES OF TAROCCHI AND SIMILAR PLAYING CARDS

BEFORE EXAMINING IN DETAIL the incomplete seventy-four-card Visconti-Sforza *tarocchi* pack, it is interesting to note various different types of packs in the *tarocchi* family, mainly Italian and French.

Visconti and Visconti-Sforza Dating from about mid-fifteenth century, the *tarocchi* packs designed for the Visconti and Visconti-Sforza families are the oldest extant *tarocchi* cards. The benefactors of these illuminated cards can be identified on the basis of the heraldic devices appearing on some of the figures in the trump and court cards. There exist today eleven versions of these incomplete groups of cards; the most nearly complete is the Pierpont Morgan–Bergamo deck, which consists of seventy-four of the original seventy-eight cards. There are in total 239 cards—or 216 if one considers the 23 Rosenthal cards of more recent date. The eleven versions totaling 239 cards are:

- 74 cards—Pierpont Morgan Library, Accademia Carrara and Casa Colleoni
- 67 cards—Cary Collection, Yale University
- 48 cards—Brera Gallery
- 23 cards—Rosenthal
- 13 cards—Von Bartsch cards: Montreal Museum of Fine Arts, J. Bartlett Morgan collection, Piero Tozzi
- 6 cards—Museo Fournier
- 4 cards—Victoria and Albert Museum
- 1 card—Guildhall
- 1 card—Andrioletti
- 1 card—Marzoli
- 1 card—Biedak

There are neither numerals nor titles on the twenty-two Major Arcana cards nor on the sixteen court cards (king, queen, knight and page in each of four suits) of the Visconti-Sforza decks.

Tarocchi of Mantegna The Tarocchi of Mantegna prints, usually described as cards, date from about 1470 and exist in two different versions. The words "Tarocchi" and "Mantegna" are misleading—the cards were incorrectly attributed to Andrea Mantegna of the school of Padua, and they do not comprise a *tarocchi* pack. The cards are also frequently and incorrectly called Carte di Baldini, but they are not the work of Baccio Baldini. Kenneth Clark, writing in 1933 in a letter in *The Burlington Magazine*, attributes these cards to Parrasio Michele of Ferrara. Some researchers believe these cards, which may be of Florentine or Venetian origin, predate the Visconti-Sforza *tarocchi* packs. The purpose of the prints or cards remains obscure; perhaps they were intended simply as a source of instruction regarding certain philosophic doctrines or precepts of morality. The cards may have been mounted in a book or, if pasted on a heavier board, may have formed part of a game.

The Tarocchi of Mantegna decks are comprised of fifty instructive cards in five classes of ten cards each that follow a carefully ordered sequence. In addition to the image, each card contains a title and a Roman numeral centered at the bottom of the card and a sequential Arabic number in the lower right corner. Additionally, a letter in the lower left corner, marked in reverse order to the numbers, divides the cards into five groups or classes. The difference between the two existing Tarocchi of Mantegna packs is that the sequence of letters in one runs E, D, C, B and A, and in the other pack, S, D, C, B and A. Thus, group E and S have numbers 1 through 10; group D, 11 through 20; group C, 21 through 30; group B, 31 through 40; and group A, 41 through 50.

It is not known with certainty which of the two sets is earlier. The E-series is technically superior in precision of outline, and the S-series is less precise in its engraving and printing. Thirty-six of the images in the S-series are fully reversed from the E-series and another seven are reversed in part. Yet only one figure, *Thalia*, fails to hold in hand the object that is found in the original E-series. *Re*, a medieval figure in the E-series, is transformed in the S-series into a classical ruler. Only six of the images face the same direction in both packs.

The highest and most important subject within each class has the highest number; the least and most subordinate, the lowest number. Thus, The Pope, the highest dignitary of the Christian world, has the last number, 10, of series E and S, while The Beggar holds number 1. The highest number of the entire sequence is 50, The First Cause.

Visconti and Visconti-Sforza tarocchi Cards Major Arcana cards from the reprinted Pierpont Morgan–Bergamo tarocchi pack. Top row: *The Fool or Beggar, The Magician, The High Priestess, The Empress.* Middle row: *The Emperor, The High Priest, The Lovers, The Chariot.* Bottom row: *Justice, The Hermit, the Wheel of Fortune, Strength.*

Tarocchi of Mantegna Cards (S-Series) *The cards illustrated are from the so-called S-series owned by the Bibliothèque Nationale, Paris. Misero 1 contains the S in the lower left corner and the picture is reversed from its counterpart in the E-series. Card No. 25, Aritmetricha, contains the board or hornbook upon which appear the numbers 1 to 10 plus either the numerals 14085 or £40s5. Card No. 29, Astrologia, for reasons not clear, sometimes is associated with The Wheel of Fortune from the tarot pack. Card No. 44, Sol, depicts Phaeton falling from a chariot while Helios holds a small sun in his left hand.*

Tarocchi of Mantegna Cards (E-Series) Pictured are the first twelve cards from the E-Series pack; group E begins with number I Misero, the lowest figure, and ends with X The Pope, the highest dignitary of the Christian world. Group D starts with XI Caliope and continues with XII Urania.

Tarocchi of Mantegna Cards (E-Series, Groups D and C) Eight cards are from group D and four cards from group C. Group D represents the nine muses plus XX Apollo, the final card of its group. XXIIII Geometria is incorrectly designated group E instead of C.

Tarocchi of Mantegna Cards. (E-Series, Groups C and B) Group C cards feature the liberal arts and group B the cosmic principles. Astrologia, really the twenty-ninth card, is incorrectly numbered 39 in both Arabic and Roman in the E-series.

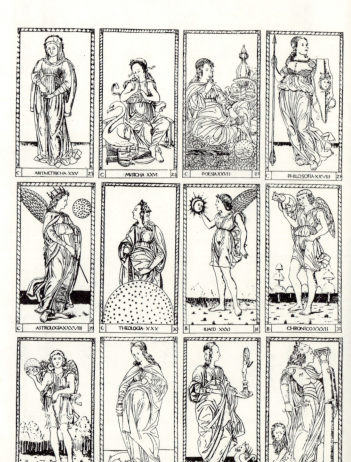

The fifty Tarocchi of Mantegna cards are as follows:

E or S (1–10)—Conditions of Man
1. *Misero* (Beggar)
2. *Fameio* (Servant)
3. *Artixan* (Artisan)
4. *Merchadante* (Merchant)
5. *Zintilomo* (Gentleman)
6. *Chavalier* (Knight)
7. *Doxe* (Doge)
8. *Re* (King)
9. *Imperator* (Emperor)
10. *Papa* (Pope)

D (11–20)—Apollo and the Muses
11. *Caliope* (Calliope)
12. *Urania*
13. *Terpsicore* (Terpsichore)
14. *Erato*
15. *Polimnia* (Polyhymnia)
16. *Talia* (Thalia)
17. *Melpomene*
18. *Euterpe*
19. *Clio*
20. *Apollo*

C (21–30)—Liberal Arts
21. *Grammatica* (Grammar)
22. *Loica* (Logic)
23. *Rhetorica* (Rhetoric)
24. *Geometria* (Geometry)
25. *Aritmetricha* (Arithmetic)
26. *Musicha* (Music)
27. *Poesia* (Poetry)
28. *Philosofia* (Philosophy)
29. *Astrologia* (Astrology)
30. *Theologia* (Theology)

B (31–40)—Cosmic Principles
31. *Iliaco* (Genius of the Sun)
32. *Chronico* (Genius of Time)
33. *Cosmico* (Genius of the World)
34. *Temperancia* (Temperance)
35. *Prudencia* (Prudence)
36. *Forteza* (Fortitude)
37. *Iusticia* (Justice)
38. *Charita* (Charity)
39. *Speranza* (Hope)
40. *Fede* (Faith)

A (41–50)—Firmaments of the Universe
41. *Luna* (Moon)
42. *Mercurio* (Mercury)
43. *Venus*
44. *Sol* (Sun)
45. *Marte* (Mars)
46. *Iupiter* (Jupiter)
47. *Saturno* (Saturn)
48. *Octava Spera* (Eighth Sphere)
49. *Primo Mobile* (Prime Mover)
50. *Prima Causa* (First Cause)

Twenty-two of the Tarocchi of Mantegna cards bear a resemblance to *tarocchi* cards.

MANTEGNA CARDS	TAROCCHI CARDS
1. *Misero*	The Fool
8. *Re*, 9 *Imperator* and 46 *Jupiter*	IIII. The Emperor
10. *Papa*	V. The Pope
20. *Apollo* and 43 *Venus*	VI. The Lovers
45. *Marte*	VII. The Chariot
23. *Rhetorica* and 37 *Iusticia*	VIII. Justice
47. *Saturno*	VIIII. The Hermit
29. *Astrologia*	X. The Wheel of Fortune
36. *Forteza*	XI. Strength
34. *Temperancia*	XIIII. Temperance
41. *Luna*	XVIII. The Moon
31. *Iliaco* and 44 *Sol*	XVIIII. The Sun
46. *Jupiter* and 50 *Prima Causa*	XXI. The World
6. *Chavalier*	Page of swords
8. *Re*	King of staves
2. *Fameio*	Page of cups

The similarities between the Tarocchi of Mantegna and the Visconti-Sforza *tarocchi* packs may be the result of the later artist, whoever he might have been, utilizing ideas from the earlier artist. Alternatively, both artists may have independently developed their ideas from some common cultural influence, or they may have worked from a series of earlier prints unknown today.

In this regard, a manuscript believed to date from the early fifteenth century, and containing a treatise on blazonry and heraldic procedures, is reported by William Hughes Willshire to contain a description of the nine muses and seven arts that are later included in the Tarocchi of Mantegna pack, thus suggesting a possible influence on the artist of the Mantegna pack. Another earlier source might be the children's instructive game, *naibi*, cited in Morelli's *Chronicle* and referred to in Chapter III.

Card number XXV (*Aritmetricha*) in the S-series depicts three rows of numerals on a hornbook. Some early researchers have sought to date this deck to 1485 by interpreting the numbers on the lowest line as the date 1485, ignoring the cipher between *4* and *8*. However, other investigators have suggested that the first sign, previously read for a *1*, should instead be interpreted as a symbol for lira, and the symbol in the fourth place, previously read as an *8*, is the symbol for *soldi*. Thus, the bottom line of the *Aritmetricha* card would read £40s5 rather than 14085. If this theory is correct, the tablet on the card, besides depicting ten numbers running from 1 to 10, also contains a practical demonstration of the monetary use of figures.

Another theory about the origin of the letters E, D, C, B and A suggests they were intended as abbreviations for *Espadone, Denari, Coppe, Battoni* and *Atutto*. The *Atutto* are the *atouts* or Major Arcana; the remaining four letters are the four suits of swords, coins, cups and batons. However, *spadone*, not *espadone*, is the Italian word for swords, though the names are in the Venetian dialect and the word form *espadone* may have been admitted at a later period.

Tarocchi of Mantegna Cards   Twelve cards, from the fifty-card Tarocchi of Mantegna S-Series, that bear a definite resemblance to twelve Major Arcana and court cards in the traditional tarot sequence. Top row: Re *(The Emperor or king of staves)*, Imperator *(The Emperor)*, Papa *(The Pope)*, Venus *(The Lovers)*. Middle row: Marte *(The Chariot)*, Iusticia *(Justice)*, Saturno *(The Hermit)*, Forteza *(Strength)*. Bottom row: Temperancia *(Temperance)*, Luna *(The Moon)*, Chavalier *(page of swords)*, Fameio *(page of cups)*.

The Encyclopedia of Tarot

The following is a description and comparison of the two Tarocchi of Mantegna sets:

E-SERIES	S-SERIES

This class (cards 1–10) represents different states, conditions and dignities of man from beggar to Pope.

E Misero I. An almost nude beggar wearing a cape leans upon a stick. His chin rests upon the back of his left hand and a dog barks at his left leg. The beggar faces toward the left and in front of him is a scrawny dog. Bare trees and a partially destroyed wall appear in the background.	*S Misero I.* The beggar and the dog barking at the beggar's right leg are both facing toward the right. In this print the beggar nestles his chin into the back of his right hand, which rests on the stick. Only one bare tree appears to the left.
E Fameio II. A valet holds aloft in both hands a wide vase and faces toward the left.	*S Fameio II.* The valet is turned toward the right.
E Artixan III. An artisan works with tools in his workshop while a young apprentice stands behind him to the right. Both figures face to the left.	*S Artixan III.* The artisan still faces left but the apprentice now faces right. In this print the ceiling is arched.
E Merchadante IIII. A merchant reads a letter and faces to the left.	*S Merchadante IIII.* The merchant reading a letter faces to the right.
E Zintilomo V. A gentleman holds a falcon on his gloved left hand and faces to the right. The falcon faces to the left. Behind the gentleman and to the left, a page holds two dogs by a leash.	*S Zintilomo V.* This print is almost the same. The gentleman faces right and holds the falcon on his left hand, but here he also holds a small rod in his right hand.
E Chavalier VI. A knight holds a dagger in his two hands and faces to his left. Behind him and to the left, a page holds a sword and faces right.	*S Chavalier VI.* The knight faces to the right while the page appears on the right, facing to the left.
E Doxe VII. The Doge of Venice, in a cap and heavy cape, faces to the left. He raises one side of his cape with his right hand.	*S Doxe VII.* The Doge of Venice faces to the right and raises part of his cape with his left hand.
E Re VIII. A king wearing a crown sits upon his throne holding a scepter in his right hand. He faces front.	*S Re VIII.* This design is entirely different. The face of the king and his crown and dress are different. The king faces to his left. He holds a scepter in his right hand. His left foot protrudes at the base of the throne.
E Imperator VIIII. A bearded emperor wearing a crown sits upon his throne holding a globe in his right hand. He faces to the left. His legs are crossed, right leg over the left, and at his foot is an eagle facing left.	*S Imperator VIIII.* The emperor holds the globe in his left hand and in this print he holds a scepter in his right hand. The crowned emperor and the eagle both face right.
E Papa X. The Pope faces front and holds the keys to the church in his right hand. The book in his left hand rests on his left leg. He wears a triple crown and his hair protrudes from under the crown in two locks that cover his ears.	*S Papa X.* The Pope also faces front with the keys in his right hand and the book in his left hand. However, his hair is pulled back behind the neck.

This class (cards 11–20) represents the nine Muses and Apollo.

D Caliope XI. Calliope plays a type of horn while facing left. A fountain is depicted on the right and a blank disc appears at her feet.	*D Caliope XI.* Calliope faces right and the fountain now appears on the left. However, the blank disc still appears at her feet on the right.
D Urania XII. Urania holds a mathematical compass in her right hand and a blank circle in her left hand. She stands before a stream on the right while facing left.	*D Urania XII.* Urania holds the blank circle in her right hand; nothing is in her left hand. She faces right and the stream is now on the left.
D Terpsicore XIII. Terpsichore plays upon a guitar. A blank circle rests at the left. She faces front while standing at a water's edge.	*D Terpsicore XIII.* Terpsichore's head is turned slightly to the left although her figure faces front. The blank circle is to the right at her feet.
D Erato XIIII. Erato plays a tambourine that touches the right edge of the print. She faces right and her lips are parted. A blank circle is at her feet at the right.	*D Erato XIIII.* Erato again faces right but the tambourine no longer touches the border of the print. Her mouth is closed. The blank circle is also at her feet at the right.

E-SERIES

D Polimnia XV. Polyhymnia plays upon a lyre. Her head is turned to the left. A blank circle appears at her feet to the right.

D Talia XVI. Thalia plays a small violin. Her right knee rests on the ground and she faces left.

D Melpomene XVII. Melpomene blows a horn, which she holds in both hands while facing to the left. A blank circle appears at her feet to the right.

D Euterpe XVIII. Euterpe plays two flageolets. She leans upon a tree and faces to the left. A blank circle appears at her feet to the left.

D Clio XVIIII. Clio stands on a swan that swims in the water. She raises her long garb with her left hand and gestures with her right hand while facing left.

D Apollo XX. Apollo sits upon two swans who face apart. His feet rest upon a globe and his right leg is uncovered to the knee. He faces front. Apollo holds upright in his left hand a branching laurel and in his right hand he points downward with a rod.

S-SERIES

D Polimnia XV. Polyhymnia's head is turned to the right. The blank circle is now at her feet to the left.

D Talia XVI. Thalia's left knee rests on the ground and she faces right while playing the small violin.

D Melpomene XVII. Melpomene faces to the right while blowing the horn. The blank circle appears at her feet to the right.

D Euterpe XVIII. Euterpe faces to the right while playing the flageolets. The blank circle appears at her feet to the right.

D Clio XVIIII. Clio raises her long garb with her right hand and gestures with her left hand. In this print she faces right.

D Apollo XX. In this print Apollo's left leg is uncovered to the knee. In all other respects this print is almost identical.

This class (cards 21-30) represents seven liberal arts and philosophy, astrology and theology.

C Grammatica XXI. Grammar is depicted as an aged woman holding a vase in her left hand and a file in her right hand. She faces to the left.

C Loica XXII. Logic is depicted as a woman facing to the right and holding in her left hand a dragon covered by a transparent veil.

C Rhetorica XXIII. Rhetoric wears a crown and faces front. She holds upright a sword in her right hand. A small winged figure on the right holds a clarion upright while on the left another small winged figure holds the clarion pointed downward.

C Geometria XXIIII. Geometry is a woman floating in the air atop a cloud. She traces geometric figures and faces to the left.

C Aritmetricha XXV. The female figure of Arithmetic is shown counting money from one hand to the other.

C Musicha XXVI. Music is a young woman seated with legs crossed, facing to the left, and playing on a flute. On the left appears a swan and around her are various musical instruments.

C Poesia XXVII. The female figure of Poetry sits before an ornate fountain and plays a flute held in her right hand. With her left hand she pours drops of water from an upturned vase. A circle at her feet contains a picture of stars and rolling hills. The figure of Poetry faces to the right.

C Philosofia XXVIII. Philosophy is a female figure standing with a lance in her right hand and a shield in her left hand. She faces to the right.

C Grammatica XXI. The aged figure of Grammar holds the vase in her left hand and the file in her right hand. Grammar faces to the right.

C Loica XXII. Logic holds the dragon in her right hand and she faces to the left.

C Rhetorica XXIII. Rhetoric holds the sword again in her right hand. The small figure on the right holds the clarion pointed down, while the winged figure on the left holds the clarion pointed upright.

C Geometria XXIIII. This print appears reversed, with the figure of Geometry facing right.

C Aritmetricha XXV. The female figure of Arithmetic is the same but she holds in her left hand a board or hornbook upon which appear the numbers 1 to 10 plus the numerals 14085.

C Musicha XXVI. The female figure of Music faces to the right and the swan is on the right.

C Poesia XXVII. Poetry faces to the left and the fountain on the left is taller and more ornate. She holds the flute in her left hand and an upturned vase in her right hand.

C Philosofia XXVIII. Philosophy again holds the lance in her right hand and the shield in her left hand but she now faces to the left.

Tarocchi of Mantegna Cards In the E-series the female figure of Aritmetricha, XXV, counts money from one hand to the other. She wears a high-waisted gown with a cape and hood. Card No. XXXXX, Prima Causa, also from the E-series, depicts the universe containing fifteen circles surrounding the earth at the center.

Tarocchi of Mantegna Cards—Poesia Card No. XXVII, Poesia, group C of the E-series, sits before an ornate fountain and plays a flute held in her right hand. The figure of Poetry faces to the right. In the S-series Poesia faces to the left; she holds the flute in her left hand and a taller, more ornate fountain is at her right.

E-SERIES	S-SERIES
C *Astrologia XXXVIIII.* This subject is incorrectly numbered 39 both in the Roman and Arabic numerals. The winged female figure of Astrology holds a rod downward in her right hand and a book in her left hand. Her wings are upraised and she faces to the right.	C *Astrologia XXVIIII.* Astrology faces to the left. She again holds the rod in her right hand but in this print the rod is upright. The book is also in her left hand. Her wings face downward.
C *Theologia XXX.* The figure of Theology has two faces; front, a woman's, and the bearded head of Janus at the back. She stands behind a large globe covered with stars. The face of the woman is turned to the left. She clasps the side of her cloak with her right hand.	C *Theologia XXX.* The face of the woman in this print is turned to the right. She clasps the side of her cloak with her left hand.

The Encyclopedia of Tarot

E-SERIES | S-SERIES

This class (cards 31–40) represents the four cardinal virtues, three theological virtues, and the three cosmic principles of Light, Time and Cosmos.

B Iliaco XXXI. The Genius of the Sun represents astronomy and holds the sun depicting a face in his right hand. The winged figure faces to the left.

B Iliaco XXXI. The figure of Astronomy holds the sun in his left hand and he faces right.

B Chronico XXXII. The Genius of Time represents chronology and is a winged figure holding in his right hand a dragon curling into a circle with its tail in its mouth. The figure faces to the left.

B Chronico XXXII. The figure of Chronology is seen in reverse with the dragon held in the left hand. The figure faces right.

B Cosmico XXXIII. The Genius of the World represents cosmology and is a winged figure holding a globe in his right hand while facing front.

B Cosmico XXXIII. The figure of Cosmology holds the globe in his left hand.

B Temperancia XXXIIII. Temperance is a female figure holding two pitchers, one in each hand. The figure faces to the left. An animal at her feet, possibly an ermine or weasel, looks at its own reflection in a mirror.

B Temperancia XXXIIII. The figure of Temperance is reversed and faces to the right. The animal appears on the right.

B Prudencia XXXV. Prudence has two faces: the bearded image of an old man and a youthful female face. She looks into an ornate mirror set on a pedestal consisting of a nude winged figure. Prudence faces to the right. A two-footed winged dragon appears at the foot of Prudence on the right.

B Prudencia XXXV. This print is the reverse with the figure of Prudence facing the left and the dragon on the left. Prudence holds the mirror in her right hand.

B Forteza XXXVI. The figure of Fortitude or Strength holds an ornate scepter in her right hand and with her other hand she appears to be breaking a marble column. The back of her head is covered with the head and neck of a lion. The upper portion of her body is exposed in the image of a lion's head. Behind her, to the left, stands a lion.

B Forteza XXXVI. The figure of Fortitude again holds the scepter in her right hand and she faces to the right. However, the lion to her rear is now on the right. Instead of a lion's head cap she wears a helmet.

B Iusticia XXXVII. Justice holds a sword upright in her right hand and the scales of justice in her left hand. She faces forward and a crane holding a stone appears at the right.

B Iusticia XXXVII. Justice appears almost identical in this print except her head is turned slightly to the right and the crane is placed forward.

B Charita XXXVIII. Charity shakes coins from an open purse. With her left hand she parts her cloak to reveal her flaming heart. A pelican feeding its young appears at the lower left.

B Charita XXXVIII. The figure of Charity appears the same but the pelican now appears at the lower right.

B Speranza XXXVIIII. The figure of Hope has her hands and eyes raised toward the sky. She faces to the left. At the upper left appears only a portion of a heavenly light. At her left a Phoenix rests upon a fire.

B Speranza XXXVIIII. This card is reversed. The figure of Hope faces the right and the Phoenix is in the lower right.

B Fede XXXX. Faith is a female figure holding a cross in her left hand and a chalice with a eucharist above it. She is barefooted and faces slightly to the left. A dog sits to the right.

B Fede XXXX. This card is reversed. The figure of Faith faces to the right while holding the cross in her left hand and the chalice in her right hand. The dog now appears on the left.

This class (cards 41–50) represents the seven planets and the three outer spheres of the Ptolemaic system.

A Luna XXXXI. The moon is depicted as Diana steering a chariot drawn by two horses to the left of the print. She holds a crescent moon in her right hand.

A Luna XXXXI. This card is reversed and the chariot is heading toward the right. Diana holds the crescent moon in her left hand.

E-SERIES

A Mercurio XXXXII. Mercury plays a flute or reed pipe which he holds with his left hand while in his right hand he holds his wand. He wears a winged hat on his head and winged boots. Mercury faces to the left where a cock rests at his feet. To his right is the decapitated head of Argus, whose face is covered with eyes.

A Venus XXXXIII. Venus is depicted bathing in a stream or sea near the shore. In her right hand she holds a seashell. Behind her stands Cupid, her son, winged and blindfolded. In front of her, to the right, are three nude young girls with long hair. Several doves circle above Venus, who faces to the right.

A Sol XXXXIIII. The Sun depicts Phaeton falling in midair from a chariot steered by the winged sun god Helios with four horses. Helios holds a small sun in his right hand. The chariot faces to the right. A crab appears in the sky above the horses.

A Marte XXXXV. Mars sits upon a chariot dressed in full armor and helmet. He holds a sword in his right hand. A dog rests at his feet.

A Iupiter XXXXVI. Jupiter is depicted seated within an oval. Above him sits an eagle on the oval facing to the right, while Jupiter faces to the left and prepares to hurl an arrow at the little figure beneath him.

S-SERIES

A Mercurio XXXXII. This design is practically the same in reverse except the headdress is without wings and Mercury's wand is in his right hand almost touching the top of the print.

A Venus XXXXIII. This print is reversed and the three nude girls appear to the left and Cupid is on the right. Venus holds the seashell in her left hand and faces to the left.

A Sol XXXXIIII. This print is reversed and the chariot faces to the left. Helios holds the small sun in his left hand.

A Marte XXXXV. This print is almost identical except the helmet is different, as is the top of the chariot.

A Iupiter XXXXVI. This print is almost the same except the eagle faces to the left and the small figures are reversed.

Tarocchi of Mantegna Cards—Iupiter   *The figure of Jupiter in the E-series, group A, No. 46, sits within an oval and prepares to hurl an arrow. The eagle at the top of the oval faces to the right. In the S-series Jupiter also faces to the left, as do the eagle and small figure sitting on the bottom of the oval. The oval in the Jupiter card is suggestive of The World or The Universe card in standard tarot packs. Jupiter also resembles The Emperor card in standard tarot packs.*

Tarocchi of Mantegna Cards—Saturno Card No. XXXXVII of group A, Saturn, is depicted as an aged, stooped man holding a scythe and a serpent that bites its own tail. In the E-series Saturn faces to the left; in the S-series he faces to the right and he appears taller. Saturn was the Roman god of agriculture who eventually became associated with the earlier Greek god, Cronus. The legend goes that Cronus, to protect himself from being dethroned by his own children, devoured the children that Rhea, his sister and wife, bore him. Both these prints apparently reflect the legend of Saturn and Cronus.

E-SERIES	S-SERIES
A Saturno XXXXVII. Saturn is depicted as an aged man, stooped, with a long beard and covered head. In his right hand he holds both a scythe and a serpent that bites its own tail. With his left hand Saturn raises a very small child in front of his face. At his feet appear four other small children.	*A Saturno XXXXVII.* This print is reversed with Saturn facing to the right but still holding the scythe in his right hand and a tiny child in his left hand. His beard is shorter.
A Octava Spera XXXXVIII. The Eighth Sphere depicts a winged angel holding a dish filled with stars. The angel faces to the left.	*A Octava Spera XXXXVIII.* This card is reversed with the winged angel facing to the right.
A Primo Mobile XXXXVIIII. The Prime Mover is a winged angel carrying a blank circle. Her left bare foot touches the earth and her right foot is raised. She faces to the left.	*A Primo Mobile XXXXVIIII.* In this print the winged angel faces the right and her wings extend to the edge of the print. Her left foot is raised.
A Prima Causa XXXXX. The First Cause depicts the universe containing fifteen circles with earth at the center surrounded by the planets, the fixed stars, the Prime Mover, and, finally, the three radiant circles of the Trinity.	*A Prima Causa XXXXX.* Here the universe is nearly identical except it includes in the lower left a seated angel reading a book, traditional symbol of St. Matthew, and a winged ox resting on a book, symbolizing St. Luke. In the upper corners a winged eagle, symbolizing St. John, and a winged lion, symbolizing St. Mark, also rest on books.

The E-series has the outline of four nail holes within the decorative border of each card; the cards in the S-series are without this mutilation. Two possible explanations are that a board was nailed over each plate to prevent scratches so that the reverse side also could be engraved to conserve metal, or that the plates were nailed down during the printing process. The British Museum in London possesses an incomplete set of forty-seven cards from a Tarocchi of Mantegna pack, and the Bibliothèque Nationale in Paris owns a complete fifty-card set.

Albrecht Dürer (1471–1528), the German painter and engraver, is credited with preparing a series of twenty-one *tarocchi* cards patterned after the so-called Tarocchi of Mantegna series. Walter Strauss, writing in 1974 in *The Complete Drawings of Albrecht Dürer*, divides the Dürer cards into two categories: ten cards drawn with a pointed pen, with contours consisting of frequently broken lines; and eleven drawn with a broad-tipped pen, with less cross-hatching and more flowing lines. Some art historians have dated the first group circa 1496 and the later group about 1506; it is possible that some of these cards were completed by Dürer's assistant.

The twenty-one Dürer cards and the so-called Tarocchi of Mantegna cards that served as the models are:

DÜRER	TAROCCHI OF MANTEGNA
Knight and Page	E *Chavalier* VI
The Doge	E *Doxe* VII
The Pope	E *Papa* X
The Muse Calliope	D *Caliope* XI
The Muse Urania	D *Urania* XII
The Muse Thalia	D *Talia* XVI
The Muse Melpomene	D *Melpomene* XVII
The Muse Euterpe	D *Euterpe* XVIII
Apollo	D *Apollo* XX
Logic	C *Loica* XXII
Rhetoric	C *Rhetorica* XXIII
Philosophy	C *Philosofia* XXVIII
The Genius of Time	B *Chronico* XXXII
Cosmos	B *Cosmico* XXXIII
Prudence	B *Prudencia* XXXV
Justice	B *Iusticia* XXXVII
Hope	B *Speranza* XXXVIIII
Faith	B *Fede* XXXX
Mercury	A *Mercurio* XXXXII
Jupiter	A *Iupiter* XXXXVI
The Angel of the Primum Mobile	A *Primo Mobile* XXXXVIIII

Sloane Collection, British Museum, London

Albrecht Dürer Tarocchi Cards   Six of the twenty-one pen drawings of tarocchi cards attributed to Albrecht Dürer and patterned after the E-series Tarocchi of Mantegna cards. Top row: Knight and Page corresponds to Chavalier VI in group E; The Doge corresponds to Doxe VII in group E; The Pope corresponds to Papa X in group E. Bottom row: Rhetoric corresponds to Rhetorica XXIII in group C; Philosofia XXVIII corresponds to the same card in group C; Jupiter XXXXVI corresponds to the same card in group A. Note that two of these six Dürer tarocchi cards, Philosofia and Iupiter, contain card titles and numbers at the bottom.

Piedmontese or Tarocchi of Venice Cards *Circa late seventeenth to mid-eighteenth century, these cards were printed from woodblocks and hand colored or stenciled. The cards with French titles are an early reintroduction of tarot from France back into Italy, with certain modifications. Top row: Le Fol (The Fool), I Le Bateleur (The Magician), II La Papesse (The Popess), III La Imperatrice (The Empress), IIII Le Emperur (The Emperor) wearing a metal hat worn by the dukes of Venice. Second row: V Le Pape (The Pope), VI L'Amoureux (The Lovers), VII Le Chariot (The Chariot), VIII La Justice (Justice), VIIII L'Ermite (The Hermit). Third row: X Roue de Fortune (Wheel of Fortune), XI La Force (Strength), XII Le Pendu (The Hanged Man), XIII untitled (Death), XIIII La Temperance (Temperance). Bottom row: XV Le Diable (The Devil), XVI La Maison Dieu (The Tower), XVII Le Toille (The Star), XVIII La Lune (The Moon); back design depicting an ostrich facing to the left with an inscription "F. in Gorizia" inside the bottom panel. The many spelling errors in card titles are due to the Italian artisans' unfamiliarity with French.*

1. *The Fool* by Johanna Sherman, 1977.
2. *The Lovers* from so-called Gringonneur pack but actually fifteenth-century Venetian pack (collection of Bibliothèque Nationale).
3. *XIII Death* from seventeenth-century minchiate pack.

Except where otherwise indicated, the cards in this section are from the collection of the author.

4. *The Magician* from Pierpont Morgan-Bergamo Visconti-Sforza tarocchi, circa mid-fifteenth-century (collection of the Pierpont Morgan Library).

5. *The Fool* from Etteilla pack, circa late nineteenth-century.

6. *XIV Temperance* from miniature Rider-Waite tarot deck, 1975.

7. *The Fool* from Fergus Hall tarot pack, 1973.

8. IIII The Grandfather from French Revolutionary tarot pack by L. Cary, circa 1791.
9. Male knight of cups from Cary-Yale Visconti-Sforza tarocchi deck, circa mid-fifteenth-century (Cary Collection of Playing Cards, The Beinecke Rare Book and Manuscript Library, Yale University).
10. II The Popess from Gassmann tarot, late nineteenth-century, Switzerland.

11. XV *The Devil from J. Galler, Belgium, late eighteenth-century.*
12. 15 *The Devil from oversize (Wirth?) tarot, late nineteenth- or early twentieth-century.*
13. VI *The Lovers from Jacques Rochias fils, Switzerland, late eighteenth-century.*
14. VII *Animal tarock by W. Sewera, Prague, 1849.*

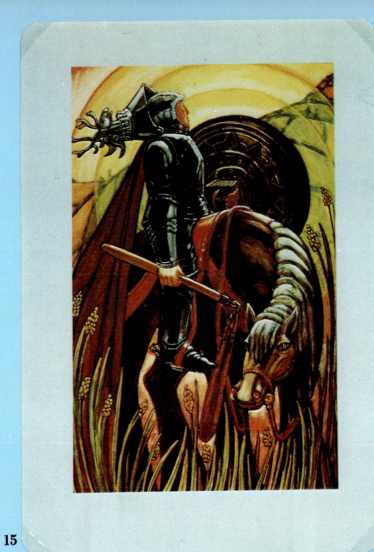

15. *Knight of Disks from Aleister Crowley Thoth Tarot, circa early 1940s.*
16. *Queen of Spades from Polish Animal Tarock pack by J. DuPont, Warsaw, early 1800s.*
17. *The Pope from J. A. Knapp tarot, 1929.*
18. *II Junon from J. Jerger tarot, Besancon, circa 1800.*

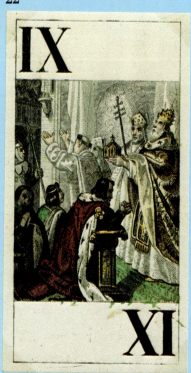

19. Queen of Batons designed by Walter Wegmuller for Zigeuner tarot deck, 1975.
20. II The Popess from Oswald Wirth tarot deck, 1974.
21. XVI The Tower by Edoardo Dotti, Milan, 1862.
22. IX Historical tarock by Gumppenberg, Milan, circa 1840.
23. XVI Ditha Moser tarock published by Berger, Vienna, 1906.

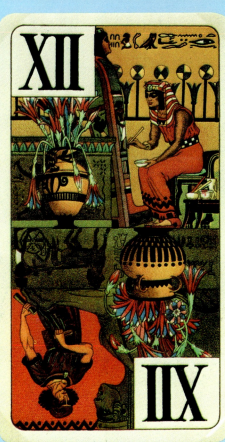

24. 17 Crowning of Empress Josephine by Napoleon, early nineteenth-century.
25. VIII Chinese tarock by Ferd Piatnik vorm a Moser, Vienna, 1860.
26. XIII Military tarock by Jos Glanz, Vienna, circa 1854.
27. XXI Notre Dame from Paris Scenic tarock by Jos Glanz, Vienna, 1855.
28. XVI Rural sçene from Ladies tarock No. 162 by Ferd Piatnik & Sohne, Vienna, nineteenth-century.
29. XII Exotic tarock for Austrian-Lloyd Shipping Lines by Modiano, Trieste, 1900.

30. XX World War I Soldaten tarock No. 217 by Ferd Piatnik & Sohne, Vienna, 1918.
31. XVII Dance tarock by E. Knepper, Austria, 1866.
32. X Revolution of 1848 tarock designed by Anton Elfinger and published by Jos Glanz, Vienna, 1848.
33. X Opera tarock by C. Titze and Schinkay, Vienna, circa 1860.
34. XIX Allegorical tarock by Joseph Estel, Vienna, 1820.
35. III Fool's tarock designed by Josef Surch and published by Ferd Piatnik & Sohne, Vienna, 1860-1865.

Tarocchi of Venice The so-called Tarocchi of Venice or Lombardi pack is more commonly known as Piedmontese tarot. Apparently Piedmontese tarot evolved from the traditional seventy-eight-card Tarot of Marseille pack. Both the Major Arcana and court cards in early Piedmontese packs were full length; modern editions generally are double-ended. Early versions of this deck had Roman numerals and introduced the figure of *La Papasse* (The Female Pope) for the card numbered II. This card in many of today's popular tarot packs is known as The High Priestess or Junon.

Tarocchini di Bologna The Tarocchini di Bologna pack comprises sixty-two instead of seventy-eight cards. The word *tarocchini* is a modification of the word *tarocchino*, or *chino* tarot, which means shortened or little tarot. There are no titles on the twenty-two *atutti* or sixteen court cards. Originally the Tarocchini di Bologna packs included The Empress, The Emperor, The Female Pope and The Pope. In the pack illustrated, the first four unnumbered *atutti* depict figures similar to Moors and satraps, probably because after 1513 the Republic of Bologna came under papal domination. The remaining twelve numbered and five unnumbered *atutti* are described as follows:

5.	Love	14.	The Devil
6.	The Chariot	15.	The Tower
7.	Temperance	16.	The Star
8.	Justice		The Moon
9.	Force		The Sun
10.	Wheel of Fortune		The World
11.	The Hermit		The Last Judgment
12.	Traitor		The Fool or The
13.	Death		Juggler

The Fool is a fancifully dressed young man simultaneously playing a horn and a drum. The Hermit is portrayed as a winged man on crutches, representing the flight of time. The World depicts a man standing on a circular wreath. The Tarocchini di Bologna is shortened to sixty-two cards by omitting the five, four, three and two in each of the four suits. The invention of the Tarocchini di Bologna deck has been incorrectly credited to Prince Fibbia of Bologna in the year 1419.

Minchiate of Florence The Minchiate of Florence deck, similar to early *tarocchi* packs, is enlarged to ninety-seven cards by the addition of twelve zodiac sign cards, four element cards, three theological virtue cards (Faith, Hope, Charity) and one cardinal virtue card (Prudence). In place of the usual four cards of The Popess, The Empress, The Emperor and The Pope, the minchiate has only three imperial cards: The Popess becomes The Grand Duke, The Empress The Western Emperor and The Emperor The Eastern Emperor. The complete minchiate pack contains forty-one trumps and fifty-six suit cards. The first five trump cards are called *papi*. The first fifteen trump cards contain Roman numerals at varying positions and the first two cards also have rosettes in the upper corners. Cards numbered XVI to XXXV have their Roman numerals on scrolls at the tops of the cards; a framed rosette is in each of the upper corners. The remaining six trumps are unnumbered. No titles are shown on the trumps, which are generally designated as follows:

I	The Juggler or Mountebank
II	The Grand Duke
III	The Western Emperor
IIII	The Eastern Emperor
V	The Lovers
VI	Temperance
VII	Force or Fortitude
VIII	Justice
VIIII	The Wheel of Fortune
X	The Chariot
XI	The Hermit or Old Man
XII	The Traitor or Hanged Man
XIII	Death
XIIII	The Devil
XV	The Tower
XVI	Hope
XVII	Prudence
XVIII	Faith
XVIIII	Charity
XX	Fire
XXI	Water
XXII	Earth
XXIII	Air
XXIIII	Libra, The Balance or The Scales
XXV	Virgo, The Virgin
XXVI	Scorpio, The Scorpion
XXVII	Aries, The Ram
XXVIII	Capricornus, The Goat
XXVIIII	Sagittarius, The Archer
XXX	Cancer, The Crab
XXXI	Pisces, The Fishes
XXXII	Aquarius, The Water Carrier
XXXIII	Leo, The Lion
XXXIIII	Taurus, The Bull
XXXV	Gemini, The Twins

The next five unnumbered cards, called *arie*, have bright red backgrounds and are arranged in the following order without titles: The Star, The Moon, The Sun, The World and The Last Judgment, sometimes depicted as Fame. The next card is The Fool.

The fifty-six suit cards, called *cartiglia*, are divided into four suits—swords, staves, cups and coins—and each suit has fourteen cards. The knights of swords and staves are represented by centaurs; the knights of cups and coins are shown as monsters, half human and half dragon. The valets, or jacks are male, as usual, in the suits of swords and batons, but in the suits of cups and coins they are female. The swords on the pip cards in the suit of swords are straight, unlike those on the court cards and the curved style on Italian *tarocchi* cards.

In the ancient game of minchiate, the forty trump cards were superior to the other suits, and The Fool apparently could not take another card nor could it be taken until all else was lost.

The origin of the term "minchiate" is not known, but it may derive from the old Italian word *menchia*, signifying game, sport, etc. The cards in the Minchiate of Florence

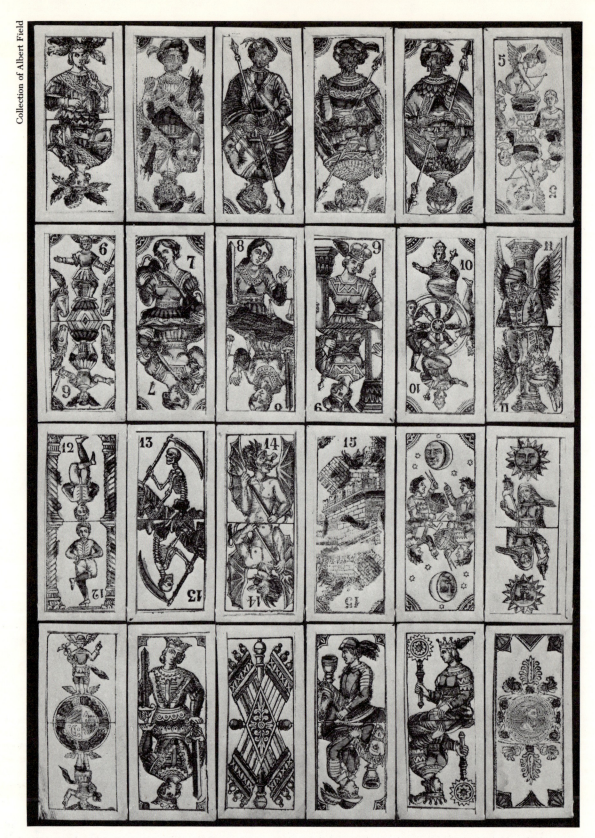

Tarocchini di Bologna Cards   Eighteenth-century Bolognese tarocchini cards measure 114 by 52 mm. and are double-ended. The Major Arcana and court cards are untitled. Each card has an extra sheet of paper wrapped from the back around the front edges. Top row: The Fool, unnumbered, is followed by four additional unnumbered cards depicting Moors and satraps; Card 5 is Love. Second row: 6 The Chariot, 7 Temperance. 8 Justice, 9 Force, 10 Wheel of Fortune, 11 The Hermit, a winged man. Third row: 12 Traitor or The Hanged Man, 13 Death, 14 The Devil, with a grotesque face and large bat wings, 15 The Tower, The Moon, The Sun. Bottom row: The World, king of swords, ten of batons, knight of cups, queen of coins and ace of coins.

Minchiate Cards from a Late-Seventeenth-Century Pack   *The cards are crudely hand stenciled; an extra sheet of paper wraps from the back around the front edges and bears a dotted pattern. Top row: I Juggler or Magician, II The Grand Duke, III The Western Emperor, IIII The Eastern Emperor, V The Lovers, VI Temperance. Second row: VII Force, VIII Justice, VIIII Wheel of Fortune, X The Chariot, XI The Hermit or Old Man, XII The Traitor or Hanged Man. Third row: XIII Death, XIIII The Devil, XV The Tower, depicting a nude figure fleeing from the tower instead of the customary falling figure, XVI Hope, XVII Prudence, XVIII Faith. Bottom row: XVIIII Charity, XX Fire and XXI Water, two of the four natural elements, XXII Earth, XXIIII Libra, the zodiac sign of the balance or scales, and a knight of swords represented by a centaur. The Libra card also has a small fleur-de-lis mark of identification between the two scales.*

Minchiate Cards from an Ornately Engraved Uncut Sheet, Circa Eighteenth Century Top row: *The Last Judgment, The World, The Sun, The Moon, The Star, XVII Prudence, XI The Hermit or Old Man.* Second row: *XVIII Faith, XVIIII Charity, Wheel of Fortune, VII Force, I The Juggler, VI Temperance, XVI Hope.* Bottom row: *XII The Hanged Man, VIII Justice, XIIII The Devil, XV The Tower, which depicts a woman fleeing from a grasping figure in a doorway.*

Collection of the author

pack are generally smaller in size than tarot packs, and up to the end of the eighteenth century most cards had wraparound edges. Some early minchiate packs comprised as many as 120 cards per deck but these decks did not gain favor because of the unwieldy quantity of cards.

Tarocchini of Mitelli The Tarocchini of Mitelli pack, an artistic rendition of the Tarocchini of Bologna pack, is comprised of sixty-two cards designed by the engraver Giuseppe Maria Mitelli in 1664. The pack consists of twenty-two *atouts* and forty suit cards. The subjects on the *atouts* and court cards are fancifully treated in a departure from the usual card designs. The *atutti* are without titles and numbers except for four numbered *atutti*, which are Moors or satraps. The female and male Popes become two bearded Popes, and The Empress and Emperor are made into the sovereigns of the West and East.

Tarocco Siciliano Tarocco Siciliano packs total sixty-four cards—twenty-two Major Arcana and forty-two Minor Arcana. The cards are short, in conformity with the regional cards of the area, and the figures are squat in appearance. The Major Arcana cards in Sicilian tarot packs are numbered in Arabic and untitled, except for the Jester, which is both unnumbered and untitled, and *Miseria*, which is unnumbered but bears its title in a ribbon at the top of the card. The trump cards contain several variations from the trumps in standard tarot packs. The Juggler sits behind a table with an open sack of gold coins instead of the usual four suit signs. Temperance pours liquid into an urn resting on the ground instead of holding both urns in her hands. The Hanged Man is suspended from a branch of a tree by a noose around his neck instead of around his ankle. The Hermit holds a flickering lamp of knowledge. The Ship is substituted for The Devil. The windowless Tower is shown undamaged and lacks the lightning bolt customarily depicted on this card in tarot packs. The Star is supported by a horseman. The Moon, partially surrounded by an ominous cloud, rises above a woman who stands near a sleeping man. The Sun, also with its ominous cloud, bears witness to two men fighting each other. Atlas supports a globe of the world encircled with zodiac signs along the equator. The highest card, Jupiter, a substitute for The Angel, is shown with lightning bolts in his hand while an eagle stands at his side. The card called *Miseria* depicts a beggar chained to a stone block and holding a bowl in his outstretched left hand. The trumps in Sicilian tarot packs are: The Fool or Jester, 1 The Juggler, 2 The Empress, 3 The Emperor, 4 Fortitude, 5 Temperance, 6 a female figure (Constancy), 7 Justice, 8 The Lovers, 9 The Chariot, 10 The Wheel of Fortune, 11 The Hanged Man, 12 The Hermit, 13 Death, 14 The Ship, 15 The Tower, 16 The Star, 17 The Moon, 18 The Sun, 19 The World, 20 Judgment and the unnumbered Beggar known as *Miseria*. The court figures are single-ended and the valets, or jacks, are female and wear shields with ornate faces. Suit marks are Italian-Portuguese.

OTHER SIMILAR PACKS

Mamluk playing cards and *trappola* packs are sometimes confused with tarot cards. In addition, although early "hunting" or falconer cards from the fifteenth century are different from *tarocchi* designs, they deserve mention since they were developed at about the same time as early *tarocchi* packs.

Mamluk Mamluk playing cards may have originated in Turkey or they may have been brought from Asia to Turkey and possibly Europe as predecessors of early Italian suited cards. There exist forty-seven hand-painted Mamluk cards from two incomplete packs that date from around the fifteenth century. Each deck totaled either fifty-two or fifty-six cards when complete.

Mamluk cards are long and narrow, measuring about 252 by 96 mm., and were first described in 1939 by L. A. Mayer, who saw them in the Treasury of the Topkapi Sarayi Museum, Istanbul. Mayer believed the pack comprised five suits: swords, polo sticks, staffs, cups and coins. However, further study indicates that the so-called staffs are polo sticks. Thus, Mamluk cards comprise the four suits of swords or scimitars, polo sticks, cups and coins or circles; the swords have double curves and some of the polo sticks are topped with elephant heads. The court or face cards total either twelve or sixteen; they contain Arabic writing on top and bottom and are represented by a king (*malik*), a governor, lieutenant or viceroy (*na'ib*), and a second governor, second lieutenant or second viceroy (*na'ib thani*). The fourth possible court card in each suit is a helper or aide (*ahad al-arkan*); however, some researchers believe these so called helper cards are in fact the kings.

Five of the forty-seven extant cards—second governor and ace of polo sticks, nine and ten of staffs and two of coins—were painted by a different hand than the others; they probably belong to the second pack but possibly they were created to replace cards missing from the main set. Some of the cards contain titles, sayings or invocations at either the top and bottom panels or only the bottom panels. According to Jan Bauwens, a Belgian researcher, the calligraphic texts were deciphered by Professor Tang of the University of Istanbul. For example, the king of cups says, "With the sword of happiness I shall redeem a beloved who will afterwards be my wife." The lieutenant of sticks says, "I am as a flower, a string of pearls is my sail." The helper of coins says, "Rejoice in the happiness that returns as a bird sings its joy."

European influence eventually caused the lieutenant of the Arabic pack to be replaced by the queen found in Italian and French packs, and the suit of polo sticks to be turned into the suit of staves or batons. According to Mayer, the ornamentation on the cards is suggestive of Circassian decoration, especially in illuminated Egyptian manuscripts. The Mamluk pack has no trump cards and it is not a *tarocchi* pack, but these cards may constitute an important link in the migration of early playing cards from the East to Europe. Richard Ettinghausen describes a fragment of a card (probably the four of cups), from a third Arabic pack that bears an arc with flower designs, ornamentation similar to that found on some of the Mamluk cards. The fragment, comprising half a card, may predate the Mamluk cards and represent early Arabic influence in Egypt. Bauwens theorizes that the words *naype* and *naibi* may derive from the Arabic word found on the lieutenant or deputy card in the Mamluk pack, thus suggesting that the name for a pack of cards actually derives from the title on one of the cards.

Trappola Trappola packs, which had their origin in the fifteenth century, are sometimes confused with tarot decks. *Trappola* cards are long and narrow, similar in shape to tarot cards, and they contain Italian suit designs of swords, staves, cups and coins, although the pictorial execution varies depending upon the artist. *Trappola* packs con-

Tarocchini of Mitelli cards   Top row: Dancing Fool, Juggler who plays and dances, bearded Emperor, Emperor, seated bearded Pope, standing bearded Pope. Second row: Blindfolded Cupid, Venus, Temperance, Justice, Strength or Force, Fortune. Third row: Old man or Father Time on crutches, a man about to strike a sleeping boy with a mallet (suggestive of The Traitor or The Hanged Man), Death holding an hourglass and a scythe, the Devil sitting upon fire, a young man struck by lightning (similar to the Lightning-Struck Tower), a rag picker with a lantern beneath a six-pointed star. Bottom row: Diana beneath the moon, Apollo highlighted by the sun, Atlas holding the world, an angel sounding its trumpet, the king and queen of swords. The ace of cups (not shown) contains a female bust in an oval shield; beneath the medallion is a pedestal containing Mitelli's name. The coat of arms of Bentivoglio of Bologna, the family for whom the hand-colored etchings were executed, also appears on the ace of cups. Several of these packs exist today in the British Museum and other depositories.

Tarocco Siciliano Cards From Modiano, Italy. Trumps are numbered in Arabic in upper right and untitled except for Miseria. In addition to the twenty-two Major Arcana cards, the eight Minor Arcana cards shown above are king, queen, knight and page (female) of swords, nine of batons, seven of cups, valet (female) and six of oros or coins.

Collection of Topkapi Sarayi Museum, Istanbul

Mamluk Cards These cards evince a style and structure—four court cards and ten numeral cards—that may be the missing link in the migration of cards into Europe. Mamluk cards date from about the fifteenth century. Cards shown are (top left) six of swords or scimitars, ten of polo sticks, staffs or staves, and the second governor or helper (ahad al-arkan malik at-tuman) in the suit of cups; (bottom right) king of coins (malik ad-darahim). The ten of staves apparently comes from another Mamluk deck because the artwork is by a cruder hand. Each of the four suits in the Mamluk deck apparently consisted of either three or four court cards and ten pip cards. Consistent with religious Islamic tradition, instead of pictures the court cards have panels with inscriptions and, as a rule, the sign of the suit appears only once on each court card, practically taking up the entire space available. If Mamluk cards are the missing link in the migration of playing cards from Asia to Europe, then it is conceivable that the fifteenth-century Italian suit signs of spade, bastoni, coppe and denari are adaptations of earlier Islamic suits of scimitars, polo sticks, cups and coins. Polo sticks, not generally recognizable in Europe, may have been stylized as staves and batons.

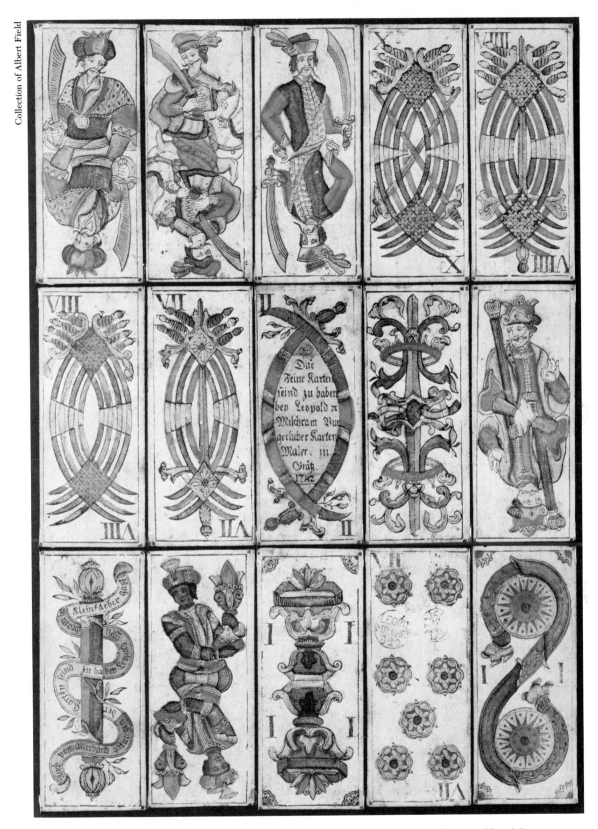

Trappola Pack   These cards were printed from woodcuts and hand stenciled in Graz by Leopold Milchram, town card maker, as evidenced by the two of swords, which shows the year 1782 as the date of the original woodcuts. However, the tax stamp on the seven of coins dates from 1829, the year the pack was actually produced and sold. The court cards are double-ended and contain Roman numerals. The pip cards are also double-ended and Roman-numbered. Cards shown are (top row) king, knight, page, ten and nine of swords; (middle row) eight and seven of swords, two of swords, ace of swords and king of staves; (bottom row) ace of staves with an inscription in a ribbon running from bottom to top of the card announcing the availability of various types of cards at Milchram's located on Kleinfarbergasse, page of cups, two of cups, seven of coins with tax stamp and two of coins. Cards measure 144 by 59 mm.

The Pack of Princely Hunting Cards of Ambras   Reprint in 1969 by Edition Leipzig, Germany, of the original Ambras Hofjagdspiel pack, circa 1440–1445, presently owned by the Kunsthistorisches Museum, Vienna. This is one of the earliest existing German packs; the pictures present a story of falconry. Top row: King of falcons carries a falcon on his red leather gauntlet; ten of falcons contains a flag bearing its suit sign; underknave shows a falcon in the lower half of the card. Middle row: King, queen and underknave of herons. The hat worn by the king of herons is similar to the one seen on The Emperor card in the Pierpont Morgan–Bergamo, Cary-Yale and Brera-Brambilla Visconti-Sforza packs. Bottom row: Knave of hounds holding a small dog (possibly an Italian greyhound) in his hand; underknave taking a stick to a dog on a leash who has run around the horse's forelegs to its right side; queen of lures tossing in the air a decoy or "feather trick" to call back the falcon who has struck a heron.

tain only thirty-six cards—king, knight, page, ten, nine, eight, seven, two and ace in each suit—and there are no trump cards. The pip cards of each suit are numbered in Roman figures. The kings are sometimes shown sitting on a low brick wall and wearing a wide-brimmed hat with a crown in the center. The figures in the court cards in the suits of swords and cups show an Oriental influence in their dress; the court figures in the suits of clubs and coins are more Western in dress.

"Hunting" Pack of Stuttgart and Ambras Hofjagdspiel The earliest German card game still preserved is the fifty-two-card "hunting" pack of Stuttgart, which dates from about 1430. The cards measure 190 by 120 mm. and there are no trumps. The suit signs are falcons, hounds, stags and ducks; the ten of each suit contains a flag or banner bearing the suit sign. The cards depict the medieval mode of fashion, including the charming dress of the ladies at court. The court cards in the suits of hounds and stags show ladies appropriately dressed in costumes of the early fifteenth century.

A second set of painted playing cards of German origin dates from about 1440–1445 and is known as Ambras Hofjagdspiel or the Pack of Princely Hunting Cards of Ambras. Dr. Herwarth Rottgen, writing in 1969, attributed this second pack to the painter Konrad Witz and his workshop at Basle. The cards measure 155 to 157 by 95 mm. and consisted originally of fifty-six cards in four suits—falcons, herons, hounds and lures—the same number of suited cards found in *tarocchi* packs. In each suit there is a king and queen who ride against golden backgrounds, a knave with its suit sign in the upper half of the card, and an underknave with the suit sign in the lower half of the card. For reasons unknown, the faces and hands of the human figures, as well as some of the horses, hounds, herons and falcons, were left unpainted with only the pen outlines remaining.

The Ambras Hofjagdspiel pack reveals in colorful pictures the art of falconry at court. The story of falconry is represented by the falcon as the hunting bird of prey, the heron as the hunted bird, the hound, which seeks out the heron after it has been struck, and the lure, which calls the falcon back to the falconer. By virtue of the subject matter, these cards are sometimes called falconer cards. Cards with falcons appear in the Victoria and Albert Museum, Rosenthal Collection, Goldschmidt cards and the Guildhall.

V

THE VISCONTI AND SFORZA FAMILIES AND THEIR HERALDIC DEVICES

The earliest tarocchi cards were hand painted and were often beautifully illuminated. Italy appears to hold the distinction of having produced the earliest such cards—the prerogative of a wealthy aristocracy. One method of dating the early Milanese *tarocchi* packs and discovering their original sponsorship and ownership is to identify the heraldic and armorial devices on the card faces. There exists today a variety of incomplete original decks painted for the Visconti and Sforza families, who dominated a wide area around Milan for over one hundred years, from the mid-fourteenth to the mid-fifteenth century.

THE VISCONTI FAMILY

Bernabo Visconti, one of the most ruthless tyrants in the latter half of the fourteenth century, was Lord of Milan. He had many children, mainly illegitimate offspring from his liaisons with various mistresses. For his daughters, he arranged good marriages with well-established *condottieri*—the popular soldiers of fortune who hired out to wage wars and defend cities.

Bernabo was married to the beautiful Beatrice, a member of the famous della Scala family of Verona. His legitimate daughters, produced by this marriage, were wedded to aristocratic kings, dukes and counts carefully selected to expand and strengthen the already broad Visconti influence.

Bernabo Visconti shared power with his brother, Galeazzo, a quiet, reserved figure in contrast to the lusty, ebullient Bernabo. Galeazzo's son, Giangaleazzo Visconti, born in 1351, did not wish to remain, as his father had, in the background. In 1385 he deposed his uncle Bernabo in a coup and became the sole ruler of Milan. Giangaleazzo married Isabelle, daughter of King John of France. For the next seventeen years he extended his dominance across northern Italy from Piedmont to the Adriatic. He brought all of Lombardy and Emilia under his rule and became known as the "Despot of Milan." In 1395 Giangaleazzo purchased from Emperor Wenceslas of Germany the hereditary title Duke of Milan, and adopted the imperial eagle as part of his coat of arms. He served as the first Duke of Milan until his death from the plague in 1402. To his credit, he established the Certosa, the great Carthusian monastery just outside Pavia. The last part of the Certosa to be completed was the facade built by the Sforzas. In a painting by Ambrogio Borgognone depicting Christ carrying the cross with monks of the Certosa, completed in 1494, the monastery is shown perched on a jagged cliff similar to the cliff depicted in such cards as Death, Temperance, The Star, The Moon and The Sun in the Pierpont Morgan–Bergamo *tarocchi* pack. The three sons of Giangaleazzo's first marriage all died in infancy, but he had two sons—Giovanni Maria and Filippo Maria—from his second marriage to his first cousin, Caterina Visconti.

The second Duke of Milan, Giovanni Maria Visconti, a vicious ruler, was assassinated in 1412. His younger brother Filippo, born in 1391, had been relegated to Pavia, but upon the murder of Giovanni, he seized power and became the third Duke of Milan. In 1413 Filippo married Beatrice di Guglielmo Ventimiglia Lascaris, Conte di Tenda, widow of Faccino Cana of Pisa. She was twice his age and Filippo allegedly married her to secure her wealth and the loyalty of her dead husband's troops. Filippo conspired to kill her, and in 1418 she was beheaded on trumped-up charges of adultery.

During Filippo's long reign, unity and authority were restored in the duchy. In 1428 he was married again—this time to Maria di Savoy—but the marriage was never consummated. Filippo's illegitimate daughter, Bianca Maria Visconti, was borne in 1423 by his mistress, Agnes del Maino. Bianca was betrothed in 1432, at age nine, to Francesco Sforza, an effective *condottiere* in the Visconti service. The marriage of Francesco and Bianca took place nine years later, in 1441, at the Church of St. Sigismund in Cremona. The bride was eighteen and the bridegroom forty, but it was a lasting and happy marriage.

The Visconti family adopted as its emblem a serpent, or dragon, half devouring a man. The Viscontis were fond of displaying divine rays on their emblems, and the king and queen of staves in the Pierpont Morgan–Bergamo deck depict a Visconti bird descending in an aureole of spires and flames.

THE SFORZA FAMILY

When Duke Giangaleazzo Visconti defeated the della Scala family in 1387, he had the skillful assistance of Alberico da Barbiano, a *condottiere* who commanded a force of men that included Muzio Attendolo. Impressed with

60

VISCONTI HERALDIC DEVICES

1. *A bird, possibly a dove, with straight, radiating lines is seen on the king, queen and page of staves. Beneath the bird is a nest containing three young birds. This device also appears in the Yale deck in the suit of coins.*

2. *The ducal crown with branches or fronds, as seen on The Empress, The Emperor and the horse's caparison on the knight of cups.*

3. *The sun, with commingled wavy and straight rays that end in a scalloped shell pattern, appears on The Hierophant, The Lovers, The Chariot, Justice, The Wheel of Fortune, Judgment, the horse's caparison on the knight of staves, the court cards of the suit of cups and all the coin cards except the ace.*

4. *The black eagle appears on The Emperor and The Empress cards and is derived from Emperor Wenceslas, 1395. This could conceivably represent the Emperor himself.*

5. *The motto A bon droyt, which Gertrude Moakley believes was suggested by Petrarch to the first Duke of Milan, Giangaleazzo Visconti, appears on the five, four, three, two and ace of swords, the five, four, three, two and ace of staves, the five, four, three and two of coins and the four of cups.*

---

young Muzio's fire, Alberico dubbed him *Sforza*, meaning force.

In addition to receiving financial rewards, Muzio became one of the most powerful *condottieri* in Italy and his military exploits won him the right to several heraldic devices. The first of these was the quince, given by the anti-Pope John XXIII, in recognition of Muzio's rank as Count of Cotignola.

At a later date Rupert III, Emperor of the Romans, successor of Wenceslas, granted Muzio Attendolo the right to bear a lion rampant on his shield. Since Sforza had been using the quince, Rupert suggested a combination of the two devices—the quince to be held in the lion's left paw and all comers to be challenged with its right paw. The Sforza helmet, a winged dragon with a human head, formed the crest.

In 1409 the Marquis of Este added a diamond ring, in recognition of Muzio Attendolo's murder of the tyrant of Parma, Ottobuono Terzo. This Sforza achievement is sometimes shown as three interlocking diamond rings repeated many times.

When Pope John failed to pay Sforza for his *condottiere* services, Sforza grew restless. Besides, he disliked serving with another commander, Paolo Orsini, so he changed sides and joined forces with King Ladislaus of Naples. This made the Pope furious and, according to Geoffrey Trease, writing in *The Condottieri* in 1971, he commissioned a caricature of Sforza dangling by one leg like a hanged traitor; the similarity to The Hanged Man in the tarot pack is obvious.

When Muzio Attendolo died in 1424, his nickname, "Sforza," was made the hereditary surname of the family by Queen Joanna II of Naples.

Muzio Attendolo's son, Francesco Sforza, was born July 23, 1401. The young Sforza inherited his father's position as a *condottiere* leader after Muzio drowned in an accident. Francesco subsequently adopted the three interlaced diamond rings as his *impresa*. In 1441 his marriage to Bianca Maria Visconti united the Visconti and Sforza families.

In 1447, six years after the marriage of Francesco and Bianca Maria, the last of the ducal Viscontis—Duke Filippo—died leaving no male heir. Milan did not pass smoothly to Francesco by inheritance, but by 1450 Francesco realized his ambitions and became the fourth Duke of Milan. He was the first Sforza to hold the title and the only *condottiere* to rise from humble origins to become a duke.

The emblem of a Saracen half devoured in a serpent's mouth was part of the ducal arms that passed into the crest of the united Visconti-Sforza family. In fact most, if not all, of the Visconti heraldic devices were taken over by Francesco Sforza.

Francesco ruled Milan peacefully and efficiently for the remaining sixteen years of his life. He and Bianca had several sons: Cardinal Ascanio Maria Sforza, Galeazzo Maria Sforza and Ludovico "il Moro" Sforza. Galeazzo succeeded his father as duke but he was a cruel and dissolute person and he was assassinated by conspirators. Galeazzo's wife, Bona of Savoy, acted as regent for their minor son, Giangaleazzo, who succeeded to the duchy on his father's death. However, in 1480, Galeazzo's brother, Ludovico Sforza, deprived his nephew of the duchy and assumed control. Ludovico and his wife Beatrice d'Este held a brilliant court and spent immense sums to further the arts and sciences. In 1499 Milan was taken by the French, and Ludovico spent the remaining years of his life as their prisoner. Two sisters of Cardinal Ascanio became nuns of the Augustinian convent founded by their mother. The French retained the Sforzas as puppet dukes until the collapse of the duchy in 1535.

HERALDIC DEVICES OF THE VISCONTI AND SFORZA FAMILIES

The identification of the Visconti-Sforza cards with the Visconti and Sforza families is based upon heraldic devices that are found on the trump, court and pip cards. The heraldic devices of the Visconti family that appear in the seventy-four-card Pierpont Morgan–Bergamo Visconti-*Sforza tarocchi* deck are shown in the illustrations on the preceeding page.

Visconti heraldic devices that do not appear in the Pierpont Morgan–Bergamo pack are writhing serpents and a serpent half devouring a Saracen. These devices do appear on The Lovers card in the sixty-seven-card Visconti-Sforza deck at Yale University and on the coat-of-arms card in the so-called Von Bartsch group. The Cary-Yale Visconti-Sforza deck has the distinction that each of the four suits is represented on the court cards by a specific design or Visconti-Sforza heraldic device. The garments worn by the figures in the suit of swords are decorated with flowers and leaves. The suit of staves depicts large fountains, the suit of cups contains the ducal crown with branches or fronds, and the suit of coins presents a pelican or dove in profile with bursting rays instead of a front view as found in the Pierpont Morgan–Bergamo pack.

SFORZA HERALDIC DEVICES

The heraldic devices of the Sforza family that appear on the seventy-four-card Pierpont Morgan–Bergamo Visconti-Sforza *tarocchi* cards are shown in the following illustration.

1. A lion, as seen on the king of swords.

2. Three interlocking rings appearing on The Empress and The Emperor cards.

3. A large fountain, as depicted on the ace of cups.

The sixty-seven-card Cary-Yale pack contains the heraldic device of a large fountain decorating the garments of the queen, female knight and male page in the suit of staves. This fountain is believed to have been a heraldic device bestowed on Francesco Sforza after he successfully completed the campaign during which his father drowned.

VI

LOCATING THE VISCONTI-SFORZA TAROCCHI DECKS

ON THE BASIS OF DIFFERENCES in size and artistic style, eleven groups of Visconti and Visconti-Sforza *tarocchi* cards can be distinguished. These incomplete groups of cards survive—as little as a single card to the most nearly complete pack of seventy-four out of seventy-eight cards. These Milanese cards are sometimes also called Lombard *tarocchi* packs because they were produced in what is now called the province of Lombardy. All the cards are hand painted and most of them seem to date from the mid-fifteenth century. The cards are generally of heavy cardboard and have either red or plain backs. The single cards are of different dimensions and, judging from variations in style and execution, do not appear to belong to the larger incomplete packs. Perhaps the single cards were renderings by apprentices or the work of artists who presented them as gifts or samples in hopes of winning the patron's designation as artist for the complete deck. Some cards have tack holes, probably attributable to the person who photographed the cards for the article by Emiliano de Parravicino that appeared in *Burlington Magazine* in 1903.

Each of the eleven distinct groups is known by one or more names, usually the name of one or several former owners or of the artist believed to have painted the cards.

Popular Name	Number of Cards	Last Known Location	Approximate Measurement (Millimeters)
1 Visconti-Sforza; Colleoni; Pierpont Morgan; Carrara; Bergamo; Cicognara; Bembo.	26 35 13 74	Accademia Carrara, Bergamo, Italy. Pierpont Morgan Library, New York. Casa Colleoni, Bergamo, Italy.	175 × 87 175 × 87 175 × 87
2 Visconti; Visconti-Sforza; Countess Gonzaga; Cary; Yale; Cicognara; Tortona; Bembo; Visconti di Modrone.	67	Cary Collection, Beinecke Rare Book and Manuscript Library, Yale University, New Haven, Connecticut.	190 × 90
3 Brera; Brambilla; Contessa di Mazzarino.	48	Brera Gallery, Milan.	178 × 90
4 Rosenthal	23	Rosenthal, London.	?
5 Von Bartsch	1 1 11 13	Museum of Fine Arts, Montreal. Cleveland Stewart-Patterson, Montreal. Previously Piero Tozzi, New York.	166 × 83 170 × 70 170 × 70
6 Museo Fournier	6	Museo Fournier, Vitoria, Spain.	171 × 88
7 Victoria and Albert	4	Victoria and Albert Museum, London.	167 × 90
8 Guildhall	1	Guildhall, London.	141 × 67
9 Andrioletti	1	Milan, Italy.	140 × 65
10 Marzoli	1	Milan, Italy.	170 × 85
11 Biedak	1	Los Angeles, California.	172 × 86
Total Cards	239		

LOCATION OF 239 EXTANT VISCONTI-SFORZA TAROCCHI CARDS

In the 74-card Visconti-Sforza deck "PM" indicates Pierpont Morgan Library, New York; "AC" Accademia Carrara, Bergamo, Italy; and "CF" the Colleoni family, Bergamo, Italy. There are 67 cards in the Visconti-Sforza deck at Yale University; 48 cards in the Brera or Brambilla pack at the Brera Gallery, Milan and 23 so-called Rosenthal cards, London. The 13 so-called von Bartsch cards are indicated by "MFA" for Museum of Fine Arts, Montreal; "CSP" for Cleveland Stewart-Patterson, Montreal; and "PT" for Piero Tozzi, New York art dealer and former owner of the remaining 11 of these cards. There are 6 cards at Museo Fournier, Vitoria, Spain; 4 cards at Victoria & Albert Museum, London; 1 card at the Guildhall, London, and single cards are owned each by Andrioletti, Marzoli and Biedak.

		Pierpont PM	AC	CF	Yale	Brera	Rosenthal	Bartsch MFA	CSP	PT	Fournier	Victoria Albert	Guildhall	Andrioletti	Marzoli	Biedak
	THE FOOL	√					√									
I	THE MAGICIAN	√														
II	THE POPESS	√			Charity?						√					
III	THE EMPRESS	√			√											
IIII	THE EMPEROR		√		√	√					√					
V	THE POPE	√			Faith?					√						
VI	THE LOVERS	√			√											
VII	THE CHARIOT	√			√					√						
VIII	JUSTICE		√				√									
VIIII	THE HERMIT	√														
X	WHEEL OF FORTUNE	√				√					√					
XI	STRENGTH	√			√											
XII	HANGED MAN	√														
XIII	DEATH	√			√							√				
XIIII	TEMPERANCE	√					√									
XV	DEVIL															
XVI	THE TOWER															
XVII	THE STAR		√		Hope?	√						√				
XVIII	THE MOON		√													
XVIIII	THE SUN	√				√										
XX	JUDGMENT	√			√					√						
XXI	THE WORLD		√		√								√			
	FAITH (THE POPE?)				√											
	HOPE (THE STAR?)				√											
	CHARITY (THE POPESS?)				√											
SWORDS	KING	√			√					√						
	QUEEN	√			√											
	MALE KNIGHT		√			√										
	FEMALE KNIGHT				√											
	MALE PAGE		√			√				√						
	FEMALE PAGE				√											
	10	√			√	√										
	9			√	√	√										
	8		√		√	√										
	7			√	√	√										
	6		√		√	√										
	5		√		√	√				√						
	4		√		√	√										
	3				√	√										
	2			√	√	√										
	ACE	√			√	√										
STAVES	KING	√			√											
	QUEEN		√		√	√										
	MALE KNIGHT		√		√	√										
	FEMALE KNIGHT				√											
	MALE PAGE		√		√	√									√	
	FEMALE PAGE				√											
	10			√	√	√										
	9	√			√	√										
	8			√	√	√										
	7		√		√	√					√					
	6		√		√	√										
	5		√		√	√	√										
	4	√			√	√										
	3				√	√										
	2			√	√	√										
	ACE	√			√	√										
CUPS	KING		√		√		√		√							√
	QUEEN	√			√											
	MALE KNIGHT	√			√	√				√						
	FEMALE KNIGHT				√											
	MALE PAGE	√			√	√		√								
	FEMALE PAGE				√											
	10		√		√	√										
	9	√			√	√										
	8			√	√	√										
	7			√	√	√										
	6		√		√	√										
	5	√			√	√	√									
	4		√		√	√										
	3	√			√	√										
	2		√		√	√										
	ACE	√			√	√	√					√				
COINS	KING	√			√	√										
	QUEEN	√			√				√							
	MALE KNIGHT				√	√										
	FEMALE KNIGHT				√											
	MALE PAGE		√		√	√					√			√		
	FEMALE PAGE				√											
	10	√			√	√										
	9		√		√	√										
	8	√			√	√				√						
	7	√			√	√										
	6			√	√	√										
	5		√		√	√										
	4			√	√											
	3				√	√	√									
	2				√	√					√					
	ACE		√		√	√	√			√						
JOKER (?)							√									
SUB TOTAL		35	26	13				1	1	11						
TOTAL		74			67	48	23	13			6	4	1	1	1	1

VII
THE PIERPONT MORGAN–BERGAMO VISCONTI-SFORZA TAROCCHI DECK

THE PIERPONT MORGAN–BERGAMO pack is the most nearly complete of all the existing decks. There are seventy-four extant cards divided among three repositories: thirty-five cards are housed at the Pierpont Morgan Library, New York; twenty-six are at the Accademia Carrara, Bergamo, Italy; and thirteen are in the possession of the Colleoni family, Bergamo, Italy. Four original cards are lost: The Devil, The Tower, the three of swords and the knight of coins.

The cards from this mid-fifteenth-century Visconti-Sforza *tarocchi* deck are believed to have belonged in the seventeenth century to a Canon Ambivero of Bergamo, who bequeathed them to the Donali family. Thereafter, the cards apparently passed to Count Allessandro Colleoni of Bergamo. Twenty-six of the cards from this pack were separated from the remainder of the deck when Count Colleoni was persuaded by his friend, Count Francesco Baglioni, to trade the cards for some objects of art including a portrait of his ancestress, Countess Cecilia Colleoni, painted in 1705 by Fra Galgario. Count Colleoni regretted the exchange, but he was never able to secure the return of the twenty-six cards (five trumps, seven court and fourteen pip cards). Upon the death of Count Baglioni in 1900, the cards were bequeathed to the Accademia Carrara in Bergamo. The existence of tack holes in the cards indicates that the damage was done before the set was broken up. In 1911 the Pierpont Morgan Library acquired thirty-five cards from Hamburger Frères, a dealer.

Several early packs contain numbers on the trump cards, including a fragmented sheet from the Metropolitan Museum of Art, New York (page 124), an uncut sheet from the Rosenwald Collection, National Gallery of Art, Washington, D.C. (page 130), and the French pack by Catelin Geofroy, which dates from 1557. Since the cards of the Visconti-Sforza pack are neither numbered nor titled, we have followed the Geoffroy sequence for presentation of the Major Arcana cards in the Visconti-Sforza pack.

THE TWENTY-TWO MAJOR ARCANA CARDS

The Fool The young man depicted as The Fool stands barefooted; his white stockings are worn and tattered. The Fool is dressed sparingly in white undergarments and a thin, ragged coat. His right hand holds a club that rests upon his right shoulder. Seven feathers protrude through his curly hair. His unshaven face has a shaggy forked beard.

The background design of this card, as in most Major Arcana cards of the Pierpont Morgan–Bergamo deck, consists of an overall gold background decorated by repeating suns with eight wavy rays within a diamond or lozenge-shaped pattern. The decorative rectangular border contains repetitive tooled dots—generally seven dots in a circle and one center dot.

The Fool Reprinted from the Pierpont Morgan–Bergamo Visconti-Sforza tarocchi *pack.*

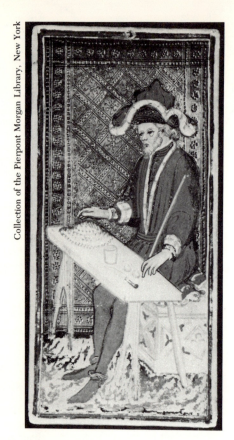

The Magician *Reprinted from the Pierpont Morgan–Bergamo Visconti-Sforza* tarocchi *pack.*

The Popess *Reprinted from the Pierpont Morgan–Bergamo Visconti-Sforza* tarocchi *pack.*

The Magician The Magician or Juggler sits at a small table on which are a knife, two coins or loaves of bread, a cup and a large white dish. His right hand is cupped over the ornate covered dish, which is speckled with gray. In his left hand The Magician holds a rod. The symbols of all four suits are depicted in this card: the knife or sword represents swords; the rod or baton, staves; the cup, cups; and the small white loaves, coins.

The Magician wears a richly colored red robe. His hat, the edge of his coat and his cuffs are trimmed with white ermine. His feet are covered with loose-fitting slippers. The floor seems to be an expanse of green grass broken by an occasional leaf pattern. The background of the card is the familiar decorative diapered or lozenge-shaped design framing the familiar sunburst—the sun emitting wavy rays. Gertrude Moakley views this card as the Carnival King in the triumphal processional before Lent.

The Popess The figure of The Popess is seated upon a gold bench on a trapezoidal platform. She is draped in a brown monastic cloak and wears a tiara over the white wimple on her head. In her right hand she holds a thin scepter topped with a cross. In her left hand, and balanced on her knee, is a sacred book. In the bottom corners of the card are floral patterns on grass. This motif is repeated throughout the deck.

Some scholars believe this card represents the legendary Female Pope. Gertrude Moakley believes her religious habit is from the Umiliata Order and that the figure is Sister Manfreda, a relative of the Visconti family who was actually elected Pope by the small Lombard sect of the Guglielmites. According to Moakley, their leader—Guglielma of Bohemia—died in Milan in 1281. Guglielma's followers believed Sister Manfreda was the incarnation of the Holy Spirit, sent to inaugurate the new age of the Spirit prophesied by Joachim of Flora.

The Empress The matronly figure of The Empress sits upon her throne. She wears a gold crown over a head scarf that drapes softly across her shoulders. In her left hand is a shield—possibly just decorative or her husband's jousting shield. It is emblazoned with the black eagle of Emperor Wenceslas, a device the Viscontis and later the Sforzas adopted. The heraldic device of three interlaced diamond rings is repeated on her royal robe; the rings symbolize eternity, and the diamonds, invincibility. The Visconti crown is depicted with two fronds or twigs, possibly a palm and a laurel. The robe is completed with a dotted border design and is lined in a rich blue.

The Emperor The aged male figure of The Emperor is seated upon an unseen throne on a trapezoidal platform. He is heavily bearded with gray hair. His robe matches the royal garment of the Empress, repeating the three interlaced diamond rings of the Sforza family and the Visconti crown. The Emperor wears a large ornate hat with the black eagle on its front. In his left hand he holds a globe with a cross—the imperial orb—as sign of his authority. In his right hand he holds a thin scepter. Several trees appear adjacent to a grassy clearing in the lower right portion of the card. Similar depictions of treed areas appear on cards throughout the deck, apparently at random.

The Empress Reprinted from the Pierpont Morgan–Bergamo Visconti-Sforza tarocchi *pack*.

The Emperor Reprinted from the Pierpont Morgan–Bergamo Visconti-Sforza tarocchi *pack*.

The Pope The aged, bearded, seated figure of The Pope is wearing a triple crown. His throne rests upon a trapezoidal platform. The Pope gives a blessing with his right hand while he holds in his left hand a long scepter that rests on the ground and extends upward with a cross at its top. The Pope's robe is lined in rich green, and a blue hexagonal ribbon pattern running throughout the robe encircles a sun pattern with mixed wavy and straight rays. The wavy rays seem to convert into straight rays as if passing through a prism. At the ends of the wavy, scalloped rays are blue dots; this may be a Visconti device.

The Lovers Some scholars believe the two figures in this card are Francesco Sforza and Bianca Maria Visconti. The male figure is shown wearing a flat hat. He is dressed in a robe decorated with the heraldic device of sun and rays. The female figure is dressed in a long robe patterned with the same wavy rays and a sun surrounded by straight prismic rays. She appears to be wearing a white hat and her gold hair protrudes slightly in front. The two figures are shaking hands; their faces are attentive and pleasant. The winged figure of Cupid, blindfolded and nude, stands on a pedestal and, without deliberation or selection, prepares to throw an arrow with his right hand. In his left hand, Cupid holds a thin rod or scepter.

The coloring of the background of this card is very much red with blue, suggesting that either the background was originally done in inferior gold, or possibly blue or

The Pope Reprinted from the Pierpont Morgan–Bergamo Visconti-Sforza tarocchi *pack*.

The Lovers Reprinted from the Pierpont Morgan–Bergamo Visconti-Sforza tarocchi pack.

The Chariot Reprinted from the Pierpont Morgan–Bergamo Visconti-Sforza tarocchi pack.

Justice Reprinted from the Pierpont Morgan–Bergamo Visconti-Sforza tarocchi pack.

The Hermit Reprinted from the Pierpont Morgan–Bergamo Visconti-Sforza tarocchi pack.

silver instead of gold. Another possibility is that the card may have been exposed to the elements for a greater period of time while on display, thus leaving the background colors so different from the other cards.

The Chariot Sitting upon a flat chariot drawn by two winged white horses seems to be the same female figure who appeared on The Lovers card. The woman wears a crown over her golden hair. In her left hand she holds a globe topped with a cross, and in her right hand, a thin scepter. The charioteer's garment is decorated with a sun emanating wavy and straight rays that terminate in a scalloped rim.

Justice A female figure holds in her left hand the scales of justice and in her right hand a two-edged sword. She seems to be the same person depicted on the previous card—The Chariot—and on several other cards, suggesting that these cards may have been intended to illustrate the many facets of Bianca Maria Visconti. The figure of Justice wears a silver garment and a gold crown, barely visible against the golden backdrop that rises in a gothic arch behind her head.

Above Justice, and as if in a dreamlike sequence, is a knightlike figure on a white stallion in rapid motion; the figure is dressed in full body armor and carries an upraised sword. The rays of the sun appear in both the upper left and upper right corners of the card. Justice is one of the four cardinal virtues to appear as a trump card; the others are Strength, The Hanged Man (Prudence?) and Temperance.

The Hermit The blue robe worn by The Hermit, or Father Time, is trimmed in gold fur, suggesting that he is a man of some means. He wears on his head a fluffy two-tiered hat also trimmed in gold fur. The Hermit has a long white beard. He appears to be wearing white gloves and white stockings; he has on the same shoes as The Magician. In his right hand The Hermit carries a large hourglass to mark time (in other popular tarot cards he is often depicted holding a lantern). In his left hand The Hermit clasps a long rod.

The Wheel of Fortune The winged female figure of Fortune within the center of the wheel is the same person previously depicted in The Lovers, The Chariot and Justice. However, in this card her robe is similar to the blue hexagonal ribbon pattern of The Pope's robe, with the exception that the color of the pattern is silver rather than gold. Straight rays emanate from a sun with scalloped smaller rays and blue dots. The placement of symbolic figures around The Wheel of Fortune is familiar in medieval art.

The young figure on a platform at the top of the wheel has ass's ears and is clothed in a gold garment with the heraldic device of the sun. The lettering near the figure reads *Regno*—I reign.

The figure descending on the right has a tail and the lettering reads *Regnavi*—I reigned.

The figure clothed in green, rising on the left side of the wheel, also has ass's ears and the lettering reads *Regnabo*—I shall reign.

The figure of an aged man on his hands and knees appears beneath the wheel. He has a heavy gray beard and is dressed in a ragged white garment. His stockings are worn through at the feet, as they are on the figure in The Fool card. The lettering by the aged man reads *Sum sine regno*—I am without reign.

The Wheel of Fortune Reprinted from the Pierpont Morgan–Bergamo Visconti-Sforza tarocchi pack.

Giulio Ferrario, compiler of *Poesie Pastorali e Rusticali* in 1808, cites in *Alcune Poesie Inedite del Saviozzo et di altri autori* how four figures engage in a monologue with the goddess Fortuna as follows:

Fortuna.—I am that Fortuna who has made and unmade kings and emperors. It is of no avail to worship me. Let him beware who sits at the top of the wheel. Let each hold fast to his treasure.

Regno.—I reign at the top of the wheel, as Fortune has destined me. But if the wheel turns I may be deprived of power. Be moderate, ye who are in power, lest you fall to earth. Behold the honor I am paid because I sit at the top of the wheel.

Regnavi.—I reigned for a while, then Fortune put me down and deprived me of everything good. Her friendship avails not. No friend remains when a man falls. Do not be confident when you are rising; Fortune makes you fall with deadly blows. Hearken to my case, how I gained and lost this honor.

Regnabo.—I shall reign if Fortune pleases and the wheel turns to the fourth place. I shall be above and rule all the world. How great is my pleasure then! Virtue moves me to speak such words, because I plan to do justice and punish those who have maliciously robbed the men of good estate. What joy I shall have to be able to punish them!

Sum sine Regno.—I am, as you see, without reign, down low in wretchedness. Fortune has disclaimed me. If I should mount on this wheel, every man would be friendly to me. Let each take warning. . . .

Strength This card, also called Fortitude, is the first of the six trump cards believed to have been painted by a different artist, possibly Antonio Cicognara. It probably served as a replacement for a lost card or to complete an unfinished deck. The figure of a strong man, perhaps Hercules, wields a club above his head. The club is green with touches of gold. The man wears a dark blue tunic with a red-violet scarf, sleeves and stockings. Both the man and the lion-like beast crouching in front of him stare intently in the same direction and share the same facial expression. The Strength card in most tarot decks depicts a man or woman controlling a lion, but in this card from the Visconti-Sforza pack the man and the animal appear poised for battle against a common enemy, although some interpretations suggest the lion is cowering under the blows of the man's club. The facial features of the man are harsher than the sweet expressions rendered in the preceding Major Arcana cards. The background of this replacement card contains a repetitive sun pattern with some straight rays rather than wavy as in the other trump cards.

The Hanged Man This card depicts a young figure hanging upside down from a wooden gallows by his left ankle. The face of the figure is similar to the face that appears in several other cards, including The Lovers and Justice. The hanging figure wears a pair of green tights with high hips and a white blouse with balloon sleeves and buttons down the center. His hands are behind his back, presumably tied, and his left leg is crossed behind his right foot, forming a triangle.

Death The animate figure of a skeleton as archer stands upon the ground. The white shrouds or fillet around his head may be a blindfold removed. The skeleton holds in his left hand a large bow; it is a weapon suggestive of the vertebrae. In his right hand is a thin arrow feathered at the top. The funereal figure of Death smiles, his piercing eyes glaring from his skull. At the bottom of the card the ground is shown with crevices and cracks as at the edge of a precipice.

Temperance This card was also done by a hand other than that of Bonifacio Bembo—the artist may have been Antonio Cicognaro. The figure of Temperance is shown as a woman pouring liquid from one ornate ceramic urn into another. Draping the figure is a deep blue peplum drawn across the bodice and hips by a fine ribbon belt and patterned with eight-rayed gold stars, the first appearance of such a decorative pattern in this deck. Her sleeves are red-violet and the red stockings on her feet are sagging. Temperance stands at the edge of a crevice or precipice and there is a decorative grass pattern at her feet.

Though the artist who painted this card did not decorate the figure's garment with any of the heraldic devices common to Visconti or Sforza; the background design is compatible with that of the other cards in this deck.

The Devil This is one of the four cards lost from the extant Visconti-Sforza *tarocchi* pack. The first five hundred Visconti-Sforza decks reproduced in 1975 by Grafica Gutenberg and U.S. Games Systems, Inc., contained a

Strength Reprinted from the Pierpont Morgan–Bergamo Visconti-Sforza tarocchi pack.

The Hanged Man Reprinted from the Pierpont Morgan–Bergamo Visconti-Sforza tarocchi pack.

Death Reprinted from the Pierpont Morgan–Bergamo Visconti-Sforza tarocchi *pack*.

Temperance Reprinted from the Pierpont Morgan–Bergamo Visconti-Sforza tarocchi *pack*.

The Devil Recreated to replace its missing counterpart in the original Pierpont Morgan–Bergamo Visconti-Sforza tarocchi *pack*.

composite line drawing of The Devil card from other popular tarot decks. The second edition of the reproduced Visconti-Sforza deck, also published in 1975, recreated the card of The Devil, shown here, as it may have appeared in the fifteenth century.

The figure of a fierce Devil—whose torso is half male and half female and whose lower body is animal—stands on a pedestal. The Devil is winged and has horns and ass's ears. It carries in its left hand a small club, while its right hand gives a sign. In front of The Devil, tied to the pedestal, are two smaller figures, both half animal and half human, one male and one female. They are clothed in loose green cloth. A heavy rope tied around their necks goes through a knot affixed to the pedestal. The male figure facially resembles The Devil. The female figure has a lighter skin tone.

The Falling Tower This is the second card missing from the trumps. In the first reproduction of five hundred Visconti-Sforza decks a line drawing of a popular Falling Tower card was substituted. In the second edition of the reproduced deck an artist recreated The Falling Tower card as it might have appeared at the time of the original Visconti-Sforza deck. A blazing red sun with scalloped rays appears in the upper right section of the card. One ray strikes the tower and separates the gold crown-shaped top from the stone battlement. Stones and debris fall to the ground, along with two figures dressed in garments similar to those worn by the two figures in The Lovers Card. How-

Collection of Grafica Gutenberg, Bergamo

The Falling Tower *Recreated to replace its missing counterpart in the original Pierpont Morgan–Bergamo Visconti-Sforza tarocchi pack.*

The Star *Reprinted from the Pierpont Morgan–Bergamo Visconti-Sforza tarocchi pack.*

ever, the facial expressions of the falling figures are tense and fearful.

The Star This is the third card of the Major Arcana not painted by Bonifacio Bembo. The female figure reaches out with her left hand to touch an eight-rayed star. The design on her blue peplum—in contrast to that pictured on the card of Temperance—depicts horizontal rays above four or five vertical rays; this suggests heavenly radiance or light from above. Her red cape is decorated with gold stars having the eight-rayed pattern, similar to the design on the Temperance card. Inside the cape is a green lining. The female figure in this card appears to be wearing some form of brown stocking footwear. Like Temperance, she is standing at the edge of a precipice.

The Moon This is the fourth trump by a different hand. The figure is that of a young woman, possibly the goddess Diana, holding a crescent moon in her right hand. She carries a broken bow in her left hand, a sign of her defeat. The classical Greek garment of Diana—a high-waisted red-violet robe without sleeves—is here worn over a long blue dress. The design on the red-violet robe consists of a series of three gold diagonal lines repeated diagonally across the garment. Interestingly, the hem of the red-violet robe lines up perfectly with the mountainscape in the distance. The figure of the goddess stands at the edge of a crevice; her feet are clearly painted, in contrast to the previous cards. A castle appears in the distance.

The Sun A winged child—*putto*—appears to be standing with his right foot on a dark blue cloud. Both hands hold aloft a radiant human head resembling the color of blood. A small purple scarf swirls around the child's neck and between his thighs. A thin beaded necklace, perhaps a good-luck charm, hangs around his neck. The foreground of this card is a cliff's edge. This card was painted by the same hand as the preceding Strength, Temperance, The Star and The Moon cards and The World card.

Judgment A godly figure similar to The Pope appears at the top of the card. Judgment holds a sword in his right hand and a globe topped with a cross in his left. He is bearded and wears a crown. His blue garment is interlaced with a silver ribbon, and a heraldic device, possibly the sun, appears beneath the waist of the garment in the center of the gold diapered background. In front of Judgment are two angels blowing trumpets with hanging banners; the lower banner shows a gold cross against a gold background. At the bottom of the card, from a marble tomb, rise two nude young figures, possibly meant to represent Francesco Sforza and Bianca Maria Visconti. Between these two figures is an aged man who appears resting at the bottom of the tomb.

The World This is the sixth and final card of the trumps painted by a different hand. Two naked children support a gigantic circular object, possibly a globe, that contains a vision of a heavenly walled city floating on a turbulent sea. In the blue sky above the city are eight-pointed gold stars, similar to the design on the garment worn by Temperance. The two winged cherubic figures have red scarves loosely draped across their shoulders.

The Moon Reprinted from the Pierpont Morgan–Bergamo *Visconti-Sforza* tarocchi *pack*.

The Sun Reprinted from the Pierpont Morgan–Bergamo *Visconti-Sforza* tarocchi *pack*.

Judgment Reprinted from the Pierpont Morgan–Bergamo *Visconti-Sforza* tarocchi *pack*.

The World Reprinted from the Pierpont Morgan–Bergamo *Visconti-Sforza* tarocchi *pack*.

THE FIFTY-SIX MINOR ARCANA CARDS

The Minor or Lesser Arcana of the Visconti-Sforza pack total fifty-six cards, comprising fifty-four extant cards and two missing cards—the three of swords and the knight of coins—which were recreated in the 1975 reproduction of the Visconti-Sforza *tarocchi* deck.

The four suits in the Minor Arcana of the Pierpont Morgan–Bergamo Visconti-Sforza *tarocchi* pack are: *spade* (swords), *bastoni* (staves, batons), *coppe* (cups) and *denari* (coins). Each suit contains fourteen cards: four court cards—king, queen, knight and page—and ten pip cards from ten to ace.

The four figures on the court cards of the suit of spades are dressed in armor and each figure carries a large sword as a symbol of his suit.

The figures on the four court cards of the suit of staves wear silver pleated garments. Each carries a long stave or rod with a large vessel at each end, except for the king whose rod has a finial only at the top.

The four figures on the court cards of the suit of cups wear gold garments decorated with the heraldic device of sun and rays. Each figure holds a large cup or chalice as a symbol of his suit.

Three figures on the court cards of the suit of coins are dressed in garments decorated with blue hexagonal ribbons that wind around circular suns with straight rays. The knight of coins has been recreated to replace the missing original. Only the king of coins fails to wear a ducal crown similar to the crown worn by the other three kings.

The court figures are viewed in varying positions—full face, left profile and right profile. With the exception of the kings, which do not have a left profile figure, at least one court figure of each type is depicted in each position. All the court figures wear gloves. The four court figures in the suit of swords are right-handed. In the suit of staves only the knight and page are right-handed, and in the suit of cups the queen, knight and page are right-handed. In the suit of coins only the queen is right-handed; since the knight card is missing, it is not known whether this figure was right- or left-handed.

The diapered diamond-shaped backgrounds on the sixteen court cards are basically similar. However, that they were done by more than one artist and possibly at different times is evidenced by the variations in execution. For example, the clarity and brightness of the diapered pattern on the kings of swords, clubs and coins contrasts with the dull gold background on the king of cups. Additionally, the wavy rays within the diapered pattern vary from clockwise to counterclockwise without apparent consistency.

King of Swords Crowned and in full armor, the king of swords sits upon a six-sided bench with a quatrefoil in a diapered pattern. The bench is on a platform that appears trapezoidal in shape. The king holds a raised sword in his right hand. His left hand rests upon a shield bearing the heraldic device, probably of Sforza origin, of a haloed lion holding a book. However, since the city crest of Venice also was a haloed lion holding a book, it is not certain this was a Sforza device. The king of swords is the only one of the four kings to have a shield beside him. The background of the card contains the same diapered or lozenge-shaped design found on the Major Arcana cards.

Queen of Swords The queen wears a crown and is dressed in a high-waisted white gown. Her arms are clad in armor. She is shown in profile and holds a sword upright in her right hand. With her left hand she seems to be giving a benediction or greeting. Along her shoulder and upper arm is the Sforza device of a lion, conferred upon Muzio Attendolo, the first Sforza, by Emperor Rupert in 1401. The lion may be a costume design intended to match the haloed lion on the king's shield.

Knight of Swords The knight of swords is shown in profile astride a white horse. Clad in full armor, he wears a pink cape with white trim. He holds an upright sword in his right hand. His hat is made of colorful peacock feathers. This is the only one of the four knights who wears a hat (assuming the missing card of the original knight of clubs is hatless). The horse wears a caparison bearing an emblematic shield known as *party per pale*—divided down the middle. Unfortunately, the design on the shield is obscure. The design around the armorial shield is an elaborate decorative quatrefoil with no apparent heraldic significance. The design of the quatrefoil border resembles the design of the platform on the king of coin's card. Some scholars believe that the division of the shield—red on the left side and

Collection of the Pierpont Morgan Library, New York

King of Swords *Reprinted from the Pierpont Morgan–Bergamo Visconti-Sforza* tarocchi *pack.*

(right)
Queen of Swords *Reprinted from the Pierpont Morgan–Bergamo Visconti-Sforza* tarocchi *pack.*

(far right)
Knight of Swords *Reprinted from the Pierpont Morgan–Bergamo Visconti-Sforza* tarocchi *pack.*

either white or silver on the right side—was added at a later date to cover a heraldic device, possibly the Visconti lion, a serpent or a plumed helmet. A second *party per pale* appears beneath the horse's neck. The horse's caparison is covered with a repetitive flower design of tooled dots within a circle.

Page of Swords The page is shown full face and dressed in armor. He wears a large colorful hat of peacock feathers. His right hand rests on the hilt of his sword. An ornamental design appears on the breastplate that he wears over a leather or mail shirt.

The Pip Cards in the Suit of Swords The pip cards ten to one are depicted by numerically repeating swords indicating the value of the card. The hilts and blades are gold and the bodies of the swords are a deep blue, except at the points where the swords intersect, which are gold. There is assorted floral decoration of flowers, leaves and branches on each card. The Visconti motto, *A bon droyt*, meaning "To the good belongs the right" or "On the side of the law,"

Page of Swords *Reprinted from the Pierpont Morgan–Bergamo Visconti-Sforza* tarocchi *pack.*

The Encyclopedia of Tarot

(far left)
Ten of Swords *Reprinted from the Pierpont Morgan–Bergamo Visconti-Sforza* tarocchi *pack.*

(left)
Ace of Swords *Reprinted from the Pierpont Morgan–Bergamo Visconti-Sforza* tarocchi *pack.*

appears within a ribbon scroll on the five, four, three, two and ace of swords.

The position of the motto *A bon droyt* indicates that the pip cards of the suit of swords are in an upright position when the sword tips point *downward*. This is the opposite of most modern tarot packs, which have the blade of the sword pointing upward to indicate the card is in an upright position, as evidenced in many packs by the ace of swords, which is depicted as a hand holding an upright sword.

The three of swords is the only pip card missing from the original Visconti-Sforza deck. In order to recreate the missing card, two inside swords have been deleted from the five of swords.

King of Staves The king of staves sits upon a hexagonal throne similar to the thrones of the other kings. The short platform beneath the throne is also hexagonal. The king wears a crown and in his left hand he holds a long regal scepter topped with an ornate vessel or finial. In his right hand he holds a small rod. The king's legs are crossed just above the ankles and he is shown full face. On the breastplate of his armor appears the Visconti heraldic device of a bird or dove with flaming rays—derived from Emperor Wenceslas in 1395. Below his belt is a nest—also a Visconti heraldic device.

King of Staves *Reprinted from the Pierpont Morgan–Bergamo Visconti-Sforza* tarocchi *pack.*

Nine through two of Swords Pierpont Morgan–Bergamo Visconti-Sforza tarocchi cards reproduced from the originals.

(far left)
Queen of Staves Reprinted from the Pierpont Morgan–Bergamo Visconti-Sforza tarocchi pack.

(left)
Knight of Staves Reprinted from the Pierpont Morgan–Bergamo Visconti-Sforza tarocchi pack.

(below)
Page of Staves Reprinted from the Pierpont Morgan–Bergamo Visconti-Sforza tarocchi pack.

Queen of Staves   Seated upon her throne, the queen of staves wears a royal crown. In her left hand she holds a regal scepter topped with an ornate vessel similar to the one held by the king. The queen wears a cape over a high-waisted gown that bears the Visconti heraldic devices of a bird with blazing rays and a bird's nest. In her right hand she holds a small rod.

Knight of Staves   The knight of staves is shown in profile mounted on a rearing white horse. In his right hand he holds a long scepter fitted at both ends with ornate vessels. The horse's caparison contains the Visconti heraldic device of a sun with blazing rays. Additionally, two escutcheons or armorial shields, similar to those on the knight of swords, are red on the left side and either silver, white or brown on the right side. Around the larger shield appears a quatrefoil less ornate than the one depicted on the caparison of the knight of swords. The smaller *party per pale* beneath the neck of the horse covers the outline of a device indiscernible on the right side.

Page of Staves   The page stands in profile and wears a short pleated coat trimmed with fur over a shirt bearing the heraldic device of the sun with rays, visible at the neck. His green-gloved right hand holds a long scepter fitted at both ends with ornate finials similar to those on the scepter held by the knight of staves.

(right)
Ten of Staves Reprinted from the Pierpont Morgan–Bergamo Visconti-Sforza tarocchi pack.

(far right)
Ace of Staves Reprinted from the Pierpont Morgan–Bergamo Visconti-Sforza tarocchi pack.

(below right)
King of Cups Reprinted from the Pierpont Morgan–Bergamo Visconti-Sforza tarocchi pack.

The Pip Cards in the Suit of Staves The ten pip cards are depicted by repeated crossed scepters or rods whose number indicates the value of the card. The scepters protrude through the ornate gold finials at both ends. The scepters are blue except at the points where they intersect; there they are gold. An assorted floral design of flowers, leaves and branches decorates the pip cards. The ten, nine, seven and six of staves have sixteen, six, two and three green crosses, respectively, within the diamonds formed by the intersected scepters. The five, four, three, two and ace of staves contain the Visconti motto, *A bon droyt*, within a scroll. Only the eight of staves contains no additional design within or around the scepters.

King of Cups The king of cups is shown in profile. He is seated upon a six-sided throne decorated with a quatrefoil in a diapered or lozenge-shaped pattern. The platform beneath his feet appears to be square rather than hexagonal, as depicted on the kings of swords and clubs. The king is wearing the ducal crown of Milan. His short coat, trimmed in fur, bears the Visconti heraldic device of a sun with wavy and straight rays that end in a scalloped pattern. His left hand holds aloft a large ornate cup or urn with a six-sided top that comes to a point like a steeple. He may be holding a small object in his right hand, but it is not distinguishable.

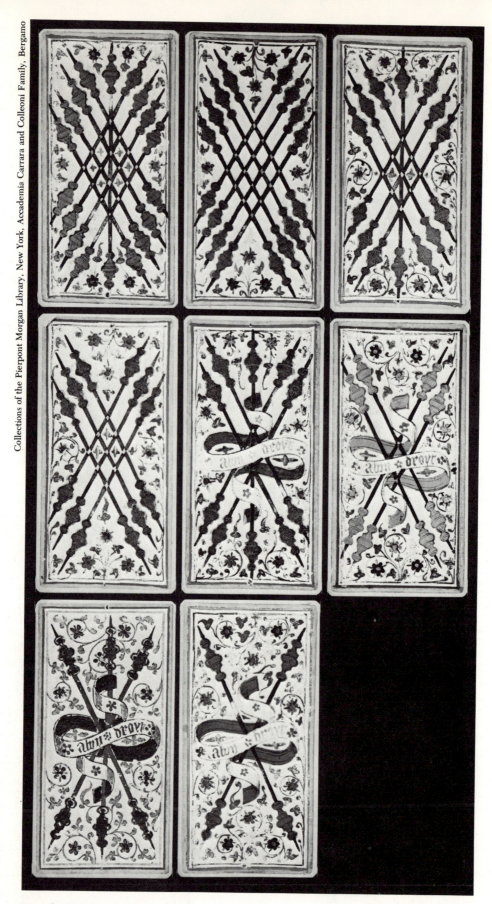

Nine through Two of Staves Pierpont Morgan–Bergamo Visconti-Sforza tarocchi cards reproduced from the originals.

Queen of Cups The queen of cups is seated upon her throne. She is shown full face and wearing a crown. Her high-waisted gown bears the Visconti heraldic device of a sun with intermixed wavy and straight rays. She wears green gloves and holds, in her right hand, a large ornate cup or urn with a pointed top. With her left hand she appears to be gesturing.

Knight of Cups The knight of cups is mounted upon a horse, the only horse in the deck painted in gold. The knight's short gold coat is trimmed with gray fur and bears the Visconti heraldic sun device. In his right hand the knight holds a large cup or urn similar to those held by the queen and king of his suit. The caparison worn by his horse bears the Visconti heraldic devices—the ducal crown of Milan with two branches or fronds and the Visconti sun with wavy rays and straight rays forming scalloped edges.

Page of Cups The page stands facing toward the left of the card. He wears a short gold coat trimmed with gray fur, similar to the frock worn by the knight of his suit, and white gloves. His right hand holds aloft a large cup or urn lacking the windows and some of the decorative dotted design of the cups depicted with the knight, queen and king of his suit. The page wears a red stocking on his right foot and a white stocking on his left foot. These colors—red and white—may be related to the colors appearing on the armorial shields depicted on the knights of swords and staves and the ace of coins.

(*above right*)
Queen of Cups Reprinted from the Pierpont Morgan–Bergamo Visconti-Sforza tarocchi pack.

(*right*)
Knight of Cups Reprinted from the Pierpont Morgan–Bergamo Visconti-Sforza tarocchi pack.

(*far right*)
Page of Cups Reprinted from the Pierpont Morgan–Bergamo Visconti-Sforza tarocchi pack.

(far left)
Ten of Cups Reprinted from the Pierpont Morgan–Bergamo Visconti-Sforza tarocchi *pack.*

(left)
Ace of Cups Reprinted from the Pierpont Morgan–Bergamo Visconti-Sforza tarocchi *pack.*

(below left)
King of Coins Reprinted from the Pierpont Morgan–Bergamo Visconti-Sforza tarocchi *pack.*

The Pip Cards in the Suit of Cups The pip cards have large ornate gold cups in the same number as the value of the card. The hexagonal bases of the cups are decorated with a trefoil in deep blue; the stems taper upward toward the bowls; the bodies are round. A gold ribbon against a deep blue turreted background runs the circumference of the vessel. The rims or lips of the cups are hexagonal. An assorted floral design of flowers, leaves and branches decorates the pip cards.

The four of cups bears the Visconti motto, *A bon droyt*, on a ribbon. The two of cups contains a ribbon proclaiming *amor myo* (my darling or my love). The use of this motto only on this card may signify the consummation of the love of husband and wife through the drinking of wine from two chalices. The ace of cups depicts a large fountain with an ornate stem rising from the center. A blue liquid flows from two spigots. The Visconti dove rests atop the fountain.

King of Coins The king of coins sits upon a six-sided throne on a raised trapezoidal-shaped platform; the platform has protruding semicircles. The king wears a large, wide-brimmed, plumed hat. His short robe resembles the garment worn by The Pope—it has interlocking, deep blue hexagonal ribbons. Although it also exhibits the familiar straight rays surrounding a sun, the sun on this robe is set within a circle of six additional suns. In his left hand the king holds a large coin that he rests on his left leg just above the knee. The coin bears the Visconti heraldic device of the sun with wavy rays and straight rays scalloped at the

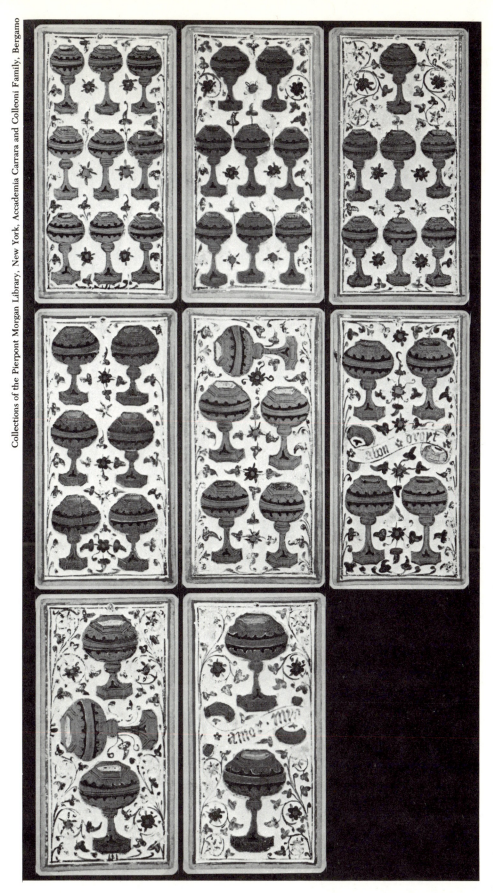

Nine through Two of Cups Pierpont Morgan–Bergamo Visconti-Sforza tarocchi cards reproduced from the originals.

Collection of the Pierpont Morgan Library, New York

Queen of Coins *Reprinted from the Pierpont Morgan–Bergamo Visconti-Sforza tarocchi pack.*

ends. A thin rod is in his right hand. His ankles are crossed. The stocking on his left leg is red on top and apparently was blue from the calf down, but the blue paint has worn off, revealing the white undercoat. The right stocking appears to have been green.

Queen of Coins The queen of coins wears a crown and is shown in profile facing to the left of the card. Her high-waisted gown and long cape bear the same design as the robe that clothes the king of her suit. With her right hand she holds a large coin—her suit sign. The rays on her coin are more delicate and less defined than those on the coin held by the king, thus suggesting that the work was completed by an apprentice artist.

Knight of Coins This is the only court card missing from the original deck. In the first five hundred Visconti-Sforza decks reproduced in 1975 by U.S. Games Systems, Inc., New York, and Grafica Gutenberg, Bergamo, Italy, a composite line drawing of a popular knight of coins was substituted. In the second edition of the reproduced deck the knight of coins was recreated by using a reversed print of the knight of cups and substituting a coin for the cup in the knight's hand. Thus, the caparison on the horse depicts the heraldic devices of the ducal crown of Milan with two branches or fronds and the Visconti sun with scallops and rays. However, the garment worn by the knight of coins in the original card, now lost, probably was similar to the short robe worn by the page of coins rather than the gold garment of the knight of cups.

Page of Coins Shown in profile facing toward the left of the card, the page wears a short robe trimmed in fur; it has the same hexagonal ribbons and floral suns shown on the king and queen cards of the coin suit. The page wears a wide-brimmed hat with curled plumes. The stocking on his left leg was probably blue below the knee; the right stocking probably red. However, now both are worn, revealing the white undercoating.

Collection of Grafica Gutenberg, Bergamo

Knight of Coins *Recreated to replace the card missing from the original Pierpont Morgan–Bergamo Visconti-Sforza tarocchi pack.*

84

The Encyclopedia of Tarot

Page of Coins Reprinted from the Pierpont Morgan–Bergamo Visconti-Sforza tarocchi *pack.*

The Pip Cards in the Suit of Coins The pip cards numbered ten through one are depicted by numerically repeating large coins that indicate the value of the card. The coins in cards ten through two contain the Visconti sun with wavy and straight rays within a blue turreted border set inside a rust-colored circle. The pip cards are further decorated with an assortment of flowers, leaves and branches. Cards five and three contain two ribbons each, bearing the words *A bon droyt*. Cards four and two contain only one ribbon each, bearing the same famous motto. The ace of coins contains an armorial device similar to the *party per pale* shown on the caparisons of the knights of swords and staves. The left side of the shield is red and the right side appears washed out but was probably white or silver. Interestingly, the right side of the *party per pale* contains the outline of a design. The hidden design may be the Sforza helmet—a winged dragon with a man's head, possibly set on top of two or three horizontal rings.

(right)
Ten of Coins Reprinted from the Pierpont Morgan–Bergamo Visconti-Sforza tarocchi *pack.*

(far right)
Ace of Coins Reprinted from the Pierpont Morgan–Bergamo Visconti-Sforza tarocchi *pack.*

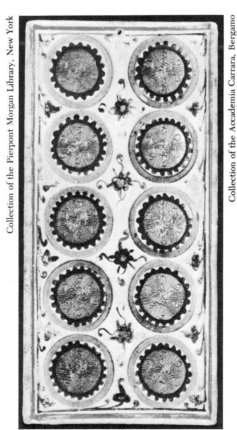

85

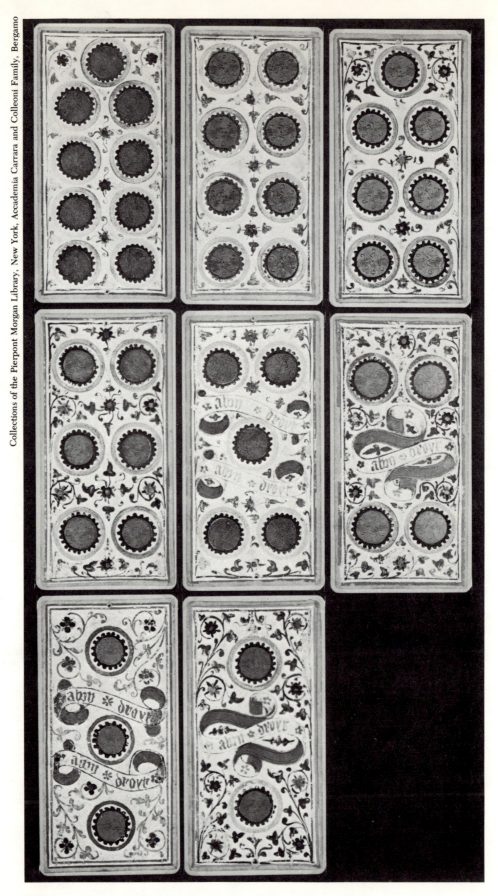

Nine through Two of Coins Pierpont Morgan–Bergamo Visconti-Sforza tarocchi cards reproduced from the originals.

VIII

THE OTHER VISCONTI AND VISCONTI-SFORZA TAROCCHI DECKS

Cary-Yale Visconti-Sforza Tarocchi Deck The cards that form this incomplete pack of Visconti-Sforza cards originally belonged to the Visconti di Modrone collection. They were acquired in 1947 by Melbert B. Cary, Jr., who subsequently bequeathed them, as part of the Cary Playing Card Collection, to The Beinecke Rare Book and Manuscript Library, Yale University, New Haven.

The Cary-Yale deck has sixty-seven extant cards, consisting of eleven Major Arcana and fifty-six Minor Arcana cards. The backs of these cards are plain without any colored ground. This unique deck has sixteen instead of fourteen cards in each of the four suits—the increase is due to two additional court cards per suit. The additional eight court cards are female counterparts to the male knight and page, also known as the mounted lady and maid. This brings the total Minor Arcana to sixty-four cards instead of fifty-six. In spite of the fact that eight Minor Arcana cards from the original pack are missing—the male knight and page of swords, the king and male knight of staves, the queen and female knight of cups, the male page and three of coins—the remaining original Minor Arcana cards ironically total exactly fourteen cards in each suit, fifty-six cards in all. At first glance this might suggest that the Minor Arcana cards are complete but, in fact, they most likely are not.

If the Yale pack in its entirety contained twenty-two Major Arcana cards and sixty-four Minor Arcana cards (as opposed to fifty-six), the pack would total eighty-six cards, of which nineteen cards would still be missing. A further complication is the presence in the Yale pack of three unusual Major Arcana cards—the three theological virtues of Faith, Hope and Charity (page 91)—which normally do not appear in tarot packs. The presence of these three cards has led some researchers to conclude, probably incorrectly, that this pack is really a minchiate deck. Other scholars believe it to be a transitional deck not yet fully developed into the minchiate pack. Faith, Hope and Charity may represent the missing Major Arcana cards of The Pope, The Star, and The Popess, respectively, though there is no positive connection between the theological virtues and these missing cards in the Yale pack.

One explanation of why the Yale pack may contain more cards than the usual seventy-eight-card *tarocchi* pack is that the artist may have been experimenting with additional court cards to please his patron. Alternatively, it is possible the artist never planned to include all the eleven or fourteen "missing" Major Arcana cards. (The difference in the number of "missing" cards depends upon whether one includes Faith, Hope and Charity as Major Arcana cards.) An additional possibility, however unlikely, is that the total number of court cards in each suit should be five—not four or six—with only the knight or the page having a female counterpart in one or more of the suits.

The king of cups in the Cary-Yale pack is depicted as a bearded, aged man in contrast to the younger kings of swords and coins (king of staves is missing) and the four youthful kings in the Pierpont Morgan–Bergamo pack. Thus, the aged king of cups in the Cary-Yale pack may represent a specific patriarch.

Another interesting aspect about the Cary-Yale pack is that the pip cards in the suit of staves are depicted by arrows, similar to the court cards in the Brera pack, rather than scepters, batons or rods. The pip cards in the suit of coins bear as their emblem the gold coins of Duke Filippo Maria, reproduced in pairs with their obverse side, except for the two and ace of coins that contain a writhing serpent.

Cary-Yale Visconti-Sforza Tarocchi Card—The Emperor The Illustration on the left is from a book of prints that accompanied Leopoldo Cicognara's work, Memorie Spettanti alla Storia della Calcografia del Commend, published in 1831. The Emperor card on the right is from the incomplete sixty-seven-card Visconti-Sforza pack at Yale University. The Emperor is seated on a throne that rests on a two-tiered platform. He is dressed in full armor and on his breastplate is the crowned imperial eagle. He wears a large plumed hat with turned-up brim on which is painted in black the imperial eagle. In his right gloved hand he holds a scepter and his left gloved hand rests on a golden orb. Around him are four youthful pages; the one at the lower right kneels with a crown in his hands, the page to the lower left has the inscription A bon droyt across the front of his garment.

Cary-Yale Visconti-Sforza Tarocchi Card—*The Lovers* The illustration on the left is from a book of prints that accompanied Cicognara's work, Memorie Spettanti alla Storia della Calcografia del Commend, *published in 1831. The Marriage or Love card on the right is from the Visconti-Sforza pack at Yale University. A winged, blindfolded Cupid in flight prepares to discharge two darts above a husband and wife. The figures may represent Duke Filippo Maria Visconti and either his first wife, Beatrice di Tenda, or his second wife, Maria of Savoy. On Filippo's wide-brimmed hat is the heraldic inscription,* A bon droyt. *Alternatively, the figures may represent Bianca Maria Visconti and Francesco Sforza; the man's short cape is decorated with a Sforza heraldic device of a fountain. Across the top of the pavilion is inscribed in letters of gold the word "Amor"; possibly on the unseen left side is the word* myo *or* mio. *The border emblems of the pavilion are composed of blazoned shields alternating the Visconti arms with those of Pavia.*

Cary-Yale Visconti-Sforza Tarocchi Cards—Death and Judgment Death is depicted as an animate skeleton, its forehead bound with a white fillet with flapping loose ends. The skeleton holds a scythe and rides a galloping black stallion over a huddled group of persons including the Pope and a cardinal. The Last Judgment depicts two winged angels on clouds playing a flute decorated with a banner and a harp. Beneath the angels are open tombs from which appear several nude persons of varying age and sex, including a male with arms crossed over his chest. In the background is a fully clothed bearded man who seems to be an observer. A high turreted castle appears along the right side, and at the top of the card are three Latin words in letters of gold, "Surgite ad judicium," which means "Stand up [or rise] to justice [or judgment]."

Cary-Yale Visconti-Sforza Tarocchi Cards—Hope and Charity The trump cards Hope and Charity (and the card Faith, which is not shown) do not appear in traditional seventy-eight-card *tarocchi* decks but are found in minchiate packs, which generally comprise ninety-seven cards. For this reason, some researchers believe the Cary-Yale *tarocchi* pack is either a minchiate deck or an intermediate game in the development and evolution of either tarot or minchiate. Hope depicts a crowned female figure in profile wearing a long robe, kneeling in prayer, with an anchor tied to her wrists. At the bottom of the card is a hunched figure of a man with a rope around his neck and with the words "Juda traditor" written in white letters on his purple garment. The despairing figure of vice is Judas. It has been suggested that the card of Hope may be a substitute for any one of several traditional Major Arcana cards missing in the Cary-Yale pack—Temperance, or The Hanged Man (suggested by the rope), or The Star with its symbolic meaning of rising new hope. Charity shows a crowned and seated female figure facing front who carries a silver torch in her right hand while supporting a suckling infant with her left arm. Charity is richly robed in an ornate gown with ermine cape. At her feet, beneath the throne at the bottom left of the card, is a crowned king suggesting King Herod. Charity may be a substitute for The Popess, but the image of a woman breast-feeding her child is inconsistent with the traditional imagery of The Popess. The Faith card depicts a female figure with a cross in her left hand; the index finger of her right hand is upraised to ward off evil spirits. Beneath her throne is a crowned king, possibly the figure of Heresy. Faith may be a substitute for The Pope or The Popess.

Cary-Yale Visconti-Sforza* Tarocchi Cards—*The World and the King of Swords   The World contains the half-length figure of a richly attired matron emerging above a large golden diadem that expands into a twisted, scalloped ornamentation of many colors. She holds a trumpet in her right hand and a smaller diadem or wreath in her left hand. Below is a large arch, and below this are ships at sea and a boat manned by two sailors. On one side of the river bank is a warrior on horseback; a fisherman is on the other side. The background is made up of towers, castles and hills surrounded by streams, fields and meadows. The king of swords sits on his throne wearing full armor. He wears a crown and his breastplate contains a decorative design, possibly the quince adopted by Muzio Attendolo Sforza. A small page stands in front of the raised platform; he wears a headdress of armor and holds a thin staff.

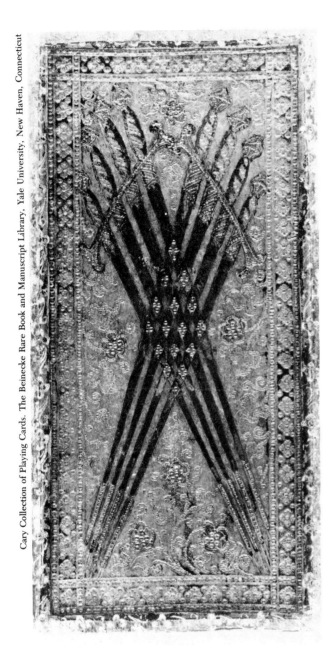 

Cary-Yale Visconti-Sforza* Tarocchi Cards—*Eight of Swords and Female Knight of Staves *The eight of swords depicts eight swords, each group of four swords joined at the handle. The female knight of staves is a unique card found only in this tarocchi pack; other knights in early tarocchi packs are male figures. The female knight sits sidesaddle on a white stallion. Her robe is decorated in a pattern of a six-sided fountain suggestive of the suit of cups in the Pierpont Morgan–Bergamo pack. At the bottom of her gown is the heraldic device of three interlocking rings. In her left hand she holds a scepter topped with a small ornate vessel.*

Cary-Yale Visconti-Sforza Tarocchi Cards—Male Page and Ace of Cups   The male page of cups is shown with his left hand near or resting on a large ornate vessel. His right hand is raised as if in a sign of greeting or benediction. The figure wears an oversized hat and both his cape and short garment display the heraldic device of the ducal crown with branches or fronds. The ace of cups is an ornate vessel or fountain that fills the entire card and possibly is a Sforza heraldic device. In the center of the vessel is the curled snake sometimes depicted in the act of partially devouring a human figure, another heraldic device. The five-lobed flowers studding the background on this card differ from the diapered pattern of a sunburst with alternating straight and wavy rays found on the Major Arcana and court cards of this pack, and the nore leafy floral design of the pip cards in the Pierpont Morgan–Bergamo pack.

Cary-Yale Visconti-Sforza Tarocchi Cards   Top row: *The six of swords; six of arrows; male knight of cups wearing a colorful hat of peacock feathers, the caparison worn by the horse bears the Visconti heraldic device of the ducal crown of Milan with branches or fronds.* Bottom row: *Female page of cups with a short, thin cape bearing the ducal crown; female knight of coins wearing a robe decorated with a pelican in profile above a ribbon panel; two of coins with the viper of the Visconti.*

The Brera Gallery or Brambilla Visconti-Sforza Tarocchi Cards Only forty-eight cards remain today of this pack. Two cards are Major Arcana—The Emperor and The Wheel of Fortune—and forty-six are suit cards. The extant suit cards include seven court cards—king, queen and knight of staves or arrows and the knights and pages in the suits of cups and coins—and thirty-nine pip cards (only the four of coins is lacking). The court figures in the suit of staves or arrows hold arrows with quill and arrowhead clearly distinguishable; the remaining pip cards in the suit of staves are depicted by pointed scepters or possibly thin quivers rather than arrows or batons. By contrast, in the Cary-Yale pack the pip cards in the suit of batons or staves are depicted by arrows while the court figures of the same suit hold batons. The presence of the arrows instead of batons suggests the possibility that the court cards of the suit of staves in the Brera pack and the pip cards of the suit of staves in the Cary-Yale pack once were part of the same pack, but this is doubtful since the border design and colors of the two packs are clearly different. It is possible that the court figures with arrows are from the suit of swords rather than staves, although that, too, is unlikely. The ace of swords carries the motto "*Phote Mantenir*," which means "We must uphold." The coins of the pip and court cards in the *denari* suit appear to be facsimiles of actual coins with figures on horseback—possibly the *fiorino* of Filippo Maria Visconti—and these also appear in the *denari* suit of the Cary-Yale pack.

Collection of Pinacoteca di Brera, Milan

Brera-Brambilla Visconti-Sforza Tarocchi Cards—The Emperor and The Wheel of Fortune *The bearded Emperor sits on a throne and wears a long robe with an ornate crescent decoration and a large hat bearing the insignia of the imperial eagle. In his left hand he holds a globe and in his right hand a thin tapered scepter. The Wheel of Fortune depicts a winged, blindfolded female figure standing inside the wheel and wearing a full-length gown decorated with repeating sunbursts. On top of the wheel and ascending its left side are two figures with ass's ears, and a fourth figure descends on the right. Supporting the wheel on his back is an aged man on his hands and knees dressed in white. This card is very similar to The Wheel of Fortune card in the Pierpont Morgan–Bergamo pack, except the descending figure is without a tail and the four figures do not have any lettering. The background design of both these cards contains a sun with eight wavy rays within a diamond or lozenge-shaped pattern. It is similar to the background designs of the Pierpont Morgan–Bergamo Visconti-Sforza tarocchi pack; however, the punch marks in the Brera pack are bolder and heavier than the more delicate punches in the Pierpont Morgan–Bergamo cards.*

Brera-Brambilla Visconti-Sforza* Tarocchi Cards—*Queen and Knight of Staves The queen of staves is seated and wears a crown. In her left hand she holds a long arrow with a quill. Her high-waisted gown contains a repeating pattern of a center flower with five surrounding petals. The knight of staves rides a rearing horse that fills the card, pressing its head against the border. The knight holds a long arrow in his right hand.

Brera-Brambilla Visconti-Sforza* Tarocchi Cards—*Knight and Page of Coins The knight of coins depicts a figure mounted on horseback. He wears an ornate hat with a large upraised rim decorated with a repeating design. His short coat lined with ermine has a feather pattern. The knight holds in his right hand a large coin. The caparison on the horse depicts the heraldic device of the ducal crown of Milan with two branches or fronds. The page of coins faces front and wears a hat and cape matching the design of the knight in this suit. The page holds in his right hand a large coin.

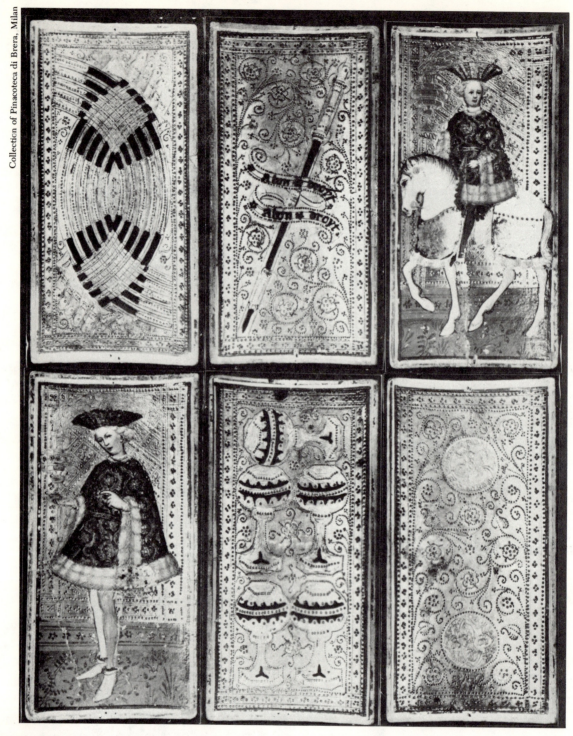

Brera-Brambilla Visconti-Sforza Tarocchi Cards Top row: *The ten of swords contains curved swords, instead of straight swords as found in the Pierpont Morgan–Bergamo pack; the ace of staves or quivers contains the Visconti motto* A bon droyt *repeated in two ribbons, and the background design is a punched pattern instead of the floral design found in the Pierpont Morgan–Bergamo pack; the knight of cups wears a large ornate hat topped with peacock feathers and holds a large ornate cup in his right hand; his horse is protected with armor.* Bottom row: *The page of cups holds an ornate cup in his right hand and wears a large ornate hat topped with peacock feathers; five of cups; two of coins is reproduced as a pair of coins with one coin and its obverse side. The coins held by the court figures and those depicted in the pip cards of the Brera pack are similar to the coins shown in the same suit in the Cary-Yale pack and are probably the fiorino of Filippo Maria Visconti. The large ornate hat with its dishlike rim topped with peacock feathers worn by the knight and page of cups differs from the hats worn by the knight and page of swords in the Pierpont Morgan–Bergamo pack (page 75), which have a much lower rim. Interestingly, in the Pierpont Morgan–Bergamo pack the knight and page of cups are hatless.*

Rosenthal Visconti-Sforza Tarocchi Cards The twenty-three so-called Rosenthal cards were offered in 1939 to a leading American collector, who declined to purchase them because he believed the cards were a much more recent rendition of fifteenth century tarocchi cards. The cards are The Fool, The Emperor, Justice, The Star, The Sun; the knight, page, five, four and ace of swords; the queen, knight, page and five of staves; the king, five and ace of cups; the king, page, five, three and ace of coins; and a joker or identification card.

Photograph from the collection of the author

Rosenthal Visconti-Sforza Cards Top row: *The Falcon card is suggestive of The Fool; The Emperor is strikingly similar to the same card in the group of six Visconti-Sforza cards owned by Museo Fournier; Justice; the Star is strikingly similar to the same card in the group of four Visconti-Sforza cards owned by the Victoria and Albert Museum; The Sun contains the word "Fortezza" in a ribbon panel beneath the castle; the knight and (second row) page of swords are similar to the same cards in the Pierpont Morgan–Bergamo pack; the five and four of swords contain the heraldic motto,* **A bon droit**; *the ace of swords is depicted as a dagger dripping blood with* **A bon droit** *in a panel at the top of the card and the word "REP(–)U(–)" and an unidentifiable word on the middle and bottom of the card; the queen of staves; the knight of staves includes a small three-turreted castle at the upper left of the card.* Third row: *The page of staves, five of staves with* 'A bon droit'; *king of cups; five of cups; ace of cups; strikingly similar to the ace of cups in the set of four cards at the Victoria and Albert Museum, except this card has unidentifiable wording on the upper ribbon behind the fountain streams and there is no precipice at the bottom of the card; king of coins.* Bottom row: *The page of coins, strikingly similar to the same card at the Victoria and Albert Museum; five and three of coins with the motto* **A bon droit**, *(the stylized design of a sun with rays on each coin is different on these two cards); the ace of coins with a picture of a cardinal and some unidentified writing in the background; and a joker or identification card depicting a crowned snake half devouring a human figure.*

Von Bartsch Visconti-Sforza Tarocchi Cards The Baron Pietro von Bartsch cards total thirteen and comprise five trumps: The Pope or Hierophant, The Chariot, The Wheel of Fortune, Temperance and Judgment. There are also the king, page and five of swords; king, knight and page of cups; queen of coins; and one unusual card bearing the coat of arms of the Visconti-Sforza family—a large crowned serpent half devouring a human figure. Some scholars have suggested this card may have been either a joker or an identification card used to establish the deck's ownership. The king of swords contains the initials A.C., which may stand for the artist Antonio Cicognara, or perhaps represent a Latinized version of Cardinal Ascani (Ascani, Cardinal), the son of Bianca Maria Visconti and the fourth Duke of Milan, Francesco Sforza. Five Von Bartsch cards—Wheel of Fortune, Temperance, Judgment and the kings of swords and cups—show marked divergences of design from the Pierpont Morgan–Bergamo pack. Seven Von Bartsch cards—The Pope, The Chariot, page and three of swords, knight and page of cups, and queen of coins—are fairly faithful copies of the originals. Only the fearsome, crowned serpent has no counterpart in earlier decks. Eleven of these cards were sold some years ago by a New York dealer, Piero Tozzi, to an unknown collector in Milan; Temperance is owned by the Montreal Museum of Fine Arts. The page of cups, formerly part of the F. Cleveland Morgan collection, and subsequently part of the J. Bartlett Morgan collection, is presently owned by Cleveland Stewart-Patterson.

Reprinted from Thirteen Tarot Cards from the Visconti-Sforza Set by M. L. D'Otrange

Von Bartsch Visconti-Sforza Cards—The Wheel of Fortune and King of Swords *The Wheel of Fortune depicts a figure perched on top of the wheel and having either ass's ears or a horned crown; the gown is adorned with an upright ladder, suggesting the heraldic device of the della Scala family. A second figure, winged, blindfolded, and with red instead of blond hair, is balanced within the wheel, and on her robes appears the design of rayed suns, each sun inset with a central motif showing a silver cross on red ground—the reverse of the arms of Savoy: a red cross on silver ground. M. L. D'Otrange, writing in 1954, rightfully asks why the della Scala family, lords of Verona until defeated in 1387 by Duke Giangaleazzo Visconti, would be honored in a set of tarot cards presumably presented to Cardinal Ascanio Sforza or another member of the Visconti-Sforza family. Two figures appear on either side of the wheel. The upright figure is thought by D'Otrange to resemble Leonello d'Este, duke of Ferrara from 1441 to 1450. The other unidentified figure has a squat nose, thick lips, bulging eyes, a long tail and is upside down. Beneath the wheel and its four figures is an aged bearded man crouching on hands and knees and supporting the wheel on his back. The lettering in small ribbon bands near each figure is discernible but the meanings unclear. The words do not seem to be the Regno, Regnabo, Regnavi and Sum sine regno that appear in The Wheel of Fortune card of the Pierpont Morgan–Bergamo deck (page 69), although the meanings may be the same.*

The king of swords sits upon his throne of gothic motif. He is clad in full armor, holds a sword, and his right hand rests on a shield emblazoned with a lion. The king has bulging eyes and an intense facial expression. The facial features of the king and the decoration of the throne differ substantially from the king of swords in the Pierpont Morgan–Bergamo pack. At the bottom of the card appear the initials A.C., suggesting to some researchers the painter Antonio Cicognara, but this seems unlikely and the initials may be a later addition.

The location of these two cards is presently unknown; they were sold in the early 1960s by Piero Tozzi, a New York dealer, to an unknown collector in Milan.

Reprinted from Thirteen Tarot Cards from the Visconti-Sforza Set by M. L. D'Otrange

Von Bartsch Visconti-Sforza Tarocchi Cards *Nine of the eleven hand-painted cards sold by Piero Tozzi to an unknown Milan collector.* Top row: *The Pope is an aged thin figure who seems almost overwhelmed by his full robes and large tiara. He gives a blessing with his right hand and in his left holds a long scepter topped by a cross. A repeating design of sunbursts with both straight and wavy rays appears on his heavy cape. The Chariot depicts a crowned female figure of small stature seated on a high throne and holding in her left hand a globe topped with a cross. She is robed in a wide-sleeved gown of rich brocade patterned with the sunburst of the Visconti-Sforza escutcheon. Judgment depicts two angels with bannered trumpets in front of a crowned figure with upraised sword; a red cross against a white background adorns one of the banners and at the bottom of the card two figures emerge from a tomb made of irregular stones.*

Middle row: *The page of swords is shown full face and dressed in silvered armor. He wears the fashionable headgear of the period—a flat wide-brimmed hat edged with peacock feathers—and his right hand rests on the hilt of his sword. The five of swords shows five swords, four pointing down and the center one pointing up, loosely bound by a band bearing the motto of the Visconti, A bon droit. The king of cups wears a ducal crown and sits upon a gothic throne. He holds the sign of his suit, a magnificently ornate covered cup, and his short coat bears the Visconti heraldic device of repeating suns with straight and wavy rays. The king sits facing to the left, the opposite facing direction of the king of cups in the Pierpont Morgan–Bergamo pack and the facial features of the king are substantially different (page 79).*

Bottom row: *The knight of cups is mounted on horseback and holds aloft a large covered cup. He faces to the right, the same facing direction as the knight of cups in the Pierpont Morgan–Bergamo pack (page 81). He wears the short, collarless, fluted tunic of the period, which here bears the heraldic Visconti sun. The caparison worn by his horse bears the Visconti heraldic device of the ducal crown of Milan with branches or fronds going through the center. The queen of coins wears a crown and is shown in profile facing to the left, the same direction faced by the queen of coins in the Pierpont Morgan–Bergamo pack. She wears a high-waisted gown and long cape with a design that resembles that on the garment worn by The Pope—interlocking ribbons surrounding a sun with straight rays. The queen holds in her lap the large coin of her suit. The final card is a fearsome crowned serpent with large green acanthus leaves clinging to its body, in the act of devouring an enemy; D'Otrange relates that, according to legend, such an occurrence took place in front of Jerusalem during one of the Crusades. The figure represents the coat of arms adopted by the Sforzas when Francesco Sforza married Bianca Visconti in 1441.*

Von Bartsch Visconti-Sforza Tarocchi Card—Temperance Painted on parchment and pasted on papier-mâché, this card is believed by some researchers to be a later rendition, copied from the substitute Temperance card in the Pierpont Morgan-Bergamo deck, but the dress worn by the figure is not adorned with stars. A tall, slender young woman with long, flowing hair pours a liquid from one pitcher into another; the pitchers are decorated with the trefoil design. The woman is clad in a high-waisted tunic of plain material with peplum folds. In the distant background are barren hills. The Temperance card measures 166 by 83 mm. and was purchased by the Montreal Museum of Fine Arts in 1949; the card is presently retired from normal exhibition.

Von Bartsch Visconti-Sforza Tarocchi Card—Page of Cups From the collection of the late F. Cleveland Morgan, Montreal. The page faces to the left and wears a coat trimmed in fur and decorated with sunbursts. He wears different colored stockings and his hands are gloved. This proud young man is depicted with heavy-lidded eyes and a faint sneer on his lips. M. L. D'Otrange, writing in 1954, suggested that Galeazzo Maria Sforza, reputedly one of the worst tyrants, and under whose reign this card allegedly was made, needed about him such servants to placate his insatiable desire for beauty and luxury, his refined corruption and his insane ferocity. This card, with the exception of the figure's facial features, bears a striking similarity to the page of cups from the seventy-four-card Pierpont Morgan–Bergamo pack.

Museo Fournier Visconti-Sforza Tarocchi Cards The six cards at Museo Fournier, Vitoria, Spain, are The Popess, The Emperor, the seven of staves, and the eight, two, and ace of coins. The backs of these cards are painted a plain dark red. The cards measure 171 by 88 mm., and there does not appear to be any previous written history of them. The background design of the face side of each card is a pierced decoration on a gold background. The faces of the two figures seem more individually designed than those on the Pierpont Morgan-Bergamo cards, and it is uncertain whether they are the work of the Bembo school.

Victoria and Albert Visconti-Sforza Tarocchi Cards The four cards at Victoria and Albert Museum, London, are Death, The Star, the ace of cups and the page of coins.

Collection of Museo Fournier, Vitoria, Spain

Fournier Visconti-Sforza Tarocchi Cards *Early Italian tarocchi cards purchased in 1975 by Museo Fournier from a dealer in Milan. Top row: The Popess or Papesse wears a long brown nun's habit and a three-tiered crown. She holds a book on her lap and with her right hand she supports a thin long rod topped with a Maltese cross. The Emperor is dressed in regal garments decorated with a pattern of blazing suns. A black eagle decorates his large hat and he holds a globe in his left hand and a short stick or rod in his right hand. The seven of staves is depicted with seven clubs having gold knobs on each end. Bottom row: The eight and two of coins contain the blazing sun design within each coin and the cards are decorated with green leaves. The two of coins contains a ribbon bearing the words, A bon droit. The ace of coins may be a presentation card; it features a large round medallion with the picture of a three-storied red castle in the middle.*

Collection of Victoria and Albert Museum, London

Victoria and Albert Museum Visconti-Sforza Tarocchi Cards Top row: *Death is depicted as an animate figure; he wears a long black shroud and a wide-brimmed black hat with long braided tassels. The skeleton of Death stands on a floor of alternating black and white squares and declares "San fine," probably a form of "Sine fine," meaning without end. The Star depicts a crowned figure with headdress and long robes with feathered sleeves who holds aloft in his right hand a thin eight-pointed star while a falcon rests on his left arm.* Bottom row: *The ace of cups is a large fountain topped by an arrow and two streams of water; two winged naked figures are at play at the fountain base. The ornate scroll in the background behind the arrow is blank, while the stem of the fountain is lettered "Nec spe nec metu" which means "Neither hope nor fear." The page of coins wears a wide-brimmed hat and a short cape decorated with the Visconti heraldic device of blazing suns; he faces left and holds aloft the sign of his suit.*

Additional Visconti-Sforza tarocchi cards are:

Guildhall Visconti-Sforza **Tarocchi Card** The single card at Guildhall, London, is The World.

Andrioletti Visconti-Sforza **Tarocchi Card** The single card, whose last known owner was Francesco Andrioletti, Milan, is the page of coins, which resembles the same card at the Accademia Carrara, Bergamo, Italy.

Marzoli Visconti-Sforza **Tarocchi Card** The single card, whose last known owner was Mrs. Marzoli, Milan, is the page of staves, much restored in the lower half but strongly suggestive of the Bembo school. This card resembles the page of staves at the Accademia Carrara, Bergamo, Italy.

Biedak Visconti-Sforza **tarocchi Card** This single card, whose last known owner was Mr. Biedak, Los Angeles, is the king of cups.

Collection of Guildhall Library, London

Guildhall Visconti-Sforza Tarocchi Card—The World *This card, circa fifteenth century, Italy, depicts two winged cherubs holding up a globe or circular panorama of a castle. The overall design is similar to that of The World card owned by Accademia Carrara, Bergamo, and forming part of the incomplete seventy-four-card Pierpont Morgan–Bergamo deck. The castle in both cards is nearly identical; however, there is a significant difference in the style and execution of the artist, the positioning of the figures and the design within the dotted squares of the background.*

***Andrioletti* Visconti-Sforza Tarocchi Card—Page of Coins** The page faces to the right in contrast to similar cards in the Victoria and Albert Museum and the Rosenthal collection, whose figures face to the left. The page of coins wears a wide-brimmed hat with a brim bearing a coin design of suns with straight rays. His short cape contains a repeating sun design with six petals and he holds aloft a large coin with the sun design featuring wavy rays. This card is one of the smallest—140 mm. in length—of the *Visconti-Sforza* tarocchi cards. The tooled dots of the background design are large holes without the ornate diapered pattern found on most other *Visconti-Sforza* tarocchi cards. Behind the page's neck and shoulders is one tooled sun with seven rays.

***Marzoli* Visconti-Sforza Tarocchi Card—Page of Staves** The page faces to the right and holds a large scepter with an ornate vessel at both its top and bottom. The page wears a short cape that bears a repeating sun design and possibly a dove with radiating lines. The cape is edged in ermine. The background of the card is a heavily tooled sun with curly rays within a paneled diapered pattern.

***Biedak* Visconti-Sforza Tarocchi Card—King of Cups** The king of cups, circa fifteenth century Italy, contains the card background illuminated in gold. The heraldic device of the Visconti sun appears on the king's cape and garments. He has bulging eyes and sunken cheeks; he gives a greeting or benediction with his right hand and holds an ornate covered cup.

THE ARTISTS

There have been many attempts to identify the painters of the different Visconti-Sforza *tarocchi* cards. It is possible that the incomplete seventy-four-card Pierpont Morgan–Bergamo pack, the sixty-seven-card Cary-Yale pack and possibly the forty-eight-card Brera Gallery pack were rendered by the same hand, with the exception of the six replacement cards in the Pierpont Morgan–Bergamo deck. All three packs have similar margin patterns, embossed with very similar punches on the rhomboid areas of the gold base. However, the figures in the Pierpont Morgan–Bergamo pack appear rounder and plumper than those in the Cary-Yale pack.

For many years it was thought the artist of the seventy-four-card Pierpont Morgan–Bergamo pack was Antonio Cicognara, a theory promoted by one of his nineteenth-century descendents, Leopoldo Cicognara, who cited as his source the *Chronicles of Cremona*, written by Domenico Bordigallo and reported in the notes of Giacomo Torresino in 1484:

> In this year our townsman Antonio di Cicognara, most skillful painter of pictures and fine miniaturist, designed and illuminated a magnificent set of cards called Tarocchi, seen by me, which he presented to the Most Illustrious and Most Reverend Monsignore Ascanio Maria Sforza, Cardinal of Holy Church, Bishop of Pavia and Novara, formerly Dean of our Cathedral and at present Commendatory of the Canonry of St. Gregory in the same, and son of the Most Illustrious and Excellent Francesco Sforza and Madonna Bianca Visconti, who was born here in Cremona. The same illuminated other games for the two sisters of the Cardinal who were Augustinian nuns in the convent founded in this town by the said Madonna Bianca.

In addition, Leopoldo Cicognara credited the sixty-seven Cary-Yale cards to Marziano da Tortona, a painter who lived at the court of Duke Filippo Maria and acted as his secretary. Cicognara believed he discerned the name of Marziano da Tortona on the bottom of the card Faith near a recumbent male figure.

Most scholars now believe that the artist was Bonifacio Bembo, a Cremonese painter supposed to have been born around 1420, who was favored with many commissions from the Sforza family of Milan. Very little remains of Bembo's work. He is mentioned several times from 1447 to 1477 as "Bonifacio, painter of Cremona" in documents, but there is no evidence of Bembo in Milan during the reign of Filippo Maria Visconti. Roberto Longhi, writing in 1928, was the first to attribute these cards to Bonifacio Bembo, and Gertrude Moakley, writing in 1966, did much to clear up the Cicognara mixup.

Interestingly, the cards of Death, Temperance, The Star and The Moon in the Pierpont Morgan–Bergamo pack each depict a sharp cliff in the foreground and, along with Strength and The World, were executed by a different artist. While this hardly suggests the identification of the artist, it is interesting to recall that the painting by Ambrogio Borgognone (1481–1523) of the Certosa also depicts the steep cliff found on the cards.

The twenty-three Visconti-Sforza cards whose last known pre-World War II owner was Rosenthal, a British dealer, vary considerably in execution and style from the three earlier packs. These cards appear to be a much later edition.

The six cards owned by Museo Fournier appear to be an early edition, although they do not match any other early pip, court or trump cards.

The several single cards in different collections appear consistent with the early style and execution of the larger incomplete decks, although the Montreal Museum of Fine Arts believes that its card, Temperance, is a copy of an earlier original.

DATING THE DECKS

There is considerable controversy about which of the Visconti-Sforza decks is the oldest. Some scholars, including Ronald Decker, believe that the incomplete forty-eight-card Brera Gallery deck is the oldest, dating from about 1445. Decker, an art teacher, has devoted considerable time to the study of the different Visconti-Sforza packs. He bases his main argument upon the style and artwork of the cards. The forty-eight-card Brera pack appears stiff and less professional than the Pierpont Morgan and Cary-Yale Visconti-Sforza packs.

Other researchers and important collectors, including Albert Field, maintain that the incomplete sixty-seven-card Cary-Yale pack is the oldest deck because of the presence of the arms of the family of Maria de Savoy on The Lovers card. Filippo Visconti, the third Duke of Milan, married his second wife, Maria de Savoy, in 1428, which suggests that the Cary-Yale Visconti pack dates from this year. If true, this pack might be called a Visconti-Savoy deck. However, according to Decker, the marriage between Filippo and Maria de Savoy was never consummated and Filippo held his bride as a political prisoner. If such was the case, one wonders whether Filippo would promote the heraldic device of his outcast wife and the Savoy family on a deck of beautiful hand-painted cards.

The device on The Lovers card in the Cary-Yale pack—a white cross on a red field—might be explained by an observation of Leopoldo Cicognara, writing in 1831, that these were the arms of Pavia. Decker observes that Francesco Sforza held two concurrent titles—Prince of Pavia, represented by the white cross on red, and Duke of Milan, symbolized in The Lovers card by a serpent crest.

The Major Arcana and court cards of the Cary-Yale pack are stylistically alike. If this pack or at least the Major Arcana and court cards were done for Francesco Sforza, then it must have been after 1450 when he assumed the titles of Duke of Milan and Prince of Pavia. Thus, what some researchers interpret as the heraldic device of the Savoy family might actually be Francesco Sforza's device for his princely duties at Pavia. Further complicating identification is the fact that the Savoy device was a popular emblem commonly used in other cities and its presence on The Lovers card might be attributable to some more remote meaning.

The suit of coins in the Brera-Brambilla and Cary-Yale packs contains coins associated with the reign of Filippo Maria Visconti, while the Pierpont Morgan–Bergamo pack utilizes the Visconti sun device. Thus, one might question why Sforza, in his subsequent reign, would use his predecessor's heraldic devices. Decker cites several plausible explanations why Visconti coins would survive in Sforza decks: Bembo was obliged to complete the decks using Filippo's currency since Francesco Sforza had not yet cast his own coins; Sforza had no objection—in fact, he saw an advantage—to associating his rule with that of Duke Filippo (the coins, after all, were synonymous with the heritage of the duchy and the duke's childhood); the pips, being common cards, might have been entrusted to apprentices who simply copied existing examples.

Based upon costume design and heraldic devices, a strong case can be made that the Brera-Brambilla pack is the oldest, followed by the Cary-Yale pack and finally the Pierpont Morgan–Bergamo pack. In the Brera-Brambilla pack, the remaining two Major Arcana and seven court cards depict figures wearing costumes decorated with crescent and floral patterns without heraldic connotation. In the sixty-seven-card Cary-Yale pack, the costumes in the suit of swords are decorated with a Sforza quince or a branch bearing leaves and flowers. A large fountain, also thought to be an early Sforza device, is used in the suit of staves. The remaining suits bear Visconti devices—crowns with branches or fronds in the suit of cups and pelicans or doves in the suit of coins. Thus, two suits in the Cary-Yale pack contain Visconti devices and two contain Sforza devices, leading one to speculate that the deck was prepared about the time of the wedding in 1441 of Francesco Sforza and Bianca Maria Visconti, each family equally represented by two suits. Furthermore, The Lovers card depicts what may be the marriage scene and the aged figure depicted as the king of cups may represent the bride's father, Filippo Visconti. The presence of Visconti coins in the Brera-Brambilla and Cary-Yale packs and Sforza coins in the Pierpont Morgan–Bergamo pack further supports the conclusion that the Pierpont Morgan–Bergamo deck is the most recent of the three Milanese packs.

The unusual use of arrows in the Brera-Brambilla pack for the pip cards in the suit of staves has been continued in the Cary-Yale pack. Subsequently, the Pierpont Morgan–Bergamo pack uses batons on the pip cards in the suit of staves, which is consistent with later tarocchi decks.

The seventy-four-card Pierpont Morgan–Bergamo pack would seem the most recent of the three decks as further evidenced by the prevalent use of Sforza heraldic devices such as three interlocking rings and Visconti heraldic emblems adopted by Francesco Sforza. For example, both The Empress and The Emperor wear garments decorated with both the interlocking rings of the Sforza family and the Visconti crown. The black eagle of Emperor Wenceslas, used first by the Viscontis and later adopted by the Sforzas, appears on the shield held by The Empress and on the hat worn by The Emperor and suggests that the Pierpont Morgan–Bergamo pack dates from sometime after the marriage of Francesco Sforza and Bianca Maria Visconti.

It is probable that hand-illuminated cards such as the Visconti-Sforza decks were commissioned to honor certain important events. Some scholars suggest that the sixty-seven-card Cary-Yale pack served as a present for the marriage of Filippo Visconti to Maria de Savoy in 1428, and the forty-eight-card Brera pack was a present for the marriage of Francesco Sforza to Bianca Maria Visconti in 1441. The seventy-four-card Pierpont Morgan–Bergamo pack might have been commissioned in celebration of Francesco Sforza's assumption of the ducal crown of Milan in 1450, or perhaps the deck served as a tenth anniversary present to Bianca Maria from Francesco Sforza.

The thirteen Von Bartsch cards were apparently painted by one artist, as evidenced by the execution and harmony of style. These cards seem to be a more recent version of the seventy-four-card Pierpont Morgan–Bergamo Visconti-Sforza pack because the artist has copied the Bembo card interpretations and the Temperance replacement card. These thirteen cards also are less graceful in style, which suggests that they are copies. The motif on the gown of the figure in the center of The Wheel of Fortune, a repeating silver cross on a red background, is similar to the design seen in the sixty-seven-card Cary-Yale pack and evidences the connection between these two packs. Perhaps these thirteen cards were originally part of a pack designed for Cardinal Ascanio Maria Sforza in the last half of the fifteenth century.

The Temperance card at the Montreal Museum of Fine Arts has been described as a nineteenth-century copy. This card has been retired by the museum from exhibition and the print shown is an old one from the museum's archives.

IX
OTHER EARLY HAND-PAINTED CARDS

Kestner Museum The Kestner Museum in Hannover, West Germany, possesses two hand-painted Italian cards, circa mid-fifteenth century. The cards are the pages of swords and coins. The page of coins holds in his left hand a large coin depicting a coiled serpent; his right hand rests upon a dagger. Since there are no existing trumps, it is not known if these cards belong to a tarot pack.

National Museum, Warsaw Two cards at the National Museum, Warsaw, are the queen of cups and the knight of coins, possibly dating from the late fifteenth century. The background of each card is a tooled floral pattern. No trump cards from this deck are known today; therefore, it is not certain if these cards belong to a tarot pack.

Castello Ursino The fifteen tarot cards at the Museo Civico, Castello Ursino, Catania, Italy, are hand painted on cardboard composed of stiff sheets of paper glued together. These cards originated in northern Italy and date from the middle to the end of the fifteenth century. Some art re-

Page of swords and page of coins from the Kestner Museum The page of swords depicts a young man resting his right hand on his sword. The page of coins holds in his left hand a large coin depicting a coiled serpent; his right hand rests upon a dagger. The page of swords is depicted outdoors; the page of coins is standing indoors on an ornamental floor.

Queen of cups and knight of coins, National Museum, Warsaw The queen of cups sits on a high-back throne and wears her crown and a long dark robe. A small female page or servant hands a large cup to the queen. The knight of coins is shown on a white horse. He wears a fur hat and holds in his right hand a large coin with an ornamental design.

The Chariot and The World, Museo Civico, Catania These are two of the remaining fifteen hand-painted cards of an incomplete set, circa middle to end of the fifteenth century, housed at the Museo Civico, Castello Ursino, Catania, Italy.

searchers believe the cards were painted by Bonifacio Bembo or under the supervision of his shop. The Castello Ursino cards comprise four trumps and two court cards—The Chariot, Father Time or The Hermit, a nude woman on a stag as Temperance(?), The World depicting a figure standing on the earthly sphere, the king of swords and page of cups—and nine pip cards—the eight and seven of swords; nine and six of staves; ten and ace of cups, and eight, seven and two of coins. Five cards—the king and eight of swords, six of staves, ten of cups and seven of coins—are part of the Benedettinis collection; the remaining ten cards belong to the Biscari collection.

Goldschmidt The nine so-called Goldschmidt cards, circa mid-fifteenth century, may have originated in either Provence or Italy. The cards measure 140 by 65 mm. and are hand painted and gilded with tooled backgrounds on parchment. The Goldschmidt cards are housed at the Deutsches Spielkarten Museum, Leinfelden, West Germany. Although they are not necessarily related to tarot, the cards bear some interesting designs for what appear to be The Fool, The Empress, The Pope, Death or the ace of swords, The Sun, a queen in prayer, the five of staves, ace of cups and a crowned sea serpent. The Fool (?) depicts a young man with a falcon on his arm, a dog barking at his feet and a wheel behind him; The Empress (?) depicts a queen or an empress looking at a small toy castle while a lady-in-waiting carries her train; the religious figure apparently is a cardinal, or possibly the Pope, and on the wall is a mysterious anchor; Death or the ace of swords (?) is shown as a short sword or dagger with a large ornate hilt, crossbones and a grinning, toothy skull chained to the sword shaft; the Sun (?) overlooks three protruding green objects bearing the initials M A C; a

Goldschmidt Cards *Nine remaining Goldschmidt cards, circa mid-fifteenth century, from a pack of cards whose original total number remains unknown. Top row: The Fool (?), The Empress (?), The Pope (?), Death or the ace of swords (?) and The Sun (?). Bottom row: A queen in prayer, five of staves, ace of cups and a crowned sea serpent.*

Guildhall Cards *Three hand-painted Italian cards, probably of the fifteenth century. The ace of swords or The Sun(?) is depicted as a flaming sun with tooled dots for facial features; beneath the sun is a large sword with an ornate hilt. The word "mia" appears in red at the top of the card and "arm(o)ur(?)" appears within a scroll in the center of the card. A serpent facing to the right encircles the sword while attempting to swallow its own tail. The dagger and serpent in this card resemble those in two of the Goldschmidt cards (page 110). The figure with crossbow may represent the page of staves, as evidenced by the single club in the background. The theme of this card is suggestive of the "hunting" cards found in the Ambras Hofjagdspiel (page 58) pack from mid-fifteenth-century Germany. The fountain in the ace of cups fills virtually the entire card. At the top of the fountain are two streams of water and an arrow. A short dagger and an anchor are placed at the upper corners of the card; the anchor design, large cup and alternating black and white square floor bear some resemblance to cards of the Goldschmidt pack (page 110). The scroll behind the ace of cups in the Guildhall card is without lettering.*

queen is in prayer with her lady-in-waiting; the five of staves appears to be of Spanish suit design with its short stumps; and the ace of cups is depicted with an arrow and two rising fountains. The ace is similar in some respects to the same card in the Visconti-Sforza collections of both the Museo Fournier and the Guildhall, with the exception that the Goldschmidt ace of cups includes a serpent facing to the left and biting its own tail while encircling the base of the cup. The crowned sea serpent, possibly an identification card, is decidedly different from the crowned snake or dragon of the Rosenthal (page 99) and Von Bartsch (page 101) Visconti-Sforza *tarocchi* cards. Not only does it look like a fish of almost humorous facial features, but it is also not in the act of devouring any human being.

Guildhall Three early Italian cards, probably of the fifteenth century, are located at the Guildhall, London. Although the cards are hand painted with gold backgrounds and are the same size as The World card from a Visconti-Sforza pack also at the Guildhall, the three cards are not suggestive of Bembo's work. The first card, either The Sun or ace of swords, depicts a large rayed sun with dotted design outlining the face. The next card appears to be the page of staves. However, the page is depicted as a hunter with crossbow, suggestive of German "hunting" cards. The final card is the ace of cups.

Gringonneur The so-called Gringonneur cards in the Bibliothèque Nationale, Paris, have been credited to Jacquemin Gringonneur who, it is alleged, painted them in 1392 during the reign of Charles VI. However, these oversized hand-painted cards are probably of mid-fifteenth-century Venetian origin. The seventeen so-called Gringonneur cards are without inscriptions, letters or numbers to indicate the manner in which the cards are to be arranged.

Nevertheless, they are readily identifiable with seventeen modern tarot symbols as well as with ten, perhaps thirteen, designs from the fifty-card Tarocchi of Mantegna pack.

Gringonneur Pack	Modern Tarot	Tarocchi of Mantegna
Le Fou	The Fool	*Misero* I
L'Empereur	III The Emperor	*Imperator* VIIII
Le Pape	V The Pope	*Papa* X
Les Amoureux	VI The Lovers	*Apollo* XX
Le Chariot	VII The Chariot	*Marte* XXXV (?)
La Justice	VIII Justice	*Iusticia* XXXVII
L'Ermite	VIIII The Hermit	*Saturno* XXXXVII (?)
La Force	XI Strength	*Forteza* XXXVI
La Tempérance	XIIII Temperance	*Temperancia* XXXIIII
La Lune	XVIII The Moon	*Luna* XXXXI
Le Soleil	XVIIII The Sun	*Sol* XXXXIIII
Le Monde	XXI The World	*Astrologia* XXVIIII (?)
Le Valet d'épée	Valet of swords	*Chavalier* VI

The following four subjects have no corresponding figures in the Tarocchi of Mantegna cards; however, they are found among the Major Arcana cards of modern tarot decks.

Gringonneur Pack	Modern Tarot
Le Pendu	XII The Hanged Man
La Mort	XIII Death
La Maison de Dieu	XVI The Tower
Le Judgment	XX Judgment

Most of the people and objects in the foreground of the Gringonneur cards are silhouetted by a lacelike pattern. The seventeen so-called Gringonneur cards have been preserved from the collection of M. de Gaignières, assistant tutor of the grandchildren of Louis XIV, who bequeathed them, together with his entire collection of prints and drawings, to the King in 1711.

Gringonneur Cards—The Fool and The Emperor *The Madman (Fool) wears a cap with ass's ears and a scalloped cape that hangs loosely from his shoulders. He holds in his hands a necklace of oversized decorated beads. Four children gather stones at his feet. The Emperor, covered in silver armor, sits on his throne and holds a globe in his left hand and a scepter ending in a fleur-de-lis spearhead in his right hand. His crown is encircled with a fleur-de-lis diadem. Two pages kneel at his side, hands crossed over their hearts in a sign of fidelity.*

Gringonneur Cards—The Pope and The Lovers The Pope, wearing a papal crown and a long robe, is seated between two cardinals. In the Pope's right hand is the key to St. Peter's and on his lap rests the Gospel. The Lovers card depicts three couples. Two couples are engaged in conversation and one couple is embracing, while two cupids launch arrows at them from the top of a cloud. The women wear medieval headdresses, a two-horned escoffin or hennin with long frontlet and a tight-fitting caul. The men wear short tunics and surcoats.

Gringonneur Cards—The Chariot and Justice The Chariot or Wagon card depicts two galloping horses pulling a wagon that carries a fully armed captain in triumph. He wears a harness and, instead of a helmet, a soft hat. In his right hand he holds a battle-ax. The seated figure of Justice holds upright in her right hand a double-edged sword and in her left hand the scales of justice. She wears a high-waisted garment with a repeating star design.

Gringonneur Cards—The Hermit and Strength The Hermit card depicts an aged bearded man in monk's robes and hooded frock. He stands near a rocky cliff and holds aloft an hourglass with his left hand. Force or Strength depicts a woman holding a column that is breaking apart. She has an aureole around her head and wears a high-waisted gown.

Gringonneur Cards—The Hanged Man and Death The Gallows or the Hanged Man reveals a gambler hanging by one foot but still holding a sack of coins in each hand. The gallows is made from two trees whose branches have been chopped off. Death rides horseback wielding a club that overturns kings, popes, bishops and other great earthly personages, as in the imagery of the Danse Macabre.

Gringonneur Cards—Temperance and The House of God Temperance is seated and, like Justice, Fortune and Strength, has an aureole around her head. She pours liquid from one vessel into another. The House of God depicts a massive stone structure whose walls are cracking while flames disintegrate the upper turrets.

Gringonneur Cards—The Moon and The Sun The Moon or The Crescent depicts two astrologers, wearing hoods and long fur robes, who measure the conjunctions of the stars and planets with astrological compasses and the aid of a book illustrating the heavens. The Sun illuminates a woman who, with disheveled hair as a sign of her innocence and virginity, is spinning wool in the midst of a meadow.

Gringonneur Cards—Judgment and The World   Judgment or The Last Judgment shows seven figures of the dead rising from their graves to the call of the trumpets of eternity sounded by two winged angels from the top of a cloud. The World depicts a female figure wearing a high-waisted gown. Her head is surrounded by an aureole and she stands on a wheel through which a landscape is depicted. In her right hand she holds a cross-topped scepter and in her left hand a globe. This card is sometimes confused with The Wheel of Fortune.

Gringonneur Card—Valet or Page of Swords   The valet or page is shown full figure, clad in a padded jerkin of gold brocade fabric with puffed sleeves and tight-fitting breeches of red wool. His hair is gathered in a bun above the nape of his neck. He rests his left hand on a shield without a coat of arms, and with his other hand he grasps an unsheathed sword.

The Encyclopedia of Tarot

D'Este Sixteen cards dating from the fifteenth century, with background illuminated in gold and framed in silver, were hand painted for the D'Este family. There are eight trumps—The Fool, The Magician, The Emperor, Temperance, The Star, The Moon, The Sun, The World—and eight court cards—king, queen and knight of swords; king, knight and page of staves; queen of cups; and king of coins. Tack holes appear at both the top and bottom borders of each card. The D'Este cards measure 140 by 78 mm. and are part of the Cary Collection housed at The Beinecke Rare Book and Manuscript Library, Yale University. The D'Este cards reprinted from D'Allemagne do not have tack holes.

Biblioteca Nazionale Universitaria, Torino The Biblioteca Nazionale Universitaria, Torino, Italy, is the custodian of fifteen hand-painted cards from the fifteenth century that were badly damaged by a fire in 1904. Since the cards consist of only courts and numerals, whether or not they belonged to a *tarocchi* pack is unknown.

D'Este Cards From the Cary Collection of Playing Cards at Yale University; sixteen cards. Top row: *The Fool, The Magician, The Emperor, Temperance.* Second row: *The Star, The Moon, The Sun, The World.* Third row: *King, queen and knight of swords and king of staves.* Bottom row: *Knight and page of staves, queen of cups and king of coins.*

D'Este Cards Reprinted from D'Allemagne, fifteenth century. Major Arcana and court cards belonged in 1906 to the Figdor Collection. The cards are heavily tooled with ornate dotted backgrounds within a panel border; the front edges are wrapped around from the back. Consistent with most early packs, the cards are without title or number. These cards do not contain the tack holes shown in the previous illustration. Top row: *The Magician, Temperance, The Star, The Moon.* Middle row: *The Sun, The World,* king of swords, queen of swords. Bottom row: Knight of swords, valet of staves, queen of cups, king of coins.

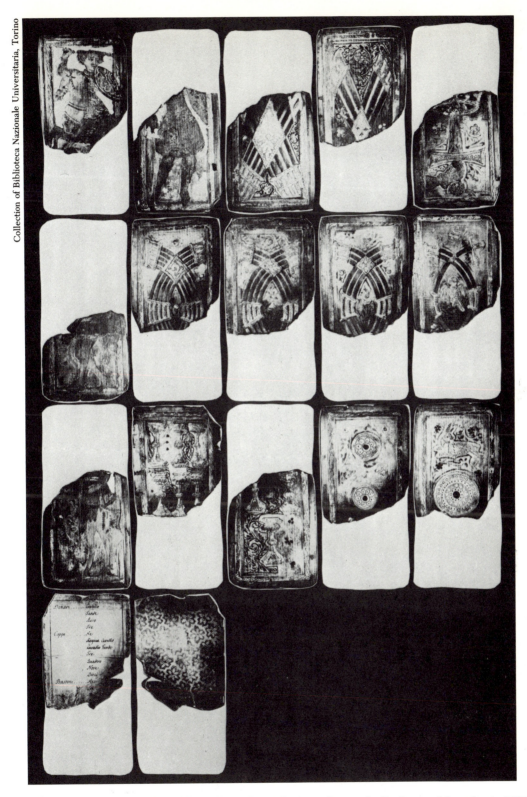

Biblioteca Nazionale Universitaria Tarocchi Cards These fifteen cards were badly damaged by a fire in 1904. The hand-painted cards probably date from the fifteenth century. Top row: Knight, page, ten, six and ace of swords. Second row: Page of staves (?); ten of staves; seven of staves with four curved staves on the left and three on the right instead of three straight staves on either side and one in the middle as found in the Tarot of Marseilles and other packs; six of staves; three of staves with one curved stave interlocking two curved staves instead of one on either side and one in the middle. Third row: Knight of cups (?), nine of cups, four of cups, three of coins, ace of coins with punched outline of a rabbit or stag over an ornate coin of Byzantine design. Bottom row: Front and back design of descriptive card with incomplete listing of cards.

Edmond de Rothschild The collection of Edmond de Rothschild at the Louvre includes eight late-fifteenth- or early-sixteenth-century Italian *tarocchi* cards, probably hand painted except for the background borders, which may be from woodcuts. The cards measure 189 by 90 mm. and comprise The Emperor and six courts. There is also one unusual card, much like a court card, but of an older standing gray-haired man—similar in facial features to The Emperor—holding a ball in his hand; this card is faintly suggestive of The World. Also from this same pack is a knight of swords located at the Museo, Biblioteca e Archivio di Bassano del Grappa.

Museo, Biblioteca e Archivio di Bassano del Grappa Knight of swords, circa late-fifteenth- or early-sixteenth-century Italy, presumed to be part of the incomplete Edmond de Rothschild pack. This single card at the Museo, Biblioteca e Archivio di Bassano del Grappa, Italy, depicts a knight slumped across his horse in a pose suggestive of the seventeenth century *Don Quixote de la Mancha*.

Museo Correr, Venice Four pip cards at the Museo Correr, Venice, dating from late-fifteenth- or early-sixteenth-century Italy, are believed to belong to an incomplete set of twenty-three numeral or pip cards in the Edmond de Rothschild collection at the Louvre. The four cards at Museo Correr are the ace of swords, two of staves, four of cups and four of coins. The twenty-three cards at the Louvre are the ten, nine and seven through two of swords, ten through three of staves, nine through five and the two of cups, and six of coins. The ten through two of swords in this set have curved swords; the staves are straight.

Museum of Bassano del Grappa Card—Knight of Swords This card measures 190 by 92 mm., which makes it slightly larger than similar cards at the Louvre. A fallen knight lies hunched across his horse. He wears tight pants and a long-sleeved gossamer shirt. In his right hand he barely holds his sword. Across his back is a large shield.

Collection of Edmond de Rothschild, Musée du Louvre, Paris

Rothschild Cards—The Emperor and The Pope   The Emperor sits upon his throne dressed in a smooth-shouldered, wide-sleeved Italian houppelande and a conical hat. He is heavily bearded and holds in his right hand a long scepter topped with a fleur-de-lis spearhead, and in his other hand a large globe or decorated coin. In front of him appear two small bearded figures facing each other. This card resembles The Emperor in the Gringonneur pack. The unidentified card on the right may represent The Pope, The Old Man or The World, although none of these titles seems entirely appropriate. The bearded standing figure wears a garment with elegant design similar to that of the one worn by The Emperor. In his right hand is a large globe. The background border of all eight cards in this series may be from woodcuts.

Collection of Edmond de Rothschild, Musée du Louvre, Paris

Rothschild Cards—King and Queen of Staves   The king of staves or batons sits on his throne and holds in his right hand a scepter with ornaments. Over his left shoulder is a cape resembling a shield. The crowned queen of staves holds a scepter matching the king's and over her left shoulder she wears a similar cape or shield. The tooled pattern in the background of all these cards follows the outline of the figure.

Rothschild Cards—Knight and Page of Staves The knight or cavalier of staves is artistically rendered. Holding an upraised scepter, he sits on a rearing horse whose front legs, neck and head follow the right border of the card. The knight readies his scepter to strike a snake or dragon, suggesting the gallantry of St. George. The page or valet of staves is a graceful figure with an upraised scepter poised to strike. He wears tight pants and a long-sleeved, almost gossamer shirt with elegant design that are practically identical to the clothing worn by the knight, except the page has a white sash at the waist.

Rothschild Cards—Queen of Swords and King of Coins The queen of swords sits on her throne and grasps upright in her right hand the sign of her suit—a large sword. In her left hand she holds a shield with no heraldic or armorial markings. She wears a high-waisted garment whose only ornate design is on the sleeves. The king of coins sits on his throne and wears elegant garments with ornate design that seems to have been superimposed over the picture because the design fails to follow the folds and pleats of the long robes. He holds a large decorative coin.

Museo Correr Cards *Ace of swords, two of staves, four of cups and four of coins. The ace of swords is encircled by a crown and pierces a heart near its narrow edge.*

X

EARLY PRINTED TAROT CARDS

IN THE FIFTEENTH CENTURY, with the advent of woodblock printing, playing cards became more popular and plentiful. Often the outline of the figures was printed from wood-blocks. The outline or design was left raised on the wood and the rest of the background was cut back so that it would not receive ink. After printing, but prior to cutting, the sheets of cards frequently were either hand colored or hand stenciled, one stencil being used for each color. Stencil-colored cards often show the color overlapping one or more of the printed outlines. Additionally, careful examination may reveal fine brush strokes in areas of solid color.

Metropolitan Museum of Art The Metropolitan Museum of Art, New York, possesses two fragmented sheets of fifteenth- or sixteenth-century Italian *tarocchi* cards from an incomplete hand-stenciled deck. The three cards from the smaller sheet are court figures; the partial fourth card is also probably a court figure. The other fragmented sheet contains both Major and Minor Arcana cards. The Tower is printed upside down on the sheet. The Wheel of Fortune card has writing near each figure, similar to that found on the same card in the Pierpont Morgan–Bergamo Visconti-Sforza deck. The Devil has a second face at its abdomen. The Minor Arcana cards shown are the knights in each suit.

Sola Busca The heavily colored Sola Busca *tarocchi* pack—the only complete extant pack of seventy-eight *tarocchi* cards engraved on metal during the late fifteenth century, possibly of Ferrarese or Venetian origin—contains trump cards featuring warriors of antiquity and Latin inscriptions. The twenty-two trumps are single figures based upon ancient history and, except for The Fool, have no counterparts in modern trumps. The name of a classical person, often barely recognizable due to misspellings by the scribe or engraver, appears on each of the trumps except for *Mato* (The Fool), and on each of the court cards of king, queen and knight except the page. The trump cards are titled as follows:

O	Mato	XI.	Tulio
I.	Panfilio	XII.	Carbone
II.	Postumio	XIII.	Catone
III.	Lenpio	XIIII.	Bocho
IIII.	Mario	XV.	Metelo
V.	Catulo	XVI.	Olivo
VI.	Sesto	XVII.	Ipeo
VII.	Deotauro	XVIII.	Lentulo
VIII.	Nerone	XVIIII.	Sabino
VIIII.	Falco	XX.	Nenbroto
X.	Venturio	XXI.	Nabuchodenasor

The court cards of the Sola-Busca pack are titled as follows:

King of swords	—Alecxandro M
Queen of swords	—Olinpia
Knight of swords	—Amone
Knave of swords	
King of staves	—L (?) Evio Plauto R
Queen of staves	—Palas
Knight of staves	—Apolino
Knave of staves	
King of cups	—Lucio Cecilio R
Queen of cups	—Polisena
Knight of cups	—Natanabo
Knave of cups	
King of coins	—R Filipo
Queen of coins	—Elena
Knight of coins	—Sarafino
Knave of coins	

A complete seventy-eight-card Sola-Busca pack housed at Palazzo Sola, Milan, Italy, contains on trump IIII Mario the additional inscription *"Senatus Venetus,"* and on trump XIIII Bocho the wording *"Anno Ab Urbe Condite MLXX,"* which refers to the founding of Venice. Uncolored impressions of the Sola-Busca cards belong to the British Museum, London, and Albertina, Vienna.

***Italian* Tarocchi Cards** *Fragmented sheets from the fifteenth or sixteenth century. The upper sheet contains one row consisting of the fragment of a seated court figure and two seated and one standing court figures. The top row of the larger sheet depicts (left to right) a fragmented card, possibly The Fool, plus the knights of swords, cups, coins and staves. The row below contains a fragmented Chariot card, XV The Tower, X The Wheel of Fortune, XIII Death and XIIII The Devil. The fragmented bottom row contains one corner of an unidentifiable card followed by what is probably a Major Arcana or court card and The Pope, III The Empress and The Emperor.*

Sola-Busca Tarocchi Cards Engraved fifteenth-century tarocchi cards featuring warriors of antiquity. Top row: *I Panfilio, II Postumio, III Lenpio, IIII Mario.* Middle Row: *V Catulo, VI Sesto, VII Deotauro, VIII Nerone.* Bottom row: *VIIII Falco, X Venturio, XI Tulio, XII Carbone.*

Sola-Busca Tarocchi Cards Top row: *XIII Catone, XIIII Bocho, XV Metelo, XVI Olivo.* Middle row: *XVII Ipeo, XVIII Lentulo, XVIIII Sabino, XX Nenbroto.* Bottom row: *Knave of swords with the sign of his suit, a sword, stuck in the ground; king of coins bearing the name R. Filipo; and queen of coins with the name Elena.*

Bibliothèque de l'Ecole Nationale Supérieure des Beaux-Arts The Bibliothèque de l'Ecole Nationale Supérieure des Beaux-Arts, Paris, owns an uncut sheet of trump cards from woodcuts dating from the late fifteenth or early sixteenth century. The six cards are The Sun, The World, The Hanged Man, The Wheel of Fortune, The Last Judgment and The Old Man, who is winged and walks with the aid of crutches.

Edmond de Rothschild The Collection of Edmond de Rothschild at the Louvre, Paris, contains a sheet of six trump cards made from woodcuts about the end of the fifteenth or beginning of the sixteenth century. These cards, which may be from a minchiate pack, were discovered in a book binding and comprise The Tower, The Star, The Moon, a bizarre rendition of a furry, winged Devil with a second face at his abdomen and clutching two figures, The Chariot and Death.

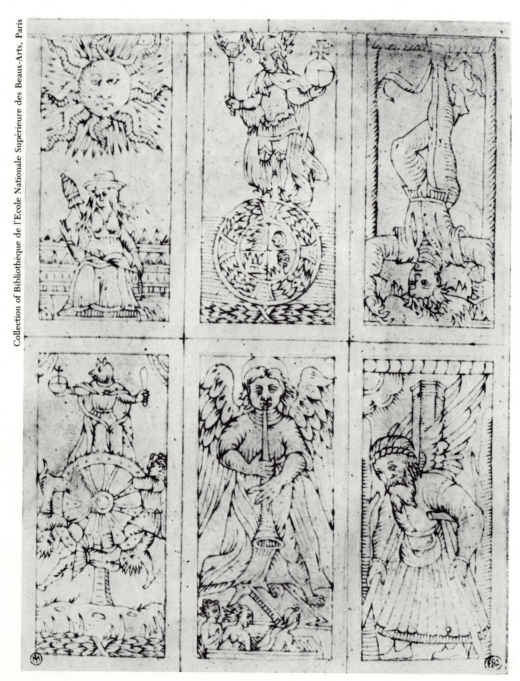

Tarot or Minchiate Cards *From an uncut sheet of six trumps, circa late fifteenth or early sixteenth century, belonging to the collection of the Bibliothèque de l'Ecole Nationale Supérieure des Beaux-Arts. Top row:* The Sun *depicts a seated female figure,* The World *shows a mythological god or warrior atop an ornate stone wheel,* The Hanged Man. *Bottom row:* The Wheel of Fortune, Judgment *and* The Hermit *or an aged man on crutches.*

Collection of Edmond de Rothschild, Musée du Louvre, Paris

Rothschild Tarot or Minchiate Cards *From an uncut sheet, circa late fifteenth or early sixteenth century, belonging to the Edmond de Rothschild Collection at the Louvre. Top row: The Tower contains a large stone structure that fills almost the entire card; The Star is suggestive of the three Magi; The Sun shows two figures holding astronomical objects. Bottom row: The Devil is a multifaced winged creature with tail, horns and claws in the act of devouring a human figure; The Chariot reveals a godlike charioteer; the animated lifelike figure of Death sits on a rearing horse and holds a scythe.*

Rosenwald The Rosenwald Collection at the National Gallery of Art, Washington, D.C., possesses an uncut sheet containing twenty-one trump cards (The Fool is lacking) and three queens (the queen of staves is missing) that probably dates from the early sixteenth century. The Magician wears a jester's hat with two ornamental pompons. Strength is depicted by a docile woman standing next to a column instead of the more customary rendition with a lion. The Hanged Man holds a sack in either hand. The awesome Devil has clawed feet; he wears a coarse garment and holds a trident in his hands. This sheet contains several Roman numerals in reverse, as evidenced by "IV" instead of "VI" for The Lovers and "IIV" instead of "VII" for Temperance. There is a duplication of number "IIIV"; it is on both Strength and Justice. It is apparent that this sheet was stenciled incorrectly because another sheet from the same stencil at the Deutsches Spielkarten Museum in Leinfelden contains the images with the correct rendition of Roman numerals.

Rosenwald Tarot Cards *From an uncut sheet dating about the early sixteenth century and belonging to the Rosenwald Collection at the National Gallery of Art, Washington, D.C. Top row: Judgment, The World, The Sun, The Moon. Middle row: The Wheel of Fortune (?), The Hanged Man, IIX (sic) The Hermit, X The Chariot. Bottom row: IIII The Emperor, III The Empress, II The High Priestess.*

Rosenwald Tarot Cards *From the same uncut sixteenth-century sheet forming part of the Rosenwald Collection at the National Gallery of Art, Washington, D.C. Top row: The Star, The Tower, The Devil, Death. Middle row: IIIV (sic) Strength, IIIV (sic) Justice, IIV (sic) Temperance, IV (sic) The Lovers. Bottom row: I The Magician, and the queens of coins, swords and cups.*

Catelin Geofroy Tarot Cards   Lyon, dated 1557 as evidenced by the name of the maker and date on the ace of falcons (cups). Thirty-eight cards remain in this pack, which contains only three suits—lions, falcons and peacocks. The Geofroy pack is the earliest set of tarot cards containing a numbered sequence for the Major Arcana; the Roman numerals are double-ended in both the top and bottom panels. Top row: I The Magician, with three onlookers around his table; III The Empress; IX The Hermit, with a cross hanging by a beaded chain from his waistband. Middle row: XII The Hanged Man; XIII Death, with a scythe and a shovel; XIIII Temperance, pouring liquid from an urn into a dish. Bottom row: XVI The Tower, with a grotesque figure suggestive of The Devil and two other figures, one of whom plays the violin in the foreground; there is a burning tower in the background; XX Judgment; ace of falcons or cups with the inscription "Catelin Geofroy 1557." The cards measure 125 by 68 mm. and are printed from woodblocks on thick cardboard and stencil colored by hand.

Catelin Geofroy   The French tarot pack made from woodcuts by Catelin Geofroy and housed at the Museum für Kunsthandwerk, Frankfurt am Main, West Germany, dates from 1557. These are the earliest Major Arcana cards numbered in the sequence that is popular today. The numeral cards in the Geofroy set are copies of Virgil Solis' copperplate cards from 1544, which also featured lions, monkeys, parrots and peacocks as the suit signs. The Geofroy courts contain double-ended identifying letters, such as "R.L." for king of lions, and the pip cards are Arabic numbered and also double-ended.

Municipal Library of Rouen The Municipal Library of Rouen, France, possesses thirty cards from an incomplete tarot pack, probably of Venetian origin and dating from the early sixteenth century, that shows figures from classical history with Latin inscriptions. The cards include Alexander the Great, king of Macedonia, and Midas, legendary Phrygian king who gained fame when Bacchus granted his wish that everything he touched turn to gold. Ninus was the son of Belus, first king of Assyria. Marcus Curtius, the Roman knight, in obedience to an oracle and to save his country, leaped armed and on horseback into a chasm that suddenly opened in the Forum. The Fool contains the inscription *Velim Fundam Dari Mihi* and depicts a fierce soldier dressed in armor and carrying an assortment of barbarous weapons. The full list of trump and court figures bear the inscriptions *Alexander Magnus rex Macedonicus, Imperator Assiriorum, Mida rex Lidorum, Ninus rex Assiriorum, Thamiris Regina Mastagetarum, Pontifex Pontificum, Marcus Curtius Romanus, Castor Amigleus, Perditorum Raptor, Omnium Dominatrix, Rerum Edax, Inclitum Sydus* and *Achilles Romanus*. The small Arabic numeral on the bottom of each trump card apparently was printed from the original woodcuts. The cards are hand colored and highlighted with gold and silver. The pip cards in the suit of swords depict Roman swords in their scabbards. The pip cards in the suit of staves are represented by branches or stalks. The cup suit is represented by decorative cups. The suit of coins depicts profiles of Roman personages on the face of each coin.

Classical Tarot Cards *By an unknown artist, early sixteenth century trump and court figures based upon classical history include* (top row) *king of swords—*Alexander Magnus rex Macedonicus, *The Emperor (?)—*Imperator Assirior, *king of coins—*Midas rex Lidor, *king of staves—*Ninus rex Assiror; (middle row) *queen of swords—*Thamaris Regina Mastagetarum, *The Pope—*Pontifex Pontificum, *knight of swords—*Marcus Curtius Romanus, *knight of staves—*Castor Amigleus. *The back design of the cards* (bottom row) *repeats the dotted border decoration that appears on the face of each card. Additionally, within the back border there is a woman holding a crossbow under her right arm and an arrow in her left hand. At her feet is a dragon, while to her left is a naked cherub. The sky is filled with clouds that surround a chariot in which a man embraces a woman. Around the chariot are several pairs of young children.*

Colonna The Colonna cards are part of two early-seventeenth-century fragmented sheets. The inscription *"Alla Colona in Piazza Nicosia"* appears on the two of swords. Each sheet contains four cards plus a portion of two additional cards. The maker of these cards probably was influenced by the Colonna family of Rome, whose arms appear on the *Fante di Spade*.

Paris Card Maker A seventeenth-century set of Parisian(?) tarot cards by an unknown Paris card maker is owned by the Bibliothèque Nationale, Paris. The cards are interesting for their articulate design and variations from standard tarot pictures.

Colonna Cards *From two uncut fragmented sheets, circa early seventeenth century. The trump cards with Arabic numbers but no titles are (top row) 10 The Chariot, 11 Wheel of Fortune; (middle row) 5 the Sultan, replacing The Hierophant or possibly The Emperor, and 6 The Lovers. Only the numbers 20 and 21 are distinguishable on the remaining two trump cards in the fragmented bottom row.*

Colonna Cards *The second fragmented Colonna sheet contains court and pip cards with identifying letters and numbers double-ended within the top and bottom borders. The cards shown are (top row) FS Fante di Spade (page of swords), FB Fante di Bastoni (page of staves), Cavallo di Denari (knight of coins); (bottom row) CB Cavallo di Bastoni (knight of staves), S2 two of swords, and S3 three of swords.*

Parisian (?) Tarot Cards Twenty-four cards measuring 125 by 69 mm. from a seventeenth-century tarot pack by an unknown card maker. The Major Arcana cards are Roman numbered and the card titles, with numerous misspellings, appear in French in a panel at the bottom of each card. All cards in this pack are decorated with an unusual border of repeating black and white squares in two parallel rows. The card numbers on the trumps and the abbreviated letter descriptions on the Minor Arcana cards appear on the top of each card in a small scroll between two facing lions.

Top row: Le Fou *(The Fool)* wears a long conical cap and holds in his hand a puppet head on a short stick; I Le Bateleur *(The Magician)* depicts three figures at a table, each with unusual headdress, and two animals resting nearby; II La Papesse *(The Popess)*; III Linperatrice *(The Empress)*; IIII Lanpereur *(The Emperor)*; V Le Pape *(The Pope)*.

Second row: VI L'Amoureus *(The Lovers)* depicts a winged Cupid above a winged female figure and a male figure with a fur hat who embraces her; VII Le Chariot *(The Chariot)* is drawn by swans instead of horses; a nude figure holds a rod with a ribbon at its end and another figure, wearing a headdress of leaves, sits on the wagon; VIIII Justice *(Justice)* is a blindfolded two-headed figure holding the scales of justice and an upraised sword; IX L'Ermite *(The Hermit)* wears a long gown and a hooded cape, and he holds a string of oversized beads in addition to a staff and a

Collection of the Bibliothèque Nationale, Paris

lantern; X La Roue de Fourtune (*The Wheel of Fortune*) depicts a figure in a short garment and cape standing on top of the wheel while the figure to the left rises, the one to the right descends, and the bottom figure lies on the ground and seems to support the wheel on his chest; XI La Force (*Strength*) depicts a female figure with flowing cape.

Third row: XII Le Pandut (*The Hanged Man*); XIII La Mort (*Death*); XIIII Atrempance (*Temperance*); XV Le Diable (*The Devil*) is a hideous winged figure with tail and taloned feet who holds a long rod and link chain; XVI La Foudare (?) (*The Tower*) depicts several figures including a naked figure with an animal's head and another figure crouching on the ground; XVII L'Estoille (*The Star*) depicts an aged scholarly man wearing a flat-topped square hat or mortarboard.

Bottom row: XVIII La Lune (*The Moon*) shows the full face of the moon and several small figures at the bottom of the card; XIX Le Soleil (*The Sun*) depicts an animal, possibly a monkey, holding a mirror in front of a cringing woman while a multirayed sun shines brightly above; XX Le Jugment (?) (*Judgment*); XXI Le Monde (*The World*) depicts a nude figure holding a large cloth behind him while balancing on a replica of the globe topped with the imperial orb; ar de cupes (*ace of cups*) and ar de deniers (*ace of coins*) showing a stag and a lion, respectively, holding a flag bearing the sign of the suit and suggestive of the ten of falcons in the Ambras Hofjagdspiel pack (page 58).

Joannes Pelagius Mayer A set of Swiss tarot cards, circa 1680, made in Constance by Joannes Pelagius Mayer, is housed at the Cincinnati Art Museum.

Tarot cards from a Swiss Pack Made in Constance by Joannes Pelagius Mayer, circa 1680. Atout *titles contain many spelling errors made by illiterate artisans.* Top row: La Maisoi Dieu *(The House of God),* Le Foille *(The Star),* La Lune *(The Moon).* Bottom row: Temperante *(Temperance),* Le Sioieil *(The Sun)* and Le Fol *(The Fool).*

XI
EIGHTEENTH- AND NINETEENTH-CENTURY TAROT DECKS

Tarot of Marseilles There are numerous varieties of the Tarot of Marseilles pack owned by museums and collectors. The Tarot of Marseilles packs, wherever they were produced in Europe, generally bore the titles of the Major Arcana cards in French and continued to use single-headed figures on the trumps and court cards rather than the double-headed figures of Piedmontese Italian packs. Frequently the trump titles were spelled incorrectly. Tarot of Marseilles packs used the Italian suit signs of swords, staves, cups and coins. The maker's name, and the city in which he worked, often appeared within a ribbon on the two of coins. French tarot packs of the eighteenth century include those decks made by J. Jerger, Renault, Cardajat, P. Madenie, J. Dodali, G. Dubesset, J. B. Benois, L. Cary, N. F. Loudier, R. Bouvard, and C. Burdel.

Court de Gebelin Court de Gebelin gave strong impetus to the theory that tarot cards were of early Egyptian origin. In his treatise *"Du Jeu des Tarots"* (see page 12) he described the titles and sequence of the Major Arcana cards as follows (numbers in parentheses indicate sequence of Major Arcana in standard tarot packs): The Fool (unnumbered); 1. The Thimble-Rigger (I); 2. The King (IV); 3. The Queen (III); 4. Chief Hierophant or High Priest (V); 5. High Priestess (II); 6. Osiris Triumphant or The Chariot (VII); 7. The Lovers (VI); 8. Force or Strength (XI); 9. Temperance (XIIII); 10. Justice (VIII); 11. Prudence (XII); 12. The Sage or The Seeker of the Truth (VIIII); 13. The Sun (XVIIII); 14. The Moon (XVIII); 15. The Dog Star or Sirius (XVII); 16. Death (XIII); 17. Typhon (XV); 18. The House of God or The Palace of Plutus (XVI); 19. The Wheel of Fortune (X); 20. Creation or The Last Judgment (XX); 21. Time or The World (XXI).

Etteilla Etteilla tarot decks total seventy-eight cards but the sequence and imagery are a departure from standard tarot packs. Etteilla, whose real name was Alliette, was an ardent follower of Court de Gebelin and popularized his unique tarot pack at the end of the eighteenth century.

The Etteilla designs are mostly full-length figures and often the subjects are accompanied by astronomical or astrological signs. Above and below each design is a title, e.g., card number 5 at the top, or *droit*, reads *Voyage* and at the bottom, or *renverse*, is *Terre*. Card number 11 is *La Force* and *Le Souverain*. The cards are numbered in succession from 1 *Etteilla* to 78 *Folie* (The Fool); some packs have the meanings on the face of each card.

Etteilla altered the imagery of the Major Arcana cards. For example, in card number 20, Fortune, the descending Typhon on the left of the wheel is replaced by a man; the ascending Hermanubis on the right is replaced by a small animal, possibly a rabbit or mouse. The traditional sphinx above the wheel becomes an ape perched on the limb of a tree.

The first twenty-one numbered cards and the last card, number 78, relate to the twenty-two Major Arcana cards of the standard tarot pack.

Seven cards in the Etteilla series represent the seven days of creation:

CARD NO. AND DESCRIPTION	DAY OF CREATION
2 *La Lumière* (Light)	1st Day
4 *Le Ciel* (The Heavens)	2nd Day
3 *Les Plantes* (Plants and Herbs)	3rd Day
6 *Les Astres* (The Sun and Moon)	4th Day
7 *Les Oiseaux et les Poissons* (Birds and Fish)	5th Day
5 *L'Homme et les Quadrupèdes* (Man and Animals)	6th Day
8 *Repos* (Repose after creation)	7th Day

These cards are followed by the four cardinal virtues:

9 *La Justice*
10 *La Tempérance*
11 *La Force*
12 *La Prudence*

Tarot of Marseilles Published by B. P. Grimaud, Paris, in 1930. On the two of coins is "1748," the year Grimaud published its first deck of cards. The titles of the Major Arcana and court cards are in French. Cards II and V use the titles La Papesse and Le Pape for Female Pope and Pope, respectively; these titles were later changed at the behest of the Church to Junon and Jupiter and The High Priestess and Hierophant, respectively. Top row: Le Mat (The Fool), I Le Bateleur (The Magician), II La Papesse (The Popess), III L'Imperatrice (The Empress), IIII L'Empereur (The Emperor). Second row: V Le Pape (The Pope), VI L'Amoureux (The Lovers), VII Le Chariot (The Chariot), VIII La Justice (Justice), VIIII L'Hermite (The Hermit). Third row: XII Le Pendu (The Hanged Man), ten of swords, ten of batons or staves, Roy de Baton (king of batons), Reyne de Baton (queen of batons). Bottom row: Cavalier de Baton (knight of batons), Valet de Baton (page of batons), two of cups, two of coins with the inscription "1748 B. P. Grimaud 1930," ace of coins.

Court de Gebelin Tarots Illustrations of the twenty-two Major Arcana and four aces from "Du Jeu des Tarots" contained in Volume 9 of Court de Gebelin's Monde Primitif, 1787. In card No. XII The Hanged Man is shown balanced on one leg and tied to a stake, suggesting the virtue Prudence. The Hermit is incorrectly numbered VIII instead of VIIII and Temperance is incorrectly shown as XIII instead of XIIII. Top row: *The Fool, I The Magician, II The High Priestess, III The Queen, IV The King.* Second row: *V Chief Hierophant or High Priest, VI The Lovers, VII Osiris Triumphant or The Chariot, VIII Justice, VIIII The Sage or The Seeker of the Truth.* Third row: *X The Wheel of Fortune, XI Force, XII Prudence, XIII Death, XIIII Temperance.* Fourth row: *XV Typhon, XVI The House of God or The Palace of Plutus, XVII The Dog Star, XVIII The Moon, XIX The Sun.* Bottom row: *XX Creation or The Last Judgment, XXI Time or The World, ace of swords, ace of staves, ace of cups, ace of coins.*

Finally, there are ten cards that signify important aspects of human life:

13 *Mariage* (Marriage): The High Priest—union.
14 *Force Majeure* (Major Force): Satan or The Devil—superior force.
15 *Maladie* (Malady): The Magician—malady.
16 *Le Jugement* (Judgment): The Last Judgment—judgment.
17 *Mortalité* (Mortality): Death—destruction.
18 *Traitre* (Treason): The Hermit—hypocrisy.
19 *Misère* (Misery): The Shattered Temple—imprisonment.
20 *Fortune* (Fortune): Fortune's Wheel—augmentation.
21 *Dissension* (Dissension): African Despot—arrogance.
78 *Folie* (Folly): Folly or The Alchemist—Folly.

The fifty-six Minor Arcana cards of the Etteilla pack comprise cards numbered 22 to 77 as follows:

4 Kings	Nos.	22, 36, 50, 64
4 Queens	Nos.	23, 37, 51, 65
4 Knights	Nos.	24, 38, 52, 66
4 Pages	Nos.	25, 39, 53, 67
4 Tens	Nos.	26, 40, 54, 68
4 Nines	Nos.	27, 41, 55, 69
4 Eights	Nos.	28, 42, 56, 70
4 Sevens	Nos.	29, 43, 57, 71
4 Sixes	Nos.	30, 44, 58, 72
4 Fives	Nos.	31, 45, 59, 73
4 Fours	Nos.	32, 46, 60, 74
4 Threes	Nos.	33, 47, 61, 75
4 Twos	Nos.	34, 48, 62, 76
4 Aces	Nos.	35, 49, 63, 77

Etteilla believed himself a learned professor of cartomancy and an interpreter of the hieroglyphics of the Book of Thoth. He made a detailed study of the ancient sciences and published many volumes dealing with cartomancy, interpretation of dreams and visions, and numerology.

COMPARISON OF ETTEILLA TAROT CARDS WITH STANDARD TAROT TRUMPS

ETTEILLA TAROT PACK	STANDARD TAROT TRUMPS
1 Etteilla *(Le Questionnant)*	V *Le Pape* or *Jupiter* (Hierophant)
2 Eclaircissement	XVIIII *Le Soleil* (The Sun)
3 Propos	XVIII *La Lune* (The Moon)
4 Depouillement	XVII *L'Etoile* (The Star)
5 Voyage	XXI *Le Monde* (The World)
6 La Nuit	III *L'Impératrice* (The Empress)
7 Appui	IIII *L'Empereur* (The Emperor)
8 Etteilla *(La Questionnante)*	II *La Papesse* or *Junon* (The High Priestess)
9 La Justice	VIII *La Justice* (Justice)
10 La Tempérance	XIIII *La Tempérance* (Temperance)
11 La Force	XI *La Force* (Strength)
12 La Prudence	XII *Le Pendu* (The Hanged Man)
13 Mariage	VI *L'Amoreux* (The Lovers)
14 Force Majeure	XV *Le Diable* (The Devil)
15 Maladie	I *Le Bateleur* (The Magician)
16 Jugement	XX *Le Jugement* (Judgment)
17 Mortalité	XIII *La Mort* (Death)
18 Traitre	VIIII *L'Ermite* (The Hermit)
19 Misère	XVI *La Maison de Dieu* (The House of God)
20 Fortune	X *La Roue de Fortune* (The Wheel of Fortune)
21 Dissension	VII *Le Chariot* (The Chariot)
78 Folie	*Le Mat* (The Fool)

Etteilla Tarot Cards Numbered in sequence from 1 Etteilla to 78 Folie. The standard and reverse titles and meanings of each card are double-ended above and below each picture. Even the card designs that resemble those of standard tarot decks vary significantly, such as 5 Voyage, a nude figure within a circle between two sailboats, similar to The World in standard packs. Etteilla's card 13 Mariage depicts an actual marriage ceremony. Card 68 La Maison (*The House*) represents the ten of coins and indicates the layout of the pip cards with the suit sign in a large rectangle above the smaller panel that often contains astrological or other symbols.

Collection of the author

Etteilla Tarot Cards, circa Nineteenth Century   These cards are more ornate than the standard Etteilla tarot designs. Top row: Card no. 1 is a sphere, suggesting the solar system; 3 is a face in the cloudy sky; 5 contains an ornate border design surrounding an oval picture with male figure leaning against a club; 8 suggests Eve and the Garden of Eden; 9 is Justice as a frugal woman with sword and scales. Middle row: 10 depicts Temperance in a gown of ornate patterns holding a large cup in her left hand and an unidentified object in her right hand; 11 shows Strength as a seated figure with a lion resting at her feet; 12 is Prudence, also wearing an ornate long gown and admiring herself in a hand mirror; 13 depicts a marriage ceremony; 14 is a fierce, even hideous, Devil with unkempt feathered wings and snake tail. Bottom row: 16 Judgment portrays a winged angel hovering above a cluster of people of whom only one raises his hands in prayer; 17 is Death; 18 The Traitor or Capucin is similar to The Hermit; 19 depicts a walled city aflame; the final card in the deck, 78 The Fool shows a court jester with hands cupped over his eyes as if to emphasize that he does not know where and in what direction he is going.

Etteilla (?) Tarot Cards, circa Nineteenth Century   The general designs in this tarot pack, probably dating from the nineteenth century, are suggestive of Etteilla cards and the cards are numbered in sequence from 1 through 78. However, the sequence of the cards and titles does not follow that of the typical Etteilla packs. The card titles and descriptions shown and the standard-type tarot cards to which they seem to apply are as follows.

Collection of the author

Top row: *1* L'Homme qui consulte, Sagesse (*reversed*—Génie)—*an Egyptian figure appears on this card rather than the usual sun and sky or circular universe;* *4* Les Etoiles, Paix (*reversed*—Intelligence)—*suggestive of Temperance;* *5* Apis, Les Saisons—Horus, Felicité (*reversed*—Misères)—*The World and The Universe;* *6* Le Firmament, Contentement—Béatitude (*reversed*—Ténèbres)—*The Sun; 7* La Mer et les Poissons, Protection (*reversed*—Réussite, L'air et les Oiseaux).

Second row: *9* La Justice, Paix (*reversed*—Dissentiments)—*Justice;* *10* La Tempérance, Santé (*reversed*—Maladie)—*Temperance;* *11* La Force, Bonheur (*reversed*—Disgrace)—*Strength or Force;* *12* La Prudence, Circonspection (*reversed*—Discours); *13* Le premier prophète gardien des divines paroles, Mariage—Union (*reversed*—Concorde)—*The Lovers or Marriage.*

Third row: *15* Le faux Devin, Mélancolie (*reversed*—Imprévoyance)—*The Magician;* *16* Jugement, Gain de Procès (*reversed*—Préjudice)—*Judgment;* *17* Destruction et Mortalité, Perte (*reversed*—Ruine)—*Death;* *18* L'ermite de la grande Thébaide d'Égypte, Repentir (*reversed*—Trahison)—*The Hermit;* *19* La Rhamesseium ou Temple funéraire de Rhamses II (Mejamoun), Catastrophe (*reversed*—Captivité)—*The Tower.*

Bottom row: *20* La Roue de fortune, Dignité. (*reversed*—Fortune)—*The Wheel of Fortune;* *21* Le tyran Busiris, Discorde (*reversed*—Indépendance)—*The Chariot;* *22* Le roi Ptolemée Lagus, Le Savoir (*reversed*—Conseil)—*king of batons;* *23* Didon, reine de Carthage, Passion des Richesses (*reversed*—Obstacles)—*queen of batons;* *78* Folie, Extravagances (*reversed*—Folie)—*The Fool.*

Etteilla Tarot circa Late Nineteenth Century The card designs in this Spanish pack are strikingly similar to the Etteilla designs from a French pack (page 142). In addition to a full-length figure, each Major Arcana card contains the applicable Hebrew letter, double-ended, and its English pronunciation. A smaller picture, usually of several persons, appears between the Hebrew letters. The cards are numbered in Arabic numerals and the upright and reversed meanings appear at the top and bottom of each card. In 1975 a reprint of this pack called Tarots Egipcios was issued in black and white by Editora y Distribuidora Mexicana and descriptions of the cards are contained in the book El Supremo Art de Echar las Cartas by Dr. Moorne.

Vandenborre Belgian Tarot Eighteenth-century Belgian tarot packs, such as the deck by F. I. Vandenborre, feature a Spanish captain, *Le'Spagnol Capitano Eracasse*, instead of The Popess, and Bacchus—the god of grape growing and wine—instead of The Pope. Captain Eracasse appears to be based on the character of Captain Fracasse in the French versions of the *Comedia dell'Arte*. He is a stock character, a braggart and swaggering soldier in the tradition that extends back to Greek and Roman satire. Bacchus, written on the card as *Bacus*, is shown astride a barrel holding a bottle to his lips; he is naked except for leaves and bunches of grapes around his waist. Card number 12, *Lepen-Du*, is reversed so that the figure is head up instead of head downward in the usual way.

Vandenborre Tarot Reprinted by Carta Mundi, Belgium, for Aurelia Books. These "Suisses" cards were originally made in the eighteenth century by F. I. Vandenborre, cartier, Brussels. Trumps II and V are Le'Spagnol Capitano Eracasse and Bacus, respectively, instead of the customary La Papesse and Le Pape.

Additional tarot packs from the eighteenth and nineteenth centuries include:

French Tarot, 1720 A French tarot pack, circa 1720, card maker unknown.

Geografia **Tarocchi** Geografia *tarocchi*, reprint of a 1725 Italian pack.

Jean Payen Tarot deck by Jean Payen, Avignon, 1743.

N. Conver Tarot pack by N. Conver, 1760, reprinted by A. Camoin.

Lando Tarot Lando tarot produced about 1760 by Giuseppe Lando, Turin.

French Tarot, Late Eighteenth Century French tarot cards of the late eighteenth century include a pack engraved by P. Voisin and made by Jean Pierre Laurent in Belfort; a tarot pack made by Nas (Nicholas) Conver, 1760; and another tarot pack published by J. Jerger in Besançon.

Jean Galler Tarot pack by Jean Galler, or his successor, published in Brussels in the late eighteenth century.

Rochias Fils Rochias Fils tarot, Neuchâtel, late eighteenth century. Deck was printed from woodblocks and hand stencil colored.

Milanese Tarot Milanese tarot pack by F. Gumppenberg, Milan, late eighteenth century or early nineteenth century.

French Revolutionary Tarot French Revolutionary tarot pack by L. Cary, Strasbourg, issued in 1791. As might be expected, the cards evince anti-Royalist sentiments.

Italian Major Arcana Cards Italian *tarocchi* cards, circa early nineteenth century.

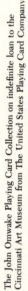

Tarot Cards from a French Pack, circa 1720. Top row: La force (*Strength*), La prudence (*Prudence*), standing on one leg, instead of the usual Hanged Man. Bottom row: *La maison Dieu* (*The House of God*), L'etoille (*The Star*) with eight large, five-pointed stars.

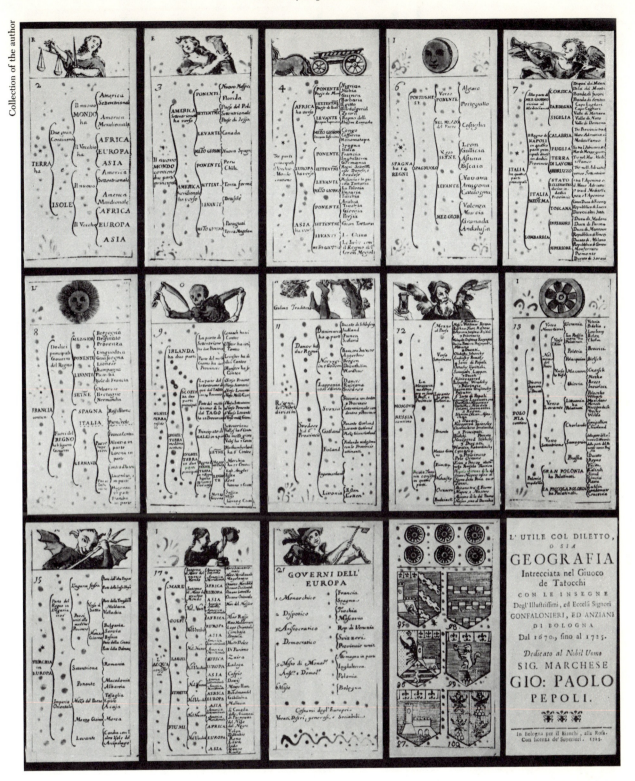

Geografia Tarocchi A 1973 colored reproduction by Vito Arienti, Lissone, of a 1725 geographical tarot pack with Italian suit marks and geographical divisions, topped with the familiar Major Arcana symbols on the trump cards. Coats of arms are shown on the pip cards with values one to six, such as the six of coins. The reproduction is limited to 250 sets. The John Omwake Playing Card Collection at the Cincinnati Art Museum owns a small volume of these cards bound in a book and containing a handwritten manuscript note at the end of the book that credits the designs to Giuseppe Maria Mitelli and cites that on September 12, 1725, a few months after publication, the book was prohibited under "penalty of from seven to ten years imprisonment for the people and five years banishment to Forte Urbano for the nobility."

Tarot Deck made by Jean Payen Made in Avignon in 1743. The titles of the Major Arcana and court figures are in French. Card 4 The Emperor contains both Roman and Arabic numerals. Top row: Le Fol *(The Fool)*, I Le Bateleur *(The Magician)*, II La Papesse *(The Popess)*, III L'Imperatrice *(The Empress)*, IIII L'Empereur *(The Emperor)*, V Le Pape *(The Pope)*. Second row: VI Les Amoureux *(The Lovers)*, VII Le Chariot (sic) *(The Chariot)*, VIII La Justice *(Justice)*, VIIII L'Hermite *(The Hermit)*, X La Roue de Fortune *(The Wheel of Fortune)*, XI La Force *(Strength)*. Third row: IIX (sic) Le Pendu *(The Hanged Man)*, XIII untitled *(Death)*, XIIII La Temperance *(Temperance)*, XV Le Diable *(The Devil)*, XVI La Maison Dieu *(The Tower)*, XVII Le Stoille *(The Star)*. Bottom row: XVIII La Lune *(The Moon)*, XVIIII Le Soleil *(The Sun)*, XX Le Jugement *(Judgment)*, XXI Le Monde *(The World)*, Chevalier de Spee (sic) *(cavalier of swords)*, Roy de Coupe *(king of cups)*.

N. Conver Tarot *Recent reprint by A. Camoin of a 1760 tarot pack originally produced by N. Conver and based upon typical Tarot of Marseilles designs. The cards are Roman numbered and bear titles in French. The two of coins contains the name and year of the original card maker.* Top row: Le Mat *(The Fool)*, I Le Bateleur *(The Magician)*, II La Papesse *(The Popess)*, III L'Imperatrice *(The Empress)*, IIII L'Empereur *(The Emperor)*. Second row: V Le Pape *(The Pope)*, VI L'Amoureux *(The Lovers)*, VII Le Chariot *(The Chariot)*, VIII La Justice *(Justice)*, VIIII L'Hermite *(The Hermit)*. Third row: X La Roue de Fortune *(The Wheel of Fortune)*, XI La Force *(Strength)*, XII Le Pendu *(The Hanged Man)*, XIII untitled *(Death)*, XIIII Temperance *(Temperance)*. Bottom row: XV Le Diable *(The Devil)*, XVI La Maison Dieu *(The Tower)*, XVII Le Toille *(The Star)*, Reyne Depee *(king of swords)*, two of coins.

Lando Tarot Woodcut designs by Giuseppe Lando, Turin, produced about 1760. The Major Arcana and court cards are titled in French with numerous misspellings; all the cards are stencil colored by hand. Top row: *The Fool; I The Magician*, incorrectly spelled *Le Batelleur; II The Popess; III The Empress; IIII The Emperor.* Second row: *V The Pope; VI The Lovers; VII The Chariot*, incorrectly spelled *La Cariot; VIII Justice; VIIII The Hermit*, incorrectly spelled *L'Eremite.* Third row: *X The Wheel of Fortune*, incorrectly spelled *La Rou de Fortunne; XI Force; XII The Hanged Man; XIII (Death); XIIII Temperance*, incorrectly spelled *La Tenperance.* Bottom row: *XV The Devil; XVI The House; XVII The Stars; XX The Angel*, misspelled *Lange;* the ace of cups with the identifying inscription "Lando Torino."

French Tarot Cards from Three Packs Late eighteenth century. Top row: King of batons; III The Empress; ace of cups with the name "P. Voisin," probably signifying the engraver; two of cups with the name "Jean Pierre Laurent A. Belfort," undoubtedly the publisher or card maker. Middle row: King of cups; page of cups with the words "France Conver;" two of coins with the inscription "Nas Conver 1760," the publisher or card maker; and two of cups with a panel at the bottom bearing the arms of France and the initials, "GM," probably the engraver. Bottom row: Queen of swords and page of swords, both with the words "France J. Jerger;" two of cups bearing the inscription "Tarots fins faites par J. Jerger, fabriquant carts a Besancon;" and Temperance with the name "France J. Jerger."

Tarot Pack by Jean Galler Similar to the Vandenborre deck, the Galler deck contains the Spanish captain, *Le' Spagnol Capitano Eracasse*, instead of the Popess, and the figure of *Bacus* instead of the Pope. Top row: I Le Bateleux (*The Magician*); II Capitano Eracasse; V Bacus (*Bacchus*), Greek and Roman god of fertility and wine; XII Le Pendu (*The Hanged Man*) here shown with head up. Middle row: XIIII Atrempance (sic) (*Temperance*) pours liquid from a vessel in her right hand while holding a long rod in her left hand; the words "Fama Sol" appear in a banner near her right arm. XV Le Diable (*The Devil*) depicts a fierce, winged devil with many heads and eyes. XVI La Foudre (*The Fire*) shows a tree struck by lightning instead of a traditional lightning-struck tower. XXI Le Monde (*The World*) depicts a nude female figure atop a globe divided into three sections: the earth, the moonlit night sky and the sun. Bottom row: XXII Le Fol (*The Fool*) is designated card number 22 instead of the traditional zero. The two of cups contains a tablet inscribed "Povr conoistre gve la plus basse de deniez et de covpes enporte les plvs havtes qvand a fait dv Jev (sic)," which indicates that the lowest value cards in the suits of coins and cups carry the highest values when played in the game of tarot. The four of coins contains the initals "I.G." for J.G. The ace of coins bears the inscription "Cartes de Taravt (sic) Faites Par Jean . . . . Dans La Rue . . . . A Brusselles." The omission of the name Galler and his street address suggests that this pack may have been issued by his successor.

Rochias Fils Tarot Swiss tarot deck, late eighteenth century. Card titles lack apostrophes and are often misspelled. Top row: Le Mat *(The Fool)*; I Le Bateleur *(The Magician)*; II La Papessa *(The Popess)*; III L'Imperatrice *(The Empress)*; IIII L'Imperatore *(The Emperor)*. Second row: V Le Pape *(The Pope)*; VI Lamoureux *(The Lovers)*; VII Le Chariot *(The Chariot)* with the initials "J.P.," possibly the name of the engraver, Jean Pierre; VIII Justice *(Justice)*; VIIII Lermite *(The Hermit)*. Third row: La Roue de Fortune *(The Wheel of Fortune)*; XI La Force *(Strength)*; XII Le Pendu *(The Hanged Man)*; XIII La Mort *(Death)*; XV Le Diable *(The Devil)*. Bottom row: XXI Le Monde *(The World)*; Roi Depee *(king of swords)*; Valet Depee *(page of swords)*; four of coins with the arms of the principality of Neuchâtel; two of coins with the inscription "Fait Par Jacque Rochias Fils a Neuchatel."

Milanese Tarot by F. Gumppenberg Milan, late eighteenth century or early nineteenth century. Card III The Empress has the advertisement "Tarocco Fino." The back design of this pack (not shown) contains the figure of a winged buffoon above the world with the inscription "Mileno." Top row: Il Matto *(The Fool)*, I Il Bagattele *(The Magician)*, II La Papessa *(The Popess)*, III L'Imperatrice *(The Empress)*, IIII L'Imperatore *(The Emperor)*, V Il Papa *(The Pope)*. Second row: VI Gli Amanti *(The Lovers)*, VII Il Carro *(The Chariot)*, VIII La Giustizia *(Justice)*, VIIII L'Eremita *(The Hermit)*, X Ruot. della For. *(Wheel of Fortune)*, XI La Forza *(Strength)*. Third row: XII L'Appeso *(The Hanged Man)*, XIII Death, XIIII La Temperanz *(Temperance)*, XV Il Diavolo *(The Devil)*, XVI La Torre *(The Tower)*, XVII Le Stelle *(The Star)*. Bottom row: XVIII La Luna *(The Moon)*, XIX Il Sole *(The Sun)*, XX Il Giudizio *(Judgment)*, XXI Il Mondo *(The World)*, Reg. di Spade *(queen of spades)*, Cav. di Bastoni *(knight of staves)*.

French Revolutionary Tarot by L. Carey Strasbourg, 1791. Top row: Le Fol *(The Fool)*, I Le Bateleur *(The Magician)*, II Junon *(Juno)*, III La Grande Mere *(The Grandmother)*. Middle row: IIII Le Grand Pere *(The Grandfather)*, V Jupiter, VI Amoureux *(The Lovers)*, VII Le Chariot *(The Chariot)*. Bottom row: VIII La Justice *(Justice)*, VIIII Le Peauvre *(The Hermit)*, Liberté de Lépée *(liberty of swords)*, Cavalier de Baatons *(cavalier of batons)*. This pack reflects anti-royalist sentiment during the French Revolution evidenced by the alteration of three of the four court cards in each suit from kings to genie, queens to liberté and valets to egalité. The crowns of the Empress (queen) and the Emperor (king) are removed and replaced by a turban and nightcap worn by the grandmother and grandfather, respectively.

Italian Major Arcana Cards Twelve cards from an Italian tarocchi pack, circa early nineteenth century. The designs are engraved with considerable detail. Top row: I Il Bagattelliere *(The Magician)*, II La Papessa *(The Popess)*, III L'Imperatrice *(The Empress)*, VI Gli Amanti *(The Lovers)*. Middle row: VII Il Carro *(The Chariot)*, VIII La Giustizia *(Justice)*, IX L'Eremita *(The Hermit)*, X La ruota della Fortuna *(The Wheel of Fortune)*. Bottom row: XI La Forza *(Strength)*, XIV La Temperanza *(Temperance)*, XV Il Diavolo *(The Devil)*, XVI La Torre *(The Tower)*.

Additional tarot decks include:

French Cartomancy Pack Tarot designs from a French cartomancy pack, early nineteenth century.

Fanciful Tarot Fanciful tarot pack by Avondo Brothers, Serravalle-Sesia, 1852. The state tax stamp, based upon the law of 1852, is marked with the year 1860.

J. Gaudais The tarot pack by J. Gaudais was created in Paris, circa 1860.

Edoardo Dotti Tarot pack by Edoardo Dotti, Milan, 1862.

Piedmontese Tarot Piedmontese tarot pack by Giuseppe Versino was done in Torino in 1862.

Doubleday Tarot Doubleday hand-colored tarot cards/Five oversize tarot cards circa late nineteenth century/Egyptian Major Arcana cards.

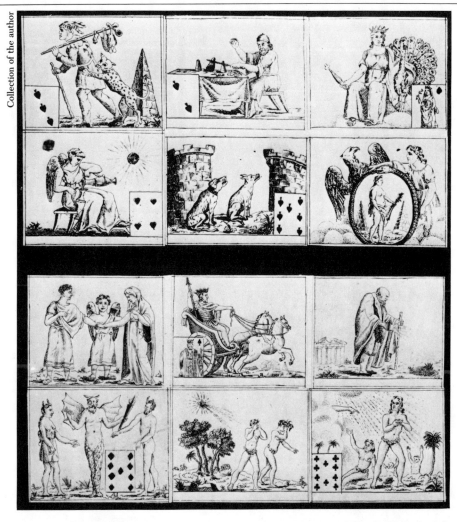

Collection of the author

Tarot Designs from a French Cartomancy Pack *The cards are from two uncut sheets published in the early nineteenth century. A similar pack (not shown) comprising forty-two cards appeared in Paris around the year 1815 under the name Le Petit Oracle des Dames and included an 82-page booklet of instructions. The blank spaces along the bottom of some cards may have been used for titles. Some of the cards contain small regular face cards in the lower left or right corners; oddly, the suit of spades is upside down in The Fool, The Magician and The Tower cards.* Top sheet, top row: *The Fool wears feathers on his head. He carries on the rod over his shoulder a bell, a spoon and the carcasses of two chickens(?) or other fowl. A leopard clings with its teeth to the back of The Fool's jacket. The Magician is an elderly man sitting before a table. The High Priestess (or possibly The Empress) is crowned and sits next to a peacock.* Top sheet, bottom row: *Temperance is a winged figure sitting on a bench performing the traditional act of pouring liquid from one vessel to another vessel. The Moon depicts two baying dogs beneath two large stone towers, but the customary moon itself is absent. The World shows a seminude female figure standing before two obelisks. The scene is encircled by an oval formed by a snake biting its tail, and a large eagle and a man appear above the oval.*

Lower sheet, top row: *The Lovers depicts a winged Cupid standing between a man dressed in Roman garb and a woman. The Chariot shows a charioteer racing in a chariot drawn by two spirited horses. The Hermit depicts an aged man wearing a heavy cowl and holding a rod and lantern.* Lower sheet, bottom row: *The Devil is a winged figure with goat's horns standing between a man and a woman also with goat's horns. The Sun depicts two nude figures resembling Adam and Eve holding their hands over their eyes for protection against the intense rays of the sun. Judgment reveals an arm emerging from a cloud above a group of scantily clad figures near a palm tree.*

Fanciful Tarot Pack Avondo Brothers, Serravalle-Sesia. The cards are ornately designed and contain both Arabic and Roman numerals in the upper panel and Italian titles in the lower panel. Top row: 0 Il Matto *(The Fool)*, I Il Bagatto *(The Magician)*, II La Papessa *(The Popess)*, III L'Imperatrice *(The Empress)*, IIII L'Imperatore *(The Emperor)*. Second row: V Il Papa *(The Pope)*, VI Gli Amanti *(The Lovers)*, VII Il Carro *(The Chariot)*, VIII La Giustizia *(Justice)*, IX L'Eremita *(The Hermit)*. Third row: X Ruota della Fortuna *(Wheel of Fortune)*, XI La Forza *(Strength)*, XII L'Appeso *(The Hanged Man)*, XIV La Temperanza *(Temperance)*, XVII Le Stelle *(The Star)*. Bottom row: XVIII La Luna *(The Moon)*, XIX Il Sole *(The Sun)*, XX Il Giudizio *(Justice)*, XXI Il Mondo *(The World)*, ace of coins.

Tarot Pack by J. Gaudais Paris, circa 1860. This unusual pack features double-ended Major Arcana and court cards divided by a diagonal bar running at approximately a forty-five-degree angle from left to right and containing short vertical lines. The designs on the Major Arcana cards are more stylized than the usual crude designs of eighteenth- and nineteenth-century packs. The numeration on the Major Arcana cards is in Arabic numbers and there are no titles. Top

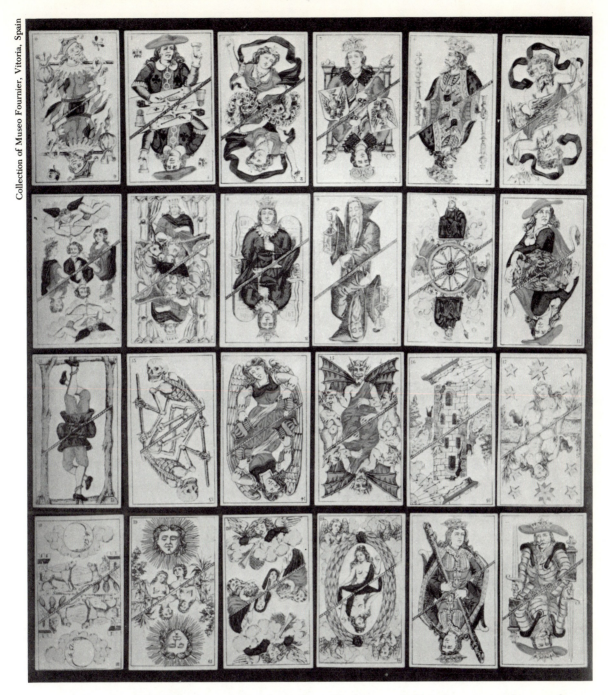

row: 0 The Fool is a bearded figure who smiles at a butterfly. 1 The Magician holds a flower pot and among the objects on the table is the ace of clubs. 2 Junon is an elegantly dressed woman with billowing sash or cape and nearby is a peacock. 3 The Empress is a crowned regal figure sitting upon her throne and holding the imperial shield and orb. 4 The Emperor is dressed in royal robes and holds his imperial orb. 5 Jupiter is a bearded figure who holds a bolt of lightning while a sash or cape billows in the background and an eagle spreads its wings.

Second row: 6 The Lovers depicts a blindfolded Cupid hovering above three figures, one of whom is crowned. 7 The Chariot depicts a crowned charioteer. 8 Justice wears a crown and sits before the tablets of laws. 9 The Hermit is an aged figure holding a lantern. 10 The Wheel of Fortune shows a sphinx figure sitting atop the wheel while a human figure falls to the left and a tiger rises to the right. 11 Strength deftly restrains a lion.

Third row: 12 The Hanged Man is tied by his left foot to the gibbet and, ironically, he is headless. 13 Death is a skeleton reaper. 14 Temperance is a female figure with large wings who pours a liquid between two vessels. 15 The Devil is a bat-winged creature. 16 The Falling Tower is struck by lightning from the sun. 17 The Star depicts a nude female figure pouring liquid from an urn.

Bottom row: 18 The Moon shows two baying dogs beneath a moon surrounded by ominous clouds. 19 The Sun depicts a holy figure hovering above Adam and Eve. 20 Judgment shows Gabriel blowing his horn. 21 The World is a female figure with a sash poised within a wreath. The queen of staves. The king of swords.

Tarot Pack by Edoardo Dotti Milan, 1862. Hand colored or stencil colored. The Major Arcana cards are neat woodblock prints titled in Italian, as are the courts. The back design is a well-engraved mounted horsewoman with a ribbon flag on a pole identifying the maker. Top row: Il Matto (*The Fool*), I Il Bagattel (*The Magician*), II La Papessa (*The Popess*), III L'Imperatrice (*The Empress*), IIII L"Imperatore (*The Emperor*), V Il Papa (*The Pope*). Second row: VI Gli Amanti (*The Lovers*), VII Il Carro (*The Chariot*), VIII La Giustizia (*Justice*), VIIII L'Eremita (*The Hermit*), X Ruot. della Fort. (*The Wheel of Fortune*), XI La Forza (*Strength*). Third row: XII L'Appeso (*The Hanged Man*), XIII Uguaglianza (*Equality*), XIIII La Temperan (*Temperance*), XV Il Diavolo (*The Devil*), XVI La Torre (*The Tower*), XVII Le Stelle (*The Star*). Bottom row: XVIII La Luna (*The Moon*), XIX Il Sole (*The Sun*), XX Il Giudizio (*Judgment*), XXI Il Mondo (*The World*), Cav. di Spade (*cavalier of swords*), back design.

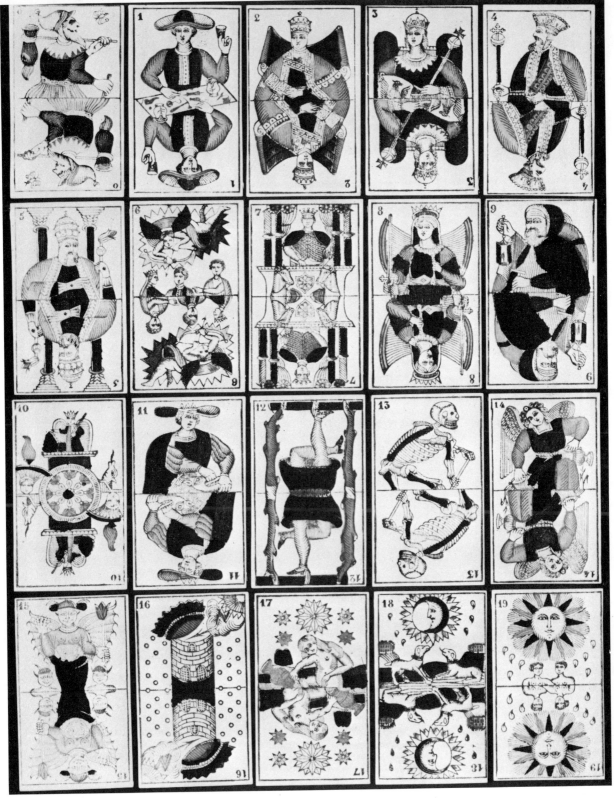

Piedmontese Tarot Pack by Giuseppe Versino Torino, 1862. The untitled Major Arcana cards are double-ended and contain Arabic numbers in the upper left corner. Top left: 0 The Fool, 1 The Magician, 2 The High Priestess, 3 The Empress, 4 The Emperor. Second row: 5 The Hierophant, 6 The Lovers, 7 The Chariot, 8 Justice, 9 The Hermit. Third row: 10 The Wheel of Fortune, 11 Strength, 12 The Hanged Man, 13 Death, 14 Temperance. Bottom row: 15 The Devil, 16 The Falling Tower, 17 The Star, 18 The Moon, 19 The Sun.

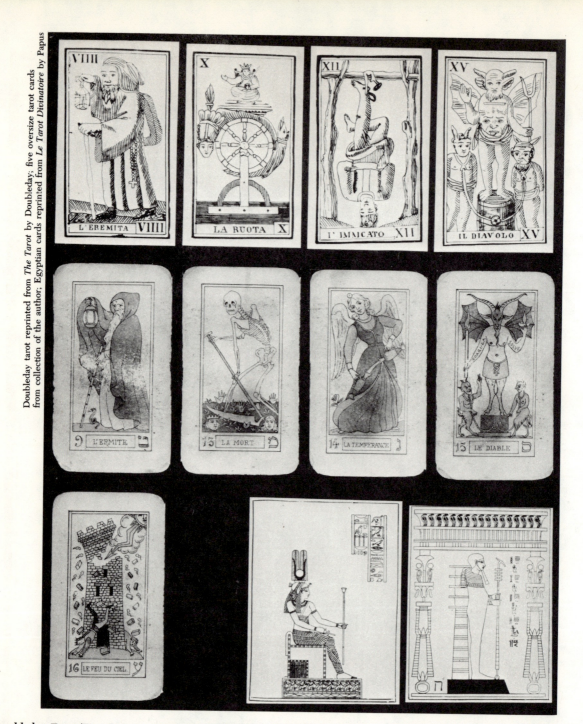

Doubleday Tarot/Five Oversize Tarot Cards/Egyptian Major Arcana Cards Top row: Hand-colored tarot cards from stenciled designs found in an unpublished handwritten manuscript believed authored by Abner Doubleday, Civil War general and the person usually credited with the founding of baseball in the United States. The designs are early-nineteenth-century tarot typical of the Varallo region and similar to the cards made by Strambo (page 165). The trump titles are in Italian. The Roman number is repeated in a box at the lower right. VIIII L'Eremita (The Hermit), X La Ruota (The Wheel), XII I'Immcato (The Hanged Man), XV Il Diavolo (The Devil).

Five oversize tarot cards, circa late nineteenth century, found by a dealer between the pages of volume I of Les Cartes à Jouer du XIV au XX Siècle by Henry D'Allemagne. Middle row: 9 L'Ermite (The Hermit), 13 La Mort (Death), 14 La Temperance (Temperance), 15 Le Diable (The Devil). Bottom row left: 16 Le Feu du Ciel (The Fire in the Sky or The Falling Tower). To the left of the card title is the appropriate Arabic number, and to the right, the Hebrew letter.

Egyptian-designed Major Arcana cards published in 1909 in Le Tarot Divinatoire by Papus and based upon original unpublished artwork from the nineteenth century credited to Eliphas Lévi. The cards (bottom row center and right) appear to be The Empress and The Hierophant. The Empress holds an ankh in her right hand and a scepter of ruling authority in her left hand. Her crown of two feathers suggests she is the ruler of Upper and Lower Egypt. In front of her feathers are the horns of Isis, suggestive of The High Priestess instead of The Empress. The figure on the right appears to be The Hierophant in a pillared temple. He holds in his hands the tet, pillar of four worldly directions. On the lower left of the card appears the Hebrew letter He, often associated with The Hierophant.

Collection of the author

Tarot Pack by Gassmann These tarot cards were woodblock printed and hand stencil colored around the year 1873 at Geneva, Switzerland. Top row: Le Mat (The Fool), I Le Bateleur (The Magician), II La Papesse (The Popess), III L'Imperatrice (The Empress), IIII L'Empereur (The Emperor). Second row: V Le Pape (The Pope), VI L'Amoureux (The Lovers), VII Le Chariot (The Chariot), VIII La Justice (Justice), VIIII L'Ermite (The Hermit). Third row: X La Roue de Fortune (The Wheel of Fortune), XI La Force (Strength), XII Le Pendu (The Hanged Man), hanging by both feet rather than the traditional one foot, XIII La Morte (Death), XIIII La Temperance (Temperance). Bottom row: XVIIII Le Soleil (The Sun), XX Le Jugement (Judgment), XXI Le Monde (The World), Roi de Denier (king of coins), two of coins with inscription "Fabriquées par Gassmann, Cartier à Genève."

Additional tarot packs from the nineteenth century include:

Gassmann Tarot pack by Gassmann, Geneva, circa 1873.

Milanese Tarot Milanese tarot pack by G. Sironi, Milan, 1882.

F. Strambo Tarocchi F. Strambo *tarocchi*, late nineteenth century, Varallo.

Vacchetta Tarocchi Vacchetta *tarocchi*, Turin, 1893.

Indian "Tarot" Indian "tarot" cards apparently based on the avatars of Vishnu.

Milanese Tarot by G. Sironi Milan, 1882. Full-length figures on the Major Arcana cards contain a Roman number at the top of each card and a title beneath the figure on the bottom. Top row: Il Matto (*The Fool*); I Il Bagattel (*The Cobbler*); II La Papessa (*The Popess*); III L'Imperatrice (*The Empress*); IIII L'Imperatore (*The Emperor*); V Il Papa (*The Pope*). Second row: VI Gli Amanti (*The Lovers*); VII Il Carro (*The Chariot*); VIII La Giustizia (*Justice*); VIIII L'Eremita (*The Hermit*); X Ruota della Fortuna (*The Wheel of Fortune*); XI La Forza (*Strength*). Third row: XII L'Appeso (*The Hanged Man*); XIII La Morte (*Death*); XIIII La Temperanza (*Temperance*); XV Il Diavolo (*The Devil*); XVI La Torre (*The Falling Tower*); XVII Le Stelle (*The Star*). Bottom row: XVIII La Luna (*The Moon*); XIX Il Sole (*The Sun*); XX Il Giudizio (*Judgment*); two of cups with inscription "Fabbrica di Milano;" ace of coins with inscription "G. Sironi, Milano," and tax stamp dated "21 Sett. 1882;" and back design of a naked male figure holding upright Neptune's pitchfork in his left hand and the reins to a sea horse in his other hand above the inscription "Milano."

F. Strambo Tarocchi *Late-nineteenth-century Major Arcana and pip cards made by F. Strambo, Varallo. The cards are hand stenciled in color and the Major Arcana cards contain Roman numerals at the upper left and lower right corners. Top row: The unnumbered card, The Fool, is entitled* Il Pazzo; *I* Bagatto *wears a work apron and his bench holds hand tools; II* La Papessa; *III* L'Imperatrice; *IIII* L'Imperatore. *Second row: V* Il Papa; *VI* L'Amore; *VII* La Carozza; *VIII* La Giustizia; *VIIII* L'Eremita. *Third row: X* La Ruota; *XI* La Forza; *XII* L'Impiccato; *XIII* La Morte; *XIV* La Temperanza. *Bottom row: XV* Il Diavolo; *XVI* La Torre. *XVII* Le Stelle, *two of cups and ace of coins.*

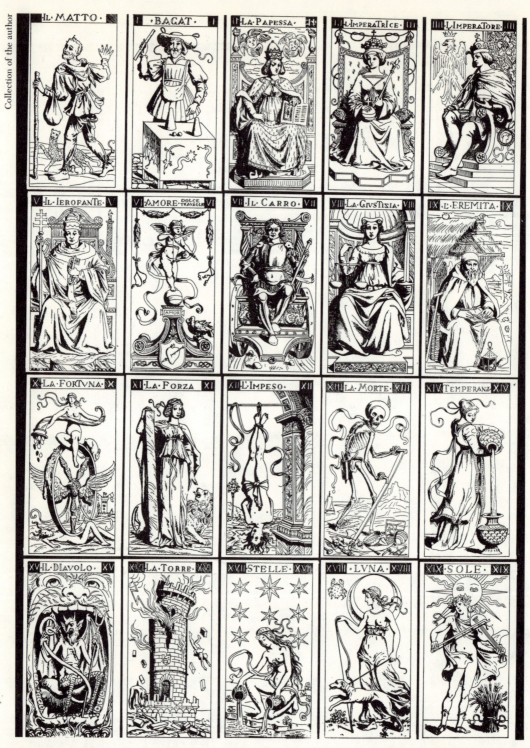

Vacchetta Tarocchi *Major Arcana cards reproduced by Edizioni del Solleone in 1976 from a black and white* tarocchi *series published in 1893 by Giovanni Vacchetta of Turin. The drawings are ornately designed and contain numerous variations from traditional cards. For example,* Il Matto *(The Fool) is hatless and carries a sack on his arm instead of across his shoulder; he is barefoot and his pants legs are tied at the cuff; a leopard prances in front of him.* I Bagat *(The Magician) stands before a magician's table.* VI Amore *(Love) depicts a blindfolded Cupid standing on a ball that rests on an ornate pedestal.* IX L'Eremita *(The Hermit) is an aged figure seated in front of a hut and reading a book.* X La Fortuna *(Fortune) shows a winged wheel of fortune resting atop a nude figure while on the upper rim of the wheel is a rabbit and a nude female figure pouring coins from a horn of plenty.* XII L'Impeso *(The Hanged Man) depicts a figure tied by both legs to a bar supported by an ornate arch.* XV Il Diavolo *(The Devil) appears inside the wide open mouth of a roaring animal.* XVI La Torre *(The Tower) depicts lightning striking from the left beneath the tower window.* XVIII Luna *(The Moon) depicts a seminude woman with a high-waisted gown holding a bow in her right hand and a dog at the leash in her other hand; in the background appears both a crab and a quarter-moon in full circle.* XIX Sole *(The Sun) depicts a figure nude, except for a flowing cape, who is playing the violin beneath a giant sun; nearby is a sheaf of wheat.*

Indian "Tarot" Cards The cards are illustrated in Papus' Le Tarot Divinatoire, 1909, and credited to an earlier, unpublished manuscript of Eliphas Levi. Each card contains a Hindu title and is Roman numbered. Adjacent to some of the human figures and animals are letters from the English alphabet probably used to identify the figures in a book or manuscript. **Card III** represents Matsya (A), the Fish incarnation of Vishnu. Matsya, crowned to signify his divine origin, is shown partially emerging from a great fish. He has four arms joined at the elbows and holds a sword in one of his right hands. Brahma (B), a four-headed figure, sits on a lotus. The horned head of a demon (C) emerges from the water, and four figures (D), representing the four Indian castes of Priests, warriors, merchants and peasants, pay homage with clasped hands. **Card IV** depicts the Boar incarnation of Vishnu (A) as a four-armed figure wearing an animal headdress and holding a double-edged sword. He stands above a fallen enemy, Kataiba (C), who is deer-headed and has talon feet. **Card VII** represents Jagannath (Lord of the Universe borne on a chariot) or Juggernaut. The tall figure of Jagannath wears a sheer garment and a long necklace. He holds above his head an effigy of himself as a sleeping Vishnu. A small child (C) or doll-like figure straddles a prone figure (B), possibly its mother. A cobra (G) crosses a stream in the direction of a dog (F) (lion?) and a bird (E). Two figures stand in the temple of Jagannath to pay homage to Vishnu, who is shown as a seated figure with sword. At the upper right of the card is a crowned priest with a rod in his right hand who straddles a wall, suggesting his presence both in this world and the divine world. **Card IX** represents Vishnu as Buddha, the seventh incarnation of Vishnu. A crowned four-armed figure is seated on a lotus with two priests in attendance. The priests wear hair tufts, confirming that they are Brahmins, followers of Brahma, the Creator. The two columns at each edge of the card support three decorative beams in a temple; beneath the seated figure is a panel containing simple flower petal designs woven in a carpet. **Card X** represents Kalki, the last incarnation of Vishnu, yet to come. A crowned figure wears a dhoti or cloth around his waist and a sacred cord around his neck indicating his high caste. His shoes are the wooden ritual shoes worn in temples. He holds a sword on his left shoulder and a sacred book in his right hand, which contains the teachings of the new age. Behind the figure is the winged horse of Kalki. At the top of the picture are two holy basil bushes and two birds, a peacock and another fowl. The last card contains an inscription along the lower right side, "Tom VI, No. 4," possibly referring to either the unknown set of books from which these pictures were taken or to a fuller description by Eliphas Lévi.

XII
TWENTIETH-CENTURY TAROT DECKS AND DESIGNS NOT READILY AVAILABLE

The following list comprises printed and hand-painted tarot decks, sketches, collages, prints, serigraphs and engravings that have been produced during the twentieth century, mainly in the past twenty-five years. The designs either are not readily available in the United States, are out of print or are available only in limited editions.

Acea Gypsy tarot
Adams/Cleveland/Hersh/MacPherson/Weiss
Alitalia tarot
Apocalypse/Bompiani/Cilento/Dykstra/Farcas/
   Izod/Kersaint/Williamson
Arcanes du Destin
Atkins/Heitmann/Klumper/Lucas/May/Picini
Balbi/Bennett/Brother Placid/Decker/Greenwich
   Library/Yves Jobert/Rivers/Sigler
Beaulieu/Laliberte/Le-Tan/Sigler
Benavides/Carter/Dorflinger/Fodera/Kloster/
   Nessim/Rota/Schlossman
Berthole tarot
British tarot
Chaboseau/Loring tarot
Cooper tarot
Dali/Gill/Iamblichus/Kaye/Littel/Metcalfe/
   Sherman/Tavaglione
Docters van Leeuwen Porcelain tarot

Fatidic Egyptian tarot
Frownstrong/Gemrod/Hoffman/Holbein/Pry/
   Saba-Telli/Scott/Skell
Glass tarot
H. J. Heinz tarot
Peter Huckerby tarot
Insight Institute tarot
Knapp tarot
De Laurence tarot
Linweave tarot
Lover's tarot
M. Lubow/N. Lubow/Sharp/Waldner/Weil
Masenghini Tarocchino Milanese
Menegazzi Seashell *tarocco*
Sergio Minero tarot
Odell tarot
Ollgaard tarot
Ortega tarot
Papus tarot
Pastor tarot
Pop/Rock tarot
Rakoczi tarot
Ravenswood Eastern tarot
Le Taro Sacerdotal
Sacred Egyptian tarot
Schikowski tarot
Scott tarot
Connie Taylor tarot
Tellurian tarot
Transitional tarot
Wollenhaupt-Brenner tarot

Collection of the artist

Acea Gypsy Tarot   Designed by Jeffrey Acea, the cards feature black figures clothed in Western and West African costumes combined with Egyptian and universal symbols. The Major Arcana cards contain Hebrew letters except for inadvertent omissions on IV Gypsy King and VIII Justice. The recurring triangles found on many cards as object shapes as well as part of the structural design signify spiritual attainment.

Top row: **0 The Fool** wears a court jester's shawl, long curling slippers and a long brimmed cap. A dog paws at his trouser leg. **I The Magician** wears a leotard; his hat and bow tie are in the form of a lemniscate or figure-of-eight nimbus. He wears a necklace with a large button topped by a crescent. **II The High Priestess** sits on her throne; the shawl around her shoulders suggests that her knowledge and wisdom are concealed. She points to a page in the book on her lap, but she guards the information from all seekers. She wears an ornamented necklace signifying her holiness. A large crescent moon—suggesting Isis—appears at her feet. **IV Gypsy King** wears an inverted crescent hat, a necklace of crescent teeth and an ornamental Egyptian beard. The shield contains an eagle superimposed with an Egyptian ankh. **V Heirophant** (sic) is a bearded figure with shoulder epaulets containing elephant heads, suggesting Buddhist influence. The two students wear shoulder robes; the feathered hats on their shaved heads symbolize the rays of the sun. One figure has his arm upraised, the other points downward, symbolizing the positive and negative forces that combine to form the universe. The heads of the three figures in this card form the vertices of an equilateral triangle.

Second row: **VII The Chariot** depicts a dominant Egyptian figure with crescent faces on his epaulets. He holds in his right hand an Indian dorje. **VIII Justice** depicts the traditional female figure holding a scale and upright sword. The iridescent symbol on her forehead suggests that the wisdom she possesses prevails during times of decision. **IX The Hermit** is a weathered figure in winter garments. He faces the darkened past, from which a strong wind howls against his bearded face. The ornamental lantern with a star in the center serves as his guiding light. **X Wheel of Fortune** depicts an eight-spoked wheel based upon the Indian wheel of life. A female figure with Egyptian headdress sits at the top of the wheel and holds a sword indicating control of the situation. The large triangle suggests spiritual attainment. **XI Strength** is an Amazon, the epitome of female strength. She controls the lion with her bare hands and feet. She wears a heavy red cape and lemniscate hat.

Third row: **XII Hanging Man** is a bare-chested figure hanging by a rope from his left foot. An aura appears around his head. **XIII** depicts a decomposing figure suggesting the metamorphosis of both its body and surrounding events. **XIV Temperance** is a winged angel with a lotus in her hair. She wears an Indian garment and a triangle pendant. **XV The Devil** is the traditional hermaphrodite signifying a combination of truths applied to evil purposes. **XVI The Tower** shows two figures toppling from a lightning-struck tower. Many of the shattered bricks are inverted triangles, symbolizing the destruction of materialism.

Bottom row: **XVIII Moon** depicts two baying dogs beneath a large moon eclipsing the sun. **XIX The Sun** shows two children beneath a huge beneficent sun with eight triangle spokes, similar to the eight spokes in the Wheel of Fortune. The **queen of swords** is an Egyptian figure, nude above the waist, holding an upright dagger suggesting wholeness of plans and contemplation of action. She sits on a rock supported by a bank of clouds, illustrating the combination of contemplation and action, thought and deed. Her earrings are triangular in shape. The **king of cups** wears a turban and sits on a high-backed chair with a fin design. The crab in his left hand signifies the water sign Cancer or the suit of cups. He holds in his other hand an elongated ceremonial cup. Around his neck hangs a large coin pendant. The **eight of pentacles** shows eight stone coins in different stages of development and not yet arranged on the bookcase shelves.

Adams/Cleveland/Hersh/MacPherson/Weiss Examples of tarot designs by contemporary artists.

Top row: Unpublished surrealistic Major Arcana cards by Frederick McLaurin Adams in which the artist seeks to guide the seeker to a deeper communion with himself, the rest of humanity and the cosmos. **Justice** (XI) is depicted as the presence of many souls in the Halls of Persephone and the Palace of Minos. In Greek mythology Persephone was the wife of Hades and queen of the underworld; Minos was king of Crete. The scene depicts numerous columns and a long staircase leading to a sunken shrine. Even while she remains on her throne, the queen of all souls rises from her pillar crypt to greet all pilgrims as they enter the Elysium or abode of the blessed after death. **The Reaper** or **Death** (XIII) depicts a nude figure who holds a young child in her right arm while simultaneously dancing and wrestling with an animate skeleton. At the upper left a Minoan eye-winged butterfly appears, while at the lower left the leaves of autumn glow and Persephone winks coquettishly as she rises from her Delphic world. **Temperance** or **Winged Victory** (XIIII) is the Greek goddess Nike. Her wings suggest those of dragonflies and even the unlikely pinions of stained-glass butterflies. Beneath the spread of her wings are two lovely infants, one male and the other female, who dance with joy as life returns from the snows of winter to the greenery of spring. The two infants hold a Samothracian version of the Tree of Life. The winged victory pours the double helix of a new DNA coding from an amphora decorated with the symbol of Aquarius.

Middle row, left and center: **The Sun** (XIX) depicts a blazing noontime disc in summer. The beak of a solar falcon lightly bites at the toe of a nude woman whose body swirls among radiant gases and solar winds. Burning vapors pass through her body into the sun's furnace of energy, while at the bottom of the card are the force-filled eye-pyramids. **The Moon** (XVIII) depicts the essence of winter as an Isis-Artemis goddess or Moon Lady, accompanied by feminine and masculine beings with bovine heads. The goddess gently embraces twin sisters who have journeyed to Earth from Hyperborean upon their moon ray. The sisters stand upon the powerful, protective back of Draco and they pour from their pitchers the genetic distillations of new Aquarian awareness. In the upper corners appear radiant "ships" from the distant constellations.

Middle row, right: *XVIII* **Luna** or **The Moon** as rendered by Jim Cleveland seeks to emphasize the mystical significance of the Triple Moon Goddess. Anubis is the jackal-headed wolf god in Egyptian mythology who conducts the dead to judgment. In this picture he is domesticated into a dog but retains his savage nature and awaits the Seeker. If Anubis recognizes the God of Essence, and passes through the spike-topped gate, he encounters Mother Kali, the Hindu goddess of creation and destruction who rules the land of the dead. When Anubis recognizes her essence, she becomes a temptress and hands him a poisoned cup. He drinks his fill and dies, remaining dormant, his existence marked by the triple cross of regeneration. The moon goddess metamorphoses into her maternal form and gives him new life so that he may journey between the crimson towers to seek the sun.

Bottom row, left: **Justice** by Helen Hersh depicts a loosely gowned figure who gently floats between ivy-covered pillars of balance. Her hands are clasped in harmony and her blank face is blindfolded by a spiritual vapor. Her hair is golden in the shape of a rainbow and the chained scales of justice stem from her mind. Bottom row, middle: **Death** by Mary Kay MacPherson is rendered in traditional form. The iridescent outline seems to illuminate the bony figure of the reaper as he mows down the people at his feet. Bottom row, right: *The Sun* by Elizabeth Sexton Weiss depicts a large burning fireball with fiery radiating rings. The tall green stalks represent young growth reaching toward the sun in competition with the delicate flowers in the center which struggle to survive. **The Sun** kindles life and growth and both the green stems and the flowers depend upon its energy for their growth. This unique Sun card represents earth in its formation prior to the beginnings of man; thus, no figures appear on it.

Alitalia tarot *Designed by Gianni Novak as a special promotional tarot pack of cubistic design for Alitalia Airlines. Top row: 0 Il Matto (The Fool), 2 La Papessa (The Popess), 5 Il Papa (The Pope). Middle row: 8 La Giustizia (Justice), 9 L'Eremita (The Hermit), 10 La Rota di Fortuna (The Wheel of Fortune). Bottom row: 14 La Temperanza (Temperance), 16 La Torre (The Tower), Cavalier di Denari (knight of coins).*

Apocalypse/Bompiani/Cilento/Dykstra/Farcas/Izod/Kersaint/Williamson

Top row: Apocalypse cards designed by David Lord Porter. The cards in this shortened twenty-eight-card pack are used in the Apocalypse Game; several of the cards are similar to Major Arcana cards in the tarot. The sinister figure of **The Magician** carries a paradoxical wand of ever-changing power. The Magician is not the controller of the wand, but rather the medium through which change takes place. His gnarled fingers show the effects of the power that surges through the wand. **The Lovers** card depicts a desert landscape broken by two profiles weathered by the sand. **The Wheel** contains twelve spokes and is decorated with eight signs or moods, commencing at the top with the sun, followed *clockwise by the ancient hand sign to ward off the evil eye, storm clouds and falling rain, a broken heart, waning phase of the moon, a spike of wheat representing fertility, lightning bursting from storm clouds and the all-seeing eye.* **The Satyr** *depicts an aphoric god with hooved feet holding in front of his face the pipes of Pan, on which he plays the harmonies of nature.*

Second row: *Bompiani Major Arcana.* **XIII Death** *and* **XXI Le Monde** *are reproductions of the Major Arcana from a tarot pack originally produced by Jean Payen in 1743 at Avignon. The reproductions were printed by Heraclio Fournier of Spain for Edizioni Bompiani of Italy.* **The Fool** *and* **The Magician** *are tarot posters by Diane Cilento published in 1972. The posters are color photographs retouched prior to printing. The Fool depicts a young man standing at the edge of a rocky precipice, his silhouette repeating itself behind him. A small dog stands nearby. Both the moon and the sun shine down; the full circle of the sun suggests the number zero of this card. The Magician is an iridescent figure who seems to float above the stones of a large courtyard where a sword, wand, cup and pentacle have been placed.*

Third row: **The High Priestess,** *also one of the Cilento posters, depicts a female figure sitting in the alcove of a temple. Palm trees and splitting pomegranates decorate the large curtain behind her. A crescent moon appears at her feet and she holds the Torah in her hands. Light radiates from her head covering and the solar cross that hangs across her breast.* **I The Magician** *and* **XIII Death** *are from a Celtic tarot deck by R. Dirk Dykstra. The cards are based upon the religious rituals of ancient Ireland. The Celtic clothing is interpreted in an art nouveau way. The Magician is an aged, bearded man representing a cross between a Celtic file or sage and a medieval magician possessed of supernatural knowledge. The Magician wears a satin crys or tunic and he holds in his lap an ancient parchment book of knowledge. The printing in the book is from the Celtic alphabet, Coelbren y Beirdo, and the open pages reveal a pentagram and a seal used to ward off evil spirits. The intersecting lines on each page follow a medieval tradition—the golden mean method—used for proportions. XIII Death is a rakish costumed figure who has wandered through the garden of the humanities. He has plucked one red rose, symbol of life and a living person, and he clutches a bunch of white roses, which represent cleansed and purified souls of the deceased. A white rose is affixed to his hat. The symbol of squat Celtic crosses is embroidered on his shirt and across his surcoat. The beckoning figure of Death promises knowledge rather than the horrors often associated with death.* 3 **The Empress** *by Laila Farcas. The tall figure of a Romanian empress with braided hair stands before a high-backed throne. She presses her right hand to her heart in a gesture of devotion and well-meaning intention. In her left hand she holds a model of the monastery of Curtea de Arges. The monastery with its four Greek crosses is a symbol of the support she receives from the church and, in turn, the support she extends to the priests and members of the Greek Orthodox Church. The Empress wears a Byzantine crown and an embroidered silk blouse called* iie. *Her gown is covered by a sleeveless cape and a colorful* catrinta *with tassles. The clothing worn by The Empress represents the costume of the people she rules and bears evidence that, even though she is Empress, she remains sympathetic to her people. The combination of a sun and a moon at the upper right represents the communion of The Empress with her people and the closeness of the people to this natural environment. To the lower right of The Empress is a medieval seal from Transylvania. The motif of a crow in the center of the seal may be linked to the Romanian legend of a prince who could not inherit his rightful throne because he had lost the imperial ring. The royal family was forced into exile by the usurper king, Alexander the Bad. One day a crow suddenly appeared bearing the ring in its beak and the prince was able to claim his inheritance. The grateful royal family granted the crow a permanent place on its coat of arms. An Arabic number 3 composed of living foliage appears at the top of the card.*

Bottom row, left: *Tarot designs by Sara Izod. These unusual tarot cards in hexagonal shape form interesting and meaningful patterns depending upon the manner in which they are placed in relation to one another. Each of the six sides of a card represents one or more subtle interpretations. The artwork is rendered in a fluid style suggesting forces in constant motion and continuous change.* **15 Vulcan,** *or The Devil, depicts the Roman fire god, originally of lightning and later of volcanoes. One story of his life relates that he was the son of Jupiter, king of the gods, and Juno, known in Greek mythology as Zeus and Hera, respectively. Vulcan was born lame and ugly, and Juno, shocked at the sight of him, threw him from Olympus. As a result, he was reared in a cave beneath the sea by nymphs and Nereids. The artist shows Vulcan with a fluid pentacle across his forehead. The* **nine of beads** *or pentacles depicts the planets of the world in harmonious transposition, suggesting that new worlds open up through adaptation. Bottom, second from right:* **1 Belier** *or Aries is from a tarot pack designed by Jean-Pol de Kersaint and published in 1974 in Tarot de Kersaint. The complete set consists of two volumes, with perforated cards in the second volume; both volumes are in English and French. The Kersaint cards include astrological symbols, flowers and diverse emotions with upright and reverse meanings printed on each card. Bottom, extreme right:* **The Hermit** *by Linda Williamson. Rendered in charcoal and pen and ink, the solitary figure of The Hermit seems to rise away from the complexities of life. He uses his raised arm to shield against invasion of his privacy. Even though he often teaches others, The Hermit chooses his own time and place to reveal his knowledge. The incomplete figure of The Hermit, as illustrated by the incomplete lower portion of the card and the stark white background, suggests the often limited insight one has of persons who are withdrawn and who may reject society. The Hermit wears a tattered cloak with a large peaked hood, which indicates his intellect. The tightly clutched lantern serves as a guide to the select paths he has chosen to travel.*

Arcanes du Destin Printed about 1950, possibly in Italy, because the double-ended Major Arcana cards are of the Piedmontese type. All the cards are numbered in sequence from 1 to 78 in Arabic and Roman numerals and bear titles in "Dog Latin." The cards are printed on a linen weave type of stock. Top row, left: 1 Praestigiator, 2 Papessae, 3 Augusta, 4 Imperator, 5 Pontifex Romanus. Second row: 6 Amore Captus, 7 Carrus, 8 Justitiae, 9 Eremita, 10 Rota Fortuna. Third row: 11 Vigoris, 12 Pendens, 13 Mortis, 14 Temperantia, 15 Diabolus. Bottom row: 16 Turris, 17 Stella, 18 Luna, 19 Solis, 69 Denarius.

Atkins/Heitmann/Klumper/Lucas/May/Picini

Top row, left: *The queen of water and the eight of earth, two cards from the Phoenix tarot deck by William Atkins in cooperation with Heather Hageman. The seventy-eight-card Phoenix tarot deck comprises five suits consisting of fifteen cards in each suit, two floating cards named The Fool and The Universe, and a Phoenix card. The five suits are called ethers, fire, earth, air and water. Twenty of the Major Arcana cards from traditional tarot are converted to court cards and aces in the Phoenix tarot. Another tarot deck developed by Hageman is called the deck of Ethers with card designs by Dorothy Sigler (page 178). The* **queen of water** *is drawn from the Moon card of the traditional Major Arcana. The malevolent image of Artemis is depicted by Hecate, Greek goddess of the dark side of the moon. She stands between a crescent moon in eclipse and an opalescent full moon. Artemis wears the tritons of Neptune in her headdress and she rules the storms of the seas and all evil. In the foreground is the beneficent image of Artemis. She wears a scarab on her finger and she cradles a conch shell to symbolize her love of life and the creatures of the water. Her diaphanous gossamer gown signifies her seductiveness. At the top border of the card is a dolphin, representing the suit of water. The* **eight of earth** *or resources depicts a man holding a chisel and hammer, symbolic of the instruments of man's inventive genius. The eight crystals in balanced order suggest energy and the productiveness of work and study.*

Top row, right: *The Fool and The Devil by Eva G. Lucas in collaboration with Mouni Sadhu. These black and white Major Arcana cards appear in* The Tarot, A Contemporary Course of the Quintessence of Hermetic Occultism, *written by Sadhu and published in 1962.* **The Fool** *is a bearded man wearing a circus fool's cap. His clothes are more decorative than suitable for travel and he carries in his bag numerous useless things. Blood flows from a leg wound inflicted by a dog and a crocodile waits for him with open jaws. The Fool turns his head away so that he doesn't see where he is going. Sadhu assigns The Fool a place between the twentieth and twenty-second Major Arcana, and to this card he designates the scientific name of furca, or fork, suggested by the shape of the Hebrew letter Shin, W.* **The Devil** *is depicted with a goat's head and legs. He sits on a cube to which are chained two naked female figures with small horns on their heads. On the right arm of the androgyne is the word "Solve," meaning to decide, cut off, dissolve. On the left arm is the word "Coagula," meaning to solidify, condense. A pentagram and waning moon appear at the top of the card.*

Second row: *Five Major Arcana cards by graphics designer Robert Charles Heitmann. The cards are rendered in full color in a phantasmagoric style and appeared on the cover of the September 1970 issue of* Greeting Card *magazine.* **II Junon, V Jupiter, XIIII Temperance, XV Le Diable, XVIIII Le Soleil.**

Third row: *Four Major Arcana cards with Egyptian motifs contained in a magazine article, "Symboliek der Getallen," by W. Tj. Klumper appeared in the October 1969 issue of* Bres. *The cards shown are* **The Magus; The Holy Marriage** *or* **The Empress; The Resurrection of the Flesh,** *suggesting that the empty grave of the new Adam is situated in the King's Room of the pyramid;* **Completion,** *with four winged figures surrounding an Egyptian woman.*

Bottom row, left: *0* **The Fool** *and XV* **Bondage** *by Wayne May in cooperation with Madilynne Mulleague. Using acrylic paints, the artist prepared these Afro tarot cards on the basis of the symbolism of tribal cultures in lower central and southern Africa; the cultures of North Africa and the desert areas were ignored in order to avoid any European or Middle Eastern influences.* **The Fool** *depicts an African youth on the path of life; he pursues a large butterfly representing foolish pleasure and he fails to heed the warning of the monkey tugging at his heels. The tall grass in the background suggests hidden dangers.* **XV Bondage** *is similar to The Devil card in traditional tarot packs and depicts two African captives. They are loosely tied to a tree, suggesting they can easily free themselves. The tree is barren and the large eye suggests the all-seeing eye of the Supreme Being. The Afro tarot deck also contains Minor Arcana cards (not shown) comprised of court cards representing tribal chiefs and other hierarchy of African tribes; the four suits each represent a specific African tribe.*

Bottom row, right: **I Il Bagatto** *(The Magician) and* **II La Papessa** *(The Popess) by Andrea Picini. The cards are decorative pattern designs with silhouetted figures in rich, vivid colors. The Magician is a feminine figure wearing a long cloak; the suit indices include a male silhouette in place of a baton, and the background of the card is an interwoven pattern of lips and hearts. La Papessa depicts a dominant female figure with elbows extended beyond the border of the card. The figure holds aloft a key and a large crook, interlacing two rings. The head of the Popess is a circle pattern whose perspective focuses into the face and contains an Arabic number 2. Along the bottom of the card appears a smaller robed figure between tall pawnlike columns.*

Atkins, May and Picini—collections of the artists: Heitmann reprinted from *Greeting Card* magazine; Klumper reprinted from *Bres* magazine; Lucas reprinted from *The Tarot, A Contemporary Course of the Quintessence of Hermetic Occultism*

Balbi/ Bennett/ Brother Placid/ Decker/ Greenwich Library/ Yves Jobert/ Rivers/ Sigler *Examples of tarot designs by contemporary artists.*

Top row, left: *Domenico Balbi engraving. Vito Arienti, one of Italy's leading playing card collectors, is depicted as the king of clubs by Domenico Balbi, Italian painter and illustrator.*

Top row, center: *Bennett Emperor card. One of a series of unpublished Major Arcana cards executed by George Bennett on scratch board. The Emperor is portrayed with the four suit signs—sword, stave, cup and coin—found in standard tarot packs.*

Top row, right: *Brother Placid print. The Emperor or Christ the King design painted by Brother Placid Stuckenschneider, O.S.B., suggests a composite of The Emperor and The Hierophant found in the Cary-Yale Visconti-Sforza tarocchi packs. Christ the King was used as the cover of Bible and Liturgy Sunday Bulletins distributed in late 1975 at Catholic churches throughout the United States. The figure of Christ with a three-pointed crown reigns over the world. He holds a globe topped with the Christian cross; in his right hand is a scepter, symbol of his rule. The scales of justice and the hands of judgment are also suggestive of the Justice and Judgment cards.*

Middle row, left and center: *Ronald Decker portrays The Popess and The Pope as examples of the virtues of Prudence and Faith, respectively. The depiction is based upon the virtues by Giotto in the Arena Chapel in Padua, Italy. The Popess is surrounded by a halo of peacock feathers with eyes that see in all directions. Since the third house relates astrologically to Virgo, the artist views The Popess as a virgin governed by Mercury, whose emblem appears on the large cross she holds. The Pope is the ninth house, the house of religion. He tramples pagan symbols, such as the bat-winged demon to his left and the Roman eagle to his right. The planetary emblem appears in the cross the Pope holds.*

Middle row, right: *Greenwich Magician design. The Greenwich Public Library, Greenwich, Connecticut, featured The Magician design on the cover of a booklet prepared in 1963 by the library staff to describe the variety of books available from the library facility.*

Bottom row, left: *The Fool, one of the engravings from copper plates on vellum paper by Yves Jobert, issued by Edition La Gravure Originale in a limited edition of sixty-two sets of the twenty-two Major Arcana cards signed by the artist. All twenty-two Major Arcana cards are represented in the complete set, fourteen on full pages and the remaining eight reduced in size and printed on two sheets.*

Bottom row, center: *Larry Rivers' The World card. First sketch and collage by noted artist Larry Rivers. The center figure standing in front of the large wreath is a sketch of Kitty Meyer in 1974, posing during the middle of the night on a deserted street in Southhampton, Long Island. In the four corners are a winged cherub, an eagle, a standing bull and a lion at rest. The oriental design in the background is part of a sketch from the acrylic painting by Rivers entitled* Heroes of Chushingura.

Bottom row, right: *Dorothy Sigler's The Fool. A youth of pure innocence with long locks of blond hair is depicted as The Fool. He wears a white garment and draws about his shoulders a loose red cloak. The white rose is a symbol of purity that emits a golden light, suggesting protective forces that will serve to guide him.*

Beaulieu/Laliberte/Le-Tan/Sigler *Examples of tarot designs by contemporary artists.*

Top row: *Puppetlike tarot cards designed by L. Beaulieu in 1970. The Fool, I The Magician, VII The Chariot, the two of pentacles. These cards were part of a series of tarot designs used by the Mary Cheney Library, Manchester, Connecticut, to present its 1969–1970 Annual Report. The back of each card contains information about library activities, services and facilities.*

Second row: *Norman Laliberte serigraphs. Three sheets in full color from a signed and limited edition of 250 sets of the Major Arcana cards by Norman Laliberte. Cards shown are XII The Hanged Man, XIII Death, XV The Devil. The paintings of these Major Arcana cards are rendered with gold lines and rich colors. All twenty-two Major Arcana cards are represented in the complete set, eighteen of them on a full page each and the remaining four (XII to XV) reduced in dimension to fit on one sheet.*

Third row: *Le-Tan tarot. Major Arcana cards by French artist Pierre Le-Tan. I The Magician wears a sweater, open-collared shirt and soft conical hat. VIIII The Hermit has a white beard and bald head. He wears a trench coat and*

179

holds a flashlight. XVI The Tower is a brick building struck by lightning. XVIII The Moon card shows baying dogs and emerging crawfish, and two low brick towers with windows. The Le-Tan prints are rendered in pen and ink and watercolors; the designs depict stylized contemporary figures against flat, uncluttered backgrounds.

Bottom row: *Dorothy Sigler tarot deck of Ethers.* The etheric tarot designs by Dorothy Sigler were prepared in collaboration with Heather Hageman. There are five suits instead of the traditional four, and each suit reflects one of the five elements: earth, air, fire, water and ether. The symbolism of the Major Arcana cards is incorporated into the court cards of the five suits. The tarot deck of Ethers totals sixty-seven cards comprised of five suits of thirteen cards each, plus two extra cards, one appearing at the beginning and the other at the end of the deck. The court cards are king, queen and child. The cards shown are: queen of ether, represented by a mandala, the oriental emblem of the universe, above the head of the winged figure who holds a reflective sphere; the king of fire, dressed in a fur-lined robe, with a five-pointed star on his forehead, a six-rayed star shining from the palm of his upraised left hand and behind him are two swords with ornately carved hilts; the king of air, with a loosely hanging toga robe, holds a large staff in his left hand; the king of water, with an almost innocent, placid facial expression, holds a cup with dolphins from which a rainbow spreads in a semicircle. The blank panels in the court cards are spaces for card identification in the form of chiseled Roman letters.

Benavides/Carter/Dorflinger/Fodera/Kloster/Nessim/Rota/Schlossman Tarot designs by contemporary artists.

Top row, left: *4 The Emperor and 15 The Devil reprinted from* The Prophetic Tarot *by Rodolfo Benavides.* **4 The Emperor** wears a large crown decorated with four small triangles symbolizing the four elements in nature: air, earth, fire and water. He holds a scepter topped with an Egyptian ankh and he sits upon a cubical stone throne beneath an eagle with outstretched wings. At the corners of the throne appear a skull, an eagle, a bull calf and a lion. **15 The Devil** *is a female figure with the head, legs and feet of a goat. Two large wings resembling those of a bat spread from its shoulders. It holds upside down a sword and a torch symbolizing injustice and venality. At its feet stand a naked man and woman, chained at the ankles, in an attitude of suffering.*

Top row, right: **22 The Wheel of Life** *was drawn by Jimmy Carter in collaboration with Simon Kasdin. According to Kasdin, the Major Arcana cards are based upon the* Sepher Yetzirah *or Book of Creation, which the Israelites brought back from exile in Babylon during the sixth century B.C. Kasdin has sought to prepare tarot images in accordance with the descriptive name of each letter in the Hebrew alphabet. 22 The Wheel of Life is based upon the Hebrew letter Tav, which means a mark. In the archaic pre-exilic Hebrew alphabet, the ancient form of the letter was an X inscribed within a circle. In ancient Greek tradition Ixion was tied to a wheel that was continuously rotated, thus causing him great suffering. In ancient Buddhist symbology the wheel of life depicts a man tied to the wheel of life, or the cycle of necessity, by the bonds of ignorance, anger and lust; to these here are added Pride at the lower left of the wheel and Fear at the wheel's center.* **XII The Hanged Man** *is a large appliqué banner sewn from silks and other colorful fabrics, and based upon the tarot design of Hans Dorflinger.*

Second row: *Four tarot designs by Hans Dorflinger from a limited edition of one hundred signed and numbered sets of the complete twenty-two Major Arcana. First published in 1975, this unique art form could be described as psychological symbolism. Several recurring features dominate the cards, including amorphous masses of particles that appear variously as spray, dust, clouds and protoplasm within geometric fields of triangles, stars, squares and circles. The identifiable objects include eggs, birds, serpents, pairs of figures and wheels. The tarot sheets were printed in twelve colors using aluminum plates in a technique called* granolitho *whereby one color is printed on top of the previous color without the appearance of dots.* **The Wheel of Fortune** *moves like a comet through space, leaving a trail of particles of fire, water, earth and air that envelop a man and woman whose mirror images reappear, their bodies joined, within the egg at the wheel's center. Radiating from the center of the wheel is a five-pointed star with holes and eggs between the pointed edges.* **Force** *is a woman whose body has an aura like a peacock's tail. Her belly is a ball of fire within which are the heads of a pair of figures who form her legs, source of her strength. She wears on her head a lion's mane crowned by an egg. The background of the Force card is an elongated star.* **The Devil** *contains a large flaming star split down the center and forming the Devil's wings. There is one wing apiece for the two bodies, which form hemispheres the Devil is pulling apart. The two figures are eating a flame and spitting it out as forked tails of fire.* **The Sun** *is depicted as a sun wheel whose inner circle is like the eye of a cyclone. Floating in the outer circle are four clouds shaped like eggs. At the bottom of the wheel is a pair of dissolving figures whose heads are in contact with a standing pair of lovers on whom the wheel is balanced and who, while supporting the sun, also form one of its rays. The other seven rays are coupled figures.*

Third row, extreme left: **King of clubs**, *one of a series of court cards designed by Vincenzo Fodera in which the tarot suit signs of swords, staves, cups and coins are interwoven into the double-ended picture. The top side of the card is distinguishable by a colored index, in this instance a black club against a white background, indicating positive meanings. The inverted index against a dark background suggests negative meanings. The king of clubs is depicted as a noble person of important stature; inverted, a critical person admonishes a young couple caught in an embrace.* Third row, center and right: *These three Major Arcana cards by Suzanne Kloster first appeared in 1949 in* Le Tarot Révélé *by Valentin Bresle.* **The Fool**, *with head high, ignores the tiger at his heels.* **VIII Justice** *sits on a brick wall and holds a double-edged sword across her lap and the scales of justice in her left hand. Her veil falls over her eyes and an owl sits at her left, while a serpent coils around her feet. The pillars in the background are named "Nizah" and "Chazed."* **XVI The Temple** *or* **House of God** *is struck by rays of destruction and the falling figures seem to float in the air. On the ground are many objects, including an overturned pedestal, a cross, a broken cup and scattered coins. At the top of the card is inscribed "Jehovah-Sabaoth."*

Bottom row: **XXII The Fool** *designed by Barbara Nessim wears a long cloak, breeches and leather knee boots; two*

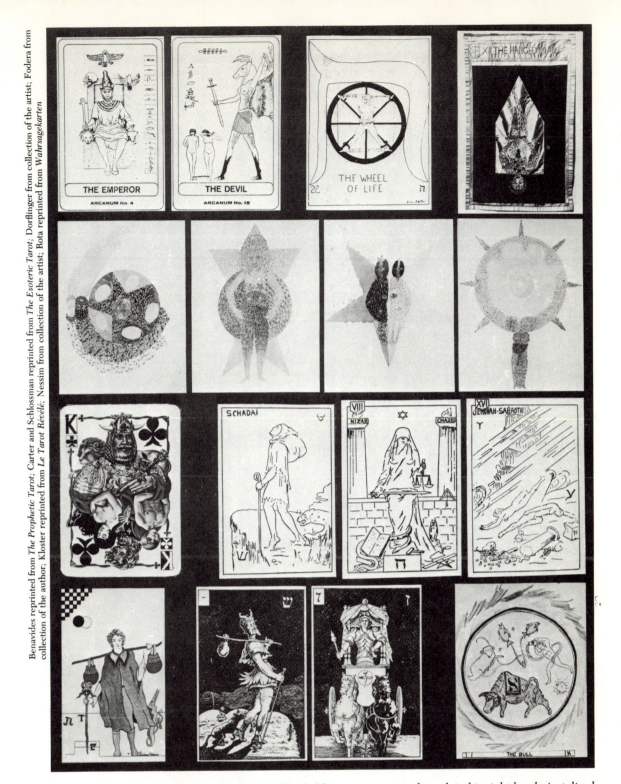

Benavides reprinted from *The Prophetic Tarot*; Carter and Schlossman reprinted from *The Esoteric Tarot*; Dorflinger from collection of the artist; Fodera from collection of the author; Kloster reprinted from *Le Tarot Révélé*; Nessim from collection of the artist; Rota reprinted from *Wahrsagekarten*

sacks hang from the scepter across his shoulders and he holds an ornate-topped crook in his right hand. A stylized serpent stands on its tail in the background while in the sky a total eclipse appears imminent. The checkerboard design at the upper left represents the game of life. The Fool appeared on the jacket of *The Book of Paradox* by Louise Cooper. Another **Fool** card, suggestive of Don Quixote, and **The Chariot** are part of a Rota deck possibly first published in Czechoslovakia. The backgrounds are black and the figures are rendered in considerable detail. The Fool has a goatee and he appears with eyes closed; the vacant, humorous expression on his face suggests he is daydreaming or in a trance. 7 The Chariot shows a charioteer in full armor and holding a scepter in his right hand while he rides in his chariot. 1 **The Bull**, was drawn by Sylvia Schlossman and appears in The Esoteric Tarot, written by Simon Kasdin. This card is a pictorial representation of the letter Aleph, which means bull or ox. Above the bull is part of the zodiac belt showing Aries, the ram, the fishes of Pisces and the water bearer of Aquarius. According to Kasdin, tarot derives from the age of Taurus, represented by the bull. The ancient bull was sacred to the early Hindu religion. A zodiac clock showing the twelve signs of the zodiac appears beneath the water bearer.

181

Reprinted from Modern Packs and Playing Card Tradition by F. Stahly

Berthole Tarot These Major Arcana and court cards are prints of colored woodcuts prepared by Jean Berthole, a French artist, and first published in 1949 in Graphis magazine. The complete pack was never published. The designs feature geometric shapes in a cubist style. Top row: *The Fool, 1 The Magician, The Emperor.* Middle Row: *The Chariot, The Moon, knight of staves.* Bottom row: *page of staves and king of coins.*

British Tarot Trumps numbered in Arabic with English titles. Pip cards contain symbolic pictures similar in general design to the Rider-Waite cards; however, there are numerous variations in each picture and the suits of staves and coins are instead called rods and pence, respectively.

Collection of the author

Chaboseau/Loring Tarot

Top row: *Major Arcana* cards by Jean Chaboseau first appeared in 1946 in Le Tarot. Le Fou (*The Fool*) is blindfolded. He holds a rod topped by a jester's face in his right hand and a violin under his left arm. A dog barks at his heels and an alligator rises from a precipice in front of him. Le Bateleur (*The Magician*) wears a headband and a long flowing cape. La Papesse (*The Female Pope*) holds two large keys and a book on her lap. The female figure of Le Monde (*The World*) is surrounded by a heavy wreath with flowers. Le Roy d'Épées (*king of swords*) is dressed in long cape and helmet; he has a large sword and shield.

Second row: Le Roy de Coupes (*king of cups*) wears a long cape and holds a cup, the sign of his suit. Sept Epées (*seven of swords*).

The Major Arcana cards by Christian Loring have a medieval style and they first appeared in 1935 in Le Tarot Médiéval by Francis Rolt-Wheeler. Second row: 0 Le Fou (*The Fool*), 1 Le Bateleur (*The Magician*), V Le Pape (*The Pope*). Bottom row: VI L'Amoureux (*The Lovers*), VIII La Justice (*Justice*), XIX Les Etoiles (*The Stars*), queen of swords, queen of staves. In the bottom panel of each Major Arcana card is the card title, Roman number and Hebrew letter.

Cooper Tarot   These modern Major Arcana tarot cards were designed by J. Cooper and published in 1969 in Eye magazine. The artist's name appears on the Wheel of Fortune and Temperance cards. The Major Arcana are unnumbered. Top row: *The Fool, The Magician, High Priestess, The Empress, The Emperor*. Second row: *The Hierophant, The Chariot, Justice, The Hermit, Wheel of Fortune*. Third row: *Strength, Death, Temperance, The Devil, The Tower*. Bottom row: *The Star, The Moon, The Sun, Judgment, The World*.

Dali/Gill/Iamblichus/Kaye/Littel/Metcalfe/Sherman/Tavaglione   *Contemporary tarot card designs. Top row, left: The card of Justice from a set of limited edition serigraphs signed by Salvador Dali. The nude figure of Justice is after a picture by the sixteenth-century German artist Lucas Cranach, the Elder. The Fool, The Empress and The Chariot by Josephine Gill in cooperation with Dolores Ashcroft-Nowicki. The fool passes in the cosmic night through a doorway from another state of consciousness; The Empress is depicted as a beautiful woman; The Chariot is an Egyptian figure wearing a zodiac belt.*

Second row: The Hermit is shown beneath a spiritual Tree of Life. Death depicts a glass boat in the sea of night with the figure casting the dice of fate for the woman. The Hermit and Death are both by Josephine Gill. 5 L'Imperatrice appears in An Egyptian Initiation *and resembles Wirth's designs. III The Empress by Jerry Kaye has a pelican and shield resembling Visconti-Sforza heraldic devices.*

Third row: The Fool and The Emperor by Sander Littel in cooperation with Gareth Knight. The Fool appears as a great clown; The Emperor is a mighty warrior figure in armor. The Queen by Andrew J. Metcalfe depicts Nefertiti, wife of Amenhotep IV or Akhnaton, from the 54-card Egyptian Temple deck. 0 The Fool by Johanna Sherman depicts a medieval, earthy figure dressed in peasant shirt and knee-length mountain pants. The Fool with a half smile across his face struts into timeless space; the rocks and earth in the background are combined into a stained glass effect and the flowers blossom through rock crevices.

Bottom row: I Il Mago, 3 L'Imperatrice, 4 L'Imperatore, 5 Il Papa and 6 L'Innamorato in black and white line drawings by Giorgio Tavaglione. The designs contain Egyptian influence, signs of the zodiac, Hebrew letters and interpretations appear in Italian at the bottom of each card.

Docters van Leeuwen Porcelain Tarot The twenty-four Major Arcana figures in this unique series were modeled in fine white clay, baked and polychromatized with oil paint and gold leaf by Onno Docters van Leeuwen of the Netherlands. The artist includes two extra figures, XXIII Jupiter and XXIV Juno, who replace in some traditional tarot packs The Pope or The Hierophant and The Popess or The High Priestess, respectively. According to Docters van Leeuwen, about the year 300 A.D. the Church unsuccessfully sought to prohibit the tarot and, especially, to ban two cards, the male principle or truth per se, expressed as Jupiter, and the female principle or inner truth, represented by Juno. These two cards correspond to the male yang and the female yin. Docters van Leeuwen believes these two cards were hidden behind The Pope and The Popess and in time they came to replace them. At the top of each picture Roman numbering follows the popular Rider-Waite sequence; however, The Fool is designated XXI. The Arabic numbering on each card designates Docters van Leeuwen's corrected sequence after reintroduction of the so-called two hidden Major Arcana. Alphabetical lettering and zodiac symbols appear at the top of each picture and at the bottom in capital letters appears a permutation of the word "taro" and the title of the arcana in Dutch. Ten Major Arcana cards are located by Docters van Leeuwen in a sequence that varies from traditional tarot. These cards are The Empress, from 3 to 6; The Emperor, 4 to 3; The Lovers, 6 to 4; Strength, 8 to 11; The Hermit, 9 to 8; Justice, 11 to 9; Death, 13 to 14; Temperance, 14 to 13; The Star, 17 to 18; The Moon, 18 to 17.

Top row: 0 (XXI TAOR) De Dwaas (The Fool), 1 (I TOAR) De Magier (The Magician), 2 (II TORA) De Hogepriesteres (The High Priestess), 3 (IV TROA) De Keizer (The Emperor), 4 (VI RTOA) De Geliefden (The Lovers). Second row: 5 (V ATRO) De Hogepriester (The High Priest or Hierophant), 6 (III OTRA) De Keizerin (The Empress), 7 (VII OTAR) De Zegewagen (The Chariot), 8 (IX RTAO) De Kluezenaar (The Hermit), 9 (VIII AOTR) De Rechtvaardigheid (Justice). Third row: 11 (XI ORTA) De Kracht (Strength), 12 (XII ARTO) De Gehangene (The Hanged Man), 13 (XIV RATO) De Gematigdheid (Temperance), 14 (XIII OATR) De Dood (Death), 15 (XV OART) De Duivel (The Devil). Bottom row: 18 (XVII AROT) De Ster (The Star), 19 (XIX AORT) De Zon (The Sun), 21 (XXII TARO) Het Universum (The Universe or The World), XXIII (ORAT) Jupiter—designated positive—and XXIV (ATOR) Juno—designated negative. After reintroducing the two hidden arcana, Jupiter and Juno, and assigning permutations of the word taro to each card, Docters van Leeuwen devised a linear structure that can be made auditive by transposition into music. Four voices, reproduced by either human being, instrument or computer, are used.

Fatidic Egyptian Tarot The designs of this Egyptian tarot appear in a book entitled Practical Astrology by Comte C. Saint-Germain, published in 1901.

Top row: *The Crocodile* depicts a sightless man with a double sack draped across his left shoulder. He has a stick in his right hand and walks toward a broken obelisk stretched on the ground, upon which a crocodile, its huge mouth open, crawls toward him. In the sky appears the sun, partially eclipsed by a dark shadow, a symbol of doubt destroying faith. The figure suggests an atheist who is unable to see the divine light and walks toward his ruin.

I The Magus stands in the attitude of willpower about to act. He is dressed in white, the emblem of purity, with a circle of gold around his brow, emblem of eternal light. He holds in his right hand a scepter tipped with a circle, the emblem of creative intelligence, which he raises toward heaven to indicate his aspirations to wisdom, science and moral force. His left hand points toward the earth to show that he is ready to dominate matter. In front of him, upon a cube of absolute solidity, are found a cup filled with human passions, a sword used by warriors who fight error, and a golden pentacle, emblem of the reward granted to voluntary labor. His belt is a snake biting its tail, the symbol of eternity. The Ibis upon the side of the cube typifies vigilance.

II The Gate of the Sanctuary. A stately woman is seated between two columns of a temple representing good and evil. The female figure is crowned with a crescent and her face is veiled as a sign that truth is not visible to the profane. She has upon her breast the solar cross, emblematic of universal generation, and in her lap a papyrus half covered by her cloak, indicating that the mysteries of the sacred science are unveiled only to the initiated. The tiara upon her head is the emblem of the power of intelligence illuminated by wisdom, as evidenced by the crescent. The figure is seated until wisdom and willpower unite to action.

III Isis-Urania. This card depicts the ancient idea of nature represented by a woman seated upon a cube covered with eyes, the emblem of the visions of the famous seer, Hermes. Her feet rest upon a crescent of the moon, the emblem of matter subjected to mind. She is crowned with twelve stars representing the twelve months and the sun serves her as a nimbus, symbolizing the creative power of intelligence. In one hand she holds a scepter tipped with a globe, the emblem of her despotic power over the world; perched on her other hand is an eagle, its head turned toward her, signifying the flight of the human soul returning to its initial principle: God.

IV The Cubic Stone. A regal man wears on his head a crowned helmet, the emblem of conquest. He sits upon a cube, which is the symbol of labor that has been completed. In his right hand he holds the scepter of the Magi as a sign of the moral power acquired through sacred studies. His left hand, pointing downward, indicates mastery over matter, while the dove on his breast symbolizes innocence, and his crossed legs signify the expansion of the power of human mind within the three dimensions of the infinite: height, width, depth. The cat upon the cube symbolizes the thought of the Magi who is able to see through the night of the ancient times.

Second row: *V The Master of the Arcanes.* The high priest of Isis is seated between the columns of the sanctuary, one hand on a long cross with three crossbars, symbolizing the penetration of the creative genius through the three

worlds: divine, intellectual and physical. The two columns represent law and the free will that permits each of us to obey or disobey. With his right hand the high priest makes the sign of meditation and silence, while at his feet kneel two men, one suggesting good and the other evil.

VI The Two Ways. The disciple or neophyte is shown hesitating between two ways, each of which is pointed out to him by a woman; the one to the right symbolizes vice, the one to the left, virtue. In the sky is a Genius holding a bow and arrow pointed toward vice as a warning of the punishment that awaits those who select the easy road to vice instead of the hard road to virtue.

VII The Chariot of Osiris. A warrior rides a cubic chariot with four columns that support a starry dais. The columns symbolize the four elements, while the cubic chariot signifies that the ambition of the warrior has been realized through his will to conquer every obstacle. The warrior has a golden band around his brow as a sign of the eternal light with which he is endowed. In one hand he holds a sword, the emblem of victory, and in the other hand, a scepter tipped with a square representing matter, a circle representing eternity and a triangle representing divinity. He wears on his breast a cuirass, the emblem of strength, adorned with three T-squares that represent good judgment, willpower and action. A winged sphere on the front of the chariot suggests the exaltation of intellectual power in the infinite spheres of space and time. Two sphinxes that pull the chariot are shown at rest; the black sphinx represents evil, the white one good. Both sphinxes are slaves of the Magus.

VIII The Balance and the Sword. A woman sits on a throne atop three steps that represent the three worlds. Her brow is encircled with a crown of iron, emblem of inflexibility, and her eyes are bandaged to indicate that she gives no preference to the social positions of the accused ones. A sword in one hand and a balance in the other, she judges and she punishes. The lion by her side symbolizes force ruled by justice. The sphinx represents the eye of God that looks into the souls of the wicked. The winged turtle at the top of the card symbolizes repentance, which may bring forgiveness in spite of the greatness of the crime. The winged divine messenger confirms that the justice of God will be the final judge of the justice of men.

IX The Veiled Lamp. An old man, symbol of wisdom, holds a lighted lamp which he covers with his mantle as a sign of discretion. He walks with little need for his stick, evidencing the inner strength he has acquired through experience.

Third row: X The Sphinx depicts an ancient drawing of the wheel of destiny turning upon its axis. Rising on the right side is the God Kne-phta, the spirit of good; on the other side is Typhon, the spirit of evil, about to be thrown off the wheel. Above the wheel presides a winged Sphinx representing the four forces of human nature: to know, to dare, to act, to remain silent. The Sphinx remains in perfect equilibrium as if the constantly revolving wheel of fortune has no influence over him. Thus, the Sphinx symbolizes the mysterious power of God disposing of human destinies according to the good or bad actions of the individual. In his claws the Sphinx holds a javelin, the emblem of supreme justice. At the foot of the supporting beam of the axis, two snakes symbolize the even forces that balance each other while struggling constantly for supremacy.

XI The Tamed Lion depicts a young maiden opening and closing, without effort, the mouth of a lion, thus confirming the power over one's self that can be acquired through educating the will and experiencing life.

XII The Sacrifice. A man hangs by one foot from a gallows stretched across the trunks of two trees whose twelve branches have been cut off. His hands are bound at the wrists and he drops pentacles or gold pieces suggesting that ideas survive those who are willing to sacrifice themselves. The twelve cut branches symbolize the signs of the zodiac, which recur regularly year after year. The crossed leg of the man, folded down and forming with the other leg a reversed triangle, reveals that he is being subjected to wicked influences.

XIII The Reaping Skeleton armed with a scythe symbolizes death mowing down human beings whose heads, feet and hands are constantly born again. A rainbow rises in the horizon, an emblem of the immortality of the soul.

XIV The Two Urns. A figure representing the sun transfers the elemental forces of nature from a golden vase into a silver vase.

Bottom row: XV Typhon is the spirit of evil, fatality and chaos. It is represented by a hippopotamus with the head of a crocodile, the feet of a goat and the characteristics of man and woman. A snake emerges from its body, to show that it begets nothing but evil. Its wings, like those of a bat, show it to be the spirit of darkness. It is depicted rising from ruins, one of its hands waving the torch of destruction and the other holding the scepter of division and hatred. At Typhon's feet are two men with goat's heads and chains around their necks, symbolizing those beings whom vice brings lower than the beast. The horn on Typhon's nose indicates rebellion against the divine spirit, which it seems to be insulting.

XVI The Thunder-struck Tower. The pinnacle of a pyramid is smashed by lightning. Two men, one of them with a crown on his head, are thrown to the ground. This symbolizes the destruction of human pride and false science by the sudden influx of astral power.

XVII The Star of the Magi. A nude young girl with one foot upon the sea and one foot upon the earth holds two cups from which flow kindness and charity, the balms that alleviate human suffering. The sea represents the bitterness of the days of sorrow. Above the young girl shines an eight-pointed star, a symbol of both the universe and the Trinity; at its center appears a white pyramid united to a black pyramid that is upside down. This is the emblem of the great occult law, which reads, "That which is above is like that which is below." Seven smaller stars represent the seven planets of ancient astrology. Next to the woman there is a flower with three blossoms and above the flower a butterfly opens its wings.

XVIII The Twilight. Two pyramids stand at the edge of a road. One of them is white, the emblem of true science; the other is black, the symbol of error. Two dogs, which represent good and evil, howl at the moon. The scorpion is the emblem of perversity, the worst feature of vice.

XIX The Dazzling Light. Under a radiant sun, a young man and woman hold each other by the hand within a circle of flowers. The sign within the sun above the couple is the symbol of universal generation.

Frownstrong/Gemrod/Hoffman/Holbein/Pry/Saba-Telli/Scott/Skell.

Top row: Frownstrong tarot cards are rendered in a mosaic pattern. **The Juggler** depicts a puppet figure wearing a dunce cap, Arabian slippers and a shirt decorated down the front with the last five letters of the alphabet. Signs of the zodiac, male and female symbols and the Hebrew star appear above his head; a cast iron table appears at his left. **The Hierophant** depicts a high priest wearing an Egyptian headdress and standing in a temple decorated by Greek crosses. Two peasants and two guards attend to the Hierophant's needs and two all-knowing eyes penetrate the temple chamber. Gemrod tarot cards are pen and ink line drawings that combine mysticism and realism. **The Lovers** depicts an evil provocator with horns and penetrating eyes that mesmerize two nude figures who hold Egyptian ankhs and walk hand in hand. Nearby are the ancient ruins of Stonehenge. A large tree is laden with tempting fruit and a butterfly, symbolizing regeneration, hovers above a wheel of continuous force. **The Hanged Man** reveals three figures hanging from different trees. The figure to the left dangles from one ankle while his money falls to the ground; the tree contains the star of David. The middle figure is tightly bound at both ankles and clothing is scattered nearby on the ground. In the sky above the center tree appears the sign of the trinity and supreme being. The last figure depicts mankind with a skull, male and female symbols and radiating spirit. **The Sun** depicts three time capsules. Six figures in the first capsule are dressed in garments worn during different eras including Greek, Roman, Medieval and contemporary, and they represent the span of recorded civilization. The center capsule depicts a seer of knowledge that serves as the link between the knowing and the unknowing. The final capsule contains mythological figures. A fiery sun radiates overhead.

Second row: **Gimel** by Douglas Hoffman. Based on Waite's association of Hebrew letters and the Major Arcana, Hoffman depicts Gimel—the camel—for The High Priestess. The camel carries goods across the barren desert and provides the means for communication between distant places. **Heh** with its Aries symbol represents The Emperor; the horned, pensive figure governs the realities of life. Reason, like rays of light, surrounds him in his solitude. Four woodcut scenes by Hans Holbein the Younger are from the **Dance of Death** series. Executed by the German Renaissance painter in the first half of the sixteenth century, the scenes probably were not meant to be tarot, but the imagery is surprisingly similar to some of the traditional Major Arcana, especially **The Emperor** and **The Pope.**

Third row: **The Chariot** and **The Last Judgment.** Each scene reveals the presence of the figure of death as an integral part of the illustration. The four Holbein prints were reissued in 1973 by Charles Pry as part of a 45-card deck of playing cards. **II The High Priestess** and **IIII The Emperor** are part of an edition of erotic Major Arcana cards limited to one hundred sets and also issued by Charles Pry. **The Emperor** and **The Chariot** are tempera illustrations by Antonio Saba-Telli in a style best described as expanded expressionism based upon phantasmagoric flashes. The imagery is without formalism and the unconventional figures are depicted in sharp and piercing brightness.

Bottom row: **IIII Imperatore** and **VIII Giustizia** are glazed enamel tarots also painted with tempera by Antonio Saba-Telli. **5 The Pope** and **6 The Lovers** by Sarah Scott. These pen and ink illustrations are a departure from the animals, reptiles and insects that were featured in another Major Arcana series by the same artist (page 220). **I Magician** and **XXI World** by Sue Skell. The imagery in these cards is based upon the work of Robert Graves in The White Goddess; each card is associated with the Druid tree calendar and alphabet. The letter B stands for tree and this is the first letter of the Celtic alphabet. I Magician depicts a birch tree at the beginning of a new lunar year. The four suits of swords, staves, cups and pentacles are represented at the base of the tree. A snake entwines the tree trunk similar to the snake that encircles the waist of the magician in other tarot packs. XXI World shows a cluster of sacred mistletoe blooming in winter as a sign of strength and regeneration. Instead of the traditional oval the artist depicts a circle comprising four smaller, overlapping circles that contain a lion, a bull, an eagle and an angel.

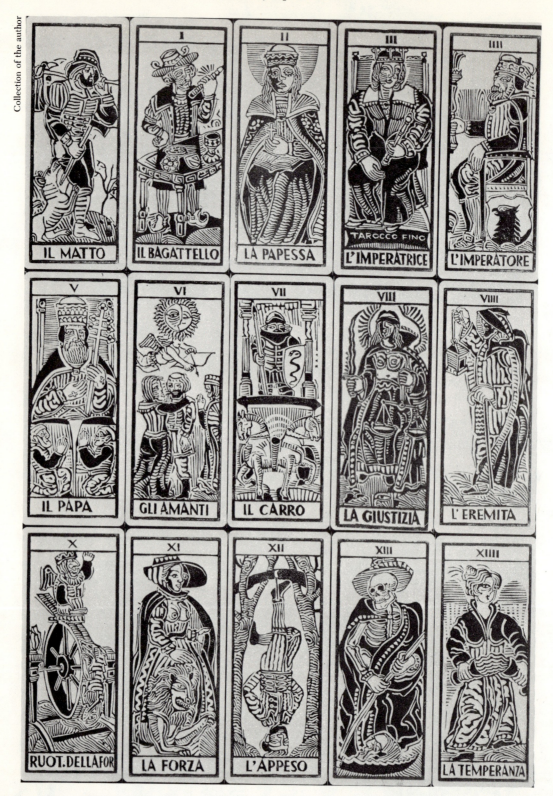

Glass Tarot Designed by a young Polish artist, Christoph Glass, this tarot deck with Italian titles was produced in a limited edition of seventy sets. The Minor Arcana cards consist of the Swiss and Italian suit signs of shields and flowers, cups and coins, respectively. Each deck is numbered and signed by the artist on a top card entitled "Tarot Tarock." Top row: Il Matto (*The Fool*), I Il Bagattello (*The Magician*), II La Papessa (*The Popess*), III L'Imperatrice (*The Empress*), IIII L'Imperatore (*The Emperor*). Middle row: V Il Papa (*The Pope*), VI Gli Amanti (*The Lovers*), VII Il Carro (*The Chariot*), VIII La Giustizia (*Justice*), VIIII L'Eremita (*The Hermit*). Bottom row: X Ruot. Della For. (*The Wheel of Fortune*), XI La Forza (*Strength*), XII L'Appeso (*The Hanged Man*), XIII (*Death*), XIIII La Temperanza (*Temperance*).

H. J. Heinz Tarot *Five Major Arcana cards and four numeral cards from a series of tarot designs by Wes Michel that was featured on the cover of the 1972 Annual Report of H. J. Heinz Company, Pittsburgh. The Major Arcana cards are (top row) Wheel of Fortune with a suit sign in each corner—tomatoes, cucumbers, potatoes and fish—and a baker sitting on top of the wheel, which reads along its rim "H. J. Heinz;" XI Justice depicts a baker holding a flour scale in his left hand and a large stirring spoon in his right hand; XIV Temperance portrays a businessman with his feet solidly on earth and his hands upraised on either side of a rainbow, and an angler with a fishing line in the water, signifying the resources derived from both land and sea. Middle row: XVIII The Moon shows a bull and a bear, and in the background a tuna; XXI The World is a long-haired figure in front of a globe of the world with some of H. J. Heinz's major products, such as Heinz vinegar, tomato ketchup and Starkist tuna; the numeral card VII of tomatoes. Bottom row: four of tomatoes; ace of cucumbers or wands; the last card, mumbered V, possibly belongs to the tomato suit.*

Peter Huckerby Tarot The Major Arcana sequence in cubist style from an unpublished set of tarot cards designed by artist Peter Huckerby of England. The designs, painted with black gouache and an airbrush, blend geometric shapes to present a novel interpretation of traditional tarot symbolism. Card 14 is entitled Art rather than Temperance, and shows a mountain peak topped with a two-faced head; Card 17 The Star depicts a figure rising from rippling water and pouring liquid from a pitcher, the flowing hair and water combining to suggest the stirring of new ideas; and Card 18 The Moon shows the moon obscured by clouds within a giant circular rim.

Insight Institute Tarot   Published in London. Trumps contain "T" above Roman number but are untitled; the heart design between the horses in VII The Chariot contains the initals "AGZ." The writing at the dogs' feet in XVIII The Moon appears to read "MA" with two vertical lines before and after. XIX The Sun, a naked child bearing a flag while riding bareback on a horse, is similar to the Rider-Waite card of the same name.

Knapp Tarot Published in 1929 by J. A. Knapp, California. The Major Arcana cards generally follow the typical tarot symbolism but vary in interpretation. The Fool is blindfolded and an alligator rises from the water in front of him. The Magician holds a winged staff. The Arabic number of the card, its title in French and its applicable Hebrew letter appear at the bottom of each card beneath the main picture. All seventy-eight cards in the pack, except for The Fool, contain a symbol or object in a shield. The card Le Monde is numbered 21 and 22, thus enabling card number 0 The Fool to be placed between cards numbered 20 and 22 or after 21. The last three cards illustrated are Minor Arcana: king of swords, king of cups and ace of cups.

De Laurence Tarot Issued by The de Laurence Company, Inc., Chicago, in 1918. The card designs were taken, apparently without authorization, from the Rider-Waite pack. The de Laurence cards are printed in heavy red, which makes their color tones inconsistent with those of the original Rider-Waite tarot pack.

Linweave Tarot Issued in 1967 as a premium deck by Brown Company, Pulp, Paper and Board Division, New York, these oversized cards measure 215 by 140 mm. and are lithographed on linweave colored stock. The designs on the cards are by several artists: David Mario Palladini (The Fool, III L'Impératrice, IIII L'Empereur, king of swords, ace of swords), Nicolas Sidjakov (I Le Bateleur), Hy Roth (II Junon), and Ron Rai (XVIII La Lune and ace of coins). Palladini is the same artist who subsequently designed the Aquarian tarot deck.

Lover's Tarot This pack of twenty-two trionfi or Major Arcana cards was painted by Juan Ballesta in Italy, circa 1975. The cards generally depict figures with oversize heads, small bodies and tiny arms and feet, and some of the cards are reminiscent of the style used by Fergus Hall in his James Bond 007 tarot pack. Stars, the sun and moon appear in many of the cards, both in the background and on the clothing and faces; for example, Il Matto (*The Fool*) contains all three celestial objects in the background; Il Mago (*The Magician*) contains repeating stars, suns and moon on his conical cap, cape and high-collared robe. Top row: Il Matto (*The Fool*), 1 Il Mago (*The Magician*), 2 La Papessa (*The Popess*), 3 L'Imperatrice (*The Empress*). Second row: 4 L'Imperatore (*The Emperor*), 5 Il Papa (*The Pope*), 6 Gli Innamorati (*The Lovers*), 7 Il Carro (*The Chariot*). Third row: 8 La Giustizia (*Justice*), 9 L'Eremita (*The Hermit*), 10 La Ruota della Fortuna (*The Wheel of Fortune*), 11 La Forza (*Strength*). Bottom row: 12 L'Impiccato (*The Hanged Man*), 13 La Morte (*Death*), 16 La Torre (*The Tower*), 21 Il Mondo (*The World*).

M. Lubow, N. Lubow, Sharp and Weil, collections of the artists; Waldner reprinted from *Predizione*

M. Lubow/N. Lubow/Sharp/Waldner/Weil
Examples of tarot cards by contemporary artists.

Top row: **The Empress** by Nancy Lubow shows Isis silhouetted by a white aura. She kneels at the water's edge in a garden. The five stairs leading from the cypress trees of Venus are the gateway to the hidden world. Two blue birds in her hair indicate the submission of the initiate's soul. Her garment is decorated with roses of longing and her veil depicts the stars of the universe she controls. Isis holds a moon in her hand, which is reflected in the water much in the same manner that Isis unveiled reflects love into the world. **The Hierophant**, also by Nancy Lubow, is a five-pointed star of human life revealing in the center the emerging figure of the Hierophant and his two disciples. The castles in the background depict ancient religious structures that are diminishing in importance in the new age. **IX The Hermit** by Katherine Sharp depicts a solitary figure at the pinnacle of a white-topped cliff. His arms are raised in hope and anticipation toward an enormous full moon that rises in the darkened sky.

Middle row: **XVI The Tower** by Nancy Lubow depicts a transparent tower suggesting an illusionary past. A nude female figure plunges with flailing arms from the tower. The top of the tower is caught in a whirlpool, while lost at the base is a dark spiral core. The **queen of cups** by Martha Lubow shows a female figure carried on a throne of water. She wears a gossamer gown and she holds a lotus cup in her hands, representing spiritual knowledge. The **knight of cups** by Katherine Sharp represents the energy of Mercury speeding across the breaking waves. He wears a winged helmet and is draped with the veil of Isis. In his right hand he holds aloft a large ornate cup, indicating the spiritual love that radiates around him. The moon has seven rays to represent the seven worlds and the seven stages of inner consciousness.

Bottom row: Highly stylized Major Arcana cards in watercolors by Francesco Waldner, reprinted from "... E ora impariamo a usare i tarocchi," Predizione, published by Fratelli Fabbri Editori. The two cards shown are **0 Il Matto** (The Fool) and **La Papessa** (The Popess). **II The High Priestess** by Susan L. Weil. Using bright colors, the artist has created The High Priestess in Shakespearean style. The female figure wears a tight-fitting medieval coif with a veil loosely hanging from a high headpiece. Her full gown is leaf pleated and she is wrapped in a huge robe. The drawing is rendered in such a manner that the circular and symmetrical lines of the clothing and the high-backed chair focus the eye on the High Priestess's stern face. The chair is decorated with a magical star and moon. The High Priestess holds in her lap a book of sacred knowledge. Her fingers are carefully placed at the book's edge, suggesting that in spite of her access to great knowledge, her actions and emotions often are inflexible.

Masenghini Tarocchino Milanese This tarocchi pack was reissued by Masenghini, Bergamo, in a limited edition of three thousand sets to commemorate the one-hundredth anniversary of the Masenghini firm. The pack was first produced by Masenghini toward the end of the nineteenth century. Although the cards are called tarocchino, which regularly totals sixty-two cards, this pack comprises seventy-eight cards. The cards are titled in Italian and they are Roman numbered. Top row: Il Matto (*The Fool*), I Il Bagatto (*The Magician*), II La Papessa (*The Popess*), III L'Imperatrice (*The Empress*), IIII L'Imperatore (*The Emperor*), V Il Papa (*The Pope*). Second row: VI Gli Amanti (*The Lovers*), VII Il Carro (*The Chariot*), VIII La Giustizia (*Justice*), VIIII L'Eremita (*The Hermit*), X La Ruota Della Fortuna (*The Wheel of Fortune*), XI La Forza (*Strength*). Third row: XII L'Appeso (*The Hanged Man*), XIII La Morte (*Death*), XIV L'Intemperanza (*Temperance*), XV Il Diavolo (*The Devil*), XVI La Torre (*The Tower*), XVII Le Stelle (*The Star*). Bottom row: XVIII La Luna (*The Moon*), XIX Il Sole (*The Sun*), XX Il Giudizio (*Judgment*), XXI Il Mondo (*The World*), Re di Spade (*king of swords*), Reg. di Spade (*queen of swords*).

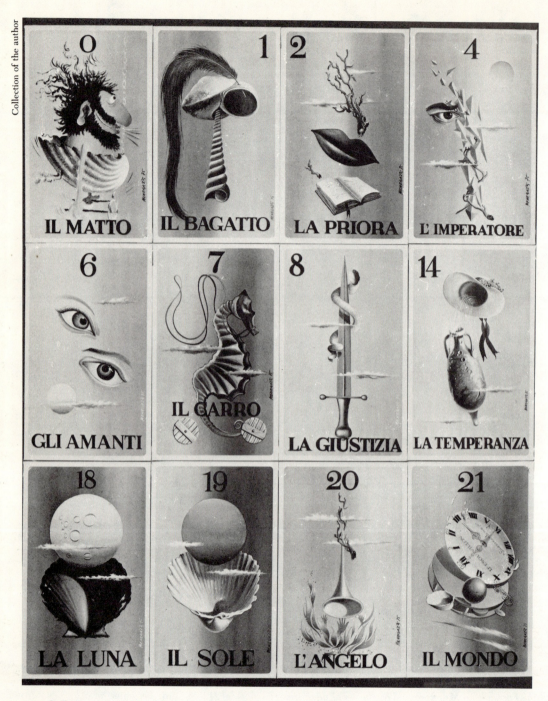

Menegazzi Seashell Tarocco The twenty-two Major Arcana cards featuring seashells and marine life were issued in 1975 by Vito Arienti as a limited edition of fifteen hundred sets with a cover sheet signed by the artist, Osvaldo Menegazzi, who for many years has loved, studied and painted seashells of all types. The artist has painted in surrealist style a vivid series of divinatory shells in the same number as the Major Arcana cards of the tarot pack.

Sergio Minero Tarot *Stylized macabre figures of the Major Arcana cards carved out of linoleum by Sergio Minero, Italy. Each card is numbered in Arabic and titled in Italian. The edition is limited to two hundred and fifty sets.* Top row: 0 Il Matto *(The Fool)*, 2 La Papessa *(The Popess)*, 3 L'Imperatrice *(The Empress)*, 4 L'Imperatore *(The Emperor)*, 5 Il Papa *(The Pope)*. Second row: 6 Gli Amanti *(The Lovers)*, 7 Il Carro *(The Chariot)*, 8 La Giustizia *(Justice)*, 9 L'Eremita *(The Hermit)*, 10 Rota di Fortuna *(The Wheel of Fortune)*. Third row: 11 La Forza *(Strength)*, 12 L'Appiccato *(The Hanged Man)*, 13 La Morte *(Death)*, 14 La Temperanza *(Temperance)*, 15 Il Diavolo *(The Devil)*. Bottom row: 16 La Torre *(The Tower)*, 17 Le Stelle *(The Star)*, 18 La Luna *(The Moon)*, 19 Il Sole *(The Sun)*, 20 L'Angelo *(The Angel)*.

Odell Tarot The cards in this tarot deck possess a magical innocence suggestive of Camelot and a children's story book. Painted by Robert Odell, the designs of the Major and Minor Arcana cards are consistently positive in expression and attitude. The four suits of the Minor Arcana comprise daggers for swords, canes for staves, gems for pentacles and the traditional suit of cups.

Top row: **The Fool** depicts a whimsical jester balanced on a high wire and wearing a large dunce cap. He clenches a dagger between his teeth while using a large cane to maintain his balance. In his left hand he holds a crystal ball suggestive of a pentacle, while at his feet a brown and white dog balances a cup on its back. Thus, the four suit symbols are intertwined in the imagery of this card. The dog peers downward at his fate while The Fool stares unhesitatingly ahead to his future. The bright sun in the background rises above the jester's shoulder but never quite reaches its zenith, much like The Fool himself, who restlessly searches for one new adventure after another. **I The Magician** depicts a long-haired figure, either female or male, dressed in a flowing robe decorated with red roses, which represent earthiness and desire, and white blossoms, which suggest purity. The Magician holds a magical wand in his left hand, an extension of the power he wields over earthly matters, while with his outstretched right hand he draws upon the heavenly powers above. The table containing the four suit symbols or elements touches the earth and The Magician clings to the earth by his toes. **II The High Priestess** shows a woman reading from a large scroll and addressing herself to her father, the moon, from whom she inherits illumination. The vegetation at her feet represents feminine grace. The black and white pillared curtains and columns indicate that all that is evil can be overcome by good. **IV The Emperor** sits on a throne decorated at the back with a ram, symbol of Mars. The Emperor is depicted as a Rip Van Winkle type of figure with combed hair and flowing beard. He holds a large scepter and a globe signifying his domain. His throne rests on a platform of four steps signifying stability and the four elements. **V The Hierophant** depicts a pontifflike figure carried on a sedia gestatoria by two celebrants who provide support from only one side. In his right hand the pontiff holds a scepter topped with an Arabic 3, symbolizing the Trinity. The crossed keys beneath the Pope's processional litter guide the way to enlightenment.

Second row: **VII The Chariot** depicts a robed figure standing in a chariot drawn by two unseen horses. The chariot represents the human personality as a vehicle for self-expression. The front of the chariot is decorated with an Egyptian figure. The border decoration of stars with alternating pluses and minuses confirms that the heavenly powers rule over negative and positive forces in the world. The wings of the chariot represent inspirational forces that lead us ahead. **VIII Strength** is a young girl dressed in a white robe of purity. She wears a garland of flowers both over her head and around her waist as a sign of her innocence. A small butterfly hovers near the eternal eight, which appears above her. The young girl calms the angry lion without fear for herself, suggesting the power of love overcomes the greatest obstacles. The lion represents the lower nature of man in contrast to the higher emotions and love of the girl. **IX The Hermit** card indicates a journey depicted by a misguided sailing ship caught in the powerful ray of a lighthouse beam. The bright light emanates from beyond the lighthouse, suggesting that guidance comes from a higher, almost blinding power that manifests itself in the light of truth. **XII The Hanging Man** is dressed in colorful tights with pointed toes. He hangs from an acrobat's swing attached to a limb heavily decorated with leaves. The acrobat displays a broad smile and his hands are clasped in pleasant repose. An aureole from the sun rings the acrobat's head. **XIII Birth** depicts a young figure reborn from death. The word "Death" appears as an inverted word fading beneath the Roman number XIII. The large black flag is decorated with an enormous red rose to indicate life's growing forces. The bands of clouds in the sky emanate from the bright sun. In the background the young woman and the pontiff represent the pleasures of life and the joys of faith, respectively.

Third row: **XIV Temperance** is God's favorite archangel, Michael, dressed in flowing white robes and blessed with immense graceful wings. The archangel pours the essence of life from a silver cup, representing the subconscious realm, into a golden cup, symbolizing the conscious mind; thus, the liquid of thought flows from unseen domains to recognizable worlds. The globe of earth is decorated with a square, to represent reality, and a triangle, symbolizing spiritual thought. An iris flower hovers in the lower sky as a pathway between the goddess of the rainbow and the realities of earth. **XV Night** replaces the fifteenth Major Arcana card, traditionally called The Devil. The black figure resembles a face with nose and eyes, which suggests the Devil or Satan is our own creation, illustrating that evil comes only to those who carelessly invite or bring it upon themselves. The dominating white background symbolizes the light that exists in the darkest moments. **XX Judgement** is the winged horn of the angel Gabriel. A seven-note scale rises from the mouth of the trumpet and several arms with open hands reach out at random. Beneath the trumpet are three tombs; a fourth ornate tomb appears behind the wings, representing spiritual presence, which rises from physical entombment. The title of the Judgment card in this tarot deck is spelled with an e because numerologically the letters total 36, and reduce to the single digit 9, which means fulfillment and completion. This is based on the numerological system of setting out the primary digits one to nine and placing the letters of the alphabet underneath them. If the title were spelled Judgment, it would total 31 before reduction to a single digit, which is an anagram for the number 13, associated with Satan and ill-fortune. The **king of daggers** is a crowned and robed figure who stands beneath a large draped throne. He wears a cross signifying human work done in accordance with the teachings of God. A male symbol appears on his chest and he holds a dagger in his left hand. The reverse figure of the king shows him with a stern face and holding a multipointed dagger of flame, suggesting the harsh side to his character. The knight's dagger or **knight of daggers** depicts a young man dressed in armor and flowing cape standing at the top of a mountain peak. He holds aloft a large banner

Collection of the artist

decorated with a white horse and several doves, symbolizing purity and the essence of one's soul. The knight holds a dagger pointed upward toward his higher ideals and he clutches to his chest his plumed helmet while surveying the vast scene below him.

Fourth row: The **six of daggers** depicts a woman bearing her own innocence, depicted as a newborn child, and fleeing on a unicycle. The large zero formed by the shape of the wheel suggests a desperate and tumultuous situation, confirmed by the erupting volcano behind her. The woman is perfectly balanced on the unicycle, displaying an agility like that of The Fool, who balances on a tightrope. Numerology suggests six is the number of love, home and family. The **four of daggers** consists of a stained-glass window depicting a knight with hands clasped to his face in prayer and contemplation. The **king of canes** shows a lion, suggestive of Leo, with a flaming crown. The cane represents his magical powers, and the salamander, beneath the symbol of man, represents the ability to survive and flourish in the sun in the midst of hardship and controversy. The ring floating to the right is a reflection of the unseen sun, suggesting the astrological belief that a person born under the sign of Leo is strongly protected by unseen forces. The **two of canes** depicts one white and one black cane striking at their tips and igniting into flames to work in unison, just as the number 2 suggests partnership. The flames are depicted as roses born of creative design and white lilies nourished by pure thoughts. The **page of cups** depicts a young man or woman holding a light bulb in one hand and a light switch in the other. Even though the bulb and switch are not connected, light appears as a sign of knowledge and enlightenment. However, the jumping fish suggests the page does not always impart his or her knowledge to others. The deep water represents a sea of psychic awareness, known to the adepts as the psiconscious, in which the page excels. The tulip represents the thoughts and messages growing nearby, which are available to those who seek them.

Bottom row: The **ten of cups** depicts a husband and wife with their two children. The figures are dressed as clowns to denote their uninhibited playfulness. The rainbow and bright clouds signify a promise of happiness. The father easily juggles ten cups over his head. The **six of cups** shows a young boy and girl playing harmoniously on a grassy knoll; a home appears in the background, behind them like the past. The two children stack the cups and the boy offers the girl the sixth cup, which signifies a loving gift. The **knight of gems** depicts a fully armored warrior holding aloft his prize of a huge gemstone. The symbol of manhood is shown above his head as he rides across fertile fields recently plowed. The black plume and masked face conceal his identity. The **ten of gems** is a bearded patriarch who gathers his grandchildren about him. The gems appear as growing fruits on the tree in the background, suggesting a prosperous person. The doorway of the home is graced with a heart within a shield representing a coat of arms. The dove and sun hover on the roof, blessing the home with prosperity, and the door is open for all to share in the good fortune. The **four of gems** shows a jeweler scrutinizing four large gemstones; he ignores their beauty and is only concerned with their value. Even possessed of such valuable gems, he cannot conceal his miserly nature, revealed by the tatters and patches on his clothing.

Ollgaard Tarot The outlines of the figures in this tarot pack were printed on manila paper and then hand-painted by Rita Ollgaard. The edition is limited to one thousand sets and the designs reflect the interpretation of the artist, who fuses traditional imagery with ancient astrological, Egyptian and religious mythology and symbolism. Top row: 0 The Fool, I the Magician, II The High Priestess, IV Emperor, V The Hierophant. Second row: VI Lovers, VII Chariot, VIII Adjustment, IX Hermit, XI Strength. Third row: XIII Death, XIIII Art (instead of Temperance), XV Devil, XIX Sun, XX Aeon. Bottom row: XXI Universe, king of swords, queen of swords, knight of wands, princess of pentacles.

Ortega Tarot   Designs from an unpublished tarot deck. Elongated cards by Spanish artist Enrique Ortega are based upon original watercolors. Top row: *The Magician, The High Priestess, The Empress, Death, The Hermit.* Middle row: *Judgment, The Moon,* queen of swords, page of swords, king of staves. Bottom row: *queen of staves, king of cups, knight of cups, queen of coins.*

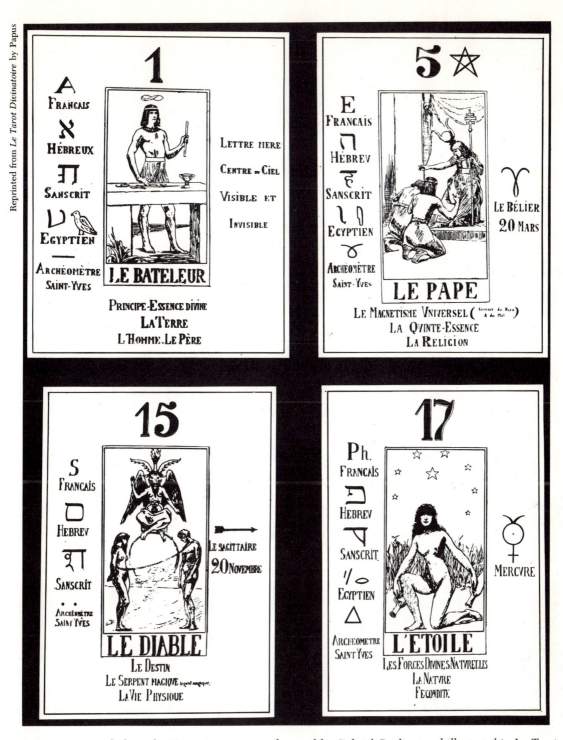

Papus Tarot Four cards from the Major Arcana series designed by Gabriel Goulinat and illustrated in *Le Tarot Divinatoire*, published in 1909. Each card contains, at top, an Arabic number; the left side of each card has French, Hebrew and Sanskrit letters, the right side of each card contains astrological signs, associations and dates, and the bottom of each card includes title of card and interpretation. Papus (and Eliphas Lévi) believed The Fool is properly placed as card number 21, between Judgment and The World, instead of at the beginning of the deck.

Pastor Tarot   Designed and published by Edouard Pastor, Paris. The twenty-two Major Arcana cards are titled in French; the number of each card appears in both Arabic and Roman numerals in a panel at the top of each card. The figures in some of the cards are almost lifelike, the facial expressions docile and attractive, such as that of The Empress. The pip cards have standard American faces.

Pop/Rock Tarot Calendar Published 1972 by Scholastic Book Services, New York. The cards were designed by Julia Noonan with accompanying text by Julia Remine Piggin. Card titles are from songs popular in the 1960s and 1970s.

Rakoczi Tarot   Four untitled Major Arcana cards, four court cards and four pip cards by Basil Ivan Rakoczi, author of The Painted Caravan.

Top row: **0 The Fool** card depicts a begging caravan dog with a butterfly fluttering overhead. The Fool's trouser leg is torn and the Hebrew letter Shin appears on his garment. He holds a pack or butterfly net on a stick and his cap is topped in front with a rooster. **II The High Priestess** has three of the four suit signs—a sword, a coin, a cup—visible on

214

the pillars of her throne, from which hang a veil; the pillars are named Jachin (Ioa from Joakim) and Boaz (Oaz), representing severity and mercy, discipline and love. She wears a white wimple with three gold tiers topped with a gold crescent; across her breast hangs a large Egyptian ankh or Cross of Life, on her lap rests the book of the Torah and across her left arm she holds two large keys while a serpent rises toward her. Against her throne a branchless tree limb rests from which grows a flower and a leaf. **VII The Chariot** depicts a youthful king or prince with a heavy crown topped by small gold beads and a gold cross. The charioteer wears a brazen breastplate embossed at the shoulders with human heads. In his right hand he holds an ornate scepter topped by a globe and cross, and in his left hand he hides a double-edged sword behind his arm. The chariot is drawn by two horses and at the top a large canopy decorated with repeating six-pointed stars is supported by four posts. The single initial "R" on the cup between the horses represents Rakoczi. At the upper left of the card is the Hebrew letter Zain. **VIIII The Hermit** is a venerable old man who walks with the aid of a staff and holds aloft a lantern with a lit candle. A snake sits nearby upon a rock and at the Hermit's feet is an hourglass. The Hebrew letter teth appears on his long robe.

Middle row: The **king of swords** depicts a man of regal stature sitting upon his throne; his crown has a wide brim in the form of a figure eight and from his upright sword emerges a leafy vine. He is dressed in a breastplate with shoulder epaulets of human faces. On his kneeplate is a spade, sign of his suit, and behind him appear the scales of justice. The crowned **queen of swords** rests the hilt of her upraised sword against her knee; the long sword is encircled by a small wreath. Her long garment is decorated with a floral pattern. On the two pillars of her throne appear the signs of her suit and on her cape is the symbol of a cross topped with a winged globe, which also appears, without the wings, on the right arm of the king's throne. The **knight of swords** is dressed in full armor and holds a large sword. His headpiece is decorated with both a five-pointed star and a crescent moon, and the horse's caparison contains a regal lion on its hind legs. The **page of swords** stands in the countryside unaware of the droplets of rain or snow. A large crab decorates the front of his cape.

Bottom row: The **nine of swords** depicts a seated woman in sorrow. The **eight of swords** depicts a blindfolded nude woman seated on a stool with hands tied behind her back and her ankles bound by a ball and chain. The **seven of swords** shows a group of men striking camp. The **six of swords** shows a man maneuvering a small boat with a pole.

Ravenswood Eastern Tarot The designs by R. Dirk Dykstra are based upon basic Waite symbolism and they incorporate East Indian and Persian decorations from the mid-nineteenth century. The designation "Ravenswood" derives from a Wiccan coven in Iowa of which the artist was originally a member. The cards do not contain titles; the Major Arcana are Roman numbered and the Minor Arcana contain Arabic numbers. The cards were issued in a limited edition of one hundred sets signed by the artist.

Top row: **0 The Fool** depicts a blindfolded fool who wears a vagabond turban and a peshwaz, an Indian garment open down the front. He holds four aces while he leans against a gambling wheel, suggesting that he takes chances without trying to control his destiny and that he enters the future without hesitation or concern for the consequences. **I The Magician** is a self-portrait of the artist dressed in a farajiygat, a long coat with wide sleeves worn by Indian judges and scholars. The brooch attached to his garment shows a moon eclipsing the sun as a symbol of the dichotomy of male and female mystical elements. The stars scattered in the background signify the presence of magical influences. The four suit symbols—sword, baton, chalice and coin—appear in the card. **II The High Priestess** sits upon an ornate brocade throne of magical stars. A dupatta, or long flowing headdress, is draped over her head. Her robe is decorated with five-pointed stars and her sash is embroidered with pomegranates. On her forehead appears a star topped by an inverted crescent moon, symbol of the moon goddess. She carefully holds the Torah in her lap. **III The Empress** wears around her head an embroidered dupatta decorated with a peacock. The strands of pearls signify her wealth and the crescent moon with a star on her forehead covers her caste mark. She holds a fan on her lap and a parrot or parakeet, popular with Indian nobility. She sits on an ornate chair with half rounded arms and in the background is a tile wall with floral

Collection of the artist

pattern. **IV The Emperor** *is a bearded and moustached figure who wears a regal turban held together with a string of pearls. A jeweled decoration hangs from his neck and the red caste mark on his forehead signifies the aristocracy. He wears a simple linen shirt and* dhoti *or plain trousers, and around his shoulders are several embroidered sashes. He sits on a throne of brocaded silk decorated with five-pointed stars and he holds a large baton. The tile wall indicates he is in the same room as The Empress.*

Second row: **V The High Priest** *wears a turban and holds a flowering baton, symbol of life. He sits in an ornate chair whose armrests contain stars that signify his mystical power. The High Priest is a regal figure and the caste mark on his forehead is white. The wide sashes across his chest and the long string of pearls hanging from the baton signify his great wealth.* **VI The Lovers** *depicts a nineteenth-century romantic melodrama. The male is an aristocrat dressed as a member of the court and wearing the high collar of the military. The swooning woman wears a lotus or lily. The setting of this card is in an alcove off a garden complete with faintly glowing lantern and crescent moon.* **VII The Chariot** *shows a military warrior with flowing turban driving a wickerwork chariot followed by a trail of dust. The warrior brandishes a large-handled whip, but his interest in warring is solely as a sport.* **VIII Strength** *depicts a young woman sharing her strength with a lion, indicated by her act of sharing the warmth of the fire. That she is a woman of high nobility is designated by the caste mark on her forehead, yet she wears simple garments and only a small ornament around her neck. The lion is seen as an intelligent beast with a long snout and mane neatly combed.* **IX The Hermit** *wears a* farajiygat *with embroidered border and large sleeves. A tassle sash is tied around his waist. He carries an ornate lantern for both guidance and identification. The open window of the building suggests that much that is unknown awaits discovery by those who are willing to seek out hidden or obscure knowledge.*

Third row: **X The Wheel of Fortune** *is an Indian mandala or circle encompassing an open eye. The decorative panel of eight winged balls of fire suggests the eight paths of Buddha, the eight different ways of achieving spiritual knowledge and perfection. In the background is one mosque with two minarets or towers from which a muezzin summons the Sudra to prayer.* **XI Justice** *depicts a male judge holding a gavel while seated at a table in front of a balance scale. He wears a half-sleeved robe over a simple white linen shirt with tight sleeves. His turban is loosely bound in the back and he wears two embroidered sashes and a small jeweled pendant.* **XII The Hanged Man** *is a Hindu mystic tied and suspended by both legs. His hands are tied behind his back and a cloth is wrapped around his waist. Though the posture is a traditional form of punishment in India, the mystic has a peaceful expression on his face, suggesting spiritual suspension rather than physical punishment.* **XIII Death** *is a hooded, sorrowful figure with a teardrop falling from its left eye. The outstretched hands and the distorted face are a pose of mourning. The empty boat diagonally across the Ganges River suggests that death is but a crossing over from one form of existence to another.* **XIV Temperance** *is a water-oriented card symbolized by the dolphin fountain. The young woman wears a long* dupatta *over a short* choli *or jacket. She holds a large chalice and covers the opening with her left hand to temper the excesses and temptations of life. The abundant water nourishes the garden of flowers that surrounds the young woman.*

Fourth row: **XV The Devil** *contains many Chinese symbols such as long fingernails popular with the aristocracy and fangs that represent evil in both Indian and Chinese mythology. A third eye on the forehead signifies strength greater than human power, and the spider necklace suggests ill will and evil intentions. The Devil has four arms; the highest hand holds a dagger, symbol of action and war; a handful of fire represents pure, raw power; a small figure signifies bondage; and the bottom right hand spits licks of flame to signify spite and hatred in physical form. On each arm The Devil wears a wrist bracelet, which reveals his susceptibility to forces of good.* **XVI The Tower** *is a stylized version of a tall minaret at the moment of total destruction. There are no falling figures because the destruction taking place is not of people but of principles and foundations. Several large fronds growing at the base of the minaret indicate the potentiality for rebirth.* **XVII The Star** *depicts a young woman with upraised arms. She is dressed in an ornate* dupatta *with an oval of cloth embroidered with pearls. She wears many brocaded sashes and strands of pearls as a symbol of her wealth. The large six-pointed star of Eastern tradition contains an image of favorable events in the future. The heavy drapes with ornate sashes suggest a large caravan tent.* **XVIII The Moon** *is a sour-faced figure denoting unpleasantness and deception entangled and tempered by an ornate sash. A caravan wagon representing travel is delayed by an ox drinking in a stream, which suggests that progress will be thwarted and plans, including voyages, delayed.* **XIX The Sun** *shows a robust and cheerful baby swathed in a brocaded sash. The smiling sun radiates its warmth and powers of growth onto the child. The cross behind the sun combines a horizontal beam, suggesting bondage to earth and material matters, and a vertical beam, denoting aspirations to spirituality. Thus, the beams represent the tensions between the physical and spiritual worlds.*

Bottom row: **XX Judgment** *depicts a six-armed Shiva in the typical dancing pose surrounded by a flaming aura or ball of fire. Below, in the Ganges River, persons who have died are rising; living persons who have not yet passed into another state stand along the shore.* **XXI The World** *is a view from an Indian palace. The ocean appears in the distance and an astrolabe hangs from the window arch. On the window sill are a baton and a jewel box with a single string of pearls leading down the sill toward the outdoors, where all the possibilities of life—power, travel, fame, fortune, etc.—await the seeker who will soon begin his journey. The* **king of batons** *holds a flowering rod. He is dressed with many sashes and beads of pearls and he wears a large medallion with a lion's head, the animal of this suit. The large feather in his turban is a Persian motif. The* **nine of chalices** *depicts a prosperous-looking man sitting on a chair of gigantic cushions. The nine cups on the shelf—three groups of three cups each—confirm his prosperous status. The* **nine of coins** *depicts a wealthy woman dressed informally and standing in the sanctuary of her garden. She wears a long, hooded gown or* farajiygat *and stares intently at a bird of fantasy, suggesting that wealth, while sometimes confining, also affords great freedom of decision and action.*

Le Taro Sacerdotal The twenty-two hand-painted Major Arcana cards of this oversized Sacerdotal tarot form part of a looseleaf book issued in 1951 by Henri Durville fils, Paris. Some of the pictures are erotic. The designs and explanations were completed by Lucien Laforge and André Godi. Top row: 1 The Magician, 4 The Emperor, 6 The Lovers, Bottom row: 20 Judgment, 21 The Fool, 22 The World. The Fool is numbered 21 and shows an alligator tearing off the leg of a shabbily dressed wanderer who seems unperturbed.

Sacred Egyptian Tarot The twenty-two Major Arcana cards of this Egyptian tarot were issued in 1949 by John H. Dequer. Although the inconography of these cards resembles the Church of Light tarot cards (page 240), there are distinct differences in the details of design. A full description of these cards is included in the book *Arrows of Light*, written and published by John H. Dequer in 1930.

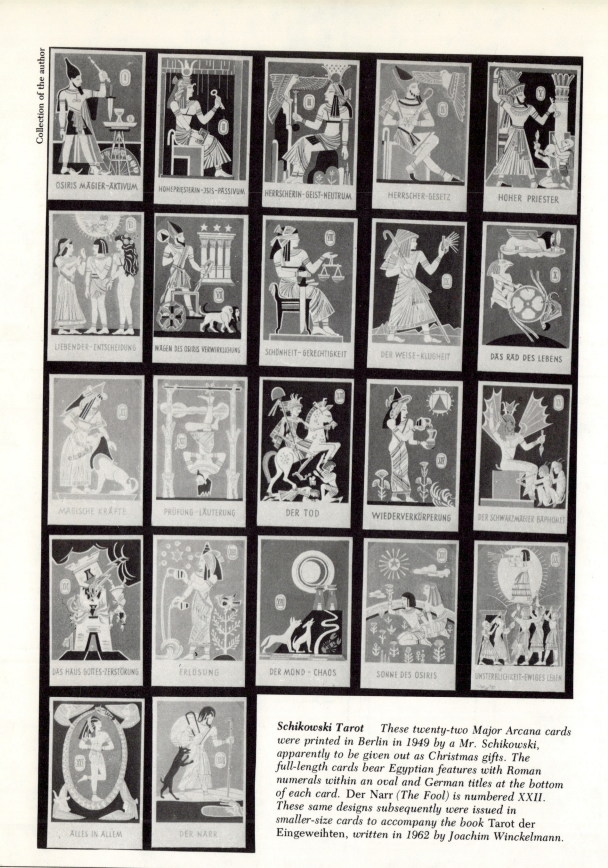

Collection of the author

Schikowski Tarot   These twenty-two Major Arcana cards were printed in Berlin in 1949 by a Mr. Schikowski, apparently to be given out as Christmas gifts. The full-length cards bear Egyptian features with Roman numerals within an oval and German titles at the bottom of each card. Der Narr (The Fool) is numbered XXII. These same designs subsequently were issued in smaller-size cards to accompany the book Tarot der Eingeweihten, written in 1962 by Joachim Winckelmann.

Scott Major Arcana Cards   Stylized pen-and-ink line drawings by Sarah Scott depict the twenty-two Major Arcana cards with insects and animals. Other cards contain reptiles and are meant to represent evil. Suit symbols of spades, clubs, hearts and diamonds are occasionally interwoven into the artwork of the card. The designs are drawn in black ink and watercolored by hand.

Top row: 0 The Fool has a dog sitting at his feet. 1 The Magician has bat wings and stands before a table covered with a cloth bearing the motif of spades, clubs, hearts and diamonds. 2 The Papess wears a toy soldier headdress. She

220

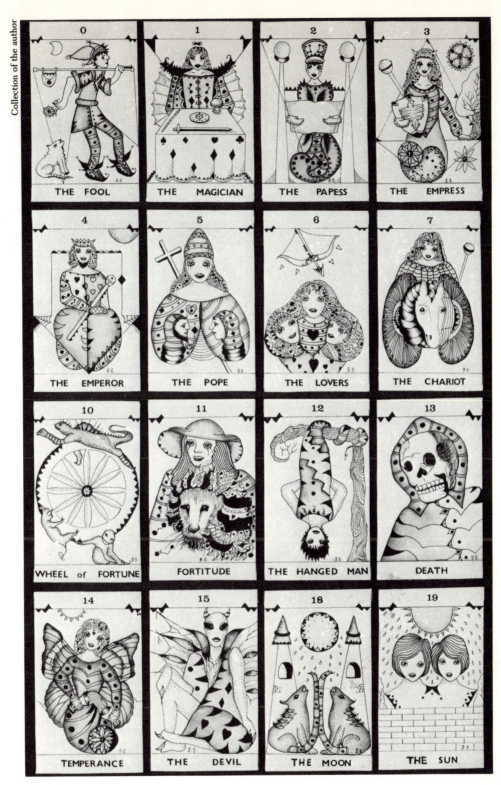

sits between two tapered posts topped by a globe and holds the holy book of knowledge. 3 The Empress holds a shield bearing an eagle. To her left is a tree symbolizing her love of the outdoors. Second row: 4 The Emperor wears his regal crown and sits upon his throne. 5 The Pope wears the papal tiara and in the background appears a cross. 6 The Lovers depicts Cupid's bow hovering above three figures. 7 The Chariot shows a female warrior whose chariot is drawn by a horse with a large mane. Third row: 10 Wheel of Fortune depicts a twelve-spoked wheel supported by a strange creature, half male and half female; a second creature hangs onto the bottom of the wheel and a lizard crawls on top. 11 Fortitude is a woman with a wide-brimmed hat and a large lion. 12 The Hanged Man depicts an evil form with cobra torso. 13 Death is a skeleton dressed in a snake-like chain. Bottom row: 14 Temperance is shown as the metamorphosis of a butterfly from its former caterpillar self. 15 The Devil is a sinister figure with bat wings and snake skin. 18 The Moon depicts two boars between two tapered towers. 19 The Sun shows a young man and woman, identical except for the coloring of their hair, standing beneath a flaming-rayed sun and behind a brick wall.

Connie Taylor Tarot Drawn in 1975 with heavy pencil shadings. III The Empress sits on her throne among the awakening flowers and butterflies of spring. VI Temptation suggests true love will be found beyond evil. VII The Chariot is represented by man the conqueror drawn by two sphinxes into his eventual destiny. X Wheel of Fortune is in perpetual motion in outer space; a sphinx and dog hang onto the top during the motion of evolving change. XVII The Star depicts a nude woman pouring water from two urns. XVIII Moon depicts two persons in a desolate area studying the cycles of the moon from an astrological chart.

The Encyclopedia of Tarot

Collection of the author

Tellurian Tarot Designed in 1971 by Flora Beresford while she was living in an ashram in the Himalayas. The card designs in this unpublished deck seek to synthesize concepts from many cultures by using the images of mythology, holy scriptures, temple carvings and paintings, religious ceremonies and sacred teachings of ancient wisdom. The word "Tellurian" was chosen to describe the cards because the symbolism pertains to the whole earth and all its inhabitants.

Top row: **The Fool** *is surrounded by faint footprints around the edge of the card, which represent the signs of Ometeotl, the invisible surrounding presence; the footprints also represent time and space, and man in the midst of both. The whorl-shape shells at the bottom of the card stand for the cyclic quality of life—birth, growth, decay, destruction, death and resurrection.* **I The Magician** *is surrounded by red roses symbolizing desire, love, the five senses, the subconscious and nature, and white lilies representing abstract thought. With heels together he stands on a checkered pavement signifying light and shadow, and near his feet are the symbols of the great work of the alchemists—sulphur (sun), salt (earth) and mercury (moon).* **II The High Priestess** *sits on her throne between the pillars of Jachin (Jakin) and Bohaz (Boaz); the pillars are crowned with the sign of the sun and the moon; an Egyptian ankh appears beneath the sun. The moons on her silver headdress, on her breast and at her feet express her connection with Diana, Hecate, Artemis, Isis, Hathor and other goddesses; her veil-becoming-water and the water lilies on her garment imply her identification with all water goddesses; she holds in her lap the secret law of the Tora or the tarot, and her fingers—three uplifted, two hidden—give the sign of sacerdotal esotericism. Reading from the bottom up, the symbols on the male pillar at the left of the card are the sun, an eagle, gold, movement or tension, a quincunx, a sun sign and a water lily; the female or opposite pillar contains a waning moon, a frog, mother pot, a shell, a fish, a tree, a crescent moon and a water lily; hanging between the columns is the veil of the temple.* **III The Empress** *sits on her throne; on her bosom is the Teotihuacan sign for the planet Venus, the horns above it represent either Venus' appearance when it is closest to the earth or the horns of Hathor; the string of seven pearls around her neck represents seven planets or seven children; the stars on her crown represent time, the rhythms of the year and the influences of the zodiac; the scepter in the left hand of the Empress is topped by a combined sign: the cross and sphere are the signs of the globe (earth), and the same sphere with a cross beneath it is the sign of the planet Venus; the web and frog suggest the opposite aspects of the dynamic, life-giving forces of The Empress; her figure is surrounded by snakes, fish, shells, flowers, jewels, feathers, trees, wheat, maize, moon and water, all of which have their specific meaning and are usually associated with female deities.* **IV The Emperor** *sits on a throne that has at its base the alchemist's symbol for sulphur, which signifies the sun, gold and the male principle; the sign on his belt is both sun and star, symbolizing day and night and the rhythms of time. The Emperor's scepter is like an Egyptian ankh, which is the tau cross, the sign of life and generation. His crown of eagle feathers symbolizes the power of the sun and fire; in his left hand he holds a globe of the world, which expresses his power and dominion. The astrological sign on his shoulders is that of Mars and signifies war, and the two rams' heads, one on either side of the throne, symbolize Aries, suggesting aggressiveness, hardheadedness and even war. In the center of the card, on the breastplate of The Emperor's armor, is the sign of the cross, which expresses union of spirit and matter.*

Second row: **V The Hierophant** *stands and with his upraised right hand gives his blessing and the sign of esotericism with two fingers. In his left hand is the triple cross, suggesting domination of the threefold nature within—thinking, feeling and the power of willing; the triple crown signifies radiant energy in the creative, formative and material worlds. Two crossed keys of wisdom appear between two ministers kneeling before the Hierophant.* **VI The Lovers** *depicts Adam and Eve beneath a winged angel; behind Adam is the Tree of Life with twelve flames, and behind Eve is the Tree of Knowledge with its good and evil, and a snake curled around its trunk. The horizontal sign of the eternal eight appears above Adam and Eve.* **VII The Chariot** *card shows the charioteer holding the snake of magic power in his right hand. The sign on his corselet suggests sacrifice, resurrection and union with light; the lingam yoni on the front of the chariot between the white and black sphinxes expresses the union of positive and negative, spirit and matter and thought and feeling.* **VIII Strength** *depicts a young woman in control of nature and her desires; the red and white roses on her white garment symbolize the purity of her desire; the serpent symbolizes power and wisdom.* **IX The Hermit** *holds a beacon inserted with a six-pointed star to shed light on the path others will follow.*

Third row: **X The Wheel of Fortune** *contains the letters T A R O or R O T A and the great Tetragrammaton Yod-He-Vau-He. In the four corners of the card are Ezekiel's four archetypal creatures—man, eagle, bull and lion.* **XI Justice** *sits between the pillars of justice and holds the unsheathed sword of justice in her right hand.* **XII The Hanged Man** *is reflected in cosmic light and he views all things from a viewpoint different from that of most men.* **XIII Death** *looms over the plane of life while the sun sets behind the distant mountains.* **XIV Temperance** *is a winged figure with one foot in the deep water of the spirit and the other foot on earth.*

Bottom row: **XV The Devil** *shows a man and woman chained to a pedestal on which rules the dominating figure of The Devil.* **XVI The Tower** *depicts lightning striking a tower and, thus, destroying ambition.* **XVII The Star** *is a nude figure personifying both maid and mother. She kneels and pours the regenerating waters of life from a gold and silver urn.* **XVIII The Moon** *depicts moonlight from a quarter-moon and the tears of Isis falling between the moon's rays. A dog and a wolf sit in the bleak plain and bay at the darkened sky.* **XIX The Sun** *is the naked and crowned figure of Horus, the child with hands clasped to his chest.*

Collection of Diane Peterson

Transitional Tarot   The twenty-two Major Arcana cards in this unpublished tarot pack were painted by Gerald Mansheim. The unnumbered and untitled cards represent the evolutionary period in time between the Piscean and Aquarian ages. The scenes on each card depict the emotional turmoil one must experience in order to expand one's awareness and consciousness. Top row: *The Fool, The Emperor, The Chariot*. Middle row: *Fortune, Hanged Man, Death*. Bottom row: *The Devil, The Sun, Judgment*. The evolution of certain cards is seen in the figure of the young Fool, who becomes The Hanged Man, The Emperor, The Charioteer, Death and is reborn as The Devil.

Wollenhaupt-Brenner Tarot The Major Arcana cards in this 1974 series by E. Wollenhaupt-Brenner of Germany are patterned after the style of medieval woodcuts. The card impressions in reddish brown and ocher were executed from linoleum blocks. Top row: 0 Le Mat (*The Fool*), I Le Bateleur (*The Magician*), II La Papesse (*The Popess*), IV L'Empereur (*The Emperor*). Middle row: IX L'Hermite (*The Hermit*), XII Le Pendu (*The Hanged Man*), XIII Le Mort (*Death*), XIV Temperance (*Temperance*). Bottom row: XV Le Diable (*The Devil*), XVI La Maison Dieu (*The House of God*), XX Le Jugement (*Judgment*), XXI Le Monde (*The World*).

XIII
POPULAR TWENTIETH-CENTURY TAROT PACKS AND REPRINTS CURRENTLY AVAILABLE

During the past ten years a large variety of tarot packs has become available to collectors, both new designs and reprints of important earlier packs. The many designs listed below reflect the personal interpretations of the artists and designers:

Tarot de Acuario
Aquarian tarot
Tarot Arista
Astral tarot
Astro tarot
Balbi tarot
Baraja Egipcia
Grand Tarot Belline
Guido Bolzani *tarocchi*
Builders of the Adytum tarot
Church of Light tarot
Tarot Classic
Aleister Crowley "Thoth" tarot
D'Epinal tarot
Il Destino Svelato Dal Tarocco
Dynamic Games tarot
Egipcios tarot
Esoteric tarot
Etteilla tarot
Fergus Hall tarot
Gentilini *tarocchi*

Golden Dawn tarot
Golden Egyptian tarot/Morgan's tarot/Praktische tarot
Hoi Polloi tarot
Tarot of Oscar Ichazo
Tarot of Marseilles
Masenghini Tarocchi Piedmontese
Mountain Dream tarot
Muchery Astrological tarot
The New Tarot Deck
The New Tarot for the Aquarian Age
Nordic tarot
1JJ Swiss tarot
Piatnik/Pointner tarot
Rider-Waite tarot
Royal Fez tarot
Sheridan/Douglas tarot
Spanish tarot
Starter tarot
Tantric tarot
Taro Adivinhatorio
20th Century tarot
Vandenborre tarot
Visconti-Sforza *tarocchi*
Oswald Wirth tarot
Xultun tarot
Yeager Tarot of Meditation
Zigeuner tarot
Zolar's New Astrological tarot

Tarot de Acuario Issued by Producciones y Ediciones Acuario, S.A., Mexico, from the book by Rene Rebetez. Trumps are a departure from standard designs; all cards are numbered in Arabic and titled in Spanish. Each trump card contains a Hebrew letter, astrological sign or other symbol. Top row: *1* El Mago *(The Magician)*, *2* La Sacerdotisa *(The Priestess)*, *3* La Emperatriz *(The Empress)*, *4* El Emperador *(The Emperor)*. Middle row: *5* El Jerarca *(The Hierarch)*, *6* La Indecision *(The Indecision)*, *7* El Triunfo *(The Triumph)*, *8* La Justicia *(The Justice)*. Bottom row: *9* El Eremita *(The Hermit)*, *10* La Retribucion *(The Retribution)*, *11* La Persuasion *(The Persuasion)*, *12* El Apostolado *(The Apostleship)*.

Aquarian Tarot Designed by David Mario Palladini and published by Morgan Press. The artist successfully combines an art deco style with ornate crowns and headgear, stoic and almost featureless faces, medieval armor, decorative triangular ornaments and heavy garments usually made from leather and decorated with overlapping layers of peacock feathers and leaves. The Major Arcana and Minor Arcana cards are titled in English and the forty pip cards—ten through ace in each of the four suits—contain a picture to facilitate interpretation. The Aquarian tarot deck was included in the Galaxy Gazer published by Karin Koal Enterprises in 1973.

Top row: *0 The Fool* wears a plumed hat with a leather scarf pulled tight across the chin. An ornament of decorative triangles hangs over his left ear and around his neck, and he wears a heavy leather jacket trimmed with a fur collar. The fingers of The Fool's right hand blend together, as is true of most of the hands in this deck. The living tree across The Fool's shoulder signifies adventure and progress and the white rose symbolizes purity of heart and soul. **I The Magician** is dressed in a leather jacket and a light gauze beret. Around his waist, as a belt, is a snake biting its tail. A lemniscate is suspended in the air above his head. The table of overlapping and interwoven peacock body feathers holds the familiar suit signs. Suspended behind The Magician are magical wind chimes and mobiles suggesting fruit ripening on the trees. **II The High Priestess** wears a robe decorated with oak leaves. The headdress covers her ears and neck and contains a large medallion that glitters in its front. In her right hand she holds a small flower with a butterfly resting on its leaf. The canopy above her head is decorated with pomegranates, and two pillar scrolls appear at her left. In the distance a turreted castle nestles in the mountains. **III The Empress** wears a metallic crown decorated with stars and peacock body feathers. She is dressed in two garments; her high-necked gown is decorated with triangles and her wide-sleeved outer robe envelops her body and arms. She holds a large rod topped with a sphere. Her headdress is decorated with stars and the shield contains the sign of Venus. Stalks of wheat flourish to her right, while, in contrast, desolate mountain ridges loom in the background, suggesting the scope of her powers.

Second row: **IV The Emperor** sits on a high throne decorated with two ram's heads. His headdress continues across his shoulders to form part of his royal robe. In his right hand he holds an ankh scepter and in his left hand a large sphere. Flowers blossom before him. **V The Hierophant** raises his gloved right hand in the sign of benediction. He wears a heavy leather chasuble and two sashes hang from his triple-crown headdress. The scepter to his left is topped with a triple cross and two keys appear near a bush of heavy overlapping leaves or armorlike plates found on an armadillo. **VI The Lovers** reveals two young figures in elegant and festive garments of peacock feathers and art deco headdress. Behind the man grow long-stemmed flowers, while near the woman a vine plant rises from a mountain peak. **VII The Chariot** depicts a warrior wearing a helmet decorated with a pentacle. Two facial epaulets appear on his shoulders and protective chain mail is depicted inside a globe that forms part of the chariot. Along the side borders are the chariot wheels.

Third row: **VIII Strength** depicts a moustached soldier resembling the artist. The soldier wears a feathered art deco headdress and shield epaulet. His sword is topped by a red ball. A saluki waits patiently at his side and an ornament of multitriangles covers the dog's headpiece. **IX The Hermit** wears a multilayered collar and pleated shawl. He is an aged, bearded figure dressed in a beggar's cowl. The Hermit holds a lantern while searching for the crystallized wall, which he passes unknowingly. **X The Wheel of Fortune** depicts a sphinx atop an eight-spoked wheel. There are actually two wheels; the inner wheel is a reflection of the outer wheel and symbolizes the opposite choices inherent in every circumstance. On either side of the wheel rise two serpents, while below the wheel a winged bull and lion face each other. **XI Justice** wears a triple-turreted crown and a heavy leather vest decorated with two emblems over a silk shirt. A ruby stone of laser light emanates from her crown. Justice rests her right hand on a large sword and with her other hand she holds aloft the balance. Her hands are gloved in protective leather to avoid any penetrating influences that might affect her judgment. Two leather quiver holders at either side nourish long-stemmed budding flowers.

Bottom row: **XII The Hanged Man** is tied by his left leg to a dead tree trunk. A living crossbar is attached to the tree, suggesting the possibility of rebirth. The figure's hands are tied behind his back. **XIII Death** depicts a skeleton with a frozen, disintegrated face. The skeleton wears a plumed helmet with leather dust flaps and peacock body feathers interwoven across his shoulders. He carries a hardwood pole with a large banner decorated with a black mourning rose. The sun hovers in the distance between two towers. **XIV Temperance** depicts a female figure clothed in a robe of short feathers. The large white wings form part of her headdress; the smaller brown wings are feathers that protect her body. The **six of swords** depicts a ferryman with a large oar. Imbedded in the boat are six swords and the prow is decorated with the carved head of an Egyptian bird.

Tarot Arista This deck, by J. M. Simon, contains Tarot of Marseilles designs, reproduced in smaller images, and both regular and reverse meanings, astrological signs and days of the week. The title in French appears at the top of each card; the number appears in Roman numerals at the upper left and in Arabic numerals at the upper right. Top row: 22 Le Fou *(The Fool)*, 1 Le Bateleur *(The Magician)*, 3 L'Impératrice *(The Empress)*, 4 L'Empereur *(The Emperor)*, 5 Le Pape *(The Pope)*. Second row: 8 La Justice *(Justice)*, 9 L'Ermite *(The Hermit)*, 10 Le Sphynx *(The Wheel of Fortune)*, 13 La Mort *(Death)*, 15 Le Diable *(The Devil)*. Third row: 21 La Couronne des Mages *(The Crown of the Mages or The World)*, 25 Cavalier de Baton *(knight of staves)*, 32 Six de baton *(six of staves)*, 39 Cavalier de coupe *(knight of cups)*, 51 Roi d'Épée *(king of swords)*. Bottom row: 65 Roi de Denier *(king of coins)*, 66 Reine de Denier *(queen of coins)*, 67 Cavalier de Denier *(knight of coins)*, 68 Valet de Denier *(page of coins)*, 69 Un de Denier *(ace of coins)*.

Astral Tarot Black line drawings issued by Mont-Saint-Johns, California. Several full-length figures in typical tarot packs are altered in the Astral tarot series, such as The High Priestess and The Hierophant. The Major Arcana and pip cards are numbered in Arabic numerals. The artist has combined modern figures with an abstract design to portray his interpretation of the Major Arcana cards. The same card designs in color were issued in a revised edition in 1971 by St. Croix Inc. as part of its The 9th Dimension Tarot game.

Astro Tarot Art Fair, New York. Each Major Arcana card is numbered in Roman numerals on the upper left and in Arabic on the lower right; titles appear in both French and English. The courts and aces are titled in both French and English with Arabic numbers on the lower right. This pack totals only forty-two cards, since pip cards ten through two in each suit are omitted.

0 LE FOU	I. LE BATELEUR	II LA PAPESSE	III L'IMPERATRICE	IV L'EMPEREUR
 THE FOOL 0	THE JUGGLER 1	 THE HIGH PRIESTESS 2	 THE EMPRESS 3	 THE EMPEROR 4
V LE PAPE	VI. L'AMOUREUX.	VII LE CHARIOT	VIII LA JUSTICE	IX. L'ERMITE
 THE POPE 5	 THE LOVERS 6	 THE CHARIOT 7	 JUSTICE 8	 THE HERMIT 9
X LA ROUE DE FORTUNE	XI LA FORCE	XII LE PENDU	XIII LA MORT	XIV TEMPERANCE
 THE WHEEL OF FORTUNE 10	 STRENGTH 11	 THE HANGED MAN 12	 DEATH 13	 TEMPERANCE 14
XV LE DIABLE.	XVI LA TOUR FOUDROYÉE	XVII L'ÉTOILE	XVIII LA LUNE	XIX LE SOLEIL
 THE DEVIL 15	 THE LIGHTNING–STRUCK TOWER 16	 THE STAR 17	 THE MOON 18	 THE SUN 19
XX. LE JUGEMENT	XXI LE MONDE	ROI DES ÉPÉES	CHEVALIER DES BÂTONS	UN DE COUPE
 THE JUDGEMENT 20	 THE UNIVERSE 21	 KING OF SWORDS 33	 KNIGHT OF BATONS 25	 ACE OF CUPS 27

Balbi Tarot The Balbi tarot pack was designed by Domenico Balbi and produced by Heraclio Fournier, Vitoria, in cooperation with U.S. Games Systems, Inc., New York. The Major Arcana cards contain titles in both English and Spanish as well as the applicable Hebrew letter and numerological attribute.

Top row: **0 El Loco** (The Fool) depicts an ageless person dressed in the colorful clothes of folly. A sack over The Fool's shoulder contains all his mistakes, and the bells hanging from his collar ring out to attract attention, while he ignores a tiger who tears at his thigh. The Fool holds a cane that has no strength and bends under his weight. **1 El Mago** (The Magician) wears a large pentagram around his neck, which is the symbol of man. The brim of his hat is shaped in the figure eight of infinity. In his left hand he holds upright a rod representing fire, and in his other hand a cup signifying water. On the table before him are several swords and coins representing air and earth, respectively. **IIII El Emperador** (The Emperor) sits upon a throne and holds in his right hand a rod topped with a small orb of the earth and a cross signifying the four elements and four directions of the world. The large eagle on his shield represents intelligence. The Emperor crosses his right leg over his left knee, demonstrating the ease of his stability. In front and to the rear of the Emperor appear the raging flames of life and energy.

Middle row: **VIII Justicia** (Justice) appears as a seated figure. Above her crown is the sign of Libra. In her right hand she holds upright a long sword and in her left hand she uses an Egyptian ankh to balance a large scale. The two long, narrow pillars of her throne represent negative and positive forces. **X La Rueda de la Fortuna** (The Wheel of Fortune) portrays Karma as a serpent in the form of a wheel that revitalizes itself by drawing nourishment from its tail. In the center of the wheel is a large head, which represents all humanity in the Age of Aquarius; a lion is to the left and a bull to the right. An eagle representing Scorpio appears within the wheel above the large head. A winged Sphinx with a third eye of solar gold watches from atop the wheel. The descending devil with fish tail represents the origins of life, which evolved from the oceans. On the right a dragon with claws and tail rises in evolution. At the lower right of the card is the symbol of Saturn above the symbol of Capricorn. **XII El Colgado** (The Hanged Man) is shown hanging by his right ankle from the Tree of Life. His left leg is crossed, evidencing that he is a person of self-control like a yogi.

Bottom row: **XV El Diablo** (The Devil) depicts a winged Devil, half male and half female. A pentagram shines from its mysterious black hat, which is topped by celestial fire. The Devil points downward with three fingers of its left hand to a black moon, which is never illuminated by the sun, and upward with three fingers of its right hand to a bright gold moon, which shines with benevolence upon the earth. **XVIIII El Sol** (The Sun) depicts a young boy and girl who play upon a multicolored lyre whose seven colors represent the creation of seven notes in music and the seven planets. Droplets of life fall from the sun and the solar rays are interspersed with swords representing life and death. **XX El Juicio** (The Judgment) depicts an angel blowing a trumpet throughout the universe, summoning all persons to rise from earth to meet their judgment. The symbol above the angel represents the planet Uranus, which suggests unending space.

Baraja Egipcia Issued by Franco Mora Ruiz, Mexico. Trump cards show Egyptian influence with letters from the English and Hebrew alphabets, astrological significances and one- or two-word meanings along the side of the card. Top row: A 1 The Magus, B 2 Isis Veiled, G 3 Isis Unveiled, D 4 The Sovereign, E 5 The Hierophant. Second row: O 6 The Two Paths, Z 7 The Conqueror, J 8 The Balance, Th 9 The Sage, Y 10 The Wheel. Third row: K 11 The Enchantress, L 12 The Martyr, M 13 The Reaper, N 14 The Alchemist, X 15 The Black Magician. Bottom row: O 16 The Lightning, FP 17 The Star, TS 18 The Moon, Q 19 The Sun, queen of diamonds. The pip cards contain reduced American and European face cards.

Grand Tarot Belline Reissued by J. M. Simon, Paris. These oversized tarot cards, designed by Magus Edmond in the nineteenth century and first published by Magus Belline, are numbered in succession from 0 The Fool to 77 the ten of coins. The appropriate letter of the English alphabet and numerological significance appear on the upper left of each card; the panel below the picture at the bottom contains the card description and interpretations. Top row: 0 The Crocodile, 1 The Magus, 3 Isis-Urania, 5 The Master of the Arcane. Middle row: 6 The Two Routes, 12 The Sacrifice, 13 The Mowing Skeleton, 15 Typhon. Bottom row: 21 The Crown of the Magi, 36 king of cups, 37 queen of cups, 74 seven of coins.

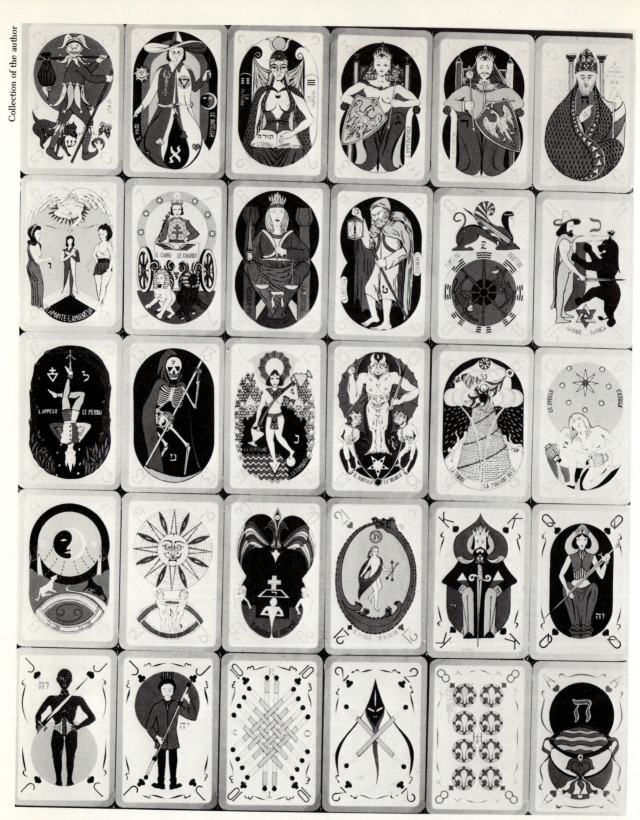

Guido Bolzani Tarocchi Issued by Edizione Europrint, Italy. Trump titles are in French and Italian; the trump and suited cards are Arabic-numbered on all four corners, except for the knights. The pictures on the cards are set within an oval or two overlapping circles; the designs reflect the artist's interpretations, such as the whimsical expression of The Fool, the sensuous gown of The Popess, the bare breasts of The Empress and the Egyptian figure of Temperance. Top row: 0 The Fool, 1 The Magician, 2 The Popess, 3 The Empress, 4 The Emperor, 5 The Pope. Second row: 6 The Lovers, 7 The Chariot, 8 Justice, 9 The Hermit, 10 The Wheel of Fortune, 11 Strength. Third row: 12 The Hanged Man, 13 Death, 14 Temperance, 15 The Devil, 16 The Tower, 17 The Star. Fourth row: 18 The Moon, 19 The Sun, 20 Judgment, 21 The World, king of spades, queen of spades. Bottom row: jack of spades, jack of clubs, ten of clubs, two of clubs, eight of diamonds, ace of hearts.

Builders of the Adytum Tarot Also known as BOTA tarot, these cards are based upon the interpretations of Paul Foster Case. They were drawn by Jessie Burns Parke either in the late 1920s or early 1930s. Some of these cards bear a striking resemblance to the Rider-Waite cards, such as The Fool and The Moon, while others are entirely different, such as Death and The Sun. The pip cards in the BOTA pack do not have descriptive pictures as do those in the Waite deck.

Church of Light Tarot *The deck relies upon Egyptian symbolism as described by C. C. Zain in* The Sacred Tarot. *Each Major Arcana card includes Arabic and Roman numbers, Egyptian, Hebrew and English letters, zodiac signs and other symbols. The uncolored* Church of Light Tarot *pack is described by Zain in a series of chapters—called serials—that deal with the scope, use, chronology, color significance and interpretation of each card. According to Zain, both the constellations in the sky—the stars, which do not offer the slightest suggestion as to the design pictured—and the tarot pictures adorning the walls of the ancient Egyptian initiation chamber make use of primitive pictograph writing to convey ancient knowledge about the human soul.*

Top row: I The Magus, II Veiled Isis, III Isis Unveiled, IV The Sovereign, V The Hierophant. Second row: VI The Two Paths, VII The Conqueror, VIII The Balance, IX The Sage, X The Wheel. Third row: XI The Enchantress, XII The Martyr, XIII The Reaper, XIV The Alchemist, XV The Black Magician. Bottom row: XVI The Lightning, XVII The Star, XVIII The Moon, XIX The Sun, XX The Sarcophagus.

A description of Arcanum I The Magus illustrates the symbolism found on the cards in this pack. Arcanum I, The Magus, represents man in full possession of his moral and physical faculties. He is standing in an attitude of will, which precedes action. His robe is white, the image of purity, either original or regained. A serpent biting its own tail serves him for a girdle; this is the symbol of eternity, which alone circumscribes his endeavors. His forehead is encircled with a band of gold, which signifies light, and the circle expresses the universal circumference in which all created things move. The right hand of the Magus holds a scepter of gold surmounted by a circle representing spirit; it is the symbol of the authority conferred by spiritual attainment. He raises it toward heaven in the sign of aspiration to science, wisdom and force. Above The Magus is a four-pointed star, its rays extending heavenward; the star suggests an overshadowing genius directing The Magus's efforts and providing guidance in his upward struggles. The left index finger is extended toward the earth to show that the mission of the perfect man is to reign over the material world. This double gesture also signifies that the human will should reflect the Divine Will in order to procure good and prevent evil. Placed before the Magus, upon a cubic stone, are a cup, a sword and a piece of gold money in the center of which is engraved a cross. The cup signifies the mixture of passions that contribute to happiness or unhappiness, depending upon whether we are the masters or slaves of our passions. The sword signifies work, struggle that overcomes obstacles and the sorrowful trials that each of us must experience. The coin, sign of determined value, is the symbol of realized aspirations, of work accomplished, and shows power conquered by perseverance and efficacy of will. The cross, seal of the infinite by which the coin is marked, announces the ascension of that power in the spheres of the future. The cube upon which these symbols rest typifies the physical world; on its side appears an ibis to indicate that eternal vigilance is necessary if physical limitations are to be surmounted. The Magus is one skilled in magic, explains Zain, and magic is performed chiefly through the creation and vitalization of mental images. The Magus, therefore, is one in whom the power of the mind has been highly developed, and since in astrology mental ability falls under the rulership of the planet Mercury, this planet corresponds to both I and the Magus of Arcanum I.

Tarot Classic Published by AGMuller & Cie, Switzerland, and U.S. Games Systems, Inc., New York, this deck is a reprint of card designs based upon woodcuts by Claude Burdel, circa 1751. The Major Arcana cards of this pack are similar to the typical Tarot of Marseilles designs. A complete description of the Tarot Classic deck is contained in the book Tarot Classic issued in 1972 by Grosset & Dunlap.

Three versions of The Magician or The Magus card painted by Lady Frieda Harris for the Aleister Crowley "Thoth" tarot pack.

Aleister Crowley "Thoth" Tarot This pack was drawn by Lady Frieda Harris, guided by Crowley's interpretations. The original Crowley paintings are housed today at the Warburg Institute, University of London. Crowley believed that the tarot trumps, or Atus of Tahuti, comprised a complete system of hieroglyphics that represented the total energies of the universe. He sought to reconstruct the tarot trumps through a combination of astrology and the Tree of Life with its ten *sephiroth* and twenty-two connecting paths. The names of four of the Major Arcana or "Atu" were changed: VIII Adjustment was substituted for Justice, XI Lust for Strength, XIV Art for Temperance and XX The Aeon for Judgment.

Top row: *0 The Fool* is shown against a background of air in an attitude of one bursting unexpectedly upon the world. He has the horns of Dionysus Zagreus, and between them is the phallic cone of white light. He is clad in green, according to the tradition of spring, but his shoes are of the gold of the sun. In his right hand he bears the wand, tipped with a pyramid of white, of the All-Father. In his left hand he bears a flaming pine cone of similar significance, but also indicating vegetable growth. From his left shoulder hangs a bunch of purple grapes, representing fertility, sweetness and the basis of ecstasy, which is shown by the stem of the grapes developing into rainbow-hued spirals. The form of the universe suggests the threefold veil of the negative manifesting into divided light. Upon the spiral whorl are other attributions of godhead: the vulture of Maut, the dove of Venus, Isis or Mary, and the ivy sacred to The Fool's devotees. There is also a butterfly of many colors and a winged globe with twin serpents, a symbol that is echoed and fortified by the twin infants embracing on the middle spiral. Above them hangs the benediction of three flowers in one. Fawning upon the figure of The Fool is a tiger, and beneath his feet, in the Nile with its lotus stems, crouches a crocodile. The whole picture is a glyph of creative light.

I The Magus is pictured in Greco-Egyptian tradition as Mercury, messenger of the gods, shown in space with the suit symbols floating nearby, which Crowley describes as weapons: "With the Wand createth He; with the Cup preserveth He; with the Dagger destroyeth He; with the Coin redeemeth He," Liber Magi vv. 7–10. His winged ankles are tied and an ape rises toward him. Above the Magus appears a caduceus with its winged staff entwined by two serpents, associated with the Greek god Hermes.

III The Empress is a regal woman with imperial crown and vestments. She is seated upon a throne whose upright arms suggest twisted blue flames symbolic of her birth from water, the feminine, fluid element. In her right hand she holds the lotus of Isis, which represents feminine or passive power, and a living form of the Holy Grail. Perched upon the flamelike uprights of her throne are two of her most sacred birds, the sparrow and the dove. On her robe are bees and dominoes surrounded by continuous spiral lines and her belt is the zodiac. Beneath her throne is a floor of tapestry embroidered with fleurs-de-lis and fishes that seem to be adoring the Secret Rose at the base of the throne. Two moons revolve on either side of The Empress.

Second row: **V The Hierophant** is shown as a smiling bearded figure surrounded by elephants, a bull and the four beasts or Kerubs, one in each corner of the card. He holds a wand interlaced with three rings representing the three aeons of Isis, Osiris and Horus. The sign of the zodiac repeated by this card is Taurus, the bull Kerub. The ruler of the sign is Venus, shown by the woman standing before the Hierophant. On the Hierophant's chest is a pentagram with the image of a dancing male child, which symbolizes the law of the aeon of the child Horus (which arrived in 1904) with its emphasis on true self or will rather than external influences. According to Crowley, there were two previous aeons in the history of the world. The first, the aeon of Isis, was the aeon of women; hence matriarchy and the worship of the Great Mother. About 500 B.C. the second aeon, of Osiris, arrived; that is, the aeon of man, the father and the paternal religions of suffering and death. The rhythm of the Hierophant is such that he moves only at intervals of two thousand years.

VII The Chariot appears to have been influenced by the trump portrayed by Eliphas Levi. The canopy of the chariot is the blue of the night sky of Binah. The pillars are the four pillars of the universe, the regimen of Tetragrammaton. The scarlet wheels represent the original energy of Geburah, which causes the revolving motions. The chariot is drawn by four sphinxes composed of the four Kerubs: the bull, the lion, the eagle and the man. The charioteer is clothed in amber-colored armor decorated with ten stars of Assiah, the inheritance of celestial dew from his mother. He bears as a crest the crab appropriate to the zodiacal sign of Cancer. The vizor of his helmet is lowered, for no man may look upon his face and live; for the same reason no part of his body is exposed. He is throned in The Chariot rather than conducting it, because the whole system of progression is perfectly balanced and his only function is to bear the Holy Grail. The most important feature of the card is the Holy Grail of pure amethyst, the color of Jupiter, though its shape suggests the full moon and the great sea of Binah. In the center is radiant blood. Spiritual life is implied as is the light that penetrates the darkness. The rays revolve, emphasizing the Jupiterian element in the symbol. The Chariot refers to the zodiacal sign of Cancer, the sign into which the sun moves at the summer solstice. Cancer also represents the path that leads from the great Mother Binah to Geburah, and is thus the influence of the supernals descending through the veil of water—which is blood—upon the energy of man, and so inspires it.

XII The Hanged Man is depicted against a background grillwork of small squares representing the elemental tables of all the energies of nature. The legs of the figure are crossed to form a right angle and the arms are outstretched to form an equilateral triangle; these shapes give the symbol of a triangle surmounted by the cross from the aeon of Osiris. The entire figure—moribund and at the same time majestic—is suspended from an ankh, while entwined around his left foot is a serpent, both the creator and destroyer who causes all transformation. A coiled serpent rests on the water below the figure.

Bottom row: The **six of swords**—Science—depicts six swords, with ornamental hilts, in the form of a hexagram. The points touch the petals of a red rose upon a golden cross of six squares, which suggests the Rosy Cross as the central secret of scientific truth. The **princess of wands** is shown leaping in a surging flame. A tiger's skin falls behind her. The princess is unclothed and carries a wand crowned with the disk of the sun. This card is said to represent the dance of the virgin priestess of the Lords of Fire, and the golden altar ornamented with ram heads symbolizes the fires of spring. The **prince of cups** is a warrior partly clad in armor. His helmet is surmounted by an eagle, and his chariot, which resembles a seashell, is also drawn by an eagle. His wings are tenuous, almost of gas. In his right hand he holds an inverted lotus flower, sacred to the element of water, and in his left hand a serpent rises from a large cup. Beneath his chariot is the calm and stagnant water of a lake upon which rain is falling.

The court cards in the Crowley pack are based upon the Hebrew system, which postulates Father and Mother from whose union issue Son and Daughter. Thus, Crowley named the four court cards knight, queen, prince and princess to represent father, mother, son and daughter, respectively. The four suits were designated by Crowley as swords attributed to air, wands attributed to fire, cups attributed to water and disks (coins) attributed to earth. The thirty-six pip cards of the Minor Arcana series (aces excluded) and their designated names in the Crowley Thoth pack are: suit of swords— ten, Ruin; nine, Cruelty; eight, Interference; seven, Futility; six, Science; five, Defeat; four, Truce; three, Sorrow; two, Peace; suit of wands—ten, Oppression; nine, Strength; eight, Swiftness; seven, Valor; six, Victory; five, Strife; four, Completion; three, Virtue; two, Dominion; suit of cups—ten, Satiety; nine, Happiness; eight, Indolence; seven, Debauch; six, Pleasure; five, Disappointment; four, Luxury; three, Abundance; two, Love; suit of disks—ten, Wealth; nine, Gain; eight, Prudence; seven, Failure; six, Success; five, Worry; four, Power; three, Work; two, Change. Crowley viewed tarot cards as living individuals that must be studied and experienced in order to be understood. To effectively use the cards, he believed it was necessary to live with them over a long period of time and to study their interplay in daily life.

D'Epinal Tarot Reprint of Tarot d'Epinal, one of the popular catchpenny tarot packs originally published in France by Pellerin during the nineteenth century. As the word "catchpenny" implies, these packs were inexpensively printed for popular distribution. This reprint was completed in 1976 by Arts et Lettres, France. Some of the Major Arcana deviate from traditional designs. Top row: Le Fou (The Fool) with a small beard; I Escamoteur (The Juggler) with plumed hat; II Junon (Juno); Impératrice (Empress) (unnumbered); L'Empereur (The Emperor) (unnumbered). Second row: V Jupiter, VI L'Amoureux (The Lovers); VII Le Chariot (The Chariot); VIII La Justice (Justice next to a tablet entitled "Lois" (Laws); VIIII Le Capucin (The Hermit). Third row: X La Roue de Fortune (The Wheel of Fortune); XI La Force (Strength); XII Le Pendu (The Hanged Man); XIII (Death); XV Le Diable (The Devil). Bottom row: XVI La Maison de Dieu (The Tower); XVIII La Lune (The Moon); XVIIII Le Soleil (The Sun); two of cups; and Le Consultant (The Consultant), an extra card found in this pack.

Il Destino Svelato Dal Tarocco Published in 1955 by S. A. Modiano, Trieste. The twenty-two Major Arcana cards in this seventy-eight-card tarot pack are a departure from typical tarot decks. The figures fluctuate from Egyptian to contemporary; each Major Arcana card contains interpretations, astrological symbols and the appropriate Arabic number in a square on the lower right. This pack was recently reissued by Modiano in an Italian edition under the name Cartomanzia 184 and an English edition called Cagliostro Tarot 184 with an instruction booklet written by a Docteur Marius.

Dynamic Games Tarot   Issued in 1973. The symbols on the Major Arcana, court and pip cards generally follow the Rider-Waite cards but the designs are by a lighter hand and the figures are depicted as younger and prettier. Some of the female figures have an almost starrylike appearance.

Egipcios Tarot *The design of this tarot pack features Egyptian symbolism based upon the writings of Professor J. Iglesias Janeiro in his work* La Cabala de Prediccion. *The deck is printed by Editorial Kier, Argentina, in attractive metallic colors. Both the twenty-two Major Arcana and fifty-six Minor Arcana cards contain descriptive pictures on each card, as well as titles in Spanish and symbols dealing with astrology, mythology, alchemy and folklore.*

Top row: **1 El Mago** (The Magician) depicts an Egyptian priest standing before an altar; his posture expresses magical will. In his left hand he holds a scepter surmounted by a circle, symbol of his authority. The other suits of the tarot are represented on the altar in front of him. His raised left hand reflects heavenly wisdom and his right hand pointing downward with finger outstretched to the earth tells that the priest rules over the material world. The cube beneath his feet signifies the earth element over which he is lord. The Uazat eyes above his head signify the eternal wisdom. **2 La Sacerdotisa** (The Priestess) depicts the figure of Isis. She is seated within a temple and wears a crown with horns encircling a moon. The Priestess is veiled and clasps against her breast the ankh of eternal life. On her knee is a papyrus book. The Priestess is the personification of occult science and she sits within the sanctuary of Isis. The veil indicates that her teachings are hidden from the profane and curious and are revealed only to the initiate. The pillars at either side and the glyphs of pillars—the tet—below her indicate that she rules over the four directions. **3 La Emperatriz** (The Empress) portrays the seated figure of an Isis type, but without a veil. She is crowned with twelve stars representing the zodiac and she sits on a cube representing matter. The serpent on her brow is a symbol of enlightenment. In her right hand she holds a scepter surmounted by a globe, evidencing that she rules over the world. Her left hand is outstretched toward an eagle, symbol of the liberated spirit. Below her is a crescent moon, indicating that her principle is lunar, the gnostic femininity. **4 El Emperador** (The Emperor) shows a seated man who wears a helmet on his head, indicating that he is a worldly ruler. His right hand holds a scepter and his left hand is clenched on his lap. He is seated on a cube that contains a cat, symbol of inner vision penetrating matter. On the Emperor's brow is a sacred serpent, symbol of his enlightenment. **5 El Jerarca** (The Hierarch) reveals the standing figure of Anubis holding a staff. His left hand points to the ground, indicating that he rules over all the things of the world. He is jackal-headed and under his feet there is a pair of scales, indicating that he is the one who weighs the souls of the dead. The Hierarch is related to the inner sanctum and he is a guardian of the sacred occult mysteries.

Second row: **6 La Indecisión** (The Lovers or Indecision) portrays the figure of a man standing at the crossroads, symbolized by the triangle, his hands crossed over his breast. Two women, one at either side, seem to be trying to influence him, and they are the symbolical figures Vice and Virtue. Above, in the spirit of justice seeking to punish wrongdoers, a male figure draws a bow and takes aim at Vice, who wears transparent clothes. **7 El Triunfo** (The Chariot of Triumph) depicts the figure of a man standing in a war chariot. Above his head is a sphere sustained by two outspread wings, symbol of the immortal soul. The charioteer wears a crown surmounted by a serpent. He holds a sword in his right hand and a scepter in his left. Two sphinxes, one white and the other black, are harnessed to the chariot, signifying positive and negative destiny. **8 La Justicia** (Justice) depicts the figure of a woman kneeling at the top of three steps. She wears a crown and in her left hand she holds a sword with its point facing upward. In her right hand she holds a balance, the symbol of justice. On her forehead is a serpent, and at the base of the steps is the serpent of eternity, Uraeus, which bites its own tail to form an endless circle. **9 El Eremita** (The Hermit) depicts the figure of a man walking in the desert. He holds a staff in his right hand and a lighted lamp in his left, which symbolizes enlightenment. He is wrapped in a long cloak and walks over the orb of the sun. Above his head another sun shines down, three rays directing themselves at his head and the flourishing tree growing in the desert. **10 La Retribución** (The Wheel of Fortune or Retribution) shows a wheel containing six spokes being turned by Hermanubis, the genius of good, and Typhon, the genius of evil. The wheel is supported below by twin serpents, symbols of sexuality. Above this wheel rests a sphinx on a platform supported by the wheel in equilibrium. The sphinx holds a staff and is winged.

Third row: **11 La Persuasión** (Strength or Persuasion) shows a woman feeding a lion. She is a virgin and wears an elaborate crown ornamented with a serpent. Below her is a glyph of an eagle riding upon a snake, suggesting the ascendency of the higher over the lower. The lion symbolizes force, here subdued by the purity of the virgin. **12 El Apostolado** (The Hanged Man or Martyr) shows a man suspended by his left foot. His two hands are tied over his head and point to the ground. His arms form a triangle pointing downward, while from his hands three pieces of gold fall to the earth. This is the sign of abrupt change, indicating that material forces have gained control. **13 La Inmortalidad** (Death or Immortality) depicts an Egyptian laborer or peasant wearing a loincloth and hard at labor reaping corn or wheat. Above his head are two entwined lotuses, indicating that there is a spirituality that survives death. **14 La Temperancia** (Temperance) depicts a male figure wearing priestly robes and having long hair. He stands with the sun above his head, indicating his divine origin. The two hands hold jars and he pours water from one to the other. Below his feet are three lotuses. A serpent emerges from the central flower, symbolizing the alchemist at work transforming one thing into another, as the combination of male and female essences. **15 La Paión** (The Devil or Passion) depicts a ram-headed figure of Typhon with horns. He stands erect and holds in his left hand a scepter staff surmounted by horns. In his right hand he holds a serpent, which rises up from his palm. On his head he has thin horns upon which rest two serpents. Below his feet is a triangular structure, symbolizing the female principle of procreation. This card is a picture of the evil magician who uses power for his own gain.

Bottom row: **16 La Fragilidad** (The Tower or Fragility) depicts an obelisk struck by lightning. A crowned and an uncrowned man fall at either side, suggesting that nature is no respecter of rank and that kings and commoners are treated alike. At the base of the obelisk are three ritual staffs or scepters, indicating that no authority is immune from heavenly wrath. **19 La Inspiración** (The Sun or Inspiration) depicts a young man and woman standing close together and holding hands. They are dressed in simple garments. Above their heads an orb of the sun emits seven rays ending in hands that reach out to the two figures below. Below the young couple appears a circle enclosing three growing flowers, which are symbols of harmony and resurrection. The entire picture is a glyph of the power and potency of the sun. **22 El Regreso** (The Fool or Regression) reveals a man standing on the back of a crocodile. Traditionally, he is blind and holds a staff in the left hand and an ankh, the symbol of eternity, in his right hand. Above his head is an eclipse of the sun.

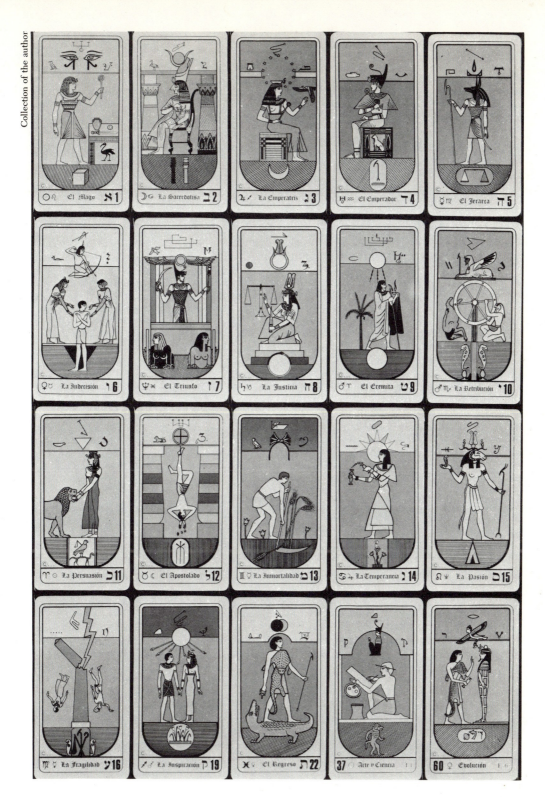

He wears animal clothing and he strides out toward his destination. This glyph is the symbol of materialism. **37 Arte y Ciencia** (Art and Science) depicts a scribe seated at his working place. He paints the glyphs of his trade. Above his head is a hieroglyph of a crowned priest holding an ankh. Under him is a monkey-headed god, patron of the arts. This is an invocation of Thoth, the founder of all knowledge. **60 Evolución** (Evolution) depicts two figures. The male figure is similar to the blind man on card 22 and he stands before an Egyptian mummy. He wears animal skins and makes a gesture of peace with his left hand. In his right hand he holds an elixir vase. Above the heads of the two figures is a bird with a human head, the Ka or released spirit, holding the sign of eternal life in its claws. Below is a glyph indicating evolution from the cosmic waters upward. This card depicts the ascent of the spirit. Cards 37 and 60 are part of the Minor Arcana.

In the Egipcios tarot pack the Minor Arcana cards are distinctive in that they contain full pictures instead of the traditional suit designations and values.

Esoteric Tarot Published in 1976 by Heraclio Fournier, Spain. The Esoteric tarot, known as El Gran Tarot Esoterico, was designed by Luis Pena Longo under the direction of Maritxu Guler. Each Major Arcana card has a Hebrew letter and some of the cards bear signs of the zodiac.

Top row: **El Loco** (The Crazy One or The Fool) is dressed in a layered garment. Three cow bells hang from his waist. In his right hand he holds upright a large corn stalk while with the other hand he holds a stick with a large handkerchief in which are coins. The conical hat on his head is topped with feathers. A cat scratches at his leg. This card symbolizes that man enslaves himself to materialistic forces. **I El Consultante** (The Male Consultant) is depicted as a young man standing before the great horizon. He is sure of his great powers. A brilliant sun shines upon him. He holds a magic wand toward the sky while in his other hand he holds an ankh that points toward earth and its pleasures. Above his head is the eternal figure eight and in front of him are evolving celestial bodies. **II La Consultante** (The Female Consultant) is a nude figure who stands between two trees in the Garden of Eden and is illuminated by the rays of the moon. One hand holds a pomegranate while the other hand is behind her back. **III La Emperatriz** (The Empress) is a winged woman wearing royal garments and a golden crown. She holds in her right hand the reflection of soul and life. Two lions sit at her feet and an ear of corn appears to her right. **IIII El Emperador** (The Emperor) is a bearded prince with large antlers protruding from his steel helmet. He is the symbol of power and conquest. His cape matches the design of the cape worn by The Empress.

Second row: **V El Maestro** (The Teacher) is the master of the Arcanas. He wears a cross and his cape is held at his neck by a button with the star symbol of wisdom. He sits before two neophytes and gives them his blessing. Above him is a darkened cloud from which seven rays and a hand in the esoteric symbol emerge. **VI Los Dos Caminos** (The Two Roads) depicts a strong man, the same person who appeared in Card I, but he now stands at a crossroad and is torn between the pressures of two women dressed in long robes. One woman has loose, long hair and the other woman wears a golden band around her forehead. **VII El Carro de Hermes** (The Chariot of Hermes) depicts two horses dragging a chariot of powerful wheels with large protruding cleats. The charioteer is crowned and he holds arrows in his left hand, symbols of victory. **VIII La Justicia** (Justice) depicts a crowned male king with upraised sword, which he is about to strike against the small child to clarify truth. The back of the throne is topped with a sphere and triangle. **VIIII El Anciano** (The Old Man) depicts a bearded figure dressed in a cloak and holding a hexagonal lantern and a wand. An antlered animal rests at his side.

Third row: **X La Rueda de la Fortuna** (The Wheel of Fortune) depicts a massive stone wheel pushed by the paw of a white bear. A crowned monkey sits on a tree branch and holds a pinwheel. At the top of the tree is a double head. **XI La Fortaleza** (Strength) shows Samson holding across his right shoulder a massive club while strolling the earth. **XII La Picota** (The Pillory) depicts a stone post topped with an iron trident. The pillory stands between two trees; each tree has six cut branches. **XIII**—This untitled card is called **La Inmortalidad** (Immortality) and corresponds to Death. A skeleton, garbed in a cloak decorated with suns, stars and moons, holds a scythe while he sits upon a strong huge dog. From the earth appear a number of plants among a female human head, an emperor's crown and a papal crown, a fallen sword, a scythe and a bishop's crozier. A mausoleum with a large golden ankh is in the background. **XIIII La Templanza** (Temperance) depicts a winged angel pouring the elixir of life from one large cup to another. In the background is the sea.

Bottom row: **XV Aker** (The Devil) is depicted as a winged and horned goat of the sabbat. A flame rises between its horns and a pentacle appears on its forehead. Its face is synthetic and with its hands it makes an esoteric sign and points to the black and white moons of evil and good. The symbol of caduceus rises from its lap in front of its scaly stomach. **XVI La Torre** (The Tower) depicts seven bolts of lightning as they strike a stone turreted tower located in Azekah. Several figures are blown into the air as flames engulf the tower. One figure leans against the archway at the main entrance. **XVII El Astro** (The Star) depicts a naked maiden pouring fluid from a gold and silver jar onto the arid earth. Her left knee rests on the earth and the toes of her right foot are in the water. A small bird perches on a tree. Above the maiden in the clear sky appears a large fiery star with three tails. In the center of the star is a large pentacle. The **queen of swords** stands on a thin moon floating upon the water. She holds a sword and behind her is the sign of Cancer, symbol of the daring woman. The **knight of swords** rides a galloping white horse. He is dressed in full armor, including helmet. In the air appears the sign of Scorpio, symbolizing a strong young man.

Etteilla Tarot   The full title of this pack issued by J. M. Simon, France, is Grand Etteilla Egyptian Gypsies Tarot Deck. The cards faithfully follow the early Etteilla designs with the added feature that the upright and reversed titles appear in both French and English.

Fergus Hall Tarot Designed by Fergus Hall, Scottish surrealist artist, and published by AG Muller & Cie, Switzerland, and U.S. Games Systems, Inc., New York. This pack was featured in the James Bond 007 movie, Live and Let Die, and is also part of the Tarot of the Witches and The Devil's Tarot packs published by U.S. Games Systems, Inc. The human figures in Hall's paintings usually have long, black, stranded hair. The men have heavy beards and a thin, long, flowing moustache tied at each end with a small bow. Both men and women have exaggerated arms and shoulders, while their legs often are undersized and covered with skinny bright-colored boots.

Top row: The Fool is a blindfolded young man dressed in colorful garments and wearing on his head a foolscap

253

comprised of four conical peaks topped with pompons; he discards eight coins while a spotted half-dog, half-cat tears at his trouser leg and the sun and crescent moon appear behind him. A large red heart is stamped on his cheek. I The Magician wears a conical hat topped with a five-pointed star and a blue blazer with wide shoulders, yellow lapels and shoulder braids. His elongated flowing moustache is tied with a bow at each end and his long black beard falls to the table, on which sits an aged striped cat near a crystal ball and one upturned card. II The High Priestess is a handsome woman with piercing eyes; she sits on a throne with a large circular backrest. In her left hand she holds a rod with lightning bolts shooting upward and her right hand holds fast to the tail of a mouse. Above her appear a bright sun and a five-pointed star, and to her right sits a docile cat. On her left cheek is the imprint of a five-pointed blue star. III The Empress is resplendent in royal robes and a jewel-studded crown in the shape of a heart, topped with a crescent moon. In her right hand she holds a globe of the world and her left hand clasps a scepter with a triad of beads topped with a crescent moon. On both cheeks appear red hearts. IIII The Emperor has a heavy, black, three-stranded beard and a long, flowing moustache. His regal crown matches the heart design of the bejeweled crown worn by The Empress, but is topped with a golden sun, as is the scepter in his right hand. The Emperor holds a volcanic planet in his left hand. The remaining cards shown are (second row) VII The Chariot, VIIII The Hermit, X Wheel of Fortune, XVIII The Moon, XVIIII The Sun; (third row) XX Judgment, XXI The World, knight of swords, king and ten of batons; (bottom row) king, queen, ten of cups, ten and ace of coins.

A complete description of the Fergus Hall cards is contained in the *James Bond 007 Tarot Book* published in 1973.

Gentilini Tarocchi   The twenty-two Major Arcana cards from the seventy-eight-card Gentilini tarot deck were painted by Franco Gentilini and published in 1975 in a limited edition of 150 sets; 120 sets numbered in Arabic and 30 sets numbered in Roman. The complete full-color seventy-eight-card Gentilini deck was issued in 1976 in a regular edition as well as two limited editions: five hundred sets with a gold plate signed and numbered by the artist, and five hundred sets with a signed and numbered silver plate. The Major Arcana cards are without numbers and the imagery reflects a blending of traditional tarot symbolism with modern scenes.

Top row: Il Bagatto (*The Magician*) depicts a cobbler in front of a workbench containing cobbler's tools. La Papessa (*The High Priestess*) is an iridescent figure wearing a papal crown and holding a book. L'Imperatrice (*The Empress*) wears a regal crown and clasps a scepter with both her hands. The Silhouette of a man wearing a hat appears to her right. L'Imperatore (*The Emperor*) wears a regal crown and holds an orb in his left hand. A young woman wearing a wide-brimmed hat appears to his left. Il Papa (*The Hierophant*) depicts a figure of religious solemnity with crook in hand.

Second row: Gli Amanti (*The Lovers*) reveals a nude woman sitting in a man's lap. Il Carro (*The Chariot*) shows a marbleized charioteer holding in his right hand a wreath while his chariot is being drawn by two marbleized horses. La Giustizia (*Justice*) is a translucent figure holding the balance scales and a double-edged sword. L'Eremita (*The Hermit*) is a solitary figure sitting near a tree and playing the guitar. A bird reposes in the menacing sky. La Fortuna (*Fortune*) is a blindfolded female figure holding a box of coins and a multileaved clover.

Third row: L'Impiccato (*The Hanged Man*) shows a painting of two hanging figures, one of whom hangs by his neck. A man and woman in the foreground observe the painting. La Morte (*Death*) shows a nude female figure admiring herself with a small hand mirror while nearby lurks the skeleton of death. La Fonte (*Temperance*) pours the traditional liquid from one vessel to another. Il Diavolo (*The Devil*) is a bearded figure dressed in formal black attire and whispering to a woman wearing a red dress and drinking wine. La Torre (*The Tower*) suggests the Leaning Tower of Pisa struck by a single bolt of lightning.

Bottom row: Le Stelle (*The Stars*) appear in the night sky above an ornate building. La Luna (*The Moon*) shows a quarter-moon reflecting its light along a deserted city street. Il Sole (*The Sun*) depicts a large rose in an open window as it flowers beneath the rays of the sun. L'Angelo (*The Angel*) reveals a winged figure created from a collage and blowing a trumpet. Il Mondo (*The World*) pictures a man reading the French newspaper Le Monde.

The Gentilini tarocchi cards are described in a book by Patrick Waldberg entitled *I Tarocchi di Gentilini*, published in 1975.

Golden Dawn Tarot These esoteric cards were painted by Robert Wang under the guidance of Francis Israel Regardie. The pictorial imagery on each card is based upon the late-nineteenth-century designs of The Order of the Golden Dawn and the notebooks of MacGregor Mathers.

Top row: 0 The Fool shows a naked child beneath a rose tree that bears yellow roses, the golden rose of joy as well as the rose of silence. While reaching to the roses, the child holds a leash in his right hand that is affixed to a collar on a gray wolf, suggesting worldly wisdom held in check by perfect innocence. The pale colors of this card suggest the early dawn of a spring day. 5 The Hierophant is a bearded figure with a crook in his right hand and a scroll of hidden truths, or the Book of the Law, in his left hand. The Hierophant wears a jeweled tiara and sits upon a throne decorated with the skulls of two bulls representing Taurus. A curtain depicting the veil of existence and representing a higher form of consciousness hangs behind the Hierophant. 6 The Lovers depicts the winged Perseus rescuing Andromeda from the dragon of fear and the waters of stagnation.

Middle row: 7 The Chariot depicts the charioteer as the spirit of man. He wears a Viking helmet and is drawn by two horses, one black and the other white. 10 Wheel of Fortune depicts the revolution of experience and progress, time and eternity, presided over by the Plutonian cynocephalus, the dog-headed ape and companion of Hermes. Above the wheel is the sphinx of Egypt. The spokes of the wheel represent the zodiac; the eternal riddle is solved only when liberation is attained. 11 Justice depicts Nephthys, the twin sister of Isis and the third aspect of Luna. Her emblems are the sword and scale. She rests her bare feet on a reposing fox.

Bottom row: 13 Death confirms that the skeleton alone survives the destructive power of time as about him are the heads and limbs of the fallen. At the top corners of the card are a funereal sun and a phoenix with a slithering serpent rising upward. 14 Temperance depicts a female figure standing between earth and water, holding two amphorae with their streams of living water. In the background is a fiery volcano. 21 The Universe depicts a nude female figure holding small rods in her hands. Around her appears the solar system and the signs of the zodiac. The string of pearls follows an oval trajectory that represents the completion of the cycle. The four cherubim in the corners are man, eagle, bull and lion.

Golden Egyptian tarot/Morgan's tarot/Praktische tarot
The Golden Egyptian tarot cards were designed by Lucia Moed, a young Belgian artist and Egyptologist, and are scheduled for publication in 1978 by U.S. Games Systems, Inc. (Left) [V] Thot [Thoth] is the god of the moon and of wisdom and learning; he is credited with inventing speech, writing and the calendar. He also assisted at the judgment of the deceased. Thot is depicted with the head and neck of the sacred bird Ibis. He corresponds to the Hierophant or Pope in standard tarot packs. (Right) Tutankhamen, the boy king, sits upon his royal throne and corresponds to one of the four suited kings.

Morgan's tarot The card designs in this tarot deck of black-and-white line drawings reflect the counterculture movement prevalent during the late 1960s. Created by Morgan Robbins and illustrated by Gordon Chorpash, the cards illustrate the personal thoughts and emotions Robbins experienced with Tibetan mysticism. Each card is presented as a mirror that the reader looks into for self-revelation and meditation. Only a few of the cards relate to the traditional Major Arcana. The cards are unnumbered and there are eighty-eight rather than seventy-eight in the complete deck. Cards that relate to the Major Arcana include (top row) Who Am I (*The Fool*), Do not meddle in the affairs of wizards for they are subtle & quick to anger (*The Magician*), Love (*The Lovers*), Heavy (*Justice*), Drug Dragged (*The Hermit*). Bottom row: untitled wheel (*Wheel of Fortune*), Death/Rebirth (*Death*), The Virgin Sun Queen (*The Sun*), If there is a judge you are it (*Judgment*), Not unfolding the way it should: The Universe (*The World or The Universe*).

Praktische Tarot The twenty-two Major Arcana cards of Praktische tarot were designed by Anneke De Diana and published in The Netherlands in De Hermetische Tarot and De Praktische Tarot, books by Dio Raman dealing with tarot symbolism and its psychological interpretations. The cards are Arabic-numbered and contain titles in Dutch. The figures have slender bodies and wide-eyed, innocent faces. The clothes are close fitting and tapered. Top row: 0 de Zwerver (The Wanderer), 1 de Magier (The Magician), 2 de Hogepriesteres (The High Priestess), 4 de Heerser (The Ruler), 5 de Hogepriester (The High Priest), 6 de Keuze (The Choice). Bottom row: 7 de Zegewagen (The Chariot), 8 de Gerechtigheid (Justice), 12 de Gehangene (The Hanged Man), 14 de Matigheid (Temperance), 18 de Maan (The Moon), 19 de Zon (The Sun).

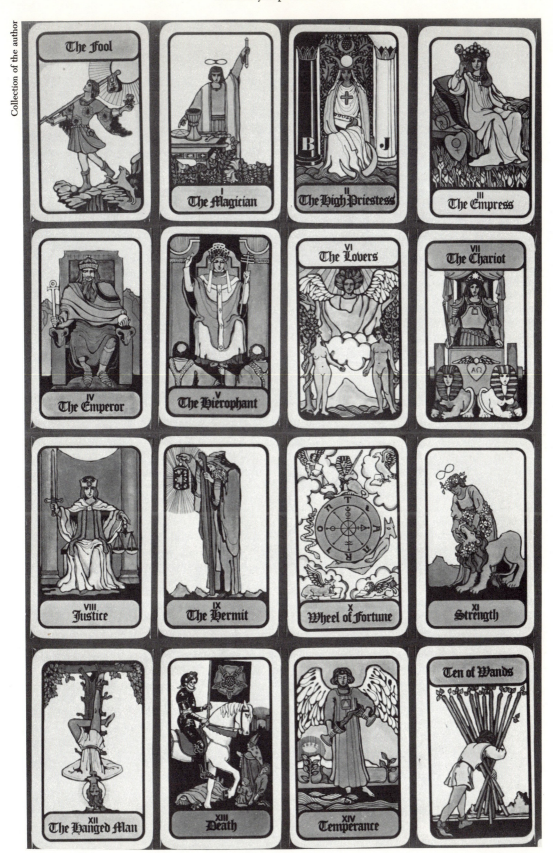

Hoi Polloi Tarot These cards follow the Rider-Waite designs and are printed in bold solid colors with emphasis on red and orange tones. The Major Arcana cards are numbered with Roman numerals and titled in English.

Tarot of Oscar Ichazo *These tarot designs were prepared by James Hanlon under the direction of Oscar Ichazo, founder of Arica, a system that teaches a scientific method for raising consciousness. The titles of some of the Major Arcana cards vary from the traditional designations. The Major Arcana are viewed as complex ideograms likened to the letters of the alphabet. The Minor Arcana open the four ways of understanding the consciousness; swords are the way of truth, wands or staves the way of wisdom, cups the way of love, and pentacles or coins the way of knowledge. Some of the figures are distinctly Egyptian in style.*

Top row: **0 The Essence,** *equivalent to the traditional Fool, depicts a young man wearing a low-waisted Egyptian kilt and holding upraised a crook. He stands at the edge of a precipice overlooking a large body of water against a background of rising cliffs. A docile alligator rests at the water's edge. A leopard entangles the young man's right leg. The eight rays of the sun represent eight principles of consciousness; the sun itself represents the ninth principle.* **3 Nature,** *equivalent to The Empress, depicts a tall woman standing in bare feet. She wears an embroidered sheath gown and a helmet crown encircled with a fillet. In her left hand she holds a flower scepter and in her right hand is a scepter of the world.* **4 The Pharaoh,** *equivalent to The Emperor, sits upon a throne decorated with cat heads. The Pharaoh wears the traditional artificial beard and atef crown of the early kings of Upper Egypt. At the front of his crown is the head of Uraeus, the sacred serpent of ancient Egyptian rulers and deities and an emblem of their sovereignty. In his crossed arms the Pharaoh holds a decorated scepter and a flail. The scepter or crook symbolizes the king's authority over the shepherds of his realm and the flail symbolizes his authority over the agricultural citizens.* **5 The Hierophant** *wears a striped headdress with a crown of stylized peacock feathers supported by goat's horns. The Hierophant's costume consists of a kilt with pendant apron in front. He holds a long crook in his right hand.*

Middle row: **6 The Lovers** *depicts two figures resting at the foot of two trees, representing vitality and the mind. Around one tree is a coiled serpent. A tall figure with cupped hands stands directly behind them.* **10 Wheel of Fortune** *depicts a nine-spoked wheel encircled by a snake that is devouring its tail. The nine spokes represent the nine domains of consciousness. The four suit signs of pentacles, cups, wands and swords appear with wings in the four corners of the card.* **11 Strength** *depicts a young naked woman. She sits astride a large docile lion and represents mind mastering the physical body.* **14 Temperance** *wears a headdress of hawk wings topped by a crown that hovers above her head, suggesting that she seeks to achieve the crown but is not yet in possession of it. Her hands are clasped and the liquid circulating between the two cups represents the blessings that flow from above to below and below to above.*

Bottom row: **19 The Sun** *depicts two naked children, hands clasped, standing beneath an eight-rayed sun within several levels of clouds. The eight rays represent eight principles of consciousness, and the sun, similar to the sun in The Essence card, represents the ninth principle.* **20 Judgment** *depicts three figures rising from earthen coffins. Their arms are outstretched toward a flaming sword, symbolic of absolute truth. The cross-bearing flag represents Christ on earth. The sky is filled with the strands from the trumpet. The* **king of cups** *sits upon his throne and wears the atef crown also worn by The Pharaoh. He is dressed in a long apron and holds in his right hand the cup of his suit. A sacred serpent of Lower Egypt rises nearby, and in the four corners of the card appear full-petaled roses, representing cups. The* **queen of pentacles** *wears an ornamented skirt. She sits upon her throne and holds a large coin in her right hand to designate her suit sign. A hawk hovers nearby and in the four corners of the card appear spikes of grain, representing pentacles.*

Collection of Oscar Ichazo

0 THE ESSENCE	3 NATURE	4 THE PHAROAH	5 THE HIEROPHANT
6 THE LOVERS	10 WHEEL OF FORTUNE	11 STRENGTH	14 TEMPERANCE
19 THE SUN	20 JUDGMENT	KING OF CUPS	QUEEN OF PENTACLES

Tarot of Marseilles Published by J. M. Simon, Paris, successor to B. P. Grimaud, one of the oldest European playing card manufacturers. The Tarot of Marseilles is also published in a separate edition with French titles on the Major Arcana cards. The same designs have been in use for several centuries and many eighteenth- and nineteenth-century hand-stenciled French tarot packs have designs patterned after these figures.

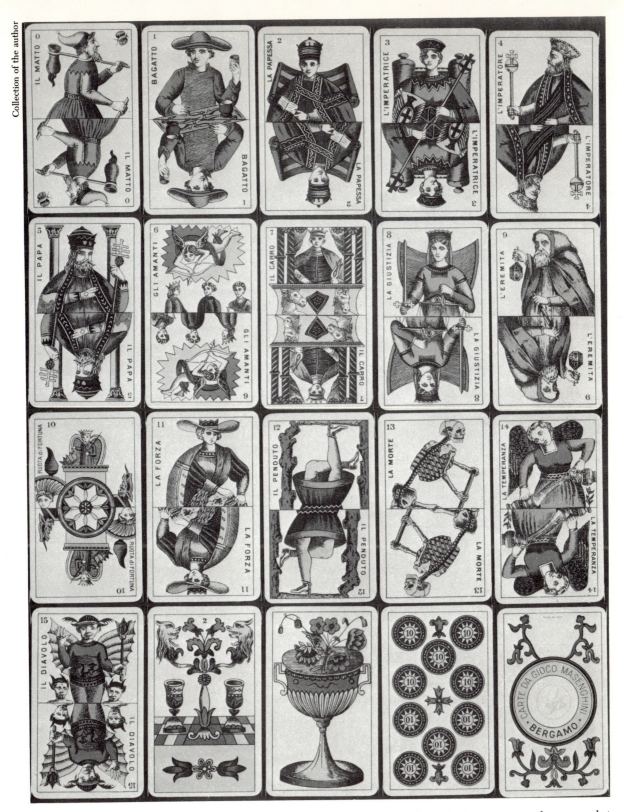

Masenghini Tarocchi Piedmontese *This Piedmontese* tarocchi *pack with double-ended Major Arcana and court cards is made by Masenghini di Lombardini, Bergamo. Top row: 0 Il Matto (The Fool) carries a butterfly net over his left shoulder while a colorful butterfly hovers nearby, 1 Bagatto (The Magician) depicts a young man holding a cup in his upraised left hand while on the bench in front of him is another cup and cobbler's tools. 2 La Papessa (The Popess), 3 L'Imperatrice (The Empress), 4 L'Imperatore (The Emperor). Second row: 5 Il Papa (The Pope), 6 Gli Amanti (The Lovers), 7 Il Carro (The Chariot), 8 La Giustizia (Justice), 9 L'Eremita (The Hermit). Third row: 10 Ruota di Fortuna (The Wheel of Fortune), 11 La Forza (Strength), 12 Il Penduto (The Hanged Man), 13 La Morte (Death) has the title printed on the card in contrast to most tarot decks, which do not contain printed titles on the Death card, 14 La Temperanza (Temperance). Bottom row: 15 Il Diavolo (The Devil), two and ace of cups, ten and ace of coins.*

Mountain Dream Tarot The pictures in this unusual tarot pack are photographs taken during a four-year period by Bea Nettles, mainly of friends and models at the Penland School of Crafts in the mountains of North Carolina. The designs are based upon the Rider-Waite tarot. Top row: **0 Fool** depicts a young man standing on a rock ledge and looking upward to the sky. A twig with a loosely hanging sack rests on his shoulder. In his left hand he holds a blossom of Queen Anne's lace or wild carrot. A small dog sits at his feet, its ears perked in readiness. **1 Magician** is a moustached man holding a bunch of golden day lilies representing the flaming torch of life. The Magician is draped with a tie-dyed cloth; he wears an embroidered V-necked shirt and a chain belt. Behind him on a table are a large coin, a twig, a small sword and a partially concealed cup. **2 High Priestess** is draped in a white robe decorated at her feet with a lace crescent moon. She wears a three-leaved tiara with the Arabic 2 designating the card number, and she holds in her lap a white cross set in a stepped base of dark wood, suggesting the Calvary. She sits in a high-backed wooden rocking chair in front of a closed doorway with glass windows. **4 Emperor** is the photographer's father. He is bearded and wears a turban and a striped royal robe. In his right hand he holds a long samurai sword and in his left hand a small marble globe. Around his neck is a strand of large beads; he is seated on a heavy wooden chair.

Second row: **5 Heirophant** (sic) is dressed in a woven poncho with rope tassels. Around his shoulders he wears an antique silk shawl. The Hierophant is seated in the same wooden chair as The High Priestess but the doorway is open to signify the presence and accessibility of knowledge and wisdom. The Hierophant holds a long, thin wooden cross with three crosspieces or arms; the top two arms and the upright pole are decorated at the ends with small jewels. With two fingers of his upraised right hand The Hierophant gives the sign of benediction. **6 Lovers** are two nude figures, a young man and woman, shown in a garden at sunrise, the rays of the sun breaking through the tree branches. The long-haired woman stands before a small fruited tree. In the sky appears an ornate angle frieze. **8 Strength** depicts a heavy-set young woman holding the collar of her Great Pyrenees dog. The woman wears a globe amulet around her neck. In the background are the Blue Ridge Mountains of North Carolina. **10 Wheel of Fortune** depicts the Taro wheel surrounded by the signs of the four evangelists and four elements; man represents the element of water, the eagle represents air, the lion symbolizes fire and the bull stands for earth.

Third row: **12 Hanged Man** is dressed in a sweater, jeans and leather boots. He hangs by a rope tied to his legs from a pine tree, the traditional hanging tree described by Frazer in The Golden Bough. The Hanged Man's upper torso rests against a clematis vine that grows at the base of the tree. Thin rays of light emanate as a nimbus around his head. **15 Devil** holds a flaming torch pointing to the ground. The fingers of his upraised right hand are spread in a V sign, the reverse of The Hierophant and suggesting malediction in contrast to benediction. In the palm of his open hand appears an inverted triangle. The Devil's hair forms two horns, and his face and feet are blotched with black spots. He wears a matted straw loincloth and crouches on a pedestal set in front of a white sheet. **17 Star** is a nude figure on one knee. She bends over a pool of rippling water. In the sky are seven small and one large star, all eight-pointed, similar to those found in the same card in the Rider-Waite deck. **19 Sun** is a nude blond girl-child riding a horse in a fenced-in pasture. The face of the sun rising above the trees is a joyous young woman with curly golden hair; the sweeping arc of the treetops suggests large wings.

Bottom row: The **eight of swords** depicts the photographer, Bea Nettles, blindfolded and bound with cord. She wears a white gauze robe and stands next to a brick column and ridged cinderblock wall. In the foreground appear the shadows of eight swords. The **queen of pentacles** shows the photographer sitting in a rocking chair. She wears a long dress decorated with white stars. From a velvet headband hangs a small cross and she holds a large pentacle in her lap. The **ten of pentacles** depicts a young married couple with their blond girl-child. They are at the doorway to their home with two Irish setters. The open screen door is decorated with ten pentacles. The **knight of cups** is a fair-haired young man wearing a peasant shirt and heavy wool cloak. In his right hand he holds aloft a metal goblet. Across the horse's mane is a small woven Greek cross, each arm of the same length.

Muchery Astrological Tarot Designed under the direction of Georges Muchery, this pack seeks to combine the advantages of astrology and tarot. It comprises twelve Major Arcana and thirty-six Minor Arcana cards and is a complete departure from the traditional tarot deck. The twelve Major Arcana cards are (top row) I Ascendant represents the consultant; the Ascending Node depicts a young girl raising aloft a torch, the Descending Node is a dragon's tail; The Part of Fortune depicts a winged wheel; The Sun is illustrated as Apollo in the prime of youth, the reverse showing the Day Luminary shining in the heavens. Middle row: The Moon depicts the goddess of night and, in reverse, moon in the nocturnal darkness of the sky; Mercury is a youthful figure carrying the caduceus or magic wand and the reverse depicts the symbol of Mercury; Venus is a nude, lithe figure; Mars is a helmeted, bearded warrior with pike in hand. Bottom row: Jupiter is sitting upon his throne and presiding over the nations; Saturn is a taciturn old man holding the scythe and hourglass; Uranus is a dejected man in a moment of meditation; Neptune stands before the sea, a trident in one hand.

The Encyclopedia of Tarot

The New Tarot Deck Issued in 1974 by William J. Hurley, Rae Hurley and John A. Horler, the New Tarot deck contains bold designs in black-and-white line drawings with a ground-reversal effect. The imagery was drawn by Horler, using a combination of modern, traditional, Egyptian, Tahitian, religious and mythological influences. The pictures reflect the archetypes of many ancient myths popularized by such authors as Joseph Campbell and Robert Graves. Gestalt principles of unified configurations are illustrated throughout the cards. The Major Arcana cards are numbered and without titles. The Minor Arcana cards are illustrated and numbered. The deck is reduced to standard poker size instead of the larger size common to most tarot cards. Top row: *The Fool, I The Magician, II The High Priestess, III The Empress, 4 The Emperor.* Second row: *5 The Hierophant, 6 The Lovers, VII The Chariot, 8 Justice, IX The Hermit.* Third row: *X Wheel of Fortune, XI Strength, XII The Hanged Man, XIII Death, XIV Temperance.* Fourth row: *XV The Devil, XVI The Tower, XVII The Star, XVIII The Moon, XIX The Sun.* Bottom row: *XX Judgment, XXI The World, king of swords, king of staves and queen of cups.*

Collection of the author

The New Tarot for the Aquarian Age The designs in this tarot pack by John Cooke, assisted by Rosalind Sharp, seek to project standard tarot into the modern age. First issued in 1968, this tarot set is also known as The Book of T and The New Tarot. The Major Arcana cards are depicted with stark realism and some of them are almost macabre in their allegorical imagery. The Major Arcana are unnumbered and titled in English. Top row: Nameless-One (The Fool) depicts a naked figure holding a book while nearby stands a two-headed cat-dog and overhead hovers a spider. Changer (The Magician) stands on a sphere with arms extended, one palm facing up and holding a flower, the other palm down. An eagle rests on his shoulder after having drawn blood, and spread on the ground in front of the sphere on a cloth of gold are a stone, a curved blade, a two-headed serpent and a pear. Mother (High Priestess) depicts a female figure astride two pillars. She holds a thunderbolt in her right hand and a flower in her other hand. Her robes are spread by two majestic birds and she is crowned by two serpents beneath a large wavy symbol. Feeler (The Empress) is a female figure who stands with open arms, her long golden tresses encircling her breasts. She is flanked by two cypress trees and the sign of Cancer hovers over her head. The remaining cards shown are (second row) Actor (The Emperor), Victorious One (Charioteer), Donor (Justice), Seeker (The Hermit); (third row) Royal Maze (Wheel of Fortune), Hanging Man (The Hanged Man), Reverser (Temperance), Virgin (The World); (fourth row) king of blades, page of serpents, knight of stones and queen of pears.

Nordic Tarot *The designs of this tarot pack, circa 1960, were drawn by Paul Mathison and are described by Rolla K. Nordic in* The Tarot Shows the Path. *The black ink line drawings feature the court figures in ornate garments. The Major Arcana cards are numbered in Roman numerals, the pip cards in Arabic.*

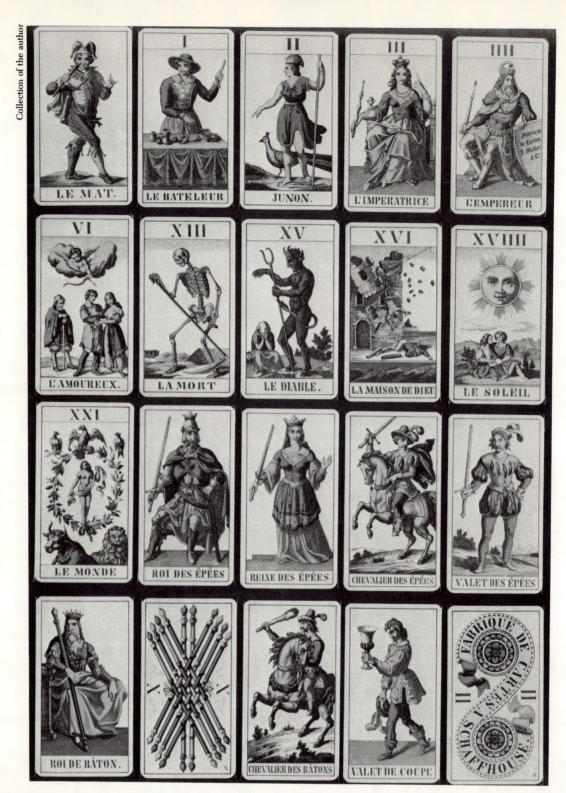

1JJ Swiss Tarot Issued by AG Muller & Cie, Switzerland, and U.S. Games Systems, Inc., New York. Major Arcana card II is entitled Junon instead of The Female Pope and includes a peacock, the symbol of Juno. XV Le Diable depicts a naked devil with wild eyes, hooked nose, horned ears, taloned hands, hooved feet and a long tail standing above a remorseful woman who holds her face in her hands. The 1JJ tarot pack is one of the most popular tarot decks today in America and Europe. Top row: Le Mat *(The Fool)*, I Le Bateleur *(The Magician or Juggler)*, II Junon *(Juno)*, III L'Impératrice *(The Empress)*, IIII L'Empereur *(The Emperor)*. Second row: VI L'Amoureux *(The Lovers)*, XIII La Mort *(Death)*, XV Le Diable *(The Devil)*, XVI La Maison de Dieu *(The House of God or The Lightning-Struck Tower)*, XVIIII Le Soleil *(The Sun)*. Third row: XXI Le Monde *(The World)*, Roi des Épées *(king of swords)*, Reine des Épées *(queen of swords)*, Chevalier des Épées *(knight of swords)*, Valet des Épées *(page of swords)*. Bottom row: Roi de Baton *(king of batons)*, ten of batons, Chevalier des Batons *(knight of batons)*, Valet de Coupe *(page of cups)*, two of coins. A complete description of the 1JJ Swiss Tarot deck is contained in the book Tarot Cards For Fun and Fortune-Telling *(1970)*.

Piatnik/Pointner Tarot Designed by Professor Rudolf Pointner, Graz, and published in 1974 by Ferd. Piatnik & Sohne, Vienna. The Major Arcana cards contain graffiti designs with ornate decorations throughout the pictures on each card. The cards shown are (top row) Le Mat *(The Fool)*; I Le Bateleur *(The Magician)* dressed in top hat and dinner jacket; VII Le Chariot *(The Chariot)* depicts a racing car with the inscription "antimony;" VIII La Justice *(Justice)*. Middle row: L'Hermite *(The Hermit)*; X La Roue de Fortune *(The Wheel of Fortune)*; XI La Force *(Strength)* depicts a weight lifter with barbells raised above his head and the numerals "1000" on his T-shirt; XII Le Pendu *(The Hanged Man)*. Bottom row: XIII La Mort *(Death)*; XVIII La Lune *(The Moon)*; XIX Le Soleil *(The Sun)*; XXI Le Monde *(The World)*.

Rider-Waite Tarot Designed by Pamela Colman Smith under the direction of Arthur Edward Waite and first issued by Rider & Company in London in 1910. Reissued in 1970 by U.S. Games Systems, Inc., New York, Hutchinson Publishing Group Ltd., London, and AG Muller & Cie, Switzerland. Other versions issued by University Press, New York, and Albano Productions, California. Miniature Rider-Waite tarot deck issued by U.S. Games Systems; the World's Tiniest Rider-Waite tarot deck issued by Merrimack Publishing Corp. The artist, Pamela Colman Smith, was an American who grew up in Jamaica and went to London where she became a member of The Order of the Golden Dawn. Working under the initiative and supervision of Arthur Edward Waite, she created the designs that became immensely popular along with Waite's book, The Pictorial Key to the Tarot. An important departure in Waite's deck as compared to typical tarot packs is the transposition of Strength and Justice. Waite, probably without adequate justification, transposed VIII Justice with XI Strength so that in the Waite pack these two cards are VIII Strength and XI Justice. In the Major Arcana series XIII Death is depicted in full armor astride a white horse and XIX The Sun is a naked child holding a large banner while riding bareback on a white horse. In the sequence of the Major Arcana cards Waite placed The Fool before I The Magician, whereas Eliphas Lévi and Papus sought to place The Fool as card number XXI, after XX Judgment and before XXI The World. The World was sometimes designated number XXII when The Fool was assigned number XXI. The attributions of the letters in the Hebrew alphabet to the twenty-two Major Arcana cards as designated by Waite, in contrast to Lévi, Papus and Oswald Wirth, is shown in the table on page 16. The Rider-Waite pack probably owes much of its success to the descriptive pictures on the forty pip cards that facilitate card interpretations.

Interestingly, both the Rider-Waite tarot pack, and the Royal Fez tarot pack designed by Michael Hobdell that closely follows the Smith-Waite designs, present a continuous story through the sequence of the cards in each suit. The three highest court cards in the suit of swords comprise a family of father, mother and eldest son. The king of swords is the father, the queen is the mother, and the son is the knight. A young lad in servitude to the knight appears as the page. In the ten of swords the son is killed and the nine of swords shows a grieving sister sitting up in bed after a dream has revealed to her the terrible fate of her brother. The sister seeks to revenge her brother's death, and in the eight of swords she is captured and shown bound and blindfolded. In the seven of swords the page appears with swords symbolizing that help is on its way, and in the six of swords the sister and her young son are rescued by the page, who is also her lover. The page is now a warrior, and in the five of swords he is shown with the swords of his craft. In time, the page is also stricken by the sword and killed, four of swords, which causes much sadness as evidenced by the broken heart pierced by three swords in the three of swords. The two of swords shows the widow in mourning with swords of defiance and her eyes blindfolded to the way of peace, for she seeks revenge. The ace of swords emerges from a cloud, emphasizing that those who live by the sword are apt to die by it.

The suit of staves or clubs depicts the story of a family divided between the traditional ways and modern methods. Its moral is that harmony and progress are best attained when the old and new work together. The suit of cups reveals the paths to happiness and the search of two brothers for companionship. The suit of coins relates the story of a wealthy family and the temptations and alternatives afforded them by the luxuries of wealth.

The Encyclopedia of Tarot

Royal Fez Tarot Suit of swords from the Royal Fez Moroccan tarot pack. Each suit reveals a story, depicted in scenes from King to ace.

Royal Fez Moroccan Tarot Issued by AG Muller & Cie, Switzerland, and U.S. Games Systems, Inc., under license from Rigel Press Ltd., London. This pack was conceived by Roland Berrill and painted by Michael Hobdell. The Major Arcana cards are Arabic-numbered in a panel at the bottom, but there are no titles on any cards. The pip cards contain symbolic pictures similar to those of the Rider-Waite tarot pack. Top row: *The Fool, 1 The Magician, 2 The High Priestess, 3 The Empress, 4 The Emperor.* Second row: *5 The Hierophant, 6 The Lovers, 7 The Chariot, 8 Strength, 9 The Hermit.* Third row: *10 The Wheel of Fortune, 11 Justice, 12 The Hanged Man, 13 Death, 14 Temperance.* Bottom row: *15 The Devil, nine of swords, three of clubs, four of cups, five of coins.*

274

Sheridan/Douglas Tarot   Designs by David Sheridan, issued by Mendragora Press, London. The cards are described in *The Tarot* by Alfred Douglas. Pip cards portray symbolic pictures. The cards are printed in bold solid colors and the faces of some of the figures, such as The Fool, have an innocent and elflike appearance.

Spanish Tarot Reprint published by Heraclio Fournier, Spain, based on an early-eighteenth-century Italian tarot deck. The trumps are titled in English and Spanish, the courts in Spanish only. The Devil has an extra face on his stomach and eyes at his knees. The smile of The Sun appears distorted.

The Encyclopedia of Tarot

Collection of the artist

THE FOOL Beginning of an adventure. Enthusiasm. Initiative. New school or job. Unlimited possibilities. Thoughtlessness. Carelessness. Extravagance. Folly. Obsession.

Reversed: Faulty choice. Bad decision. Apathy. Hesitation. Indecision. Failure to diligently proceed. Ignoring opportunities. Shyness.

I THE MAGICIAN Creativity. Free will. Self-reliance. Skill. Spontaneity. Willpower. Self-confidence. A good salesman. Dexterity. Ingenuity. Deception. Trickery. Sleight of hand.

Reversed: Weakness of will. Ineptitude. Insecurity. Disquiet. Delay. Lack of imagination. Willpower applied to evil ends. Disgrace.

III THE EMPRESS Feminine progress. Action. Fertility. Marriage. Mother. Sister. Wife. Girl friend. Feminine influence. Female guiles. The motivation behind a successful partner.

Reversed: Vacillation. Inaction. Lack of concentration. Anxiety. Loss of material possessions. Vanity. Delay in progress.

IIII THE EMPEROR Worldly power. Accomplishment. Confidence. Father. Brother. Husband. Male influence. Wealth. Maturity. Stability. Authority. Leadership. Conviction.

Reversed: Immaturity. Ineffectiveness. Lack of strength. Indecision. Weak character. Failure to control petty emotions.

V THE HIEROPHANT Ritualism. Goodness. Kindness. Compassion. Well—meaning person. Platonic friend. Inactivity. Lack of conviction. Timidity. Captive to one's own ideas.

Reversed: Over-kindness. Foolish exercise of generosity. Repeated errors. Susceptibility. Vulnerability. Frailty. Renunciation.

VI THE LOVERS Love. Beauty. Perfection. Harmony. Trust. Honor. Beginning of a romance or friendship. Deep feeling. Freedom of emotion. Testing of sincerity. Marriage.

Reversed: Unreliability. Failure to meet the test. Separation. Frustration. Interference by others. Fickleness. Unwise plans.

VII THE CHARIOT Fortitude. Perseverance. Major effort. Possible voyage or journey. Escape. Rushing to decision. Trouble. Adversity. Conflicting influence. Turmoil. Vengeance.

Reversed: Failure. Defeat. Sudden collapse of plans. Conquered. Overwhelmed. Failure to face reality. Time to rest. Unexpected loss.

VIIII THE HERMIT Counsel. Knowledge. Solicitude. Self-illumination. Prudence. Discretion. Caution. Vigilance. Circumspection. Self-denial. Withdrawal. Regression. Desertion.

Reversed: Imprudence. Hastiness. Rashness. Immaturity. Foolish act. Incorrect advice. Failure resulting from inactivity. Dullness.

X WHEEL OF FORTUNE Destiny. Fortune. Fate. Outcome. Advancement for better or worse. Culmination. Conclusion. Approaching the end of a problem. Unexpected events may occur.

Reversed: Failure. Ill luck. Broken sequence. Unexpected bad fate. Outside influences not contemplated. Wait and then try again.

XII THE HANGED MAN Suspension. Transition. Change. Reversal of one's way of life. Apathy. Boredom. Abandonment. Renunciation. Sacrifice. Readjustment. Regeneration. Rebirth.

Reversed: Unwillingness to make necessary effort. Preoccupation with the ego. False prophecy. Useless sacrifice. Ineptitude.

XIII DEATH Transformation. Clearing away the old to make way for the new. Alteration. Abrupt change. Bad omen. Illness. Mishap. Loss of financial security. Bad investment.

Reversed: Stagnation. Immobility. Slow or partial change. Inertia. Ending of a friendship.

XVI THE FALLING TOWER Complete and sudden change. Abandonment of past relationships. End of a long friendship. Unexpected events. Downfall. Undoing. Loss of stability. Setback.

Reversed: Continued oppression. Following old ways. Living in a rut. Unhappy marriage. Inability to affect any worthwhile change.

XVIIII THE SUN Satisfaction. Accomplishment. Favorable social relationships. Love. Joy. Devotion. Engagement. Happy marriage. Pleasure in daily existence. Exuberance. Sincerity.

Reversed: Unhappiness. Loneliness. Broken engagement or marriage. Cancelled plans. Clouded future. Lack of friendship.

XX JUDGMENT Atonement. Judgment. Need to repent and forgive. Time to account for our actions. Improvement. Development. Promotion. Outcome of past effort. Rebirth.

Reversed: Delay. Frustration. Failure to face facts. Indecision. Procrastination. Theft. Alienation of affection. Deep worry.

XXI THE WORLD Perfection. Recognition. Honor. Ultimate change. Fulfillment. Capability. Triumph in undertakings. Just rewards from hard work. Success. Ultimate change.

Reversed: Imperfection. Failure to complete the task one starts. Lack of vision. Disappointment. Futile effort. Broken heart.

Starter Tarot The cards in the Starter tarot deck consist of twenty-two Major Arcana based upon traditional designs from the Tarot of Marseilles pack with modifications by George Bennett. Each card contains Roman number, title and meanings in both upright and reversed positions for reading the cards.

Tantric Tarot Collage assembled in London in 1976 by Penny Slinger, Nik Douglas and Meryl White, based upon the Tantric tradition of the transformation center of the human body. The cards, also called Secret Dakini Oracle cards, reveal the secret teachings of mystical yoga through the portrayal of sixty-four archetypal energies in contemporary symbols. The complete pack of Tantric tarot totals sixty-five cards; twenty-two correspond to the twenty-two Major Arcana, and forty, divided into four groups of ten, correspond to air, fire, water and earth or the forty numeral pip cards in the playing card pack. The final three cards represent Time and are called Past, Present and Future.

Top row: 0 The Joker corresponds to The Fool in traditional tarot packs. The Joker is depicted standing on the orb of the sun, his back to the earth as viewed from space. He is in the form of Brahma, the Creator, with eleven heads signifying the unity of all things, and he wears the traditional dunce's hat ornamented with a lotus blossom, the symbol of spiritual Enlightenment. The body of The Joker is composed of a double swastika symbol, suggesting the combination of positive and negative, and he possesses movement in both directions. He holds a pen in his right hand to show that he is the writer of destiny and the maker of the Akashic records. His left hand holds a rosary of pearls indicating his concern that the links in the chain of destiny be maintained. The rest of his body is cosmic, bearing auspicious symbols and containing all worlds. His right foot rests on a volume of the I-Ching, the Chinese Book of Changes, upon which is a die bearing the number of Saturn, indicating that The Joker rules over fate and destiny. His left foot playfully kicks the ball of the world, for he is Lord of the Game.

Card 1 Mercury corresponds to The Magician. Two serpents are shown entwined around a central staff or wand of Mercury, the whole forming the mystic caduceus, the symbol of magical transformation. The snakes wind around the staff three and one-half times, resembling the coiled Kundalini serpent and suggesting that energy emanates from the base or sexual center. The staff symbolizes the backbone, the spine, through which the raw energy of the serpent travels and is transformed. The aim of awakening Kundalini energy is to draw the most potent inner forces upward so they can pierce and illuminate the psychic subtle centers—known as Chakras—and finally be distilled as droplets of wisdom in the region of the head, which is the home of the higher intellect. This card represents the primordial energy—the inner Shakti—transformed alchemically into the elixir depicted as fluid mercury and harnessed as four stable pools (related to the four main psychic centers at the navel, heart, throat and head) in the subtle body. This card is also a symbol of the realization and fulfillment stage of Tantric practice, as is suggested by the crowns on the heads of the snakes. The background is revealed as a black sun, suggesting the mystery of energy transformed into something beyond worldly concepts.

Card 2 Isis corresponds to The High Priestess. The head and shoulders of Isis, also known as Ishtar the High Priestess, are seen as if rising through a nebulous veil of a night sky. She is considered to be guarding the doorway to occult knowledge, her position being that of a wisdom holder, attendant and guardian of the Great Secret Dakini realm. The night sky symbolizes the limitless nature and awe-inspiring qualities of her territory, the wisdom that she guards so carefully. Traditionally, Isis is portrayed as revealing only her bared head and shoulders, for, like the sleeping Venus, if her full nakedness and potency are exposed prematurely or without adequate psychic preparation, there is the danger of misunderstanding the subtleties of her knowledge. Her two eyes are rubies, indicating her firelike inner nature, and at her forehead there is an open third eye, which points to her function as a distiller of occult wisdom and indicates her deep intuitive penetration. She wears ornaments signifying her exalted position and on her head are two golden horns forming the shape of a crescent moon that is upturned, indicating that she catches drops of wisdom from the cosmos.

Card 3 Scarlet Woman corresponds to The Empress. The two large eyes of the Scarlet Woman as a goddess stare out over a cluster of small red flowers. In the foreground there is a large open red poppy, relating her to the earth in its fruitfulness and fecundity. She represents the threefold play of the goddess or the Shakti in her sensual and sexual aspects through her magnetic form. She is the seductive Yogini—the female aspect of yoga fulfillment, which teaches that one should not hesitate to perform potent acts provided one is prepared to handle the consequences. The red color

Collection of the author

indicates the sulphurous nature of her energy as the female principle in the alchemical process of self-realization. The open poppy is a manifestation of the womb of the goddess open in mystic invitation. On her brow is a ruby, related to her firelike transcendental nature; she wears her potency as an ornament, so sure is she of her position of authority.

    Middle row: 4 The Hot Seat corresponds to The Emperor. An ornately carved wooden throne is depicted in space, surrounded by solar flares and balls of fire. The throne itself has a base of carved lions, symbolizing the position of power and responsibility of any person sitting on its exalted place. From the seat of the throne great flames issue forth, indicating tremendous masculine transforming power, which is related to spiritual and secular authority. It is the seat of the Master of the Universe, and persons wishing to hold such a position should prepare for the responsibility. Under the seat is depicted the mystic Stone of Scone, over which many battles have been fought and many lives lost; it has a practical function of support once the flames have been overcome.

Card 10 Wheel of Great Time corresponds to The Wheel of Fortune. This card bears the number 10, signifying the completion of a cycle of time and the coming together of the digits "1," representing unity, and "0," representing the void from which all things emerge and into which all things dissolve. In the center of a clock face the form of Mahakali, the Great Time Mother, is depicted in divine union with her consort Shiva Mahakala, the Great Time Father. In one hand she holds a sword, symbolizing her function as the power of Shakti that cuts through the three times of Past, Present and Future. Her other two hands hold a skull bowl filled with blood, symbolizing the integration of renunciation and compassion. She has three arms, indicating that she rules over the three times of Past, Present and Future. The fire indicates the burning of past Karma in the completion of a cycle of time, and the burning and transforming of destiny itself. The eyes and skulls around the clock face denote that Mahakali rules over the cycles of lives beyond death, and that she is the guardian of the Great Time Wheel, which includes but is not limited to linear time structures. The eye at the center is the all-seeing eye of Horus, reminding us that there is a constant, unchanging center to all changing phenomena. Two eyes take fluid form at the base of the circle, representing the fluidity and mutability of the world of fate and fortune.

Card 13 Death/Transfiguration corresponds to Death. This card bears the number 13; the combination of "1," unity, and "3," trinity, indicate the perpetuity of the creative movement, and the position at the center of all time cycles. A skeleton is shown in the traditional pose of Death the Reaper, but here he holds a staff instead of a scythe, symbolizing the spinal column through which the psychic centers or Chakras are threaded. The branch sprouting from the staff suggests that organic life is still present and there is a possibility of regeneration. Cosmic white light emanates from behind the head of the skeleton to show that death, the loss of the physical temple of the soul, is an experience that brings one a step nearer the pure light of consciousness. The card depicts the transcendent spirit, freed from the body, renewed and reborn. Beneath the feet of Death are the things of the world, abandoned.

Card 15 The Ally corresponds to The Devil. Standing on the shores of a lake of molten lava, the figure of The Ally is depicted breathing out fire from jaws filled with spikelike teeth, symbolizing his power to destroy and devour. In both hands he holds double hooks, revealing his function as a catcher of men (twofold, as both flesh and spirit) and also tormentor. His body and head have all the marks of the lower orders of beings: ears, horns, scales, etc., which form his armor. His head is adorned with six grotesque bestial heads, his epaulets are animal heads and his nether regions are composed of another demonic face. His function here is a destroyer of enemies; only those who have something to hide or fear can be caught.

Bottom row: Card 16 The Holocaust corresponds to The Tower. A house is depicted in a state of demolition by fire. Rubble is heaped on the ground as the material edifice of reality crumbles and burns. This is an unpredicted event, breaking down the ego roles of everyday existence. As the transforming fire of the base center takes control, along with the flames, there bursts forth from the building a cascade of eyes, symbolizing the loss of ego and the shedding of preconceptions brought about by the sudden traumatic event.

Card 19 The Phoenix corresponds to The Sun. From an alchemical fire of transformation there arises an eternal flame consuming the past and all illusion. From the flame is born a cosmic couple in divine union, the Celestial Buddha Vajradhara and his consort, rising as a phoenix from the ashes of the temporal body. The cosmic couple are blue, symbolizing the complementary aspects of wisdom and means in the celestial void, and are winged to show their transcendent spiritual nature. They are the alchemically produced philosopher's stone, described in the classical texts of the school of Agrippa as "fed with the fire of the Father and the ether of the Mother, the first of which may be understood allegorically as 'food' and the second as 'drink,' without which the phoenix will not attain to full glory." The text continues: "feed thy bird and it will move in the nest and then rise up like a star of the firmament." On the Secret Dakini card the red star ruby suggests this concept.

Card 20 Transformation corresponds to Judgment. The lower part of this card depicts awakened serpent power, the Kundalini energy commencing a journey through the subtle centers of the body. The lower part of the card shows the raw Shakti as energy in its gross form, and the upper part shows the same energy in a transformed and elevated state. The intersection of the two states is marked by a rainbow band of light, indicating the threshold where striving becomes attainment. On the rainbow the Cosmic Goddess, known as Chinnamasta, is seated in the lotus posture. She has four hands and her body is the color of the inner central psychic subtle nerve. She represents the channeling of energy upward to the fulfillment stage where psychic balance is all-important. She holds a Kundalini serpent, which indicates that she has harnessed the raw energy of the base center; a skull bowl filled with blood, symbolizing her position of renunciation and compassion; an elixir fruit, suggesting the transformation into the realm of eternity; and a plate supporting her own decapitated head, symbolizing her egoless self-transcendence. From her neck flow three streams of blood, indicating that the three main psychic arteries are opened to receive the fulfillment. Around her neck she wears a garland of skulls, telling of her evocation of the subtle primordial matrix vibrations of which the whole universe is comprised. In the position of her head, at the neck, there is placed a fine sapphire, meaning that the Original Void is inherent in her. This card is the visual representation of the process of alchemy in balance and is reflected in the Transformation Body of Fulfillment.

Card 21 Earth Bound corresponds to The World. The surface of the earth is viewed from space. Above the horizon the orb of a new earth is seen as if suspended in the darkness of the night. This symbolizes the beginning inherent in every completed cycle. As we step out of one situation, beyond existing roots, as suggested by the surface of the earth, the next moment manifests itself in new perspective.

Taro Adivinhatorio The designs in this Brazilian tarot pack published in São Paulo in 1974 are based upon the series created by Gabriel Goulinat that originally appeared in 1909 in Le Tarot Divinatoire by Papus (page 211). The left side of each card has a letter of the alphabet in Portuguese, Hebrew, Sanskrit and Egyptian. Along the right side of each card is an astrological sign; the bottom of each card includes the card's title and a brief interpretation. Top row: 1 O Mago (*The Magician*), 2 A Papisa (*The Popess*), 3 A Imperatriz (*The Empress*), 4 O Imperador (*The Emperor*), 5 O Papa (*The Pope*). Second row: 6 O Namorado (*The Lovers*), 7 O Carro (*The Chariot*), 8 A Justiça (*Justice*), 9 O Eremita (*The Hermit*), 10 A Roda da Fortuna (*The Wheel of Fortune*). Third row: 11 A Fôrça (*Strength*), 12 O Enforcado (*The Hanged Man*), 13 A Morte (*Death*), 14 A Temperança (*Temperance*), 15 O Diabo (*The Devil*). Fourth row: 16 Casa de Deus (*House of God*), 17 A Estrèla (*The Star*), 18 A Lua (*The Moon*), 19 O Sol (*The Sun*), 20 O Julgamento (*Judgment*). Bottom row: 21 O Louco (*The Fool*), 22 O Mundo (*The World*), 23 Senhor do Bastao (*king of batons*), 24 Senhora do Bastao (*queen of batons*), 61 Quatro Gladios (*four of swords*).

20th Century Tarot These cards were issued by Skor-Mor Corp., California. The black line drawings are depicted against a shaded gray background. The Major Arcana and court cards bear titles in English. The majority of the figures are shown in profile rather than full face. Some of the facial expressions appear whimsical, such as 0 The Fool and 4 The Emperor, or innocent, such as 2 The High Priestess and 5 The Hierophant. Card 12 The Hanged Man depicts a man hanging by a noose around his neck. Card 13 Death is a shrouded figure and 14 Temperance depicts a knight slashing a cup down the middle with his sword. Card 16 The Tower shows a giant hand ripping off the top of the tower.

Vandenborre Tarot Cards from the 1974 reprint of the eighteenth-century Vandenborre tarot pack (see also page 145). XIII La Mort *(Death)* wears a cape; XIIII La Tempérence *(Temperance)* is pouring water from an urn in her right hand into an urn on the ground; XV Le Diable *(The Devil)* has numerous eyes; XVI La Foudre *(The Lightning)* shows lightning striking a burning tree instead of the customary tower; XVII Le Toille *(The Star)* shows a male figure seated before a three-storied tower, observing the stars with an astronomical instrument; XVIII La Lune *(The Moon)* depicts a seated figure next to a palm tree instead of the customary two baying dogs, or one dog and a wolf, between two towers; XIX Le Soleil *(The Sun)* shows a figure on horseback holding a flag; XX Le Jugement *(Judgment)*; XXI Le Monde *(The World)* depicts a nude figure holding outstretched a large cape while standing on a large globe of the world divided into three sections—the moon and stars in the heavens, the sun, and the earth with a castle or walled city—and topped with an ornate cross; Le Fou *(The Fool)*, numbered XXII instead of unnumbered; Roi des Épées *(king of swords)* and ace of coins with identification of the card maker: "Swiss cards fabricated by F. I. Vandenborre, card maker, Brussels." The alternating black and white border design on all the cards, and the upper panel of two lions on either side of the Roman numeral XXI in The World card, are somewhat similar to the seventeenth-century tarot cards (page 134) by an unknown card maker.

Visconti-Sforza Tarocchi   *Reproduction in 1975 by Grafica Gutenberg, in cooperation with U.S. Games Systems, Inc., New York, of the extant* tarocchi *deck, circa mid-fifteenth century. A complete description of this beautifully illuminated deck will be found elsewhere in this book.* Top row: *The Hanged Man, Death, Temperance, The Devil.* Middle row: *The Falling Tower, The Star, The Moon, The Sun.* Bottom row: *Judgment, The World, king of swords, queen of coins.*

Oswald Wirth Tarot Reproduction in 1975 by U.S. Games Systems, Inc., under license from Tchou Productions, Paris. This deck is based upon Wirth's book Le Tarot des Imagiers du Moyen Age, written in 1927. Trumps contain Hebrew letters on lower right. The deck is printed in unusual metallic colors. Note the grotesque figure of The Fool and the Egyptian influence in the two sphinxes in The Chariot. The Emperor wears a helmet instead of a crown, while Justice wears a crown. A serpent appears in front of The Hermit.

Xultun Tarot Pronounced Shoul-toun, *the Xultun tarot deck was painted by Peter Balin based upon sketches drawn by the artist at Tikal, Guatemala, during the summer of 1972. Much of the card imagery reflects the beliefs and customs of pre-Columbian Indians, especially the Maya.*

The twenty-two Major Arcana cards are without titles; however, at the extreme bottom center of each card is a number based upon the traditional Mayan numbering system, which uses a dot for one unit and a bar or dash for five units. When positioned in sequence, the entire mosaic of twenty-two Major Arcana cards and two decoration cards reveals a complete scene with the glyphs and designs on each card interlocking with the remainder of the design on the adjoining cards.

Six Mayan figures—The Fool, The Sorcerer, The Priestess, The Consort, The Ruler and The Priest—are taken from wooden lintels principally found at Temple III at Tikal. The upper row of glyphs running across the bottom of three Major Arcana cards—The Consort, The Ruler and The Priest—is also patterned after lintels at Temple III; the lower row of glyphs comes from Stela 26, presently housed at the Tikal Museum. Additional designs are taken from Stelas 1 and 31. The sequence of the Major Arcana cards is based upon Waite; the eighth numbered card is titled Cactus instead of Strength, and the eleventh numbered card is titled The Balance instead of Justice. According to Balin, there are many links between the Xultun tarot deck and the teachings of Don Juan, the Yaqui sorcerer and man of knowledge in several books by Carlos Castaneda.

Each of the Major Arcana cards, excepting The Fool and The Sorcerer, is named after one day of the Mayan month and represents one of the twenty steps to enlightenment that The Fool must take in order to reach attainment. The Fool and The Sorcerer are in reality the same person; The Fool begins his journey as The Priestess and travels through the experience and circumstances represented by each Major Arcana card until finally he fully understands himself and he returns as The Sorcerer.

Card titles are (top row) the Xultun decorative card, The Fool, who faces to the right; The Sorcerer, who faces to the left and suggests I The Magician of traditional tarot packs; the Tarot decorative card. The two decorative cards depict a hummingbird drinking from the nectar of a water lily; Second row: The Priestess; The Consort, instead of III The Empress found in traditional tarot; The Ruler for IIII The Emperor; The Priest for V The Hierophant; The Lovers. Third row: The Warrior instead of VII The Chariot; The Cactus for VIII Strength; The Sage for VIIII The Hermit; The Wheel for X The Wheel of Fortune; The Balance for XI Justice. Fourth row: The Hanged Man; The Dead Man for XIII Death; The Temperate Man for XIIII Temperance; The Bound Man for XV The Devil; The Divided Man for XVI The Tower. Bottom row: The Star; The Moon; The Sun; The Planet Venus for XX Judgment; The Planet Earth for XXI The World.

The day names in Yucatec dialect of the Mayan month and the Major Arcana cards to which they relate are as follows: Imix—The Priestess, Ik—The Consort, Akbal—The Ruler, Kan—The Priest, Chicchan—The Lovers, Cimi—The Warrior, Manik—The Cactus, Lamat—The Sage, Muluc—The Wheel, Oc—The Balance, Chuen—The Hanged Man, Eb—The Dead Man, Ben—The Temperate Man, Ix—The Bound Man, Men—The Divided Man, Cib—The Star, Caban—The Moon, Etz'nab—The Sun, Cauac—The Planet Venus, Ahau—The Planet Earth.

Top row: **The Fool** is a young person; he wears a crown of feathers decorated at the top with a large skull and at the back with a budding water lily. His feet are covered with the traditional Mayan leather sandals; the cummerbund around his waist is used to carry small objects and possessions. The white flower in his right hand symbolizes openness, while the sun in the background of this card and the adjoining card suggests the mysteries of the ancients, which may be visible but are often not fully comprehensible. The Fool stands upon the open mouth of a jaguar, indicating his confidence in the future and his willingness to start his journey as apprentice to The Sorcerer. **The Sorcerer** is taken from Stela 31 at Tikal. The Sorcerer stands at the source of all knowledge and that which is known—tonal—while facing toward The Fool and that which remains unknown—nagual. Both The Fool and The Sorcerer are the same person at different moments of experience. The Sorcerer is dressed in ceremonial costume and the girdle around his waist represents the yoke worn by players in the ceremonial Mayan ball game where players hit or propel a large solid rubber ball without touching the ball with hands or feet. The Sorcerer holds a magical wand of jade disks and a living staff. The white platform beneath him is taken from a bone drawing found at Tikal depicting a canoe carrying three men and four animals. The headdress of the man in the center of the canoe is the same headdress worn by The Fool. The four animals represent the four cycles of time prior to the present or fifth Maya cycle of man. The first cycle, represented by a fish, was creation based solely upon emotion, which could not survive alone and thus was destroyed. The second cycle, represented by the monkey, was creation based upon action; the third cycle, shown as a bird or parrot, was creation based upon the intellect; and the fourth cycle, represented by the jaguar, was creation based upon spirit. Each of these cycles could not survive alone and was dependent upon the arrival of the fifth cycle, of man, who controls the animals and maintains the proper balance between emotion, action, intellect and spirit. The young man at the front of the canoe and the old man at the back suggest the journey of life itself from youth to old age. The empty pot at the base of the mountain symbolizes all the emotions that have been drained from The Sorcerer during his arduous voyages.

Second row: The cards in this row deal with the spirit of man. **The Priestess** represents the bridge The Fool must cross in his journey through the tonal or known experiences in order to reach the knowledge of The Sorcerer. The Priestess sits on a throne between the black pillar of the conscious mind and the white pillar of the unconscious mind. She wears a crescent moon hat with feathers and her robe is decorated with circles of four dots representing the cycles of the past. Her canopy is made of straw thatch and she is surrounded by the fragrance of wisteria. **The Consort** sits upon a throne covered with a jaguar skin. Her massive headdress, taken from a lintel at Tikal, is decorated with jade beads

Collection of the artist

288

and green Quetzal feathers, symbolic of the richness of life. She holds a shield and the two darts of opposites, and between the shield and her chin is the lower jaw and tongue of a serpent. An elaborate red sash hangs across her lap and her feet are bare. The giant sun is the source of power, which she shares with The Ruler. **The Ruler** is taken from Stela I at Tikal Museum. The elaborate headdress is topped by a golden cup pouring Quetzal feathers. In his arms The Ruler clutches mexquimilli, the ceremonial bundle containing the bones and ashes of either his father or a revered person. He wears across his shoulders an immensely ornate back pack of light wood decorated with feathers and beads. His waist is decorated with colorful tassles hanging from a ball player's yoke. **The Priest** is taken from a lintel at Temple III. The Priest is the guardian of tradition; he is dressed as a jaguar, the fire animal, to represent the spirit of man, and on his head are three cups pouring Quetzal feathers. He holds a living staff with yellow tassles. Behind him are three colorful drapes hanging from an Itzamna mask representing the important Mayan deity. The three figures of The Consort, The Ruler and The Priest stand upon a framework of two rows of Maya glyphs. **The Lovers** depicts a young boy and girl holding a mirror indicating that they can know each other only by reflective images. The boy stands beneath a canopy attached to a living tree that is supported by a slab pillar. The tree possesses the knowledge he will learn from The Priest. The girl stands under a star-filled sky, suggesting she is open to new friendship.

Third row: The next five cards deal with the mind of man. **The Warrior** is based upon a drawing found in Codex Nuttall. The Warrior is seated in a litter and he wears a jaguar mask. Two savage jaguars, one black and the other white to represent opposites, are tied to the litter; although they bare their sharp teeth, they are under the control of the warrior. A large banner decorated with stars confirms the link between this card and The Priestess. **The Cactus** is taken from a bone drawing at Tikal Museum. A large cactus grows in a pot decorated with the design of a temple. The cactus represents endurance and it blossoms as well as provides a home for birds. **The Sage** is shown pointing upward toward an ornate lintel depicting two men in a canoe facing in opposite directions. In the center is the mask of Itzamna surrounded by water lilies. The Sage also points downward toward a large vessel burning with copal, food of the gods. Thus, The Sage indicates that the confusion of his life is now under control. The open doorway shows the path through the realm of the unconscious to the star-filled sky of the conscious. **The Wheel** contains designs taken from the Great Calendar Stone of the Aztecs originally found near the main temple enclosure at Tenochtitlan. The stone reveals the calendric knowledge of the Mayas and the legend of the four suns or cycles. The center mask depicts a man's face with his tongue hanging out. Behind the face is a glyph in the shape of St. Andrew's cross and representing movement, direction and the prophecy of the end of the world in a great earthquake or terrible cataclysm. The third underlying Mayan glyph—a pointed triangle above the face with two circles or zeros at each side—represents time. The combined glyphs—nahui ollin—symbolize the four cycles or suns previously destroyed in great cataclysms, and the present sun is the center. The twenty Mayan days are depicted by glyphs around the border of the inner stone; beneath the wheel a serpent swallows its tail. The white glyphs around the outer border of the wheel are taken from a ceremonial plate discovered in the grave of a high priest. The parrot atop the border symbolizes knowledge gained, memorized and repeated, yet not necessarily understood. The cat nurturing the kitten represents development and progress. The entire wheel is held fast between two stones suggesting that now is a great pool that is bound between the past when time began and the future when all things will end. **The Balance** is based upon the figure of a spear thrower carved along the

Major Arcana cards from Xultun tarot. Identification of each card by title and number corresponds to the illustration (opposite). The end cards on the top row are decorative cards which complete the composite painting.

		The Fool	The Sorcerer	
The Priestess	The Consort	The Ruler	The Priest	The Lovers
The Warrior	The Cactus	The Sage	The Wheel	The Balance
The Hanged Man	The Dead Man	The Temperate Man	The Bound Man	The Divided Man
The Star	The Moon	The Sun	The Planet Venus	The Planet Earth

side of Stela 31. The Balance depicts a judge wearing a Quetzal feather headdress and holding a sword made of wood and obsidian tips. The judge wears a helmet around his head that covers his mouth and suggests that true judgment requires action, not necessarily speech. The weighing pot hangs from only one side of the rigid beam in accordance with the needs of each man. The lightning-struck skull represents the loss that must result from any division or act of injustice.

Fourth row: *The cards in this row deal with emotions indicated by the flaming clouds that descend from The Sage card.* **The Hanged Man,** based upon an upright Toltec figure found in Codex Nuttall, depicts a figure hanging upside down between a gibbet consisting of a dead tree (the past) and a living tree with flowering branches (the now). The figure is tied securely at wrists and ankles. **The Dead Man** represents a way out of the present predicament and the beginning of a new circumstance. The flowers of the future spring up between the past, represented by the skulls upon which Death is balanced. The two darts carried by the skeleton symbolize the opposites of life and death and the beginning and end; the shield represents conciliation. The tied bundle of bones on the ground is related to the sacred ashes and bones held in the mexquimilli by The Ruler. **The Temperate Man** is taken from a lintel at Temple III; the figure is one of two acolytes standing before a priest. The figure's hair is bound in the style of corn silk. He is shown pouring star-filled water, representing his emotions. The sun glyph rises directly above his head and the rainbow provides his source of energy. This card is positioned after Death and confirms that rebirth is possible after one's emotions and substance have been drained. **The Bound Man** is taken from the decoration on an ornate vase at Tikal Museum. The man and woman are loosely bound to Xipe-Totec, god of sacrifice and liberation who holds a serpent and a torch in his outstretched hands. Xipe wears a mask of flayed skin and the lines on his face represent the seams of the mask cutting across his eyes. The tail of the feathered serpent, Quetzalcoatl, rises from The Planet Venus below them. **The Divided Man** shows a large temple with twenty-two steps of knowledge representing the twenty-two Major Arcana. The temple is struck by lightning emanating from the card of Justice. The Divided Man is the last card of the emotion series, which began as The Hanged Man of the past and ends in the now or present; both the past and the present are flung from the temple and separated from their previous ties. The temple contains a tower with the great eye of the ego in the center and the two eyes of the subconscious in the background. There are no stars in the sky and the open tunnel previously seen in The Sage card is now closed.

Bottom row: *The cards in this row deal with the physical life of man and his material existence.* **The Star** depicts a female figure sitting on a plinth or altar and pouring water from two vases. A macaw flies overhead and the star has eight points. The lower panel of this card and the remaining four cards in the bottom row depict a traditional Indian stepped fret. **The Moon** shows two erupting volcanoes in a deceptive light of flaming serpents. The eye-moon with its eight spikes is tempered by the star-filled water seeping down from The Temperate Man. **The Sun,** depicted by the Mayan glyph Etz'nab, means perfection attained. Four dots form the four past suns or cycles. Rays of energy burst forth from the center sun of the present to nourish the roots of the living tree growing down from The Temperate Man card. **The Planet Venus** is represented by the feathered Quetzalcoatl serpent surrounded by a halo. The two erupting volcanoes appear again, this time in the light of awareness and realization. **The Planet Earth** depicts the Yaqui or Toltec symbol of earth with eight living trees, an echo of the mirror previously seen in The Lovers card. The lightning of decision is grounded in the altar where a small vessel of burning copal adds its fragrance to the air. Across the altar lies the white flower of The Fool, left behind because now The Fool has entered the world of the tonal or The Sorcerer.

Yeager Tarot of Meditation From a surrealistic series of paintings of the Major Arcana cards by Marty Yeager.

Top row: 2 The High Priestess, with the horns of Isis protruding above her temples, sits erect on her throne in the midst of turbulent waters from a large waterfall. Two palm trees topped by open palms rise behind the throne; a veil hangs between the trees with a repeating design of red pomegranates against a green background. The High Priestess wears a wristwatch and holds a scroll in her left hand; on both her right arm and wrist she wears gold bands that match her collar, hair band and the oval frame surrounding the moon atop her hair. Her facial expression appears as a distorted male reflection in the water in front of her gown. Near her right hand is a translucent cross topped by a bird, and to her left, floating at an angle in the water, is the Egyptian symbol for The High Priestess. Additional cards shown are 3 The Empress, 4 The Emperor, 5 The Hierophant.

Second row: 7 The Chariot, is depicted as a young bare-chested figure drawn through the shallow water by two galloping horses, the darker horse representing material forces and the white horse symbolizing spiritual and ethereal forces. The charioteer wears around his neck a small vial containing sacred Hebrew words from the Torah and a gold coin with a dot in its center symbolizing the beginnings of time and Christian civilization. In his right hand the charioteer holds a long scepter topped with different geometric shapes. The chariot has four torches and in the front two torches are horizontal theatrical masks of a grinning, happy face and a saddened face. 9 The Hermit is depicted as an aged bearded figure wearing long white robes. He stands at the precipice of a jagged cliff above a misty gorge in a serene setting of snow-capped towering cliffs glistening in the moonlight beneath a star-studded sky. The Hermit holds in his right hand a tapered staff entwined by a snake, and in his left hand he carefully holds a glowing sphere of knowledge. 11 Strength is shown as a beautiful naked red-haired young woman who sits astride a large lion in a serene jungle. The symbol known as the eternal or infinite eight appears above her head. The lion's right paw rests on a floating blue sphere, symbol of the totality of one's own self. 14 Temperance.

Third row: 16 The Tower, 17 The Star, 18 The Moon, 19 The Sun.

Bottom row: 20 Judgement, 21 The World, king of wands, queen of cups.

Zigeuner Tarot Card designs by Walter Wegmuller, published 1975 by AG Muller & Cie, Switzerland. Rendered in a style described as phantastic popular art, the twenty-two Major Arcana cards were originally silk-screened in twenty-two different color tones; the Minor Arcana cards were prepared with felt-tipped pens. The designs are characterized by the application of small dots and dashes—pointillistic in style—that create an effect of luminosity. At the bottom of each card are two flowers; the left flower holds the Arabic number assigned to the card, the other flower contains the appropriate Hebrew letter. Between the flowers appears the hand-lettered title in German.

Top row: **0 Der Narr** (The Fool) depicts a bearded figure with head upraised toward the cosmos. The Fool perceives but he does not always understand. Droplets containing the earthly symbols of the Minor Arcana shower around him but The Fool fails to recognize the signs of reality. A serpent entwines the Fool's cap and the animal tearing at his legs simultaneously chases The Fool while also holding him back. The sagging tulip at the bottom right of the card, its cup facing down, indicates that the Fool is not totally aware of his freedom. The pennons on both sides of the card are composed of hanging balls decorated with esoteric gypsy symbols. **1 Der Gauklen** (The Magician) depicts a youthful figure holding a baton that contains a cosmic eye at the top to penetrate the future; the plant growing at the center of the baton represents the present and the roots at the bottom indicate the past. The cosmic egg on the table receives the energy of the Magician through his baton. At the center of the table beneath the four suit symbols flourish the roots of sustenance which nurture the suit symbols; beneath the roots is an embryo by which the Magician holds the power to create life. The tulip at the left is open and faces up—in contrast to the sagging flower in the Fool card—and confirms the unlimited possibilities commanded by the Magician who reigns over the past, present and future represented by three buds growing in the tulip. The sign of the eternal eight appears in the Magician's hat and in the shape of the table. On the Magician's chest is the cosmic eye and face of death evidencing that the Magician reigns over life and death. The cosmic snake entwines around the Magician's hat and the seven levels of knowledge and wisdom with their all-perceiving eyes emanate above him. **2 Hohepriesterin** (The High Priestess) depicts the sacred priestess beneath the cosmic egg and a large quarter moon. The High Priestess is the goddess of the night and the guardian of secrets. She wears a cosmic cape decorated with stars and she holds a long baton of two keys, one male and the other female, with a cosmic eye.

Middle row: **6 Die Entscheidung** (Decision or The Lovers) depicts a bearded man and two females. Cupid hovers overhead and a rainbow appears in the cosmic sky. The flower buds and pomegranates decorating the man's shirt symbolize spring, autumn and nature; the tree of life confirms the control he possesses over his own future. The tall flowers at the bottom of the card represent spring and autumn. The female figure on the right wears the cosmic band of shakti around her right ankle. The cosmic bands at the top and bottom of the card confirm the presence of four avenues of consciousness and the alternatives open to the man. **9 Der Weise** (The Hermit) is a bearded, cloaked figure beneath his third eye. The aura behind him symbolizes all the experiences of his past; the steps behind him, at the bottom of the card, represent the long road he has traveled. The Hebrew star in the Hermit's lantern symbolizes the powers of night and day that combine into the six-pointed star; the circle within the star is the symbol of manna, holy bread and spiritual nourishment of divine origin. **18 Der Mond** (The Moon) has two faces, the face unseen during the day and the nighttime face reflected by the rays of the sun. In this card, the sun and moon are shown in partial eclipse. The black droplets decorated with stars represent the consciousness that prevails during the night. The tower on the right has two windows and is guarded by a sheep; the other animal is a wolf ready for attack. The towers are a phallic symbol for the lingam. The crab approaches the fork in the road by which passive and active elements must part and go their separate ways. The oval black background behind the towers is a dark opening that engulfs the secrets of the night.

Bottom row: **Schwert-Konig** (king of swords) depicts a king in armor seated in a winged, cosmic vehicle and holding a large sword; his left hand covers his heart confirming his good intentions. The arrow on his garment derives from his past and his crown is winged to assist his approach to a higher level. He sits on a chair which is also a window to the past and the future; the seven stars in the distance symbolize the seven levels of consciousness. **Konigin-Stab** (queen of batons) sits in a high-backed throne beneath drapes decorated with heart symbols for luck and love. She wears a multi-pointed crown and holds a large, living baton which is also an instrument on which she plays the game of love. From the crystals of life at the bottom of the instrument ferment the chromosomes that rise up for purposes of fertility. The columns at the sides of the card are part of the queen's chariot; the layered bands in the background are part of the floor of her vehicle. **Zwei-Munzen** (two of pentacles) is a mirrored reflection of a large coin with altered interpretations. The two faces at the top center of the card represent two powerful figures who play with the coins; the single figure at the bottom of the card is a reflection of the two upper figures. The fishes in the upper, male coin represent the material world surrounded by drapes decorated with clouds. The lower, female coin contains the core of the cosmos surrounded by a snake.

The Zigeuner tarot cards are described in the book by Sergius Golowin entitled Die Welt des Tarot, published in 1975 by Sphinx Verlag Basel. A limited edition of one hundred signed and numbered sets of the twenty-two Major Arcana with two Minor Arcana cards was issued as full color lithographs.

Zolar's New Astrological Tarot Zolar Publishing Co., Inc., New York. The designs used in these cards are the same as those on the Rider-Waite pack. Brief interpretations, including regular and reverse meanings, are printed on each card. The Minor Arcana cards contain standard corner indices of spades, clubs, hearts and diamonds. The color tones in Zolar's tarot are inconsistent with the color tones of the original Rider-Waite tarot pack.

XIV
TAROCK PACKS

THE GAME OF TAROCK probably dates from the sixteenth century, possibly even the fifteenth century, and it continues in popularity today in certain sections of southwestern Germany, Austria and Switzerland. Early trumps were often highly artistic and depicted animals, either single-ended or double-ended, or full-length figures and scenes including operas, dancers, costumes, weddings, proverbs, mythology, folklore, genre, buildings and monuments, cities, and military and historical people and events. Many of these early cards were hand stenciled. Tarock packs usually comprise seventy-eight cards, though sometimes only fifty-four. In the fifty-four-card deck the suited cards total only thirty-two instead of fifty-six and comprise four courts and four pip cards in each suit: the black suits of swords and staves each contain the ten, nine, eight and seven, and the red suits of cups and coins each contain four, three, two and ace.

The game of tarock may be played by either two or three players. One early-nineteenth-century description of the game runs as follows:

The full pack of seventy-eight cards is shuffled and cut in the ordinary manner. The dealer deals them out in three hands, one card at a time, and places the remaining three cards face down on the table at his own right-hand side. Thus, there will be three hands of twenty-five cards each, and three cards on the table. The players sort their hands, and the dealer discards the three most useless cards in his own hand and exchanges them for the before-mentioned three cards from the table. The deal is taken in rotation by each player. The method of dealing is the same whether two or three players participate, three hands being dealt out in each instance. However, if only two players contend with each other, the third hand is untouched by either party. When a fifty-four-card tarock deck is used, each player is dealt eighteen cards and there are no cards placed on the table or exchanged.

The points constituting the game are one hundred, which may be marked on paper or a cribbage board.

Before the hands are played out their score is reckoned in the following way:

The twenty-two trumps are not all of the same value.

Twenty-one, twenty, nineteen, eighteen and seventeen are called the Five Greater Trumps. One, two, three, four and five are called the Five Lesser Trumps.

Whoever has three of the Greater or three of the Lesser Trumps in his hand scores five points for the same, ten points if he has four, and fifteen points if he has all five. If the player has *any* ten trumps in his hand they will score ten points, *any* thirteen trumps fifteen points. It does not matter if Greater or Lesser Trumps, which have been already scored, form part of such ten or thirteen; all scores are independent of other combinations. Furthermore, for any cards to be scored they must be shown to the adversary at the time of scoring. This rule holds good in all cases. The nondealer scores and leads first. If three play, the player to the dealer's left begins.

Seven cards bear the distinguishing title of Tarot Trumps (although the four kings are usually known as court cards): 21 The World or The Universe; The Fool; 1 The Magician, Pagad or Juggler; and the four kings of swords, staves, cups and coins.

If the player has any two of these Tarot Trumps, he can ask his opponent for a third; if the latter cannot reply by showing a third Tarot Trump, the former can score five points; but if he has the third it must be given up to the asker, who then does not score, but gives him some card of small value in exchange. For every three Tarot Trumps actually held in hand, the holder marks fifteen points.

Sequences of trumps or of cards of the same suit count; for every four cards in sequence, five points; for every seven cards, ten points; for ten cards, fifteen points. All cards forming these scores must be shown to the other players.

The Fool is the lowest card in the pack in playing the hand; it cannot take a card of any suit, and may be played to a card of any suit. For instance, if one player leads a king, and another player has only the queen of that suit remaining in his hand, but he also has The Fool, he can play The Fool instead of the queen, and thus save the queen from being taken. A king cut counts 5 points to whoever cuts it. In each suit king is highest, then come queen, knight, page, ten, nine, etc., down to ace, which is the lowest and can only take The Fool. The Trumps reckon from 21, which is highest, to 1, which is lowest. Players must follow suit if they can; if not, they may trump. Each trick should be kept separate for counting afterward. Of course, the principal care of the player should be directed toward saving his own important cards, and taking those of the adversary. The player who takes a trick leads next. When all the hand is played out, the tricks on either side are counted as follows:

For every trick in which there is a Tarot Trump, five points (The Fool counts to its *original* possessor, while The Magician counts to the player who takes it). For every trick with a queen, four points; with a knight, three points; with a page, two points; for every other trick one point.

At the end of each hand the points made by each player are added up separately, then the lesser is taken from the greater, and only the *excess* points of the more fortunate player are scored. When three play the game, only the player who has most should score, and then only the amount by which he exceeds the player who comes second. The other players do not score at all. The same is done in each hand, and the player who, in this way, first reaches one hundred points (or over in the final hand) wins the game.

The following table summarizes the points which can be scored:

SCORED IN HAND	Points
For any three of the Greater Trumps held in hand	5
For any four of the Greater Trumps held in hand	10
For all five of the Greater Trumps held in hand	15
For any three of the Lesser Trumps held in hand	5
For any four of the Lesser Trumps held in hand	10
For all five of the Lesser Trumps held in hand	15
For any ten Trumps held in hand	10
For any thirteen Trumps held in hand	15
For any three Tarot Trumps called unanswered	5
For any three Tarot Trumps actually held in hand	15
For every sequence of four cards	5
For every sequence of seven cards	10
For every sequence of ten cards	15
SCORED IN PLAY	
For a king, cut	5
For each Trick containing a Tarot Trump	5
For each Trick containing a queen	4
For each Trick containing a knight	3
For each Trick containing a Page	2
For every Trick of two plain cards	1

The following nineteenth- and twentieth-century tarock and tarock-type packs, including a Cego deck, are illustrated in this chapter.

Gobl tarock	Chinese tarock	Ditha Moser tarock
Napoleon tarock	Fool's tarock	Soldaten tarock
Allegorical tarock	Dance tarock	Piatnik tarock
Turkish Costume tarock	Theatrical tarock	Willer tarock
Pfluger Scenic tarock	Proverb tarock	Paris Scenic tarock
Historical tarock	Dondorf tarock no. 246	Ladies tarock no. 162
Animal tarock (Bohemia)	Military tarock (circa 1882)	Tarotrump and tarock no. 4
Animal tarock (Germany)	Nejedly tarock	Coffee House tarock no. 9a
Military tarock (circa 1854)	Habsburger tarock no. 146	Piatnik tarock no. 36a
Opera and Operetta tarock	Exotic tarock	Cego pack

Gobl Tarock This engraved series of hand-colored wedding tarocks was designed by Andreas Benedictus Gobl of Munich in 1780. The odd-numbered trumps depict a well-dressed figure with plumed hat riding a show horse, and the even-numbered cards contain an ornate wagon drawn by two horses, decorated with flowers and laden with food and drink, which various people nearby are savoring. The appropriate Roman number appears at the top of each trump and a two-line descriptive verse appears at the bottom. Top row: Trump I reads, "Ye wedding guests come hither, so that the joy may be complete." Trump II, "With such nice hosts and hostesses, it is easy to go to a wedding feast." Trump III, "A rustic person am I by the way I dress, but henceforth I am great of nobility." Middle row: Trump IV, "Here is the bridegroom, familiar with the bride, but not so far as in the bridal chamber." Trump V, "Be only new, only gay, only aware, while the time itself commands." Trump VI, "Minister, why are you so well dressed today; are you on your way to see your wife?" Bottom row: Trump IX, "Hunting is my greatest pleasure, especially hunting for a marriageable girl." Trump X, "Here on this hunter's wagon, one can expect a good feast of game." Trump XI, "Bavarian, Bavarian, it's got to be; then everything agrees with me."

Napoleon Tarock These rare tarock cards, circa 1812, are hand stenciled in full color and depict important events in the life of Napoleon I. The trump cards are full figured with large double-ended Arabic numbers within a circle set in a panel. Card 1, entitled Pa-gat, suggests a fortuitous leader; Card 2 depicts the French military school at Brienne-le Château where Napoleon was educated; Card 3 probably illustrates Napoleon commanding the French Republican artillery at the siege of Toulon in 1793; Card 6 appears to depict Napoleon in 1796 at the Bridge of Arcola when he seized the falling flag and rallied his troops to victory; Card 8 portrays Napoleon either in Egypt in July 1798 at the time of the Battle of the Pyramids, or in the following year when he defeated a Turkish force at Abukir; Card 17 depicts the crowning in 1804 of Empress Josephine by Napoleon at the time of his own "coronation" as Emperor by Pope Pius VII.

Allegorical Tarock From a fifty-four-card pack by Joseph Estel, Vienna. Tax stamp on ace of hearts indicates year 1820. The cards are hand stenciled in color. The double-ended trumps depict a variety of oriental scenes. The court figures are also double-ended.

Turkish Costume Tarock This pack was made in Germany in 1826 by H. F. Muller. The Roman numbers on the Major Arcana are double-ended and the identification of each figure appears along the side of the card. Top row: IX Une Femme Grècque de l'Ile de Marmara (*A Greek Woman from the Island of Marmara*); X Le Kislaraga (*An Army Officer*); XIII Un Derwisch (*A Dervish*). Bottom row: XIV Un Officier du Grand Seigneur (*An Officer of the Nobility*); XV Le Porteur de la Cuillier (*The Porter of the Spoon*); XVI Un Turc dans une pelisse (*A Turk in a Fur-Lined Coat*) Un Jchlogan.

Pfluger Scenic Tarock Published in Strasbourg, France, early to mid-nineteenth century. The double-ended trumps are hand colored and depict a variety of scenes—military, boating, hunting, theater, gardens, volcanoes, etc. The court figures are double-ended. The aces also are double-ended and illustrate famous buildings such as the ace of clubs with the Palais Royal and La Douane.

Historical Tarock From a seventy-eight-card pack published circa 1840 by Gumppenberg, Milan. The twenty-two trump cards depict artistic and well-engraved historical figures and events apparently dealing with the Holy Roman Empire. The Fool is called Excusée or Excuse. The court cards are historical figures such as king of spades, Carlo Magno Incoronato 775, presumably Charles the Great, better known as Charlemagne, and the queen of spades, Ermengarda.

Animal Tarock (Bohemia) From a fifty-four-card pack woodblock printed in Bohemia and stencil colored by hand. Trump I contains the name of the card maker, "W. Sewera in Prag" (Prague), and the year 1849 appears on the tax stamp in the lower left and upper right corners. The designs on the trump and court cards are double-ended; the subjects on the trumps are animals except the unnumbered card and Card I, which are a fanciful figure in colorful hat and costume playing the flute and a well-dressed figure. Trump XXI contains the wording "Industrie und Gluck," which is found on Trump II in most packs. The crowned king of spades holds a small rod and the king of hearts holds an upright sword and a globe topped with the imperial orb, in contrast to the kings of swords and staves who usually are depicted with a sword and stave, respectively.

Animal Tarock (Germany) From a fifty-four-card pack probably made in Germany, circa mid-nineteenth century. The atouts contain double-ended pictures of animals except Trump I, which depicts the double figure of a young boy. The Arabic numbers are in an oval within a panel of repeating vertical lines. The courts are also double-ended.

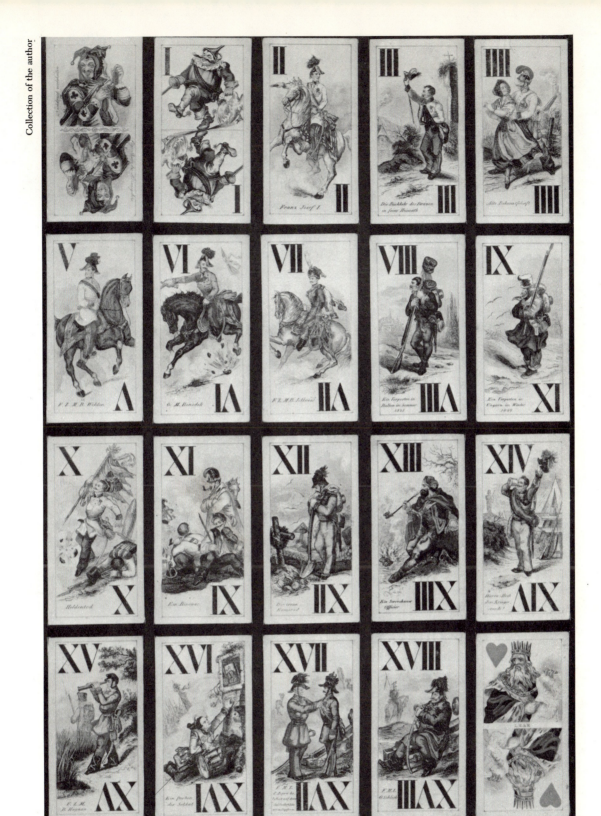

Military Tarock   From a fifty-four-card pack by Jos. Glanz, Vienna, circa 1854. This is the first of four packs in a series of military tarocks that depict on the atouts full-length figures of a military nature, including Emperor Franz Josef I on atout II. On this pack the Emperor is shown as a young, clean-shaven officer. Later packs show him with a moustache and a heavy beard. The court cards are double-ended historical characters including Shakespeare's King Lear on the king of hearts. Other cards shown are (top row) unnumbered Jester or Harlequin, I A jovial swordsman, II Franz Josef I, III The return of the brave soldier to his home, IIII An old acquaintance. Second row: V, VI and VII Officers on horseback, VIII An outpost in Italy during the summer of 1848, IX An outpost in Hungary during the winter. Third row: X A hero's death, XI Bivouac, XII The true comrade, XIII A Saracen officer, XIV Harrah for the Armistice. Bottom row: XV An officer, XVI Death of a soldier, XVII An officer promotes a brave soldier on the battlefield, XVIII An officer.

Opera and Operetta Tarock This beautiful pack was made by C. Titze and Schinkay, Vienna, about 1860 as evidenced on the ace of hearts by the tax stamp, which was valid from 1858 to 1877. The cards are stencil colored and the faces are hand colored. The scenes featured on the trump cards in this pack are from the following operas and operettas, some of which are obscure: II Landfrieden, III Afrikanerin, IIII Hugenotten, V Lohengrin, VI Tulipatan, VII Sardanapal, VIII Frou-Frou, IX Sardanapal, X Schach dem Konig, XI Judith, XII Schone Helene, XIII Orpheus, XIV Pariser Leben, XV Satanella, XVI Romeo u. Juliet, XVII Schone Mullerin, XVIII Grobherzogin von Gerolstein, XIX Ein Wort an den Minister, XX Banditen and XXI Grafin Orsini. The court figures are double-ended as evidenced by the king of spades.

Chinese Tarock From a fifty-four-card pack by Ferd. Piatnik vorm A. Moser, Vienna, circa 1860. The atouts are double-ended scenes of oriental life; usually one side has a standing figure and the other side a seated figure.

Fool's Tarock From a fifty-four-card pack designed by Josef Surch of Vienna, whose name appears on Trump I, and engraved by someone with the initials "I.F." appearing on Trump V. This pack was published by Ferd. Piatnik & Sohne, Vienna, between 1860 and 1865. The trump cards contain satirical titles in German, mainly of a contemporary political nature; the satire of the remaining trumps is more general. For example, Trump II depicts A Dangerous Fool; III The Game Fool; V The Ballet Fool; VI The Inflated Fool (or Inflated Ego); VIII A Patient Fool, depicted as a young man with the imperial eagle on his shirt and the caption strife on the sign behind him, who waits for the unity of Germany; X A Politician Fool and XI A Carnival Fool.

Dance Tarock Hand-colored pack by E. Knepper, Austria, comprises fifty-four cards. The trumps are in full costume and depict various dance steps, exercises and poses. The courts are double-ended and the pack was made in 1866 as evidenced by the tax stamp appearing on the ace of hearts (not shown).

Theatrical Tarock From a fifty-four-card pack by Josef Glanz, Vienna. The tax stamp on the ace of hearts was valid from 1858 to 1877. Cards are hand stenciled in color and faces are hand colored. The Roman numerals on the Major Arcana cards are double-ended; the scenes are full-length figures except for Trump I, which is a double-ended swordsman. At the top of each Major Arcana card, except Trump I, is the name of a playwright, and at the bottom is the name of the play from which the depicted scene is taken; the authors selected are for the most part obscure today. The Major Arcana shown include VIII Adan Gottlob Oehlenschlager, a Danish playwright, author of Correggio; X Johann Wolfgang von Goethe, author of Faust; XV August von Kotzebue, author of Misanthropy and Repentance; and XIX Heinrich von Kleist, author of Kitty of Heilbrun.

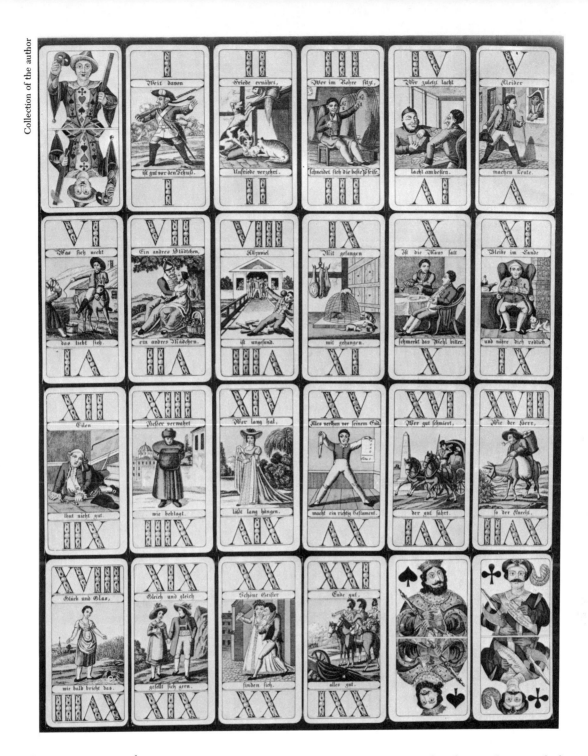

Proverb Tarock   *Designed (?) by Baumgartner and manufactured by Vereinigte Stralsunder Spielkarten Fabriken, Stralsund. Since the Stralsunder combine was formed in 1872, these cards probably date circa 1875. The trump cards depict illustrated proverbs with German titles; the Roman numerals are double-ended. The court cards with French suit signs are also double-ended. The illustrated trumps and their corresponding American meanings are as follows: I Discretion is the better part of valor (to be far away from the shooting is good); II Money that harmony earns, discord spends; III He who stays closest to the fire, warms himself best; IV He who laughs best, laughs last; V Clothes make the person, or fine feathers make fine birds; VI Rallying is dallying (while the girl throws a bucket of water into the boy's face, he gently whips her); VII Another town, another girl, or a girl in every port; VIII One can have too much of a good thing; IX They all come in the same box, or the same fate befalls everyone caught in the same act; X When the mouse has eaten its fill, the flour tastes better; XI Utopia may be far away, or stay in your own country and feed yourself in a reasonable way; XII Haste makes waste; XIII Better to be envied than pitied; XIV Those who have a good store of butter may lay it thick on their bread, or if you've got it, flaunt it; XV Spending everything before your end makes the best testament; XVI Good oiling makes easy riding; XVII As the master, so the valet; XVIII Happiness and glass easily fall to pieces; XIX Birds of a feather flock together; XX Great minds think alike, or great minds find each other; XXI All's well that ends well.*

Dondorf Tarock Pack 246 Published by B. Dondorf, Frankfurt, in the second half of the nineteenth century. The older editions contain Arabic numbers on the double-ended trumps. The unnumbered card is called Excuse. The upright view of each trump can be determined from the monogram in the center panel of a small "B" within a larger "O." The reverse scene in each trump differs from the upright picture. Trump 1 shows a woman reaching for a bouquet of flowers held by the "pagat" or jester. Trumps 2 to 5 depict objects of great value such as jewels, armor, chinaware and porcelain. Trumps 6 to 9 are tradesmen and artists such as a sculptor, maker of boats, poet and man of medicine. Trumps 10 to 13 are royalty and military persons. Trumps 14 to 17 depict scenes and pleasures of persons who are well off. Trump 18 shows the perquisites of the wealthy. Each trump also is designated with the name of a country. The king of clubs is Leopold I and the other kings (not shown) are all past monarchs, the queens are consorts, the cavaliers are political leaders, the pages are literary and scientific leaders and the aces depict the palaces of Europe.

Military Tarock   From a fifty-four-card pack by Ferd. Piatnik & Sohne, Vienna, circa 1882. Trumps depict military battles and camp scenes with brief titles in German. The courts are named historical figures and all the cards are hand stenciled in color. Trump III Homecoming of the reservist, V Field Marshal Rodetzky, VIII Halt! Who's there? XV The Duke von Wurtemberg, and XVII Decorating the grave. The king and queen of spades are Karl VII and Agnès Sorel.

Nejedly Tarock Published by Johann Nejedly, Vienna, circa 1881 to 1900. The atouts are conventional scenes such as Card I depicting Harlequin and Columbine playing a harp and a tambourine; the next card is an imperial eagle with the motto "Industrie und Glück." Each double-ended atout has a Roman number plus a curious inset Arabic number.

Habsburger Tarock No. 146 By Ferd. Piatnik & Sohne, Vienna, circa 1900. The atouts are rendered in soft colors and depict a variety of scenes from foreign countries and different periods including rural scenes, outdoor events in the country and the desert, religious pictures and scenes of domestic life.

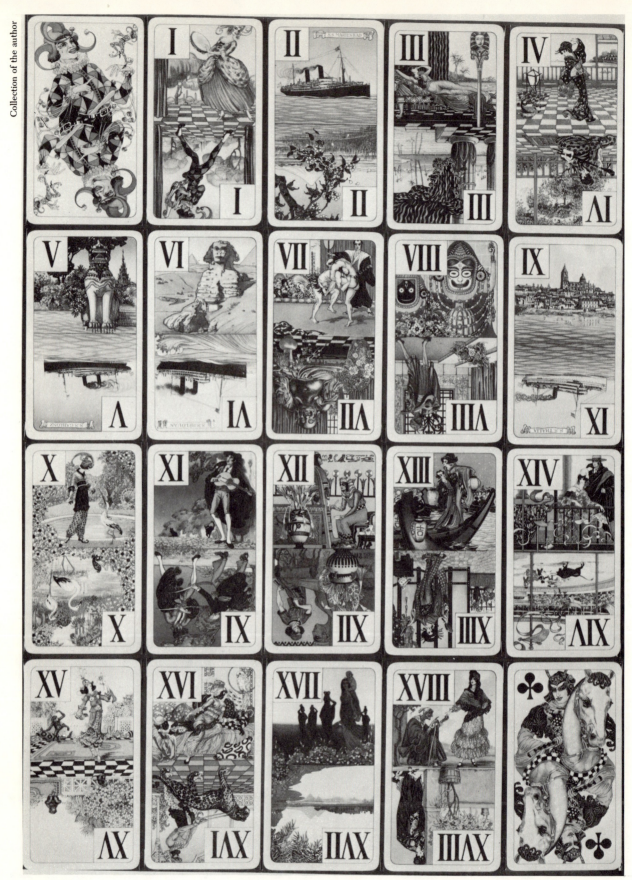

Exotic Tarock From a fifty-four-card promotional pack made by S. D. Modiano, Trieste, circa 1900, for the Austrian-Lloyd Steamship Lines. The cards are richly colored; the atouts include, besides steamships, exotic scenes from ports of call. The courts are double-ended figures from Europe, the Middle East and Asia.

Ditha Moser Tarock 1972 reprint by Ferd. Piatnik & Sohne, Vienna, of a fifty-four-card tarock designed by Moser and published in 1906 by Berger, Vienna, for the benefit of a Viennese charity. Trumps are double-ended scenes of stiff little people, animals and houses. The court cards are painted almost in a stained-glass effect and picture Assyrians, knights, royalty and Egyptians.

Soldaten Tarock No. 217 From a fifty-four-card pack by Ferd. Piatnik & Sohne, Vienna, issued in 1918. Trumps depict war scenes from World War I, except for Card I, which portrays the usual Columbine and Harlequin. Women in various social and charitable roles are shown on the queens, such as a Red Cross nurse on the queen of hearts. Soldiers and commissioned officers are depicted on the valets and jacks. Trump VII depicts the Siege of Antwerp, VIII Field kitchen, X Belgrade, XI Attack, XII Pilots over Venice, XIII German U-Boat Captain Vonig, XIV Homecoming, XVI Captain Lieutenant Konjovicz.

Piatnik Tarock Deck of genre scenes by Ferd. Piatnik & Sohne. The atouts in this fifty-four-card pack are double-ended and the Arabic numbers appear in large size within ornate panels on both ends. The courts are unnamed historical figures.

Willer Tarock Designed by Willer, Paris, twentieth century. The double-ended trumps portray a variety of scenes including street vendor and puppet show (1), marketplace (2), Roman and Greek mythology (2, 3, 4, 5, 6), Napoleon's march during the Russian winter (4), sheepherder (9), tank warfare (13), Boy Scout campout (14) and playing at the beach (19). Card 21 depicts a globe of the world and the figures in each corner represent a different race.

Paris Scenic Tarock From a fifty-four-card pack by Josef Glanz, Vienna. The horizontal full-color scenes consist of Paris landmarks including IIII Palais-Royal, V Tuilerien, X Vendome-Saule, XVIII Pantheon, XIX Triumphbogen der Etoile and XXI Notre-Dame. Court cards are double-ended historical figures. Tax stamp on the ace of hearts is dated 1855.

Ladies Tarock No. 162 From a fifty-four-card pack by Ferd. Piatnik & Sohne, Vienna; it is designated Ladies Tarock because the cards are slightly smaller in size than standard tarock cards. The atouts contain double-ended conventional scenes of rural life. The court cards are double-ended as shown by the king of clubs and queen of hearts.

Tarotrump and Tarock No. 4 By AG Muller & Cie, Switzerland. The trump cards depict double-ended folk scenes and contain double-ended Arabic numbers in the upper left and lower right squares.

Coffee House Tarock No. 9a By Ferd. Piatnik & Sohne, Vienna. *The double-ended scenes on these oversized cards depict genre folklore. Trump II contains the usual "Industrie und Gluck."*

Tarock No. 36a By Ferd. Piatnik & Sohne, Vienna. This fifty-four-card tarock pack features folklore scenes of Austrian life. The jack of clubs has a double-ended page with the name Ferd. Piatnik & Sohne, Vienna.

Cego Pack Modern version of a fifty-four-card Cego pack published by Altenburger und Stralsunder Spielkarten Fabriken A. G., Leinfelden. The seventy-eight-card Cego pack was used throughout Bavaria in the nineteenth century to play the game of Cego. Today the popular Cego deck comprises fifty-four cards—twenty-two trumps and thirty-two suited cards. The twenty-two double-ended trumps, except The Fool, are numbered in Arabic numerals and generally depict animals, as shown in the illustration, genre or nineteenth-century rural scenes of persons at work or play. The thirty-two suited cards contain eight cards per suit—four court cards (king, queen, knight and valet) and four numeral cards. The numeral or pip cards use French suit signs and comprise ten, nine, eight and seven in the black suits of spades and clubs. The red suits of hearts and diamonds each contain four, three, two and ace.

XV
INTERPRETING TAROT CARDS

TAROT IN ITS PURE FORM is a universal language that crosses all barriers. Persons of different backgrounds who do not speak or read the same language can communicate through tarot symbolism. Numerous varieties of tarot packs have developed during the past five centuries, with slight variations in the symbolism of the twenty-two Major Arcana cards. Some packs, such as the Visconti-Sforza, do not have titles or numbers on the Major Arcana cards; others may contain titles in one or more languages, plus Arabic and/or Roman numerals and occasionally Hebrew letters. The following section summarizes the general symbolism found on each of the twenty-two Major Arcana and the divinatory and reverse meanings.

THE TWENTY-TWO MAJOR ARCANA CARDS

The Fool A young man carries a staff and bundle upon his shoulder. He walks with the aid of a stick at the edge of a precipice while a dog tears at his tight-fitting trouser leg. In the Rider-Waite pack the boy holds a rose instead of a walking stick and the dog plays nearby. The 1JJ tarot pack depicts The Fool as a gaily dressed jester in conical foolscap with ornamental pompons. His cap, shirt, pants, leggings and shoes are divided into two colors—red and blue—signifying extravagance. In some Italian tarot packs The Fool holds a butterfly net and a butterfly hovers nearby. In most tarot packs The Fool wears a hat, sometimes a conical cap, but in the Visconti-Sforza *tarocchi* he has seven feathers protruding from his hair. The Tarocchi of Mantegna shows a beggar leaning on a crooked staff while two dogs bark at his feet. The Etteilla tarot designs usually show The Fool blindfolded or with his hands cupped over his eyes. In most tarot packs The Fool uses a stick to carry his possessions as he strides toward the right of the card and into the future. By contrast, The Hermit uses his stick for support while he searches to the left suggesting the past; The Empress and The Emperor use their sticks or scepters topped with an imperial orb to defend and maintain the position and possessions they have attained through conquest or inheritance. In the Egyptian-type tarots an alligator replaces the dog. The Gringonneur tarot depicts The Fool surrounded by four young boys.

DIVINATORY MEANINGS: Beginning of an adventure. Enthusiasm. Initiative. New opportunities beckon. Unlimited possibilities. Pleasure. Passion. Craze. Rashness. Frenzy. Obsession. Mania. Folly. Thoughtlessness. Extravagance. Lack of discipline. Immaturity. Foolishness. Irrationality. Insecurity. Frivolity. Inconsiderateness. Delirium. Spontaneity. Levity. Exhibitionism. Unrestrained excess. Ridiculous expenditure or act. Carelessness in promises. Inattentiveness to important details. Infatuation. Indiscretion. Tendency to start a project without carefully considering all the details. Reluctance to listen to advice from other people.

REVERSE MEANINGS: Faulty choice or a bad decision. Indecision. Apathy. Hesitation. Failure to diligently proceed. Ignoring opportunities.

I The Magician A man seated at a table wears a hat with a double nimbus in the form of the eternal figure eight and the cosmic lemniscate. In his left hand is a rod, the sign of one of the four suits, pointing to the heavens, while his other hand points downward toward the earth. This suggests that emanations from heaven may be put to use on earth by those persons who are aware of the wonders surrounding them. On the table are placed examples of the remaining suit signs: a sword, a cup and coins. In the Pierpont Morgan–Bergamo Visconti-Sforza *tarocchi* pack the objects on the table include small loaves of bread and a large white dish. In some Italian tarots The Magician holds a cup in his hand and the table has cobbler's tools. Egyptian tarots depict The Magician with a golden band around his forehead.

DIVINATORY MEANINGS: Originality. Creativity. Free will. Ability to utilize one's capabilities in order to accomplish a task. Imagination. Self-reliance. Spontaneity. Skill. Willpower. Self-confidence. Dexterity. Ingenuity. Flexibility. Craft. Guile. Masterfulness. Self-control. Trickery. Deception. Sleight of hand. Bewilderment. Unity of thought and emotion. Ability to choose one's own actions. Determination to see a task through to completion. Capability to influence other people.

REVERSE MEANINGS: Weakness of will. Ineptitude. Insecurity. Disquiet. Delay. Lack of imagination. The use of one's skills for destructive ends. Willpower applied to evil ends.

327

II The Popess or The High Priestess A woman clothed in impressive robes is seated on a throne with a high veil or canopy between two pillars and with a double wimple behind her head. In some packs the pillars bear the inscription on the left *B* or *Boaz* and on the right *J* or *Jachin*. The Popess wears a crown similar to the papal crown with two or three diadems and sometimes topped by a lunar crescent, while in her lap rests the Torah or book of infinite wisdom. This figure has been associated with the legend of the female Pope Joan. Egyptian tarots show The Popess veiled. In minchiate packs she holds a globe and a scepter. Eighteenth-century tarot packs in southern France substituted Juno or Junon for The Female Pope or The Popess. In the 1JJ pack a peacock appears in the background. The Popess is sometimes shown with a masculine face. She represents the self-motivated, intellectual person with perception and understanding.

DIVINATORY MEANINGS: Wisdom. Sound judgment. Serene knowledge. Common sense. Learning. Serenity. Objectivity. Penetration. Education. Foresight. Intuition. Comprehension. Perception. Self-reliance. Hidden emotion. Purity. Virtue. Apparent emotionlessness. Inability to share. Lack of patience. Spinster. Platonic relationships. Avoids emotional entanglements. Occasionally talks too much. Practical. Teacher.

REVERSE MEANINGS: Ignorance. Shortsightedness. Lack of understanding. Selfishness. Acceptance of superficial knowledge. Improper judgment. Shallowness. Conceit.

III The Empress The female figure of the crowned, winged Empress sits on a throne and holds the symbol of power in her hand—a scepter with a globe at the end topped with the imperial orb. The Empress frequently is shown holding a shield in her right hand decorated with an eagle. In some packs she appears outdoors and is surrounded by the beauties of nature. Many packs show her left foot or both feet resting on a crescent. Instead of being crowned, or in addition to it, she is surrounded by a diadem of stars. The Empress is a forceful, strong-willed person whose marriage to The Emperor completes the dual sign of authority.

DIVINATORY MEANINGS: Feminine progress. Action. Natural energy. Development. Fruitfulness. Fertility. Attainment. Accomplishment. Interest in day-to-day details. Mother. Sister. Wife. Marriage. Children. Feminine influence. Material wealth. Evolution. Female guile. Harassment. Spendthrift. Capable of motivating others. A leader. Makes decisions founded upon all the facts at hand. The motivator of a successful partner or husband. Businesswoman. Level-headed. Practical. Decisive. Intuitive.

REVERSE MEANINGS: Vacillation. Inaction. Lack of interest. Lack of concentration. Indecision. Delay in accomplishment or progress. Anxiety. Frittering away of resources. Loss of material possessions. Seduction. Infertility. Infidelity. Fickle love. Vanity.

IIII The Emperor A bearded, mature male figure sits on a throne; he is dressed in regal robes and sometimes wears a pointed crown shaped like a coal scuttle. The Emperor holds the symbol of power in his hand and usually alongside him is a shield decorated with the imperial eagle, the design derived from the heraldic device first appearing on the fifteenth-century Pierpont Morgan–Bergamo Visconti-Sforza *tarocchi* pack. Sometimes his throne is a cubical stone and The Emperor appears in full armor. The figure of The Emperor is a strong-willed man of accomplishment and power.

DIVINATORY MEANINGS: Worldly power. Accomplishment. Confidence. Wealth. Stability. Authority. Indomitable spirit. Leadership. Maturity. War-making tendencies. A go-getter. Paternity. Father. Brother. Husband. Male influence. Direct pressure. Conviction. Domination of intelligence and reason over emotion and passion. Strength. Patriarchal figure. Attainment of goals. Achievement. Desire to increase domination in every direction. Strong masculine development. Worthy of exercising authority. A capable person who is knowledgeable and competent. Willing to listen to counsel.

REVERSE MEANINGS: Immaturity. Ineffectiveness. Lack of strength. Indecision. Inability to make progress. Weak character. Feebleness. Failure to control petty emotions.

V The Pope or The Hierophant A man of great stature and wisdom sits upon a throne, usually on a raised platform between two pillars. He wears a triple crown and holds a scepter topped with a triple cross. He is clothed in heavy robes. In many packs two figures kneel in reverent attitude near his feet and receive his benediction. This card is also sometimes called Jupiter. It expresses instruction and it is usually associated with some religious meaning or accepted practice and custom.

DIVINATORY MEANINGS: Ritualism. Ceremonies. Mercy. Humilities. Kindness. Goodness. Forgiveness. Inspiration. Alliance. Compassion. Servitude. Inactivity. Lack of conviction. Timidity. Overt reserve. Captivity to one's own ideas. Tendency to cling to former ideas and principles even if outdated. A person to whom one has recourse. Conformity. A religious or spiritual leader. At times this person is unable to adapt to new circumstances and changing conditions. A person with a sense of historical importance.

REVERSE MEANINGS: Foolish exercise of generosity. Overkindness. Repeated errors. Susceptibility. Impotence. Vulnerability. Frailty. Unorthodoxy. Renunciation. Unconventionality.

VI The Lovers A sun or flaming cherub appears in the sky above two figures, a man and woman, often both naked. Sometimes there are three figures, a young man in the middle torn with indecision between two females representing good and evil. In some packs the figures stand in a flowering garden before a stone wall and Cupid is blindfolded. Nearby is a tree bearing fruits and entwined by a serpent. This card is also known as Marriage and in the Cary-Yale Visconti-Sforza *tarocchi* pack it depicts a marriage ceremony. Several packs indicate the figures are Adam and Eve. This card expresses interaction between people, perhaps the result of some unexpected event or meeting. Mainly, this is a card of choice and friendship.

DIVINATORY MEANINGS: Love. Beauty. Perfection. Harmony. Unanimity. Trials overcome. Confidence. Trust. Honor. Possibly the beginning of a romance. Infatuation. Deep feeling. Development. Optimism. Oblivious to possible consequences. Letting oneself go. Freedom of emotion. The necessity of testing or subjecting to trial. Struggle between sacred and profane love. Putting to the proof. Examining. Yearning. Tempting. Possible predicaments. A person deeply involved in the emotions and problems of a friend or relative. A meaningful affair.

REVERSE MEANINGS: Failure to meet the test. Unreliability. Separation. Frustration in love and marriage. Interference by others. Fickleness. Untrustworthiness. Unwise plans.

VII The Chariot A warrior or princess stands in a chariot drawn by either two horses or sphinxes, one black and one white and sometimes without bridle or reins. Usually the chariot or wagon has a canopy hung from four pillars and the standing figure often carries a rod or scepter. Sometimes the warrior is bare-chested while in other packs he is dressed in full armor with a metal breastplate ornamented with pauldrons and shoulder plates decorated with lunar crescents or facial profiles looking upward. In older tarot decks the initials of the designer of the pack frequently appear on the front of the chariot. This card symbolizes adversity that can be overcome and the accomplishments that can be realized when effort and physical resources are brought into harmony and strong direction.

DIVINATORY MEANINGS: Fortitude. Perseverance. Major effort. Possible voyage or journey. Escape. Rushing to decision. Riding the crest of success or popularity. Perplexity. Trouble. Adversity, possibly already overcome. Conflicting influence. Turmoil. Vengeance. Need for supervision. Need for attention to details. Urgency to gain control of one's emotions. This card suggests that one can achieve greatness when physical and mental powers are maintained in balance.

REVERSE MEANINGS: To be unsuccessful. Defeat. Failure. At the last minute to lose something otherwise within your grasp. Sudden collapse of plans. Conquered. Overwhelmed. Failure to face reality.

VIII Justice The figure of Justice is a woman, sometimes blindfolded, who is seated and vested in the robes of a judge. In many packs she holds in her left hand the scales of justice and in her right hand the upraised, double-edged sword of justice. The female figure seems to easily hold the heavy sword because it is supported by all that is good and righteous. Sometimes Justice is crowned; other times she has long, flowing hair, occasionally topped with a garland of flowers. In the Tarocchi of Mantegna pack the figure of Justice is depicted standing, while in many packs she is seated on a raised throne.

DIVINATORY MEANINGS: Fairness. Reasonableness. Justice. Proper balance. Harmony. Balanced conduct. Equity. Righteousness. Virtue. Honor. Virginity. Just reward. Sincere desire. Good intentions. Well-meaning actions. Firmness of character. Advice. Self-satisfaction. The eventual outcome, whether favorable or unfavorable, will truly be fair for the person concerned. Equilibrium. Poise. Impartiality. Capability of perceiving temptation and avoiding evil. This card suggests a person who responds favorably to the good nature of others. A considerate person.

REVERSE MEANINGS: Bias. False accusations. Bigotry. Severity in judgment. Intolerance. Unfairness. Abuse.

VIIII The Hermit The aged, bearded figure of The Hermit is dressed in long robes and usually carries a lamp, lit with a candle or star, in one hand and a staff in the other. He is often robed in a monk's habit and cowl and occasionally leans heavily upon his staff or crutches. Some cards show a pointed hood pulled over his head; other packs show his hood resting on his bent shoulders while his head leans forward. In Mitelli's *tarocchino* pack The Hermit appears as a beggar with a basket slung across his shoulder. In the Egyptian tarots The Hermit holds a lamp in front of his rectangular cape. Generally, The Hermit faces to the left of the card, or is shown in profile toward his left, as he perceives the past. Sometimes a serpent lies at his feet. This card is also known as The Old Man, The Aged Man, The Poor Man, The Beggar and The Aged Man on Crutches. The Hermit suggests a quiet, withdrawn person, intent upon self-reflection and meditation.

DIVINATORY MEANINGS: Counsel. Knowledge. Solicitude. Inner strength. Self-illumination. Prudence. Discretion. Caution. Vigilance. Patience. Circumspection. Self-denial. Withdrawal. Under certain circumstances this card also represents recession and regression. Desertion. Annulment. Insincerity. Expressionless. A loner or person incapable of interaction with another person. Misleading. Misguided. Tendency to withhold emotion. Fearful of discovery. Failure to face facts. Possessor of secrets. Complacency. Unutilized knowledge.

REVERSE MEANINGS: Imprudence. Hastiness. Rashness. Prematurity. Foolish acts. Incorrect advice. Failure resulting from inactivity. Overprudence resulting in unnecessary delay. Immaturity. Excessive isolation.

X The Wheel of Fortune Seated on the top of a large wheel is either a sphinx or a winged crowned animal holding a sword. On the left side of the wheel is a descending figure with a human face and lionlike tail, while another figure rises on the right; probably the figures are meant to represent Anubis and Typhon, the principles of good and evil. Sometimes the ascending figure clings to the rim of the wheel with its claws. In the Visconti-Sforza and 1JJ packs the wheel turns in a clockwise direction, whereas in the Tarot of Marseilles and Rider-Waite packs the wheel revolves in a counterclockwise direction. Sometimes a fourth figure appears in the center of the wheel or beneath it, as in the Visconti-Sforza *tarocchi* packs. Depending upon the pack, the figures on the wheel vary from allegorical beasts to humans with animal extremities such as ass's ears and a tail. In a recent Etteilla pack The Wheel of Fortune is an unbroken chain, and in an older Etteilla version a blindfolded woman stands on the wheel. The spokes of the wheel usually number from six to eight and occasionally the wheel bears the inscription "Taro." Waite represents Typhon in his serpent form and includes four living creatures in the corners of the card. The wheel is a never-ending and forever-changing field of motion in which all manner of experiences, events, opportunities and future possibilities rise and fall in terms of dual opportunities such as birth and death, good and evil, abundance and poverty, hope and despair.

DIVINATORY MEANINGS: Destiny. Fortune. Fate. Outcome. Felicity. Godsend. Special gain or unusual loss. Culmination. Conclusion. Result. Approaching the end of a problem. The influences affecting the outcome of a problem. Inevitability. Unexpected events may occur. The entire sequence of the wheel suggests the course of things from beginning to end. Advancement for better or worse. Progress. Good or bad luck depending upon other nearby cards.

REVERSE MEANINGS: Failure. Ill luck. Broken sequence. Unexpected bad fate. Interruption or inconsistency due to unexpected events. Outside influences not contemplated.

XI Strength A woman exerts little effort to close or open the jaws of a lion (there is much controversy as to what the figure is really doing). Sometimes a man representing Hercules appears in place of the woman. In some packs Strength wears a crown or hat in the form of a lemniscate. The seemingly effortless strength of the figure suggests that much can be accomplished by the combined application of mental and physical effort.

DIVINATORY MEANINGS: Control over a situation. Strength. Courage. Fortitude. Conviction. Energy. Determination. Resolution. Defiance. Action. Awareness of temptations and the mental and physical abilities to overcome them. Confidence. Innate ability. Zeal. Fervor. Physical strength. Matter over mind and, alternatively, mind over matter, depending upon the circumstances. Accomplishment. Attainment at considerable peril. Conquest. Hidden forces at work are challenged. Heroism. Virility. Strength to endure in spite of all obstacles.

REVERSE MEANINGS: Weakness. Pettiness. Impotence. Sickness. Tyranny. Lack of faith. Abuse of power. Succumbing to temptation. Indifference.

XII The Hanged Man A man hangs upside down, usually tied by his left ankle to a horizontal beam or gibbet supported by two tree trunks, often branchless and leafless; his other leg is usually bent at the knee so as to form a triangle. The hands of this figure are often behind his back, so that his arms form another triangle, and other times they hold two sacks of coins. The figure usually seems relaxed and occasionally smiles; the face has no expression of pain. In Tarot Classic the figure is shown hanging from both ankles, and in a few packs the figure is hanging by his neck. On rare occasion, this figure is shown standing on one foot —Court de Gebelin thought the design represented Prudence cautiously reaching out for a place to put the other foot. The rectangular border depicted in this card is replaced in The World card by an oval. Interestingly, in some tarot packs the hanging figure with crossed right leg and hands behind his back is changed to an upright figure in The World card who stands with left leg crossed and arms apart; thus the Major Arcana card is altered pictorially and numerically from 12 to 21.

DIVINATORY MEANINGS: Life in suspension. Transition. Change. Reversal of the mind and one's way of life. In a passive sense, apathy and dullness. Boredom. Abandonment. Renunciation. The changing of life's forces. Events of an uncertain nature. The period of respite between significant events. Sacrifice. Repentance. Readjustment. Efforts may have to be undertaken toward the success of a goal, which still may not be attained. Regeneration. Improvement. Rebirth. The approach of new life forces. This is the time to condition oneself for new experiences. Surrender. Lack of progress. Oversacrifice. An unappreciated person.

REVERSE MEANINGS: Lack of sacrifice. Unwillingness to make the necessary effort. Failure to give of one's self. Preoccupation with the ego. False prophecy. Useless sacrifice.

XIII Death The figure of an animated skeleton either stands in a field or rides a horse and mows down with a scythe the heads, hands and feet of various people, which remain in attitudes of movement. In some packs the decapitated heads include the Pope, a cardinal, a man and a woman. Several packs show the figure of Death in an incomplete state of decomposition with skin covering some part of the bones. In the Etteilla pack he wears a shroud, and in the Pierpont Morgan–Bergamo Visconti-Sforza deck, the card of Death is shown with white shrouds around his head and holding a large bow. In some packs this card resembles the medieval *Danse Macabre*. Sometimes Death has cut off his own foot with the scythe, as shown in the Tarot of Marseilles pack. When the figure of Death faces to the left he represents past change; when he faces to the right he suggests the future and approaching events yet unfulfilled. Frequently the title Death is omitted from the card.

DIVINATORY MEANINGS: Transformation. Clearing away the old to make way for the new. Risk for renewal. Unexpected change. Loss. Failure. Alteration. Abrupt change of the old self, though not necessarily physical death. The ending of a familiar situation or friendship. Loss of income or financial security. Beginning of a new era. Illness, possibly even death. Streak of bad luck. A loan that will not be repaid.

REVERSE MEANINGS: Stagnation. Immobility. Slow changes. Partial change. Inertia. Narrowly avoiding serious accident.

XIIII Temperance A young female figure, usually winged and wearing a long gown, continuously pours measured water from one urn to another, but no water is lost through spilling. Frequently the figure of Temperance is shown with one foot on earth and the other in water. In the Egyptian tarots the figure appears to be male. The mixing and transference of the liquid suggests a uniting of abilities and forces coupled with self-control, patience, supervision and consistency.

DIVINATORY MEANINGS: Moderation. Temperance. Patience. That which can be accomplished through self-control and frugality. Accommodation. Harmony. The mixing or bringing together into perfect union. Management. Compatibility. Good impression. Fusion. Adjustment. Good influence. Fortunate omen. Consolidation. Successful combination. Ability to recognize and utilize the material and intellectual manifestations available to oneself. Possibly a person without excessive tendencies. Well-liked. Highly regarded. Mother image. Father image. Worldly image. Exudes confidence and placidity. Possibly too temperate and moderate to achieve a goal presently out of reach.

REVERSE MEANINGS: Discord. Disunion. Conflict of interest. Hostility. Inability to work with others. Difficulty in understanding others. Impatience. Sterility. Frustration.

XV The Devil A grotesque creature, usually with the horns of a ram or deer, the breasts and arms of a woman, the body of a man, the hairy legs and hooves of a goat, and a tail and batlike wings, stands on a cubic stone to which are chained two small figures or satyrs. In some tarot packs, The Devil has many eyes and faces on his body. The Egyptian tarots show The Devil as a winged, large-jawed creature representing Typhon. Minchiate packs show a bare-chested winged figure with a band of snakes around its waist. Some packs bear the inscription "*Solve*" and "*Coagula*" on The Devil's arms, and in an old Etteilla series The Devil appears on top of a mountain. In the 1JJ tarot pack a seated woman near The Devil holds her head in a bowed position, hands covering her eyes, in an attitude of suffering.

DIVINATORY MEANINGS: Subordination. Ravage. Bondage. Malevolence. Subservience. Downfall. Lack of success. Weird experience. Bad outside influence or advice. Black magic. Unexpected failure. Seeming inability to realize one's goals. Dependence upon another person that leads to unhappiness. Controversy. Violence. Shock. Fatality. Self-punishment. Temptation to evil. Regression. Self-destruction. Disaster. Astral influence. The tearing apart of one's self-expression to such an extent that the person becomes ineffectual. An ill-tempered person. Lack of humor except at another's expense. Lack of principles.

REVERSE MEANINGS: Release from bondage. Throwing off shackles. Respite. Divorce. Recognition of one's needs by another person. Overcoming insurmountable handicaps. The beginning of spiritual understanding. The first steps toward enlightenment.

XVI The Falling Tower This card is customarily shown as a narrow brick or stone tower with two or three windows. The tower's crown pinnacle is struck by lightning emanating from the sun. Two figures fall from the tower; sometimes one figure is shown already on the ground. In the Grand Tarot Belline pack one of the figures falling head over heels is a king who wears a crown. Besides the falling figures, other objects plunge earthward; these vary from pack to pack and include gold coins, bricks, stones and droplets of water and fire. In the Egyptian tarot the apex of the pyramid is shattered by a lightning bolt. An old Etteilla pack depicts a walled city engulfed in flames with buildings toppling over.

DIVINATORY MEANINGS: Complete and sudden change. Breaking down of old beliefs. Abandonment of past relationships. Severing of a friendship. Changing of one's opinion. Unexpected events. Disruption. Adversity. Calamity. Misery. Deception. Bankruptcy. Termination. Havoc. Downfall. Undoing. Ruin. Disruption. Loss of stability. A sudden event that destroys trust. Loss of money. Loss of security. Loss of love and affection. Setback. Terrible change. Unforeseen accident.

REVERSE MEANINGS: Continued oppression. Following old ways. Living in a rut. Inability to effect any worthwhile change. Entrapped in an unhappy situation. Imprisoned.

XVII The Star A naked young woman is usually portrayed kneeling with one foot in water and one knee on the ground. She pours water from two urns onto the earth and sea. Some scholars suggest that this card allegorizes the sacrament of baptism. Above the girl's head are eight stars; one central large star, possibly representing Sirius, and the other smaller stars, suggesting the planets, grouped around the center star. In the background are bushes and nearby rests a bird or sometimes a butterfly, suggesting the Tree of Life, fruits of life and rebirth. In Egyptian tarots the star encircles a large triangle divided into black and white halves, while the female figure pours water on a small bush. The Church of Light tarot has an additional seven stars trailing in the distance.

DIVINATORY MEANINGS: Hope. Faith. Inspiration. Bright prospects. Mixing of the past and present. Promising opportunity. Optimism. Insight. Good omen. Spiritual love. Ascending star. Rebirth. Influence of the stars on one's birth. Astrological influence. Accumulation of past knowledge for use in the present. Results that will soon come to pass from energies expended. Fulfillment. Satisfaction. Pleasure. The proper balancing of desire and work, hope and effort, love and expression. A favorable card suggesting that desire and energy are essential to happiness.

REVERSE MEANINGS: Unfulfilled hopes. Disappointment. Pessimism. Bad luck. Lack of opportunity. Stubbornness. Bullheadedness. Imbalance. Conclusion of an unsatisfactory business experience or friendship.

XVIII The Moon The Moon or Luna, generally full but sometimes crescent, is seen rising between two towers while a dog and wolf bay in the night. In the foreground a large red crayfish emerges from its hiding place in a pool of water. The Gringonneur pack shows two figures with astrological instruments observing the heavens. The Tarocchi of Mantegna pack depicts a female figure riding a horse-drawn chariot in the sky and holding in her right hand a crescent moon. In the 1JJ tarot pack a figure is shown serenading a young woman on a balcony. Egyptian tarots usually show two pyramids and sometimes a white and black dog. Fergus Hall depicts The Moon card without towers; instead, a large face with a heart on its left cheek emerges from the inside of a crescent moon that hovers above a thinly wooded hilltop.

DIVINATORY MEANINGS: Deception. Twilight. Obscurity. Trickery. Dishonesty. Disillusionment. Danger. Error. Caution. Warning. Bad influence. Ulterior motives. Insincerity. False friends. Selfishness. Deceit. Double dealing. Craftiness. False pretenses. Disgrace. Slander. Liability. Being taken advantage of. An insincere relationship. Superficiality. Unknown enemies. The meeting of many divergent influences. Falling into a trap. Being misled. Failure to avoid dangers. Unforeseen changes in plans.

REVERSE MEANINGS: A minor deception recognized before damage is done. Trifling mistakes. Overcoming bad temptations. Gain without paying the price. Taking advantage of someone.

XVIIII The Sun There are two types of illustrations prevalent for The Sun card. One frequent Sun card depicts two figures, a boy and girl, standing in a garden in front of a stone wall; usually they are naked or scantily clad and above them shines a rayed sun with golden droplets or tears. The other typical card depicts a naked boy, riding horseback and holding a large banner. The child's head is adorned with a chaplet of flowers and above him shines a brilliant sun. Frequently a face is painted on the round sun. In the minchiate pack the two figures are usually older, the man bearded. In the Egyptian tarot the figures are a maiden and a young Egyptian youth standing beneath a solar nimbus with a phallic symbol of a line piercing a rayed circle. The 1JJ tarot pack shows a young boy and girl arm in arm and sitting on the ground with a book in their laps.

DIVINATORY MEANINGS: Satisfaction. Accomplishment. Contentment. Success. Favorable social relationships.

Love. Joy. Devotion. Unselfish sentiment. Engagement. Favorable omen. A happy marriage. Pleasure in daily existence. Earthly happiness. The contentment derived from extending oneself toward another human being. A good friend. High spirits. Warmth. Sincerity. The rewards of a new friendship. Pleasures derived from simple things. Achievement in the arts. Liberation. Appreciation of small favors. Acceptance of life.

REVERSE MEANINGS: Unhappiness. Loneliness. Possibly a broken engagement or marriage. Canceled plans. Triumph delayed although not necessarily completely lost. Clouded future. Lack of friendship.

XX Judgment The winged angel Gabriel with a halo is shown floating on a cloud and blowing a trumpet, sometimes with a banner hanging from the trumpet. Three or more figures rise from partially concealed tombs. The Rider-Waite deck depicts several persons rising from tombs floating on water. Etteilla depicts a crowd of figures surrounding the scene of a miracle performed by the angel. The Egyptian tarot portrays three mummies rising from a mummy case. The Aquarian tarot depicts a trumpeter who plays his instrument and its sound is heard throughout the countryside. Sometimes the figures on the ground seem to be drawn up toward the angel in heaven, and in other cards they appear to be praying and pleading for forgiveness.

DIVINATORY MEANINGS: Atonement. Judgment. The need to repent and forgive. The moment to account for the manner in which we have used our opportunities. The possibility that present conduct toward other people is unfair and unkind. Rejuvenation. Rebirth. Improvement. Development. Promotion. Effort that ends in just reward. The desire for immortality. The possibility exists that someone is taking unfair advantage, which they will come to regret. Legal judgment. The outcome of a lawsuit or personal conflict. One should carefully consider present actions as they affect other persons.

REVERSE MEANINGS: Delay. Disappointment. Failure to face facts. Indecision. Divorce. Procrastination. Theft. Alienation of affection. Deep worry.

XXI The World A female figure, almost naked except for a thin scarf blown by the wind, stands within an elliptical wreath. She holds a wand, sometimes in only one hand and occasionally in both hands. Usually, her left foot crosses behind her right leg. Sometimes she appears to be dancing. In the corners of the card appear the winged cherubim represented by a man, eagle, bull and lion; the figures occasionally are shown with halos. Some packs show a large globe to signify earth or the world. The Belgian tarots depict a nude winged figure standing on a large globe.

DIVINATORY MEANINGS: Attachment. Completion. Perfection. Recognition. Honors. Ultimate change. The end result of all efforts. Success. Assurance. Synthesis. Fulfillment. Capability. Triumph in undertakings. The rewards that come from hard work. The path of liberation. Eternal life. The final goal to which all other cards have led. Admiration of others. Inheritance. The outcome of events in spite of other signs. This is a very favorable card, especially if surrounded by other favorable cards.

REVERSE MEANINGS: Imperfection. Failure to complete the task one starts. Lack of vision. Failure. Disappointment.

THE FIFTY-SIX MINOR ARCANA CARDS

THE SUIT OF SWORDS

King of Swords

DIVINATORY MEANINGS: An active and determined person. Experienced. Authoritative. Controlled. Commanding. A professional person. Someone proficient in his field. Highly analytical. Justice. Force. Superiority. A person having many ideas, thoughts and designs.

REVERSE MEANINGS: A person who may pursue a matter to ruin. Cruelty. Conflict. Selfishness. Sadism. A dangerous or wicked person. One who causes unnecessary disturbance and sadness. Perversity.

Queen of Swords

DIVINATORY MEANINGS: Sharp. Quick-witted. A keen person. Intensely perceptive. A subtle person. May signify a widow or woman of sadness. Mourning. Privation. Absence. Loneliness. Separation. One who has savored great happiness but who presently knows the anxiety of misfortune and reversal.

REVERSE MEANINGS: Narrow-mindedness. Maliciousness. Bigotry. Deceitfulness. Vengefulness. Prudishness. A treacherous enemy. An ill-tempered person.

Knight of Swords

DIVINATORY MEANINGS: Bravery. Skill. Capacity. The strength and dash of a young man. Heroic action. Opposition and war. Impetuous rush into the unknown without fear. The surrounding cards indicate the influences around the knight in his gallant pursuit.

REVERSE MEANINGS: Incapacity. Imprudence. Dispute or ruin due to a woman. Impulsive mistakes. Conceited fool. Simplicity. Disunion.

Page of Swords

DIVINATORY MEANINGS: This card symbolizes a person adept at perceiving and uncovering the unknown or that which is less than obvious. The quality of insight. Vigilance. Agility. Spying. A discreet person. An active youth. A lithe figure, alert and awake to unknown dangers.

REVERSE MEANINGS: Revealed as an imposter. The unforeseen. Illness is also possible. Powerless in the face of stronger forces. Lack of preparation.

Ten of Swords

DIVINATORY MEANINGS: Ruin. Pain. Affliction. Sadness. Mental anguish. Desolation. Tears. Misfortune. Trouble. Disappointment. Grief. Sorrow.

REVERSE MEANINGS: Benefit. Profit. Temporary gain. Improvement. Passing success. Temporary favor. Momentary advantage.

Nine of Swords

DIVINATORY MEANINGS: Misery. Concern. Quarrel. Unhappiness. Miscarriage. Anxiety over a loved one. Worry. Despair. Suffering.

REVERSE MEANINGS: Doubt. Suspicion. Slanderous gossip. Shame. Scruple. Timidity. Shady character. Reasonable fear.

Eight of Swords

DIVINATORY MEANINGS: Crisis. Calamity. Conflict. Domination. Imprisonment. Turmoil. Bad news. Censure. Criticism. Sickness. Calumny.

REVERSE MEANINGS: Treachery in the past. Difficulty. Hard work. Depressed state of mind. Disquiet. Accident. Fatality.

Seven of Swords

DIVINATORY MEANINGS: New plans. Wishes. Fortitude. Perseverance. Attempt. Endeavor. Hope. Confidence. Fantasy. Design.

REVERSE MEANINGS: Arguments. Quarrels. Uncertain counsel or advice. Circumspection. Slander. Babbling.

Six of Swords

DIVINATORY MEANINGS: A trip or journey. Travel. Voyage. Route. Headstrong attempt to overcome difficulties. Expedient manner. Success after anxiety.

REVERSE MEANINGS: Stalemate. Unwanted proposal. No immediate solution to present difficulties. Confession. Declaration.

Five of Swords

DIVINATORY MEANINGS: Conquest. Defeat. Destruction of others. Degradation. Adversaries may arise. Revocation. Infamy. Dishonor.

REVERSE MEANINGS: Uncertain outlook. Chance of loss or defeat. Weakness. Possible misfortune befalling a friend. Seduction. Burial.

Four of Swords

DIVINATORY MEANINGS: Respite. Rest after illness. Repose. Replenishment. Solitude. Exile. Retreat. Temporary seclusion. Abandonment.

REVERSE MEANINGS: Activity. Circumspection. Precaution. Economy. Guarded advancement. Desire to recover what is lost.

Three of Swords

DIVINATORY MEANINGS: Absence. Disappointment. Strife. Removal. Dispersion. Diversion. Opposition. Separation. Delay.

REVERSE MEANINGS: Distraction. Confusion. Disorder. Error. Mistake. Incompatibility. Mental anxieties. Loss. Alienation.

Two of Swords

DIVINATORY MEANINGS: Balanced force. Harmony. Firmness. Concord. Offsetting factors. Stalemate. Affection.

REVERSE MEANINGS: Duplicity. Falsehood. Misrepresentation. Disloyalty. Dishonor. Treachery. False friends. Lies.

Ace of Swords

DIVINATORY MEANINGS: Great determination. Initiative. Strength. Force. Activity. Excessiveness. Triumph. Power. Success. Fertility. Prosperity. Deep emotional feeling. Love. Championship. Conquest.

REVERSE MEANINGS: Debacle. Tyranny. Disaster. Self-destruction. Violent temper. Embarrassment. Obstacle. Infertility. Hindrance.

SUIT OF STAVES

King of Staves

DIVINATORY MEANINGS: An honest and conscientious person. Mature. Wise. Devoted. Friendly. Sympathetic. Educated. A gentleman. Generally married. Fatherly.

REVERSE MEANINGS: Severity. Austerity. Somewhat excessive and exaggerated ideas. Dogmatic. Deliberate.

Queen of Staves

DIVINATORY MEANINGS: A sympathetic and understanding person. Friendly. Loving. Honorable. Chaste. Practical. Full of feminine charm and grace. Capable of meaningful expression and love. Gracious hostess. Sincere interest in others.

REVERSE MEANINGS: Jealousy. Deceit. Possible infidelity. Unstable emotions. Fickleness. Resistance. Obstacles. Opposition.

Knight of Staves

DIVINATORY MEANINGS: Departure. A journey. Advancement into the unknown. Alteration. Flight. Absence. Change of residence.

REVERSE MEANINGS: Discord. Interruption. Unexpected change. Quarreling. Breakup of personal relationships. Rupture. Discontinuance.

Page of Staves

DIVINATORY MEANINGS: A faithful and loyal person. An envoy. Emissary. Entrusted friend. A stranger with good intentions. A consistent person. A bearer of important news.

REVERSE MEANINGS: Indecision in proceeding. Reluctance. Instability. Inability to make decisions. A gossip. Bearer of bad tidings. A person who may break one's heart. Displeasure.

Ten of Staves

DIVINATORY MEANINGS: Overburdened. Excessive pressures. Problems soon to be resolved. Striving to meet a goal or to maintain a certain level or position. Possibly using power for selfish ends.

REVERSE MEANINGS: Difficulties. Intrigues. Duplicity. Treachery. A traitor. Deceiver. Subterfuge. Some losses will occur.

Nine of Staves

DIVINATORY MEANINGS: Expectation of difficulties and changes. Awaiting tribulation. Anticipation. Hidden enemies. Deception. Discipline. Order. A pause in a current struggle.

REVERSE MEANINGS: Obstacles. Adversity. Problems. Delays. Displeasure. Calamity. Disaster. Barriers to overcome. Ill health.

Eight of Staves

DIVINATORY MEANINGS: Swift activity. Sudden progress or movement. Speed. Hastily made decisions. Too rapid advancement.

REVERSE MEANINGS: Thorns of dispute. Jealousy. Harassment. Quarrels. Discord. Delay. Stagnation. Domestic quarrels.

Seven of Staves

DIVINATORY MEANINGS: Success. Gain. Overcoming obstacles and challenges. Surmounting overwhelming odds. Advantage. Victory.

REVERSE MEANINGS: Consternation. Anxiety. Embarrassment. Indecision. Hesitancy causing losses. Uncertainty. Perplexity. Doubt.

Six of Staves

DIVINATORY MEANINGS: Conquest. Triumph. Good news. Gain. Advancement. Expectation. Desires realized. The results of efforts.

REVERSE MEANINGS: Indefinite delay. Fear. Apprehension. Disloyalty. Superficial benefit. Inconclusive gain.

Five of Staves

DIVINATORY MEANINGS: Unsatisfied desires. Struggle. Labor. Endeavors. Violent strife. Conflict. Obstacles.

REVERSE MEANINGS: Trickery. Contradictions. Complexity. Involvement. Caution against indecision.

Four of Staves

DIVINATORY MEANINGS: Romance. Society. Harmony. Newly acquired prosperity. Peace. Tranquility. The fruits of labor. Rest after peace.

REVERSE MEANINGS: Loss of full tranquility. Unfulfilled romance. Insecurity. Tarnished beauty. Incomplete happiness.

Three of Staves

DIVINATORY MEANINGS: Practical knowledge. Business acumen. Strength. Enterprise. Negotiations. Trade. Commerce. Undertaking.

REVERSE MEANINGS: Assistance with an ulterior motive. Treachery. Diminishing adversity. Beware of help offered.

Two of Staves

DIVINATORY MEANINGS: Mature individual. Ruler. Attainment of goals and needs. Boldness. Courage in undertakings. A dominant personality.

REVERSE MEANINGS: Sadness. Trouble. Restraint caused by others. Loss of faith. Unexpected surprise.

Ace of Staves

DIVINATORY MEANINGS: Creation. Beginning. Invention. Start of an undertaking. Fortune. Enterprise. Gain. Inheritance. Birth of a child. Beginning of a meaningful experience. An adventure. Escapade.

REVERSE MEANINGS: False start. Cloudy outlook. Unrealized goal. Decadence. Empty existence. Vexation. Cancellation of plans.

SUIT OF CUPS

King of Cups

DIVINATORY MEANINGS: Responsibility and creativity. Learned person. Professional. Businessperson. Lawyer. Religious person. Scientist. A considerate person. Kindly. Reliable. Liberal in manner. Artist. Interested in the arts and sciences. Generous.

REVERSE MEANINGS: Artistic temperament. Double-dealing. Dishonesty. Scandal. Loss. Ruin. Injustice. A crafty person without virtue. Shifty in dealings.

Queen of Cups

DIVINATORY MEANINGS: A warmhearted and fair person. Poetic. Beloved. Adored. Good friend and mother. Devoted wife. Practical. Honest. Possesses loving intelligence. Gift of vision.

REVERSE MEANINGS: Inconsistency of honor. Possible immorality. Dishonesty. Unreliability. Vice. Not to be trusted.

Knight of Cups

DIVINATORY MEANINGS: An invitation or opportunity may soon arise. Arrival. Approach. Advancement. Attraction. Inducement. Appeal. Request. Challenge. Proposal. Proposition.

REVERSE MEANINGS: Subtlety. Artifice. Trickery. Deception. Fraud. A sly and cunning person. A person capable of swindling.

Page of Cups

DIVINATORY MEANINGS: A studious and intent person. Reflective. Meditative. Loyal. Willing to offer services and efforts toward a specific goal. A helpful person. A trustworthy worker.

REVERSE MEANINGS: Inclination. Deviation. Susceptibility. Temporary distraction. Seduction. A flatterer.

Ten of Cups

DIVINATORY MEANINGS: Home. Abode. Happiness. Joy. Pleasure. Peace. Love. Contentment. Good family life. Honor. Esteem. Virtue. Reputation.

REVERSE MEANINGS: Loss of friendship. Unhappiness. Family quarrel. Pettiness. Rage. Combat. Strife. Opposition. Differences of opinion.

Nine of Cups

DIVINATORY MEANINGS: Success. Material attainment. Advantage. Well-being. Abundance. Good health. Victory. Difficulties surmounted.

REVERSE MEANINGS: Mistakes. Material loss. Imperfections. Misplaced truth. False freedom. Opposition. Differences. Dispute.

Eight of Cups

DIVINATORY MEANINGS: Discontinuance of effort. Disappointment. Abandonment of previous plans. Shyness. Modesty. Abandoned success.

REVERSE MEANINGS: Happiness. Effort continued until full success is attained. Festivity. Joy. Gaiety. Feasting.

Seven of Cups

DIVINATORY MEANINGS: Fantasy. Unrealistic attitudes. Imagination. Daydreams. Foolish whims. Wishful thinking. Illusionary success.

REVERSE MEANINGS: Desire. Determination. Strong willpower. A goal nearly attained. Intelligent choice. Desire. Will. Resolution.

Six of Cups

DIVINATORY MEANINGS: Memories. Past influences. Things that have vanished. Childhood past. Nostalgia. Faded images. Longing.

REVERSE MEANINGS: The future. Opportunities ahead. Coming events. New vistas. Plans that may fail. That which will shortly arrive.

Five of Cups

DIVINATORY MEANINGS: Partial loss. Regret. Friendship without real meaning. Marriage without real love. Imperfection. Flaw. Delayed inheritance. Incomplete union or partnership.

REVERSE MEANINGS: Hopeful outlook. Favorable expectations. New alliances. Affinity. Return of an old friend. Reunion.

Four of Cups

DIVINATORY MEANINGS: Weariness. Aversion. Disgust. Disappointment. Unhappiness. Bitter experience. Stationary period in one's life.

REVERSE MEANINGS: New possibilities. New relationships. New approaches to old problems. New acquaintance. New knowledge.

Three of Cups

DIVINATORY MEANINGS: Resolution of a problem. Conclusion. Solace. Healing. Satisfactory result. Partial fulfillment. Compromise.

REVERSE MEANINGS: Excessive pleasures. Overabundance. Superfluity. Loss of prestige. Delays. Unappreciation.

Two of Cups

DIVINATORY MEANINGS: Love. Friendship beginning or renewed. Passion. Union. Engagement. Understanding. Cooperation. Partnership. Marriage.

REVERSE MEANINGS: Unsatisfactory love. False friendship. Troubled relationship. Divorce. Separation. Crossed desires. Opposition. Disunion. Misunderstanding.

Ace of Cups

DIVINATORY MEANINGS: Great abundance. Fulfillment. Perfection. Joy. Fertility. Opulence. Fullness. Happiness. Productiveness. Beauty and pleasure. Goodness overflowing. Favorable outlook.

REVERSE MEANINGS: Change. Alteration. Erosion. Instability. Sterility. Unrequited love. Clouded joy. False heart. Inconsistency.

THE SUIT OF COINS

King of Coins

DIVINATORY MEANINGS: An experienced and successful leader. A person of character and intelligence. Business acumen. Mathematical ability. Loyal friend. Reliable in marriage. Successful businessperson. Wise investments. Ability to acquire money and valuable possessions.

REVERSE MEANINGS: Corruption. Using any means to achieve the desired end. Vice. Avarice. Unfaithfulness. An old and vicious man. Peril. Danger. Thriftlessness.

Queen of Coins

DIVINATORY MEANINGS: Prosperity and well-being. Wealth. Abundance. Luxury. Opulence. Extreme comfort. Generosity. Security. Liberty. Magnificence. Grace. Dignity. A rich person who is generous and charitable. A noble soul.

REVERSE MEANINGS: False prosperity. Suspense. Suspicion. Responsibilities neglected. Vicious person. Untrusting person. Fearful of failure.

Knight of Coins

DIVINATORY MEANINGS: A mature and responsible person. Reliable. Methodical. Patient. Persistent. Able to conclude a task. Laborious. Organized. Capable. A dependable person.

REVERSE MEANINGS: Stagnation. Carelessness. Inertia. Lack of determination or direction. Narrow-mindedness. Limited by dogmatic views. Idleness.

Page of Coins

DIVINATORY MEANINGS: Deep concentration and application. Study. Scholarship. Reflection. Respect for knowledge. Desire for learning and new ideas. A do-gooder. Bearer of news.

REVERSE MEANINGS: An unrealistic person. Failure to recognize obvious facts. Dissipation of ideas. Illogical thinking. Rebelliousness. Wastefulness. Loss. Unfavorable news.

Ten of Coins

DIVINATORY MEANINGS: Prosperity. Riches. Security. Safety. Family. Family matters. Ancestry. Inheritance. Home. Dwelling.

REVERSE MEANINGS: Poor risk. Bad odds. Possible loss. Hazard. Robbery. Loss of inheritance. Dissipation. Gambling.

Nine of Coins

DIVINATORY MEANINGS: Accomplishment. Discernment. Discretion. Foresight. Safety. Prudence. Material well-being. Love of nature.

REVERSE MEANINGS: Threat to safety. Roguery. Dissipation. Danger. Storms. Bad faith. Possible loss of a valued friendship or a treasured possession.

Eight of Coins

DIVINATORY MEANINGS: Apprenticeship. Craftsmanship. Fast to learn. Candor. Frankness. Modesty. Handiwork. Personal effort.

REVERSE MEANINGS: Lack of ambition. Vanity. Conceit. Disillusionment. Usury. Hypocrisy. Flattery. Intrigue.

Seven of Coins

DIVINATORY MEANINGS: Ingenuity. Growth. Hard work. Progress. Successful dealings. Money. Wealth. Treasure. Gain.

REVERSE MEANINGS: Anxiety. Impatience. Uneasiness. Imprudent actions. Loss of money. Unwise investments.

Six of Coins

DIVINATORY MEANINGS: Generosity. Philanthropy. Charity. Kindness. Gratification. Gifts. Material gain.

REVERSE MEANINGS: Avarice. Selfishness. Envy. Jealousy. Ungiving of one's self. Bad debts. Unpaid loans.

Five of Coins

DIVINATORY MEANINGS: Material trouble. Destitution. Loss. Failure. Error. Impoverishment. Mistress. Lover. Misaffection.

REVERSE MEANINGS: Reversal of bad trend. New interests. Overcoming disharmony in marriage or love.

Four of Coins

DIVINATORY MEANINGS: Love of material wealth. Hoarder. Usurer. Skinflint. Miser. Ungenerous person. Inability to share.

REVERSE MEANINGS: Setbacks in material holdings. Obstacles. Opposition to further gain. Suspense and delay. Spendthrift.

Three of Coins

DIVINATORY MEANINGS: Great skill in trade or work. Mastery. Perfection. Artistic ability. Dignity. Renown. Rank. Power.

REVERSE MEANINGS: Sloppiness. Mediocrity. Lower quality. Money problems. Commonplace ideas. Lack of skill. Preoccupation.

Two of Coins

DIVINATORY MEANINGS: Difficulty in launching new projects. Difficult situations arising. New troubles. Embarrassment. Worry. Concern.

REVERSE MEANINGS: Literary ability. Agility in handling matters. Simulated enjoyment. Enforced gaiety. Letter. Message. Missive.

Ace of Coins

DIVINATORY MEANINGS: Perfection. Attainment. Prosperity. Felicity. Great wealth. Riches. Bliss. Ecstasy. Gold. Valuable coins or artifacts. Treasures. The combination of material and spiritual prosperity.

REVERSE MEANINGS: Prosperity without happiness. Misused wealth. Wasted money. Corruption by money. Miserliness. Greed. Fool's gold.

XVI
SPREADING THE TAROT DECK

THE KNOWN METHODS of spreading the twenty-two Major Arcana cards are numerous and some of them are exceedingly complicated. Nothing written in mid-fifteenth-century Italy about spreading the Visconti-Sforza packs for divination has descended to us. The ten-card spread explained here, which dates back several centuries, is one of the earliest and most effective methods. After a few practice readings this method will become quite natural and easy to use.

TEN-CARD SPREAD WITH TWENTY-TWO MAJOR ARCANA CARDS

The ten-card spread may be used with the entire seventy-eight-card *tarocchi* deck or with a lesser number of cards. The following explanation involves only the twenty-two Major Arcana cards.

The fifty-six Minor Arcana cards are set aside. The diviner, also known as the reader or interpreter of the deck, places the twenty-two Major Arcana cards in numerical sequence. The unnumbered card, The Fool, is placed either at the beginning of the deck, in the middle of the deck, between the twentieth and twenty-first numbered cards, or at the end of the deck. Generally, The Fool is best placed at the beginning of the deck, preceding The Magician, facing out. Arrange the pack so that upon placing the twenty-two Major Arcana cards face down on the table, The Fool is closest to the table.

The person seeking an answer to a question is known as the questioner. The questioner sits at a table opposite the diviner and both persons maintain a serious mental attitude. The questioner puts all other thoughts and desires from his mind except the specific question, which he states aloud to the diviner, while simultaneously shuffling the face-down deck. The person who handles the cards impregnates them with his own personal magnetism and thereby creates a rapport between his subconscious and the cards. The cards may be shuffled either hand over hand or by riffling (separating the deck into two parts and riffling with the thumb so the cards intermix). The shuffling must be done by the person who wishes to have an interpretation or prediction concerning himself—not by the interpreter. When the questioner is satisfied with his shuffling, he places the deck face down in front of the diviner. The cards are always viewed from the diviner's position. Beginning with the top card as number one, the second card as number two and so on, the diviner turns up the first six cards and places them face up on the table in the sequence shown in the diagram.

The diviner should turn the cards over from left to right, thereby assuring that the cards continue to point in the same direction as placed on the table by the questioner. The cards that face the diviner are said to be positioned for a strong, positive reading. The cards that face the questioner are said to be upside down or inverted and, therefore, have a weak, delayed or even reversed meaning. In the event the first card turned over by the diviner is upside down, the diviner should reverse the first card so that it is upright. The remaining nine cards should be turned over from the bottom to the top in such a manner as to reverse the direction of each of the cards since the questioner may have inadvertently placed the entire pack upside down before the diviner. Similarly, if during a spread the majority of the cards are reversed, the diviner may elect to place the cards upright if it seems more natural and gives a more meaningful reading.

The correct manner of turning over the cards is illustrated in the following diagram:

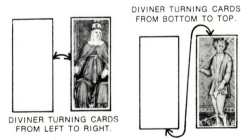

Sequence and Meanings The sequence of laying out the cards in the ten-card spread is as follows:

CARD NUMBER 1—PRESENT POSITION: Atmosphere in which the questioner is presently working and living. Shows the area of influence in which the questioner presently exists and the atmosphere in which other currents are working. This card represents the questioner.

CARD NUMBER 2—IMMEDIATE INFLUENCE: Shows the nature of the influence or immediate sphere of involvement or obstacles that lie just ahead. This card crosses the questioner.

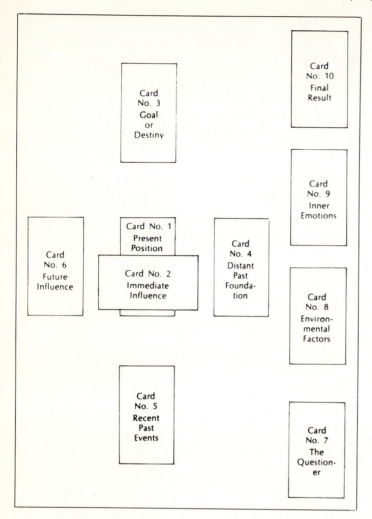

CARD NUMBER 3—GOAL OR DESTINY: Shows the ultimate goal or destiny of the questioner. Indicates the best that can be accomplished by the questioner based upon existing circumstances. This card may also represent the questioner's aim or ideal within his present frame of reference. This card crowns the questioner.

CARD NUMBER 4—DISTANT PAST FOUNDATION: Shows the broad and basic events and influences that existed in the distant past and upon which the present events are taking place. It is the basis of fact already passed into actuality and which is embodied within the questioner. This card is behind the questioner.

CARD NUMBER 5—RECENT PAST EVENTS: Shows the most recent sphere of influence or events that have just passed or are just passing. This card may also represent distant past influences of an inordinately strong nature that exert pressures on recent influences. This card is beneath the questioner.

CARD NUMBER 6—FUTURE INFLUENCE: Shows the sphere of influence that is coming into being in the near future, in a broad sense. This card is before the questioner.

After the diviner has read the foregoing six cards, he then proceeds to turn over the next four cards from the deck. They are placed one above the other, in a line to the right of the previous six cards, as shown in the diagram.

CARD NUMBER 7—THE QUESTIONER: Shows the questioner in his present position or attitude within the circumstances surrounding him. This card attempts to place the questioner in proper perspective.

CARD NUMBER 8—ENVIRONMENTAL FACTORS: Shows the questioner's influence on other people and his position in life. Reveals those tendencies and factors that exist with respect to other persons who may have an effect on the questioner.

CARD NUMBER 9—INNER EMOTIONS: Shows the inner hopes, hidden emotions and secret desires, fears and anxieties of the questioner including those thoughts that will come to the mind of the questioner in the future. This card may also reveal secrets the questioner keeps from other people and ulterior motives that concern the questioner.

CARD NUMBER 10—FINAL RESULT: Shows the culmination and results that will be brought about from all the influences as revealed by the other cards in the divination, provided events and influences continue as indicated.

After reading each individual card the diviner should go back and interpret the cards as they relate to each other. For example, Card Number 4, Distant Past Foundation, may show a similarity to Card Number 5, Recent Past Events. Likewise, a striking connection may exist between Card Number 1, Present Position, and Card Number 7, The Questioner. Card Number 6, Future Influence, and Card Number 3, Goal or Destiny, may reveal a trend in future possibilities. Card Number 9, Inner Emotions, frequently reveals an insight about the inner emotions, fears and anxieties of the questioner that helps explain the significance of the other cards. The relationship between several cards may indicate a trend or pattern. The cards may reveal the changing life pattern of the questioner and the areas of new direction into which he is advancing.

Interpretations The interpretations revealed in the ten-card spread may vary slightly from reading to reading, since the questioner may have one or more overlapping influences. Thus, the diviner should seek to interpret the cards, as spread, in the manner that feels most comfortable. Always bear in mind that the titles on the cards, the divinatory suggestions for each card and the descriptive name of each of the ten sequential spaces in the card spread are meant as *suggestive* references. The cards frequently reveal considerably more about the questioner than solely a response to the original question. Therefore, the diviner, through practice and intuition, should read the cards freely, allowing special interpretations and ideas to come to mind.

The symbolic cards may suggest emotions, feelings and desires. They may stand for objects and persons. They may indicate circumstances and duration of time. The interpretation of each card, singularly and in connection with other cards, is limited only by the total responsiveness and capability of the diviner or interpreter.

After a reading is completed, and before starting a new reading, the diviner should remember to place the cards back in their original sequence, in order to wipe away the currents and influences remaining in the cards from the completed reading. A questioner should be allowed no more than one reading per day so as to avoid any confusion that may arise due to continuously adjusting currents and influences. This is not meant to suggest that a second reading produces an interpretation inconsistent with the previous reading. Rather, influences and currents at one moment may vary in intensity from the vibrations of the next moment and thus cause confusion. One interpretation per day, per questioner, yields the most perceptive and concise reading.

TEN-CARD SPREAD WITH FORTY-TWO CARDS

The ten-card spread may also be employed with a forty-two-card pack—using the Major Arcana cards, the sixteen court cards and the four aces in each suit. Thus, the diviner should eliminate from the pack the thirty-six pip cards from ten to two in each of the four suits.

Before the questioner shuffles the forty-two-card pack, the diviner should arrange the cards in the following sequence: the ace of swords, followed by the page, knight, queen and king of that suit; the ace of staves, followed by the court cards in the same sequence; the ace of cups and its court cards, and the ace of coins and its court cards. The Fool follows the king of cups and is followed by the Major Arcana cards from I to XXI. Thus, the ace of swords lies face down on the table before shuffling.

THE NAME SPREAD

This spread utilizes that important aspect of an individual with which he has been associated and known since birth, his full name. The name spread utilizes the full tarot deck.

After the questioner shuffles the cards while simultaneously stating his question aloud, the diviner spreads the cards face up in the same number as the full name of the questioner.

For example, if the questioner's full name, comprising twenty-one letters, is ROBERT EDWIN SOUTHWORTH, the diviner spreads the first twenty-one cards in three rows from left to right as follows:

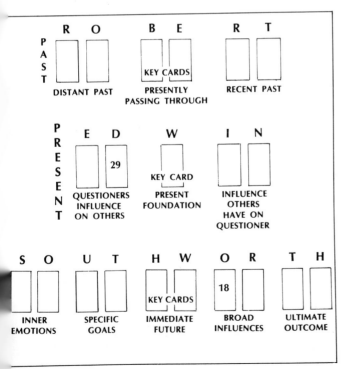

If the questioner does not have a middle name, the number of cards in the first row is repeated in the middle row. If the questioner's first or middle name does not contain a minimum of three letters, or the last name a minimum of five letters, the rows are spread with three, three and five cards representing the first, middle and last names, respectively. The center card in each row (or two cards if the row is even numbered) is the key card.

The top row represents the past influences and experiences the questioner has experienced. To the left of the center key card are those influences from the distant past that represent the previous broad background of the questioner. To the right of the key card are those influences the questioner has passed through during the relatively recent past, possibly during the past days, weeks or months. The key card represents those influences that are the most recent, either just past or just being completed.

The middle row of cards represents the period of present influences. To the left of the key card are those influences the questioner exerts upon other people with whom he comes into contact. The cards also may show the impressions and opinions held by others about the questioner. To the right of the key card are those influences and pressures that other people exert upon the questioner. The center key card represents the foundation and environment in which the questioner is presently living and working.

The bottom row of cards relates to the future and ultimate outcome. To the left of the key card are the inner emotions and specific goals of the questioner. To the immediate right of the key card are the broad influences or spheres of influence that are coming into being in the near future. To the extreme right are the ultimate outcome and final results that will be brought about from all of the influences as revealed by the other cards. The key card represents the questioner's immediate future. This card may represent obstacles that will have to be met and overcome, or it could represent opportunity, good fortune or progress toward a goal the questioner is seeking to attain.

The name spread has one additional interesting feature, the *age card*. The age of the questioner is used to determine the *age card*, which has strong meaning. For example, if the questioner, Robert Edwin Southworth, is eighteen years of age, then the diviner counts eighteen cards from left to right beginning at the top row, and the *age card* is found on the bottom row, seventh card from the left. If the questioner is twenty-nine years of age, then the *age card* is the second card in the second row (see name spread illustration). The *age card* is usually a very strong and influential card. Its meaning is generally very important and a significant key to the past, present or future of the questioner.

THE HORSESHOE SPREAD

The full deck of seventy-eight cards is shuffled face down by the questioner. The diviner then deals out the first card face down to his right on a part of the table designated pile A, and two cards face down on a part of the table designated pile B. The diviner continues to deal out the deck face down at the rate of one card on pile A and two cards on pile B until the entire deck is dealt out, leaving two piles consisting of twenty-six cards in pile A and fifty-two cards in pile B.

Pile A remains where it is for the moment. Pile B is picked up by the diviner and dealt face down into two new

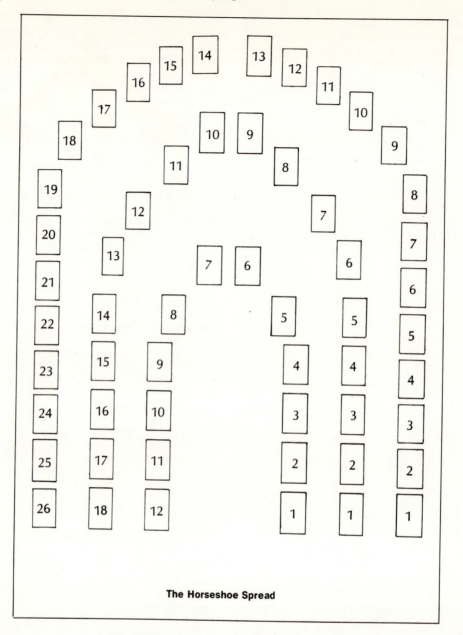

The Horseshoe Spread

piles designated C and D at the rate of one card on pile C and two cards on pile D until the full fifty-two cards are dealt out. Now there are three piles: A = 26 cards, C = 18 cards, and D = 34 cards.

The diviner takes up pile D and deals face down two new piles designated E and F at the rate of one card on pile E and two cards on pile F until the full thirty-four cards are dealt out. Now there are four piles: A = 26 cards, C = 18 cards, E = 12 cards and F = 22 cards.

The diviner puts pile F aside, as these twenty-two cards are not to be used for reading. Pile A is picked up and the diviner deals out the twenty-six cards face up from *right* to *left* in the shape of a horseshoe, the first card being at the lowest right-hand corner of the horseshoe, and the twenty-sixth card being at the lowest left-hand corner, as illustrated.

The diviner reads the cards from *right* to *left* in a connected manner. When this is completed, the diviner reads the first and twenty-sixth cards together, the second and twenty-fifth cards together, etc., and so on until all the pairs have been read.

After completing the above reading, pile A is put aside and pile C is spread out and read exactly in the same way, and then pile E last.

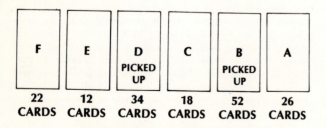

Six Card Piles for Horseshoe Spread

THE ROYAL SPREAD

This spread involves fifty-four cards: the Major Arcana cards, sixteen court cards (king, queen, knight and page), four aces, and pip cards numbered two, three and four in each suit.

To prepare this spread, the diviner first removes the twenty-four pip cards numbered five through ten in each of the four suits.

The diviner then lets the questioner select from the court cards any one key card representing himself or herself and any one to four additional cards representing either those persons who have had in the past, or who presently have, the greatest influence upon the questioner, or who are most involved in the question to which an answer is sought.

Generally, swords represent dark-complexioned persons; coins not so dark; cups rather fair people; and staves those much fairer. In making his selection, the questioner also considers those personal factors described under each of the cards in the previous section.

A man usually takes one of the kings to represent himself; a woman, generally, one of the queens. If the questioner is a youth or boy, he may select one of the knights; while a young girl may select a page. After the questioner selects the additional cards, he places face up the key card and the one to four additional court cards as shown.

The questioner then shuffles the remaining cards and the diviner places the cards face up (fifty-three to forty-nine cards, depending upon whether the questioner placed one to five cards on the table) beginning at the top row from *right* to *left*. The diviner proceeds to read the cards, combining groups of cards to form a series or sequence of events.

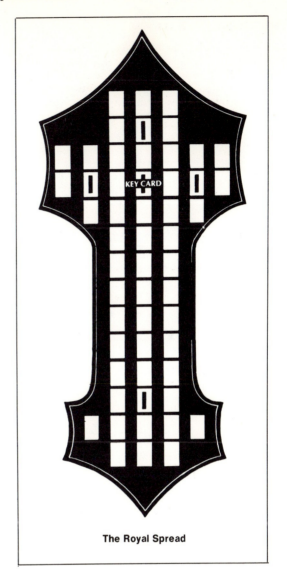

The Royal Spread

THE SEVENTH-CARD SPREAD

The questioner removes from the full deck one court card (king, queen, knight or page) representing himself and places this key card on the table face upward, leaving room to the left for seven more cards.

The questioner shuffles the cards face down and hands the pack to the diviner, who places the top card face up to the left of the key card. The diviner then counts off six cards and transfers them, in the same order, to the bottom of the pack. The seventh card is removed from the pack and placed to the left of the last spread card. This process is continued—six cards to the bottom of the pack and the seventh added to the spread—until the diviner has drawn a total of twenty-one cards and the twenty-one cards are arranged in three rows of seven cards each from *right* to *left*, always to the left of the key card.

The diviner reads the meaning of each card, and group of cards, in sequence from *right* to *left*.

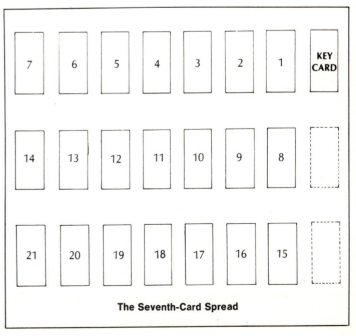

The Seventh-Card Spread

THE GYPSY SPREAD

The diviner removes the Major Arcana cards from the tarot pack and gives to the questioner the fifty-six Minor Arcana cards. The questioner shuffles the Minor Arcana and separates, into a pile face down, the first twenty cards. These twenty Minor Arcana cards are then put together with the Major Arcana cards to form a forty-two-card pack. The remaining thirty-six cards are set aside.

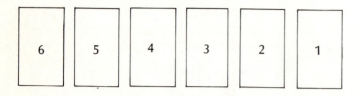

Six Card Piles for Gypsy Spread

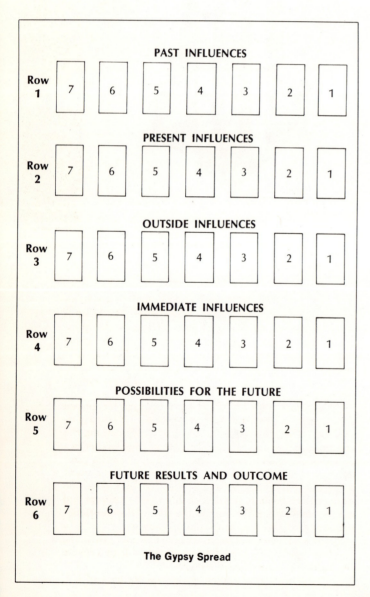

The Gypsy Spread

The questioner shuffles the forty-two-card pack and separates the cards into six piles of seven cards each, placing them face down, from *right* to *left*, so that the first seven cards form the first pile, the second seven cards form the second pile and so on.

The diviner takes up each pile, beginning with the first, and deals out the cards, face up, beginning from *right* to *left* in rows of seven until there are six rows containing seven cards each, as shown.

In this card spread, the questioner—if of the male sex—is represented by any one of the following Major Arcana cards of his choice: The Fool, The Magician, The Emperor. If the questioner is of the female sex, she is represented by The Fool, The High Priestess or The Empress.

After forty-two cards have been spread into six rows as previously directed, the card representing the questioner is removed and placed a slight distance above and to the right of the first horizontal row. The questioner then draws at random from the unused thirty-six-card pack one card to fill the vacant position.

The cards are then read from *right* to *left* beginning at the top row and continuing through each of the rows to card number 7 on the bottom row. This reading will reveal a general and continuous story of the questioner's past, present and future. Generally, instead of reading each card individually, this spread is best interpreted if the diviner takes into account adjoining cards or even an entire row of cards. Sometimes it is worthwhile to run through the cards quickly, so that the mind receives an overall general impression of the trend of the cards, and then the diviner reads the cards again in more detail. The interpretations of cards should be adapted to harmonize with the circumstances of the questioner such as age, sex and marital status. The diviner should also bear in mind that the Major Arcana cards, and then the sixteen court cards, represent stronger and more compelling forces than the Minor Arcana cards.

The meanings for each of the rows are as follows:

Row 1—PAST INFLUENCES. Those past influences and experiences that have played a part in the life of the questioner.

Row 2—PRESENT INFLUENCES. Those influences and experiences in which the questioner is involved at the present time.

Row 3—OUTSIDE INFLUENCES. Those influences, environmental factors, pressures and other outside events that are now taking place and over which the questioner has no control.

Row 4—IMMEDIATE FUTURE INFLUENCES. Those events and influences that are approaching the questioner or into which he is presently entering, including unexpected events.

Row 5—POSSIBILITIES FOR THE FUTURE. Those events and influences that are available, attainable and avoidable by the questioner if he wishes to prepare for them or avoid them.

Row 6—FUTURE RESULTS AND OUTCOME. Those events and circumstances that will ultimately result in the future of the questioner.

The Encyclopedia of Tarot

SAMPLE TAROT CARD READING

The following sample card reading illustrates the Ten-Card spread which uses the twenty-two Major Arcana cards.

The tarot pack of seventy-eight cards is separated into two sections: the twenty-two Major Arcana cards and the fifty-six Minor Arcana cards. The Minor Arcana cards are set aside. The diviner or person who will read the cards places the twenty-two Major Arcana in numerical sequence, The Fool through to The World. The cards are given to the questioner, the person who seeks to learn from the cards an answer to a specific question or the general outlook. The questioner shuffles the twenty-two Major Arcana cards while stating aloud a question. At the conclusion of the shuffle, the questioner places the twenty-two Major Arcana cards in a pile face down on the table.

The diviner turns over the top six cards and places them face up, one at a time, in the positions numbered 1 to 6 as illustrated in the ten-card spread. After interpreting and reading each of these six cards, the diviner turns over the next four cards and places them face up in the positions numbered 7 through 10. These last four cards are then interpreted by the diviner.

For this sample reading, a young woman of twenty-two years is about to graduate from college. She is uncertain as to her future. She is thinking about an acting career. Her current boyfriend seeks her hand in marriage but she is uncertain whether he would make a good husband and if they would be happy together.

After shuffling the twenty-two Major Arcana cards and placing them face down in a pile on the table, the questioner turns over the first six cards one at a time.

The first card turned up is I The Magician and it is placed at card position number 1, Present Position. This card position represents the present atmosphere of the questioner and her current circumstances. The Magician indicates that the questioner is a creative and skillful person with considerable self-reliance. She is capable of accomplishing the tasks she sets for herself. She is also a talented person who often influences other people.

The second card turned up is XVI The Tower and it is placed at card position number 2, Immediate Influence. This card position crosses the questioner and indicates the sphere of involvement or obstacles that lie just ahead. The Tower indicates a sudden and abrupt change and the termination of important past relationships. It is likely the questioner will find her emotional feelings and opinions wavering in the near future.

The third card turned up is VI The Lovers and it is placed at card position number 3, Goal or Destiny. This card position shows the ultimate goal or destiny of the questioner. The Lovers card confirms that the questioner is a warmhearted person who looks forward someday to marriage. The questioner soon will have to make important decisions about her personal life and career; she should maintain an open mind and carefully consider all possibilities before reaching a final decision.

The fourth card is XVII The Star and it is placed at card position number 4, Distant Past Foundation. This card position reveals the broad and basic influences that existed in the distant past and upon which present events are taking place. The Star is a positive card; it suggests the questioner comes from a happy home where one or both of her parents were theatrically or musically talented.

The fifth card is XVIII The Moon and it is placed at card position number 5, Recent Past Events. This card posi-

tion shows events and influences just passed or which are just passing through the life of the questioner. The Moon is a card of deception. The attentions offered by the questioner's suitor may not be entirely sincere and the questioner would be wise to view her current relationship with caution. Additionally, the possibility of a theatrical career, while attractive on the surface, may prove disappointing in the long run.

The sixth card is XII The Hanged Man and it is placed at card position number 6, Future Influence. This card position shows the sphere of influence that is approaching the questioner in the near future. The Hanged Man forebodes a period of uncertainty and change in the questioner's present way of life. She will soon recognize that her current suitor is not the ideal person for marriage and, once she expresses her feelings, it will probably signal an abrupt end to their relationship. The current life-style of the questioner will soon undergo suspension and transition.

The questioner now turns over the next four cards, one at a time, and places them face up on the table in a row to the right of the previous six cards.

The seventh card turned up is VIII Justice and it is

placed at card position number 7, The Questioner. This card position shows the questioner in her present position or attitude within the circumstances surrounding her. Justice confirms the questioner's need to resolve her problems so that she can move on to the important new relationships that are coming into her life. This card suggests that while the decisions the questioner soon will make are fair and reasonable, at first they will cause some embarrassment and unpleasantness.

The eighth card is V The Hierophant and it is placed at card position number 8, Environmental Factors. This card position shows the questioner's influence on other people. The Hierophant is a kindly person but prone to inactivity and lack of decision. She does not like to hurt people. The questioner's tendency to cling to old relationships makes it difficult for those around her to break away. The questioner should not be afraid to express her true feelings.

The ninth card is VII The Chariot and it is placed at card position number 9, Inner Emotions. This card position shows the inner hopes, hidden emotions and the fears and anxieties held by the questioner. The Chariot is a strong card and it reveals that the questioner is a strongly motivated person. At the same time, the questioner recognizes that she is prone to rush into a friendship or act impulsively. She would be wise to view people as they really are and not as she would like them to be.

The tenth card is XV The Devil and it is placed at card position number 10, Final Result. This card position shows the culmination and results that will be brought about from all the influences as revealed by the preceding nine cards. The Devil, consistent with The Moon, which appeared in card position 5, confirms that marriage to her current suitor would be unfavorable. The questioner would not receive the love and companionship she desires. It would be best to break off from her present suitor. The questioner should try to pursue her acting career for a specific period of time and, if unsuccessful, she should enter another field of employment where she would undoubtedly succeed.

Tarot card reader

XVII
CONCLUSIONS

The history of playing cards began many centuries ago in an obscure time and place; the theories are numerous and unproven. It seems likely that the court and pip cards of the so-called Minor Arcana were devised separately from the twenty-two allegorical *trionfi* or Major Arcana and at a later date they were combined for reasons of convenience into the seventy-eight-card *tarocchi* pack. The earliest extant tarot cards are the beautifully illuminated Lombard packs known as the Visconti-Sforza cards and hand painted in the mid-fifteenth century for a favored few Italian families and nobility.

The Visconti-Sforza *tarocchi* cards must have been an important commission as evidenced by their artistic execution; yet the precise purpose of these early cards remains unknown. It seems safe to conclude that the allegorical imagery of the twenty-two Major Arcana was drawn from some of the persons and events of fifteenth-century Milan, thus resulting in a pictorial representation of the Visconti-Sforza family complete with heraldic devices. The Visconti-Sforza cards may well have been a gift from the ruling duke to his wife—probably the fourth duke of Milan, Francesco Sforza, to his wife, Bianca Maria Visconti.

There are no records to indicate that *tarocchi* cards were used for fortune-telling in the fifteenth century. The earliest illustrations of the use of regular cards for fortune-telling appear in *Mainzer Kartenlosbuch* (Mainz Fortune-telling Book), which Helmut Rosenfeld believes is the work of a book illustrator who lived in Ulm about 1487. The regular cards are illustrated with meanings, four cards to each sheet. Another early work is Marcolino's *Le Sorti*, published in Venice in 1540, which depicts cards from the suit of coins that are not drawn from a *tarocchi* pack. The impetus to occult interpretations of tarot cards was started by Court de Gebelin in France in the late eighteenth century; prior to this date *tarocchi* cards appear to have been used mainly as a game or as pictorial representations of noble families and their surroundings.

The earliest list of the Major Arcana or *trionfi* appears in the Latin manuscript entitled *Sermones de Ludo Cumalis* dating from about 1500. It is interesting to note that the listing and titles of some of the cards vary from the standard sequence used today: The Empress is second, The Popess is moved to fourth place, The Arrow is substituted for The Tower and The Angel for Judgment. Several early packs contain numbers on the trump cards, including two uncut sheets from the early sixteenth century and the Catelin Geofroy cards dated 1557. Therefore, it is likely that the sequence of the Major Arcana used today differs from the original listing of *trionfi* in the fifteenth century.

In 1977 most European playing card companies celebrated the six-hundredth anniversary of the history of playing cards based upon Brother Johannes' reference to *ludus cartarum*, which allegedly dates from the year 1377. There are other early references, although not necessarily proven, that suggest the existence of cards in the latter part of the fourteenth century, such as Justinger and the Canton of Bern, 1367; the decree of Florence, 1376; Covelluzzo's reference to Saracens of Viterbo, 1379; Archives of Marseilles, 1381; ordinance of the city of Lille, 1382; Gringonneur, 1392; and the Chronicle of Morelli, 1393.

It is likely that some artistic individual, probably of Eastern origin, "invented" card designs in the fourteenth century, as evidenced by the Mamluk cards bearing Islamic influence. These court cards, which lack pictures, and the pip cards were probably brought across the Mediterranean to enter Europe through either Spain or Italy. Subsequently, in the early fifteenth century another creative person devised the twenty-two *trionfi*. It is conceivable, although doubtful, that early court and pip cards were influenced by chess and dice; similarly, it seems doubtful that the *trionfi* derives from the Kabbalah, the Hebrew alphabet, or the so-called last vestige of the great Egyptian library of Alexandria about which Court de Gebelin wrote in 1781.

Whatever the true origin, playing cards and the *trionfi* have enjoyed a remarkable development during the past six hundred years. Thus, to some unknown artistic genius of the medieval ages we are indebted for the birth of a fascinating art form that combines pictorial art and allegorical imagery. Some people view cards as arcane and mysterious, while others simply enjoy them for many hours of gaming pleasure. Perhaps what compels most of us is the knowledge that what we see in the symbology of tarot derives in large measure from our own intuition and, once revealed, reflects back upon each of us to further enrich our lives.

ANNOTATED BIBLIOGRAPHY

THIS COMPREHENSIVE LISTING comprises over one thousand seven hundred books, incunabula, manuscripts and magazine articles selected from published and unpublished works dealing with tarot cards and playing cards in their many aspects. Subjects include the origin, history, development, symbolism, art form, attributes, occult meanings and interpretations of tarot and playing cards from the fourteenth century to the present. The bibliography does not include books devoted to card tricks, card sharping, gambling and rules of card games with the exception that a few of the earliest and noteworthy rule books are included such as Hoyle and Cotton; also included are books containing rules for the games of tarock, tarocco and minchiate, and rule books which contain references to the history of playing cards. Books designated with an asterisk (*) are from the private collection of the author; double asterisk (**) denotes facsimile edition.

A

*ANONYMOUS. *Academie des Jeux.* Paris. 1659. 12mo. Rules of card games and other gambling games.
ANONYMOUS. *Academie dos Jogos.* Lisbon. 1806.
*ANONYMOUS. *Academie Universelle des Jeux.* Paris. Thirty-nine editions of this rule book were issued between the years 1717 and 1859.
ANONYMOUS. *An Act for Granting to His Majesty an Additional Duty on Cards and Dice.* London. 1756. 9 pp.
ANONYMOUS. *An Act for Granting to His Majesty Several Additional Stamp Duties . . . on Cards and Dice.* London. 1789. 10 pp.
ANONYMOUS. *Les Amusements des Allemands, or the Diversions of the Court of Vienna . . . Fortune Telling by laying out the cards* [etc]. London. 1796. 31 pp. Fortune telling with 32 cards.
ANONYMOUS. *Antico manuale per fare le carte e leggere la mano.* Rome. 1970.
ANONYMOUS. *L'art de tirer les cartes,* [etc]. Paris, 1798. Lyon, 1815.
ANONYMOUS. *L'art de tirer les cartes et de lire dans l'avenir ou le nouvel Etteilla, etc.* Rouen. n.d. 24mo. Ill.
ANONYMOUS. "Arte Lombarda dai Visconti agli Sforza," *Palazzo Reale.* Milan. 1958. Exhibition catalog.
ANONYMOUS. *L'avenir devoilé. Traite complet de l'art de la divination.* 1838. 444 pp. Ill.
ANONYMOUS. *Bibliotheca Esoterica.* Paris. 1940. *Reprinted 1975. 660 pp. Ill. Annotated bibliography of 6707 books on the occult sciences including cartomancy, the kabbalah and tarot.
ANONYMOUS. *The Card Fortune Book. For the Benefit of Young Men and Blooming Maidens.* Dublin. Circa 1820. 16mo. 8 pp.
*ANONYMOUS. *The Card-Player's Companion: A Description of the United States Playing Cards and Popular Games.* Cincinnati. 1887. 24mo. 64 pp. Description and rules of popular card games in the United States.
ANONYMOUS. "Card Revelation," *Young Ladies' Journal.* London. 1887. Folio. 3 pp. Supplement to Christmas issue.
ANONYMOUS. [*Cartes*]. *Predictions par les cartes a jouer.* Circa 1780. 32 pp. Predicts favorable numbers for lotteries held in Lille, Paris, Lyon, Bordeaux and Strasbourg.
ANONYMOUS. *La cartomancie complete ou l'art de tirer les cartes,* [etc]. Circa 1865. 263 pp.
ANONYMOUS. *Catalogo alfabetico di Libri di Scacchi e altri giuochi.* Firenze. 1886. 22 pp. Bibliography on books dealing with games including playing cards.
ANONYMOUS. *Catalogue annote d'ouvrages anciens et modernes relatifs aux Sciences Occultes: alchimie, astrologie, cartomancie,* [etc]. 1909. Bibliography of 1576 volumes dealing with the occult.
*ANONYMOUS. *De La Rue Journal.* London. Winter 1957. No. 29. Describes playing card conference and exhibition sponsored by Thomas de la Rue and Co. Ltd. in 1957 (p. 1–15).
ANONYMOUS. *Les destins ou les tarots francais precede de la cartomancie ordinaire ou moyen de tirer les cartes.* Paris. 1845.
ANONYMOUS. *Diccionario de la Academia Espanol.* 1734. Proposes that the word *naipes* derives from N. P., the initials of Nicolas Pepin, alleged inventor of playing cards.
ANONYMOUS. *Dictionnaire de l'art et de la curiosite.* Paris. 1883. Ill. Contains article about tarot.
*ANONYMOUS. *Edinburgh Heraldic Exhibition. The Memorial Catalog.* Edinburgh. 1892. 4to. Ill. Privately printed. Contains fifteen plates of playing cards.
ANONYMOUS. *Elementi (Primi) e regole del giuoco de'tarocchi.* Torino. 1787. 16mo. 100 pp.
ANONYMOUS. *Encyclopedia de la Divination.* Preface by Gilbert Durand. Paris. 1965. Contains chapter on tarot cards.
ANONYMOUS. *Encyclopedia ou dictionnaire resume des sciences.* Paris. 1771. Ill.
ANONYMOUS. *Encyclopedia methodique. Arts et metiers mecaniques.* Paris. 1782. Ill.

**ANONYMOUS. *Encyclopedie methodique. Dictionnaire des jeux familiers, ou des amusemens de societe.* Paris. n.d. Discusses cards (p. 28–32) and tarot (p. 156–158).
*ANONYMOUS. *Entertaining with Cards.* The United States Playing Card Co. Cincinnati. 1892. sm 12mo. 48 pp. Ill. Describes card party themes.
ANONYMOUS. *Explication morale du jeu de cartes, anecdote curieuse et interessante, sous le nom de Louis Bras-de-fer* [etc]. Brussels and Paris. 1768. 12mo. Soldier in church uses playing cards as prayer book.
*ANONYMOUS. *Fortune-Telling For Everyone. A complete manual of fortune-telling by astrology, cards,* [etc]. Manchester n.d. 192 pp. Ill.
ANONYMOUS. "Games and Amusements of the Middle Ages," *The Art Journal.* London. 1859. Vol. 5. (p. 9 and 79).
*ANONYMOUS. *Ganjappa Playing Cards.* India. 24mo. 8 pp. Describes Indian game of Ganjappa.
ANONYMOUS. "Ganjifa," *Bombay Gazetteer.* Volume IX. Part 2. p. 173.
ANONYMOUS. [Geographie and Des Reynes Renommees.] Bound volume of two packs of French cards.
*ANONYMOUS. *Giochi di Carte.* Milan. 1969. 4to. Ill. Volume I contains a brief summary of the origin of cards.
ANONYMOUS. *Giochi di Carte.* 1974.
ANONYMOUS. *Il Giuocatore de'tarocchi che da le regole colle quali non solo si fissano le penali corrispondenti ai falli che si puonno commettere in questo giuoco,* [etc]. Milano. 1817. 16mo. 116 pp.
ANONYMOUS. *Il Giuocatore di tarocchi al tavoliere operetta divisa in due parti raccolta ed ordinata da L. B. Parte prima.* [etc]. Torino. [1846]. 16mo. 58 pp.
ANONYMOUS. *Il Giuocatore in conversazione che da preçetti sul tarocco,* [etc]. Milano. n.d. 8vo. 128 pp. Several enlarged editions of this work were published between 1820 and 1848.
ANONYMOUS. *Il Giuocatore in conversazione, che da regole e precetti sul tarocco* [etc]. Milano. 1843. 24mo. 72 pp.
ANONYMOUS. *Giuochi di Carte bellissimi, di regola e di memoria, e con secreti particolari, composti e dati in luce per il Cartaginese.* Verona. 1597.
ANONYMOUS. *Il Giuoco delle minchiate capitolo.* Livorno. 1752. 22 pp.
*ANONYMOUS. *La Grande Cartomancie ou l'art de faire les cartes aux autres et a soi-meme.* Paris. Circa 1860. 24mo. 108 pp. Ill. Fortune telling with a 32-card pack.
*ANONYMOUS. *Le grand et le petit Etteilla, ou l'art de tirer les cartes.* Brussels. Circa 1860. Etteilla system of cartomancy.
ANONYMOUS. "Gregory King's Peerage Cards, Temp. James II," *The Herald and Genealogist.* October 1865. Part 16. p. 366.
ANONYMOUS. "Heraldic Cards by Richard Blome," *The Herald and Genealogist.* May 1865. Part 14. p. 180.
ANONYMOUS. "Hindostanee cards," *Calcutta Magazine.* 1815. Volume 2. Describes Hindostanee playing cards.
ANONYMOUS. "Historical and Heraldic Cards," *The Herald and Genealogist.* London. March 1865. 8vo. Part 13. p. 67.
ANONYMOUS. "The History of Playing Cards," *Bradshaw's Journal.* Manchester. April 1842. No. 23. p. 363.
ANONYMOUS. "History of Playing Cards," *Irish Quarterly Review.* Dublin. 1859. Vol. 8. p. 437.
ANONYMOUS. *Indian Card Reading. The Art of Fortune Telling by means of ordinary Playing Cards.* Blackpool. 1899. 8vo. 35 pp.
ANONYMOUS. "Invention des cartes a jouer en Chine," *Magasin pittoresque.* 1850. p. 106.
*ANONYMOUS. *Istruzioni necessarie per chi volesse imparare il giuoco dilettevole delli Tarocchini di Bologna.* Bologna. 1754. 124 pp. Rules for the game of tarocchini of Bologna.
ANONYMOUS. "Jeux d'hier et jeux d'aujourd'hui," *Gazette Dunlop.* June 1937. No. 202. Ill. Illustrates several 18th and 19th century playing card decks manufactured by G.-P. Grimaud, France (p. 10–11).
ANONYMOUS. *Katalog der in Germanischen Museum Befindlichen Kartenspiele und Spielkarten.* Nurenberg. 1886. 35 pp.
**ANONYMOUS. *The Knave of Clubs. Otherwise called, A Game at Cards, and Clubs Trump.* [etc]. London. 1643. 6 pp. Describes card game played by Prometheus and explains the knave of clubs.

*ANONYMOUS. *El Libro negro.* Edited by Manuel Sauri. Barcelona. n.d.
ANONYMOUS. *Le Livre du Thot. Circulaire adressee aux illustres membres de toutes les societes litteraires et philosophiques* [etc]. 1790.
ANONYMOUS. *Mainzer Kartenlosbuch.* [Mainz Fortune Telling Book] Ulm. Circa 1487. Ill. Earliest evidence of ordinary playing cards used for fortune-telling. The questioner selects a card from the pack and opens the book to the appropriate page to read his fortune.
ANONYMOUS. *A manual of cartomancy. Fortune telling and occult divination* [etc]. London. 1909. 8vo. Ill.

ANONYMOUS. "Memoires et communications sur les cartes a jouer," *Bulletin de la societe archeologique historique et artistique.*
ANONYMOUS. *Le Mirascope et ses 36 cartes.* Paris. 1972. 91 pp. Fortune-telling with 36 picture cards similar to Seni-Horoskop.
ANONYMOUS. *La mort aux pipeurs, ou sont contenues toutes les tromperies et piperies du jeu, et le moyen de les eviter.* Paris. 1608.
*ANONYMOUS. "Motive for Motifs — Those Playing Cards," *The Ambassador.* 1950. No. 6. p. 117–125. Origin and development of playing cards.
ANONYMOUS. *Mysteres des Sciences Occultes* [etc]. Circa 1892.
ANONYMOUS. *The new and complete fortune teller* [etc]. Buffalo. 1822. 8vo. From Arabic manuscript of Ibrahim Ali Mohamed Hafez.
ANONYMOUS. *Le nouvel Etteilla ou moyen infaillible de tirer les cartes* [etc]. Paris. 1806. From manuscript of Pythagoras.
ANONYMOUS. *Observations on Card Playing, with an Address to the Clergy.* London. 1758. 4to. 34 pp.
ANONYMOUS. *Oracle parfait ou le passetemps des dames. Art de tirer les cartes . . . d'apres les plus celebres cartomanciens: Mlle Lenorman, Etteilla, etc.* Circa 1860. Ill.
ANONYMOUS. (Orient, Grand). *Manuel de Cartamancie.* n.d. Includes one chapter about tarot.
*ANONYMOUS. "The Origins of Playing Cards," *British Stationer.* October 1957. 7 pp. Ill. Brief history of playing cards prepared on the 125th anniversary of Thomas De La Rue, the playing card firm.
ANONYMOUS. "A Pack of Cards," *Household Words.* London. December 1852. Vol. 6. p. 328.
ANONYMOUS. "Packs of Cards, Old and New," *All The Year Round.* London. December 28, 1878. Vol. 21. p. 38.
ANONYMOUS. *The Platonist.* St. Louis. 1884–1885. Vol. II. Article about tarot (p. 126–128).
*ANONYMOUS. "Playing Cards," *Art in America.* New York. 1962. 4to. Vol. 50. No. 4. Ill. Describes several playing card packs including tarot designs of Jean Berthole (p. 80–83).
ANONYMOUS. "Playing Cards," *Chambers' Journal.* Edinburgh. September 1871. p. 593.
ANONYMOUS. "Playing Cards," *The Home Companion.* London. 1852. Vol. 1. p. 220.
*ANONYMOUS. "Playing Cards Make Distinctive Collectibles," *Collectors News.* Grundy Center, Iowa. March 1973. Reprinted October 1976. Ill. Summarizes hobby of collecting playing cards.
ANONYMOUS. *Plume (Numero exceptionnel de la), consacre a la magie.* Paris. 1892. Ill. Reproduces ten tarot cards.
ANONYMOUS. *The private companion: Alchemy, Astrology, Cartomancy, etc.* London. n.d. 8vo.
*ANONYMOUS. "Putting our Cards on the Table," *World of Wonder.* London. May 8, 1971. Describes cards from various countries (p. 23–26).
ANONYMOUS. *Recueil des actes sur la regie du droit des cartes a jouer.* Paris. 1774.
ANONYMOUS. *Regeln des Minchiatta-spiels.* Dresden. 1798. 64 pp. Rules and description of minchiate pack.
ANONYMOUS. *The Romance of playing cards. History on pasteboard.* New York. [1941]. 12 pp.
*ANONYMOUS. *The Royal Fortune-Teller, or True Telling Gypsy . . . Fortune-Telling by Cards, etc.* London. 1817. 12mo. 30 pp. Ill. Fortune telling with a 52-card pack.

ANONYMOUS. *Satire Contre le joueurs de Cartes.* Strasbourg. 1543.
*ANONYMOUS. *Les Science mysterieuses . . . les secrets des cartes.* Paris. 1899. 317 pp. Ill. Fortune telling with 32-card pack.
*ANONYMOUS. *Seni-Horoskop mit 36 Karten.* Leipzig. 1870. 16mo. 80 pp. Fortune-telling game with 36 cards.
ANONYMOUS. *Sermones de Ludo Cumalis.* Circa 1500. Earliest written list of the atouts.
*ANONYMOUS. "Some unusual playing cards," *Royal Globe Group Bulletin.* England. May/June 1956. No. 74. Ill. Describes English playing cards related to insurance (p. 22–23).
*ANONYMOUS. *Spelkorten Genom Tiderna.* [Sweden]. 1932. 12 pp. Describes origin of cards and mainly nineteenth century decks.
*ANONYMOUS. *Taro Advinhatorio.* Sao Paulo. 1974. 171 pp. Ill. Booklet describes 78-card tarot deck.
ANONYMOUS. *Taroc. — Tappspiel, in einem Lehrdicht vorgetragen.* Vienna. 8vo.
ANONYMOUS. *Taroc (Anweisung zur Erlernung des), Piquet, Whist, und Batonspiels.* Luneburg. 1787.
ANONYMOUS. *Taroc, l'Hombre eines der feinsten Kartenspiele u.s.w.* Nuremberg. 1795. 8vo.
ANONYMOUS. *Taroc (Das verbesserte) a l'Hombre und Bostonspiel.* Berlin. 1801. 8vo.
ANONYMOUS. *Taroc (Das deutsche oder grosse); eine Anleitung seibiges zu lernen.* Leipzig. 1816. 8vo.
ANONYMOUS. "Taroc. Tarok," *De Navorscher.* 1856. T. VI. p. 131–132.
ANONYMOUS. "Tarocchi Cards," *Gentleman's Magazine.* 1849. Part I. p. 491–493. Reprinted in *The Gentleman's Magazine Library: Bibliographical Notes.* 1889. Extract from Chatto's book with further notes.
ANONYMOUS. *Tarokspiele, Regeln bei dem Tarokspiele.* Leipzig. 1754.
ANONYMOUS. *Tarokspiele, Neueste Art das mit dreierlei Karten wohl zu spielen.* Nuremberg. 1770. 8vo.
*ANONYMOUS. "Tarot Cards. What Tarot Cards Say," *Fijingaho.* Japan. 1972. Text in Japanese. Ill. Short story about tarot cards (p. 212–219).
*ANONYMOUS. "Le tarot," *Le Voile d'Isis.* August-September 1928. Nos. 104–105. Special issue on tarot (see Auriger, Caslant, Clavelle, Darc, Deloserai, L'Isle, Maxwell, Mongoi, Osmont, Paulnord, R., Tidianeuq and Trarieux).
*ANONYMOUS. "Tarot personnel d'Eliphas Levi," *Le Voile d'Isis.* August-September 1928. Nos. 104–105. p. 640. Ill. Two curious tarot designs by Eliphas Levi, *22 Le Supplicie* and *27 La Vierge* (p. 640).
ANONYMOUS. *Tarots. Explication du jeu des Tarots.* Leipzig and Dresden.
ANONYMOUS. *Thoughts on Card Playing.* London. 1791. 8vo. 23 pp.
*ANONYMOUS. "To the Patrons and Encouragers of Rowley's New Designed Patent Copper-Plate Cards," *The Journal of The Playing-Card Society.* Manchester. May 1973. Vol. 1. No. 4. p. 2–3.
ANONYMOUS. *Tours de Cartes (Les) les plus amusants rendus faciles par un grand nombre de figures gravees.* Circa 1840.
ANONYMOUS. *Tours de Cartes: recueil complet des plus jolis tours que l'on puisse faire avec les cartes* [etc]. Circa 1850.
ANONYMOUS. *Il Traditor.* 1550. Poem against playing cards.
ANONYMOUS. *Traits historiques concernant les superstitions des anciens peuples . . . avec les differentes interpretations donnees aux cartes a jouer* [etc]. Warsaw. 1794. 2 Volumes, 223 and 455 pp. Ill. Also published in Polish language, 1794. Volume II includes 52 woodcuts of cards and interpretations for fortune telling.
ANONYMOUS. *T'u-shu-chi-ch'eng Encyclopedia.* Emperor Mu Tsung, in the year 969, made reference to the game of cards played in the house of Duke Ch'ien; two months later the duke was murdered and the emperor associated cards with an evil omen.
*ANONYMOUS. *L'Utile Col Diletto o sia Geografia Intrecciate nel Giuoco de' Tarocchi Un Giuoco Di Tarocchi Andato Al Rogo In Bologna Nel Settembre 1725.* Milan. 1725. 4to. 74 pp. Ill. Geographical tarot pack with tarot symbols.
ANONYMOUS. "A Visit to Messrs. De La Rue's Card Manufactory," *Bradshaw's Journal.* Manchester. April 1842. No. 24. p. 369.
*ABEL-REMUSAT. "D'un second Memoire sur les Relations politiques des Rois de France, avec les Empereurs Mongols," *Journal Asiatique.* September 1822. Author claims cards were created by the Chinese in the year 1120 (p. 137).
ABUL, Fazl Allami. *Ain-i-Akbari.* Calcutta. 1973. Vol. I. Describes Indian card game of 144 cards with twelve suits changed by Akbar into a game of 96 cards with eight suits (p. 306–308).
*ACHAD, Frater (pseudonym of Charles Stansfeld Jones). *The Egyptian Revival or The Ever-Coming Son in the Light of the Tarot.* Chicago. 1928. 120 pp. Limited edition of 1,001 copies. *Reprinted New York, 1973. Allocates the tarot trumps according to the paths of the Tree of Life.
ACKERMANN, Rudolf. "Beatrice or The Fracas," *Ackermann's Repository of Arts.* London. 1819. Ill. Transformation cards.
● ADAMETZ, F. "Um die Geheimnisse der Spielkarten-fabriken," *Graphische Revue Osterreichs.* Vienna. 1952. p. 166–168.
● ADAMETZ, F. "Uber die Geheimnisse der Spielkartenherstellung," *Der Druckspiegel.* Stuttgart. 1953. p. 228–232.

*ADAMS, Richard. *The Tyger Voyage*. New York. 1976. 30 pp. Illustrated by Nicola Bayley. Story for young readers about two young tigers who learn to read tarot from gypsies.

*ADY, Cecilia M. *A History of Milan Under the Sforza*. London. 1907. sm 8vo. 351 pp. Ill. Reference book on Sforza family but no mention of cards.

*AGFA-GEVAERT. "Playing Cards," *Reprorama 39*. International Bulletin for Graphic Information 39/1974. Ill. Describes history of cards (p. 1–16).

*AGRELL, Sigurd. *Die pergamenische Zauberscheibe und das Tarockspiele*. Lund. 1936. 130 pp.

AGRIPPA, Henry Cornelius. *La Philosophie occult*. La Haye. 1727. 2 vols.

AGRIPPA, Henry Cornelius. *Three Books of Occult Philosophy*. London. 1651. Reprinted 1897, 1971 and 1973. 288 pp. Ill. Contains a table of the tarot and kaballah.

*ALAN, Jim. "Kabbalah: The Roots of the Magickal Tree," *Gnostica*. St. Paul. April/May 1977. Vol. 5. No. 6. Whole number 42. Ill. Describes the ten sephiroth of the Tree of Life (pp. 36–38, 70–73).

ALARI, Claudio. *Gli Arcani Maggiori e Minori del Tarocco*. Rome.

ALBERICI, Clelia. *Un Mazzo di Carte Istruttivo Tedesco*. Milan. 1974. 24 pp. Ill.

*ALBY, Albert D'. *L'Oracle parfait ou nouvelle maniere de tirer les cartes* [etc]. Paris. 1802. 12mo. 92 pp. Ill. Fortune-telling with a 32-card pack.

ALCOCER, Francisco De. *Tratado del juego*. Salamanca. 1543.

*ALEXANDRE, Alexandre. "Kunstlerische Kartenspiele im Dienste der Werbung und der Eleganz," *Gebrauchs-graphik*. 1958. No. 3.

*ALEXANDRE, Alexandre. "Italien liebt seine alten Spielkarten," *Gebrachs-graphik*. 1959. No. 2. p. 44–49.

ALFARO Fournier, Felix. *Catalogo del Museo de Naipes Heraclio Fournier*. Vitoria. 1972.

*ALI, Mohammed. *Telling Fortunes by Cards* [etc]. New York. 1914. 12mo. 159 pp. Fortune telling with a 52-card pack.

ALLEMAGNE (see D'Allemagne).

ALLIETTE (see under pseudonym Etteilla).

*ALTA, Elie [pseudonym of Gervais Bouchet]. *Le Tarot Egyptien* [etc]. Vichy. 1922. 8vo. 311 pp. Ill. Includes information about Etteilla, Egyptian origin of tarot and reproduction of work by d'Odoucet, *Science Des Signes, Ou Medecine de l'Esprit, connue sous le nom d'Art de tirer les Cartes*.

AMBELIN, Robert. *Le Tarot, Apercu historique. Signification des Arcanes*. Paris. 1906. 12mo.

AMBELIN, Robert. *Les Tarots, comment apprendre a les manier*. Paris. 1950.

AMMAN, Jost. *Charta Lusoria* [etc]. Nurnberg. 1558. *Reprinted in facsimile edition, Munich, 1880, and Leipzig, 1967 (see Kohlmann). 8vo.

*ANGELINI, Sandro. *I 33 Giochi*. Bergamo. 1976. Folio. Loose sheets. Reproduces 42 decks and games designed by Giuseppe Maria Mitelli between the years 1687 and 1712.

*ANNO, Mitsumasa. *Upside-Downers*. New York. 1971. 28 pp. Ill. Children's fantasy about the upside down world of double-ended playing cards.

ANTHONY, Saint. *Treatise of Theology*. 1457. Refers to playing cards and tarot.

ANTON, Friedrich. *Enzyklopädie der spiele*. Leipzig. 1884. 650 pp.

ANTROBUS, Robert. *The Square of Sevens, an authoritative system of Cartomancy* [etc]. New York, 1896. London, 1900. 8vo. 72 pp.

**AQUARIUS. *German and French Games at Cards*. London. 1888. 143 pp. Rules for German tarock.

*ARETINO, Pietro. *Le Carte parlare col Padovano Cartaro in Fiorenza*. London. 1589. Small 8vo. Dialogue about card games with descriptions of the suits, numeral cards and tarot trumps.

ARIENTI, Vito. *170 Carte di Tarocchi e Minchiate Fiorentine*. Lissone. 1969. Edition limited to 100 copies. Series of card reproductions by Edizioni del Solleone also includes: *172 Carte Regionali Italiane, Les Tables de Geographie reduites en un jeu de cartes, Pasquins Windkaart, Giuoco D'Arne, Giuoco del Passatempo di Giuseppe M. Mitelli, Geografia nel Giuoco dei Tarocchi.*

ARIENTI, Vito (see *La Voce del Collezionista*).

ARINY Y ALBIZU, Santiago. "De Vitoria, barajas," *Gazteiz*. Vitoria. August 1959. No. 2.

ASENJO MARTINEZ, Jose Luis. *El papel en los naipes*. Barcelona. 1967.

*ASHCROFT-NOWICKI, Dolores. *The S.O.L. Major Arcana Slides for Meditation*. St. Helier, Jersey. April 1977. 9 pp. Describes 22 Major Arcana cards designed by Josephine Gill and photographed by Robin Clapham for the Servants of the Light, Great Britain.

ASSOCIATION OF AMERICAN PLAYING CARD MANUFACTURERS. *The Romance of Playing Cards*.

AUCTION CATALOGS (see Auktionshaus Wendt, Christie's, Gibbons, Nebehay, Numismatica, Sotheby, and U.S. Games Systems, Inc.).

*AUKTIONSHAUS WENDT. *Auktionskatalog XIV. Alte Spielkarten, Spielkartenboegen, Gebrauchsgegenstaende fuer den Kartenspieler*. Vienna. 1976. Ill. Describes playing card auction held November 1976.

*AUKTIONSHAUS WENDT. *Auktion XX. Spielkartenauktion*. Vienna. 1977. Ill. Describes playing card auction held November 1977.

*AURELIA GAMES. *Aurelia Games Index*. Brussels. 1976. Detailed index in Dutch, French and English of playing cards from Belgium and the Netherlands.

*AURELIA GAMES. *Le Jolly Joker* (see Borveau).

*AURIGER. "L'Alchimie devant le Tarot," *Le Voile d'Isis*. August-September 1928. Nos. 104–105. pp. 563–583. Ill. Origin of cards and treatises on alchemy which relate to the tarot. Includes The Magician designed by M. F. Sedivy.

"AURO." *Fortune Telling by Cards, Numbers and Tea Leaves*. New York. 1925. 108 pp. Ill. Fortune telling with 36 cards.

AVELINE, Cl. *Le code des jeux*. Paris. 1963.

AWTKINSON, Rogy. *La cartomante in casa*. Torino. 1975. Second edition. 156 pp. Fortunes are determined by combination of numbered card and lettered card; sleeve in back of book contains 26 cards.

B

BABA, Ichiro, Koichi Kansaku, Toru Mori, Koichi Yoshida, Kaname Sato and Kakutaro Yamaguchi. "Hyakunin-Isshu," *The Sun*. Japan. 1975. sm 4to. 284 pp. Ill. Depicts several editions of antique Hyakunin-Isshu cards. Fujiwara-Sodail, 13th century Japanese poet, selected poems from 100 poets of the Heian period that describe changing seasons, love, etc.

**BACHE, Paul Eugene. *Jacquemin Gringonneur ou l'invention des cartes a jouer*. Algiers. July 1846. 137 pp. Illustrated with hand-painted court and pip cards tipped in book. Edition limited to 100 copies. Origin of playing cards and story about Jacquemin Gringonneur.

*BACHMANN, Kurt. *Die Spielkarten. Ihre Geschichte in 15 Jahrhunderten*. Altenburg. 1932. 24 pp.

*BACHMANN, Kurt. "Neue Forschungsergebnisse zur altesten Geschichte der Spielkarten und des Kartenspiels in Asien und Europa," *Forschungen und Fortschritte*. 1950. pp. 63–66.

*BACHMANN, Kurt. "Von der Spielkarte und ihrer Herstellung in Vergangenheit und Gegenwart," *Das Buchgewerbe*. 1949. pp. 315–320.

*BACHMANN, Kurt. "Zur Entwicklung der Spielkarten und der Kartenspiele und deren Beziehungen zur Skatstadt Altenburg," *Beitrage zur Sprachwissenschaft und Volkskunde*. 1951. pp. 308–373.

BACHTOLD-STAUBLI. *Handwortenbuch des Deutschen Aberglaubens*. Berlin and Leipzig. 1931.

BAILEY. *Astrology and the Cards*. London. 1931.

*BALBI, Domenico. *Tarot Balbi. Book of Instructions*. Spain. 1976. 55 pp. Instruction booklet accompanies the Balbi tarot deck.

*BALBI, Domenico. "Il Diavolo: Demonologia e cabala," *Vitalita*. Torino. October 1973. Anno 12. No. 132. Ill. Interpretation of card XV The Devil from Balbi pack. (p. 48–49).

BALIN, Peter. "The Flight of Quetzalcoatl, The Feathered Serpent." Unpublished manuscript. 1977. Ill. Describes the Xultun tarot deck based upon Mayan art and imagery.

BALIN, Peter. *The Journey of The Fool*. Children's coloring book based upon the Xultun tarot deck.

*BALLARD, Martha C. *Shakespeare on Poker*. Denver. 1906. 16mo. 28 pp. Shakespearian scenes illustrated with playing cards.

*BALLESTA, Juan. *I Trionfi d'Amore*. Perugia. Circa 1975. 22 pp. Describes the 22 Major Arcana cards entitled I Trionfi d'Amore.

BALMFORD, James. *A Short and Plain Dialogue concerning the unlawfulness of playing at Cards or Tables, or any other game consisting in chance*. London. 1593. Reprinted 1607. 8vo.

BARA, A., and L. Crick. "Un jeu de cartes en argent," *Musees Royaux d'Art et d'Histoire Bulletin*. Brussels. September, 1942. Vol. 14. p. 98–105.

BARBE, J. J. "Les cartes a jouer a Metz," *Annales de la Societe d'histoire et d'archeologie de la Lorraine*. 1926. T. XXXV.

BARBETRAC, Jean. *Traite du jeu. Ou l'on examine les principales questions de droit natural et de morale qui ont du rapport a cette Matiere*. Amsterdam. 1737. 2nd edition. 3 volumes. 896 pp. Discusses various moral questions about games including playing cards.

*BARBIERI, Gino. *Aspetti Dell'Economia Lombarda Durante La Dominazione Visconteo-Sforzesca*. Milano. 1958. 72 + 50 pp. Ill. Contains documents from 15th century Visconti-Sforza reign.

BARETTI. *An Account of the Manners and Customs of Italy*. London. 1768. Vol. II. The author contends that the Italian games of minchiate and taroccho are superior in play to the popular English game of whist, the French game of piquet and the Spanish game of ombre (p. 217).

*BARGAGLI. Girolamo. *Dialogo de Giuochi che nelle Vegghie Sanesi si usano di fare.* Siena. 1572. 8vo. 223 pp. Also issued in 1575 and 1581. Contains reference to the game of Tarocchi (p. 77).

BARLANDI, Hadriani. *Dialogi omnes.* 1542.

BARLET, F. Ch. [Pseudonym of Albert Faucheux]. "Le Nom Divin dans le Tarot," *Le Tarot des Bohemiens.* Paris. 1889. Ill. The author places the tarot pack in a sphere and interprets the divine world from the cards (p. 282-298).

BARLET, F. Ch. [Pseudonym of Albert Faucheux]. *Saint-Yves d'Alveydre, comprenant une table raisonee de la Mission des Juifs et des notions precises sur l'Archeometre.* Paris. 1910. 218 pp. Presents an adaptation of the 22 Major Arcana.

BARLET, F. Ch. [Pseudonym of Albert Faucheux]. "L'Initiation," *Le Tarot des Bohemiens.* 1889. p. 262-281. Reprinted in *La Science Secrete*, Paris, 1890, Vol. 4, No. 12, p. 222-245. Describes the 22 Greater Arcana as the entire sequence from involution through evolution and initiation.

BARONI, C., and S. Samek Ludovici. *La pittura lombarda del Quattrocento.* Messina. 1952. Contains transcriptions of documents by or about Bonifacio Bembo.

*BARRINGTON, Daines. "Observations on a picture of Zuccaro from Lord Falkland's collection supposed to represent the game of Primero," *Archaeologia.* Society of Antiquaries. 1787. 4to. Vol. 8. A paper read before the Society of Antiquaries of London on May 5, 1785 dealing with the game of Primero.

BARRINGTON, Daines. "Observations on the Antiquity of Card-playing in England," *Archaeologia.* Society of Antiquaries. London. 1787. 4to. Vol. 8. p. 134-146. Reprinted in *The European Magazine*, 1788, volume 14, and *The Universal Magazine*, December 1788. Describes early development of playing cards in European countries including Spain where author believes they were probably invented.

BARTSCH, Adam. *Le peintre graveur.* Leipzig, 1803. Vienna, 1811. Leipzig, 1821 and 1824. 12mo. 426 pp. Comparison of the two extant Tarocchi of Mantegna packs. (Vol. 13, p. 120-138); additional references to cards Vol. 6, p. 55, 302 and 377; Vol. 10, p. 70-120; Vol. 13, p. 120-138.

*BASILIDE, T. *Le profond mystere du tarot metaphysique.* Paris. 1929. 12mo. 63 pp. According to Basilide, the 22 Major Arcana cards represent 3 primordial events, 12 signs of the zodiac and 7 planets.

*BAUDOUIN, Marcel. *Le Jeu d'Alluette* [etc]. Paris. n.d. sm 8vo. 70 pp. Ill. Describes the game of Alluette or La Vache, the cow.

*BAUWENS, Jan. *Alexander Mayr's zilveren speelkaarten van 1594.* Brussels. 1975. 24 pp. Describes silver playing cards of Alexander Mayr.

*BAUWENS, Jan. *Cartes de Suisses.* Brussels. 1975. Accompanies Vandenborre tarot deck; includes summary of 18th century cards in Austria and the Netherlands.

*BAUWENS, Jan. *Commedia dell' Carte.* Brussels. 1977. 32 pp. Accompanies Commedia dell' Carte deck of Belgian politicians.

*BAUWENS, Jan. *Muluk wanuwwab.* Brussels. 1972. sm 8vo. 63 pp. Ill. Booklet accompanies reproduction of Mamluk cards.

*BAUWENS, Jan and Eugeen Van Autenboer. *Turnhout Bongout.* Brussels. 1976. 64 pp. Accompanies reprint of two Bongout decks.

*BAUWENS, Jan. "Van devotieprent naar bidprent," *Bidprentjes in de Zuidelijke Nederlanden.* Brussels. 1975. p. I-VII. Describes card playing among Flemish Catholics in Northern Belgium and French Flanders during 18th century. Cards were also used as death notices similar to the earlier French custom of writing communications on backs of cards.

*BAYLEY, Harold. *The Lost Language of Symbolism.* London. 784 pp. Ill. Describes ancient and modern symbols of East and West.

*BEAL, George. *Discovering Playing Cards & Tarots.* United Kingdom. 1972. 16mo. 56 pp. Guide to playing cards of the world.

BEAL, George. *Playing Cards and Their Story.* New York. 1975. 8vo. 116 pp. Ill. History and development of playing cards and methods of identification.

*BEALE, A. J. "A Further Note on Thomas Tuttell," *The Journal of The Playing-Card Society.* Cranbrook. November 1976. Vol. 5. No. 2. Contains information on Tuttell not included in Wayland's article (p. 25-26).

BEALE, A. J. "In Search of Cards," *The Journal of The Playing-Card Society.* Birmingham. August 1975. Vol. IV. No. 1. Describes playing card collections at European museums and libraries (p. 19-23).

*BEALE, A. J. "Sammlung Deutsches Spielkartenmuseum Leinfelden," *The Journal of The Playing-Card Society.* Cranbrook. November 1975. Vol. IV. No. 2. p. 8-15.

*BEALS, Kathie. "It's all in the cards. . . . ," *Westchester Weekend.* New York. April 16, 1976. Playing card exhibition of the Stuart and Marilyn R. Kaplan Collection (p. 5)

BEAUDOIRE, Th. *Genese de la Cryptographie Apostolique, et de l'Architecture Rituelle.* Paris. 1902.

*BECK, Fritz. *Tarock Komplett Alle Spiele.* 1970. 176 pp. Ill. Rules for game of tarock.

*BEHMAN, Patricia. "The Golden Dawn Method of Tarot Divination. Part I. Tarot: Beyond Reason, Beyond Time," *Gnostica.* St. Paul, April/May 1977. Vol. 5. No. 6. Ill. Brief history of tarot in six-week study plan (pp. 6-12, 74-75).

**BELL, William. "The origin and nomenclature of playing cards," *The Art-Journal.* London. 1861. Vol. 23. Ill. Proposes that the word *naipes* or *naib* derives from a gnome or *turnip* counter in a German fairy tale; the word *turnip* is reduced to *nip* or *nib* and ultimately to *naipes* and *naib* (pp. 249, 270, 301, 337, 369).

*BENAVIDES, Rodolfo. *The Prophetic Tarot.* Mexico. 1969. 378 pp. Ill. Major Arcana are described in relation to the Apocalypse.

*BENHAM, W. Gurney. *Playing Cards. History of The Pack and Explanations of Its Many Secrets.* London and Melbourne. 1931. Reprinted London, 1957. 8vo. 196 pp. History of cards including tarot.

*BENHAM, W. Gurney. *A Short History of Playing Cards.* Bristol. [1938]. 16mo. 55 pp. Ill. Limited edition. History of cards including how English pack began and names of each court card.

*BENNETT, Sidney (Ms.). *More Tarot Secrets for the Millions.* Los Angeles. 1970. 8vo. 149 pp. Tarot meditation and card readings.

*BENNETT, Sidney (Ms.). *Tarot For The Millions.* Los Angeles. 1967. 8vo. 157 pp. Card spreads, meanings and sample tarot readings.

*BENVENISTE, Asa. *The Atoz Formula.* London. 1969. 64 pp. Poems of the 22 Major Arcana cards.

*BERESFORD, Flora. "Tellurian Tarot Cards." Unpublished MS. Himalayas. 1971(?). Ill. Describes the Tellurian tarot pack designed by Flora Beresford.

● BERG, Siegfried. "Kinderspielkarten," *Offset-Buch und Werbekunst.* 1925. Heft 10. Describes children's playing cards (p 643-645).

*BERLOQUIN, Pierre. *Regles du jeu de tarot.* Paris. 1973. 12 mo. 77 pp. Ill. Bibliography. Rules for tarock and early published card references.

*BERLOQUIN, Pierre. *Regles du jeu de tarot.* Paris. 1973. 12mo. 77 pp. Ill. Rules for 100 card games including tarock.

BERNAT, Juan B. *Cartomagia. El mundo maravilloso de los naipes.* Barcelona. 1953.

BERNHARDI, A. "4 Konige. Beitrage zur Geschichte der Spiele," *Baessler-Archiv.* 1937. pp. 148-180.

*BERNI, Francesco. *Capitolo del Gioco della Primiera.* 1526. Possibly earliest printed reference to game of tarocchi.

BERNOULLI, Rudolf. "Zur Symbolik geometrischer Figuren und Zahlen," *Eranos-Jahrbuch 1934.* Zurich. 1935. Symbolism of tarot systems (p 369-415).

BERNSTROM, John. *Spelkort.* Stockholm. 1959. 8vo. 90 pp. Ill. Development of Swedish cards.

BERSIER, J. "Les cartes a jouer," *Almanach d'Estienne.* 1958. p 25-31.

BERTARELLI, A. *Le Meisioni di G. M. Mitelli.* Milan. 1940.

BERTARELLI, A *L'Imagerie Populaire Italienne.* Paris. 1929.

[BERTARELLI, A.] *Raccolta delle stompe A. Bertarelli.* Milan. 1970.

BERTELSSON, A. "Spielkarten-Werbung," *Offset-Buch und Werbekunst.* 1925. Heft 10. p 636-643. Ill. Advertising playing cards.

BERTET, Adolphe. *Apocalypse du Bienheureux Jean, apotre* [etc]. Paris. 1861. Introduction devoted to tarot.

BERTET, Adolphe. *Apocalype du Bienheureux Jean, devoilee* [etc]. Chambery. 1870. 362 pp. Later edition of Bertet's work.

**BERTONI, G. "Tarocchi Versificati," *Poesie leggende costumanze del medio evo.* Ferrara. 1550. Reprinted Modena, 1917. Poem associates the ladies of the court of Ferrara with the tarocchi trumps.

*BERTRAND, Romain. *Votre Psychanalyse par Les Tarots.* 6 pp. Tarot cards in psychoanalysis.

BETTINELLI, L'Abbe Saverio. *Il giuoco delle carte, poemetto, con annotazioni.* Cremona. 1775. Venice, 1778 and 1799. 8vo. 63 pp. An Italian pack of cards illuminated in a manuscript prior to 1500 for Alfonso III, Duke of Ferrara.

BEUCLER, A. "Les cartes a jouer," *Arts et Metiers Graphiques.* Paris. 1934. No. 41. pp. 9-15.

BIANCHINI, Francesco. *Carta da giuoco in servizio dell' istoria e della cronologia.* Bologna. 1871.

BIANCONI, J. Joseph. "[Lettre sur les] Cartes a jouer," *Bulletin du Bibliophile belge*. Brussels. 1870. Tome IV. pp 343–345.
*BIBLIOTHEQUE Nationale. *Cinq Siecles de Cartes a Jouer en France*. Paris. 1963. sm 4to. 93 pp.
*BIEDERMANN, Hans. *Handlexikon der Magischen Kunste von der Spatantike bis zum 19, Jahrhundert*. Graz. 1968. 12 mo. 432 pp. Bibliography. Brief explanation of kabbalah and tarot.
BIERDIMP, K. A. *Die Sammlung der Spielkarten des baierischen Nationalmuseums*. Munich. 1884. 240 pp. Description of cards including tarots.
BIERDIMP, K. A. *The Collection of Playing Cards in the Bavarian National Museum*. MS. translation of portion of preceding work.
BIGG (Miss). "Experiments in cartomancy," *S.P.R.*, *J.X.* p. 47.
BILLIOUD, Joseph. "La carte a jouer. Une vieille industrie Marseillaise," *Revue municipale de Marseilles*. 1958. Nos. 34 & 35.
*BLAKELEY, John D. *The Mystical Power of the Tarot*. London. 1974. 8vo. 193 pp. Ill.
BLAVATSKY (Mme). *Isis Unveiled: A Master-Key to the Mysteries of ancient and moderne Science and Technology*. New York. 1884. 8vo. 2 vols.
*BLAVATSKY (Mme). *The Secret Doctrine: The synthesis of science, religion and philosophy*. London. 1893. 3 vols. plus index. Blavatsky believes that tarot symbology derives from ancient Babylonian cylinders, or antediluvian rhombs, which were covered with sacred signs (Vol. III).
BLOESCH, Hans. "Ein altes bernisches Kartenspiel," *Pro Arte*. 1943. No. 9.
BLOME (see Anonymous, Heraldic Cards by Richard Blome).
**BLUM, Andre. *Les origines du papier, de l'imprimerie et de la gravure*. Paris. 1935. 252 pp. Ill. Discusses early French card making and the beginning of xylography (89–96).
BOCHELLI [Bouchel], Laurentii. *Decreta ecclesiae Gallicanae*. Paris. 1609. Cites the Synod of Langres in 1404 which forbade clergy from playing games and cards.
BOCK, Robert. "Das Geistliche Kartenspiel des Andreas Strobl," *Bayerisches Jahrbuch fur Volkunde 1955*. Ragensburg. 1955. pp. 201–210.
BOIARDO, Matteo Maria. *Tutte le opere*. Describes tarot pack in a set of verses, two sonnets and seventy-eight *terzine*, one for each of the tarocchi cards.
BOIS, George. *Le peril occultiste, Les theses de l'occultisme [etc]*. Paris. 1899. 315 pp.
BOIS, Jules. *Le Satanisme et la Magie*. Paris. n.d.
BOISSONNADE. *Journal de l'Empire*. August 23, 1811. Origin of cards and the word *naipes*.
*BOITEAU, P[aul] d'Ambly. *Les Cartes a Jouer et La Cartomancie*. Paris. 1854 and 1859. 16mo. 390 pp. Ill. History of playing cards, tarot and cartomancy.
BOLTON, Henry Carrington. "Fortune-Telling in America To-day," *Journal of American Folk-Lore*. Boston. 1896. pp. 299–397.
BOND, E. A. "History of Playing Cards," *Athenaeum*. 1878.
BORDIGALLO, Domenico. "Le cronache di Cremona" [The Chronicles of Cremona]. Unpublished manuscript. The Bordigallo manuscript, presently housed at the Biblioteca Treccani, Milan, contains no references to either Antonio Cicognara or tarocchi as claimed by Leopoldo Cicognara.
*BORVEAU, Alain. *Le Jolly Joker*. Paris. January/February 1970, No. 1–May 1974, No. 15. Newsletter for collectors of playing cards. Aurelia Games resumed publication 1976, No. 16.
*BORVO, Alain (pseudonym of Alain Borveau). *Anatomie D'Un Jeu De Cartes: L'Aluette Ou Le Jeu De Vache*. Nantes. 1977. 82 pp. Ill. Describes game of L'Aluette.
BOTTARI, S. "I tarocchi di Castello Ursino di Bonifacio Bembo," *Emporium*. September 1951. CXIV. No. 681. 110–124.
BOUCHET, Gervais (see Elie Alta).
BOUCHOT, H. "A Newly Discovered Pack of Lyonese Playing Cards (1470)," *Burlington Magazine*. March–May, 1903. Vol. 1. p. 296–305. Ill.
BOURGEAT, J. -G. [Jean Gaston] *La Magie*. Paris. 1895. Reprinted 1904 and 1909. Includes section on tarot.
*BOURGEAT, J. -G. [Jean Gaston] *Le Tarot*. Paris. 1906. Reprinted 1913, 1918, 1923 and 1936. 126 pp. Ill. Describes Major Arcana and card spreads.
BOUTET, Frederic. *Dictionnaire des sciences occultes*. Paris. 1937. Ill. Contains tarot (p 316–326).
BOUVIER, J. "Les cartiers et la fabrication des cartes a jouer a Romans," *Bulletin de la Societe d'archeologie de la Drome*. 1955–1957. T. 73.
BOWDOIN, W. G. "Playing Cards of All Nations," *The Metropolitan Magazine*. 1928.
BOWDOIN, W. G. "Playing Cards, Their History and Symbolism," *Art & Archaeology*. March 1921. Vol. II. No. 3.
*BOWLE, John. "Observations on Card-playing," *Archaeologia*. London. 1786. Vol. 8. p. 147–151. Cites omissions of the word *cards* by early authors.
*BRAHMAN-STAR. *L'Avenir Devoile Par Tous Les Moyens Connus*. Paris. Circa 19th century. 12mo. 384 pp. Fortune telling with tarot and 36 card pack.
BRAINVILLE (see Fine).

BRALEDA [Vicomte]. *La Patrie, la Langue maternelle, la Vraie religion. Etudes psychologiques*. Luxembourg. 1894. Refutes some of Papus' theories.
*BRAUN, Franz. *Playing Card Information Service*. Cologne. 1970– . Ill. Description of over 1,400 decks of all types. Text in English/German.
*BRAUN, Franz. *Die Spielkarte–The Playing Card*. Germany. 1967. 19 pp.
*BRAUN, Franz. *Spielkarten und Kartenspiele*. Hannover. 1966. 227 pp. Ill. Development of playing cards.
**BREITKOPF, Johann Gottlob Immanuel. *An Inquiry Into the Origin of Playing Cards—1784*. Translated from the German by I. W. May and transcribed by Charles Bond. Gravesend. 1815. 44 pages plus plates. Limited to 25 copies. Handwritten English translation of Breitkopf's work.
**BREITKOPF, Johann Gottlob Immanuel. *Versuch den Ursprung der Spielkarten die Einfuehrung des Leinenpapieres [etc]*. Leipzig. 1784. 136 and 218 pp. 8vo. Ill. History of playing cards. Breitkopf believes cards originated in the East; the word *naipes* being derived from the Arabic *Nabaa*, signifying divination.
*BRENNAN, J. H. *Astral Doorways*. New York. 1971. 115 pp. Ill. Describes the Major Arcana.
BRENT, Cecil. "On a Pack of Cards of the Sixteenth Century, found in the cover of an old book," *The Journal of the British Archaeological Association*. London. 1881. Vol. 37. p. 89–91. Ill.
*BREPOLS & DIERCKX ZOON. *Cartes a Jouer (Book of Samples)*. Circa 1850. 82 pp. Wrappers and sample cards made by Brepols & Dierckx Zoon (B.D.Z.), Turnhout, Belgium; and used as sample book by M. Cresta & Co., Hamburg.

*BRESLE, Valentin. *Le Tarot Revele Dans Son Integralite Theorique Et Pratique*. Paris. 1949. 223 pp. Ill. Edition limited to 1,000 copies. Tarot from theoretical and practical viewpoints.
BRIDGET. *The True Fortune Teller, or Universal Book of Fate [etc]*. London. Circa 1800. 8vo. 60 pp.
*BRITISH MUSEUM. *Playing Cards of Various Ages and Countries. Selected from The Collection of Lady Charlotte Schreiber*. Introduction by Sir A. W. Franks. London. 1892–1895. Folio. 3 volumes. Illustrated, 447 plates. Vol. I, English and Scottish, Dutch and Flemish. Vol. II, French and German. Vol. III, Swiss, Swedish, Russian, Polish, Italian, Spanish and Portuguese. Profusely illustrated documentary on cards.
*BRITZ, Meredith. "Tarot Cards: Black Magic, or the Symbols of Man's Experience." Unpublished MS. Scarsdale High School. New York. 1972. 65 pp. High school research paper deals with history and development of tarot.
BROCKHAUS, Heinrich. "Ein edles Geduldspiel. Die Leitung der Welt oder die Himmelsleiter. Die sogennanten Taroks Mantegnas vom Jahre 1459-60," *Miscellanea di Storia dell'arte in onore di Igino Benvenuto Supino*. Florence. 1933. Tarocchi of Mantegna cards are viewed as containing astrological connotations (p. 397–416).
BRODIE-INNES, J. W. "The Tarot Cards," *The Occult Review*. February 1919. Critique of Waite's views (p.90–98).
BRODIE-INNES, J. W. "The Problem of the Tarot Cards," *The Occult*

Review. August 1920. Letter stimulated by previous article in *The Occult Review*, "The Problem of the Tarot Cards," by Julius L. Lachner.

BROMAGE, B. "The Tarot," *Occult Observer*. 1950. No. 5. p. 267–275.

BRONSART, H. von. "Astronomische Kartenspiele," *Die Sterne*. 1964. No. 40. p. 241–244.

*BROWN, Philip. "St. Barbara and the Tower: a Conjecture," *The Journal of The Playing-Card Society*. Birmingham. February 1976. St. Barbara was shut in a tower by her father to protect her from opportunist suitors. She converted to Christianity and constructed in the tower three windows symbolizing the Trinity. This so enraged her father that he put her to death and thereupon he was killed by lightning; thus suggesting one legend of The Tower card.

*BROWN, Wenzell. *How To Tell Fortunes With Cards*. New York. 1969. 12mo. 128 pp. Ill. Fortune telling with 52 cards.

BRUNET, G. Fils. *Notice bibliographique sur les cartes a jouer*. Paris. 1842. 12 pp. French translation by Brunet of J. G. H. Graesse's bibliographical summary of playing cards (see Graesse).

BRUNET y BELLET, Joseph. *Lo joch de naibs, naips o cartes*. Barcelona. 1886. sm 8vo. 280 pp. Ill. Development of playing cards in Spain.

BRUNET y BELLET, Joseph. "Quatre paraulas sobre la fulla d'un joch de cartas trobada a Gerona per D. Enrich C. Girbal," *L'Avens*. Barcelona. November 30, 1890. Number II. p. 253–262.

BRUNET y BELLET, Joseph. *Mes sobre'l joch do naips o cartas de jugar*. Barcelona. 1898.

BRUNETTI DA CORINALDO, Francesco Saverio. *Giuochi delle minchiate* [etc.] Rules and commentary about Minchiate. Rome. 1747. 128 pp.

*BRYDEN, Dean. *Fun with Cards*. New York. 1927. 165 pp.

*BUCHAN, A.P. *A conjecture concerning the origin of playing cards and the game of whist*. Printed in Singer's *Researches into the History of Playing Cards*. London. 1816. Describes analogies between origin of playing cards and certain astrological phenomena in ancient Egypt.

*BUDGE, Sir E. A. Wallis. *The Book of the Dead* [etc]. London. 1928. 12mo. 2 Vols. Ill. Egyptian hymns, religious texts, litanies, etc.

BUE [Hector Joseph]. *La main du general Boulanger* [etc]. Paris. 1889. 73 pages. Ill. Contains curious tarots.

*BUESS, Lynn M. *The Tarot and Transformation*. Lakemont, Georgia. 1973. sm 8vo. 256 pp. Ill. Tarot cards are described based upon different levels of human development. Card illustrations are a mixture of Egyptian and contemporary imagery.

*BUILDERS OF THE ADYTUM (BOTA). *Introduction to Tarot*. Los Angeles. Introductory mail order instruction on tarot based upon the work of Paul Foster Case.

*BUILDERS OF THE ADYTUM (BOTA). *Seven Steps in Practical Occultism*. Los Angeles. Mail order instruction dealing with the use of subconscious and conscious power to better our lives.

*BUILDERS OF THE ADYTUM (BOTA). *Tarot Fundamentals*. Los Angeles. Mail order instruction on all aspects of tarot based upon Case.

*BULLET, Jean Baptiste. *Recherches historiques sur les cartes a jouer avec /des notes critiques & interessantes*. Lyon. 1757. 12mo. 163 pp. Proponent of the French origin of cards originating during the reign of Charles V, circa 1375.

BULTHUIS, Rico. *Open kaart*. Zwolle. 1967. 8vo. 158 pp.

BUONINSEGNI, Father M. Tommaso. *Del Giuoco Discorso*. Florence. 1585. 39 pp. Reference to St. Bernardin's sermon against cards in 1423.

*BURDICK, Jefferson R. *The American Card Catalog. The Standard Guide On All Collected Cards and Their Values*. Syracuse. 1953. 8vo. 168 pp. Ill. New edition published East Shoudsbury. 1960. 8vo. 240 pp. Primarily advertising and picture post cards with a short section on playing cards.

BURT, Professor. *The Popular Fortune Teller by Cards*. London. Circa 1900. 12mo. 30 pp.

*BUSSI, Feliciano. *Istoria della Citta di Viterbo*. Rome. 1742. 4to. 478 pp. Refers to Covelluzzo, fifteenth century chronicler, who claimed playing cards were brought to Viterbo in 1379 (p. 213).

*BUTLER, Bill. *Dictionary of the Tarot*. New York. 1975. 12mo. 254 pp. Ill. Summarizes card interpretations based on Case, Crowley, Douglas, Grey, Kaplan, Thierens, Waite, etc.

BYNNEMAN, H. *A Treatise wherein Dicing, Dauncing, Vaine Playes, and Enterludes, with other idle Pastimes, commonly used on the Sabbath day, are reproved by the Authoritie of the Word of God and Auntient Writers*.

C

*CAILLET, Albert L. *Manuel Bibliographique des Sciences Psychiques ou Occultes*. Paris. 1912. Reissued 1964 in edition limited to 300 copies. 8vo. 3 Vols. Bibliography of the occult including tarot, divination and kabbalah.

CAILLOIS, Roger. "Jeu de cartes," *Jardin des Arts*. December 1960/January 1961. No. 74. pp. 33–40.

CALMET, Dom A. "De l'origine du jeu de cartes," *Bulletins de la Societe Philomatique Vosgienne*. Saint-Die. 1876. Brief references to cards.

CALVINO, Italo. *Il Castello dei destini incrociati*. 1973.

*CALVINO, Italo. *The Castle of Crossed Destinies*. Translated by William Weaver. New York. 1977. 129 pp. Ill. English translation of *Il Castello dei destini incrociati*, a novel with characters struck mute who communicate through the pictures and symbols on a pack of tarot cards.

*CALVINO, Italo. *Tarocchi Il Mazzo Visconteo di Bergamo e New York Analisi di Sergio Samek Ludovici* [etc]. Italy. 1969. 165 pp. Folio. Ill. Commentary with reproductions of the Pierpont Morgan-Bergamo Visconti-Sforza tarocchi deck.

*CALVINO, Italo. *Tarots. The Visconti Pack in Bergamo and New York*. Critical examination by Sergio Samek Ludovici. Translation by William Weaver. Parma. 1975. 161 pp. Ill. English translation of Italian edition.

CAMINITO, Claudia. *La Bibbia del Diavolo*.

CAMMERLANDER, Jacob. *Kartenlosbuch*. Strassburg. 1543. Ill. Text in rhyme describes pip cards in terms of Bible and religious themes.

CAMPARI, G. *Le carte da giuoco dipinte per gli Estensi nel Secolo XV*. Mantova. 1875.

*CANDAMO, Luis G. de. "El Museo de Naipes de Heraclio Fournier," Madrid. 1975. No. 12.

CANNEGIETER, H. E. "Kaartenspelen en speelkaarten," *Op de hoogte*. Noel 1932. pp. 357–372.

CARDAN, Jerome. *Subtility*. 1550. According to Papus, this treatise by Cardan is based upon the keys of the tarot.

CARNARIUS, Rusty Smith. "Self Discovery Through the Tarot." Unpublished manuscript. Lancaster. 1977. Ill. Interpreting Rider-Waite cards from the subconscious.

CARNY, Lucien. *Le tarot de Charles VI chemin royal de la vie* [etc]. 1964. 136 pp.

*CARR, John Dickson. *The Eight of Swords*. 1934. 220 pp. Murder mystery with dead man clutching eight of swords from tarot pack.

CARRERAS CANDI, Francisco. "Naipes y ruletas," *La Vanguardia*. Barcelona. September 8, 1932.

CARROLL, Lewis. *Alice in Wonderland*. 1865. Classic story of Alice with the queen of hearts and her entourage of card people.

CARTAGINESE. *Giuochi di carte bellissimi, dati in luce per il Cartaginese*. Verona. 1597.

CARTER, F. W. "Playing Cards — 'The Devil's Picture Book,'" *Chambers' Journal*. December, 1948. pp. 638–640.

CARTER, Thomas Francis. *The Invention of Printing in China and its Spread Westward*. New York. 1925. 282 pp. Ill. Suggests ancient Taoist seal-charms may be the ancestors to playing cards or cards may derive from early Chinese dice; T'u-shu-chi-ch'eng Encyclopedia allegedly states Emperor Mu Tsung referred to playing cards in the year 969.

CARY, Melbert Brinckerhoff, Jr. "Playing Cards of Past and Present," *Gutenberg Jahrbuch*. 1938. pp. 37–52.

*CARY, Melbert Brinckerhoff, Jr. "A Stencil Sheet of Playing Cards of the Late 15th Century with two related uncut sheets of cards," *The Print Collector's Quarterly*. Kansas City. December 1939. Vol. 26. No. 4. Pages 392–423. Describes rare 15th century card stencil (p. 392–423).

*CARY, Melbert Brinckerhoff, Jr. "War Among the Playing Cards," *Antiques*. Concord. July, 1937. 4to. Vol. XXXII. No. 1. Ill. Cards with war themes (p. 15–17).

*CARY, Melbert Brinckerhoff, Jr. *War Cards*. New York. 1937. 8vo. 92 pp. Ill. Edition limited to 250 copies. Describes 89 packs of cards including tarot commemorating wars, battles and heroes.

*CARY, Melbert Brinckerhoff, Jr. "When a Spade is not a Spade," *Antiques*. Concord. January, 1936. 4to. Vol. XXIX. No. 1. Ill. Origin and development of card suit signs (p. 26–28).

*CASE, Carleton B., editor. *Gypsy Witch Fortune Teller* [etc]. Chicago. 1914. 160 pp. Ill. Fortune telling with 32 cards.

*CASE, Paul Foster. *The Book of Tokens: Tarot Meditations*. California. 1934. 12mo. 200 pp. Ill. *Separate edition of 191 pages also published in 1934, Washington D.C. Meditations on the 22 Major Tarot Keys.

*CASE, Paul Foster. *A Brief Analysis of The Tarot*. New York. 1927. 8vo. 102 pp. Same text as *The Tarot: A Key to the Wisdom of the Ages*.

*CASE, Paul Foster. *Highlights of Tarot*. Los Angeles. 1931. 16mo. 51 pp. Tarot symbolism and coloring instructions for BOTA tarot.

*CASE, Paul Foster. *The Tarot: A Key to the Wisdom of the Ages*. Virginia.

1947. Reprint. 12mo. 214 pp. Ill. Describes the Major Arcana for divination.

CASE, Paul Foster. *Two Courses in the Tarot.* Washington, D.C. 1928.

CASE, Paul Foster. (see *The Word*).

*CASLANT, E. "Le Tarot," *Le Voile d'Isis.* August–September 1928. Nos. 104–105. pp. 535–540. Tarot as it relates to occult sciences.

*CASTANEDA, Carlos. *Journey to Ixtlan: The Lessons of Don Juan.* New York. 1972. 315 pp.

*CASTANEDA, Carlos. *A Separate Reality: Further Conversations with Don Juan.* New York. 317 pp.

CASTANEDA, Carlos. *Tales of Power.*

*CASTANEDA, Carlos. *The Teachings of Don Juan: A Yaqui Way of Knowledge.* California. 1968. 276 pp.

*CASTELLI, Alfredo. *Viaggio curioso nel mondo delle carte.* Milan. 1975. 159 pp. Ill. Development of cards including tarot.

CASTELOT, Jollivet [F.]. *Comment on devient alchimiste, traite d'hermetisme et d'art spagyrique base sur les clefs du tarot.* 1897. 417 pp. Hermiticism and spagyric art based upon tarot.

*CASTELOT, Jollivet [F.]. *Les Destin ou les Fils d'Hermes, roman esoterique.* Paris. 1920. 612 pp. Book is divided into 22 chapters corresponding to the 22 Major Arcana.

CASTELOT, Jollivet [F.]. "Le tarot alchimique," *L'Initiation.* November 1896. Vol. 33. No. 2. pp. 151–159.

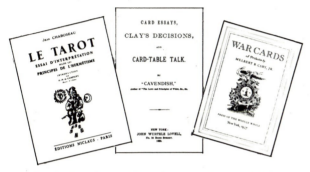

*CAVENDISH (pseudonym of Henry Jones). *Card Essays, Clay's Decisions and Card-Table Talk.* New York. 1880. 16mo. 257 pp. Rules, anecdotes and miscellanea relating to card origins and games.

CAVENDISH, Richard. *The Black Arts.* London. 1967. 373 pp. Ill. Tarot correspondences to the Tree of Life.

*CAVENDISH, Richard. *The Tarot.* New York. 1975. 4to. 191 pp. Ill. Origins and legends about tarot.

*CHABOSEAU, Jean. *Le Tarot, essai d'Interpretation selon les principes de L'Hermetisme.* Paris. 1946. 12mo. 93 pp. Appendix.

CHACORNAC, Paul. *Eliphas Levi, renovateur de l'Occultisme en France (1810–1875)* [etc]. Paris. 1926. Ill. The life and writings of Eliphas Levi with 42 portraits of Levi and other 19th century occultists.

CHANOINE-DAVRANCHES. *Histoire du jeu de cartes en Normandie.* Rouen. 1892.

CHARAVAY, Etienne. "Cartes numerales a jouer," *Revue des Documents Historiques I.* 1873–74 pp. 24–26.

[CHARROT, J., le baron de Spedalieri, Aubin Gauthier, Christian fils, J. Reynoud, etc.]. *Lettres autographes de disciples d'Eliphas Levi.* 1872–1890. 143 pp. Letters about Eliphas Levi by his disciples and a section on tarot.

*CHATTO, William Andrew. *Facts and Speculations on the Origin and History of Playing Cards.* London. 1848. 8vo. 343 pp. Ill. Origin and development of playing cards.

CHATTO, William Andrew. *A Treatise on Wood Engraving* [etc]. London. 1839. 8vo. 749 pp. Ill. Early German playing cards from wood engravings (Chapter II).

CHENEVIER, A. "Le Tarot," *Le Voile d'Isis.* 1908. No. 30, April, pp. 50–51. No. 31, May, pp. 67–68.

CHENEVIER, A. "Le Tarot moderne," *Le Voile d'Isis.* June 1908. No. 32 pp. 83–85.

CHENEY, Mrs. E. D. *Patience: A Series of Thirty Games with Cards.* Boston, 1870. 96 pp. Ill. Rules for the game of Patience including terms.

CHESNEY, Hettie. "Secrets of the Tarot," *Fate Magazine.* February 1955. Vol. 8. No. 2. Issue No. 59. Tarot and the 22 Major Arcana (pp. 37–45).

CHEW, Samuel C. *The Virtues Reconciled. An Iconographic Study.* Toronto. 1947. 163 pp. Ill.

*CHICAGO PLAYING CARD COLLECTORS INC. *Deck Reference Guide.* 1968. Identifies playing cards.

*CHICAGO PLAYING CARD COLLECTORS INC. *CPCC Bulletin.* Chicago. Monthly bulletin for members of Chicago Playing Card Collectors Inc.

*CHIRO, Madam. *Fortune Telling by Cards.* Chicago. 1901. 80 pp. Ill. Fortune telling with 32 and 52 cards.

CHOBAUT, H. "Les Maitres-cartiers d'Avignon du XVeme siecle a la Revolution," *Memoires de l'Acad. de Vacluse.* Vaison-la-Romaine. 1955. 84 pp.

CHONEBARY. "Die Spielkarten des Ostenreichischen Museums fur Kunst und Industrie," *Mitteilungen des Museums.* 1882. p. 265.

CHRISTIAN, Paul (pseudonym of Jean-Baptiste Pitois). *Carmen Sibyllum. Prediction de la naissance du fils de Napoleon III* [etc]. Paris. 1854. 2nd edition, 1856.

*CHRISTIAN, Paul (pseudonym of Jean-Baptiste Pitois). *Histoire de la Magie.* Paris. 1870. Description of the tarot trumps (p. 112–131).

*CHRISTIAN, Paul (pseudonym of Jean-Baptiste Pitois). *The History and Practice of Magic.* Translated from French by James Kirkup and Julian Shaw. New York. n.d. 602 pp. English translation of Christian's *Histoire de la Magie* includes section on tarot (p. 94–112).

CHRISTIAN, Paul (pseudonym of Jean-Baptiste Pitois). *L'homme rouge des Tuileries.* Paris. 1863. 464 pp. Ill. Commentary on the tarot trumps.

CHRISTIAN [P.] fils. *La reine Zinzarah. Comment on devient sorcier.* Paris. n.d. The author, son of Paul Christian, compares The Empress and The Emperor cards to the Church of the Albigenses and Henry VII (ruler of Germany from 1309 to 1313) respectively.

CHRISTIE, James. *An enquiry into the ancient Greek game supposed to have been invented by Palamedes* [etc]. London. 1801. 4 to. Analogies between chess and cards suggest that cards may derive from the early Indian game of chess called *chaturanga*.

*CHRISTIE'S. *Printed Books and a Choice Collection of Playing Cards.* London. 1971. 76 pages. Ill. Catalog of card auction held in November 1971.

CHURCHWARD, James. *The Sacred Symbols of Mu.* Binghamton. 1933. 12vo. 258 pp. Ill. Describes early religions and ancient Egyptian gods who sometimes are associated with the 22 Major Arcana.

*CICOGNARA, Leopoldo. *Memorie Spettanti Alla Storia della Calcografia del Commend.* Prato. 1831. 8vo. 262 pp. Folio, 18 pp. Origin of playing cards including early tarocchi decks. Separate folio includes Italian cards.

*CIRLOT, Juan Eduardo. *A Dictionary of Symbols.* Translated from *Diccionario de Simbolos* by Jack Sage. New York. 1962. 400 pp. Ill. Tarot symbolism and the 22 Major Arcana.

CLARK, Frieda. *Hobbies Magazine.* The author wrote many articles dealing with playing card collecting.

CLARK, Frieda. *Playing Card Collector's Handbook.* Chicago. 1954. 8vo. 64 pp. Describes cards by Worshipful Company of Makers of Playing Cards.

CLARK, Kenneth. Frieda Clark. A letter in *The Burlington Magazine.* 1933. p. 143. The author attributes the 50-card Tarocchi of Mantegna series to Parrasio Michele, Ferarra, who died in 1578.

CLAVELLE, M. "Essai de bibliographie francaise du Tarot," *Le Voile d'Isis.* August–September 1928. Nos. 104–105. pp. 627–640.

CLERC de TROYES (Le). *Le roman de Renart le Contrefait.* 1319–1322 and 1328–1342. The first version of this poem of 32,000 verses, housed at the Bibliotheque Nationale, Paris, does not contain the words *cards* or *playing cards;* however a copy dating from the second half of the fifteenth century allegedly contains the word *cards.*

CLERICI, P. "Il Perrama, il Toschi, Il Cicognara. Il giuoco del Tarocchi e un quadretto del Montegna," *La Bibliofilia.* XIX. 1917–1918. pp. 97–113.

CLERK, S. I. "The Art of Ganjifa Cards," *Modern Review.* Calcutta. December 1946. pp. 435–436.

CLODIUS, Henrici Ionath. *Bibliothecae Lusoriae sive notitia Scriptorum de Ludis.* Lipsiae. 1761. 166 pp. Annotated bibliography on games, playing cards and several references to tarocchi cards.

CLOUZOT, H. "La fabrication des cartes a jouer," *La renaissance de l'art francais.* 1927. pp. 179–187.

CLULOW, George. "Origin and Manufacture of Playing Cards," *Journal of The Society of Arts.* 1889.

*CLULOW, George. "Peculiar Playing Cards," *The Strand Magazine.* January/February, 1893. 12 pp. Ill. Brief description of playing cards including tarot.

*COBWEBS PRESS. *Dear Dragon.* London. 1976. 93 pp. Ill. Meditations on the Major Arcana.

*COHEN, Daniel. *The Magic Art of Foreseeing the Future.* New York. 1973. 8vo. 192 pp. Mentions tarot and includes illustrations of French Revolutionary tarot cards by L. Cary.

COHEN, J. *Origine des cartes.* 1826.

COHEN, Julie. *Research Paper on Tarot.* Unpublished manuscript. New York. 1977. Briefly defines tarot, describes history and uses in fortune-telling, and influences on modern culture.

**COHEN, Stanley A. *Some Interesting Facts about the Origin and History of Playing Cards.* New York. 1916. 31 pp. The author believes playing cards are of Hindustan origin, probably having developed around the 7th century from the game of chess; the oldest extant deck of cards is a circular pack of 120 pieces from the kingdom of Visnupur, circa 900 A.D.

*COLDWELL, Joan, and Ann Saddlemyer. *Pamela Colman Smith — An Exhibition.* Hamilton, Ontario. February 1977. 12 pp. Ill. Catalog of an exhibition of Pamela Colman Smith's work held February 1977 at McMaster University, Hamilton, Ontario.

COLDWELL, Joan. "Pamela Colman Smith and the Yeats Family," *Canadian Journal for Irish Studies.* December 1977.

*COLLETT, Maurice. "The Royal Masonic Playing-Cards," *The Journal of The Playing-Card Society.* Birmingham. November 1974. Vol. III. No. 2. pp. 25–26.

COLLIJN, Isak. *Nagra Gamla Spelkort Fran Medeltiden.* Upsula. 1905. 8 pp. Ill. Describes pack of 15th century hunting cards.

COLLIN, Rodney. *The Theory of Celestial Influence.* 1954. The author proposes that the Cathedral of Chartres, a pack of tarot cards, and certain multi-armed and multi-headed bronzes of Tibetan deities are formulations of exactly the same ideas and thus are directly comparable.

*COLLISON-MORLEY, L. *The Story of the Sforzas.* New York. 1934. 8vo. 312 pp. Ill. Traces history of the Sforza family of Milan.

COLOCCI, A. *Gli Zingari.* Torino. 1880. According to Colocci, the gypsies or *Romanichals* called the four suits of playing cards by the names *pal, pohara, spathi* and *rup* which represent the four seasons of the year.

COLVILLE, W. J. *Kabbalah. The Harmony of Opposites [etc].* New York. 1916. sm 12mo. 189 pp. Discusses inner significance of the 22 Letters of the Hebrew alphabet.

COMELLI, G. B. "Il governo 'misto' in Bologna dal 1507 al 1797 a la carte di giuoco del can. montieri," *Atti e memorie della reale deputazione di storia patria per le provincie della romagna.* 1909. Series 3. Volume XXVII.

*PAR MME LA COMTESSE DE***. *Grand Jeu de Societe. Pratiques Secretes. De Mlle Le Normand [etc].* Paris. 1845. 16mo. 66 and 169 pp.

*CONNIE [Taylor]. "Tarots and Carats." Miami. Unpublished MS. Esoteric teaching methods for tarot cards.

CONSIL-LACOSTE, M. "Figures du jeu," *L'Oeil.* Noel 1958. No. 58. Ill. Summary of the history of playing cards.

CONSTANT, Alphonse Louis (see under pseudonym Eliphas Levi).

COOKE, John (see also Rosalind Sharpe).

COOKE, John, and Rosalind Sharpe. *The New Tarot. The Tarot for the Aquarian Age.* California. 1968. 16mo. 150 pp. Ill. Describes the New Tarot also known as the Royal Maze, painted by John Cooke.

*COOPER, Louise. *The Book of Paradox.* New York. n.d. 8vo. 244 pages. Ill. Novel about a young man's trials and adventures, each characterized by a tarot card.

CORDONNIER-DETRIE. "Jacques Gaugain, maitre-cartier-dominotier-imagier... du Mans au XVIII[e] siecle," *Le Mans.* 1928.

*COROLEU, Jose. *La Superstiaciones de la Humanidad.* Barcelona. 1880–1881. 2 Vols. 856 and 1007 pp. Ill. Description of Major Arcana based upon P. Christian's *Histoire de la Magie* (Vol. 1, p. 280–293). Illustration by R. Marti depicts Mlle Lenormand in her Paris apartment at 5 Rue de Tournon reading the cards for Napoleon I (Vol. II, p. 355).

COROMINAS, Joao. *Diccionario Etimologico de la Lengua Espanola.* Buenos Aires. 1954. Contains playing cards (Vol. III, pp. 494–498).

*CORWIN, Arthur. *The Tarot and the Tapestry of Myth.* Connecticut. 1975. 500 pp. Ill. Iconographic analysis on the function of tarot as a primer of prehistoric thought.

COTTON, Charles. *The Compleat Gamester [etc].* London. 1674. 12mo. 232 pp. *Reprinted.

COTTON, Charles, and Theophilus Lucas. *Games and Gamesters of the Restoration: The Compleat Gamester and Lives of the Gamesters.* London. 1930. 281 pp.

COURT de GEBELIN, Antoine. "Du Jeu des Tarots," *Le Monde Primitif, analyse et compare avec le monde moderne.* Paris. 1775–1784. 9 volumes. Describes Egyptian origin of tarot and the meaning of each card (Vol. 9).

COUSTE, Alberto. *El Tarot o la maquina de imaginar.* Barcelona. 1972.

*COUSTE, Alberto. *Il Tarocco. Ovvero: La macchina per immaginare.* Milano. 1974. 199 pp. Includes 22 Major Arcana cards with book.

COVARRUBIAS, Fray Pedro de. *Remedio de Jugadores.* Madrid. 1543.

COVARRUBIAS y HOROZCO. *Tesoro de la Lengua Castellana o Espanola.* Madrid. 1611. Folio.

COVELLUZZO, Giovanni (see Bussi).

CRICK, Lucien. "Cartes a jouer: usages secondaires et note complementaire," *Bulletin Musees des Royaux d'Art et d'histoire.* Belgium. 1941–1942. 3rd series. Nos. 2 & 6. pp. 30–35 and 137–138.

CRICK, Lucien, and Aline Bara. "Un jeu de cartes en argent," *Bulletin Musees des Royaux d'Art et d'Histoire.* Belgium. 1942. No. 5. 8 pp.

*CRISWELL. *Criswell's Forbidden Predictions. Based on Nostradamus and the Tarot.* Atlanta. 1972. sm 8vo. 128 pp. Ill. Criswell believes *tarot* is the Druid word for *truth* and the tarot pack comprises 22 cards of the Grand Gallery (Major Arcana) and 56 cards of the Hall of Shadows (Minor Arcana).

*CROFT, Colin. [Narbeth] "Games: Cards of the Past," *Antique Collector.* London. September 1976. pp. 20–23. Ill. Brief description of card games including tarot.

*CROFT, Colin. "Playing-Cards and Money," *The Journal of The Playing-Card Society.* Birmingham. Nov. 1974. Vol. III. No. 2. pp. 8–12. Ill.

*CROSBY, C. Russell, Jr. *Die Flotnerschen Spielkarten und andere Curiosa der Musikuberlieferung des 16. Jahrhunderts aus Franken.* Weisbaden. 1967. 8vo. 99 pp. Ill. Describes the pack of playing cards by Peter Floetner, circa 1540–1545.

*CROW, W. B. "The Symbolism of Chess and Cards," *Mysteries of the Ancients.* London. 1944. 12mo. No. 13. 38 pp. Symbolic interpretations of cards and chess.

*CROW, W. B. *The Arcana of Symbolism.* New York. 1970. 96 pp.

*CROWLEY, Aleister. "A description of the cards of the tarot, with their attributions; including a method of divination by their use," *The Equinox.* September 1912. Vol. I. No. VIII. pp. 143–210. Meanings of the Major Arcana cards and meanings and descriptions of the Minor Arcana.

*CROWLEY, Aleister. *The Book of Thoth (Egyptian Tarot).* 1944. Edition limited to 200 copies. New York. Reprinted 1969. 8vo. 287 pp. Ill. Discusses tarot and Crowley's interpretation.

*CROWLEY, Aleister. *Magick.* London. 1973. 511 pp. Ill. According to Crowley, tarot symbols are mathematically precise and possess an artistic significance which helps the diviner to understand them by stimulating asthetic perceptions.

*CROWLEY, Aleister. *Tarot Divination.* San Francisco. Reprint. 1973. 12mo. 79 pp. Ill. Describes Crowley tarot pack and card interpretations.

*CROWTHER, Arnold and Patricia. *The Secrets of Ancient Witchcraft with The Witches Tarot.* Introduction and Notes by Dr. Leo Louis Martello. Secaucus. 1974. 218 pp. Ill.

*CSELENY, L. "The Devil's Invention. Playing Cards in the ROM," *Rotunda.* Toronto. Spring 1976. Volume 9. Number 1. Ill. Describes several early decks including tarot and minchiate in the collection of the Royal Ontario Museum, Toronto (p. 4–13).

CUELLO MARTINELL, Maria Angeles. *La Renta de los Naipes en Nueva Espana.* Seville. 1966.

*CULIN, Stewart. *Chess and Playing-Cards [etc].* Washington. 1898. Extract from the Report of the U.S. National Museum for 1896, p. 665–942. Ill. According to Culin, both chess and playing cards derive from divinatory arrows; and the basis of all divinatory systems arises from the classification of all things according to Four Directions.

CULIN, Stewart. *Games of the Orient.* 1895 Reprinted Tokyo, 1958.

CULIN, Stewart. "Origin of Playing Cards," *Journal of American Folklore.* July 1895.

CUMING, H. Syer. "Why is the Nine of Diamonds called the Curse of Scotland?," *Journal of the British Archaeological Association.* London. 1874. 8vo. Vol. 30. p. 207–212.

*CUNDALL, H. M. "Playing Cards," *The Studio.* London. 1927. sm 4to. pp. 85–89. Origin and development of playing cards.

*CUNNINGHAM, Donna. "Safety Rules for Amateur Tarot Readers," *Your Personal Astrology.* Winter 1975. pp. 115–117. Suggestions to improve tarot card readings.

CURRIE, Geraldine. "The Call of the Card. Playing Cards Through the Ages," *Edinburgh Tatler.* March 1967. Vol. 9. No. 71. 2 pp. Ill. Describes cards used as markers for debts and legal documents.

*CURTISS, Harriette Augusta and F. Homer. *The Key to the Universe.* 1917. Reprinted San Gabriel, 1974. 392 pp. Ill. Description of ten Major Arcana cards, I The Juggler to X The Wheel of Life including comparisons of Wirth, Tarot of Marseilles, Church of Light and Rider-Waite decks.

*CURTISS, Harriette Augusta and F. Homer. *The Key of Destiny.* London. 1923. 328 pp. Ill. Description of Major Arcana cards XI Strength to XXI The World, and The Fool, including comparisons of decks.

D

D.A. *Observaciones sobre los juegos de naypes* [etc]. Madrid. 1807.

D'ADDA, Marchese. *Indagini storiche, artistiche e bibliografiche sulla Libreria Visconteo-sforzesca del Castello di Pavia.* Milan. 1875.

*****D'AGOSTINO**, Joseph. *Tarot, The Royal Path to Wisdom*. New York. 1976. 148 pp. Delineates meditative symbolism inherent in the 22 Major Arcana cards of the Rider-Waite pack.

D'AGUILAR, Jackson Lewis. *Tarocco and Tresillo*. New York. 1886.

D'AIGLE, Jean. *Less XXII Arcanes symboliques d'Hermes*. Locarno. n.d.

*****D'ALLEMAGNE**, Henry René. *Causerie sur les cartes a jouer*. sm 4to. Ill. Origin and development of playing cards (p. 168–180).

*****D'ALLEMAGNE**, Henry René. *Le cartes a jouer Lyonnaises*. *Revue d'Histoire de Lyon*. 1906.

*****D'ALLEMAGNE**, Henry René. *Les Cartes a Jouer du Quatorzieme au Vingtieme Siecle. Contenant 3200 reproductions de cartes, dont 956 en couleur, 12 planches hors textes coloriees a l'aquarelle, 25 phototypies, 116 enveloppes illustrees pour jeux de cartes et 340 vignettes et vues diverses.* Paris. 1906. 2 Vols. 504 and 640 pp. Folio. Ill. Reprinted 1975. Authoritative work on the history of cards; profusely illustrated including tarot.

[**DALLET**, Gabriel (pseudonym Plytoff)]. *Mysteres des Sciences occultes . . . cartomancie* [etc]. 1894.

D'AMBLY, P. Boiteau (see Boiteau).

DAMMARTIN, Moreau de. *Origine de la Forme des caracteres alphabetiques de toutes les nations, des clefs chinoises, des hieroglyphes egyptiens* [etc]. Paris. 1839. Relates Major Arcana to early hieroglyphics.

DANEAU, Lambert. *Remonstrances sur les jeux de sort ou de hazard et principalement de dez et de cartes*. Geneva. 1575. 8vo.

DANEAU, Lambert. *Deux traictez nouveaux tres-utiles pour ce temps, le premier touchant les sorciers, le deuxieme contient une breve remonstrance sur les jeux de cartes et de dez*. Paris. 1579.

DANIEL, Père Gabriel. "Memoire sur l'origine du jeu de piquet trouve dans l'histoire de France sous le regne de Charles VII." Extract from the *Journal of Trevoux*. May 1720. pp. 934–968. Pere Daniel, a reverend Father of the order of Jesuits, believes the game of piquet was devised in France about 1430 during the reign of Charles VII; each court card is explained in terms of its symbolic, allegoric, military, political and historical significance.

*****DARC**, P. S. "Arcanes mineurs," *Le Voile d'Isis*. August-September 1928. Nos. 104–105. pp. 591–600. Ill. Describes Minor Arcana and includes original designs by Eliphas Levi for 10 of cups, 10 of coins and ace of swords.

DARCEL, Alfred. "Sur une ancienne forme a imprimer des cartes a jouer," *Revue de Rouen et de la Normandie*. Rouen. 1846.

DASHWOOD, George Henry. "Notice of Three Engraved Plates for a Pack of Heraldic Playing Cards," *Norfolk Archaeology*. Norwich. 1859. 8vo. Vol. 5. pp. 1–7.

*****DAVERIO**, Michele. *Memorie Sulla Storia Dell' Ex-Ducato di Milano Risguardanti Il Dominio Dei Visconti, etc*. Milano. 1804. 277 pp. Describes domination of Visconti and Sforza families in fifteenth-century Milan.

*****DAVIES**, Frederic. *Ancien tarot de Marseille*. London. 1975. 95 pp. Ill. Manual on reading tarot cards.

DAVIS, Andrew McFarland. *A Few Additional Notes on Indian Games*. Salem. 1887. 8vo. 23 pp.

DAVIS, Andrew McFarland. *Indian Games. An Historical Research*. Salem. 1886. 8vo. 58 pp.

DAVIS, Dorothy Salisbury. *A Death In the Life*. New York. Novel about a young lady who takes up fortune-telling with tarot cards.

D'AVRANCHES, Chanoine L. *Histoire du jeu des cartes en Normandie* [etc]. Rouen. 1892. 8vo.

D'AVRANCHES, Chanoine L. *Notes sur l'origine et l'histoire des jeux*. Rouen. 1917. 307 pp. Origins of playing cards and early French card makers (Chapters IV and V).

*****DAY**, Harvey. *Occult Illustrated Dictionary*. New York. 1975. 156 pp. Ill. People and subjects in the occult including tarot and the kabbalah.

De ALCALA, Pedro. *Vocabulista arauigo en letra castellana*. Granada. 1505.

*****DECKER**, Ronald. "The Early Illuminated Tarots from Milan." Unpublished MS. 1974. 33 pp. Ill. Tarocchi packs painted by Bonifacio Bembo.

*****DECKER**, Ronald. "Two Tarot Studies Related," *The Journal of the Playing Card Society*. Birmingham. Parts I & II, May 1975, Vol. III, No. 4, p. 13–20. Part III, August 1975, Vol. IV, No. 1, p. 46–52. Discusses sequence and meanings of early tarot trumps including virtues triumphant over vices and astrological associations.

*****DECKER**, Ronald and Charlotte. "The Visconti-Sforza Cards in the Cary Collection." Unpublished MS. 1975.

*****DECKER**, Ronald and Charlotte. "The Visconti-Sforza Cards in the Cary Collection," *The Journal of The Playing-Card Society*. Cranbrook. November 1975. Vol. IV. No. 2. p. 27–32. Discusses the Visconti-Sforza pack at Yale University.

DECRESPE [Marius]. *La Main et ses mysteres*. Paris. n.d. 2 vol. Includes references to tarot.

DECRESPE [Marius]. *Manuel de Graphologie appliquee*. Paris. n.d. Includes references to tarot.

De JONG, Jan. H. N. *Tarot, Prentkaartenboek der Bybel Profetien (Tarot, Picture Book of the Bible Prophecy)*. Middenmeer. 1977. Ill. Tarot theory based upon the Bible; Major Arcana illustrations painted by Piet Meyer and Jan H. N. de Jong.

DELAAGE. *Le monde prophetique ou moyen de connaitre l'avenir employe par les sybilles, les pythiques, les tireuses de cartes, etc.* Paris. 1853. 12mo.

De LAENNAC, Sophie. *La Mystere du Tarot*. Description of the trumps with one-word meanings.

*****DELCAMP**, Edmond. *Le Tarot Initiatique Symbolique et Esoterique*. Paris. 1972. 8vo. 475 pp.

*****DELOSERAYE**, H. "Remarques sur le tarot," *Le Voile d'Isis*. August-September 1928. Nos. 104–105. Compares the Hebrew alphabet and the Major Arcana (p. 584–588).

DELPHA. *L'art de tirer les cartes*.

DENNING, Trevor (Ed). *Ace of Spades*. Birmingham. 1969. 47 pp. Ill. A single-issue publication served as a link between collectors before the formation of the Playing-Card Society.

*****DENNING**, Trevor (Ed). "Alphabetical List of Playing-card Makers (Spanish and Latin-American) in the Catalogue of Fournier's Museo de Naipes, Vitoria," *The Journal of The Playing-Card Society*. Cranbrook. August 1976. Vol. V. No. 1. Lists Spanish and Latin-American card makers (p. 26–35).

DENNING, Trevor (Ed). "The Hidden Design of Playing Cards," *Design*. London. January, 1968. Ill. Contemporary playing cards and the differences between evolved and "designed" cards (p. 40–43).

DENNING, Trevor (Ed). "In Search of the Tarot," *Prediction*. London. November 1967. Ill. Survey of tarot in Great Britain (p. 20–22).

*****DENNING**, Trevor (Ed). "Kimberley's Patriotic Playing-Cards," *The Journal of The Playing-Card Society*. Manchester. August 1973. Vol. II. No. 1. Four editions of Kimberley's Patriotic Playing Cards (p. 2–6).

*****DENNING**, Trevor (Ed). "Style and the Spanish Pattern," *The Journal of The Playing-Card Society*. Cranbrook. May 1976. Vol. 4. No. 4. Spanish playing card classification (p. 15–19).

DENNING, Trevor (Ed). *Translucent Playing-Cards*. Birmingham. 1976. 51 pp. Ill. Erotic "transparent" playing cards. Limited signed edition of 300.

DEPPING. "Note sur l'histoire des Cartes, a l'occasion des Recherches de Singer." Extract from *La Revue encyclopedique*. Paris. 1819. 8vo.

*****DEQUER**, John H. *Arrows of Light from The Egyptian Tarot*. New York. 1930. 263 pp. Interpretation of the Major Arcana based upon Egyptian symbolism and the teachings of BOTA.

DEQUER, John H. "The Tarot as I use it," *The Seer*. June 1931. Vol. 3. No. 6. pp. 256–264.

DESMARETS, Jean. *Les jeux de Cartes des Roys de France, des Reines Renommees, de la Geographie, et des Fables*. Paris. 1664. 60 pp.

DESSENTELLES, N. N. *Apercu sur le jeu des Tarots, son origine reconnue egyptienne, son antiquite de 3500, 7 ou 800 ans*. Brunswick. 1800.

D'ESSLING, Prince, and Eugene Muntz. *Petrarque; ses etudes d'art, son influence sur les artistes, ses portraits et ceux de Laure*. Paris. 1902. 293 pp. Ill. Profusely illustrated with representations of Petrarch's triumphs from the fourteenth to seventeenth century, but no mention of tarocchi cards.

DEVAUX, A. "Le papier des cartes a jouer," *Le vieux papier*. No. 10.

De VIGNY. "Memoire sur l'origine de L'imprimerie," *Journal Economique*. Paris. March 1758. 8vo.

****DE VINNE**, Theodore L. *The Invention of Printing* [etc]. London. 1877. 8vo. Early playing cards and methods to print them (Chapter V).

D.F.B. y B. *El Recreo de las Tertulias. Coleccion de juegos que comprende los de los naipes* [etc]. 1864.

*****DIETRICH**, Margot. "History of the Deutsches Spielkarten Museum," *The Journal of The Playing-Card Society*. Cranbrook. November 1976. Vol. V. No. 2. Describes playing card museum at Leinfelden (p. 4–14).

DIGNEF, L. *Cartes a jouer et jeux de cartes a Turnhout*. Louvain. 1970. Unpublished MS. Thesis on playing cards and card games in Turnhout.

*****DINAGO**, F. *Publication des oeuvres inedites de Dom A. Calmet*. 1876. 4to. Article on the origin of cards (p. 81–92).

*****DIO RAMAN** [pseudonym from anagram of Italo De Diana, his wife, and

George Hulskramer]. *De Hermetische Tarot.* Netherlands. 1976. 278 pp. Ill. Origin, symbolism and interpretation of tarot.

*DIO RAMAN [pseudonym from anagram of Italo De Diana, his wife, and George Hulskramer]. *De Praktische Tarot.* Netherlands. 1976. 105 pp. Ill. The 22 Major Arcana are described as archetypes representing the sum total of human experience. Sleeve at back of book contains 22 Major Arcana cards designed by Anneke De Diana.

*DIRF, Benno. "Von der spielkarte und com kartenmacherhandwerk," *Offset-Buch und Werbekunst.* 1925. Heft 10. Ill. Development and art of making playing cards (p. 624–636).

*DOANE, Doris Chase, and King Keyes. *Tarot-Card Spread Reader.* New York. 1970. Reprint. 8vo. 207 pp. Ill. Reprinted under the title *How to Read Tarot Cards.* Explains how to use and read tarot cards.

DODGSON, Campbell, and Sidney M. Peartree. *The Durer Society.* Facsimiles. London. 1906. Ser. 9. The author dates ten Durer tarocchi cards circa 1494 and the remaining eleven cards circa 1506.

*D'ODOUCET, M. *Science des signes et medicine de l'esprit connue sous le nom d'Art de tirer les cartes* [etc]. Paris. Circa 1804. Tarot based upon the works of Etteilla (see also Alta).

**DOERING, Dr. Oskar. "Die Spielkarten," *Velhagen & Klasing's Neue Monatshefte.* Bielefeld & Leipzig. March 1891. Vol. 5. Describes early playing cards (p. 601–613).

DONOGHUE, Denis. *W.B. Yeats Memoirs. Autobiography–First Draft and Journal.* New York. 1972. 318 pp. According to Yeats, the sword, stone, spear and cauldron relate to the four suits of the Minor Arcana.

DORNIK-EGER, Hanna. *Playing Card Catalog of the Vienna Museum of the Applied Arts.* 1975.

*DORNIK-EGER, Hanna. *Spielkarten und Kartenspiele. Schriften der Bibliothek des Oesterreichischen Museums fuer angerwandte Kunst 10.* Vienna. 1973. 25 pp. Ill. Catalog of playing cards.

*D'OTRANGE, M. L. "Thirteen Tarot Cards from the Visconti-Sforza Set," *The Connoisseur Magazine.* March 1954. Vol. CXXXIII. No. 535. Ill. Describes the 13 Von Bartsch Visconti-Sforza tarocchi cards (p. 54–60).

*DOUBLEDAY, Abner. "The Tarot." Unpublished MS. Circa 1870. 257 pp. Handwritten manuscript contains notes, illustrations and translation of works by Levi and Papus. Signed letter on page 175 bears signature *Abner Doubleday,* Civil War general and founder of baseball in America.

*DOUGLAS, Alfred. *The Tarot. The Origins, Meaning and Uses of the Cards.* New York. 1972. sm 8vo. 249 pp. Ill. Bibliography. Origin, meaning and divination with tarot cards illustrated by David Sheridan. Game of tarocco is also described.

DOUGLAS, Nik. *Chakra; An Anthology of Tantra and Yoga.* New Delhi. 1971. 250 pp. Ill. Anthology of articles by scholars in Tantric Art and Yoga.

DOUGLAS, Nik. *Tantra Yoga.* New Delhi. 1970. 120 pp. Ill. Tantric art and symbolism including the meaning of Indian philosophical images and cosmology.

DOUGLAS, Nik. *Tibetan Tantric Charms and Amulets.* New York. 1976. Ill. Meaning and symbolism of Tantric charms and amulets.

DOUGLAS, Nik, and Meryl White. *Karmapa; The Black Hat Lama of Tibet.* London. 1976. 220 pp. Ill. Occult history of the Tibetan Tantric hierarch with bibliographies of the Lamas of the Kargyudpa sect.

DOWNES, Gwladys V. "W. B. Yeats and the Tarot," *The World of W. B. Yeats: Essays in Perspective.* Victoria, B.C. 1965.

*DOYON, Rene Louis. "La petite histoire des cartes a jouer," *Gazette Dunlop.* June 1937. 4to. No. 202. Ill. Discusses methods of manufacture and suit signs in playing cards (p. 4–5).

*DOYON, Rene Louis. "Petite histoire des cartes a jouer. Du casse-tete au prophetisme," *Carnets du Mandarin.* September, 1962. No. 8. pp. 37–46.

DRAGONI, Antonio (falsified the Bordigallo passages; see Bordigallo).

*DRAYSON, Martin. "A Brief History of Playing Cards," *Mankind.* August 1968. Vol. 1. No. 8. Ill. Brief development of playing cards (p. 50–55).

*DUBEN, C. G. F. von. *Talisman des Glucks oder der Selbstlehrer fur alle Karten-Schach-Billard-Ball und Kegel-Spiele.* Berlin. 1816.

DUBEN, C. G. F. von. *Das Tarotspiel.* Berlin. 1819. 42 pp. Rules for the game of tarock.

DU BLED, V. *Histoire anecdotique et psychologique des jeux de cartes, des echecs.* Paris. 1919.

**DUBUC, R. "Classification Decimale Universelle. Cartes a Jouer." Unpublished MS. Evreux. 1975. Text in English, French and German. 19 pp. Classification system for playing cards based on universal decimal system.

DUCHARTRE, Pierre Louis. "Cartes a jouer," *Ce-Temps-Ci. Cahiers d'Art contemporain.* 1931. No. 11. pp. 327–330.

*DUCHARTRE, Pierre Louis. "Tarot Packs. Tarockspiele. Jeux de Tarots," *Graphis Magazine.* Zurich. 1949. Vol. 5. No. 26. Describes the graphic development of French tarot cards (p. 168–173).

*DUCHESNE, Maine. *Jeux de Cartes Tarots et de Cartes Numérales, du quatorzième au dix-huitième siècle. Publiés par la Société des Bibliophiles Français.* Paris. 1844. Folio. 100 pp. Hand illustrated. Limited to 32 copies on *grande papier* and 100 copies on *petit papier.* Contains hand-illuminated reproductions of the 17 tarot cards in the Bibliotheque Nationale, Paris, and 50 Tarocchi de Mantegna cards.

*DUCHESNE, Maine. *Observations sur les cartes a jouer. Extrait de l'annuaire historique pour 1837, publie par la societe de l'histoire de France.* Paris. 1836. 16mo. 46 pp. Describes the 17 Gringonneur and 50 Tarocchi of Mantegna cards (p. 172–213).

DUHAMEL du MONCEAU (see Monceau).

*DUMMETT, Andy. "The Spanish Captain," *The Journal of The Playing-Card Society.* Birmingham. November 1974. Vol. III. No. 2. the author believes the braggart captain frequently appearing in 16th and 17th century European plays is the same figure represented in Belgian tarots as trump number II, Capitano Eracasse (p. 7–8).

*DUMMETT, Michael. "A Note On Cicognara," *The Journal of The Playing-Card Society.* Manchester. August 1973. Vol. II. No. 1. Discusses the evolution of the shortened 62-card tarocchino pack from the present game of tarocco (p. 14–17).

*DUMMETT, Michael. "15th Century Card Games and the Hofaemterspiel," *Hofaemterspiel.* Vienna. 1976. Describes characteristics common to early card games (p. 62–79 and 123–137).

*DUMMETT, Michael. "More about Cicognara," *The Journal of The Playing-Card Society.* London. November 1976. Vol. V. No. 2. Identifies the 17th century portrait of Prince Fibbia described in detail by Cicognara in 1831 (p. 26–34).

*DUMMETT, Michael. "Notes on a 15th-Century Pack of Cards From Italy," *The Journal of The Playing-Card Society.* Manchester. February 1973. Vol. 1. No. 3. pp. 2–6.

*DUMMETT, Michael. "The Order of the Tarot Trumps," *The Journal of the Playing-Card Society.* Manchester. Part I, February 1974, Vol. II, No. 3, pp. 1–17. Part II, May 1974, Vol. II, No. 4, pp. 33–50. Analytical summary of the possible sequence of the 22 Major Arcana cards in early tarocchi packs.

*DUMMETT, Michael, and John McLeod. "Cego," *The Journal of The Playing-Card Society.* Birmingham. August 1975. Vol. IV. No. 1. Ill. Rules for the game of Cego (p. 30–46).

DUMMETT, Michael, and John McLeod. "A Note on Some Fragments in the Benaki Museum," *AARP 4.* December 1973.

*DUMMETT, Michael, and Kamal Abu-Deeb. "Some Remarks on Mamluk Playing Cards," *Journal of the Warburg and Courtauld Institutes.* London. 1973. Volume XXXVI. Ill. Analysis of Mamluk playing cards (p. 106–128).

DURAND, *Apercu du jeu des tarots, ou jeu de la vie, etc.* Metz. 1813. 12mo.

*DURAND, Dominique. *Le Jeu de la Vme.* Designs by Pino Zac. Nancy. 1977. Political figures of the fifth French Republic; die cut cards.

*DUREN, Rev. Stephen. *Cards, Bible, Church, Religion.* Chicago. 1912. 16mo. 430 pages. The Bible through pictures, numbers and suit signs of a 52-card deck.

DURRIEU, P. *Michelino de Besozzo et les relations entre l'art italien et l'art francais.* 1911. Cites sixteen early cards described in a letter dated 1449 from Jacobo Antonio Marcello, a servant of King Rene, to Isabelle of Lorraine, first wife of King Rene of Anjou.

E

EBELING, F. *Zur Geschichte der Spielkarten.*

*EBERHARD, von Balz. "Spielkarten und Spielkartensteuer in der Helvetischen Republik 1798–1803," *Zeitschrift fur Schweizerische Archaoologie und Kunstgeschichte.* Zurich. 1973. Band 30. Doppelheft 3/4. pp. 169–184. Ill.

*ECCLESTON GALLERIES. *Playing Cards by The Worshipful Company and Others.* n.d. Catalog. Supplement 72.

*ECCLESTON GALLERIES. *Playing Cards for Collectors.* n.d. Catalog. Supplement 74.

*EDINDUSTRIA EDITORIALE. *Antiche Carte Italiane da Tarocchi.* Rome. 1961. Folio. 26 pp. Ill. Second edition limited to 300 copies. Brief history of Italian tarot cards and reproductions of early tarot, tarocchino and minchiate cards.

*EDITORA PENSAMENTO. *Taro Adivinhatorio.* Sao Paulo. 1974. 171 pp. Ill. A 78-card tarot deck based on Papus is packaged with the book.

*EDMUNDS, Sheila. "A Note on the Art of Joseph Ibn Hayyim," *Studies in Bibliography and Booklore.* 1976. Vol. XI. pp. 25–40. Reveals parallels among colophons with animal themes in the Kennicott Bible, a 15th century Spanish Hebrew work of art, and animal designs for cards prepared by the Master of the Playing Cards.

EICHENBERG, Fritz. "Playing Cards," *Print Collector*. No. 12. March/April, 1975.

*****EIMERL**, Sarel. *The World of Giotto c. 1267–1337*. New York. 1967. 199 pp. Ill. The Arena Chapel, Padua, contains Giotto's frescoes which include vices and virtues suggestive of the Major Arcana.

EISTIBUS, Nitibus. "Astrologie onomantique," *L'Initiation*. August 1895. Vol. XXVIII. No. II. pp. 121–144. Explanations of several tarot cards.

******EITELBERGER** v. **EDELBERG**, R. *Die Aufgaben des Zeichenunterrichtes. Das Portrat Goethe als Kunstschriftsteller. Uber spielkarten*. Vienna. 1884. 390 pages. Ill. Describes early playing cards (p. 262–322).

EITELBERGER v. **EDELBERG**, R. *Memoir on Playing Cards, with special reference to examples of old packs existing at Vienna*. Vienna. 1860.

ELIOT, T. S. *The Waste Land*. 1922. Madame Sosostris, a clairvoyant, reads several Rider-Waite tarot cards.

ELIOT, T. S. *Sweeney Agonistes*. Fragment of a Prologue. Fortune telling with a regular pack of cards.

*****ELLETSE**, Madame. *The Tarot According to Mme. Elletse*. New York. 1970. 32 pp. Ill.

*****EMMERING**, S. *Catalogue of a Collection of Playing Cards*. Amsterdam. June 1977. Catalog of 58 rare decks for sale.

ENCAUSSE, Gerard (see under the pseudonym Papus).

ENCAUSSE, Philippe. *Papus (Dr. Gerard Encausse), sa vie, son oeuvre*. 1932. Ill. The life and work of Papus including bibliography of his writings.

ENCYCLOPEDIE METHODIQUE. *Dictionnaire des jeux. Familiers, ou des amusements de societe*. Paris. 1796. 172 pp. Includes cards and tarot.

EPHRUSSI, Charles. *Albert Durer et ses Dessins*. Paris. 1882. The author credits Durer with two of the 21 known Durer tarocchi cards, the others to his assistant.

ESCAR LADAGA, Mariano. "La industria del papel. La resma, los naipes y las filigranas," *Gaceta de las Artes Graficas*. Barcelona. 1928. No. VI

ESMAEL. *Manuel de cartomancie, ou l'art de tirer les cartes, mis a la portee de tous*. Paris. 1875. Ill. Fortune telling with tarot.

ESSENWEIN, A. *Katalog der im Germanischen Museum befindlichen Kartenspiele und Spielkarten. Mit Abbildungen*. Nurnberg. 1886.

ESTEVE BOTEY, Francisco. *Historia del grabado*. Barcelona. 1935.

*****ETTEILLA** [pseudonym of Alliette]. *Apercu d'un rigoriste sur la cartomancie et sur son auteur*. Circa 1785. 24 pp.

*****ETTEILLA** [pseudonym of Alliette]. [Cartes a jouer.] Circa late 18th century. Bound volume of hand-colored illustrations of the 78-card Etteilla tarot pack.

ETTEILLA [pseudonym of Alliette]. *Code pratique de la cartomancie egyptienne ou les principes de la permutation des 78 feuillets du Livre de Thot*. n.d. 16 pp.

ETTEILLA [pseudonym of Alliette]. *Cours theorique et pratique du Livre de Thot, pour entendre avec justesse l'Art, la Science et la Sagesse*. 1790.

ETTEILLA [pseudonym of Alliette]. *Dictionnaire synonimique du Livre de Thot ou synonimes de significations primitives tracees sur les feuillets du livre de Thot [etc]*. 1791. 104 pp.

*****ETTEILLA** [pseudonym of Alliette]. *Fragment sur Les Hautes Sciences, [etc]*. Amsterdam. 1785. 60 pages. Egyptian origin of tarot cards and methods of interpreting them.

*****ETTEILLA** [pseudonym of Alliette]. *Jeu des Tarots ou Le Livre de Thot, ouvert a la Maniere des Egyptiens [etc]* 12 pp.

*****ETTEILLA** [pseudonym of Alliette]. *Les Sept Nuances de L'Oeuvre Philosophique [etc]*. 1772. 48 and 60 pp.

*****ETTEILLA** [pseudonym of Alliette]. *Livre de Thot*. 4 pp.

*****ETTEILLA** [pseudonym of Alliette]. *Maniere de se Recreer avec le Jeu de Cartes Nommees Tarots . . . premier Cahier [etc]*. Amsterdam. 1783. 182 pp. *Quatrieme Cahier, Amsterdam, 1785, 256 pp. *Second Cahier, Amsterdam, 1785, 202 pp. *Troisieme Cahier, Amsterdam, 1783, 142 pp.

*****ETTEILLA** [pseudonym of Alliette]. *Philosophie des Hautes Sciences [etc]*. Amsterdam. 1785. 189 pp.

ETTEILLA [pseudonym of Alliette]. *Science Lecons Theoriques et Pratiques du Livre de Thot*. 1787. 24 pp.

*****ETTEILLA** [pseudonym of Alliette]. *Sciences Lecons Theoriques et Pratiques du Livre de Thot. Moyennes Classes*. Amsterdam. 1787. 94 pp.

ETTINGHAUSEN, Richard. "Further Comments on Mamluk Playing Cards," *Gatherings in Honor of Dorothy E. Miner*. Baltimore. 1974. Ill. Discusses Mamluk playing cards and related Islamic material (p. 51–78).

*****ETTINGHAUSEN**, R., and O. Kurz. *Mamluk Playing Cards*. Leiden. 1971. sm 8vo. Ill. Reprint of original article by L. A. Mayer, plus new research on the Mamluk cards.

EYE. "Spielkarten vom 15. and 16. Jahrhundert," *Anzeiger fur Kunde der deutschen Vorzeit*. 1858.

F

FABRE d'OLIVET, Antoine. *La Langue hebraique restituée [etc]*. Paris. 1815–16. Second Edition, Paris, 1905. Reprinted 1931.

*****FABRE d'OLIVET**, Antoine. *Les Vers dores de Pythagore expliqués [etc]*. Paris. 1813. Reprinted 1932. 8vo. 409 pp.

FABRE d'OLIVET, Antoine. *The Hebraic Tongue Restored*. New York. 1976. 860 pp. English translation of Fabre d'Olivet's work; contains analysis of the Hebrew language and explanation of Biblical mysteries.

*****FALCONNIER**, R. *Les XXII Lames Hermetiques du Tarot Divinatoire [etc]*. Paris. 1896. 12mo. 104 pp. Ill. Egyptian origin and meaning of tarot; card designs by Maurice Otto Wegener.

*****FALGAIROLLE**, Prosper. *Recherches sur les cartiers et les cartes a jouer a Montpellier et a Nimes avant 1790*. Nimes. 1904. 29 pp. Ill. Development of cards in Montpellier and Nimes.

FANT, M. *Lecons sur l'histoire universelle, depuis le commencement du XVI Siecle*. 1780–1793. The author believes the engraving of cards led to the invention of printing.

FANTI, Sigismondo. *Trionfo della Fortuna*. 1526. Fortune-telling book uses dice for predictions.

*****FARINHA**, Ramiro. *Imprensa Nacionale de Lisboa*. Lisbon. 1969. 77 pp.

FERENC, Gabnay. "Legregibb kartyaink," *Magyar Iparmuveszet*. Vol. XII. 1909.

FERGUSON, George. *Signs and Symbols in Christian Art*. 1961.

FERRARIO, Giulio (see Howard R. Patch).

FIELD, Albert (See Yale University Library).

*****FIELD**, Albert. "Printing Methods Used in the Manufacture of Playing-Cards," *The Journal of The Playing-Card Society*. Birmingham. May 1975. Vol. III. No. 4. Printing methods for producing cards (p. 9–13).

*****FIGUEROA**, Moses Anthony. *The Court Cards of the Tarot*. 1971. Folio. Contains 16 court cards plus The Fool in black and white line drawings.

FINARTE (see Istituto Finanzierio per L'Arte).

*****FINE**, C. Oronce. *Giuoco d'Armi dei Sovrani e stati d'Europa per apprendere l'Armi [etc]*. 1677. sm 16mo.

*****FINE**, C. Oronce. *Jeu d'Armoiries des Souverains [etc]*. Lyon. 1697. 24mo. 188 pp. Deck of educational cards for learning heraldic devices, etc.

FINE, C. Oronce. (Brainville). *Wapen-Karten oder Herolds-Spiel, etc*. Hamburg. 1695.

FISHER, Margaret Sargent. "The Devil's Picture Books," *The Yale University Library Gazette*. 1946. Volume 20. No. 3. 7 pp.

FISHER, Mrs. Samuel. "The Devil's Picture Books — An Address read by Mrs. Samuel Fisher," *Litchfield Enquirer*. 1933. 12mo. 18 pp. Describes history and development of playing cards in Europe.

FLAMAND. *Le Petit Etteilla. L'art de tirer les cartes [etc]*. Circa 1880. Ill.

FLETCHER, W. M. "More Old Playing Cards Found in Cambridge," *The Proceedings of the Cambridge Antiquarian Society*. 1907. Vol. XII. 11 pp.

******FLETCHER**, W. M. "On Some Old Playing Cards found in Trinity College," *The Proceedings of the Cambridge Antiquarian Society*. XLVII. 1907. 11 pp. Ill. Describes several 16th and 17th century playing cards found in a stairwell (p. 454–464).

FLOBERT, R. *Curiosities des anciennes cartes a jouer*. Lille. 1902.

*****FLORENCE**, W. J. *The Gentlemen's Hand-Book on Poker*. New York. 1892. 195 pp.

FOLEY, Martin. "The Art of Playing Cards," *Design for Industry*. June 1959. pp. 20–23.

*****FOLI**, Professor P. R. S. *Fortune Telling by Cards*. Baltimore. n.d. 12mo. 122 pp. Ill. Fortune telling with 52 cards and short section on tarot.

FONS-MELICOG (le baron de). "Le jeu de cartes defendu en 1382," *Annales Archeologiques*. XV. March-April 1855. pp. 130–131.

FONTENAY, Harold de. "Notice sur un jeu de cartes inedit du temps de Louis XII," *Bibliotheque du musee des Arts decoratifs*. Paris. 1865.

FORMAGGIO, Dino and Carlo Basso. *A Book of Miniatures*. N.Y. 1962. 143 pp. Ill. Reproduction of page of staves from Pierpont Morgan-Bergamo tarocchi deck (p. 82).

*****FORSTER**, Dr. Carl. *Abdrucke eines Vollstandigen Kartenspieles auf Silberplatten Gestochen Von Georg Heinrich Bleich*. Munich. 1881. 12mo. 33 pp. + 36 plates. Comprises 36 handmade reprints from silver cards originally etched circa 1696 by Georg Heinrich Bleich, goldsmith and engraver at Nurnberg.

*****FORTUNE**, Dion (pseudonym of Violet Firth). *The Mystical Quabalah*. London. 1935. 327 pp. Ill. Correlates tarot to kabbalah and Tree of Life.

FOUBERT, Thomas. *The Literary Cards, being a new Invention to learn to Read, etc*. London. 1758. 25 pp. + 10 sheets.

*FOURNIER, Heraclio. *Annual Calendar*. 1968 through 1977 inclusive. Folio. Calendars issued each year with full color reproductions of antique playing cards.

*FOURNIER, Heraclio. *Museo de Naipes — Catalogo*. 1868–1968 Centenario de Heraclio Fournier S. A. 1968. Ill. Catalog of playing cards at Fournier Museum.

*FOX, James M. *Tarots*. Original Story by Rafael Azcona & Jose Maria Forque. 121 pp.

*FRANCOIS, Andre. *Histoire de la carte a jouer*. Ivry, France. 1974. 4to. 355 pp. Ill. Origin and development of cards with a section on tarot.

FRANCK, Adolphe. *La Kabbale ou La Philosuphie des Hebreux*. Paris. 1843.

*FRANCK, Adolphe. *The Kabbalah. The Religious Philosophy of the Hebrews*. New York. 1967. Reprint. 12mo. 224 pp. Origins of the kabbalah and two principal works, *Sefer Yetzirah* and the *Zohar*.

FRANKS, Sir Augustus Wollaston, K.C.B. "Account of Two Packs of Old English Cards [etc]," *Proceedings of the Society of Antiquaries*. London. February 25, 1892. 8vo. Vol. XIV. Cards illustrate the Meal Tub Plot and the South Sea Bubble (p. 72–89).

FRANKS, Sir Augustus Wollaston, K.C.B. (see also British Museum, Schreiber Collection).

*FRATELLI FABBRI EDITORI. *Predizione. Il gioco dei tarocchi* [etc]. Milan. 1974. 125 pp. Ill. Describes Major and Minor Arcana cards.

*FRAZER, Sir James George. *The Golden Bough: A Study in Magic and Religion*. New York. 1911–15. 3rd edition. 13 vols. T. S. Eliot in "The Waste Land" associates The Hanged Man with Frazer's hanged god, Attis, Phrygian god of fertility (Part IV, Vol I).

FRAZER, William. *Description of the series of Playing Cards relating to the Political History of Rev. Dr. Sacheverell in the Reign of Queen Anne*. Dublin. 1885. Privately printed.

FREEDMAN, Anne. "The Occult." Unpublished MS. 1977. Ill. One chapter deals with tarot.

*FRERE, Thomas. *Hoyle's Games. Containing all the modern methods of playing the latest and most fashionable games*. Boston. n.d. 365 pp.

*FREY, Albert R[omer]. "A Bibliography of Playing Cards compiled by Albert R. Frey of the Astor Library," *The Bookmart*. Pittsburgh. August 1886. 8vo. 24 pp. Bibliography of 270 volumes dealing with the history of playing cards and card games.

FRICHET, Henry. *Le Tarot divinatoire et le livre de Thot*. Paris. 1924. 12mo. 156 pp.

FUGAIRON. "Essai d'une reconstruction des 22 arcanes majeurs du Tarot," *L'Initiation*. August 1893. Vol. 20. No. 11. pp. 123–151.

FUGAIRON. "L'Origine du Tarot," *L'Initiation*. July 1895. Vol. 28. No. 10. pp. 53–56.

*FULLWOOD, Nancy. *The Song of Sano Tarot*. New York. 1929. 12mo. 206 pp. According to the author, tarot means royal road and there are seven royal roads which are the seven realms of being and primal forces that govern life.

G

*GABRIELLI, Alexandra. "Tarot in keramiek van Onno Docters van Leeuwen," *Bres*. The Hague. March/April 1976. Pages 56–65. Describes 24 porcelain figures by Onno Docters van Leeuwen that depict 22 Major Arcana plus Juno and Jupiter (p. 56–65).

GAGNE. *L'histoire des miracles renfermant l'histoire de ma mort, la cartomancie* [etc.]. Paris. 1860. 12mo. 72 pp.

GALASSO, Orazio. *Giuochi di Carte bellissimi di Regola e di Memoria e con secreti particolari. Composti e dati in luce per il Cartaginese*, 1597.

GALEOTTUS, Martuis. *De doctrina promiscua*. Lugduni. 1558. (Written in 1488). Chapter XXXVI. pp. 477–478.

GALICHON, Emile. *Gazette des Beaux Arts*. Paris. 1861. The author views the Tarocchi of Mantegna series not as a game of cards, but as a book in five cantos based upon Dante.

*GALLIEN, Solin (see Neroman, *Grand Encyclopedie*).

GARCIA RAMILA, Ismael. "Del Burgos de antano. Debilidades humanas: los naipes," *Diario de Burgos*. August 16, 1970.

*GARDNER, Richard. *Evolution Through The Tarot*. England. 1970. Reprint of previous title *Accelerate Your Evolution*. 8vo. 112 pp. Ill. Describes the Major Arcana in metaphysical terms.

*GARDNER, Richard. *The Tarot Speaks*. London. 1971. 8vo. 99 pp. Ill. Fortune telling with tarot.

*GARNIER, Jacques Marie. *Histoire de l'imagerie populaire et des cartes a jouer a chartres*. Chartres. 1869. sm 8vo. 448 pp. Ill. Edition limited to 624 copies. Describes card making in Chartres.

*GARRETT, Eileen J. *The Sense and Nonsense of Prophecy*. New York. 1950. 279 pp. Contains brief chapter on cartomancy and tarot.

GARSONNIN, Dr. *La collection de cartes a jouer du musee historique et les cartiers orleanais*. Orleans. 1917.

GARZONI, Thomaso. *La Piazza universale di tutte le Professioni del Mondo, e nobili et ignobili*. Venice. 1589. 4to. Cites tarot among tavern games.

GAZAN, Francisco. *Baraja del Blason*. Madrid. 1748.

GEISBERG, Max. *Das alteste gestochene deutsche Kartenspiel vom Meister der Spielkarten vor 1466*. Strasbourg. 1905.

GEISBERG, Max. "Franzosische und deutsche Spielkarten," *Der Turmer*. 1933/34. pp. 487–493.

GEISBERG, Max. *Das Kartenspiel der Staats und Altertumersammlung in Stuttgart*. Strasbourg. 1910/1911. 48 pp. + 49 plates.

GEISBERG, Max. *Das Kupferstich-Kartenspiel der k. und k. Hofbibliothek zu Wien mitte des XV Jahrhunderts*. Strasbourg. 1918.

GERVER, Frans. *Le Guide Marabout de tous les jeux de cartes*. Verviers. 1966. 315 pp.

*GETTINGS, Fred. *The Book of Tarot*. London. 1973. 4to. 144 pp. Ill. Tarot symbolism from the standpoints of graphic art and structure.

**GHENO, Antonio. *Di un' Antica Carta da Giuoco Incisa in Legno Esistente nel Civico Museo di Bassano*. Brescia. 1890. 8 pp. Describes a single knight of swords from a 15th or 16th century tarocchi pack.

*GIBBONS, Stanley, Auctions. *Playing Cards for sale by auction 1 June 1977*. London. 1977. 20 pp. Ill. Auction catalog.

*GIBBONS, Stanley, Auctions. *Playing Cards for sale by auction 27 October 1977*. London. 1977. 18pp. + 16 plates. Auction catalog.

*GIBSON, Walter B. *The Complete Illustrated Book of Divination and Prophecy*. Garden City, N.Y. 1973. sm 8vo. 336 pp. Ill. Several chapters deal with fortune telling with 36, 52, and 78 cards.

*GIBSON, Walter B. and Litzka R. *The Complete Illustrated Book of the Psychic Sciences*. New York. 1966. 447 pp. Ill. Contains chapter on cartomancy.

*GILBERT, George, and Wendy Rydell. *The Great Book of Magic*. New York. 1976. Ill. Briefly includes tarot.

GILKIN, Iwan. *Stances dorees. Commentaire sacerdotal du Tarot*. Paris and Brussels. 1893. 8vo. Ill.

GILLOT, M. *Le Tarot initiatique et symbolique*. 16mo. 112 pp.

*GINSBURG, Christian D. *The Essenes. Their History and Doctrines. The Kabbalah. Its Doctrines, Development and Literature*. London. 1863–1864. Reprint 1970. 12mo. 245 pp. Origin, development and application of the kabbalah and Tree of Life.

*GIPSY QUEEN, A. *The Zingara Fortune Teller*. Philadelphia. 1901. 183 pp. Ill. Fortune telling with cards.

**GIRAULT, Francis. *Mlle Le Normand. Sa Biographie, Ses Prédictions Extraordinaires* [etc]. Paris. 1843. 16mo. 191 pp. Ill. Life of Mlle Le Normand and description of tarot cards.

*GIRAULT, Francis. *Mlle Le Normand. Her Biography*. Translation of Girault's book about Mlle Le Normand, famous French sibyl during the time of Napoleon.

GIRGOIS de la PLATA. "Le theme des Sephiroth," *L'Initiation*. January 1891. Vol. X. No. 4. Relates the 10 sephiroth to the Major Arcana (pp. 377–381).

GIRIDHARA. "Ganjifa Khelana (Sanskrit Poem)," *Kavyamata Gucchakas*. No. 13. Refers to the Persian origin of Ganjifa (p. 81–84).

GIVRY, Emile Grillot de. *Le Musee des Sorciers, Mages et Alchimistes*. Paris. 1929. 450 pp. Describes tarot and explains Marcolino da Forli's *Le Sorti* (Chapter VII).

*GIVRY, Emile Grillot de. *Picture Museum of Sorcery, Magic and Alchemy*. New York. 1963. 8vo. 394 pp. Ill. Translation of *Le Musee des Sorciers, Mages et Alchimistes*.

*GLAHN, A. Frank. *Das Deutsche Tarotbuch*. 1958. 8vo. 324 pp. Ill. Tarot from the standpoints of symbolism, astrology, kabbalah, Hebrew alphabet and fortune telling.

*GLAHN, A. Frank. *Wissenschastlichen Prophetie aus Karten mit bem Buche Thot Oder Tarot*. 1925. 8vo. 68 pp.

*GODWIN, David F. "Tzaddi Is The Star," *Gnostica*. St. Paul. February/March 1977. Vol. 5. No. 5. Ill. Discusses Crowley's opinion that the Hebrew letter Tzaddi does not correspond to The Star, as taught by the Order of the Golden Dawn (p. 56–61).

GOLDSCHMIDT, Victor. *Farben in der Kunst, eine Studie von Dr. Victor Goldschmidt*. Heidelberg. 1919. 210 pp. Ill. Reproductions of old cards.

*GOLDSMID, Edmund. *Explanatory Notes on a Pack of Cavalier Playing Cards*. Edinburgh. 1886. 23 pp. Ill. Facsimile of 17th century political satire deck.

GOLEBIOWSKI, Lukasz. *Gry i zabawy roznych stanow*. Warsaw. 1831. Tome 3. p. 40–63.

*GOLOWIN, Sergius. *Die Welt des Tarot. Geheimnis und lehre der 78 karten der Zigeuner.* Basel. 1975. sm 8vo. 390 pp. Ill. Describes the Zigeuner tarot pack designed by Walter Wegmuller.

*GOOCK, Roland. *Freude am Kartenspiel. Spielregeln fur die 100 Beliebtesten Kartenspiele und Spielarten.* Germany. 1970. 12mo. 190 pp. Ill. Photographs and descriptions of playing cards and card game rules.

GOOCK, Roland. *Il grande libro dei giochi.* 1967.

*GOREN, Charles. "Fancy faces for a familiar deck," *Sports Illustrated.* Chicago. September 17, 1962. Ill. Anecdotes about cards (p. 56–58).

*GOSHAWK, Evelyn. "The Fool in the Tarot," *The Journal of The Playing-Card Society.* Cranbrook. May 1976. Vol. IV. No. 4. pp. 1–8.

*GOSHAWK, Evelyn. "The Royal Servant, A study of the Knave in European Playing-Cards," *The Journal of The Playing-Card Society.* Birmingham. Part I-Vol. II, No. 2, November 1973, pp. 20–21. Part II-Vol. II, No. 3, February 1974, pp. 29–33.

GOSSELIN, Jean. *La Signification de l'ancien jeu des Chartes pythagoriques.* Paris. 1582.

*GOUGH, Richard. "Some observations on the Invention of Cards and their Introduction into England," *Archaeologia.* 1787. Vol 8. Describes 52 cards, known as Dr. Stukeley's cards, found in the pasteboard of an old book printed prior to 1500 (pp. 152–174).

*GRAD, A. D., Jean-Marie Lhote and Pierre Boujut. *La Tour de feu. Le Nouveau tarot de jarnac.* 182 pages.

GRAESSE, Dr. J. G. Hofrath. *Lehrbuch einer Literargeschichte der beruhmtesten Volker des Mittelalters.* Dresden and Leipsig. 1842. 8vo. Bibliographical summary of the history of playing cards (see G. Brunet for French translation).

**GRAESSE, Dr. J. G. Hofrath. "Zur Geschichte der Spielkarten," *Zeitschrift fur Allegmeine Museologie.* May 1 to December 1, 1878. Series of articles on the history of playing cards.

GRAND-CARTERET, John. *Papeterie et Papetiers de L'Ancien Temps.* Paris. 1913. Ill. Edition limited to 500 numbered copies. Paper and stencils used in card manufacture.

*GRAND ORIENT (pseudonym of Arthur Edward Waite). *A Handbook of Cartomancy, Fortune-Telling and Occult Divination.* London. 1891. 114 pp. Ill. Fortune telling with 52 cards.

*GRAPHISCHE SAMMLUNG ALBERTINA. *Spielkarten Ihre Kunst und Geschichte in Mitteleuropa.* Vienna. 1974. 256 pp. Ill.

*GRAVES, F. *Companion Book to the Aquarian Tarot.* Dobbs Ferry. 1975. 29 pp. Booklet accompanies Aquarian tarot deck (see Morgan Press).

*GRAVES, F. D. *The Windows of Tarot.* Dobbs Ferry, N.Y. 1973. 8vo. 95 pp. Ill. Tarot meanings based upon the Aquarian tarot deck.

*GRAVES, Robert. *The White Goddess.* London. 1959.

*GRAY, (Ms.) Eden. *A Complete Guide to the Tarot.* New York. 1970. Reprint. 156 pp. Ill. Fortune telling and tarot including numerology, astrology and kabbalah.

*GRAY, (Ms.) Eden. *Mastering The Tarot. Basic Lessons in an ancient, mystic art.* New York. 1971. 8vo. 160 pp. Ill. Beginner's tarot book with sample card readings.

*GRAY, (Ms.) Eden. *The Tarot Revealed: A Modern Guide to Reading the Tarot Cards.* New York. 1969. Reprint. 12mo. 239 pp. Ill. Fortune telling with tarot cards.

GRAZZINI, Antonio Francesco. *Tutti i trionfi . . . dal tempo del magnifico Lorenzo de' Medici fino all' anno 1559.* Lucca. 1750. Refers to the tarocchi trumps.

*GREENWICH TIME. "April Fools' Day Appropriate Opening Time For Fortune-Telling Card Exhibit at Library." April 1, 1976. Tarot exhibition in April 1976 (p. 14).

GREGORIETTI, Guido. "Una serie di tarocchi Viscontei per Milano," *Antichita viva.* January-February, 1972. Vol. II. No. 1. pp. 46–53. Ill.

GRESHAM, William Lindsay. *Nightmare Alley.* Mystery story based upon tarot and its mysticism.

*GRIMAUD, B. P. *Ancien Tarot de Marseille.* France. n.d. sm 24mo. 80 pp. Describes the Tarot of Marseilles pack.

*GRIMAUD, B. P. *Grand Etteilla Egyptian Gypsies Tarot.* Paris. 1969. 48mo. 118 pp. Booklet accompanies Grand Etteilla cards.

*GRIMAUD, B. P. *Tarot of Marseilles.* Paris. 1969. 48mo. 48 pp. Booklet accompanies Tarot of Marseilles deck.

GRIMSHAW, Bayard. "The Devil's Picture Book," *Dunlop Gazette.* 1958 pp. 24–25.

GRINGONNEUR (see Bache).

GROSCHWITZ, von. "Playing Card Design," *Art in America.* Springfield. 1962. No. 4. pp. 80–83.

GROSLEY. *Memoirs historiques et critiques pour l'Histoire de Troyes.* 1774. Author erroneously credits invention of the game of piquet to a mathematician named Picquet who lived in Troyes during the reign of Louis XIII, 1610 to 1643.

GRUBE, Ernst. *Islamic Paintings and the Arts of the Book.* 1976. Describes playing card fragments found in Cairo and believed to date circa 13th century.

*GRUNWALD, Edgar A. "Card Game," *The American Legion Magazine.* New York. January 1957. Vol. 62. No. 1. Pages 10, 11. Ill. Describes playing card manufacture and brief history of cards (p. 49–51).

*GRUPP, Claus D. *Spielkarten und Ihre Geschichte.* Stuttgart. 1973. 8vo. 88 pp. Ill.

GUAITA, Stanislas de. *Catalogue de sa Bibliotheque occulte.* Paris. 1899. 299 pp. Ill. Bibliography includes 2,227 occult works.

GUAITA, Stanislas de. *Essais de Sciences maudites. I, II and III. Le Serpent de la Genese [etc].* Paris. 1897. Reprinted 1920. Ill. Seven chapters describe Major Arcana cards VIII through XIV (Vol. III).

GUAITA, Stanislas de. "Exemple d'Application du tarot a la kabbale. L'hierogramme d'Adam," *Le Tarot des Bohemiens.* Paris. 1889. Applies tarot keys to the kabbalah.

GUALAZZINI, U. "Contributo alla questione Dragoniana," *Atti della reale accademia delle scienze di Torino.* 1930–1931. Vol. 66. Notes of Giacomo Torresino (see Bordigallo) have no basis of fact (p. 397–425).

GUEVARA, Anthony. *Epistolas Familares.* Valladolid, 1539. Anvers, 1538(?). Venice, 1558. Lyons, 1558. Paris, 1570 and 1573. London, 1575, 1582 and 1584. Interpolation of the word *cards.*

GUILLEVILLE, William de. *Le Pelerinaige de l'Homme.* Circa 1330. Interpolation of playing cards.

*GULER, Maritzu. *El Gran Tarot Esoterico.* Vitoria. 1976. 63 pp. Ill. Booklet accompanies the El Gran Esoterico tarot deck.

*GULER, Maritzu. *The Great Esoteric Tarot.* Vitoria. 1976. 71 pp. Ill. Translation of *El Gran Tarot Esoterico.*

*GUNDELLA [Marion Clark Kuclo]. "Witch Watch," *Observer & Eccentric.* Detroit. 1976. Weekly newspaper column of occult including tarot.

GUNTHER, E. "Alte deutsche Spielkarten," *Das Werk.* Dusseldorf. 1940. pp. 209–212.

H

H., H.D.V. *Easy Method of Fortune Telling by Cards [etc].* London. n.d.

HABERLAND, F. L. W. *Anleitung das deutsche oder Gross-Taroc spielen zu lernen.* Jena. 1803. 8vo.

*HADES. *Manuel complet d'interpretation du tarot.* Paris. 1968. 8vo. 143 pp. Origin of cards and their association to religious events; includes Grenadier Richard Midaleton' reading of cards as a prayer book.

*HADIN. *Histoire du jeu de cartes du Grenadier Richard ou explication du jeu de cinquante-deux cartes.* Paris. 1811. 16mo. 228 pp. The 52-card prayer book of Grenadier Richard.

**HAGA, Enoch. "TAROsolution." Unpublished MS. 31 pp. Utilizes tarot cards and layout board for multi-level interpretations.

*HAICH, Elisabeth. *Sagesse du tarot les vingt-deux niveaux de conscience de l'etre humain.* Lausanne. 1972. 12mo. 199 pp. Ill. French translation of Haich's work; includes 22 Major Arcana cards from Wirth pack in book sleeve.

*HAICH Elisabeth. *Tarot. Die Zweiundzwanzig Bewuss tseinsstufen des Menschen.* Stuttgart. 1969. 12mo. 189 pp. Describes Major Arcana from many viewpoints plus Wirth's Major Arcana are in book sleeve.

HAICH, Elisabeth. *Wisdom of the Tarot.* New York. 1975. 174 pp. English translation of Haich's work plus Wirth's Major Arcana in book sleeve.

*HALBERT (d'Angers). *Cartomancie ancienne et nouvelle [etc].* Paris. 1865. 16mo. 192 pages. Etteilla's methods of reading 36 and 78 cards and describes cartomancy methods used by Mlle Lenormand, Mme Clement, Mme Mouginet and Moreau.

HALEVI, Z'ev ben Shimon (pseudonym of Warren Kenton). *Tree of Life. An Introduction to the Cabala.* London. 1972. sm 8vo. 200 pp. Ill. Principles of the kabbalistic Tree of Life.

*HALL, Adelaide S. *A Glossary of Important Symbols in their Hebrew, Pagan and Christian Forms.* Boston. 1912. 12mo. 103 pp. Symbols and their meaning.

*HALL, Angus. "Revealing the Tarot's Secrets," *Signs of Things to Come.* London. 1975. 8vo. pp. 74–93. Ill. Tarot cards and fortune-telling.

*HALL, Manley P. *An Encyclopedic Outline of Masonic, Hermetic, Qabbalistic and Rosicrucian Symbolical Philosophy.* San Francisco, 1928. Fifth edition. Reprinted in several editions. Large folio. Illustrated by J. Augustus Knapp. Concise analysis of tarot (Chapter CXXIX).

*HALL, Manley P. *An Essay on the Book of Thoth.* Los Angeles. 1929. 24mo. 47 pp. Booklet accompanies Knapp tarot cards. According to Hall, tarot cards are the leaves of an ancient, sacred book from the pagan world which eventually circulated through Rosicrucian, Templar and Freemason societies.

*HALL, Manley P. *Man, the Grand Symbol of the Mysteries.* Los Angeles. 1932. Relates the 10 avatars of Vishnu to 10 of the Major Arcana (Chapter VII).

HAMMER, P. *Die Deutsches Kartenspiele.* Leipzig. 1811.

HANKEY, S. A. "Remarks upon a Series of Forty-seven Historical Cards . . . of Titus Oates," *The Archaeol. Journal.* London. 1873. Vol. 30. p. 185

*HARGRAVE, Catherine Perry. *A History of Playing Cards and a Bibliography of Cards and Gaming.* New York. 1930. Reprinted New York, 1966 and later. 4to. 468 pp. Ill. Origin and development of playing cards based upon collection of United States Playing Card Company.

*HARGRAVE, Catherine Perry. "Playing Cards Through the Ages," *Auction Bridge Magazine.* March 1929. Ill. Brief origin and history of playing cards (p. 24–27).

*HARPER, George Mills, editor. *Yeats and The Occult.* Canada. 1975. 322 pp. Ill. Yeats and his investigations into the occult; includes diagram of the "Tree of Life in Tarot" from the Golden Dawn notebook of Georgie Hyde-Lee, Yeats' wife.

*HARPER, George Mills, editor. *Yeats's Golden Dawn.* New York. 1974. 322 pp. Describes the Order of the Golden Dawn and a tarot reading by Christina Mary Stoddart that prophesized the Order's difficulties.

**HARRIS, Lady Frieda. "Tarot Lecture." Unpublished manuscript. 1945. 7 pp. Lecture by the artist on the Crowley tarot pack.

**HARRIS, Frieda. *Exhibition of 78 Paintings of the Tarot Cards.* London. 1942. 23pp. Booklet accompanied exhibition at Berkeley Galleries of Crowley Thoth tarot paintings by Frieda Harris.

*HARTLEY, Christine. "Tarot," *Man, Myth & Magic. An illustrated encyclopedia of the supernatural.* London. 1970. 4to. Ill. Describes tarot cards and Major Arcana of Waite's pack (p. 2789–2794).

HARTMAN, William C. *Who's Who in Occult, Psychic and Spiritual Realms.* 1925.

*HARTMAN, William C. *Who's Who in Occultism, New Thought, Psychism and Spiritualism.* Jamaica. 1927. 350 pp. Lists the names, addresses and biographical sketches of over 1500 persons and 600 principal societies in the world of the occult during 1927.

*HASBROUCK, Muriel Bruce. *Pursuit of Destiny.* New York. 1941. 8vo. 270 pp. Ill. Tarot cards are assigned time cycles within the solar year.

HASE, Martin von. "Neues uber alte Spielkarten," *Borsenblatt.* 1965. pp. 1540–1542.

*HASE, Martin von. *Spielkarten aus Aller Welt.* Stuttgart. 1968. Folio. 104 pp. Ill. Catalog of 115 decks displayed at the Vereinigten Altenburger und Stralsunder Spielkartenfabriken Exhibition.

*HASE, Martin von. *Spielkarten aus Funf Jahrhunderten.* Stuttgart-Leinfelden. Abridged exhibition catalog.

HASE, Martin von. "Spielkarten aus sechs Jahrhunderten," *Archiv fur Buchgewerbe und Gebrauchsgraphik.* 1935. pp. 319–324.

HASE, Martin von. "Zur Geschichte der Spielkarten," *Borsenblatt fur den Deutschen Buchhandel.* Frankfurter Ausgabe. 1959. pp. 395–397.

*HAVEN, Marc. *Le Tarot, L'alphabet hebraique et les nombres.* Lyon. 1937. 8vo. 251 pp. Ill. Tarot symbolism and attributes to numbers and the Hebrew alphabet with card spreads based upon M. D'Odoucet.

*HAWTHORNE, Diana. *Laurie's Complete Fortune Teller.* London. 1946. 256 pp. Contains chapter on fortune telling with cards.

HAYMES, Wendy, and Kenneth J. Morris. "The 'Angelus' Tarot For Man." Unpublished MS. 1975.

HAZARD, Berthe MacMonnies. "The Tarot and the Accomplishment of the Great Work," *Spring 1942.* New York. 1942. Reprinted Nendeln, Liechtenstein, 1975. Ill. The Major Arcana cards are used in psychological methods of study; and illustrations by Courtland Hoppin (p. 31–42).

**HEATHER, H. E. *Cards and Card Tricks, containing A Brief History of Playing Cards [etc].* London. [1876]. 8vo. Ill. Brief history of cards.

HECKETHORN, Ch. W. *The Secret Societies of all ages and countries [etc].* London. 1897. 2 Vols. Describes 160 secret societies worldwide.

HEIDRICK, Bill. "Understanding the Tarot," *Gnostica.* St. Paul. Feb/March 1977. Vol. 5. No. 5. Ill. Describes Temperance card (p. 47).

*HEINECKEN, Le Baron de. *Idee Generale D'Une Collection Complete D'Estampes [etc].* Leipzig and Vienna. 1771. 8vo. 520 pages. Ill. Advances German claim to the origin of the first *printed* playing cards at Ulm (pp. 237–246, 455, 468).

*HEITZ, J. H. Ed. *Das Alteste Deutsche Kartenspiel Vom Meister der Spielkarten Vor 1446 in Kupfer Gestochen.* Strassburg. Reprint of 32 Meister playing cards mounted on Japanese paper.

HEITZ, P. "Italienische Einblattdrucke," *Einblattdrucke des funfzehnten Jahrhunderts.* Bassano and Berlin. 1933.

*HELINE, Corinne. *The Bible and the Tarot.* California. 1969. 8vo. 237 pp. Ill. Principles of tarot and correlation of Major Arcana to Hebrew alphabet and verses from the Bible; card illustrations similiar to Comte C. Saint-Germain's *Practical Astrology.*

HELLER, Joseph. *Geschichte der Holzschneidekunst; nebst zwei Beilagen enthaltend den Ursprung der Spielkarten und ein Verzeichniss der samt xylographischen Werke.* Bamberg. 1823. 8vo. 457 pp. Origin of playing cards (p. 299–337).

HENDERSON, Joseph L., and Maud Oakes. *The Wisdom of the Serpent.* N.Y. 1963. 290 pp. Ill. Description of Death card as Skeleton Mower.

HERLOSSOHN, Carl. *Vier farben das heint die deutschen spielkarten in ihrer symbolischer Bedeutung beschriehen [etc].* Leipzig. 1828. 8vo. Ill.

HERMANSEN, J[ens] V[illads] V[aldemar]. "Gamle danske spillekort," *Kulturminder.* 1942/43.

*HERMANSEN, J[ens] V[illads] V[aldermar]. *Spille kort 1350–1950.* Copenhagen, 1950. 8vo. 51 pp. Ill. Origin and development of cards.

HERMANSEN, J[ens] V[illads] V. *Tarok.* Copenhagen. 1943. 8vo. 32 pp.

HERVEY, George F. *The Hamlyn Illustrated Book of Card Games.* London. 1973. 240 pp.

HEUERTZ, M. "Survivance de signes prehistoriques," *Les cahiers luxembourgeois.* 1953.

*HIND, Arthur M. *An Introduction to a History of Woodcut with a Detailed Survey of Work Done in the Fifteenth Century.* New York. 1963. sm 8vo. 2 volumes. Ill. Hind concludes that the production of playing cards from woodblocks must have been a thriving industry by the end of the 14th and beginning of the 15th centuries, especially at Ulm (Vol. I, p. 80–89).

*HIND, Arthur M. *Early Italian Engraving [etc].* New York. 1938. Reprinted 1970. 4 Vols. Ill. Describes two series of Tarocchi of Mantegna prints and complete pack of Sola-Busca tarocchi cards (Vol. I) with illustrations (Vol. II).

HIND, Arthur M. "Elizabethan pack of playing cards with maps of countries of England and Wales," *British Museum Quarterly.* Feb, 1939. pp. 2–4.

*HIRTH, Georg. *Jost Amman's Kartenspielbuch. Charta Lusoria [etc].* Munich and Leipzig. 1880. sm 8vo. 64 pp. Ill.

HISEY, Lehmann. *Keys to Inner Space [etc].* New York. 1974. 250 pp. Ill. Includes chapter on tarot symbology.

HISEY, Lehmann. "The New Cosmic Tarot with Keys to Meditation." Unpublished MS. Ill. Metaphysical interpretations of Major Arcana cards as they pertain to the questioner during the last period of the Piscean Age, 1978 to 2011.

HOBSON, Rev. Tilman. *The Secret Language of a Deck of Cards and the Dance of Death.* Chicago. 1911. 12 mo. 81 pp. Invective against gambling which the author calls "the devil's bible."

*HOCHMAN, Gene. *Encyclopedia of American Playing Cards.* New Jersey. 1976–1977. 4 Parts. Illustrated. Describes antique American playing cards including souvenir, political, war, railroad, transformation, advertising and fortune-telling packs.

*HOELLER, Stephan A. *The Royal Road.* Wheaton. 1975. sm 8vo. Ill. Describes the Major Arcana cards and their attributes.

*HOFFMANN, Detlef. *Die Kartenalmanache der J. G. Cotta'schen Buchhandlung.* Germany. 1970. 4to. Ill. Describes transformation packs (suit signs form integral part of each picture) produced between the years 1805 and 1811 by J. G. Cotta, bookseller of Tubingen (p. 117–134).

*HOFFMANN, Detlef. "Ein Kartenspiel Alfred Rethels [etc]," *Schriften des Historischen Museums Frankfurt am Main.* Germany. 1972. Heft XIII. pp. 141–167. Ill.

*HOFFMANN, Detlef. *Die Welt Der Spielkarte. Eine Kulturgeschichte.* Germany. 1972. 4to. 96 pp. Ill. Describes cultural history of playing cards.

*HOFFMANN, Detlef. "Fortune-Telling Cards," *The Journal of The Playing-Card Society.* Translated by Fred Taylor. Manchester. Part I — Vol. I, No. 2, November 1972, pp. 5–8. Part II — Vol. I, No. 3, February 1973, pp. 12–13. Part III — Vol. I, No. 4, May 1973, pp. 4–6.

*HOFFMANN, Detlef. *Froezoesische Spielkarten des XX. Jahrhunderts.* Bielefeld. 1966. 8vo. 66 pp. Twentieth century playing cards by Bertholle, Cassandre, Delaunay, Fini, Francois and Picart le Doux; Bertholle cards are tarots.

*HOFFMANN, Detlef. "The Hofaemterspiel and its position in the historical development of gaming," *Hofaemterspiel.* Vienna. 1976. Ill. Describes gambling popular during 14th and 15th centuries and cites early references to playing cards (p. 45–54 and 108–116).

*HOFFMANN, Detlef. *Le Monde de la Carte a Jouer.* Leipzig. 1972. 4to. 198 pp. Ill. French edition of Hoffmann's *Die Welt der Spielkarten.*

*HOFFMANN, Detlef. *The Playing Card, An Illustrated History.* New York. 4to. 192 pp. Ill. English edition of Hoffmann's *Die Welt der Spielkarten.*

*HOFFMANN, Detlef. *Spielkarten. Inventar katalog der Spielkarten-*

sammlung des Historischen Museums Frankfurt am Main. Frankfurt am Main. 1972. 8vo. 316 pp. Ill. Catalog of playing cards, wrappers and books in the collection of the Historischen Museums, Frankfurt am Main; includes some tarot.

*HOFFMANN, Detlef. *Spielkartensammlung Piatnik. Eine Auswahl.* Vienna. 1970. 8vo. 52 pp. Ill. Describes 52 packs of playing cards, mainly tarot and tarock packs, from the Piatnik collection, Austria.

*HOFFMANN, Detlef. "Vier Spielkarten aus Lyon und ein Kabinettschraenkchen aus Spanien," *Alte und Moderne Kunst.* Vienna. 1971. Heft 116. pp. 18–21. Ill.

*HOFFMANN, Detlef and Erika Kroppenstedt. *Die Cotta'schen Spielkarten-Almanache 1805–1811.* Bielefeld. 1968–1969. 8vo. 114 pp. Ill. Describes and illustrates each card in the six Cotta transformation packs.

*HOFFMANN, Detlef and Erika Kroppenstedt. *Wahrsagekarten — Ein Beitrag zur Geschichte des Okkultismus.* Bielefeld. 1972. 8vo. 191 pp. Ill. Exhibition catalog of 118 decks including tarot at Bielefeld Playing Card Museum.

*HOFFMANN, Detlef, Z. Freiburg and Erika Kroppenstedt. *Tarocke mit franzoesischen Farben. Don Quichote, Pelikan, Vitzliputzli.* Bielefeld. 1967. 8vo. 60 pp. Ill. Describes 327 trump cards from 22 tarock decks dating from the 18th and 19th centuries and displayed at The Deutsches Spielkarten Museum, Bielefeld.

*HOFFMANN, Detlef and Jan Bauwens. *Van den Borre Taravt* (sic). Brussels. 1977. Ill. Summarizes animal tarots.

**HOFMEISTER, Ad. *Eyn loszbuch ausz der karten gemacht.* Rostock. 1890.

*HOLY ORDER OF MANS. *Jewels of the Wise.* San Francisco. 1974. sm 8vo. 197 pp. Ill. Describes Major Arcana cards.

*HOLY ORDER OF MANS. *Keystone of Tarot Symbols. An Outline of Tarot Symbology [etc].* San Francisco. 1971. sm 8vo. 108 pp. Describes and defines the Major Arcana and provides instructions for coloring.

HONL, Ivan. *Z minulosti karetni hry vcechach.* Prague. 1947. 8vo. 112 pp. Includes short English summary.

*HORR, Norton T. *A Bibliography of Card Games and of the History of Playing Cards.* Cleveland. 1892. Reprinted Montclair, 1972. sm 4to. 79 pp. Limited to 250 numbered copies signed by the author. Bibliography of 1,348 books and articles dealing with playing cards.

*HOTEMA, Hilton. *Ancient Tarot Symbolism Revealed.* Lakemont. 1969. 213 pp. Ill.

*HOTEMA, Hilton. *Land of Light.* Mokelumne Hill, Calif. 1959. Reprinted 1972. 157 pp. Interpretation of tarot based upon ancient philosophy.

HOWE, Ellic. *The Magicians of The Golden Dawn.*

*HOY, David. *The Meaning of Tarot.* Tennessee. 1971. 8vo. 168 pp. Ill. Describes tarot and methods of divination.

[HOYLE, Edmund]. *A short Treatise on the Game of Whist [etc].* Bath and London. 1743. 8vo. Original edition of celebrated rule book, subsequently reprinted in hundreds of editions worldwide.

*HUBER und HERPEL. *Bologneser Tarockspiel des 17. Jahrhunderts. Giuseppe Maria Mitelli.* Germany. 1970. Folio. 8 pp. Edition limited to 150. Reproduces the Tarocchino of Bologna cards designed in the 17th century by Giuseppe Maria Mitelli.

HULTON, P. H. "A Volume of Drawings by Francis Barlow," *The British Museum Quarterly.* 1955. Vol. XX. No. 1. 3 pp.

*HUMPHREYS, Henry Noel. *The Origin and Progress of the Art of Writing.* London. 1855. 178 pp. Ill. Describes history of writing including ancient alphabets.

*HUSON, Paul. *The Devil's Picturebook. The Compleat Guide to Tarot Cards.* New York. 1971. 8vo. 256 pp. Ill. Origin of tarot and meanings of each card with methods of reading the pack.

I

*IAMBLICHUS. *An Egyptian Initiation.* Translated from original MS by P. Christian. Preface by Edward Leon Bloom. Denver. 1965. 105 pp. Ill. Describes Major Arcana in terms of divine, intellectual and physical worlds once concealed and preserved in sacred Egyptian temples; illustrations resemble Oswald Wirth cards.

*ICHAZO, Oscar. *The Human Process for Enlightenment and Freedom.* New York. 1976. 120 pp. Ill. Lectures by Oscar Ichazo, founder of Arica Institute; the Major Arcana cards are viewed as complex ideograms likened to the letters of the alphabet, the Minor Arcana open the four ways of understanding the consciousness.

IGLESIAS JANEIRO, Professor J. *La Cabala de Prediccion.*

INGOLD. *Das Guldin Spil* (Das Guildin Spiel). Augsburg. 1472. The author, a Dominican friar, describes the principal games in vogue, and claims playing cards were brought to Germany in 1300.

INITIE,(un). *Physionomie, cartomancie, loi des sciences occultes [etc].* Paris. n.d. 8vo. Ill.

*INNES, Brian. *The Tarot: How to Use and Interpret the Cards.* London. 1977. 88 pp. Ill. Describes tarot history and development, compares Major Arcana cards and relationship to the kabbalah and astrology.

*ISTITUTO FINANZIARIO PER L'ARTE. *48 Tarocchi di Bonifacio Bembo.* Milan. 1971. 8vo. Ill. Description with illustrations of the 48 tarocchi cards from the Brera Brambilla pack.

J

J., D. "Cartes," *La Grande Encyclopedie de Diderot et d'Alembert.* 1751.

JACKSON, F. *The Scholler's Practical Cards. Containing instructions by means of cards how to spell, cypher and cast accounts [etc].* London. 1656.

JACKSON, Mrs. F. Nevill. "Children's Playing Cards," *Connoisseur.* December 1910. 5 pp.

**JACKSON, John. *A Treatise on Wood Engraving, Historical and Practical.* London. 1839. Ill. Early wood engraving including playing cards.

JACKSON, Lewis d'Aguilar. *English Tarocco, or The Allies.* London. 1884. 16mo. 46 pp.

JACKSON, Lewis d'Aguilar. *Tarocco and Tresillo.* London. 1886. 106 pp.

JACOB, Dr. "Origines des cartes a jouer," *Les Cahiers de Marottes et Violons d'Ingres.* December 11, 1952. No. 22. pp. 45–63.

**JACOB, P. L. *Curiosites de l'histoire des arts.* Paris. 1858. 410 pp. Origin and development of playing cards (p. 17–73).

JACOB, P. L. [Paul Lacroix]. "Origine des cartes a jouer," *Dictionnaire de la Conversation.* Reprinted in *Mon Grand Fauteuil*, pp. 147–160. Reprinted 1835.

JACOBS (see under pseudonym d'Ely Star).

*JACOBY, Oswald, and Albert Morehead. *The Fireside Book of Cards.* New York. 1957. 8vo. 364 pp. Ill. Anecdotes, short stories and poems about playing cards.

JACOTIN de ROSIERES. *La fabrication des cartes a jouer au Puy.* Paris. 1909.

JAGOT, P. C. (see under pseudonym Thylbus).

JAKSTEIN, Werner. "Das Spiel mit Konig, Dame und Bube," *Der Druckspiegel.* 1953. pp. 222–228.

JAKSTEIN, Werner. "Geheimnisse der Spielkarten," *Velhagen und Klasings Monatshefte.* 1941/42. pp. 168–176.

JAKSTEIN, Werner. "Konige aller Volker. Eine kleine Spielkartenschau," *Westermanns Monatshefte.* 1949. Heft 8. pp. 71–74.

*JAKSTEIN, Werner. *Spielkarten Aus Funf Jahrunderten.* Bielefeld. Circa 1950s. 12mo. 30 pp. Ill. Catalog of the playing card collection of Werner Jakstein acquired by Deutsches Spielkarten Museum, Bielefeld.

JAKSTEIN, Werner, and Eberhard Pinder. *Des Duivels Prentenboek.* Bielefeld. [1957?]. 32 pp. Catalog of an exhibition of playing cards at the Deutsches Spielkarten Museum.

JANER, Florencio. "Naipes o cartas de jugar y dados antiguos," *Museo español de Antiquedades.* III. pp. 43–63.

JANNONE, M. Christina. "I Tarocchi Bembeschi." Unpublished MS. Milan. 1970-71.

*JANSEN, Henri, *Essai sur l'origine de la gravure en bois . . . Ou il est parle aussi de l'origine des cartes a jouer [etc].* Paris. 1808. 8vo. 2 Vols. Ill. Jansen believes playing cards were invented in Germany and, following the theory of Heinecken, views the game of *landsknecht* or *lansquenet* as the earliest card game, derived from the German word for foot soldier.

*JANSSEN, Han. *Speelkaarten.* Bussum. 1965. 8vo. 120 pp. Ill. Development of playing cards.

*JAPAN PUBLICATIONS. *Hanafuda. The Flower Card Game.* Japan. 1970. 94 pp. Ill. Describes popular card game of Hanafuda or Flower Cards.

JAVANE, Faith, and Dusty Bunker. "Numerology and the Divine Triangle." Unpublished MS. Rockport. Uses the Pythagorean triangle and numerology to discover life patterns and potential; contains sets of four delineations for each number, 1 through 78, corresponding to the 78 tarot keys.

*JEAN-RICHARD, Pierrette. *Les Incunables de la Collection Edmond de Rothschild.* Paris. 1974. 64 pp. Ill. Tarots and uncut card sheets exhibited at the Louvre (p. 27–31).

JELALEL, H. (pseudonym of Hugand). *Cartomancie, ou l'art de developper la chaine des evenements de la vie [etc].* Lyon. 1791.

JELALEL, H. *Cours complet theorique et pratique du livre de Thot.* Paris.

JENNINGS, Hargrave. *The Rosicrucians, Their Rites and Mysteries.* London. 1870. 12mo. 339 pp. Ill. History of the Order of the Rose-Cross.

*JENSEN, K. Frank. *Tarot.* Denmark. 1975. 8vo. 201 pp. Ill.
*JESSEL, Frederic. *Bibliographies of Works on Playing Cards and Gaming.* London. 1905. Reprinted Montclair, 1972. 8vo. 311 + 79 pages. Reprints of bibliographies on playing cards and gaming by Frederic Jessel and Norton T. Horr.
JOBES, Gertrude. *Dictionary of Mythology, Folklore and Symbols.* 1961. N.Y. 3 vols. Includes symbols from tarot, kabbalah, and occult sciences.
JOHANNEAU, Eloi. *Melanges d'origines etymologiques et de questions grammaticales.* Paris. 1818. Claims the Spanish word for cards, *naipes,* derives from the Latin word *mappa.*
JOHANNES (von RHEINFELDEN), Brother. *Tractatus de moribus et disciplina humanae conversationis.* 1377. Often cited as earliest published reference to cards; describes game called *ludus cartarum.*
JOLLY JOKER, le (see Alain Bourveau).
JOLY[us], Adolphus. *Le grand art de tirer les cartes* [etc]. 1864. 70 pp. Fortune-telling with cards and predictions for the year 1864.
JONES, Charles Stansfeld (see under pseudonym Frater Achad).
JOSEPH OF ST. BARBARA, Father. *Het Gheestelyck kaert-spel met Herten Troef, oft het Spel der Liefde door den e'erw pater F. Joseph a S. Barbara.* Antwerp. 1666. 16mo. 528 pp. Ill. Spiritual game with heart trumps; however, hearts were popular 17th and 18th century representations of the soul, not necessarily of playing cards.
JOSEPH OF ST. BARBARA, Father. *Het Gheestelyck kaert-spel met Herten Troef, oft 'spel der liefde door den e'erw pater F. Joseph a S. Barbara.* Antwerp. 1676. 16mo. 538 + 21 pp. Ill. A later edition of preceding book.
JUNG, Carl Gustav. *Symbols of Transformation.* Deals with dreams and archetypal imagery.
JUNG, Carl Gustav. *Psychological Types.* London. 1964. Jungian typology includes the four functions of thinking, sensation, intuition and feeling.
JUNG, Carl Gustav. *Synchronicity. An Acausal Connecting Principle.* Translated by R. F. C. Hull. Princeton. 1973. 135 pp. Jung's work in parapsychology includes ESP cards and I Ching cards.
JUSSELIN, Maurice. "Imagiers et cartiers a Chartres," *Memoires de la Societe archeologique d'Eure-et-Loire.* 1957. XXX. 281 pp.

K

*KAHN, Yitzhac. *Tarot and the Game of Fate.* San Francisco. 1971. 24 mo. 80 pp. Ill. Meanings of each tarot card and description of Game of Fate.
*KAISER, John Boynton. *I. British Playing Card Stamp Duties* [etc]. *II. The Laws Relating to United States Playing Card Revenue Stamps 1862–1883 and 1894–1960.* State College. 1960. 8vo. 62 pp. Ill. Tax and duty stamps on playing cards in the United Kingdom and the United States.
KAMMENTHALER, J. *L'Oracle chez soi, contenant tous les moyens de connaitre l'avenir par les lettres magiques, par les cartes* [etc]. 1907. Ill.
**KAMMER LANDER, Jacob. *Kartenlosbuch.* Strasbourg. 1543. 24mo. Ill. Satire about playing cards with movable, directional figure.
*KAPLAN, Stuart R. *Commentary on the Oswald Wirth Tarot Deck.* New York. 1976. 12 pp. Booklet accompanies the Oswald Wirth tarot deck.

*KAPLAN, Stuart R. *The Devil's Tarot Deck Instructions.* New York. 1974. 41 pp. Booklet accompanies the Fergus Hall tarot deck with rules for The Exorcist Tarot Game.
*KAPLAN, Stuart R. (see *Greenwich Time*).
*KAPLAN, Stuart R. *I Tarocchi.* Translated by Francesca Romana Pontani. Milan. 1973. 12mo. 238 pp. Ill. Italian translation of *Tarot Classic.*
*KAPLAN, Stuart R. "I tarocchi," *Cosmopolitan.* August 1974. No. 17. Ill. Reprint from *Tarot Classic* in Cosmopolitan Magazine (p. 35–55).
*KAPLAN, Stuart R. *James Bond 007 Tarot Book.* New York. 1973. 16mo. 96 pp. Ill. Also published in German and Spanish editions. Describes Fergus Hall tarot deck featured in James Bond 007 film, "Live and Let Die."
*KAPLAN, Stuart R. *Official Rules of the Tarotrump Card Game.* New York. 1971. 88 pp.
*KAPLAN, Stuart R. *The Rider Tarot Deck Instructions.* New York. 1971. 44 pp. Booklet accompanies Rider-Waite tarot deck.
*KAPLAN, Stuart R. *The Royal Fez Moroccan Tarot Deck Instructions.* New York. 1975. 36 pp. Booklet accompanies Royal Fez Moroccan tarot deck.

*KAPLAN, Stuart R. *Spanish Tarot Deck Instructions.* New York. 1975. Bilingual English and Spanish. 106 pp. Accompanies Spanish tarot deck..
*KAPLAN, Stuart R. *The Starter Tarot Deck.* New York. 1976. 16 pp. Booklet accompanies Starter tarot deck.
*KAPLAN, Stuart R. *Stuart and Marilyn R. Kaplan Collection, The.* Connecticut. 1976. 4 pp. Brochure describes playing card exhibit in 1976.
*KAPLAN, Stuart R. *Stuart R. Kaplan Collection, The.* New York. 1975. 24 pp. Catalog of tarot and cartomancy decks.
*KAPLAN, Stuart R. *Tarot Cards For Fun And Fortune Telling.* New York. 1970. 8vo. 96 pp. Ill. Guide to the IJJ Swiss tarot pack.
*KAPLAN, Stuart R. "Tarot Cards For Fun And Fortune Telling." Original manuscript with author's corrections and IJJ cards pasted on pages.
*KAPLAN, Stuart R. *Tarot Classic.* New York. 1972. 8vo. 240 pp. Ill. Origin and development of tarot cards and guide to Tarot Classic deck.
*KAPLAN, Stuart R. *Tarot of the Witches Instructions.* New York. 1974. 28 pp. Booklet accompanies the Fergus Hall tarot deck.
*KAPLAN, Stuart R. *The Visconti-Sforza Tarocchi Deck Instructions.* New York. 1975. 38 pp. Booklet describes the Pierpont Morgan-Bergamo Visconti-Sforza tarocchi deck.
KARRASCH, Alfred. "Bube, Dame, Konig, As!" *Berliner Lokalanzeiger.* April 1931.
KASDIN, Simon. *Cabala: A definition of Man.* Phamphlet includes reference to tarot as a commentary on the Sepher Yetzirah.
*KASDIN, Simon. *The Esoteric Tarot.* New Jersey. 1965. 8vo. 96 pp, Ill. Tarot related to Hebrew alphabet and Sepher Yetzirah.
KASDIN, Simon. *Mantra Yoga.* Includes verses relating to tarot from Case's *The Book of Tokens.*
KATZENELLENBOGEN, Adolf. *Allegories of the Virtues and Vices in Mediaeval Art.* Hamburg. 1939. 102 + 48 pp. Describes virtues and vices popular during medieval ages.
KAUFMAN, Gerald Lynton. *When Bards Play Cards.* New York. 1952.
**KAY, Jerry. *The Book of Thoth: The Ultimate Tarot.* Los Angeles. 1968. 64 pp. Describes a series of tarot cards of which a few resemble Crowley designs.
*KELLER, William B. "The Cataloguing of the Cary Collection of Playing Cards," *The Journal of The Playing-Card Society.* Birmingham. May 1974. Vol. II. No. 4. pp. 2-3.
KELLER, William B. *(Catalog of The Cary Collection of Playing Cards, Yale University Library.)* New Haven. Ill. A catalog of the Cary Collection currently is in preparation by William B. Keller. As presently envisioned, the catalog will contain detailed descriptions of over 3,000 items including playing card packs, uncut sheets, wood blocks and metal plates.
KEMMIS, J.H. "The Devil's Picture Books," *Pearson's Magazine.* London. March 1898. Vol. 5. p. 277.
KENDALL, Maurice G. "Studies in the History of Probability and Statistics: II. The Beginnings of a Probability Calculus," *Biometrika.* XLIII. 1956. The 21 trumps (omitting the unnumbered Fool) and the 56 suit cards, allegedly are based upon the 21 possible combinations from two dice, 56 possible combinations with three dice.
*KENT, Cicely. *Telling Fortunes by Cards.* New York, 1922. 12mo. 192 pp. Ill. Fortune telling with 52 and 78 card packs.
KERDANCE de Pornic. "Le Livre des XXII feuillets hermetiques: 1° dont chacun devoile un arcane spagyrique et montre clairement une des 22 operations ou portes de la vraie pratique" (etc). Unpublished MS. Circa 1763. Ill. The 22 figures represent different symbols of the transmutation.
*KERSAINT. Jean-Pol de. *Tarot De Kersaint.* Paris. 1974. 2 Vols. 8 vo. Ill. Presents a new tarot pack based upon astrological influences (Vol I); contains 78 cards perforated for removal and use as a deck (Vol. II).
KHARE, G. H. "The Game of Ganjifa and its Variations (Marathi)," *Bharata Itihasa Samshodhaka Mendala.* Poona. 1942. Vol. XXII No. 3/4.
KING, Francis, and Stephen Skinner. *The Techniques of High Magic.* London. 1976. Includes section on tarot.
KIRCHER, Athanasius. *Oedipus Aegyptiacus.* Rome. 1652-1654. 3 Vols usually bound in four. Description of ancient Egypt includes the Bembine Table, *Mensa Isiaca* (Vol.III).
*KLAUS, Barbara. "O Seer, Can you Say?", *Westchester.* Mamaroneck. January 1977. Vol. 9. No. 1. Experiences with methods of fortune-telling (pp. 76-79, 91-94).
KLEIN, Robert. "Les Tarots Enlumines du XVe Siecle, "*L'Oeil.* January, 1967. No. 145. Describes hand-painted tarots of the 15th and 16th centuries including Visconti-Sforza (pp 11-17, 51-52).
KLOK, J.A.F. *De tarot als raadsvrouw onzer toekomst.* Den Haag.
*KLUMPER, W. Tj. "Symboliek der Gatellen," *Bres Planete.* Gravenhage. October 1969. Ill. Tarot symbolism including the 22 Major Arcana with Egyptian designs (p.99-116).
KNAPP, J.A. *Divination with Tarot Cards.* Los Angeles 1936. 31pp. Fortune telling with tarot.
KNAPP, J.A. *The Tarot Cards in Divination.* Los Angeles. 1935. 31 pp. Same as *Divination with Tarot Cards.*
**KNIGHT, Gareth (pseudonym of Basil Wilby). "The Fool's Journey," (etc.), *New Dimensions.* 1963-1964. Vol. I. Nos. 1-6. Ill. Series of six articles describing The Fool, The Magician, The Priestess, The Empress, The Emperor, The High Priest.

*KNIGHT, Gareth (pseudonym of Basil Wilby). *A Practical Guide to Qabalistic Symbolism.* England. 1965. 2 Vols. 249 and 291 pp. Ill. Application and theory of kabbalistic symbolism; analyzes Major Arcana cards from standpoint of tarot symbols, Hebrew letters and astrological signs (Vol II).

KNORR de ROSENROTH, W. *Kabbala denudada.* Salzbach. 1677.

KOHLMANN, Erwin. "Eine Naumburger Spielkartenfabrik des Biedermeier," *Marginalien, Blatter der Pirckheimer-Gesellschaft.* Aug. 1960. pp. 26-32.

*KOHLMANN, Erwin. *Kartenspiel des Jost Amman.* Leipzig. 1967. 36 pp. Brochure accompanies reproduction of Jost Amman cards.

*KOHLMANN, Erwin. *Kartenspiel des Meisters PW.* Munich. 1974. 58 pp. Booklet accompanies reproduction of round cards originally engraved in the 15th century by the *Master of Playing Cards.*

KOHLMANN, Erwin. "Kinderwelt und Spielkarten," *Marginalien.* June 1966. pp. 46-49.

KOHLMANN, Erwin. "Peter Mafferts Boek oder Wissenschaftliche Anmerkungen zu Laurembergs Scherzgedichten," *Marginalien.* December 1965. pp. 59-63.

*KOHLMANN, Erwin. "Remarks on the Early History of Playing Cards in Europe and the Low Countries," *In de kaart gekeken.* Amsterdam. 1976. Text in Dutch and English. Ill. Forward to catalog of playing card exhibition in 1976 at Museum Wilet-Holthuysen.

*KOLB, Eugene. *Old Playing Cards from the Fifteenth to the Nineteenth Century.* Budapest. 1940. 80 pp. Ill. Translation of Kolb's *Regi Jatekkartyak Magyar.*

*KOLB, Eugene (Jeno Kolb). *Regi Jatekkartyak Magyar Es Kulfoldi Kartyafestes XV-XIX Szazad.* Budapest. 1939. sm 8vo. 79 pp. Ill. Origin and development of playing cards including tarot.

*KONICEK, Mona. *The Art of Card Reading.* 1974. Reprinted 1976. 4 pp. Fortune telling with 32 cards.

KONRAD, W. "Hildesheim Spielkarten aus dem 18 Jahrhundert," *Alt-Hildesheim.* 1957. pp. 39-42.

*KONSTAM, Kenneth W. "Cartes a jouer modernes," *Graphis.* 1957. No. 77. pp. 262-263.

*KONSTAM, Kenneth W. *Enquire Within. A History and Guide to Card Playing.* (1955?) 72 pp. Ill. Brief description of early playing cards and rules of several card games.

*KOPP, Peter F. "Basel und die Spielkarten im 19. Jahrhundert," *Zeitschrift fur Schweizerische Archaologie und Kunstgeschichte.* Zurich. 1973. Band 30. Doppelheft 3/4. pp. 162-168. Ill.

*KOPP, Peter F. "Die fruhesten Spielkarten in der Schweiz," *Zeitschrift fur Schweizerische Archaologie und Kunstgeschichte.* Zurich. 1973. Band 30. Doppelheft 3/4. pp. 130-145. Ill. History of playing cards.

KOPP, Sheldon. *The Hanged Man.* Palo Alto. 1974. Autobiographical account of author's life as a therapist and teacher of psychotherapy.

*KORENY, Fritz. "The Hofaemterspiel: The Ambras Castle Collection," *Hofaemterspiel.* Vienna. 1976. Text in German and English. Ill. Describes the 48 cards of the Hofaemterspiel pack (pp. 15-44, 88-107).

*KORENY, Fritz. *Zirkus des Lebens.* Vienna. 1977. 140 pp. Ill. Booklet accompanies the Circus of Life fortune-telling cards by Alfred Kubin.

KRISTELLER, Paul. *Die Tarrocchi des XIV Jahrhunderts.* Berlin. 1890.

KRISTELLER, Paul. *Graphische Gesellschaft. Die Tarocchi, zwei italienische kupferstichfolgen aus dem XV jahrhundert.* Berlin. 1910.

KRISTELLER, Paul. *Kupferstich und Holzschnitt in vier Jahrhunderten.* Berlin. 1905. Origin of graphic art and early playing cards (p. 19) and Tarocchi of Mantegna cards (p. 179).

*KROPPENSTEDT, Erika and Detlef Hoffmann. *Inventar Katalog Der Spielkarten Sammlung Des Stadtmuseums Linz.* Bielefeld. 1969. sm 8vo. 86 pp. Ill.

*KRUPINSKI, Doris Ann. "Pursuing Playing Cards Through History," *Hobbies Magazine.* U.S.A. July 1954. Ill. Describes playing card collection of Evelyn Boeyer (pp. 12-15, 59-61).

KRZYSZTOFOWISZ, Stefania. "Polskie karty do gry," *Mowia wieki.* Warsaw. 1967. pp. 24-28.

*KUGLER, Georg. "15th Century Europe and the Hofaemterspiel," *Hofaemterspiel.* Vienna. 1976. pp. 55-61 and 117-122. Ill. Describes Europe in the 15th century when the Hofaemterspiel cards were printed by woodblocks and hand colored.

*KUGLER, Georg. "What is a Hofamt?" *Hofaemterspiel.* Vienna. 1976. Text in German and English. Ill. Describes court life during the Middle Ages represented in the Hofaemterspiel pack (pp. 11-14, 83-87).

KUMPEL, Heinrich. "Rund um die Spielkarte," *Librarium.* 1958. 8 pp.

KUMPEL, Heinrich. "The Fabulous Story of Cards," *The American Abroad.* February 1960. pp. 16-18, 44.

KURTZAHN, Ernst (pseudonym Daitynus). *Der Tarot.* Leipzig. 1920.

*(KURZROK, Lawrence. *United States Playing Cards Priced Catalog.* New York. 1965. 21 pp.

KVMRIS. "Les Arcanes majeures du Tarot," *Branche du Groupe independant d'Etudes Esoteriques (etc).* Brussels. 1891-1895.

L

L.C.*** *Academie Universelle Des Jeux, ou Dictionnaire Methodique et Raisonne.* Paris. 1825. 12mo. 460 pp.

LA BLEAU, Mme. *Fortune Telling by Cards or Card Reading Made Easy.* Chicago. 1920. 12mo. 78 pp. Ill. Brief history of cards and fortune telling with 32 and 52 cards.

LACHNER, Julius L. "The Problem of the Tarot Cards," *The Occult Review.* May 1920. Vol. XXXI. No. 5. pp. 262-268.

LACOUR, P. I. *Essai sur les hieroglyphes egyptiens.* Bordeaux. 1821. Edition limited to 300 copies. Describes hieroglyphics of the sacred language of the priests of Egypt.

*LACROIX, M. Paul. *Le Moyen Age et la Renaissance.* Paris. 1869. sm 4to. 5 Vols. Reprinted in several editions. Ill. Origin and development of playing cards and description of Gringonneur cards (Vol II).

*LACROIX, Paul. *Les Arts au Moyen Age Et a L'Epoque de La Renaissance.* Paris 1869. 548 pp. Ill. Origin and development of cards (p 229-256).

*LACROIX, Paul. *The Arts in the Middle Ages and the Renaissance.* London. n.d. *Reprinted New York, 1964. sm 4to. 464 pp. Ill. Translation of *Les Arts au Moyen Age Et a L'Epoque de La Renaissance.*

LACROIX, Paul. *Moeurs, Usages et Costumes au Moyen Age et a l'epoque de la Renaissance.* Paris. 1878. 12mo. 603 pp. Ill. Brief reference to card playing (p. 255).

LACURIA, F.G. *Harmonies de l'Etre exprimees par les nombres.* Paris. 1847. 2 Vols.

LAFORGE, Lucien. *Le Tarot sacerdotal (etc).* Paris. 1951. 8vo. 22 pp. Ill. Edition limited to 200. Lithographs of the 22 Major Arcana with brief descriptive text.

*LAGERBERG, Guy de. "Cards for Kings and Kibitzers," *Antiques.* Orange. 1942. 4to. Vol. XLII, No. 3. pp. 124-126. Ill. Describes playing cards and card games sought by collectors.

LAGERBERG, Guy de. "Notes on the History of Playing Cards," *Hobbies.* April, 1942.

LA GRANGE (Frederic de) (pseudonym of J.P. Pitois, alias P. Christian). *Le grand livre du destin. Repertoire general des sciences occultes d'apres . . . Agrippa, Etteilla, Mlle Lenormand (etc).* Paris. 1845. Reprinted Paris, 1850.

LAING, Caroline. *Cosmopolitan's Guide to Fortune-Telling.* New York. 1974. 169 pp. Includes section on tarot cards.

*LAMBERT, Latham. *The Red Rabbit.* Quarterly. Auction list of playing card decks and books.

LANCELIN Charles. *La Sorcellerie des campagnes.* Paris. 1910. Reprinted Paris. n.d. Ill. Summary of the work of Vaillant, Papus and Falconnier.

LANDI, Vincenzio. *Regole Generali del Giuoco delle Minchiate (etc).* Florence. 1781. 8vo. 70 pp. Rules for the game of minchiate.

LANGE, E. *Das grosse Buch der Kartenspiele.* Berlin. Describes tarot cards (Chapter 10).

**LANRA, Maurice (Maguelone). *Le Tarot de la Reyne. Histoire de Catherine di Medicis suivie des Sept Pensees de Nostradamus.* Paris. 1911. 158 pp. Ill. Cards illustrate events in the life of Catherine de Medici ending with her death in 1589, represented by card *70 La Mort.*

LANSLOTS, R. *De Speelkaartnijverheid in Turnhout.* Antwerp. 1969. Unpublished MS. Thesis on playing card industry in Turnhout.

LANTIEZ, D. "La carte a jouer est-elle d'origine europeenne?" *La France graphique.* 1958. No. 144.

LANZI, Luigi. *Storia pittorica dell' Italia.* Bassano, 1795-1796, or Milan, 1809 (?). Refers to the Tarocchi of Mantegna series.

LAPADU-HARGUES, F., and G. H. Riviere. "Imagerie, cartes a jouer, toiles imprimees," *Arts et traditions populaires.* July-December, 1965.

*LARUSSON, R. F. "A Souvenir With A Difference," *The Journal of The Playing-Card Society.* Manchester. Feb. 1973. Vol. I. No. 3. p. 10-11.

LASSALE, Antoine de. *Chronicle du Petit-Jehan de Saintre.* 1459. Claims the pages of Charles V, king from 1364 to 1380, played at the game of cards.

LASZLOE, Elizabeth. *De geheimen van de Tarot.* Amsterdam. 1954. 8vo.

LATIMER, Hugh. *Sermons on the Card.* London. 1886. 12mo. Sermon on cards from 1529.

LAURAIN, E. *Ouvriers d'art lavallois.* Laval. 1941.

*LAURENCE, L. W. de. *The Illustrated Key to the Tarot.* 1971. Reprint of *The Key to the Tarot* (see Waite).

*LAURENCE, Theodor. *How the Tarot Speaks to Modern Man.* Harrisburg, Pa. 1972. 12mo. Ill. Tarot symbology on physical, psychological, spiritual, and philosophical planes for deeper self-understanding.

*LAURENCE, Theodor. *The Sexual Key to the Tarot.* New York. 1971. 8vo. 121 pp. Ill. People consult cards for guidance in health, wealth and sex, not necessarily in that order; sexual symbolism and interpretations are presented for each card.

LAURENT, Dominican. *The Book of Vices and Virtues.* London. 1942. 378 pp. Translation of several manuscripts that deal with virtues and vices.

LAZZARELLI, Ludovico. *De Imaginibus gentilium Deorum.* 1471. Ill. Early codex containing illustrations from the Tarocchi of Mantegna pack.

LEBER, M. C. [Jean Michel Constant]. "Bibliographie de l'histoire des cartes a jouer, d'apres les documents ecrits [etc]." Unpublished MS. After 1842(?). Documents and research on playing cards by other authors.

*LEBER, M. C. [Jean Michel Constant]. *Catalogue des livres imprimes manuscrits, estampes, dessins et cartes a jouer de la collection de C. Leber.* Paris. 1839 and 1852. 4 Vols. sm 8vo. Ill. Catalog of playing card collection of M. C. Leber at Library of Rouen.

LEBER, M. C. [Jean Michel Constant]. *Collection des meilleues dissertations et traites particuliers relatifs a l'Histoire de France [etc].* Paris. 1838. 8vo. 20 vols. Contains articles on playing cards by Bullet, Daniel, Rive, etc.

**LEBER, M. C. [Jean Michel Constant]. "Etudes historiques sur les cartes a jouer, principalement sur les cartes francaises," *Memoires de la Societe royale des antiquaires de France.* T.XVI. Paris. 1842. Origin and development of cards including tarot; Leber appears the first to point out the passage by Bussi about Covelluzzo and cards brought into Viterbo in 1379.

LEBON, Editor. "Over Speelkarten en Kaartspelen," *Kerstboek Panorama.* 12/1949. pp. 34–39.

LEBRUN. *Manuel du Cartonnier, du Cartier, et du Fabriquant des Cartonnages.* Paris. 1830 or 1845(?). Ill.

LE GENDRE, l'Abbe. *Moeurs des Francais.* The author believes Lydians invented playing cards and dice.

*LEHMANN-HAUPT, Hellmut. *Gutenberg and the Master of the Playing Cards.* New Haven and London. 1966. sm 4to. 83 pp. Ill. Gutenberg, inventor of printing with movable metal type, may have been associated with early copper engravings used to produce playing cards with animals as suits.

*LEHNER, Ernst. *The Picture Book of Symbols.* New York. 1956. Includes reproduction of Major Arcana and aces from Tarot of Marseilles pack (p. 76–77).

*LEHNER, Ernst. *Symbols, Signs & Signets.* New York. 1950. 221 pp. Ill.

*LEHNER, Kurt, and Sigrun Wyss. "Zur Geschichte der Spielkarten im Raume Schaffhausen," *Zeitschrift fur Schweizerische Archaologie und Kunstgeschichte.* Zurich. 1973. Band 30. Doppelheft 3/4. Ill. History of the playing|card|firm AG Muller & Cie from the 18th century to the present (p. 185–204).

LEHRS, Max. *Die altesten deutschen Spielkarten des Kupferstichkabinets zu Dresden.* Dresden. 1885.

LEHRS, Max. *Geschichte und kritischer Katalog des deutschen, nederlandischen, und franzosischen Kupferstichs im funfzehnten Jahrhundert.* Vienna. 1908. Lists early manuscripts which the author identifies with playing card motifs.

LEHRS, Max. *Die Spielkarten des Meisters ES von 1466.* Berlin. 1892.

LEHRS, Max. "Der Meister der Spielkarten," *Jahrbuch der preussischen Kunstsammlungen.* 1888–1897. Describes extant playing cards from the 15th century with motifs of animals, birds and flowers that are also found in early manuscripts (T.IX, p. 239–242, T.XI, p. 53–55; T.XVIII, p. 46–58).

LEHRS, Max. *Die altesten deutsche Spielkarten. Meister vom Jahre 1462.* Dresden.

LEMOINE, J.-G. "La 'Machine a penser' de Raymond Lulle et l'astrologie arabe," *Bulletin de la Societe de Philosophie de Bordeaux.* August, 1950.

*LEMYNE, Margot. *Fortune Telling by Cards [etc].* Chicago. 1928. 12mo. 127 pp. Fortune telling with 52 cards.

LENAIN. *La Science kabbalistique ou l'art de connaitre les bons genies.* Amiens. 1823. 8vo. Explanation of the Tetragrammaton.

*LE NORMAND, Madame. *The Unerring Fortune-Teller: containing the celebrated Oracle of Human Destiny, or Book of Fate [etc].* New York. 1866. 16mo. 146 pp. Ill. Fortune telling with 32 cards.

*LE NORMAND, Madame [Camille]. *Fortune-Telling By Cards: or Cartomancy Made Easy.* 12mo. 192 pp. Ill. Fortune telling with regular cards.

*LE NORMAND, Mlle M. A. [Marie-Anne]. *Les Souvenirs Prophetiques D'Une Sibylle, Sur les Causes Secretes de son Arrestation, Le II Decembre 1809.* Paris. 1814. 590 pp. Describes events leading to the arrest of Mlle Le Normand, French sibyl; and contains account of Richard Midaleton, the soldier who used cards as a prayer book (p. 340–356).

*LE NORMAND, Madame [Victorine]. *The Oracle of Human Destiny: or, The Unerring Foreteller [etc].* London. 1825. 12mo. 105 pp. Ill. Future telling with cards in conjunction with oracle table.

**LENSI, Alfredo. *Bibliografia Italiana di Giuochi di Carte.* Firenze. 1892. 46 pp. Bibliography of 187 Italian books on history of playing cards and rules of card games.

LE SCOUEZEC, Gwen. *Cartomancia y Chiromancia.* Traduccion de Elisenda Guarro. Barcelona. 1974.

LE SCOUEZEC, Gwen. "La Cartomancie ordinaire" and "Le Tarot symbolique," *Encyclopedie de la Divination.* Paris. 1965. pp. 251–331.

LE SCOUEZEC, Gwen. *Diccionario de las Artes Adivinatorias.* Barcelona. 1973.

LETONNELIER, G., and L. Vidal. "Sur la technique de la fabrication des cartes a jouer en Dauphine sous l'Ancien Regime," *Bulletin de la Societe Scientifique du Dauphine.* 1935. pp. 596–602.

LETTSOM, John Coakley. *Hints addressed to Card Parties.* London. 1798.

LEVENSON, Jay A. *Prints of the Italian Renaissance. A Handbook of the Exhibition.* Washington, D.C. 1973. 4to. 34 pp.

*LEVENSON, Jay A., Konrad Oberhuber and Jacquelyn L. Sheenan. *Early Italian Engravings from the National Gallery of Art.* Washington, D.C. 1973. 4to. 587 pp. Ill. Describes 15th century Tarocchi of Mantegna cards and two codices at the Biblioteca Vaticana.

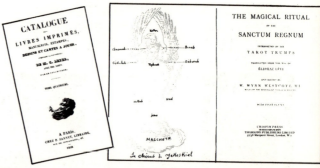

LEVI, Eliphas (pseudonym of Alphonse Louis Constant). *La Clef des Grands Mysteres.* Paris. 1861. According to Levi, tarot is a sacred alphabet attributed by the Hebrews to Enoch, the Egyptians to Thoth or Hermes Trismegistus, and the Greeks to Cadmus and Palamedes; moreover, Levi proposes chess is derived from tarot and some symbols in the French game of goose are taken from the Major Arcana.

LEVI, Eliphas (pseudonym of Alphonse Louis Constant). *Clefs Magiques et Clavicules de Salomon.* 1895. Reprinted Paris, 1926. The kabbalistic tarot is generally credited to Levi.

LEVI, Eliphas (pseudonym of Alphonse Louis Constant). *Cours de Philosophie occulte. Lettres au baron Spedalieri.* Paris. 1932–1933. Several letters describe tarot cards.

LEVI, Eliphas (pseudonym of Alphonse Louis Constant). *Le Dogme et Rituel de la Haute Magie.* Paris. 1854. Reprinted 1861. Application of the Major Keys to the tarot pack.

LEVI, Eliphas (pseudonym of Alphonse Louis Constant). *Le Grand Arcane ou L'Occultisme Devoile.* Paris. 1898.

LEVI, Eliphas (pseudonym of Alphonse Louis Constant). *Histoire de la Magie.* Paris. 1860. 8vo. The Bembine tablet is described as a record of hieroglyphic knowledge with references to tarot.

*LEVI, Eliphas (pseudonym of Alphonse Louis Constant). *The History of Magic.* Translated by Arthur Edward Waite. London. 1913. 536 pp. Ill. Translation of *Histoire de la Magie.*

LEVI, Eliphas (pseudonym of Alphonse Louis Constant). *Le Livre des Splendeurs.* Paris. 1894. 8vo. Tarot is viewed as a hieroglyphical book of 32 paths of kabbalistic theosophy in the Tree of Life.

LEVI, Eliphas (pseudonym of Alphonse Louis Constant). *The Magical Ritual of the Sanctum Regnum, Interpreted by the Tarot trumps.* Edited by W. Wynn Westcott. London. 1896. Ill. Informal commentary and description of the 22 Major Arcana.

LEVY, Yves. *L'Empereur et le Mat.*

LEWANDOWSKI, Gerhard. "Die Spielkarte im Wandel der Zeiten," *Der Druckspiegel.* 1967. p. 812–822.

LEWES, M. L. "Fortune-Telling By Cards," *Occult Review.* London. January 1915. Vol. XXI. No. 1. Fortune telling with 52 cards (p. 100–108).

*LEWIS, Lester A. *Ancient Secret Wisdom.* San Diego. 1961. 58 pp. Ill. Describes ancient traditions and symbols including tarot cards.

*LEYDON, Rudolf von. "A Note On Certain Suit Signs of Indian Playing-Cards," *The Journal of The Playing-Card Society.* Birmingham. February 1975. Vol. III. No. 3. pp. 33–36.

LEYDON, Rudolf von. "A Set of Ivory Playing Cards in the Baroda Museum," *The Bulletin of the Museum and Picture Gallery.* Baroda. 1953–1955. Vol. X-XI. 7 pp.

LEYDON, Rudolf von. Chad. *The Playing Cards of Mysore (India).* Vienna. 1973. 32 + 23 pp.

*LEYDON, Rudolf von. "Ganjifa, The Playing Cards of India," *Marg.* Bombay. 1949. Vol. III. No. 4. pp. 36–56. Ill. Describes numerous Indian and Hindu playing cards.

**LEYDON, Rudolf von. "Indian Playing Cards," *Graphis.* 1950. French and German. Vol. 6. No. 33. pp. 386–395. Ill. Describes Indian playing cards.

LEYDEN, Rudolf von. *Indische Spielkarten.* Leinfelden. 1977. Ill. Catalog of the collection of Indian playing cards at the Deutsches Spielkarten Museum.

LEYDON, Rudolf von. "The Playing Cards of India," *B.B.&C.I. Annual*. Bombay. 1946. pp. 57–62.

*LEYDON, Rudolf von. "The Playing Cards of India," *The Journal of The Playing-Card Society*. Birmingham. Part I — Vol. II, No. 2, November 1973, pp. 4–9; Part II — Vol. II, No. 3, February 1974, pp. 35–36.

LEYDON, Rudolf von. "The Playing Cards of South India," *The Illustrated Weekly of India*. October, 1954.

LEYDON, Rudolf von. "Raritat fur Spezialisten: Indische Spielkarten," *Sammler Journal*. Schwabisch Hall. July 1976. No. 7. Ill. Indian playing cards (p. 276–279).

*LEYDON, Rudolf von. "Tibetan and Mongol Playing-Cards," *The Journal of The Playing-Card Society*. Cranbrook. August 1976. Vol. V. No. 1. Ill. Describes Mongolian playing cards (p. 29–31).

*LHÔTE, Jean-Marie. *Proposition pour un tarot prophetique et pour une eventuelle metamorphose des lames mineures du tarot*. France. 1974.

*LHÔTE, Jean-Marie. "Shakespeare dans les tarots [etc]." *Bizarre Magazine*. June 1967. Nos. 43–44. 100 pp. Analogies between the characters in Shakespeare's "Midsummer Night's Dream" and tarot figures.

*LHÔTE, Jean-Marie. *Le symbolisme des deux*. Paris. 1976. 349 pp. Ill. Describes symbolism found in children's games, dice and playing cards including tarot.

*LHÔTE, Jean-Marie. *Le Tarot. Discours en forme de catalogue a propos d'une exposition sur les Tarots realisée par la Maison de la Culture d'Amiens*. Paris. 1971. 4to. 55 pp. Ill. Describes exhibit on tarot held at Maison de la Culture, Amiens, France.

LHOTZKY, H. *Das Geheimnis der Spielkarten*. Ludwigshafen am Bodensee. 1922.

*LIDSTONE, R[onald] A. *Studies in Symbology*. London. 1926. 93 pp. Ill. Presents thesis that symbology of Major Arcana is identical with that of the crucifix.

*LILLARD, J.F.B. *Poker Stories*. New York. 1896. 251 pp.

*LIND, Frank. *How To Understand The Tarot*. London. 1969. 63 pp. Ill. Fortune telling with tarot.

LINDE. *Geschichte und Litteratur des Schachspiels*. Discusses relationship between cards and chess.

*L'ISLE-ADAM, Villiers de. "L'Ermite," *Le Voile d'Isis*. August-September 1928. Nos. 104–105. Ill. Brief description of The Hermit as a symbol of the fool (p. 561–562).

LITART, John. *A Pack of Cards and a Pack of Nonsense; etc. containing the history authentic of each card in the Pack*. London. 1889. 4to. 118 pp.

LITTA, Pompeo, conte. *Famiglie celebri italiane*. Milan. 1819. Heraldic devices of Italian families.

*LLANO GOROSTIZA, Manuel. *Naipes Espanoles*. Vitoria. 1975. 183 pp. Ill. History of playing cards and development of Spanish cards; includes chapter on tarot.

LLORENTE de LARY, J. *La Baraja Pedagogico-Alfabetica*. Mollerusa. 1917.

*LODGE, Ken. "The English Pattern (known also as Rouen or Anglo-American)," *The Journal of The Playing-Card Society*. Birmingham. May 1974. Vol. II. No. 4. pp. 25–28. Ill.

LOLLIO, Flavio Alberti. *Invettiva Di Flavio Alberti Lollio Ferrarese contra Il Giuoco del Tarocco*. Venice. 1550. 24mo. 12 pp. Invective against tarocco and gaming.

LONG, Max Freedom. *Selections from Kahuna Vistas on Tarot Card Symbology*. Missouri. 1972. 83 pp. Ill. The author believes Kahuna priests of Hawaii had a hand in inventing tarot; includes illustrations from Rider-Waite tarot.

LONGHE, R., editor. *Arte lombarda dai Visconti agli Sforza*. 1958.

LONGHI, Roberto. "Me Pinxit." I resti del polittico di Cristoforo Moretti. La restituzione di une trittico d'arte cremonese. *Pinacotheca*. pp. 17–33, 55–87.

*LONGUEVILLE, Adhemar de. *Manuel Complet de tous les Jeux de Cartes suivi de L'Art de Tirer Les Cartes [etc]*. Paris. n.d. 12mo. 209 pp. Fortune telling with 52 cards.

LONGUEVILLE, Adhemar de. *Manuel Complet de tous les jeux de cartes contenant les regles des jeux connus anciens et nouveaux*. Paris. 1873.

LOYARTE, Adrien de. *Las Veladas en los caserios y en los pueblos y su transcendencia social en el Pais Vasco*. San Sebastian. 1905.

LOZZI, Carlo. "Le Antiche Carte da Giuoco," *La Bibliofilia*. Florence. 1899–1900. Vol. 1. pp. 37–46, 181–186. Describes 15th century Italian deck of cards with suits of arrows, vases, eyes and whips.

LULLY [LULLE], Raymond. *Ars Magna*. Circa late 13th century. According to Papus, Lully developed a system of logic based upon application of the tarot.

LUQUE FAXARDO, Francisco. *Fiel desengano contra la ociosidad y el juego*. Madrid. 1603.

LUTGENS, H. "Spielkarten und Kartenspiele," *Marburger Beitrage zum Blindenbildungswesen*. 1943. pp. 59–65.

LUYKEN, Barbara (see Sylvia Mann).

M

*M***, M. Le C de. "Recherches sur les tarots, et sur la divination par les cartes de tarots." Paris. 1781. Appended to Court de Gebelin's *Monde Primitif*, Vol 9, pp. 395–410. The author contends tarot pack is the ancient Book of Thoth from Egypt and when the 22 Major Arcana cards are placed in correct order, they retrace the events of early history.

*MACDOUGALL, Michael. "Almanac or Devil's Prayer Book," *True Magazine*. Connecticut. January 1950. Anecdotes about playing cards and their uses (p. 22–23, 72–74).

MACEDWARD, G. K. "The History of Playing Cards is the History of Graphic Arts," *Adcrafter*. 1955.

MACHAU, Guillaume de. *Confort d'Amy*. 1364. Prohibition against dice but makes no mention of cards.

*MACKENZIE, George M. *The Story of Each Playing Card*. Glasgow. 1945. 8vo. 16 pp. Nicknames and anecdotes about the 52-card pack.

MACKENZIE, Kenneth. *The Royal Masonic Cyclopaedia*. 1877.

MACLEOD, Malcolm, D.D. *The Key of Knowledge; or Universal Conjurer [etc]*. London. 1796. Includes cartomancy.

*MADURELL MARIMON, Jose Maria. "Notas documentales de naipes barceloneses," Instituto municipal de Historia. Barcelona. 1961. Vol. IV. History and development of Spanish playing cards.

MAFFEI, Raphaelus (see Volaterrani, Raphaelis).

**MAGGS BROS. *A Selection of Books, Manuscripts, Engravings [etc]*. London. 1928. 357 pp. Ill. Describes 16th century court cards, probably from the workshop of Pierre Gayon (1485-1515), Lyons. (p. 236–237).

*MAGNUSSON, Gudbrandur. "The Playing-Cards of Iceland," *The Journal of The Playing-Card Society*. Birmingham. 1974–1975. Parts I-IV. Vols. III and IV. Ill. History of Icelandic playing cards.

*MAGNUSSON, Gudbrandur. *Un Spil a Islandi*. Reykjavik. 1961.

MAGRE, M. *La clef des choses cachees*. Paris. 1953.

MAGRE, Maurice. *Valse des Bohemiens*. Paris. 1933.

MAGUS, Antonio. *L'art de tirer les cartes avec toutes les explications [etc]*. Paris. 1875. 12mo. 320 pp. Fortune telling with cards including tarot.

*MAIGNIEN, Edmond. *Recherches sur les cartiers et les cartes a jouer a Grenoble [etc]*. Numero IX. Grenoble. 1887. 8vo. 34 pp. Ill. Edition limited to 200. History and development of card making in Grenoble.

MAJOR, Emil. *Die Kartenmacher, Briefmaler und Heiligenmaler zu Basel*.

MALCHONT. "Le Tarot social," *Mysteria*. July 1913. Vol. 3. No. 7. pp. 48–57.

MALONE, Marisol. "Guide to Symbols (?)," *Astrology Superspecial*. New York. January 1977. No. 2. Ill. Symbols used in the Major Arcana.

*MANAS, John H. *Divination, Ancient and Modern [etc]*. New York. 1947. 298 pp. Ill. Early methods of divination by seers, sibyls and oracles.

MANDARIN, Le. "Les jeux de cartes en France (types et varietes)," *Gazette Dunlop*. June 1937. No. 202. Ill. Describes playing cards popular in France including tarots (p. 20–23).

*MANDEL, Gabriele. *I Tarocchi dei Visconti*. Bergamo. 1974. 32 pp. Booklet describes the Pierpont Morgan-Bergamo Visconti-Sforza tarocchi pack.

**MANDROVSKY, Boris. "Catalog of the Collection of Playing Cards in the Library of Congress." Unpublished MS. Describes playing cards in the collection of the Library of Congress.

*MANDROVSKY, Boris. "Comments On Terminology and Classification," *The Journal of The Playing-Card Society*. Manchester. May 1973. Vol. I. No. 4. pp. 13–14.

*MANDROVSKY, Boris. "Early Italian Playing-Cards in the Rosenwald Collection, The National Gallery of Art, Washington, D.C.," *The Journal of The Playing-Card Society*. November 1972. Vol. I. No. 2. p. 8. Ill.

*MANDROVKSY, Boris. "The Paris Pattern In Exile," *The Journal of The Playing-Card Society*. Birmingham. May 1974. Vol. II. No. 4. pp. 29–32, 22, 23. Ill.

*MANDROVSKY, Boris. "A Roman Pattern?", *The Journal of The Playing-Card Society*. Cranbrook. August 1976. Vol. V. No. 1. pp. 9–10. Describes a pack of cards published in Italy in 1973.

*MANDROVSKY, Boris. "600 Years of Playing Cards [etc]," *Print Magazine*. New York. January/February 1973.

*MANN, Sylvia. "A Choice Collection of Playing Cards," *The Journal of The Playing-Card Society*. Manchester. Aug. 1972. Vol. 1. No. 1. pp. 4–7. Ill.

*MANN, Sylvia. *Collecting Playing Cards*. New York. 1966. 8vo. 215 pp. Ill. Reference work on playing cards including tarot.

*MANN, Sylvia. "The Exhibition in Amsterdam," *The Journal of The Playing-Card Society*. Cranbrook. August 1976. Vol. V. No. 1. Describes the playing card exhibition held in 1976 at the Museum Willet-Holthuysen in Amsterdam (p. 1–6). (see also Willet-Holthuysen Museum)

*MANN, Sylvia. "Memory Cards," *The Journal of The Playing-Card Society*. Birmingham. February 1974. Vol. II. No. 3. pp. 34–35.

*MANN, Sylvia. "The Neapolitan Pattern," *The Journal of The Playing-Card Society*. Birmingham. August 1975. Vol. IV. No. 1. pp. 52–56. Ill. Neapolitan suited cards.

*MANN, Sylvia. "Pattern Numbers," *The Journal of The Playing-Card Society*. Cranbrook. November 1975. Vol. IV. No. 2. pp. 37–44. Classification system for cards.

*MANN, Sylvia. "Some Thoughts on the Albertina Exhibition," *The Journal of The Playing-Card Society*. Birmingham. November 1974. Vol. III. No. 2. pp. 36–40. Describes exhibition of playing cards as graphic art.

*MANN, Sylvia. "Terminology," *The Journal of The Playing-Card Society*. Manchester. February 1973, Vol. I, No. 3, pp. 13–14; May 1973, Vol. I, No. 4, pp. 11–12. Discusses terminology of playing cards.

*MANN, Sylvia. "When the Fighting Stopped," *The Journal of The Playing-Card Society*. Manchester. May 1975. Vol. III. No. 4. pp. 1–9. Ill. Card designs after the Napoleonic wars.

*MANN, Sylvia. *The William Penn Collection of Playing Cards*. England. 1966. Folio. 93 pp. Ill. Description of the William Penn collection of playing cards and books.

MANN, Sylvia, and David Kingsley. "Playing Cards: Depicting maps of the British Isles [etc]," *The Map Collector's Guide*. London. 1972. No. 87. 35 + 22 pp. Cards depict geographical locations.

*MANN, Sylvia, and Barbara Luyken. *Humanist Playing Cards*. Amsterdam. 1977. Ill. Facsimile edition of humanist card game with Latin texts originally published in 1544 by Christian Wechel, Paris.

*MANN, Sylvia, and Virginia Wayland. *The Dragons of Portugal*. Farnham. 1973. 74 pp. Describes dragon cards of Portugal which spread to the East in the 16th century.

MANNI (see Morelli).

MANSER, Ann, and Cecil North. *Pages of Shustah*. 140 pp. Ill. Interprets tarot from four levels: material, emotional, mental, and spiritual.

MANZI, R. "Le carte," *Pagina*. 1963. No. 2. pp. 94–95.

MARC, J. "L'histoire des cartes a jouer," *Typographische Schweizer Monatsblatter*. 1958. No. 77. pp. 461–464.

*MARCOLINI, Francesco. *Le Ingeniose Sorti composte per Francesco Marcolini da Forli [etc]*. Venice. 1550. 206 pp. Ill. Second edition of Marcolino's work published in 1540; note altered spelling of author's name.

MARCOLINO, Francesco. *Le Sorti di Francesco Marcolino da Forli [etc]*. Venice. 1540. Reprinted 1550. 206 pp. Ill. New edition 1784. One of the earliest books employing cards for divination; depicts king, knight, knave, 10, 9, 8, 7, 2 and ace of coins. Questions are answered based upon the drawing of one or two cards and the reading of an oracular triplet.

MARGIOTTA. *Le Palladisme*. Grenoble. 1895.

MARIUS, Docteur. *Il Destino Svelato dal Tarocco*. Italy. n.d. 77 pp. Ill.

MARLE, Raimond van. *Iconographie de l'art profane au Moyen Age et a la Renaissance*. The Hague. 1932.

*MARTEAU, Paul. *Le Tarot de Marseille*. Paris. 1949. 4to. 281 pp. Ill. Describes the Tarot of Marseilles pack; cards are pasted to pages.

MARTEAU, Paul. "Propos d'un cartier," *Le vieux papier*. June, 1937.

MARTELLO, Leo Louis. *It's In The Cards. The Atomic-Age Approach to Card Reading Using Psychological & Parapsychological Principles*. U.S.A. 1964. 8vo. 95 pp. Fortune telling with tarot including numerology, astrology and proper names.

MARTELLO, Leo Louis. *Understanding the Tarot*. U.S.A. 1972. 12mo. 192 pp. Ill. Fortune telling with the Rider-Waite deck.

*MARTIN, Kevin. *The Complete Gypsy Fortune-Teller*. New York. 1970. 8vo. 315 pp.

*MARTIN, Kevin. *Il Futuro Con Le Carte*. Italy. 1973. 8vo. 172 pp. Translation of *The Complete Gypsy Fortune-Teller*.

MARTIN, Kevin. *Telling Fortunes With Cards: A Guide to Party Fun*. England and New York. 1970. 8vo. 155 pp.

MARTIUS, Calcottus. *De Doctrina Promiscua*. Written 1488 to 1490. Published circa 1552. Allegorical meanings of the four suits.

MARINUS, L. *Groot Kaartspelenboek*. [Great Playing Card Book]. Delft and Brussels. 1977. 164 pp. Ill. Describes playing card games and rules.

MASPERO, G. *Manual of Egyptian Archaeology [etc]*. New York and London. 1895. 360 pp. Ill.

*MATEU, Francisco F., and Carmen Guerro. *Enciclopedia de la Magia y del Misterio*. Barcelona. 1969. 404 pp. Ill.

*MATHERS, S. L. MacGregor. [Golden Dawn Notebook.] London. Circa 1898. 101 leaves. Handwritten lecture notes on tarot based upon Cypher M.S.S. by V. H. Frater S. Reoghail Mo. Dhream (S. L. MacGregor Mathers); also references to Court de Gebelin, Eliphas Levi and tarot trumps including Justice and Strength.

*MATHERS, S. L. MacGregor. *The Tarot, Its Occult Signification, Use in Fortune-Telling, and Method of Play*. London. 1888. Reprinted in the 1970s. 24mo. 60 pp. Supports the kabbalistic-Egyptian origin of tarot.

MAUGER, G.-E. *Quelques considerations sur les jeux en Chine*. Paris. 1917.

MAXWELL, J. *Le Tarot. Le Symbole Les Arcanes La Divination*. Paris. 1933. sm 8vo. 327 pp. Fortune telling with tarot.

*MAXWELL, J. "Symbolisme des Arcanes majeurs," *Le Voile d'Isis*. August-September 1928. Nos. 104–105. Ill. Symbolism of the Major Arcana (pp. 541–558).

*MAXWELL, Joseph. *The Tarot*. London. 1975. sm 8vo. 223 pp. Translation of *Le Tarot*.

*MAYANANDA. *The Tarot For Today [etc]*. London. 1963. 8vo. 255 pp. Ill. Fortune telling with tarot.

*MAYER, L. A. "Mamluk Playing Cards," *Bulletin de l'Institut Francais d'Archeologie Orientale du Caire*. 1939. Vol. 38. Describes Mamluk playing cards (pp. 113–118).

*MAYOR, A. Hyatt. "Old Calling Cards," *The Metropolitan Museum of Art Bulletin*. New York. October 1943. Vol. II. No. 2. Ill. Describes 18th century French custom of using blank backs of playing cards for calling cards (p. 93–98).

MAYOR, A. Hyatt. "Painters' Playing Cards," *Art in America*. Springfield. 1963. No. 2. pp. 39–42.

McCAULLY, Stephen Abbott. "Tarot: Questions & Answers," *Gnostica*. St. Paul. Bi-monthly. Question and answer column on tarot.

*McCAULLY, Stephen Abbott. "Tarot: Ritual Meditation on the Major Tarot Trump: The Moon, Key 18," *Gnostica*. St. Paul. April/May 1977. Vol. 5. No. 6. pp. 51.

McCORMACK, Kathy. *How to Read Tarot Cards*. England.

McILVAINE, Nancy. "Let the Secret of the 'Tarot Cards' See Into Your Future," *Beyond Reality Magazine*. October 1972. pp. 33–39.

*McINTOSH, Christopher. *Eliphas Levi and the French Occult Revival*. London. 1972. 8vo. 238 pp. Describes French occult movement with much information about Eliphas Levi, his contemporaries and disciples.

*McLEOD, John. "Ulti," *The Journal of The Playing-Card Society*. Cranbrook. May 1976. Vol. IV. No. 4. pp. 8–15.

*McLEOD, John, and Michael Dummett. "Hachi-Hachi," *The Journal of Playing-Card Society*. Birmingham. Feb. 1875. Vol. III. No. 3. pp 21–33.

*McLEOD, John, and Michael Dummett. "Jass," *The Journal of The Playing-Card-Society*. Birmingham. Feb. 1975. Vol. III. No. 3. pp. 21–33. 21–33.

*McMILLAN, Alec. *Portentous Prophets and Prophetesses*. London. 1897. 125 pp. Generally unfavorable comments about the works of Eliphas Levi.

MEERMAN, Gerard. *Origines typographicae*. The Hague. 1765. 2 Vols. Claims playing cards date from 1367 based upon the Chronicle of Petit-Jehan de Saintre.

MEISS, Millard, and Edith W. Kirsch, Editors. *The Visconti Hours*. New York. 1972. 8vo. 262 pp. Ill.

**MEISSENBURG, Egbert. "Spielkartenliteratur seit 1930," *Borsenblatt* *fur den Deutschen Buchhandel.* September 24, 1968. No. 77. Bibliography of 79 books and 174 magazine articles published between the years 1930-1968. Most deal with playing cards (p. 2534–2542).

MENESTRIER, Pere C.F. (Claude Francois). *Bibliotheque curieuse et instructive de divers ouvrages anciens et modernes de litterature & des arts.* Trevoux. 1704. 12mo. 2 vols. The author cites the entry in the account books of Charles VI of France that Jacquemin Gringonneur was paid 60 *sols parisis* for three packs of cards (Vol II, p. 174).

MENESTRIER, Pere C.F. (Claude Francois). *Jeu de Cartes du blason.* Lyon. 1692. 224pp.

MERLIN, R. *Les Cartes A Jouer* (etc). Brussels 1857. sm 8vo. 36 pp. History of playing cards.

*MERLIN, R. *Origine des Cartes à Jouer* (etc). Paris. 1869. 4to. 144 and 74 pp. Ill. Origin and development of cards including tarot plus reproductions of Tarocchi of Mantegna, minchiate and tarot.

*MERY, J. *L'Art de Tirer Les Cartes* (etc). Paris. (1925.) 12mo. 228 pp. Ill.

*MESURET, R. *La carte a jouer en languedoc des origines a 1800.* France. 1971. 8vo. 119 pp. Ill. Development of cards in French provence of Languedoc.

*METROPOLITAN MUSEUM OF ART. *The Secular Spirit: Life and Art at the End of the Middle Ages.* New York. 1975. 287 pp. Ill. Description of several playing cards including tarot.

*METZNER, Ralph. *Maps of Consciousness.* New York. 1971. sm 4to. 160 pp. Ill. Includes description and meaning of the Major Arcana.

MEYRINK, Gustav. *The Golem.* New York. 1976. 196 pp. Author contends that the word tarot has the same meaning as Torah (the Law), or may be connected with the Egyptian word *Taruth* (One who is consulted), or may derive from the ancient Zend word, *Tarisk* (I demand the answer).

*MIALL, Agnes M. *Complete Fortune Telling.* London. 1958. 12mo. 334 pp. Ill. Includes fortune telling with 52 cards.

MICHAUX, M. Clovis. *Les douze Heures de la nuit, esquisses en vers.* Paris. 1825. 8vo. The eleventh verse of this poem describes court figures in a deck of cards.

MICHELET, V.E. "La tireuse de cartes," *Les Portes d'Airain.* Derain. 1934.

MIGNE, Abbe. *Dictionnaire des Sciences Occultes* (etc). 1860–1861. 2 Vols. Dictionary of occult sciences.

*MILANO, Alberto. "La Civica Raccolta Delle Stampe A(chille) Bertarelli," *The Journal of the Playing-Card Society.* Cranbrook. May 1977. Vol V. No. 4. Discusses the Bertarelli card collection housed at Milan's Castello Sforzesco (p. 1-5).

MILLET-SAINT-PIERRE (J.B.). *Recherches sur le dernier sorcier et la dernier ecole de Magie.* Le Havre. 1859. Etteilla and his work.

MILLIN, M. *Le Dictionnaire des Beaux Arts.* Paris. 1806. 3 Vols. Early French and Italian playing cards.

**MINER, Dorothy. "A Sheet of Fifteenth-Century Playing Cards," *The Bulletin of the Walters Art Gallery.* Baltimore. March 1959. XI. No. 6. Describes an uncut sheet of French playing cards from Lyon, circa 1500, with the name of the maker, Andre Perrocet.

*MINER, Dorothy. *The Giant Bible of Mainz: 500th Anniversary.* Washington. 1952. 31 pp. Describes similarity between animals, human figures and flowers found in the illuminated borders of the Mainz Bible and an early set of 15th century copper-engraved German playing cards.

MINETTA. *Fortune-Telling Cards and How to Use Them.* London. 1897. 16mo. 29 pp.

MINETTA. *What the Cards Tell.* London. 1896. 8vo. 67 pp.

MINGUET e IROL, Pablo. *Enganos y Diversiones.* Madrid. 1733.

MISTLER, Jean, Francois Blaudey and Andre Jacquemin. *Epinal et l'imagerie populaire.* Paris. 1961. 190 pp.

MITELLI, Giuseppe Maria. *Giuoco di Carte, con nuova forma di Tarocchine.* Rome. 1725. Folio. Ill. *Reprinted in a limited edition of 150 sets. Reproduction of 62 Tarocchino di Bologna cards originally engraved for the family of A. Bentivoglia, Bologna.

M.L.A. *Le jeu des Tarots.* Paris. n.d.

*MOAKLEY, Gertrude. *The Tarot Cards Painted by Bonifacio Bembo for the Visconti-Sforza Family.* (etc). New York. 1966. 8vo. 124 pp. Ill. Describes the 74-card Pierpont Morgan-Bergamo pack painted by Bonifacio Bembo and suggests the tarocchi trumps are popular triumphs celebrated in carnival processions prior to Lent.

*MOAKLEY, Gertrude. "The Tarot Trumps and Petrarch's Trionfi." *Bulletin of the New York Public Library.* Vol. 60. No. 2. 15 pp. Discusses the Major Arcana and Petrarch's *Trionfi.*

*MOAKLEY, Gertrude. The Waite-Smith "Tarot," *Bulletin of The New York Public Library.* New York. October 1954. 12mo. Vol. 58. No. 10. Ill. Describes T.S. Eliot's poem *The Waste Land* and references to the Rider-Waite tarot pack (p. 471-475).

*MOED, Lucia. "The Golden Egyptian Tarot." Unpublished MS. 1978. 12 pp. Ill. Describes tarot deck comprised of Egyptian gods and pharaohs.

*MOFFET, Samuel. "The Psychic Boom," *1973 Encyclopedia Britannica Yearbook of Science and the Future.* Chicago. 1972. sm 4to. Ill. Reproduces Major Arcana from IJJ tarot (p. 66-83).

*MOKUSEIOH, Alexand (pseudonym of Junya Suzue). *Gipsy Fortunetelling: The First Step to Tarot Card Reading.* Osaka. 1974. 152 pp. Ill. Tarot decks and first steps to their use.

*MONCEAU, Duhamel de. "Art du Cartier," *Encyclopedie des Arts et Metiers.* Paris. 1761. 4to. Vol. I. Part II. Ill. Origin of cards based upon Menestrier; and methods of card manufacture in 18th century France (p. 465-481).

*MONCKTON, O. Paul. *Pastimes in Times Past.* London. 1913. 12mo. 256 pp. Ill. Chess and playing cards (Chapter IX) and the history of cards (Chapter XI).

*MONGOI, Lan. "Digressions sur la cartomancie, les cartomanciennes et le tarot," *Le Voile d'Isis.* August-September 1928. Nos. 104–105. pp. 529–534. Ill.

*MONNIER, Antoine. *Symbolisme des cartes a jouer. Histoire occulte de leurs quatre Rois.* Paris. 1921. sm 8vo. 94 pp. Ill.

*MONREAL y TEJADA, Luis. *Los Dichos del Taroco.* Spain. 1966. sm 4to. 19 pp. History of playing cards and tarot.

*MONREAL y TEJADA, Luis. *Museo de Naipes.* Vitoria. 1972. 48mo. 162 pp. Ill. Centenary catalog of the Playing Card Museum of Heraclio Fournier. Spain.

MONTAGUE, Nell St. John. *The Red Fortune Book.* London. 1924. 12mo. 126 pp. Ill.

MONTANDON, Pat. *The Intruders.* New York. Novel deals with tarot and the supernatural.

MONTMIRAIL, J. "Les cartiers; leur organisation professionelle," *La France graphique.* 1958. No. 144.

*MOORE, Rev. Ralph M., Lawrence Kornfeld and James F. Colaianni. *The Jesus Deck. Book of Instructions.* New York. 1972. 123 pp. Booklet accompanies the Jesus deck.

*MOORNE. *El Supremo Arte de Echar Las Cartas.* Mexico. 1972. 8vo. 248 pp. Ill. Fortune telling with Etteilla tarot.

*MORA, P.E. *Tous les jeux de cartes et leurs regles.* Paris. 1969. 12mo. 149 pp. Rules for 40 card games including tarock.

MORELLI, Giovani. *Chroniche di Giovani Morelli.* (1393). First published in Florence, 1728, in *Historia Antica di Ricordano Morelli* by Manni.

*MORETTI, Ugo. *I Tarocchi di Andrea Picini.* Italy. 1975(?). 47 pp. Ill. Limited to 990 signed and numbered sets. The Major Arcana cards by Andrea Picini are pasted on separate pages with descriptions of each card.

MORGAN, Bryan. *Playing with History.*

*MORGAN, Lester B. "Tarot Cards: A Market Analysis," *The Journal of the Playing-Card Society.* Birmingham. May 1974. Vol. II. No. 4. pp. 3-13. Discusses popular tarot decks and their comparative sales.

*MORGAN PRESS. *Aquarian Tarot Instruction Book.* Dobbs Ferry. 1975. 21 pages. Booklet accompanies Aquarian tarot deck.

MORIN, Louis. *Recherches sur la fabrication des cartes a jouer a Troyes.* Troyes. 1899. Ill. Development of card making in Troyes (p. 63-124).

MORITA, Seigo. *Mukashi Iroha-Karuta.* Tokyo. 1970. 4to. 200 pp. Ill. History of Japanese cards and description of Iroha-Karuta packs that comprise 48 cards containing proverbs.

*MORLEY, H.T. *Old and Curious Playing Cards* [etc]. London. 1931. 8vo. 235 pp. Ill. History of playing cards.

*MORNAND, Pierre. "Cartes et Tarots du Cabinet des Estampes," *France Illustration Magazine.* France. 1946. 17 pp. Ill. Brief history of tarot.

MORRISON, J.A.S. "Gambler's Printed Art," *Penrose Annual.* 1959. Vol. 32. pp. 51-56.

MOTT-SMITH, Geoffrey. *The Tarot.* Fortune telling with tarot.

MOULTH, Nathaniel. *Petit manuel du Devin et du Sorcier, contenant . . . l'art de tirer les cartes, le traite des tarots, etc.* Paris. 1854.

MOULTON, S. A. & L. V. *Pahlavi/Cartomancy or Card Reading* [etc]. Revised. Grand Rapids. 1904. 64 pp. Ill.

MOURIER, Paul. *Recherches sur la fabrication des cartes a jouer a Angouleme.* Angouleme. 1904. 54 pp. Ill. Edition limited to 100. Development of playing cards at Angouleme.

*MUCHERY, Georges. *The Astrological Tarot (Astromancy).* New York. n.d. 8vo. 312 pp. Ill. Combines tarot with astrology in 48-card pack.

*MUCHERY, Georges. *La synthese du tarot* [etc]. Paris. 1927. 8vo. 159 pp. Ill. Fortune telling with tarot based upon astrology, a person's name, date of birth and numerology.

*MUCHERY, Georges. *Le Tarot Astrologique*. 1927. 8vo. 350 pp. Ill. Describes Muchery's Astrological tarot pack.
*MUCHERY, Georges. *Les Tarot Astrologique*. Chartres. n.d. 24mo. 46 pp. Translation of *Le Tarot Astrologique*.
*MUCHERY, Georges. *Le Tarot Divinatoire [etc]*. Paris. 1955. 255 pp. Ill.
MUCHERY, Georges. *Votre Destin par le jeu du tarot astrologique*. Paris. 1936.
MUNTZ, Eugene. *Histoire de l'art pendant la Renaissance*. Paris. 1889. 3 vols. Ill. Reprinted 1895. Includes section on the Sforza family of Milan (V. I, pp. 175–191) and references to Bembo, but no mention of tarocchi cards.
MUNTZ, Eugene (see D'Essling).
MURATORI, Ludovico Antonio. *Rerum Italicarum Scriptores*. Milan. 1725–1751. Describes Visconti Tarocchi (Vol. 20, p. 986–1019).
MURNER, Thomas. *Chartiludium Institute Summarie*. Strasburg. 1518. Instructive cards containing twelve suits.
MURNER, Thomas. *Logica memorativa chartiludium logice [etc]*. Cracow 1507(?). Strasburg, 1509. Paris edition published in 1629 by Jean Balesdens. 12mo. Ill. Reprinted in Netherlands, 1967, Vol. II *Homo Ludens*, limited to 500 copies. To stimulate interest among his students, Murner devised a card game with sixteen suits.
MURR, G. G. von. *Journal zur kunstgeschichte*. Nuremberg. 1776. Vol. 2. Murr believes cards were known in Nuremberg during the years 1380 to 1384 based upon city bylaws (pp. 89–92, 98, 200).
*MUSEE du VIEUX-MARSEILLE. *Donation Camoin et Cie Exposition du Tarot de Marseille*. Marseilles. 1975.
*MUSEUM WILLET-HOLTHUYSEN. *In de kaart gekeken. Europese speelkaarten van de 15de eeuw tot heden*. Amsterdam. 1976. 131 pp. Ill. Catalog of playing card exhibition held in 1976 at Museum Willet-Holthuysen, Amsterdam (see also Mann).
MUTES. *Liber Maugetus*.
*MYER, Isaac. *Qubbalah. The Philosophical Writings of Solomon Ben Yehudah Ibn Gebirol or Avicebron and their connection with the Hebrew Qabbalah and Sepher ha-Zohar, etc*. Philadelphia. 1888. Reprinted 1970, 1972 and 1974. 497 pp. Describes the kabbalah.

N

N . . . v. d. "Het Kaartspel," *De Navorscher*. Jg. 3. pp. 74–75.
**NARAYANA, Maha Yogi A. S. [pseudonym of Alfred Schmielewski]. "The Space Age Tarot." Unpublished MS. Toronto. 1977. 159 pp. Ill. Ancient tarot system combines Von Daeniken's *Chariots of the Gods* and Tolkien's *Lord of the Rings* into 12 Major Arcana and 60 Minor Arcana.
NAVARRETE y RIBERA, Francisco de. *La casa del jeugo*. Madrid. 1644.
*NEBEHAY, Christian M. *List 85 — Old Playing Cards*. Vienna. [1964]. 65 pp. Ill. Describes 101 card packs from 1570–1860 offered for sale.
*NEROMAN, D., editor. *Grande Encyclopedie Illustree des Sciences Occultes*. Strasbourg. 1937. 2 Vols. 474 and 578 pp. Ill. Symbolism and interpretation of tarot (Vol. I, p. 61–154); text prepared by Solin Gallien and Oswald Wirth.
NEVILL, Lady Dorothy. *Under Five Reigns*. Playing cards were used as calling cards.
*NEWMAN, Emanuel S. *The Playing Card Information Circle*. Richmond. 1967–. Quarterly newsletter about history and development of cards.
*NEWMAN, Emanuel S. "Why Do You Collect Playing Cards?" *The Journal of The Playing-Card Society*. Manchester. August 1973. Vol. II. No. 1. pp. 12–13.
*NICHOLS, Sallie. "Hung Up . . . Or Redemption," *Psychological Perspectives*. Los Angeles. Fall 1976. Vol. 7. No. 2. Review of Sheldon Kopp's book, *The Hanged Man* (p. 237–241).
*NICHOLS, Sallie. "La Papesse," *Psychological Perspectives*. Pasadena. Fall, 1973. Ill. Describes the Popess tarot card (p. 135–149).
*NICHOLS, Sallie. *A Tarot Trip Into Jung's Psychology*. Unpublished MS. The Major Arcana are depicted as Jungian archetypes.
*NICHOLS, Sallie. "The Wisdom of the Fool," *Psychological Perspectives*. Pasadena. Fall, 1974. Ill. Describes The Fool card (p. 97–116). This article and "La Papesse" are part of a tarot book in preparation.
*NICOLAI, Alexandre. *Histoire de la carte a jouer en Guienne [etc]*. 1892. Bordeaux, 1911. sm 8vo. 132 pp. History of playing cards in the French region of Guienne.
NIEIASLAND. *Lectiones Memorabiles*. Vol. I.
NIEIASLAND. *Les Maitres cartiers de Bordeaux*. Bordeaux. 1905.
NOEL, M. "La fin de l'industrie cartiere lunevilloise au XVIIIe siecle," *Annales de l'Est*. 1966. No. 3.
*NORDHOFF, Charles. "Cards and Dice," *Harper's Monthly*. 1863. Vol. 26. Ill. History of playing cards with emphasis on gambling (p. 163–176).
*NORDIC, Rolla. *The Tarot Shows The Path [etc]*. England. 1960. 12mo. 127 pp. Ill. Fortune telling with Nordic tarot.
*NORRISS, Ruth Moore. "It's in the cards," *The Mentor*. Springfield, Ohio. March 1930. Vol. 18. No. 2. Ill. Anecdotes about playing cards (pp. 26–29, 58–61).
NOSTRADAMUS, Casar. *Historique et Chronique de Provence*. 1614. The author believes the first cards appeared in 1361 in Provence.
NOVATI, F. "La vita e le opere di Domenico Bordigallo," *Archivio Veneto*. 1880. Vol. XIX. pp. 5–45.
NOVATI, F. "Per la storia delle carte da giuoco in Italia," *Il libro e la stampa*. Milan. March-April, 1908. Ill. Origin and development of Italian playing cards (p. 54–69).
NOWOTNY, Fausta. "Die indischen Spielkarten des Museums fur Volkerkunde," *Archiv fur Volkerkunde*. Vienna. 1947. Vol. 2. pp. 1–25.
*NUMISMATICA. *Auktion XI. Spiele, Kartenspiele, Siegel*. Vienna. 1975. Ill. Auction catalog of antique playing cards.

O

THE OCCULT REVIEW. Edited by Ralph Shirley. London. Monthly magazine of super-normal phenomena includes articles on fortune-telling with cards (see Lewes) and tarot.
*O'DONOGHUE, Freeman. M. *Catalogue of The Collection of Playing Cards Bequeathed to the Trustees of the British Museum by the Late Lady Charlotte Schreiber*. London. 1901. 8vo. 228 pp. Includes description of several hundred tarot packs in the Schreiber Collection (see also British Museum).
OLDFIELD, Margaret. "Playing cards — The Surprising World of Print," *British Printer*. January/February 1955. pp. 46–48.
*OMWAKE, John. [Untitled booklet]. Cincinnati. 1928. 24mo. ob. 12 pp. Ill. Booklet contains facsimile of cards from the Clulow collection acquired in 1898 by the United States Playing Card Company.
*ORSINI, Julia. *Le Grand Etteilla ou L'Art de Tirer les Cartes [etc]*. Paris. Circa 1850. 12 mo. 209 pp. Ill. Fortune telling with Etteilla tarot cards.
*OSMONT, Anne. "Le Fou," *Le Voile d'Isis*. August-September 1928. Nos. 104–105. Ill. Short poem about The Fool (p. 559–561).
OSTROW, Albert A. *The Complete Card Player*. New York and London. 1945. 771 pp.

OSTUNI. *Novantanove Chimere*.
OTTLEY, W. G. *An Inquiry into the Origin and Early History of Engraving [etc]*. London. 1816. 2 Vols. Section on playing cards (Vol. I, p. 63–79).
*OUSPENSKY, P. D. "The Symbolism of the Tarot. Philosophy of Occultism in Pictures and Numbers," *A New Model of the Universe*. Translated by A. L. Pogossky. St. Petersburg. 1913. Reprinted London, 1938, and New York, 1976. Ill. 8vo. 65 pp. Describes the 22 Major Arcana.

P

*P.A. *Historische Entwicklung der Praktischen Regeln des Zigo-Taroc-Spieles [etc]*. Mannheim. 1860. 44 pp. Rules for game of tarock.
PABAN, Gabrielle (see Perenna).
PAPILLON, J. M. *Traite historique et pratique de la gravure en bois*.
*PAPUS (pseudonym of Dr. Gerard Encausse). "L'Annee 1913 et le Tarot," *Le Voile d'Isis*. January 1913. No. 37. pp. 3–4.
PAPUS (pseudonym of Dr. Gerard Encausse). "The Divinatory Tarot. Unpublished translation of *Le Tarot Divinatoire*.
*PAPUS (pseudonym of Dr. Gerard Encausse). *La Kabbale [etc]*. Paris. 1892. 8vo. 188 pp. Ill. Description of kabbalah, sephiroth and Tree of Life.
PAPUS (pseudonym of Dr. Gerard Encausse). *Le Livre de la Chance bonne ou mauvaise [etc]*. Paris. n.d. 150 pp.
*PAPUS (pseudonym of Dr. Gerard Encausse). *Le Tarot des Bohemiens*. Paris. 1889. Ill. Supports Egyptian origin of cards and describes tarot in terms of numerology, Tree of Life and the sacred Tetragrammaton known as Yod-He-Vau-He.
*PAPUS (pseudonym of Dr. Gerard Encausse). *Le Tarot Divinatoire: Clef du Tirage des Cartes et des Sorts*. Paris. 1909. Ill. Reconstitution of tarot symbols for divination with card illustrations by Gabriel Goulinat.
*PAPUS (pseudonym of Dr. Gerard Encausse). "Le Tarot divinatoire," *Le Voile d'Isis*. January 1909. No. 39. pp. 3–4.
PAPUS (pseudonym of Dr. Gerard Encausse). "Le Tarot divinatoire," *L'Initiation*. October 1907. Vol. 79. No. 1. pp. 5–8.
PAPUS. (pseudonym of Dr. Gerard Encausse). "Le Tarot divinatoire," *L'Initiation*. November 1908. Vol. 81. No. 2. pp. 102–105.
*PAPUS (pseudonym of Dr. Gerard Encausse). *The Tarot of the Bohemians. Absolute Key to Occult Science*. Preface by Arthur Edward Waite. Lon-

don. 1929. Many editions in print. 352 pp. Ill. Translation of *Le Tarot des Bohemiens*.

*PAPUS (pseudonym of Dr. Gerard Encausse). *Traité Elémentaire de Science Occulte Mettant* [etc]. Paris. 1888. 12 mo. 219 pp. Ill. Elementary text on occult science.

*PAPUS (pseudonym of Dr. Gerard Encausse). *Traite Methodique de Science Occulte*. Paris. 1891. Reprinted Paris, 1928. 8vo. Includes tarot, the Hebrew alphabet, and reproduction of Oswald Wirth tarot cards.

*PARLETT, David. "Romania Today," *The Journal of The Playing-Card Society*. Cranbrook. November 1976. Vol. V. No. 2. Playing cards of Romania (p. 23–25).

*PARLETT, David. "600 Years of Playing Cards," *Games & Puzzles*. London. March 1977. No. 58. pp. 4–7. Ill. One in a series of monthly articles that deals with history of playing cards and rules of card games.

PARLIAMENT ROLLS. England. 1464. Playing cards are mentioned among other articles not permitted for importation into England.

*PARRAVICINO, Emiliano di. "Three Packs of Italian Tarocco Cards," *Burlington Magazine*. London. December 1903. Vol. III. No. 9. Ill. Describes three incomplete Visconti-Sforza tarocchi packs: the 74-card Pierpont Morgan-Bergamo pack, 67-card Cary-Yale pack, and 48-card Brambilla-Brera pack (p. 237–247).

*PARSONS, Melinda Boyd. *To All Believers — The Art of Pamela Colman Smith*. Wilmington. 1975. 28 pp. Ill. Describes art of "Pixie" Smith in conjunction with exhibit at Delaware and Princeton Art Museums.

PASSAVANT, J. D. *Le Peintre graveur*. Leipzig. 1860. 8vo. Passavant doubts cards were known in 14th century Spain because a manuscript dating from 1321, composed by the order of Don Alphonso the Wise, fails to mention cards.

PASTEUR, Claude. "D'ou viennent les cartes a jouer," *Miroir de l'Histoire*. January 1964. No. 164. p. 64.

*PATCH, Howard R. *The Goddess Fortuna in Mediaeval Literature*. Cambridge. 1929. 215 pp. Ill. Describes the figure and symbolism of *Fortune* found in medieval literature.

*PAULNORD. "Le Tarot et la foi," *Le Voile d'Isis*. August-September 1928. No. 104-105. Ill. Briefly discusses tarot (p. 603–608).

PAWLOWSKI, G. "Cartes a jouer," *La Grande Encyclopedia* [etc]. Paris. 1885–1901. T. IX. p. 570.

*PEABODY INSTITUTE. *The Cardboard Court Playing Cards Through History*. Baltimore. 1960. 4to. Catalog of playing card exhibition.

PEARTREE (see Dodgson).

PECKELL, M. L. "The Evolution of Cards," *Connoisseur*. June 1913. 5 pp.

PEETERS, R. "De Turnhouste Speelkaartenindustrie," *Turnhout, Wereldcentrum van de Speelkaart*. 1965. p. 4-9.

**PEIGNOT, Gabriel. *Recherches historiques et litteraires sur les Danses des Morts, et sur l'origine des cartes a jouer* [etc]. Dijon and Paris. 1826. 8vo. 367 pp. Ill. Summarizes research on history and development of playing cards by Menestrier, Daniel, Bullet, Heineken, Bettinelli, Rive, Court de Gebelin, Breitkopf, Jansen, Ottley and Singer (p. 197–334).

PELADAN, Josephin. *La decadence Latine, Ethopee*. Paris. According to Papus, the works of Peladan include references to the tarot.

PELLEGRIN, E. *La bibliotheque des Visconti et des Sforza Ducs de Milan au XVe siecle*. Paris. 1955.

*PELLEGRINI, Amalia. "Le scienze ermetiche nei 'Tarocchi' di Domenico Balbi," *Vitalita*. May 1973. Anno 12. No. 128. Ill. Describes the Major Arcana painted by Domenico Balbi (p. 40–43).

PENN, William, Collection of Playing Cards (see Mann).

*PENN, William, "The Playing Card Collector," *The Antique Collector*. London. October 1957. Vol. 28. No. 5. Ill. Brief identification of playing cards (p. 177–182).

PERCIVAL, H. W., Ed. *The Word*. New York. 1904–1918. 25 Vols. Monthly magazine devoted to philosophy, religion, eastern thought and occultism including articles on the tarot by Paul Foster Case entitled "The Secret Doctrine of The Tarot".

PEREIRE, A. "Les cartes a jouer," *Revue de l'Art XX*. 1906. pp. 308–316. 316.

PERENNA, Aldegonde, Sibylle polonaise. *L'art de tirer les cartes et les Tarots* [etc]. Paris. 1826. 211 pp. Fortune telling with 52 and 78 cards.

PERENNA, Gabrielle (pseudonym of Gabrielle Paban). *L'art de dire la bonne aventure dans la main . . . aussi l'art de tirer les cartes* [etc]. Paris. 1818. Ill.

PERENNA, Gabrielle-Radegonde. *L'Art de dire la Bonne Aventure dans le marc de cafe, . . . de l'Art de tirer les cartes* [etc]. 2nd ed. Lerouge. 1819.

PERROUT, Rene. *Les Images D'Epinal*. Nancy. 1912. Folio. Ill. Edition limited to 300 sets. Includes reproduction of several 18th century tarot cards by Pellerin.

PETIBON, Andree. *Le Tarot. La Cabbale* [etc]. Paris. 1959. 12mo. 157 pp. Tarot in terms of the kabbalah and numerology.

PETIBON, Andree. *Le Tarot. L'Alchimie Mystique* [etc]. Paris. 1968. 12mo. 94 pp. Tarot in terms of astrological applications and alchemy.

PETIBON, Andree. *Le Tarot. Origine Mystique Des Arcanes* [etc]. France. 1953. 12mo. 110 pp. Ill. Edition limited to 1000. Tarot from the standpoint of mysticism, numbers, ancient alphabets and theology.

*PETRARCA, Francesco [Petrarch]. *Li sonetti Canzone e Triumphi*. Venice. 1513. 184 leaves. Ill. Describes six triumphs — Cupid, Chastity, Death, Fame, Time and Eternity — which Gertride Moakley associates with the tarot trumps.

*PETRARCA, Francesco. *The Triumphs of Francesco Petrarch*. Translated by Henry Boyd. London and Cambridge, Mass. 1906. Ill. Edition limited to 200 copies. English translation of Petrarch's *Trionfi*.

PETTIGREW, Thomas Joseph. "On the origin and antiquity of playing cards [etc]. and (The Knavery of the Rump)," *The Journal of the British Archeological Association*. London. 1853. Vol. IX. pp. 121–154, 308–329. Ill.

PEYRINS, Beneton Moranges de. "Dissertation sur l'origine des Jeux de Hasard [etc]," *Mercure de France*. Reprinted Vol. X; *Collection des meilleures dissertations* [etc]. (see Leber). September 1738. pp. 1908–1925.

PHILIPPE, A. "Plus anciennes cartes a jouer fabriquees a Epinal," *L'Art Populaire en France*. 1933. pp. 67–72.

*PHILLIPS, Henry D. *Catalogue of The Collection of Playing Cards of Various Ages and Countries*. London. 1903. 8vo. 125 pp. Describes tarot, tarocchino and minchiate packs in the British Museum.

*PIATNIK. *150 Jahre Piatnik 1824–1974*. Vienna. 1974. 61 pp. Describes 150 years of playing cards published by Ferd Piatnik & Sohne, Vienna.

PICARD, Eudes. "Le Tarot," *L'Annee occultiste et psychique*. 1908. No. 2.

*PICARD, Eudes. *Manuel Synthetique et Pratique du Tarot*. Paris. 1909. 8vo. 189 pp. Ill. Describes the tarot pack based upon astrological and numerological correspondences.

*PICARD, Eudes. *Manuale Sintetico e Pratico del Tarocco*. Rome. 1968. 8vo. 106 pp. Ill. Italian edition of *Manuel synthetique et pratique du tarot*.

PICART, Bernard. *Religious Ceremonies and Customs of the Several Nations of the World*. London. 1731. Contains incarnations of Vishnu which some occultists relate to Major Arcana cards.

PIGNORIUS, Laurentius. *Mensa Isiaca*. 1669. Reproduction of the Bembine Tablet.

PIKE, Albert. *Morals and Dogma of the Scottish Rites*. Reference to cards.

*PILZ, Kurt. *Tarok-Skat-17+4. Spielkarten in Nurnberg*. 1970. Catalog describes 188 decks.

PINCHART, Alexandre. "Recherches sur les cartes a jouer et sur leur fabrication en Belgique depuis l'annee 1379," *Le Bibliophile belge*. T. 4, 1869, pp. 5–13, 37–45, 69–75. T. 5, 1870, pp. 285–313. Early references to playing cards and development of Belgian cards.

PINDER, Eberhard. "Bube, Dame, Konig, As," *Merian*. 1955. Heft I. pp. 43–47.

PINDER, Eberhard. *Charta Lusoria. Spielkarten Aus Aller Welt Und Sechs Jahrhunderten*. Germany. 1961. 95 pp. Ill.

PINDER Eberhard. "Das Deutsche Spielkarten-Museum in Bielefeld," *Der Ravensberger*. 1955. Vol. 27. pp. 88–89.

PINDER, Eberhard. "Das Deutsche Spielkartenmuseum in Bielefeld," *Kulturarbeit*. 1962. Vol. 14. No. 8. p. 151.

PINDER, Eberhard. "Deutsches Spielkartenmuseum," *Der helle Kopf*. 1961. Vol. 9. No. 3. p. 14.

PINDER, Eberhard. "Das Deutsche Spielkarten-Museum in Bielefeld," *Graphische Woche*. December 21, 1964. No. 35/36. pp. 1538–1540.

PINDER, Eberhard. "Die Spielkarten des Israel van Meckenem im Rahmen der Kupferstichspiele des 15. Jahrhunderts," *Unser Bocholt*. 1964. No. 4. pp. 16–21.

PINDER, Eberhard. "Spielkarte und Kartenspiel," *Salve Hospes, Braunschweig*. July 1953. pp. 59–61.

PINDER, Eberhard. *Spielkarten Aus Funf Jahrhunderten*. Bielefeld. 1957(?) 12mo. 30 pp. Ill. Describes exhibition of 151 packs of playing cards at Deutsches Spielkarten Museum.

*PINDER, Eberhard. *Spielkarten Aus Sechs Jahrhunderten*. Bielefeld. n.d. 12mo. 10 pp. Ill. Early Asian and European playing cards including several tarots.

*PINDER, Eberhard. "The Development of European Playing Cards," *Graphis Magazine*. Zurich. 1955. Development of European playing cards including tarots and minchiate packs (p. 242–257).

PINDER, Eberhard. "Von Karo 7 bis Kreuz As," *Kriegsblinden-Jahrbuch 1957*. pp. 124–129.

PINTO, Isidore. *Lettre a Diderot sur le jeu de cartes*. Paris. 1768.

PIOBB [Pierre]. [Pseudonym of Comte Vincenti]. *Formulaire de Haute-Magie.* Paris. 1907.

PIOBB, P.V. *Clef universelle des sciences secretes.* Paris. 1950. Tarot and its symbolism.

PISARRI, Ferdinando. *Istruzioni necessario per chi volesse impare il giuoco dilettevole delli tarocchini di Bologna.* Bologna. 1754. 124 pp. Rules for the 62-card tarocchino di Bologna pack.

PITOIS, Jean-Baptiste (see Christian).

PLANCHE, James Robinson. "Notes on New Theories respecting the Fairford Window and early Wood-Engraving [etc]," *Journal of the British Archaeological Association.* London. 1871. 8vo. Vol. 27. pp. 103–109. Origin and antiquity of playing cards.

PLATINA, Baptista. *De Honesta Voluptate.* Venice. 1475. Reprinted 1480. Platina cites playing cards as a game to divert gentlemen's minds.

*PLAYING-CARD SOCIETY. [Bibliography of Books in the Collection of Sylvia Mann.] Rye [1973?] 10 pp. Lists 119 books in the Sylvia Mann Collection.

*PLAYING-CARD SOCIETY. *Journal of the Playing-Card Society.* Birmingham. 1972–. Quarterly journal on scholarly playing card research.

PONCE, Charles. *The Game of Wizards; psyche, science, and symbol in the occult.* Middlesex annd Baltimore. 1975. 240 pp. Ill.

POPE, Alexander. "The Rape of the Lock." 1712. Pope's famous poem on the game of ombre.

POPENOE, Cris. *Books For Inner Development.* Washington. 1976. 383 pp. Ill. Bibliography of 8,000 books in print dealing with all branches of esoteric wisdom including tarot.

POSTEL, Guillaume. *Clavis absconditorum a Constitutione Mundi.* 1546. Claimed discovery of the key to tarot but failed to disclose the secret.

POTTIER, Andre. "Sur une ancienne forme a imprimer des cartes a jouer," *La Revue de Rouen et de la Normandie.* June 1846. 5 pp.

POWELL, Nathan. *The New Universal Fortune Teller, or Complete Book of Fate: containing . . . Telling Fortunes by Cards, Dice, etc.* London. Circa 1800. 8vo. 92 pp.

*POWILLS, Dorothy. "Playing Cards," *Hobbies Magzine.* Popular articles deal with card collecting as a hobby.

P.R. "Un jeu de tarots peu connu," *Le Voile d'Isis.* August-September 1928. Nos. 104–105. pp. 183–184.

PRANGLEY, Ida B. *Fortune Telling by Cards* [etc]. London. 1899. *Reprinted London, 1975. 8vo. 80 pp. Ill. Fortune telling with 52 cards.

PRANGLEY, Ida B. *Ye Booke of Ye Cards. By Zuresta.* London. 1897. 89 pp. 89 pp.

PR[IMISSER]. "Spielkarten im 15. Jahrhundert," *Wiener Moden-Zeitung.* II. 1817.

PROBE. *Das astronomische Kartenspiel.* 1656, 1663, 1668, 1674.

PROVENZANO, Ferdinando. *La Voce del Collezionista (L'Uniforme).* Rome. 1972. 8vo. Ill.

*PRUNNER, Gernot. *Ostasiatische Spielkarten.* Bielefeld. 1969. sm 8vo. 149 pp. Ill. Catalog of an exhibition of antique Japanese, Chinese and Korean playing cards held at three German museums from December 1969 through June 1970.

**PUIGGARI, Joseph. "Joch de Nayps Catala del sigle XV," *L'Avens, Literari, Artistich, Cientifich.* Barcelona. October 1890.

*PULITZER, Walter. *Cupid's Pack of Cards.* Boston. 1908. 12mo. Ill. Contains an epigram for each card in the 52-card pack.

*PUPPI, Lionello. "A proposito di Bonifacio Bembo e della sua bottega," *Arte Lombarda.* Milano. 1959. Vol. IV. No. 2. Describes artwork of Benifacio Bembo including Visconti cards (p. 245–252).

*PUSHONG, Carlyle A. *The Tarot of the Magi.* London. 1967. 8vo. 111 pp. Ill. Fortune telling with tarot.

R

*R., P. "Un jeu de Tarots peu connu," *Le Voile d'Isis.* August-September 1928. Nos. 104–105. Credits the design of several tarot cards to Franciscus Bentivoglio, 1803, after the work of Joseph M. Mitelli (p. 583–584).

RABELAIS, Francois. *Gargantua.* Circa 1535. Includes list of games played by Gargantua but tarot is not one of them.

*RADL, Shirley L., and Carol A. Chetkovich, eds. *. . . And the Pursuit of Happiness.* Palo Alto. 1976. 224 pp. Ill. Describes 12 tarot decks and 7 books.

*RAGG, Ernst Rudolf, Editor. *Hofaemterspiel. Beruehmte Kartenspiele. Famous Packs of Playing Cards.* Vienna. 1976. 137 pp. Ill. Edition limited to 1000. Describes 15th century Hofaemterspiel cards of Ambras Castle and includes related articles by Michael Dummett, Detlef Hoffmann, Fritz Koreny and Georg Kugler.

*RAINE, Kathleen. *Yeats, The Tarot and the Golden Dawn.* Dublin. 1972. 8vo. 60 pp. Ill. Includes poems and mythologies by Yeats that contain symbols found in the tarot.

*RÁKÓCZI, Basil Ivan. *The Painted Caravan: A Penetration Into the Secrets of the Tarot Cards.* Holland. 1954. 8vo. 119 pp. Ill. History and development of tarot.

*RÁKÓCZI, Basil Ivan. *La Roulotte Initiatique. Initiation Bohemienne et Tarot.* Paris. 1967. 12mo. 254 pp.

RAMBAUD, P. "Les fabricants de cartes a Poitiers," *Bulletin de la Societe des Antiquaires de l'Ouest.* 1921. T. IV.

*RANDALL, Edith L., and Florence Evylinn Campbell. *Sacred Symbols of The Ancients.* North Hollywood. 1970. 198 pp. Significance of the 52-card deck and individual birth dates.

RANDALL, Edith L. *Your Place in the Cards.* Los Angeles. 1974. 8vo. 530 pp. Ill.

RANKING, D. F. del'Hoste. "The Graal Legend [etc]," *Transactions of the Royal Society of Literature.* 1918. Vol. 36. Refers to tarot trumps and the Grail Hallows.

*RANKING, D. F. dé L'Hoste. "The Tarot," *Journal of The Gypsy Lore Society.* Liverpool. July 1908-April 1909. Vol. II. Ill. Summarizes 18th and 19th century writers who researched the origin and meaning of tarot (p. 14–37).

RANSOME, Arthur. *Bohemia in London.* London. 1907. Includes chapter devoted to Pamela Colman Smith.

*RAWLINSON, George. *The Story of Ancient Egypt.* N.Y. 1888. 408 pp. Ill.

*RAWSON, Philip. *The Art of Tantra.* Greenwich. 1973. 216 pp. Ill. The Tantric *chakra* system and the tarot trumps may both derive in part from Indian Tantra.

*RAYMOND, Jane. "Italian Greyhounds Pictured on Fifteenth Century Playing Cards," *The Italian Greyhound.* Tallahassee. March-April 1977. Vol. XVIII. No. 6. Ill. Describes the use of Italian Greyhounds on four court cards of the Ambras Hofjagdspiel pack (p. 5–6).

REAVIS, Betsy. "A Pictorial Guide to the Tarot," *Probe The Unknown.* Burbank. January 1977. Ill. Fortune telling with tarot (pp. 30–37, 66).

*REBETEZ, Rene. *Tarot de Acuario.* Mexico. 1971. 16mo. 230 pp. Ill. Booklet accompanies the *tarot de acuario* pack.

*THE RED RABBIT (see Latham Lambert).

REEVES, James. *How to Read or Divine by the Cards.* London. [1898]. 8vo. 38 pp.

*REGARDIE, Israel. *A Garden of Pomegranates. An Outline of the Qabalah.* 2nd edition. St. Paul. 1970. 8vo. 160 pp. Describes the kabbalah.

*REGARDIE, Israel. *The Golden Dawn* [etc]. St. Paul. 1971. 8vo. Ill. 4 Vols. 226, 300, 276 and 368 pp. Description of the 78 tarot symbols with sample readings (Vol. 4, Book 8, p. 137–257).

REGLA, Paul Desjardin de. *El Ktab, ou le livre des choses connues et cachees* [etc]. Paris. 1911. 450 pp. Ill. Preface contains the Book of Thoth and Arab tarot; also includes explanation of tarot keys.

*REIF, Rita. "Antiques: Tarot Cards Reflect Changing Art Styles," *The New York Times.* April 3, 1976. Describes playing card exhibition in 1976.

*REIFF, Stephanie Ann. *Visions of the Future: Magic Numbers and Cards.* New York. 1977. 48 pp. Ill. Introduction to tarot and numerology for children.

REIFFENBERG, Fred. "De quelques professions relatives a l'imprimerie [etc]," *Le Bibliophile belge.* 1845. T. I. Playing cards and early printing (p. 290–299).

REIFFENBERG, Fred. *Sur d'anciennes cartes a jouer,"* *Bulletin de l'Academie royale des Sciences* [etc]. 9 octobre 1847. T. 14. No. 10. pp. 270–278.

REIFFENBERG, Fred. "Sur l'antiquite des cartes a jouer," *Bulletin de l'Academie royale des Sciences* [etc]. Brussels. 14 janvier 1838. T. 4. No. 2. pp. 66–68.

*REISIG, Otto. *Deutsche Spielkarten.* Leipzig. 1935. sm 12mo. 58 pp. Ill. Brief history of early playing cards with description of German cards including tarock.

*REISIG, Otto. *Die Kartenruckseiten in ihrer Bedeutung fur die zeitliche Festlegung der Spielkarten.* Altenburg. 1936. sm 8vo. Describes playing card back designs.

*REISIG, Otto. "Spielkarten," *Atlantis.* 1941. Heft 1. pp. 17–21.

RENIER, Ridolfo. "I tarocchi del Conte Matteo Maria Boiardo," *Rassegna Emiliana.* 1889. Vol. 1.

RENIER, Ridolfo. "Tarocchi di M. M. Boiardo," *Studi su Matteo Maria Boiardo.* Bologna. 1894.

REPTON, John Ady. "On the Costume of Coat Cards," *Gentlemen's Magazine.* November, 1843.

REY. "Origine francaise de la boussole et des cartes a jouer," *Nouvelles annales des voyages.* Paris. 1836. 8vo. Contends that the presence of fleur-de-lys on European playing cards confirms their French origin.

*RHEINHARDT, Rudolf H. "Fortunetelling with Regular Cards," *The Fireside Book of Cards* (see Jacoby). Fortune telling with 52 cards.

*RHEINHARDT, Rudolf H. *Whist Scores and Card-Table Talk with A Bibliography of Whist.* Chicago. 1887. 310 pp. Ill. History of playing cards and description of early European and Asian cards.

*RICCIULLI, Luigi, and Antonio Brunori. *Cartomanzia e Solitari.* Rome. 1948. 109 pp. Ill. Includes interpretation and symbolism of the Major Arcana.

RICHARDSON, Alan. *An Introduction to the Mystical Qabalah.* Liverpool. 1974. 63 pp. Brief mention of tarot cards relating to magical visualization.

*RICHMAN, Robert. *Richman's Book of Luck.* New York. 1970. 192 pp. Ill. Includes chapter on fortune telling with cards.

*RICHMOND, Olney H. *The Mystic Test Book or The Magic of the Cards.* Chicago. 1946. sm 8vo. 339 pp. Ill.

*RICHTER, Emil H. "The Tarocchi Prints," *Print Collector's Quarterly.* 1916. Describes the Tarocchi of Mantegna prints (p. 37–88).

*RICKWOOD, Gypsy. *Gypsy Rickwood's Fortune-Telling Book.* New York. n.d. 12mo. 125 pp.

RIJNBERK (see Van Rijnberk).

*RIJNEN, Lex. "Makers of Playing-Cards in the Netherlands," *The Journal of The Playing-Card Society.* Cranbrook. November 1975. Vol. IV. No. 2. pp. 34–37.

*RINGHIERI, Innocentio. *Cento giuochi liberali e d'ingegno.* Bologna. 1551. Reprinted Venice 1553 and Bologna 1580. 4to. References to playing cards (p. 131–133).

RINTCHEN, Biambyn. "Mongol kojur, le jeu de cartes mongol [etc]," *Studia Orientalia Edidit Societas Orientalis Fennica.* XVIII, 4. Helsinki. 1955. 7 pp.

RIOLS, J[ules] de. *Cartomancie ou art de tirer les cartes.* Circa 1903. 32 pp. Ill. Discusses tarot pack and cartomancy based upon Etteilla.

RIOLS, Jules. *Le Satanisme et La Magie.* The author believes tarot cards were brought to Europe by the gypsies.

RITCHIE, David Mac. "Tarot," *Encyclopedia of Occultism.* Edited by Lewis Spence. London. 1920.

•RIVE, M. l'Abbe [Jean Joseph]. *Eclaircissements Historiques et Critiques Sur L'Invention des Cartes a Jouer.* Paris. 1780. 16mo. 48 pp. Edition limited to 100 copies on large paper and 4 copies on vellum. Summarizes the origin and history of playing cards.

RIVE, M. l'Abbe [Jean Joseph]. *Historisch Onderzoech over de Speelkaarten.* Utrecht. 1781. 8vo. Dutch translation of Rive's treatise.

RIVE, M. l'Abbe [Jean Joseph]. *Notices historiques et critiques de deux manuscrits . . . de nouvelles conjectures sur l'epoque de l'invention des cartes à jouer [etc].* Paris. 1779. 4to. Edition limited to 100.

ROBA, Jean-Paul. *Tarots et cartes a jouer.* Port de Bouc. 1978. Ill. Catalog of tarot and playing card exhibition at Port de Bouc.

*ROBERTS, Richard. *Tarot & You.* New York. 1971. 8vo. 295 pp. Ill. Fortune telling with tarot.

ROBERTSON, A. A. "The Devil's Picture Book," *Scotland Magazine.* November 1954. pp. 40–41.

ROBINS, J. R. *Suggestions on the Origin of Playing-Cards [etc].* Brussels and London. 1870. 8vo. 71 pp.

*ROBINSON, Annalice. *Secrets of the Cards.* London. 1954. 95 pp. Ill.

ROBINSON, B. W., Editor. *Islamic Paintings and the Arts of the Book.* London. 1976. Describes Egyptian playing card fragments.

*ROBINSON, Mrs. Joe. *Playing Card Collector's Handbook Description and List. Bicycle Brand Playing Cards.* 1955. 8vo. 48 pp. Ill. Identifies Bicycle brand playing card back designs.

*ROGERS, Susan. "The 1970's? — It's In the Cards," *New York Post.* July 9, 1970. Newspaper article about tarot.

ROLT-WHEELER, Francis. *Cabbalisme Esoterique. I. Tarot esoterique, Arcanes majeurs et mineurs.* Nice.

*ROLT-WHEELER, Francis. *Le Tarot Medieval.* Nice. 1939. 8vo. 160 pp. Describes tarot pack based upon illustrations by Christian Loring.

ROLT-WHEELER, Francis. "Le Tarot Medieval," *L'Astrosophie.* Nice. July 1935 to November 1939. Illustrated by Christian Loring. The material in *Le Tarot Medieval* appeared in the *L'Astrosophie* magazine.

ROLT-WHEELER, Francis. "The Tarot I-XII," *The Seer.* Vol. 1. No. 1–6. Vol. 2. 1930.

RONDOT, N. *Les graveurs sur bois et les imprimeurs a Lyon au XVe siecle.* Lyon. 1896. References to playing cards (Chapter III).

RORET, Manuel. *Nouveau manuel complet du cartonnier, du cartier et du fabricant de cartonnages.* Paris. 1845.

*ROSART, Jacques-Francois. *The Type Specimen of Jacques-Francois Rosart. Brussels. 1768.* Amsterdam. Reprint 1973. 8vo. Ill. Tarotee back designs.

ROSENFELD, Hellmut. "Das Alter der Spielkarten in Europa und im Orient," *Borsenblatt.* 1960. Vol. 16. No. 14a. pp. 250–258.

ROSENFELD, Hellmut. "Das Alter des Kartenspiels und die Spielkarten bei den Juden," *Borsenblatt.* 1967. No. 102. pp. 3095–3097.

ROSENFELD, Hellmut. "Das Mainzer Kartenlosbuch von 1503/10 und die Spielkartentradition," *Gutenberg-Jahrbuch.* 1962. pp. 212–218.

ROSENFELD, Hellmut. "Das Schwein im Volksglauben und in der Spielkartenillustration," *Borsenblatt.* 1962. Vol. 18. pp. 622–625.

ROSENFELD, Hellmut. "Der Meister der Spielkarten und die Spielkartentradition und Gutenbergs typographische [etc]," *Borsenblatt.* 1964. Vol. 20. No. 61. pp. 1481–1484.

ROSENFELD, Hellmut. "Die altesten Spielkarten und ihre Farbzeichen," *Borsenblatt fur den Deutschen Buchhandel, Frankfurter Ausgabe.* 1956. No. 38a. pp. 636–642.

ROSENFELD, Hellmut. "Die Beziehung der europaischen Spielkarten zum Orient und zum Ur-Schach," *Archiv fur Kulturgeschichte.* 1960. XLII. pp. 1–36.

ROSENFELD, Hellmut. "Figurliche Ruckdrucke der Spielkarten des 16. und 17. Jahrhunderts," *Gutenberg-Jahrbuch.* 1964. pp. 312–319.

ROSENFELD, Hellmut. "Gab es im Mittelalter schablonierte Graphik und Spielkarten?" *Philobiblon.* 1958. Vol. 2. pp. 275–287.

ROSENFELD, Hellmut. *Munchner Spielkarten um 1500 ein Beitrag zur Datierung der Spielkarten des 15. und 16. Jahrhunderts.* Bielefeld. 1958. 27 pp. Ill.

ROSENFELD, Hellmut. "Neues uber alte Spielkarten," *Borsenblatt.* 1965. Vol. 21. pp. 2236–2237.

ROSENFELD, Hellmut. "Spielkarten als volkstumliche Massenkunst," *Borsenblatt.* 1961. No. 17. pp. 206–208.

ROSENFELD, Hellmut. "Zur Datierung der Spielkarten des 15. und 16. Jahrhunderts," *Borsenblatt.* 1958. Vol. 14. pp. 453–464.

ROSENFELD, Hellmut. "Zur Geschichte der Spielkarten Forschungsbericht 1965–1975," *Antiquariat.* 1976. pp. 286–297.

*ROSENFELD, Hellmut, and Erwin Kohlmann. *Deutsche Spielkarten Aus Funf Jahrhunderten.* Frankfurt and Leipzig. 1964. 51 pp. Ill. Development of cards from the 15th century to the present including tarock.

ROSENTHAL, Jacques. *Bibliotheca Magica et Pneumatica [etc].* n.d. 682 pp. Bibliography of 8875 books on occult sciences.

*ROSIERE, Gabrielle. *Fortune Telling and Character Reading.* New York. 1928. 243 pp. Contains several chapters on fortune-telling with cards.

*ROSS, Alan S. C., and F. G. Healey. "Patience Napoleon [etc]," *Proceedings of the Leeds Philosophical and Literary Society.* Leeds. September 1963. Volume X. Part V. Ill. Origin, development and rules for the game of patience (p. 137–190).

ROTH, H. "Spielkartendruck auf der offsetmaschine," *Offset-Buch und Werbekunst.* 1925, Heft 10. Ill. Offset printing of cards (p. 666-669).

ROTTGEN, Herwarth. "Das Ambraser Hofjagdspiel," *Jahrbuch der Kunsthistorischen Sammlungen in Wien.* 1961. Vol. 57. Describes the Ambras hunting pack (p. 39–68).

*ROTTGEN, Herwarth. *The Pack of Princely Hunting Cards of Ambras.* Leipzig. 1969. Text in German and English. 63 pp. Ill. Booklet accompanies the Ambras hunting cards.

ROWLANDS, Samuel. *The Four Knaves: A Series of Satirical Tracts.* London. 1611. Reprinted 1843. 136 pp. Ill. Reprint of four tracts dealing with English playing cards.

ROWLANDS, Samuel. *The Knave of Harts. Haile Fellow, Well Met.* London. 1612. Reprinted 1613. Ill.

ROWLANDS, Samuel. *A Mery Meetinge, or 'Tis Mery When Knaves Mete.* 1600. Reissued as *The Knave of Clubbs,* London, 1609. Reprinted 1615.

ROWLANDS, Samuel. *More Knaves Yet? The Knaves of Spades and Diamonds.* London. [1613?]. Ill.

RUFFY, Arthur G. "The Origins of Playing Cards," *Geographical Magzine.* December 1951. pp. 380–387.

RUMPF, Fritz. "Beitrage zur Geschichte der Fruhen Spielkarten," *Festschrift fur Adolph Goldschmidt zu seinem 70. Geburtstag.* Berlin. 1935. pp. 77–91.

RUMPF, Fritz. "Spielkarten," *Jahrbuch fur historische Volkskunde, III/IV.* Berlin. 1934. pp. 311–347.

RUMPF, Marianne. "Zur Entwicklung der Spielkarten in der Schweiz, in Deutschland und in Frankreich," *Schweizerischen Archiv für Volkskunde.* Basel. 1976. Heft 1–2.

RUMPLER, Susanna. *Vier Farben, das heisst: Die Deutschen Spielkarten in ihrer symbolischen Bedeutung beschrieben und erklart.* Leipzig. 1829. 345 pp. Ill. Meaning and symbolism of German playing cards.

*RUTHVEN, Noel. "Cards," *Frank Leslie's Popular Monthly*. July 1889. Ill. Origin and development of playing cards (pp. 21, 23–30).

*RYAN, Dr. Allan J. "Cards for Play and Profit," *Antiques*. December 1956. Vol. LXX. No. 6. Ill. Educational playing cards from the 16th to 20th centuries (p. 570–572).

RYAN, Mary E. *Telling Fortunes by Cards* [etc]. N.Y. 1927. Reprinted 1943.

*RYDELL, Wendy, with George Gilbert. *The Great Book of Magic.* New York. 1976. 271 pp. Ill. Brief mention of tarot and cartomancy.

S

*S.M.R.D. & Others. *The Tarot Book: The Secret Workings of the Golden Dawn*, Book "T". England. 1967. 8vo. 149 pp. Ill. Description of tarot by G. H. Soror based upon Order of the Golden Dawn.

SACHS, Paul J., Compiler. "The Tarocchi Cards," *A Loan Exhibition of Early Italian Engravings*. Cambridge. 1915. Ill. Describes Tarocchi of Mantegna exhibited at Fogg Art Museum (p. 103–153).

*SADHU, Mouni. *The Tarot. A Contemporary Course of The Quintessence of Hermetic Occultism.* London. 1968. 8vo. 494 pp. Ill. Describes the Major Arcana in 101 lessons.

SAINT-BONNET, Georges. *Le Tarot des Rose-Croix.* 1963. 12mo. 150 pp. Ill. Describes the Major Arcana.

SAINT-FOXE, Poullain de. *Oeuvres completes*. Paris. 1777. 12mo. 5 Vols. Includes dissertation on origin of playing cards.

SAINT-GENIES, Jehan. *Les cartes divinatoires provencales* [etc]. Paris. 1941.

*SAINT-GERMAIN, Comte C. de. *Practical Astrology. The Language of the Stars easily comprehended.* Binghamton. 1901. Reprinted 1931 and later editions. 12mo. 292 pp. Ill. Includes tarot pack with Egyptian symbolism (p. 168–257).

SAINT-LAMBERT, R. "La fabrication des cartes a jouer," *La France graphique*. Noel 1958. No. 144.

SAINT-LOUIS, P. Pierre de. *La Magdeleine au desert de la Sainte-Baume en Provence* [etc]. Lyon. 1668. 12mo. 216 pp. Playing cards and terminology popular in mid-17th century France.

*ST. MARTIN, Louis Claude de. *Tableau natural des Rapports* [etc]. Edinburgh. 1782. 8vo. 2 Vols. Allegedly St. Martin, founder of the Martinist order, based this book upon the 22 keys of the tarot.

SAINTRE, Petit-Jehan de (see Lasalle).

SALISBURY, James Louis. "The Tarot in Verse." Unpublished MS. Meanings set in verse of 22 Major Arcana and 40 of the Minor Arcana.

SALMI, Mario. *Italian Miniatures*. London. 1957. 214 pp. Ill. Reproduction of queen of swords and page of coins from Pierpont Morgan-Bergamo tarocchi deck.

SALMI, Mario. "Nota su Bonifacio Bembo," *Commentari*. 1953. pp. 7–15.

SALVERTE, Eusebe. *Des sciences occultes* [etc]. Paris. 1829. History of magic, initiation, and related subjects.

SAMUEL, Marcus. "British Playing Card Duties, 1711–1828; Further Information and Observations," *American Philatelist*. Phoenix. 1964. Volume 77, No. 12, and Volume 78, No. 1.

SAMUEL, Marcus. "Perkins, Heath, Bacon and Petch, Stamp Printers 1828–40," *The Philatelic Journal of Great Britain*. June 1972. 5 pp.

SANDRO, Pipozzo di. *Trattato del governo della famiglia*. Circa 15th century. Interpolation on playing cards.

SAULNIER, J.-P. "Histoire et reglementation de la carte a jouer," *La France graphique*. Noel 1958. No. 144.

SAULNIER, R. "Une lignee de Cartiers-Dominotiers bisontins," *L'Art Populaire en France*. 1934. pp. 69–75.

SAUNIER, Baudry de. "L'Enigme de la carte a jouer," *Gazette Dunlop*. June 1937. 4to. No. 202. Ill. Brief commentary on playing cards (p. 3).

SAUNIER, Marc. *La Legende des symboles, Philosophiques, religieux et maconniques*. Paris. 1911. Believes Major Arcana represent the knowledge of the universe.

SAWICKA, Slanislawa. *Dwie wloskie kartz "tarocchi" w zbriorach muzeum narodowego w Warszawie.* Warsaw. Describes two 15th century Italian cards at the National Museum of Warsaw and includes information about Visconti-Sforza tarocchi packs (p. 605–624).

*SCARNE, John. *Scarne's Complete Guide to Gambling.* New York. 1961. 714 pp. Brief history of playing cards.

SCHADENDORF, Wulf. "Peter Flotners Spielkarten fur Francesco d'Este," *Anzeiger des Germanischen Nationalmuseums 1954–1959*. Nurnberg. pp. 143–169.

SCHAER, Sidney C. "A Full House is One of a Kind," *Newsday*. February 24, 1976. Describes playing card collection of Dr. J. Richard Block (p. 4A–5A).

*SCHEMAHNI. *La Cartomancie Scientifique* [etc]. Paris. Circa 1923. sm 8vo. 340 pp. Ill.

SCHEMAHNI. *Le Tarot egyptien* [etc]. Paris. n.d.

SCHEMAHNI. *Precis de sciences magiques*. Tome II. Divination. Cartomancie. Paris. n.d.

SCHINDLER, R. "Die Spielkarte mit den vier himmlischen Tieren," *Historisches Jahrbuch der Stadt Linz*. 1957. pp. 379–381.

SCHLOSSER, J. V. "Giotto's Fresken in Padua [etc.]," *Jahrbuch der Kunstsammlungen* [etc]. Vienna. 1896. T. XVII. Describes Tarocchi of Mantegna cards (p. 13–100).

SCHMALZ, John Barnes. *Nuggets From King Solomon's Mine*. Boston. 1908. 12mo. 141 pp. Ill. Compares origin of cards to mathematical proportions of the Great Pyramid of Egypt.

SCHMIDT, Adolf. "Ein Schweizer Kartenspiel [etc]," *Quartalsblatter des Historischen Vereins* [etc]. 1899.

SCHMIELEWSKI, Alfred (see Maha Yogi A. S. Narayana).

SCHNEITER, Eugen. "Heraldik und Spielkarten," *Schweizer Archiv fur Heraldik*. 1943.

SCHOLEM, Gershom G. *On the Kabbalah and Its Symbolism*. Zurich. 1960. 12mo. 216 pp. Discusses the Tree of Life and symbolism of the kabbalah.

SCHOOLING, J. Holt. "Fortune Telling by Cards," *Pearson's Magazine*. London. May 1897. Vol. 3. p. 536.

SCHOTEL, G. D. J. "Lets over het kaartspel," *Noordbrabantsche volkmanak*. 1844. No. 2. pp. 77–92.

SCHREIBER, Lady Charlotte, Collection (see British Museum).

*SCHREIBER, W[ilhelm] L[udwig]. *Die altesten Spielkarten* [etc]. Strassburg. 1937. 8vo. 176pp. Early history and development of cards.

SCHRODER, Edward. "Das guldin Spiel von Meister Ingold," *Elsassische Litteraturdenkmaler aus dem XIV-XVII Jahrhundert*. Strassburg. 1882.

*SCHROEDER, Horst. "The Playing-Cards of Vital Berthin," *The Journal of The Playing-Card Society*. Birmingham. November 1974. Vol. III. No. 2. p. 12–18.

SCHROETER, Timon. *Spielkarte und Kartenspiel*. Leipzig. 1883. 140 pp. Includes German cards pasted on each page with explanatory poem.

SCHULZE, Kurt. "Spielkarten aus 5 Jahrhunderten," *Sachsische Heimatblatter*. Dresden. 1967.

SCHULTZ-JACOBI. "Tarok," *De Navorscher*. Vannee. 1855. pp. 321–328.

SCHUTZ, F. A. "Alte Spielkarten," *Serapeum*.

SCOTT, Amouret and Christoph. "From Tarot Packs to Modern Cards," *Country Life*. December 1960. pp. 1305–1307.

SCOUEZEC, Gwen Le. "La Cartomanzie," *Encyclopedie de la Divination-Cartomancie*. 1973.

**SEABURY, William Marston. *The Tarot Cards and Dante's Divine Comedy*. New York. 1951. Privately printed. 28 pp. Proposes that symbolism of tarot cards and Dante's *Divine Comedy* derive from same source.

 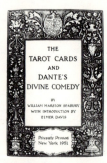 

*SEQUIN, Jean-Pierre. "Cinq Siecles de Cartes a Jouer en France," *Le vieux papier*. Paris. September 1963. 94 pp. Ill. Catalog of exhibition at Galerie Mansart.

SEQUIN, Jean-Pierre. "Fernande et le roi de pique," *Janus*. 1965. No. 8.

*SEQUIN, Jean-Pierre. *Le Jeu de Carte*. Paris. 1968. 8vo. 344 pp. Ill. Iconographic history of playing cards.

*[SEQUIN, Jean-Pierre, Cecile de Jandin and Marie-Therese Gourdon]. *La carte a jouer. Donation faile a la Bibliotheque Nationale*. Paris. 1966. 44 pp. Catalog of the Paul Marteau collection at the Bibliotheque Nationale.

*SELIGMANN, Kurt. *The Mirror of Magic* [etc]. Massachusetts. 1948. 8vo. 504 pp. Ill. Describes tarot (p. 409–434).

SEMAINE (La). *Histoire des cartes a jouer*. Text in French.

SEPHARIAL. *A Manual of Occultism*. London. 1910. Reprinted 1972. 8vo. 356 pp. Describes the Major Arcana in terms of spiritual, intellectual, psychic and physical applications.

SERGE. "Tireurs et Tireuses de Cartes," *Gazette Dunlop*. June 1937. No. 202. Ill. Brief discussion of card fortune-tellers (p. 6–7).

*SEVERN, Bill. *Packs of Fun, 101 Unusual Things to Do with Playing Cards and to Know about them*. New York. 1967. 8vo. 170 pp. Ill.

SEZNEC, Jean. *The Survival of the Pagan Gods*.

*SHADEGG, Stephen. "Cards, Gentlemen." 4 pp.

*SHAH, Idries. *The Sufis*. New York. 1964. 451 pp. Suggests tarot cards derive from the word *turug*, meaning four sections or ways (p. 449–450).

SHARPE, Rosalind (see also John Cooke).

SHARPE, Rosalind, and John Cooke, editors. *The Word of One: Aquarius Tarot Notes*. 414 pp. Ill. A series of teachings based upon 106 sessions using the ouija board and keyed to tarot cards.

SHASTRI, Haraprasad. "Note on Vishnupur Circular Cards," *As. Soc. Beng.* Calcutta. 1895. Vol. LXIV. p. 284.

*SHAW, Charles G. "The Versatile Playing Card," *Antiques.* February 1951. Vol. LIX. No. 2. Ill. Brief description of several European packs of cards (p. 120–121).

*SHENANDOAH VALLEY HIGH SCHOOL. *1977 Mirror.* Edited by Tim Twardzik. Shenandoah. 1977. 136 pp. Ill. High school yearbook features illustrations of tarot cards.

SHOWERS, Paul. *Fortune Telling For Fun and Popularity.* N.Y. 1942. 349 pp.

SICULO, Lucio Marinero. *Parallele entre la Jurisprudence espagnole et celle de France, relativement aux Jeux de Cartes.* 1686.

**SIEBER, Ludwig. "Thomas Murner and sein juristisches Kartenspiel," *Beitrage zur vaterlandischen Geschichte X.* Basel. 1875. Discusses Thomas Murner's educational cards (p. 273–307).

*SILVA, Henriques da, and Egas Moniz. *Tratado do jogo do Boston com a historia das cartas de jogar.* Lisbon. 1942. 8vo. 324 pp. Ill. History of playing cards.

*SIMON, J. M. *Know Your Future By Cartomancy.* Paris. Circa 1970. Tarot and cartomancy decks published by J. M. Simon, successor to B.-P. Grimaud.

*SINGER, Samuel Weller. *Researches into the History of Playing Cards with Illustrations of the Origin of Printing and Engraving on Wood.* London. 1816. 4to. 373 pp. Ill. Edition limited to 250. Origin and development of playing cards including appendix: (1) Extracts from poem on the game of Tarocco; (2) Reprint of Court de Gebelin's "*Du Jeu des Tarots, etc*"; (3) Reprint of Rive's "*Eclaircissements Historiques et Critiques sur l'Invention des Cartes à Jouer*"; and (4) Reprint of "*Recherches Sur Les Tarots, et Sur La Divination Par Les Cartes des Tarots,*" by M. Le C. de M. . . .".

SIVRY, L. de et Champagnac. *Dictionnaire des Pelerinages anciens et modernes [etc].* Paris. 1850. 2 Vols. According to Papus, Sivry describes the symbolism of the Major Arcana based upon gypsy lore.

*SMITH, Robert. "Account of the Italian Game of Minchiate," *Society of the Antiquaries of London.* November 1803. Describes the 97-card minchiate pack and rules of play based upon Vincenzio Londi, 1781 (p. 140–144).

SNIJDERS, C. J. *Beginselen der astrologie.* Amsterdam. 1940. Comparisons between the influence of the stars and tarot.

[SOLMS, Reinhard, Graf zu]. *Das sibend Buch ist ein Kartenspiel genant . . .* 1559. Ill.

SOMMI-PICENARDI, G. *Cremona durante il dominino de' Veneziani.* Milan. 1866.

SONEPUR, H. H., The Maharaja of. "A note on Ganjifa [etc]," *Journal of Bihar & Orissa Research Society.* Bihar. 1924. Vol. X. Pt. III. pp. 221–226.

*SONZOGNO, Edoardo. *Almanacco Della Commedia Umana Per Il 1886.* Milan. 1886. 12mo. 126 pp. Ill. Comical and satirical tarot scenes.

SORBELLI, A. "Un' antica stamperia de carte da giuoco", *Gutenberg-Jahrbuch.* 1940. pp. 189–197.

SOROR, G. H. [Sister G. H.]. "The Tarot Trumps," *The Secret Working of the Golden Dawn, Book "T", The Tarot.* England. 1967. 8vo. Description of the Major Arcana as glyphs of cosmic forces based upon the Golden Dawn (p. 89–99).

*SOTHEBY & CO. *The Celebrated De La Rue Collection of Playing Cards.* London. 1970. 40 pp. Ill. Auction catalog of playing card collection for sale.

*SPENCE, Lewis. *Arcane Secrets and Occult Lore of Mexico and Mayan Central America [etc].* Detroit. 1973. 8vo. 288 pp. Ill. Previously published as *Magic and Mysteries of Mexico,* London, 1930.

*SPENCE, Lewis. *An Encylopaedia of Occultism.* London. 1920. 451 pp. Ill. Summary of tarot and related occult subjects.

SPORHAN-KREMPEL, L[ore]. *Eine Handvoll Gluck. Plaudereien um Spielkarten und Kartenspieler.* Munich. 1958. 8vo. 108 pp. Ill. History of playing cards.

SPORHAN-KREMPEL, L[ore]. "Das Stuttgarter Kartenspiel," *Borsenblatt.* 1959. Number 76a. pp. 1151–1154.

SPORHAN-KREMPEL, L[ore]. "Nurnberger Kartenmacher," *Borsenblatt.* April 1962. Number 27a. Vol. 4. pp. 625–628.

*STAATSGALERIE STUTTGART. *Spielkarten aus aller Welt vom Mittelalter bis zur Gegenwart, aus dem Museum der Vereinigten Altenburger und Stralsunder Spielkarten-fabriken, Leinfelden bei Stuttgart, und aus deutschen Sammlungen.* Stuttgart. 1968. Folio. 104 pp. Ill. Describes playing card exhibition including tarots.

*STAHLY, F. "Modern Packs and Playing Card Tradition," *Graphis Magazine.* Zurich. 1949. Describes playing cards with surrealistic designs (pp. 174, 175, 194–197).

*STAR, Ely (pseudonym of Jacobs). *Les mysteres de l'Etre [etc].* Paris. 1902. Contains one chapter on tarot.

STAR, Ely. *Les Mysteres de l'horoscope [etc].* Paris. 1888. 383 pp. Reprinted Paris, 1925.

*STARKIE, Walter. *Carmen.* Edited by Dorle J. Soria. Italy. n.d. Ill. Describes tarot and Carmen.

*STARKIE, Walter. *In Sara's Tents.* New York. 1953. 323 pp. Ill. Includes origins of tarot and associations to gypsies.

**STEELE, Robert. "A Notice of the Ludus Triumphorum and some Early Italian Card Games with some Remarks on the Origin of the Game of Cards," *Archaeologia.* London. 1900. LVII. Series 2. Vol. III. References to playing cards including Sermones de Ludo Cumalis and description by Cicognara of the Visconti-Sforza and Gringonneur cards (p. 185–200).

**STEELE, Robert. "Early Playing Cards, Their Design and Decoration," *Journal of the Royal Society of Arts.* March 22, 1901. Vol. 49. Origin of playing cards and comparison of trump cards in Cary-Yale Visconti-Sforza tarocchi, Tarocchi of Mantegna and minchiate packs (p. 317–323).

*STEIGER, Brad, and Ron Warmoth. *The Tarot.* New York. 1969. 16mo. 168 pp. Ill. Describes in story form several methods of tarot divination.

STENRING. *Book of Formation.*

*STEVENSON, E. Irenaeus. *The Square of Sevens. An Authoritative System of Cartomancy.* New York. 1897. 72 pp. Fortune telling with 52 cards.

STRAPAROLA, Giovanni Francesco. *Les facetieuses nuits de Straparole.* Paris. 1857. French translation of 16th century poem with a riddle of the four suits and vague references to tarot trumps.

STRAUSS, Walter L. *The Complete Drawings of Albrecht Durer.* New York. 1974. 6 Vols. Ill. Reproduction of 21 tarocchi of Mantegna cards credited to Durer (Vol. I).

STROBL, Andreas. *Das Geistliche Teutsche Karten-Spil [etc].* Sultzbach. 1691. 4to.

**STRUTT, Joseph. *The Sports and Pastimes of the People of England.* London. 1876. Ill. Early references to cards and games (pp. 47, 423–437).

*STUART, Micheline. *The Tarot: Path to Self-Development.* Boulder & London. 1977. 58 pp. Ill. Describes 22 Major Arcana cards in terms of self-development; illustrations are from the Tarot of Marseilles pack.

STURZAKER, Doreen and James. *Colour and the Kabbalah.* 287 pp. Meanings and concepts of colors related to tarot trumps and the kabbalah.

*STURZAKER, James. *Kabbalistic Aphorisms.* London. 1971. 118 pp. The kabbalah and the tarot trumps.

*SUMA, Wolfgang. "German-suited Hunting-cards and Single-figure Cards of the Prussian Patterns," *The Journal of the Playing-Card Society.* Birmingham. February 1976. Volume IV. No. 1. Ill. Discusses hunting cards of German and Prussian origin (p. 1–7).

*SUMA, Wolfgang. "The Prussian Pattern," *The Journal of The Playing-Card Society.* Birmingham. February 1975. Vol. III. No. 3. pp. 1–21. Ill.

*SUMA, Wolfgang. "The Spielkarten Museum, Altenburg," *The Journal of The Playing-Card Society.* February 1974. Vol. II. No. 3. pp. 27–29.

SUSIO, Giambattista. ___. Circa 1570. Poem associates ladies of the court of Mantua with the tarocchi trumps.

SUZUE, Junya (see Alexand Mokuseioh).

SZCZEPANSKI, J. *Tarok. Zasady i sposob gry.* Krakon. 1910. 47 pp.

T

*TAYLOR, Rev. Ed. S. *The History of Playing Cards with Anecdotes of their Use in Conjuring, Fortune-Telling, and Card-Sharping.* London. 1865. 16mo. 529 pp. Ill. Origin and development of playing cards including chapter on cartomancy and tarot. This book is practically a translation of the earlier work by P. Boiteau D'Ambly.

*TAYLOR, Fred G. "Playing Cards As Reflectors of the Passing Scene," *The Journal of The Playing-Card Society.* Manchester. August 1972. Vol. I. No. 1. pp. 8–10. Ill.

*TAYLOR, Fred G. "Some Sober Thoughts on Austrian Playing Card Tax Stamps." Unpublished MS. Prague. 1960. 5 pp.

[TAYLOR, Joseph?]. *Curiosities for the Ingenious.* London. 1821. 16mo. 192 pp. Includes references to origin of playing cards.

TESTE d'OUET. *Jacquemin Gringonneur et Nicolas Flamel.* Paris. 1855. 64 pp. Research on Gringonneur and Charles VI.

TEXTOR RAVISIUS. *Theatrum poeticum.* L. IV. C. 49. Suggests playing cards were invented by "perditis hominibus" or the heathens.

THACKERAY, William Makepeace. *The Orphan of Pimlico.* London. 1876. 10 pp. Ill. Transformation cards by Thackeray.

THIERENS, A. E. *The General Book of the Tarot [etc].* London. n.d. Philadelphia. 1928. 8vo. 158 pp. Discusses tarot and astrology.

THIERS, M. Jean Baptiste. *Traite des Jeux et des Divertissemens.* Paris. 1686. 12mo. 481 pp. Cites the Synod of Langres which forbade the playing of dice, trictrac and cards by the clergy.

*THORPE, C. *Card Fortune Telling.* London. 1972. 63 pp. Ill. Fortune telling with 52 and 78 cards.

THYLBUS [pseudonym of P. C. Jagot]. *Les cartes et les tarots [etc].* Paris. n.d. 12mo. 222 pp.

*TIDIANEUQ. "Utilisation du Symbolisme du Tarot dans la voyance," *Le Voile d'Isis.* Aug.-Sept. 1928. Nos. 104–105. Ill. Tarot symbolism (p. 614–624).

*TILLEY, Roger. *A History of Playing Cards.* London. 1973. sm 4to. 191 pp. Ill. Origin and development of cards.

*TILLEY, Roger. *Playing Cards.* New York. 1967. 8vo. 120 pp. Ill. Early playing cards including tarot and minchiate packs.

*TISSOT. *Tours de cartes recueil complet.* Paris. sm 8vo. 152 pp.

TJAN, Tjoe-Siem. *Javaanse kaartspelen.* Bandoeng. 1941. 8vo. 168 pp.

TOESCA, Pietro. *La pittura e la miniatura nella lombardia.* Milan. 1912.

TOESCA, Pietro. *Uffizióla Visconteo Landau-Finaly.* Florence. 1951.

**TOPPAN, George L., Hiram E. Deats and Alexander Holland. *An Historical Reference List of the Revenue Stamps of the United States including

the Private Die Proprietary Stamps. Boston. 1899. Includes American playing card revenue tax stamps used 1864–1895 (p. 108, 326–332).
TORREBADELL MORTES, Carles. *Fets d'un jugador o vuits i nous i cartes que no lliguen*. Barcelona. 1935.
*****TORRENS**, R. G. *The Golden Dawn. The Inner Teachings*. New York. 1973. 12mo. 208 pp. Includes tarot cards.
*****TORRENS**, R. G. *The Secret Rituals of the Golden Dawn*. New York. 1973. 12mo. 304 pp. Ill. Describes secret rituals and ceremonies of the Golden Dawn.
TORRESINO, Giacomo. [Notes]. Contains Bordigallo's *Chronicles*.
TOUCHE, Francois. "Les cartes ne servent-elles qu'a jouer," *Gazette Dunlop*. June 1937. Number 202. Ill. pp. 14–16. Brief description of cards in 18th and 19th centuries used for purposes other than playing cards, such as calling cards.
*****TRARIEUX**, Gabriel. "La divination par le Tarot," *Le Voile d'Isis*. August-September 1928. Nos. 104–105. The success of tarot for fortune telling is because of the multiple interpretations of each card (p. 609–613).
TREASE, Geoffrey. *The Condottieri. Soldiers of Fortune*. N.Y. 1971. 376 pp. Describes 15th century Italy and Visconti and Sforza families.
TREMEAU de ROCHEBRUNE, Alphonse. "Notice sur un jeu de cartes ... regne de Francois 1er et sur un jeu de 1760," *Revue de l'Aunis, de la Saintonge et du Poitou*. Niort. August 25, 1867. Ill. Describes two packs of 18th century playing cards (p. 74–84).

TRIMM, Timothee [pseudonym of A. J. N. Lespes]. *Histoire authentique et complete de tous les moyens de lire l'Avenir* [etc]. Paris. 1892.
TRISMEGISTE, Johannes (pseudonym of Lorambert). *Bibliotheque du Destin, l'art de tirer les cartes* [etc]. 1843.
TRISMEGISTE, Johannes (pseudonym of Lorambert). *L'art de tirer les cartes francaises* [etc]. Paris. Circa 1860. Reprinted 1867.
TRISMEGISTE, Johannes (pseudonym of Lorambert). *L'art de tirer les cartes, revelations complete sur les destinees au moyen des cartes et des tarots illustres*. Paris. 1849. 1850.
*****TRISMEGISTE**, Johannes (pseudonym of Lorambert). *Manuel Illustre de Cartomancie* [etc]. Paris. 1867. 24mo. 192 pp. Ill. Fortune telling with tarot cards of Egyptian design.
TRITHEME [Jean]. *Traite des causes secondes precede d'une vie de l'auteur* [etc]. Paris. 1897. Contains commentary on Major Arcana.
TRUMPF, Peter (pseudonym of Rolf Staedale). "Cartes a jouer de notre temps," *Typographische Schweizer Monatsblatter*. 1958. Vol. 77. p. 465.
●***TRUMPF**, Peter (pseudonym of Rolf Staedale). *Die Spielkarte*. Germany. 1957. sm 8vo. 48 pp. Ill. History of cards in celebration of 125th anniversary of Altenburger und Stralsunder Spielkarten.
●**TRUMPF**, Peter (pseudonym of Rolf Staedale). *Kartenspiele und Spielkarten*. Munich. 1966. 8vo. 159 pp.
●**TRUMPF**, Peter (pseudonym of Rolf Staedale). *Spielkarten und Kartenspiele*. Heidelberg and Munich. 1958. 8vo. 187 pp.
*****"TRUMPS."** *The American Hoyle* [etc]. New York. 1864. 491 pp. Ill.
TUMMERS, Louis. "Les cartes a jouer," *Bulletin de l'Amicale du Personnel du Ministere des Communications*. Anderlecht. [1957]. 8vo. 59 pp.
TUMMERS, Louis. "De geschiedenis van der speelkaarten in Belgie," *Ons Heem*. XXI. Brussels. 1968. p. 193–230. History of playing cards in Belgium.
TUMMERS, Louis. *De geschiedenis der speelkaart in Belgie*. Brussels. 1968.
TUMMERS, Louis. *History of Playing Cards in Belgium*. Turnhout. 1957. 8vo. 32 pp.
*****TUMMERS**, Louis. "The History of Playing-Cards in Belgium," *The Journal of The Playing-Card Society*. Birmingham. Part I — Vol. IV, No. 1, August 1975, pp. 1–19. Part II — Vol. IV, No. 2, November 1975, pp. 15–27. Ill. Enlarged and reprinted, Brussels. History of Belgian cards.
TUMMERS, Louis, and J. M. Berjani. "Cinq siecles de cartes a jouer," *La Cite*. 1957.

U

U.S. GAMES SYSTEMS, INC. [Catalog]. New York. 1970–1977. Annual catalog published by U.S. Games Systems, Inc. Describes popular tarot decks, tarot books and cartomancy products.
U.S. GAMES SYSTEMS, INC. *Mail Bid Auction Catalog*. July, 1971. Vol. I, No. 1. Decks and books offered for sale.
U.S. GAMES SYSTEMS, INC. *Mail Bid Auction Catalog*. November, 1971. Vol. I. No. 2. Decks and books offered for sale.
*****U.S. PLAYING CARD CO.** *The Official Rules of Card Games*. 29th edition. Cincinnati. 1926. 240 pp. Rules for popular card games.
*****U.S. PLAYING CARD CO.** *Fortune Telling With Playing Cards*. Cincinnati. 1921. 12 pp. Fortune telling with cards.
●**ULMANN**, S. *Illustrirtes Wiener Tarokbuch Leitfaden zur Erleenung aller Arten des Tarokspiels*. Leipsig. Circa 1888. 180 pp. Ill. Tarock rules.
UNBEGAUN, B. O. "Cards and Card-Playing in Muscovite Russia," *Slavonic and East European Review*. December 1962. Vol. 41. pp. 25–30.
●**UNGER**, Von Franz. *Tarock*. Vienna. 24mo. 32 pp.
USPENSKIJ [Ouspensky], Piotr Demaianovic. "El simbolismo del Tarot," *Un nuevo modelo del Universo*. Mexico. 1950. pp. 223–259.
USSHER, [Percy] Arland. *The XXII Keys of the Tarot*. Dublin. 1957 and 1969. 54 pp. Ill.

V

*****VAILLANT**, J. A. *Les Rômes, histoire vraie des vrais Bohémiens*. Paris. 1857. 8vo. Describes tarot designs as heirlooms of Hindustani wisdom.
VALLANCE, Aymer. "The Modern Playing Card and its Possibilities," *The Artist*. London. December 1896. Vol. 27. pp. 568–573.
VALOUX, G. du. "Les Arcanes majeurs du Tarot," *Le Voile d'Isis*. January 1920. Origin of tarot and analogy between cards and zodiac signs (p. 20–43).
VAN AUTENBOER, Eugeen. *Turnhout Great Mogul*. Brussels. 1975. Text in Dutch, French and English. 64 pp. Describes the *Great Mogul* pack issued originally by Van Genechten, Turnhout, circa 1900.
VAN AUTENBOER, Eugeen. *Turnhout Playing Cards 1826–1976*. Brussels. 1976. 152 pp. Ill. History of playing card manufacturer at Turnhout.
VAN AUTENBOER, EUGEEN. "Verboden kaartenspel in vroegere tijden," *Turnhout, Wereldcentrum van de Speelkaart*. Turnhout. 1966. Card games prohibited in olden times.
VAN AUTENBOER, EUGEEN. *Waaryeggerijen Speelkaart*. Turnhout. 1973. Fortune-telling and plaving cards.
VAN BUREN, Anne H. and Sheila Edmunds. "Playing Cards and Manuscripts: Some Widely Disseminated Fifteenth-Century Model Sheets," *The Art Bulletin*. 1974. I/LVI. Describes 15th century manuscripts and engravings that contain playing card motifs of animals, birds and flowers.
*****VAN RENSSELAER**, Mrs. John King. *The Devil's Picture Books. A History of Playing Cards*. New York. 1895. 8vo. 207 pp. Ill. History of playing cards including brief section on tarot.
VAN RENSSELAER, Mrs. John King. "Playing Cards from Japan," *Science Magazine*. June 5, 1891.
*****VAN RENSSELAER**, Mrs. John King. *Prophetical Educational and Playing Cards*. Philadelphia. 1912. 8vo. 392 pp. Ill. History of tarot cards from Egyptian origins.
*****VAN RIJNBERK**, Gerard. *Le Tarot. Histoire Iconographie Esoterisme*. Lyon. 1947. 8vo. 367 pp. Ill. Tarot iconography and symbolism, origin of cards, plus extensive bibliography.
VAN TENAC, Prof. *Academie des Jeux* [etc]. Paris. 1858.
VAN TENAC, Prof. *Album des jeux de hasard* [etc]. Paris. 1850. 12mo. 2 Vols. Rules for the games of piquet (Vol. I.) and whist (Vol. II).
VAN TENAC, Prof. *Bibliotheque des jeux de cartes, ou Regles des principaux jeux* [etc]. Paris. 1854. 6 Vols.
VERNEUIL, Marianne. *Dictionnaire Practique des Sciences Occultes*. Monaco. 1950. 8vo. 489 pp.
VEYRIER, H. *Encyclopedie de la divination*. Madrid. 1973.
VEZE, J. Marcus de. "A propos d'un Tarot persan," *L'Initiation*. September 1889. Vol. 4. No. 12. pp. 264–265.
VIDAL, L. "Sur la composition des cartons pour cartes a jouer au XVIII siecle." *Contribution a l'histoire de la Papeterie en France*. Vol. I.
VIEUX PAPIER, LE. *Bulletin de la Societe Archeologique et Artistique*. Paris. 1900–1929, 1961–. Includes articles on playing cards (Vols. I–IV, VII–XI, XIV–XVII, XX, XXIII and XXIV).
VILLARET. *Histoire de France*. Paris. 1770. Reference to cards (p. 308).
VINOLA y LARDIES, V. *Manual de Barajas Mitologicas*. Barcelona. 1901.
VIRESWARA. *Ganjifa Khelana (Sanskrit Poem)*. MS. No. 3843 at Bikaner Library. Describes Persian origin of game of Ganjifa with rules of play.
VIVES, Ludovico (Joan Ludovicus?). *Ludus Chartarum, Dialogus*. 1545. 12mo. Contains one of earliest published references to game of tarocchi.
LA VOCE DEL COLLEZIONISTA. Rome. Bi-monthly magazine. Ill. Monthly feature article by Vito Arienti, leading Italian playing card collector, reviews new decks and books.
VOISIN, H. "Bandes et enveloppes de jeux de cartes," *Le vieux papier*. 1919. No. 3.
VOLATERRANI, Raphaelis. [Il Volterrano and Raphaelus Maffei]. *Commentariorum (Volateranus Commentariorum Urbanorum)*. 1506. Later editions 1511, 1515, *1530, 1544, 1552. Folio. Brief reference to cards (p. 347) but no mention of tarot.
●**VOLCKMANN**, E. *Alteste Deutsche Spielkarte von 1475*. Altenburg. 1927.

VOLGUINE, A. *Utilisation du tarot en astrologie judiciaire.* Paris. 1933. 8vo. 30 pp. Tarot based upon astrology and the zodiac.

**VOORHIS, Harold V. B. *Arthur Edward Waite: A Check List of His Writings.* New Jersey. 1932. 14 pp. Ill. Lists the works of which Arthur Edward Waite either was author, compiler, translator, editor, or writer of preface or foreward.

VOREL, Irys. "How the Gypsies Use the Tarot," *Fate Magazine.* February 1955. Vol. 8. No. 2. No. 59. Ill. Fortune telling with tarot (p. 26–36).

W

*WAGER-SMITH, Elizabeth. *Skat. Principles and Illustrative Games.* Philadelphia and London. 1910. 16mo. 225 pp. Rules of the game of Skat derived from games known to the Wends, wandering Slavonic tribe which appeared in Germany in the 6th century.

WAITE, Arthur Edward. *The Brotherhood of the Rosy Cross.* London. 1924. 649 pp. Brief reference to tarot trumps and the Hebrew alphabet.

WAITE, Arthur Edward. "The Great Symbols of the Tarot," *The Occult Review.* February 1926. T. 43. No. 2. pp. 83–91.

*WAITE, Arthur Edward. *The Hidden Church of the Holy Graal: Its Legends and Symbolism.* London. 1909. 714 pp. "The Hallows of the Graal Mystery Rediscovered in the Talismans of the Tarot," (Chapter IX), deals with the symbolism of tarot cards; Chapter IX was rewritten as an appendix in *The Holy Grail.* Waite associates wands with diamonds (instead of clubs) because the diamond shape is similar to the head of a weapon.

WAITE, Arthur Edward. *The Holy Grail.* London. 1933. Waite suggests the four sacred objects of the Grail legends — cup, lance, dish and sword — reappear as tarot suits of cups, batons, coins and swords.

*WAITE, Arthur Edward. *The Holy Kabbalah* [etc]. New York. 1960. Reprint. 8vo. 636 pp. Comprehensive history of kabbalah.

*WAITE, Arthur Edward. *The Key to the Tarot. Being Fragments of a Secret Tradition under the Veil of Divination.* London. 1910. 24mo. 212 pp. Reprinted many times. Fortune telling with the Rider-Waite tarot pack.

WAITE, Arthur Edward. *The Mysteries of Magic.* London. 1886. sm 8vo. 349 pp. Digest of the writings of Eliphas Levi includes mysticism of the Major Arcana (p. 236–265).

*WAITE, Arthur Edward. *The Pictorial Key to the Tarot. Being Fragments of a Secret Tradition under the Veil of Divination.* London. 1910. Ill. Same as *The Key to the Tarot* but includes black and white illustrations of the Waite cards.

WAITE, Arthur Edward. "Review of *Le Tarot des Imagiers du Moyen Age* by Oswald Wirth," *The Occult Review.* May 1928. Vol. XLVII. No. 5. Review of Wirth's famous work on tarot (p. 347–348).

WAITE, Arthur Edward. *Rituals of the Holy Order of the Golden Dawn.* 1910. Privately printed. The Ceremony of Advancement contains explanation of the 21st tarot key (p. 25–27); the 20th tarot key with diagrams (p. 37–38) and the 18–16th tarot keys (p. 26–30).

*WAITE, Arthur Edward. *Shadows of Life and Thought.* London. 1938. 288 pp. Ill. Autobiography of Waite includes events surrounding Pamela Colman Smith's preparation of the Rider-Waite pack.

WAITE, Arthur Edward. "The Tarot: A Wheel of Fortune," *The Occult Review.* December 1909. Vol. X. No. 6. Discusses the 4th edition of *A Manual of Cartomancy* by Grand Orient (Waite) (p. 307–317).

WAITE, Arthur Edward. "The Tarot; an Antique Method of Divination," *Walford's Antiquarian Magazine.* October 1887. Vol. XII. No. 4. Introductory article on tarot for the layman (p. 210–213).

WAITE, Arthur Edward. "The Tarot and the Secret Tradition," *The Occult Review.* March 1919. Vol. XXIX. No. 3. pp. 157–161. Contain an article on tarot stimulated by an earlier article, "The Tarot Cards," by Brodie-Innes which appeared in *The Occult Review* for February 1919 and which in part is a critique of Waite's views.

WAITE, Arthur Edward. "The Tarot and the Secret Tradition," *The Occult Review.* November 1920. Vol. XXXII. No. 5. Reply (p. 303) to a previous letter by Brodie-Innes entitled "The Problem of the Tarot Cards" which appeared in *The Occult Review* for August 1920.

WAITE, Arthur Edward. (see also Grand Orient).

WAITE, Arthur Edward. (see also introductions by Waite to Levi's *Le Dogme et Rituel de la Haute Magie,* Papus' *Tarot of the Bohemians,* Stenring's *Book of Formation* and Thieren's *General Book of the Tarot.*)

WAITE, Arthur Edward. Also see Voorhis.

*WALDBERG, Patrick. *I Tarocchi di [Franco] Gentilini.* Rome. Circa 1975. 20 pp. Ill. Booklet describes the Major Arcana cards of Franco Gentilini.

*WALDBERG, Patrick. *I Tarocchi di Gentilini.* Torino. 1975. Ill. Brief description of the history of tarot cards and the Gentilini tarocchi deck with photographs of the artist at work.

*WANG, Robert. "The Golden Dawn Tarot," *Gnostica.* St. Paul. February/March 1977. Vol. 5. No. 5. Ill. Brief description of the Golden Dawn tarot deck (p. 18–19).

WANG, Robert. *An Introduction to the Golden Dawn Tarot.* New York. 1977. Ill. Brief introduction to the Golden Dawn tarot.

WANG, Robert. "The Last Secret of The Golden Dawn: The Tarot," *New Dimensions.* London. December 1976. Ill. Describes the Golden Dawn tarot deck.

WANG, Robert. *The Mystical Tarot: A Treatise on the Qabalistic System of the Hermetic Order of the Golden Dawn.* Comprehensive work on the Golden Dawn tarot deck.

WANG, Robert. *Notes on the Golden Dawn Tarot.* New York. 1977. Booklet accompanies the Golden Dawn tarot deck.

WARNER, Rebecca Micca. *Tarot.* New York and London. 1974. 87 pp. Ill. Fortune telling with tarot cards.

WARTON. *History of English Poetry.* Vol. II. The author claims the Arabians were inventors of cards, which they communicated to the Greeks at Constantinople (p. 316).

*WASSERMAN, Jim. *The Book of Thoth.* New York. 1977. Booklet accompanies Crowley's Thoth tarot.

WATSON, Julie A. "Beginner's Tarot Class." Unpublished MS. Hialeah. 1975. 48 pp. Six lectures on tarot with interpretations drawn from Waite and Gray.

*WAYLAND, Harold and Virginia. "John Lenthall: Purveyor of Playing Cards," *The Journal of The Playing-Card Society.* Manchester. August 1972. Vol. I. No. 1. Describes the life of John Lenthall who reissued many 17th and 18th century playing cards (p. 2–3).

*WAYLAND, Harold and Virginia. [The Lenthall Packs]. Articles on Lenthall Packs in *The Journal of The Playing-Card Society*: 1 Heraldry Cards (Vol. I, No. 2.); 2 Traveling Cards (Vol. I. No. 3); 3 Navigation Cards (Vol. I, No. 4); 4 Map Cards (Vol. II, No. 1.); 5 Astronomical Cards (Vol. II, No. 2); VI Geographical Cards (Vol. II, No. 4); VII Mathematical Cards (Vol. II, No. 3); VIII Geometrical Cards (Vol. III, No. 2); IX Cosmographical Cards (Vol. III, No. 4); X Cookery and Pastry Cards (Vol. IV, No. 3); XI Carving Cards (Vol. IV, No. 4); XII British Cards (Vol. V, No. 1); XIII Historiographical Cards (Vol. V, No. 2); XIV Grammatical Cards (Vol. V, No. 4).

WAYLAND, Virginia (see also Mann).

*WAYLAND, Virginia (see also Mann). "Apache Playing Cards," *Expedition.* The Bulletin of the University Museum of the University of Pennsylvania. Philadelphia. 1962. Vol. 4. No. 3. Ill. Describes two 19th century Apache Indian playing cards (p. 34–39).

*WAYLAND, Virginia (see also Mann). "Apache Playing Cards," *Southwest Museum Leaflets.* Los Angeles. 1961. No. 28. 18 pp. Ill. Describes 19th century Apache Indian playing cards.

*WAYLAND, Virginia (see also Mann). *Apache Playing Cards from the Wayland Collection.* Wayland Playing Card Monograph No. 3. Pasadena. 1972. 8vo. 10 pp. Ill. Describes 19th century Apache Indian playing cards.

WAYLAND, Virginia (see also Mann). "The Indian Looks at the White Man," *Expedition.* The Bulletin of the University Museum of the University of Pennsylvania. Philadelphia. Spring 1972. Ill. Examines American Indian playing cards with court figures of soldiers, padres, Mexicans and other Indians (p. 15–24).

*WAYLAND, Virginia (see also Mann). "The Moxon Family," *The Journal of The Playing-Card Society.* Birmingham. August 1974. Vol. III. No. 1. pp. 1–10. Ill. Describes the Moxon family, publishers of 4 packs of 17th century playing cards: Astronomical, Carving, Geographical and Geometrical (p. 1–10).

WAYLAND, Virginia and Harold. *Apache Playing Cards.* Pasadena. 1961. 12mo. 20 pp. Ill. Describes 19th century Apache Indian playing cards.

WAYLAND, Virginia and Harold. *Francis Barlow's Sketches for the Meal Tub Plot Playing Cards.* Pasadena. 1971. 41 pp. Ill. Describes the Meal Tub Plot playing cards.

WAYLAND, Virginia and Harold. "Japanese Playing Cards." Typed MS. Pasadena. 1975. 37 pp. Published 1976 in Supplement of *The Playing-Card Journal.* Describes Japanese playing cards including Iroha, Hyakunin-isshu and Hana Fuda cards.

*WAYLAND, Virginia and Harold. *of Carving, Cards & Cookery or The Mode of Carving at the Table.* Arcadia. 1962. 123 pp. Ill. Edition limited to 275. Deals with carving and cookery cards by Moxon, London, 1676–1677.

*WAYLAND, Virginia and Harold. "Princeton's Apache Playing Cards," *Princeton University Library Chronicle.* Princeton. Vol. XXXIV. No. 3. Ill. Describes 19th century Apache Indian playing cards owned by Princeton University (p. 147–157).

WAYLAND, Virginia and Harold. "A Puzzle Solved," *UCLA Librarian.* Los Angeles. February 1966. Vol. 19. No. 2. pp. 11–15.

*WAYLAND, Virginia and Harold. *The Winstanley Geographical Cards.* Pasadena. 1967. 8vo. 75 pp. Ill. Edition limited to 514. Describes 17th

century pack of geographical cards designed and published by Henry Winstanley.
WEHMAN, Henry J. *Wehman's Fortune-Telling by Cards, or Cartomancy made Easy*. New York. 1898. 8vo. 192 pp. Ill.
WEIGEL, Klaus. "Kartenspielfragmente," *Libri*. Copenhagen. 1964/1965. pp. 40–43.
WEIGEL, T. O. *Die Spielkarten der Weigel'schen Sammlung*. Leipzig. 1865. Folio. 45 pp. Ill. Edition limited to 100. Describes early playing cards.
WEIGLE, C. F. *Deck of Cards*. 1939.
*WEISS, Hans [etc]. *Focus On Switzerland*. Lausanne. 1975. 4 Vols. Ill. Reproduces several old Swiss playing cards including 15th century cards depicting secular music.
WELDING, Patsy Ruth. *Let E.S.P. Work for You!* Tarot cards in the subconscious.
WERNER, K. *Das Moderne Tarokspiel*. Leipzig. n.d. 12mo. 150 pp.
WESTCOTT. *Aesch Mezareph (Purifying Fire)*.
*WESTCOTT, W. Wynn. *The Isiac Tablet or The Bembine Table of Isis*. Los Angeles. 1976. Facsimile reprint of 1887 edition. 20 pp. Ill. Cites Bembine Tablet as key to tarot.
WESTCOTT, W. Wynn, editor (see Levi, *The Magical Ritual of the Sanctum Regnum*).
*WESTON, Jessie L. *From Ritual to Romance*. 1920. Reprinted New York, 1957. 217 pp. The ceiling of one of the halls of the palace of Medinet Abou allegedly is supported by 22 columns corresponding to the keys of the tarot.
*WHEATLEY, Dennis. *The Devil and All His Works*. New York. 1971. 4to. 302 pp. Ill. Traces the interaction of good and evil throughout history and includes several pages on tarot.
WHITING, J. R. S. *A Handful of History*. Dursley. 1978. 300 pp. Ill. History of England as depicted on 14 packs of 17th and 18th century playing cards.
*WHITNEY, Elizabeth. "Tarok Tarot or Taroc," *Spring 1942*. New York. Ill. Reprinted Nendeln, Lichtenstein, 1975. History of tarot with illustrations drawn by Alda Oertly (p. 13–30).
*WIEGMINK, Alan. *The Game of Regain Paradise*. Chicago. 1975.
WIENER, Lucien. *Jean Volay et les cartiers Lorraine*. Nancy. 1884.
WIENER, Lucien. *Recherches sur l'histoire et l'industrie cartiere en Lorraine*. Nancy. 1884.
*WILKINSON, Sir J. Gardner. *A Popular Account of the Ancient Egyptians*. New York. n.d. 2 Vols. 419 and 436 pp. Ill.
WILKINSON, William Henry. "The Chinese Origin of Playing Cards," *American Anthropologist*. Washington. January 1895. Vol. 8. p. 61.
WILLEFORD, William. *The Fool and His Scepter. A Study in Clowns and Jesters and Their Audience*. 1969. Ill. Includes references to The Fool of the tarot pack.
WILLET-HOLTHUYSEN MUSEUM. *In de kaart gekeken*. Amsterdam. 1976. Text in Dutch and English. Catalog of playing card exhibition in 1976 at Museum Willet-Holthuysen.
*WILLIAMS, Charles. *The Greater Trumps*. London. 1964. Reprinted. 12mo. 230 pp. The Major Arcana cards are described in a story of modern times.
*WILLSHIRE, William Hughes. *A Descriptive Catalogue of Playing And Other Cards in the British Museum [etc]*. London. 1876. 4to. 360 pp. Ill. Supplement 87 pp. Origin and history of playing cards including tarot.
*WILSON, Colin. *The Occult*. New York. 1971, Reprinted 1973. 601 pp.
WILSON, T. *Catalogue Raisonne of the Select Collection of Engravings [etc]*. Illustrations by G. Cruikshank and others. London. 1828. 4to. 274 pp. Ill. Edition limited to 125 copies privately printed. Refers to playing cards (p. 87–91).
*WINCKELMANN, Joachim. *Tarot Der Eingeweihten*. Berlin. 1962. 12mo. 135 pp. Ill. Describes the Major Arcana and includes cards designed by Erich and Liesel Mutze in sleeve at back of book.
WINNIE, Thelma. "The History of Playing Cards," *The Western Collector*. January 1967, pp. 16–19. February 1967, pp. 18–21.
*WIRTH, Oswald. *Introduction a l'etude du Tarot. Collection du Symbolisme*. Paris. 1931. 12mo. 51 pp. Ill. Describes the Major Arcana for fortune-telling.
WIRTH, Oswald. *Le livre de Thot. Les 22 arcanes du Tarot . . . de Stanislas de Guaita*. Paris. 1889. Ill. Edition limited to 100. Describes the 22 Major Arcana which are hand colored in the book.
*WIRTH, Oswald. *Stanislas de Guaita — Souvenirs de son Secretaire*. Paris. 1935. 265 pp. Ill. Contains several illustrations of tarot cards.
*WIRTH, Oswald. *Le Tarot, des Imagiers du Moyen Age*. Paris. 1927. Reprinted, Paris, 1969. 8vo. 374 pp. Ill. Origin and history of tarot with 22 Major Arcana in sleeve at back of book.
*WIRTH, Oswald. "Les origines du Tarot," *Le Voile d'Isis*. February 1912. No. 26. pp. 37–41.
WIRTH, Oswald (see also Neroman, D. *Grande Encyclopedie*).
WOLFF, Martha. "Bonifacio Bembo and the *Minchiate* Cards Painted for Filippo Maria Visconti." M.A. Thesis. Yale University. New Haven. April 1974. 80 pp. + 84 plates. Iconographic and artistic aspects of the Cary-Yale Visconti-Sforza tarocchi cards.

THE WORD (see Percival).
WORLD ALMANAC. *World Almanac of the Strange and Unusual*. New York. 1977. 540 pp. Ill. Includes section on tarot.
WRIGHT, Basil. "The Queen of Spades — and a Joker," *Britain Today*. 1948. No. 158. pp. 138–141.
WRONSKI, Hoene. *Le Messianisme, ou Reforme Absolue du Savoir Humain*. Paris. 1825. 3 Vols. According to Papus, the writings of Wronski agree with the principles and conclusions found in the tarot.
*WUTHRICH, Lucas. "Spielkarten des 16. Jahrhunderts im Schweizerischen Landesmuseum," *Zeitschrift fur Schweizerische Archaeologie und Kunstgeschichte*. Zurich. 1973. Band 30. Doppelheft 3/4. pp. 146–161. Ill.
WYNNE, Marjorie G. (See Yale University Library).

X

*XANTO, Madame. *Fortune Telling*. Philadelphia. 1908. 140 pp. Includes fortune telling with 52 cards.

Y

*YALE UNIVERSITY LIBRARY. *The Art of The Playing Card: The Cary Collection*. Forward by Marjorie G. Wynne. Introduction by A. Hyatt Mayor. Card documentation and description by Albert Field. New Haven. 1973. 44 pp. Ill. Describes 39 packs and books featured at the 1973 exhibition of the Cary Playing Card Collection.
YALE UNIVERSITY LIBRARY. (see also William B. Keller).
YAMAGUCHI, Kakutaro V. and Hiroaki Hamaguchi. *Nihon No Karuta (Playing Cards of Japan)*. Osaka. 1973. 16mo. 152 pp. Ill. Describes playing cards of Japan including The Song Game of the Hundred Poets and matching card games.
YAMAGUCHI, Kichirobei IV. *Un-Sun Karuta*. Edited by Kakutaro Yamaguchi V. Osaka. 1961. 4to. 256 pp. Ill. Describes the history of Japanese playing cards which are believed to have descended from sixteenth century Portuguese cards; Un-Sun refers to the two court cards in each suit.
YEATS (see Donoghue, Harper and Raine).
YOSHIDA, Yuki. *Whispering Leaves in Grosvenor Square*. Describes the Japanese game of *Hyakunin-Isshu* or 100 Poems.

Z

*ZAC[CARIA], Pino. *Le Cartes du Vatican*. Paris. 1973. Ill. Features satirical cards with religious theme.
ZAIN, C. C. *The Sacred Tarot*. Los Angeles. 1969. 416 pp. Ill. Comprises 13 serials that deal with the scope, use, color and interpretation of tarot.
ZAINI, R. Fulgi. *Giochi di Carte*. 6th edition. Milan. 1968. 162 pp. Rules for the game of tarocchi.
*ZANCIG, Madame. *How to tell Fortunes by Cards*. Chicago. [1902]. 8vo. 150 pp. Ill. Fortune telling with 52 cards.
*ZANI, D. Pietro. *Materiali per servire alla storia dell' origine e de' progressi dell' incisione in rame e in legno [etc]*. Parma. 1802. 8vo. 248 pp. Early references to playing cards and description of tarocchi of Montegna series (pp. 78–84, 149–193).
ZANI, D. Pietro. *Enciclopedia metodica critico-ragionata delle Belle-Arti*. Parma. 1819–1828. 29 Vols. References to playing cards.
ZDEKAUER, L. "Il giuoco in Italia nei secoli XIII-XIV e specialmente in Firenze," *Archivio storico italiano*. 1886. Serial IV. Vol. 18. pp. 20–74.
ZDEKAUER, L. *Sull' organizzazione publica del giuoco in Italia nel medio evo*. Bologna. 1892.
ZEE, P. E. "Speelkaarten," *De Navorscher. III*. Bijblad (?) 1853. pp. LXXV-LXXVII.
*ZOLAR. *Encyclopedia of Ancient and Forbidden Knowledge*. Los Angeles. 1970. sm 8vo. 472 pp. Fortune telling with tarot cards.
*ZOVELLO. *History and Origin of Playing Cards*. New York. 1935. sm 8vo. 18 pp. Ill. Playing cards are viewed as an allegorical development from the early Egyptian calendar devised over 6000 years ago.
*ZSOLDOS, Ben. "Cardmakers in Hungary," *The Journal of the Playing-Card Society*. Manchester. August 1973, Vol. II, No. 1 and May 1975, Vol. III, No. 4.
*ZSOLDOS, Ben. *Directory of 18th and 19th Century Hungarian Playing Cards*. Budapest. May 1975. 10 pp. Describes 85 Hungarian decks and 39 card makers from the 18th and 19th centuries.
**ZSOLDOS, Ben. "Kartyafestok Pesten," *Budapest Magazine*. Budapest. September 1976. pp. 39–41. Ill. Describes Pest cardmakers and their cards.
**ZSOLDOS, Ben. "Regi korok kartyai," *Magyar Grafika*. Budapest. 1975. Vol. XIX. No. 4. pp. 76–78. Ill. Describes old Hungarian playing cards.
*ZSOLDOS, Ben. "The House of Piatnik," *The Journal of The Playing-Card Society*. Manchester. May 1973. Vol. I. No. 4.
*ZSOLDOS, Ben. "The Seasons Pattern," *The Journal of The Playing-Card Society*. Manchester. May 1973, Vol. I, No. 4 and August 1973, Vol. II, No. 1.
*ZSOLDOS, Ben. "The Sopron/Oedenburg Pattern," *The Journal of The Playing-Card Society*. Manchester. August 1974. Vol. III. No. 1.

INDEX

A

A bon droyt 61, 75, 76, 77, 79, 80, 82, 83, 85, 86, 88, 89, 98, 99, 101, 103
A. C. 100
A Notice of the Ludus Triumphorum 26
Accademia Carrara 1, 35, 63-65, 67, 68, 72, 73, 75, 78-80, 82-86, 104
Acea Gypsy Tarot 169
Acea, Jeffrey 169
Acuario Tarot 8, 228
Adam 11, 176
Adam and Eve 157, 159, 224
Adams, Frederick McLaurin 170, 171
Adjustment 208, 209, 243
Aeon, The 208, 209, 243
Aeons 244
African culture 169, 176
Age of Aquarius 234
Ages of the world 14
AGMuller & Cie 161, 164, 242, 253, 270, 274, 292
Agnes del Maino 60
Agrippa 281
AGZ 197
Ahad al-arkan 53, 56
Ahriman 18
Ailsa Mellon Bruce Fund 45, 46
Air 279
Ajedrez 19
Akhnaton 186
Albano Productions 272
Alberico de Barbiano 60
Albertina 124, 126
Alchemist, The 219, 236
Alchemists 7
Alecxandro M 124
Aleister Crowley Thoth Tarot (see Crowley)
Alexander 7, 133
Alexander Magnus 133
Alexander the Bad 174
Alitalia Airlines 172
Alitalia Tarot 172
Allegorical Tarock 299
Alliette (see Etteilla)
Alphabets 15
Alphonse XI 31
Altenburger und Stralsunder Spielkarten 326
Ambika 18
Ambivero of Bergamo, Canon 65
Ambras Hofjagdspiel 12, 58, 59, 111, 135
Amenhotep IV 186
Amigleus, Castor 133
Amone 124

Amor myo 82, 83, 89, 111
Andrioletti 35, 63, 64, 104, 105
Andromeda 256
Angel of the prime mobile 47
Angel, The 53, 54, 150, 254, 255
Angels 90
Animal Tarock 303, 304
Anno Ab Urbe Condite MLXX 124
Antoine de Lassale 32
Antwerp, siege of 318
Anubis 170
Apocalypse 173, 174
Apollo 27, 38, 39, 42, 47, 54, 112, 266
Aquarian Tarot 1, 8, 9, 200, 229
Aquarius 170, 181, 225
Arabian Nights 34
Arabic cards 53
Arcana 1
Arcanes du Destin 175
Ardhanari 7, 18, 19
Arena Chapel 20, 178
Aretino, Pietro 28
Argine 7
Arica 260
Arie 49
Arienti, Vito 147, 178, 204
Aries 173, 174, 181
Arista Tarot 230, 231
Aritmetricha 37, 38, 39, 42, 43
Armorial shields 78, 81
Arrows 87, 96, 97, 107
Arrows of Light 219
Ars Amatoria 33
Art 196, 208, 209, 243
Art and Science 249
Art deco 230
Artemis 176, 224
Arthur, King 7
Artixan 38, 39, 41
Arts et Lettres 245
Ashcroft-Nowicki, Dolores 186
Assiah 7
Assyria 133, 317
Astral Tarot 232
Astro Tarot 232, 233
Astrologia 37, 38, 39, 43, 112
Astrology 4, 42, 115, 140, 174, 191, 208, 211, 219, 222, 224, 228, 230, 236, 246, 248, 266, 282, 294
Astronomy 115, 129
Atkins, William 176
Atlas 53, 54
Ator 1
Atouts XVI, 1, 39, 53
Attalo 29
Attendolo, Muzio 60, 61, 74, 92
Atu 243

Atus of Tahuti 243
Atutti 26, 49, 53
Atutto 39
Atziluth 7
Augsburg 33
Augustinian convent 62
Aurelia Books 145
Austrian-Lloyd Steamship Lines 316
Avignon 146, 148
Avondo Brothers 157, 158
Aycardi, Laurent 24
Azekah 250
Aztecs 19

B

Bacchus 145, 152
Back designs 8, 48, 133, 160, 164
Bacus (see Bacchus)
Bagat 166
Bagatino, Il 22
Baglioni, Count Francesco 65
Balance, The 190, 191
Balbi, Domenico ii, 1, 178, 234, 235
Balbi tarot 234, 235
Baldini, Baccio 35
Baldini, Carte di 35
Balin, Peter 19, 287-290
Ballesta, Juan 201
Banners 180, 181
Bar, Cardinal Louis de 26
Baraja Egipcia 236
Bargagli, Girolamo 30
Bartsch (see Von Bartsch)
Basilide, T. 4
Bassetta 29
Bathsheba 11
Batons 4, 28
Baumgartner 311
Bauwens, Jan 20, 53
Beatrice della Scala 60
Beatrice di Tenda 60, 89
Beaulieu, L. 179
Beggar, The 35, 39, 41, 53, 55
Beinecke Rare Book and Manuscript Library 63, 87-95, 117
Belier 173, 174
Belus 133
Bembine Tablet 14
Bembo, Bonifacio 1, 20, 63, 72, 106, 107, 110, 111
Bembo, Cardinal 14
Benavides, Rodolfo 180, 181
Benedettinis Collection 110
Benjamine, Elbert (see Zain)
Bennett, George 178, 278
Benois, J. B. 137

Bentivoglio of Bologna 32, 54
Beresford, Flora 223, 224
Bergamo 63
Berger 317
Bern 24
Berni, Francesco 28, **29**
Berrill, Roland 274
Berthole, Jean **182**
Bertoni, G. 30
Besancon 151
Bhairavi 18
Bible 11
Biblioteca Nazionale Universitaria 117, 119
Biblioteca Treccani 33
Biblioteca Vaticana **26**, **27**
Bibliotheque de l'Ecole Nationale Superieure des Beaux-Arts 128
Bibliotheque Nationale 21, 37, 40, 47, 111, 112-116, 135
Biedak 35, 63, 64, 104, **105**
Binah 244
Bird heraldic device 60, **61**, 72, **76**, **82**
Birth 206
Biscari Collection 110
Bishop of Florence 26
Bishop of Langres 26
Blavatsky, Madame 23
Blindfolded Cupid **54**
Blue Ridge Mountains 264
Boar **167**
Boaz 214, 215, 224
Boccaccio, Giovanni 34
Bochelli, Laurentii 26
Bocho 124, **127**
Bohemia 303
Bohemians 21
Boiardo, Count Matteo Maria 28
Bologna 26, 32, 49
Bologneser Tarockspiel 54
Bolzani, Guido 238
Bompiani **173**, **174**
Bona of Savoy 62
Bond, James (see James Bond)
Bondage 176, **177**
Book of Creation 16, 180
Book of Paradox, The 181
Book of Splendors 16
Book of T 268
Book of Tarot 12
Book of the Law 256
Book of the Leaves of Gold 12
Book of Thoth 12, 140
Books of Moses 10
Bordigallo, Domenico 33, 106
Borgognone, Ambrogio 60, 106
BOTA (see Builders of the Adytum)
Bouvard, R. 137
Boy Scout campout 320
Brabant 24
Brahma 18, 167, 279
Brambilla 63
Brera-Brambilla Visconti-Sforza tarocchi 58, 64, 87, **96-98**, 106, 107
Brera Gallery 35, 63, 64, **96-98**, 106
Bres Magazine 176
Bresle, Valentin 180
Briah 7
Briefes 21
Briefmahlers 21
British Library **25**
British Museum 47, 54, 124
British Tarot 8, **182**, **183**

Bronze Age 14
Brother Placid Stuckenschneider **178**
Brown Company 200
Buddha 18, 167, 217, 281
Buddhist symbology 180
Builders of the Adytum 23, **239**
Bull, The **181**
Bullet, Jean Baptiste 32
Burdel, Claude 137, 242
Burlington Magazine, The 35, 63
Bussi, Feliciano 32
Bynneman 30

C

Cabala de Prediccion, La 248
Cactus, The **288**, **289**
Caduceus 250, 266
Caesar 7
Cagliostro tarot 246
Calendar comparisons to cards 9, 10
Calendric counters 12
Caliope 38, 39, 41, 47
Calvary 264
Camelot 206
Cammerlander, Jacob 10
Camoin, A. **149**
Campbell, Joseph 267
Cana of Pisa, Faccino 60
Cancer 250
Caparison 61, **75**, **78**, **81**, **84**, **95**, 97, **101**
Capitolo del gioco della primiera 28, **29**
Capucin **142**
Carbone 124, **126**
Card Spreads (see Spreading the tarot deck)
Cardajat 137
Cardinal virtues 4, 44, 49, 69, 137
Cards as children's game 24, 26
Carey, L. **8**
Carlino 28
Carnival King 22, 66
Carrara (see Accademia Carrara)
Carta Mundi 145
Carten 32
Carter, Jimmy 180, **181**
Cartes a jouer du XIV au XX siecle, Les 38, 117, 118, 162
Cartes parlantes, Les 28
Carthusian monastery 60
Cartiglia 49
Cartomanzia 184, 246
Cary, L. 137, 146, **155**
Cary, Melbert B., Jr. 87
Cary Playing Card Collection 35, 87, **88-95**, 117
Cary-Yale Visconti-Sforza Tarocchi 58, 61-64, 87, **88-95**, 96, 98, 106, 107, 178
Case, Paul Foster 20, 23, 239
Castaneda, Carlos 287
Castello Ursino 108, 109, 110
Castile 21, 31, 32
Catchpenny Tarot **245**
Catelin Geofroy (see Geofroy)
Catholic Church 18, 22, 178, 189
Catone 124, **127**
Catulo 124, **126**
Cavalier 9
Cego **326**
Celtic alphabet 173, 174, 192
Celtic tarot **173**, **174**
Centaurs 49, 51
Cento giuochi liberali et d'ingegno 30

Central American Indians 19
Certosa 60, 106
Chaboseau tarot **184**
Chad 20
Chahar-Taj 18
Chakras 279, 281
Champollion, Jean Francois 14
Chamundeswari 20
Chariot of Osiris, The **190**, **191**
Chariot, The xvi, 2-5, 15-17, 30, 33, 36, 39, **40**, 48, 49, **50**, **51**, 53, **55**, 61, 64, 68, 69, 100, **101**, 109, 110, 112, **113**, 125, 128, 129, 130, 134, 135, 137, **138**, 139, 140, 143, 145, 147-150, 153-161, 163-166, 169, 170, 175, 179, **182**, **183**, **185**, **186**, **187**, **188**, **189**, **190**, **191**, 192, 193, 194, 196-199, 201, 203-205, 206, 207, 208, 209, 212-214, 216, 217, 219-225, 228, 229, 230, 232, 233, 236, 238, 239, 240, 241, 243, 245-247, 248, 249, 250, 251, 253, 254, 255, 256, 258, 259, 263, 267-269, 271, 275-278, 282, 283, 288, 289, 290, 291, 294, 329
Charita 39, 44
Charity 49, **51**, **52**, 64, 87, **91**
Charlemagne 7, 30, 302
Charles V 24, 32, 34
Charles VI 21, 24, 32, **34**, 111
Charles VII 7
Chartarum 33
Chastity 21
Chatto, William Andrew 18, 20
Chaturanga 18, 19
Chaucer, Geoffrey 34
Chavalier 38, 39, 40, 41, 47, 112
Chazed 180
Chess 18, 19, 33
Chinese Book of Changes 279
Chinese dominoes 20
Chinese mythology 217
Chinese symbols 217
Chinese tarock **307**
Ching-tsze-tung 20
Chinnamasta 281
Chorpash, Gordon 257
Christ 11, 260
Christ the King 178
Christian Church 11, 33
Christian faith 4
Christian, Paul 14, 22
Christian world 38, 290
Chronicle of Morelli 24, 39
Chronicles of Cremona 33, 106
Chronico 38, 39, 44, 47
Chronique du Petit Jehan de Saintre 32
Church of Light tarot 9, 23, 219, 240, **241**
Church of St. Sigismund 60
Church of San Petronio 26
Cicognara, Antonio 33, 63, 70, 100, 106
Cicognara, Leopoldo 32, 88, 89, 106
Cilento, Diane **173**, **174**
Cincinnati Art Museum xvi, 136, 146, 147, 156, 297, 300
Circassian decoration 53
Cité de Dieu 32
Clark, Kenneth 35
Classic Tarot (see Tarot Classic)
Cleveland, Jim 170, **171**
Clio **27**, 38, 39, 42
Clubs 7, 8, 180, **181**
Coagula 176
Coate cards 5, 7, 30

Cobbler, The **160, 164**
Code of Nuremberg 34
Codex at the Vatican **27**
Codex Nuttall 289, 290
Coelbrin y Beirdo 174
Coffee House Tarock **324**
Coins 4, 5, **6, 7**, 28, 49, 53, **82, 84-86,** 96, **97-99, 103, 105,** 106, **108, 109,** 110, **117-119,** 120, **122-124, 125, 131, 133-135, 138, 139,** 141, **149, 151-153, 158, 163, 165, 169,** 170, **172, 174, 175, 179, 182, 183, 200, 206, 208, 209, 210, 217, 218, 230, 231, 236, 237, 240, 242, 245, 247, 252, 253, 254,** 260, **261-263, 264, 265, 269, 270, 273, 275,** 292, **293,** 335, 336
Collecting Playing Cards 21
Colleoni 1, 35, 63-65, 79, 80, 81
Colleoni cards **134**
Colleoni, Count Allessandro 65
Colleoni, Countess Cecilia 65
Comedia dell'Arte 145
Commentariorum Urbanorum 33
Complete Drawings of Albrecht Durer, The 47
Conclusions 345
Conditions of Man 38, 39, 41
Condottieri 32, 60
Condottieri, The 61
Confort d'Amy 34
Conquerer, The **219**
Consort, The 287, **288**
Constance 136
Constancy 53, **55**
Constant, Alphonse Louis (see Levi, Eliphas)
Contignola, Count of 61
Conver, Nas (Nicholas) 146, **149, 151**
Cooke, John 268
Cooper, J. 185
Cooper, Louise 181
Cooper Tarot **185**
Copperplate cards 132
Correr (see Museo Correr)
Corwin, Arthur 12
Cosmic principles 38, 39, 44
Cosmico 38, 39, 44, 47
Cosmos 47
Costume cards 5
Council of Worcester 33
Country loaves 28
Court cards 7, 53, 64
Court de Gebelin, Antoine 1, 12, 13, 14, 20, 22, **137, 139**
Covarrubias 7
Covelluzzo, Giovanni 32
Cranach the Elder, Lucas 186
Creation **137, 139**
Cremona 60, 106
Cross heraldic device 100, **101,** 107
Crowley, Aleister 5, 18, 23, **243,** 244
Crowley Thoth Tarot 1, 9, 18, **243**
Crusades 101
Cupid 21, 45, **54,** 67, 89, 113, 157, 159
Cups 4, 5, **6, 7,** 28, 49, 53, 79, **81-83, 98, 99,** 103, **105, 109,** 110, 111, **117-119,** 120, **123,** 124, **125, 131, 135, 138, 139, 148, 150-152, 165, 169,** 170, **183, 202, 206,** 210, **230, 231, 233, 237, 240, 242, 243, 244, 245, 247, 252, 253, 254,** 260, **261, 263, 264, 265, 267, 269, 270, 273, 275, 286, 291,** 334, 335
Curtius, Marcus 133

◆ D ♠

Dali, Salvador 1, 186, **187**
D'Allemagne, Henry Rene 24, 38, 117, 118, 162
Dance tarock **309**
Dancing Fool **54**
Daniel, Père Fabriel 7
Danse Macabre 114
Das Guldin Spil 31
David, King 7, 11, 15
De Doctrina Promiscua 28
De Hermetische Tarot 258
De Honesta Voluptate 26
De Imaginibus gentilium Deorum 26, 27
De Laurence tarot (see Laurence tarot)
Death xvi, 3-5, 15-17, 21, 30, 33, **48,** 49, **50, 51, 54, 55,** 60, 64, 70, **71,** 90, 103, 104, 106, 110, 112, 114, **125,** 128, **129-132,** 135, **137, 139, 140, 141, 142, 144, 147-150, 153, 154, 159-166, 169, 170, 171, 173, 174, 175, 179, 183, 185,** 186, **187, 188, 189, 190, 191, 194, 196-198, 201, 203, 205, 206, 207, 208, 209, 210, 212, 213, 216, 217, 219-221, 223,** 224, **225, 226, 229,** 230, **231-233, 236-239, 240, 241, 245-247, 248, 249, 250, 251, 252, 254, 255-257, 259, 262, 263, 267, 269-271, 272, 273, 275-278, 280, 281, 282-285, 288,** 290, **294,** 330
Decembrio 26
Decker, Ronald 20, 106, **178**
Decreta ecclesial Gallicanae 26
Della Scala 100
Deotauro 124, **126**
D'Epinal tarot **245**
Dequer, John H. 219
Despot of Milan 60
D'Este, Beatrice 62
D'Este cards 117, 118
D'Este, Duke Borso 26
D'Este, Isabella 30
D'Este, Leonello 100
D'Este, Marquis 61
Deutsches Spielkarten Museum 110, 130
Devil, The xvi, 3-5, 15-17, 30, 33, **48,** 49, **50-52,** 53, **54,** 64, 65, 70, **71,** 124, **125,** 128, **129,** 130, **131, 132, 135, 139, 140, 141, 142, 144, 147-150, 152-154, 156, 157, 159-162, 164-166, 169,** 170, **173, 174, 175, 176, 177, 179,** 180, **181, 183, 185, 188, 189, 190, 191, 196-198, 203, 205, 206, 207, 208, 209, 211, 213, 216, 217, 220, 221, 223,** 224, **225, 226, 231-233,** 234, **235-239,** 240, **241, 245-247, 248, 249, 250, 251, 252,** 254, **255, 263, 264, 265, 267, 269,** 270, **275-277,** 280, 281, **282-286, 288,** 290, 330, 331
Devil's Bible 2
Devil's Picture Book 2
Devil's Tarot, The 253
Dialogo da Givochi 30
Diamond rings heraldic device (see Rings heraldic device)
Diamonds 7, 8
Diana **54,** 72, 224
Diana, Anneke De 258
Dice 19, 28, 31-34, 186
Die Welt des Tarot 292
Dionysus Zagreus 243
Ditha Moser tarock **317**

Docters van Leeuwen Porcelain tarot **188,** 189
Docteur Marius 246
Dodali, J. 137
Dog Latin 175
Dog Star, The 137, **139**
Doge 47
Doge of Venice 41
Dogma et Rituel de la Haute Magie 14, 22
D'Olivet, Fabre 22
Domitian 29
Don Juan 287
Don Quixote 120, 181
Donali family 65
Dondorf, B. 312
Dondorf tarok no. 246 **312**
Dorflinger, Hans 180, **181**
D'Otrange 100, 101, 102
Dotti, Edoardo 157
Doubleday, Abner 162
Doubleday tarot 157, **162**
Douglas, Alfred 276
Douglas, Nik 279
Dove heraldic device (see Bird heraldic device)
Doxe 38, 39, 41, 47
Dragon heraldic device 60
Dragoni, Antonio 14, 33
Du Jeu Des Tarots **13,** 137, **139**
Dubesset, G. 137
Ducal crown heraldic device 61, 62, 66, **79,** 81, 84, **94, 95,** 97, 107
Duke of Urbino 26
Dukes of Milan 26, 60, 61, 100, 106
Dummett, Michael 33
Durer, Albrecht 47
Durga 18
Durrieu, P. 26
Durville fils, Henri 218
Dykstra, R. Dirk **173,** 174, **215-217**
Dynamic Games tarot 8, **247**

♥ E ♣

Eagle heraldic devices 61, 66, 88, **103,** 107, **314**
Earliest references to cards 24-34
Early hand-painted cards 63-123
Early playing cards, their design and decoration 32
Early printed tarot cards 124-136
Early types of tarocchi and similar playing cards 35-59
Earth **51,** 279
Eastern Emperor, The 49, **51,** 53
Echecs 19
Edition La Gravure Originale 178
Edition Leipzig 58
Editora y Distribuidora Mexicana 144
Editorial Kier **248-250**
Edizione Europrint 238
Edizioni del Solleone 166
Edward I 33, 34
Egipcios tarot 8, 144, **248, 249,** 250
Egypt 162, 260
Egypt Minor 21
Egyptian card designs **143**
Egyptian gods and goddesses 1
Egyptian Initiate, An 186, **187**
Egyptian libraries 131
Egyptian Major Arcana cards 157, **162,** 180, **181,** 186, **187,** 189, **190, 219, 220, 236, 240, 241, 249, 260, 261, 282**

Egyptian origin of cards 7
Egyptian pantheon 12
Egyptian symbols 169, 192, 206, 208,
    209, 214, 215, 224, 246, 248-250, 267,
    290, 317
Egyptian words 1
Eighteenth-century tarot decks 137-155
El Supremo Art de Echar les cartas 144
Elements 7, 49, 51, 279
Elena 124, **127**
Eliphas Levi and the French Occult
    Revival 22
Emperor of the Romans 61
Emperor, The xvi, 2, 4, 5, 15-17, 30,
    33, 36, 39, **40**, 45, 48, 49, 53, **54**, **55**,
    58, 61, 64, 66, 67, 88, 96, 99, 103, 107,
    112, 117, 120, 121, **125**, 130, 133, 134,
    135, 137, **138**, 139, 140, 145, 148-150,
    153-155, 158-161, 163-166, 169, 178,
    180, 181-183, 185, 186, 187, 188, 189,
    190, 192, 193, 194, 196-201, 203-205,
    206, 207, 208, 209, 210, 212, 213, 216, 217,
    218-221, 223, 224, 225, 226, 228, 229,
    230, 231-233, 234, 235, 236, 238, 239,
    240, 241, 245-247, 248, 249, 250, 251,
    253, 254, 255, 258, 259, 260, 261-263,
    264, 265, 267-270, 275-278, 280, 282,
    283, 288, 289, 290, 291, 294, 328
Empress, The xvi, 2-5, 15-17, 30, 33,
    36, **48**, 49, 53, **55**, 61, 64, 66, 67, 107,
    110, **125**, 130, **132**, 134, **135**, 137, **138**,
    139, 140, 145, 148, 151, 156, 158-161,
    163-166, 169, 173, 174, 175, 183, 185,
    186, 187, 188, 189, 190, 194, 196-203,
    205, 210-212, 215, 216, 219-223, 224,
    228, 229, 230, 231-233, 236-239, 240,
    241-243, 245-247, 248, 249, 250, 251,
    253, 254, 255, 259, 260, 261-263,
    267-271, 275-278, 279, 280, 282, 283,
    287, 288, 290, 291, 294, 328
En Soph 17
Enamel tarot 192, **193**
Encausse, Gerard (see Papus)
Eracasse, Captain **145**, **152**
Erato 38, 39, 41
Ermengarda 302
Escutcheon 78, 101
Esoteric tarot, The 181, **250**
Essence, The 260, **261**
Este (see D'Este)
Estel, Joseph 299
Estense, Isabella 30
Eternity 21
Ethers tarot 180
Etteilla 4, 5, 22
Etteilla tarot 8, 137, 140, **141-144**,
    252
Ettinghausen, Richard 53
Euterpe 26, **38**, 39, 42, 47
Eve 11
Evio Plauto R, L. 124
Evolution **249**
Excuse 302, 312
Exotic tarock **316**
Eye Magazine 185
Ezekiel 224

♠ F ♦

Faith 47, 49, **51**, **52**, 64, 87, 91, 106
Falco 124, **126**
Falconer 53, 59
Falcons 58, 59, 132, 135
Fama Sol 152

Fame 21, 49
Fameio 38, 39, **40**, **41**
Familiar Epistles 31
Fanciful tarot 157, **158**
Fano tarot 1
Fanti, Sigismondo 28
Farcas, Laila **173**, **174**
Father Time **54**, 110,
Fatidic Egyptian tarot 189, **190**
Faust 310
Fede 39, 44, 47
Female Pope 49, **66**
Fergus Hall tarot **253**, **254**
Ferrara 26, 30, 35, 100
Ferrario, Giulio 69
Fez 20
Fibbia, Prince 32, 33, 49
Field, Albert 50, 57, 106
Fifteen hundred gold pieces for cards 26
Fifty-two-card deck 8-11
Figure cards 5
Filipo, R 124, **127**
Fiorino 96
Fire 51, 279
Fire, The 152
Firmaments of the universe 39
Five books of Moses 10
Five wise virgins 11
Fleur-de-lis 21, 51, 112, 121
Florence 24
Fodera, Vincenzo 180, **181**
Folium 18
Folklore 248
Fool, The 2-5, 15-17, 30, 33, 36, 39, **48**,
    49, **50**, 53, **54**, **55**, 64, **65**, 99, 110, 112,
    117, **124**, **125**, 130, 133, 134, **135**, **136**,
    137, **138**, 139, 140, **141-144**, 147-150,
    152-155, 157-161, 163-166, 169, 172,
    173, 174, 176, 177-179, 180, 181-185,
    186, **187**, 188, 189, 190, 192, 193, **194**,
    196-205, 206, 207, 208, 209, 211,
    212-214, 215, 216, 218-221, 223, 224,
    225, 226, 229, 230, 231-233, 234, 235,
    238, 239, 242, 243, 245-247, 248, 249,
    250, 251-253, 256-259, 260, 261-263,
    264, 265, 267-271, 273, 275-278, 279,
    280, 282-284, 287, 288, 292, 293, 294,
    295, 296, 327
Fool's tarock 308
Force 49, **51**, **52**, **54**, 137, 180, **181**,
    271
Formschneiders 21
Forte Urbano 147
Forteza 38, 39, **40**, 44, 112
Fortitude 53, **55**, 70, 276
Fortuna 69
Fortune **54**
Fountain heraldic device 62, 89, 93, 94,
    99, 104, 107, 110, 111
Four Kings 18, 19, 33
Fournier, Heraclio 234, 235, 250, 277
Fourteenth-century designs 21
Fracasse, Captain 145
Franz Josef I, Emperor 305
Fratelli Fabbri Editori 202
Frazer, Gordon 264
Freemasons 22
French Cartomancy pack **157**
French Pack, circa 1720 **146**
French Revolutionary tarot 146, **155**
French tarot cards 146, **151**
Frownstrong tarot 192, **193**
Fullwood, Nancy 1

♥ G ♣

Gabriel 159, 206
Gaignières, M. de 112
Galary Gazer 229
Galba 29
Galgario, Fra 65
Galler, Jean **8**, 146, **152**
Game of the King 30
Ganges River 217
Gano tarot 1
Garden of Eden 250
Garzoni, Thomaso 30, 33
Gassmann **8**, **163**
Gaudais, J. 157-159
Gauri 18
Gebelin, Court de (see Court de Gebelin)
Geburah 244
Gemrod 192, **193**
Genius of the sun 44
Genius of the world 44
Genius of time 44, 47
Gentilini, Franco 254
Gentilini tarocchi 254, **255**
Geofroy, Catelin 65, **132**
Geografia tarocchi 146, **147**
Geometria 38, 39, 42
Gestalt principles 267
Ghibellines 20
Gill, Josephine 186, **187**
Giotto 20, 178
Givry, Emile Grillot de 4
Glanz, Josef 305, 310, 321
Glass, Christoph 194
Glass tarot **194**
GM 151
Gobl, Andreas Benedictus 297
Gobl tarock **297**
God Kne-phta 191
God, man and the universe 14
Godeffroi de St. Omer 22
Godi, Andre 218
Goethe 310
Golden Age 14
Golden Bough, The 264
Golden Dawn tarot **256**
Golden Egyptian tarot **257**
Goldschmidt Cards 59, 110
Golowin, Sergius 292
Gonzaga, Countess 63
Gorizia, F. in **48**
Gospel 113
Goulinat, Gabriel 211, 282
Governor 53
Graffiti 271
Grafica Gutenberg 70, 71, 72, 84, 285
Grammatica 38, 39, 42
Grand Duke, The 49, **51**
Grand Etteilla Egyptian Gypsies tarot
    (see Etteilla tarot)
Grand Tarot Belline 9, 237
Grandfather, The **155**
Grandmother, The **155**
Granolitho printing 180, **181**
Graphis Magazine 182
Graves, Robert 192, 267
Graz 57
Grazzini, Francesco Antonio 30
Great Calendar Stone of the Aztecs 289
Great deluxe 11
Great Priest **183**
Great Priestess **183**
Great Time Wheel 281

Greater Arcana 1
Greater Trumps 295, 296
Greek alphabet **15**
Greek Cross 264
Greek Orthodox Church 174
Greenwich Public Library **178**
Greeting Card Magazine 176, 177
Grimaud, B. P. 138, **262**
Gringonneur, Jacquemin 21, 24, 111, 112, 121
Grosset & Dunlap 242
Guaita, Stanislas de 23
Guelphs 20
Guevara 31
Guglielma of Bohemia 66
Guglielmites 66
Guido Bolzani tarocchi **238**
Guildhall 35, 59, 63, 64, **104**, 111
Guillaume de Machau 34
Guldin Spil, Das 31
Guler, Maritxu 250
Gumppenberg, F. 146, **154**, **302**
Guterrey 31
Gypsies 21
Gypsy king 169, 170
Gypsy symbols 292

♦ H ♠

H. J. Heinz tarot **195**
Habsburger tarock No. 146 **315**
Hageman, Heather 176
Hall, Fergus 1, 201, **253**
Hall, Manley Palmer 14, 18, 23
Halls of Persephone 170
Ham 11
Hanged Man, The xvi, 3-5, 15-17, 30, 33, **48**, **50-52**, 53, **54**, **55**, 61, 64, 69, 70, 91, 112, **114**, **128**, **130**, **132**, **135**, **138**, **139**, 140, **145**, 147-150, **152-154**, **158-166**, 169, 170, **175**, **179**, 180, **181**, **183**, **185**, 188, 189, **190**, 191, 192, **193**, 194, 196-198, 201, 203, 205, 212, 213, 216, 217, 219-221, 223, 224, **225**, **226**, 228, 229, 230, **232**, 233, 234, **235-239**, 240, **241**, 243, **245**, 246, 248, **249**, 250, 251, 254, **255**, 258, 259, 262, 263, 264, 265, 267-269, 271, 275-278, **282**, **283**, 288, 290, 294, 330
Hanlon, James 260
Harlequin and Columbine 314
Harris Brisbane Deck Fund 125
Harris, Lady Frieda 1, 23, 243
Hathor 1, 224
Hearts 7, 8
Hebraic occultism 22
Hebrew alphabet 7, **15**, **16**, 22, 23, **144**, 162, 169, 180, **181**, **184**, 186, **187**, 192, **193**, **198**, **211**, 214, 215, **228**, 234, **235**, **236**, 240, **241**, 250, **251**, 272, 282
Hebrew star 192
Hebrew system 244
Hebrew words 1
Hecate 176, 224
Hector 7, 30
Heineken, Baron 21
Heinz Company, H. J. 195
Heitmann, Robert Charles 176
Helie de Borron 32
Helios **37**, **45**
Henry VII 26
Hera 174
Heraldic devices 35, 39, 60-62, 66, 67, 70-72, 74, 76, 78, 79, 81, 82, 84, 89, 93-95, 97, 99-101, 104-108, 110, 111, 186
Hercules 70
Heresy 91
Hermanubis 137, 248
Hermes 189, 244, 256
Hermes Trismegistus 12
Hermit, The xvi, 2-5, 15-18, 30, 33, **36**, 39, **40**, **48**, 49, **50**, **52**, 53, **55**, 64, **68**, 69, 110, 112, **114**, **128**, **130**, **132**, 134, **135**, **138**, **139**, 140, **141-143**, **145**, **147-150**, **153-166**, 169, 170, **172**, **173**, 174, **175**, **179**, 180, **183**, **185**, 186, **187**, 188, 189, 190, 191, **194**, **196-199**, **201-203**, 205, 206, **207**, 208, **209**, 210, 212-214, 216, 217, **219**, **220**, 223, 224, **226**, 228, 229, 230, **231-233**, 236, **238**, 239, 240, 241, **242**, **245-247**, 248, **249**, 250, **251-253**, 254, **255**, **257-259**, 263, 267-269, 271, **275-278**, **282**, **283**, **288**, 289, 290, **291**, **292**, **293**, **294**, 329
Hermopolis 12
Herod, King **91**
Heroes of Chushingura 178
Herons 58, 59
Hersh, Helen 170, **171**
Hieroglyphic books 12
Hieroglyphic paintings 14, 18
Hieroglyphic writing 14, 140
Hierophant, The 137, 162, 170, 192, **193**, 208, **209**, **229**, 230, 240, **241**, **256**, 260, **261**, 264, 265, 269, 273, 328
High Priest, The 216, 217, **219**, **277**
High Priestess, The 49, 137, 140, **157**, **173**, 174, 210, 214, 215, 216, **229**, 230, **258**, **259**, 277, 292, **293**, 328
Hindu mythology 18
Hindustani language 18, 20
Hindustans 19, 217
Hire (see La Hire)
Historical tarock **302**
Historique et Chronique de Provence 32
History of Viterbo 32
Hobdell, Michael 272, 274
Hoffman, Douglas 192, **193**
Hogier 7
Hoi Polloi tarot 8, **259**
Holbein the Younger, Hans 192, **193**
Holy Grail 244
Holy Land 22
Holy Marriage, The 176, **177**
Holy Roman Emperor 302
Holy Spirit 66
Hope 47, 49, **51**, **52**, 64, 87, **91**
Horler, John A. 267
Hornbook 37, 39
Horus 143, 244, 281
House of God, The **115**, 137, **139**, 140
Htou-Tjyen 20
Huckerby, Peter 196
Huckerby tarot **196**
Hugues de Payns 22
Humberger Frères 65
Humphreys, Henry Noel 15
Hunting Pack 12, 53, **58**, 59, 111
Hurley, Rae 267
Hurley, William J. 267
Hutchinson Publishing Group Ltd. 272

♥ I ♠

I.F. 308
I.G. 152
I Tarocchi di Gentilini 254
Iamblichus 186, **187**
Ichazo, Oscar 260
Ichazo, Oscar, tarot of 260, **261**
I-Ching 279
Il Destino Svelato Dal Tarocco 8, **246**
Iliaco **38**, 39, 44
Imperator **38**, 39, **40**, 41, 112
Imperial eagle heraldic device (see Eagle heraldic device)
Imperial orb 66
Indian tarot 163, **167**
Industrie und gluck 303, 314, 324
Ingold 31
Insight Institute tarot 23, **197**
Interpolations 31-33
Interpreting tarot cards 327-336
Introduction to tarot cards 1-11
Invettiva contra il giuoco del tarocco 29
Ipeo 124, **127**
Isabel of Bavaria 7
Isabelle of Lorraine 26, 60
Ishtar 279
Isis 14, 162, 189, **190**, 224, **236**, 240, 241, 243, 244, 248, 257, 279, 290
Isis-Artemis 170
Isis Urania 189, **190**, 237
Istanbul, University of 53
Italian Major Arcana cards 146, **156**
Italian-Portuguese suit marks 53
Itzamna mask 289
Ixion 180
Izod, Sarah 173, 174

♣ J ♦

J.G. 152
Jachin 214, 215, 224
Jack 8
Jagannath **167**
Jakin 224
James Bond 007 1, 201, 253, 254
James IV of Scotland 26
Janeiro, Professor J. Iglesias 248
Janus 43
Japheth 11
Jean, Jacques 24
Jehovah-Sabaoth 180
Jerger, J. 8, 137, **151**
Jerusalem 11, 101
Jester 53, 206
Jewish theosophy 15
JHVH 7, 18, 22
Joachim of Flora 66
Joakim 214, 215
Joan of Arc 7
Joanna II of Naples, Queen 61
Jobert, Yves **178**
Jochai, Rabbi Simon Ben 16
Johannes von Rheinfelden, Brother 24, **25**
John 11
John of France, King 60
John of Salisbury 33
John Omwake Playing Card Collection xvi, 136, 146, 147, 156, 297, 300
John I 32
John II 32
Joker 9, 99, 279
Josephine, Empress 298
Juda traditor 91
Judas **91**
Judgment xvi, 3-5, 15-17, 30, 33, 49, **52**, 53, **55**, 61, 64, 72, **73**, **90**, 100, **101**,

112, **116**, **128**, **130**, **132**, **135**, 137, **139**, 140, **141-143**, **147**, **148**, 154, **157-160**, 163, 164, 178, 183, **185**, **190**, 191, 192, **193**, **198**, **203-205**, 206, **207**, 210, 211, 216, 217, **218**, **220**, 225, **226**, **233**, 234, **235**, **237**, 240, **241**, **252**, 253, 254, 255, **257**, **267**, **269**, 273, 278, 280, 281, **282**, 284, 285, 288, 290, **291**, 332
Judith 7, 28
Juggernaut 167
Juggler, The 49, **51**, **52**, 53, **54**, **55**, 66, 192, **193**, 269, 295
Junon 49, **155**, **159**, 174, 176, **177**, **189**, 269
Jupiter 39, **45**, **47**, 53, 140, **155**, **159**, 174, 176, **177**, **189**, 244, 266
Jupites 27
Justice xvi, 2-5, 15-17, 30, 33, 36, 39, **40**, **47**, 48, 49, **50-52**, **54**, **55**, 61, 64, 68-70, 99, 112, 113, 115, 130, **131**, 134, **135**, 137, **138**, **139**, 140, **141**, **142**, **145**, **147-150**, **153-156**, **158-161**, 163-166, 169, 170, **171**, **172**, **175**, 178, 183, **185**, 186, **187**, **188**, 189, **190**, 191, **194-199**, **201**, **203-205**, **212**, **213**, **216**, **217**, **219-221**, **223**, **224**, **228**, **229**, 230, **231-233**, 234, **235**, **236**, **238**, **239**, 240, **241**, **245-247**, 248, **249**, **250**, **251**, **252**, **254**, **255-259**, 263, **267-269**, 271, 272, **275-277**, **282**, **283**, **288**, 289, **294**, 329
Justicia 39, **40**, 44, **47**, 112
Justinger, Konrad 24, **25**

Kabbalah 15, 16, 22
Kabbalistic Order of the Rose-Cross 23
Kabbalists 7
Kali 170
Kalki 18, **167**
Kaou-tsung 20
Karin Koal Enterprises 229
Karma 234, 281
Karten 21
Kasdin, Simon 180
Kataiba 167
Kaye, Jerry 186, **187**
Kersaint, Jean-Pol de **173**, 174
Kestner Museum 108
King 7, 9, 39, 50, 54, 55, **57-59**, 74, 76, **79**, 87, 92, 96, 99, 100, **101**, 105, 110, 117, 118, 121, 122, **127**, 137, 138, 139, 148, 151, 159, 169, 178, 179, 180, 181, 182, 206, 207, 208, 209, 210, 214, 230, 231, 233, 237, 242, 247, 250, **251-253**, 254, 257, 260, 261, 262, 264, **265**, **267-270**, 273, 274, 282, 286, 291, 292, **293**
King and queen, game of 33
Kings of France 34
Kircher, Athanasius 14
Kloster, Suzanne 180, **181**
Klumper, W. Tj. 176
Knapp, J. A. 23, 198
Knapp tarot **198**
Knaves 7, 58, **127**
Knepper, E. **309**
Knight 7, 8, 9, 50, 55, 57, 59, 74, **75**, **78**, **79**, 84, 87, 96, **97**, **98**, 99, 100, **101**, **108**, **109**, **117-119**, 122, **124**, **125**, 134, **138**, 148, 154, **155**, **160**, **172**, 182, **183**, **207**, **208**, **209**, **210**, **214**, 230, **231**, **233**, **253**, 254, **262**, **268-270**, **273**, **274**, 286

Knight, female 87, **93**, **95**
Knight, Gareth 186
Konig 9
Koran 20
Korean Arrow 20
Krishna 18
Kundalini 281
Kunsthistorisches Museum 58
Kurma 18

La Hire 7
Ladies tarock No. 162   **322**
Ladislaus of Naples, King 61
Laforge, Lucien 218
Laliberte, Norman **179**
Lancelot 7, 30
Lando, Giuseppe **150**
Lando tarot 146
Langres (see Synod of Langres)
Last Judgment, The 49, **52**, **128**, 137, 192, **193**
Latin inscriptions on cards 124, 133
Laura 21
Laurence, L. W. de 199
Laurence tarot, de 8, **199**
Laurent, Jean Pierre 151
Laws of the kingdom of Spain 32
Lazzarelli, Ludovico 26, 27
Leber, Michel Constant 18
Lenain 22
Lenpio 24, **126**
Lent 22, 66
Lentulo 124, **127**
Leo 208
Leopold I 312
Lepen-Du **145**
Lesser Trumps 295, 296
Le-Tan, Pierre **179**, 180
Levi, Eliphas 14, 15, 16, **22**, 162, 167, 211, 272
Leyden, Rudolf von 20
Liberal Arts 38, 39, 42
Liberte 155
Libra 51
Lille, ordinance of 24
Lingam yoni 224
Linweave tarot **200**
Lion heraldic device 61, **62**, 74
Littel, Sander 186, **187**
Little Egypt 21
Live and Let Die 253
Logic 47
Loica 38, 39, 42, 47
Lollio, Flavio Alberti 29
Lombardi 49
Lombardy tarocchi 63
Longhi, Roberto 106
Longo, Luis Pena 250
Loring, Christian **184**
Loudier, N.F. 137
Louis XIV 112
Louvre Museum 120-122, 128, 129
Love 49, **50**
Lover's tarot **201**
Lovers, The xvi, 2-5, 15-17, 30, 33, 36, 39, **40**, 48, 49, **50**, **51**, 53, **55**, 61, 62, 64, 68-70, **71**, 89, 106, 112, 113, **131**, 134, **135**, 137, **138**, **139**, 140, **141-143**, **145**, **148-150**, **153-161**, 163-166, **169**, 170, **173**, **175**, 183, **185**, 186, **187**, **188**, 189, **190**, 191, 192, **193**, **194-199**,

201, **203-205**, 208, **209**, **212**, **213**, **216**, **217**, **218-223**, 224, **228**, **229**, 230, **232**, **233**, **236-239**, 240, **241**, **242**, **245-247**, 248, **249**, **250**, **251**, **252**, **254**, **255-259**, 260. **261**, 263, 264, **265**, **267**, **269**, **270**, **275-278**, **282**, **283**, **288**, 289, 292, 293, **294**, 328, 329
Lower Egypt 260
Lubow, Martha **202**
Lubow, Nancy **202**
Lucas, Eva G. 176
Ludus cartarum 24, **25**
Ludus chartarum dialogus 28
Luke 11
Luna **27**, 39, **40**, 44, 112
Lust 243

M A 197
M A C 110
Macedonia 133
Mackenzie, Kenneth 22
MacPherson, Mary Kay 170, **171**
Madenie, P. 137
Maffei, Raphaelus 33
Magasin Pittoresque 32
Magi 129, 189, **190**, 237
Magician, The xvi, 2, 4, 5, 15-17, 30, 33, **36**, 48, **51**, **52**, 53, **54**, **55**, 64, 66, 117, 118, 130, **131**, **132**, 134, **135**, 137, **138**, **139**, 140, **143**, **145**, **148-150**, **152-161**, 163-166, 169, 173, 174, **175**, 176, **177-179**, 182-185, 186, **187**, **188**, 189, **190**, 194, **196-201**, 203, 204, 206, **207**, **208**, **209-213**, 215, **216**, **218-221**, **223**, **224**, **226**, **228**, **229**, 230, **231-233**, 234, **235-239**, 240, **241-243**, **245-247**, 248, **249**, **250**, **251**, **253**, 254, **255**, **257-259**, **262**, 263, 264, **265**, **267-271**, 273, **275-278**, 279, 280, **282**, **283**, 287, **288**, 292, 293, **294**, 295, 296, 327
Magus Belline 237
Magus Edmond 237
Magus, The 176, **177**, 189, **190**, 236, 240, **241**, **243**, 244
Mahakala 281
Mahakali 280, 281
Mainz 31
Major Arcana 1-5, 14, 15, 17, **48**, **50-52**, 53, **54**, **55**, **65-73**, 87, 124, 137, 169-226, **228-294**
Major Arcana card titles 2, 3, 5, 30, 33
Major Arcana related to astrology 4, 5
Major Arcana related to suit signs 4
Malik 53
Maltese cross 103
Mamluk 53, **56**
Manfreda, Sister 66
Mann, Sylvia 21
Manni 24
Mansheim, Gerald 225
Mansueto 30
Mantegna (see tarocchi of Mantegna)
Mantegna, Andrea 35
Mantua 30
Marcello, Jacobo Antonio 26
Marcolino, Francesco 28
Maria di Savoy 60, 89, 106, 107
Mario 124, **126**
Mark 11
Marriage **141**
Mars **27**, 206, 266

Marschalli 24
Marseilles, archives of 24
Marte 39, **40**, 45, 112
Martinists 23
Martius, Galcottus 7, 28
Martyr, The **219**
Mary 243
Mary Cheney Library 179
Mary of Anjou 7
Marziano da Tortona 26
Marzoli 35, 63, 64, 104, **105**
Masenghini tarocchino **203**, **263**
Mason 23
Mat 20
Mathers, MacGregor 1, 5, 23, 256
Mathers, Samuel Liddell
  (see Mathers, MacGregor)
Mathison, Paul 269
Mato, O 124
Matsya 18, **167**
Matthew 11
Maut 243
May, Wayne 176
Mayan tarot (see Xultun tarot)
Mayer, Joannes Pelagius **136**
Mayer, L. A. 53
Mazzarino, Countessa di 63
McGuire, James Clark 125
McIntosh, Christopher 22
Medici, Lorenzo 30
Medieval style tarot **184**
Meliadus de Leonnoys, roi 31
Melpomene **38**, 39, 42, 47
Memorie Spettanti alla Storia della
  Calcografia del Commend 88, 89
Menchia 49
Mendragora Press 276
Menegazzi, Osvaldo 204
Menegazzi Seashell tarocco **204**
Mensa Isiaca 14
Merchadante **38**, 39, 41
Mercurio 39, 45, 47
Mercurius **27**
Mercury 47, 202, 240, 244, 266, 279
Merrimack Publishing Corp. 272
Metcalfe, Andrew J. 186, **187**
Metelo 124, **127**
Metropolitan Museum of Art 65, 124, 125
Mexican Indians 19
Mexquimilli 289, 290
Meyer, Kitty 178
Michael, Archangel 206
Michel, Wes 195
Michele, Parrasio 35
Michelino de Besozzo et les relations
  entre l'art italien et l'art francais 26
Midas 29, 133
Middleton, Richard 11
Milanese tarocchi 60, 163
Milano 154
Milchram, Leopold 57
Military tarock **305**, **313**
Minchiate 28, 49, **51**, **52**, 53, 128, 129
Minero, Sergio 205
Minero tarot **205**
Miniature Rider-Waite tarot 9, 272
Minoan 170
Minor Arcana 1, 5-8, 14, 53, 74-87, 124
Minos 170
Miseria 53, **55**
Misero 37, **38**, 39, 41, 112
Mistletoe 192

Mitelli, Giuseppe Maria 53, 54, 147
Moakley, Gertrude 20, 61, 66, 106
Modiano, S. D. 55, 246, 316
Modrone, Visconti di 63
Moed, Lucia 257
Monde Primitif 1, 12, **13**, 139
Monsters 49
Mont-Saint-Johns 232
Montreal Museum of Fine Arts
  35, 63, 64, 100, 102, 106, 107
Moon Lady 170
Moon, The xvi, 3-5, 15-17, 30, 33, 39,
  40, 49, **50**, **52**, 53, **54**, **55**, 60, 64, 72,
  73, 106, 112, **115**, **117**, **118**, 128, **130**,
  135, 136, 137, 139, 140, **141**, **147**, **148**,
  154, **158-161**, 164, 166, 169, 170, **171**,
  175, 179, 180, **182**, **183**, **185**, **190**, 191,
  195-198, 200, **203-205**, 210, 213, 216,
  217, **220-223**, 224, 232, 233, 236, **238**,
  239, 240, 241, **245**, 246, **252**, **253**, 254,
  255, **258**, 267, 269, 271, 273, **276**, **277**,
  282-285, **288**, 290, **291**, 331
Moorne, Dr. 144
Moors 49, **50**, 53
Morelli, Giovani 24, 39
Morgan, F. Cleveland 100, 102
Morgan, J. Bartlett 35, 100
Morgan Press 229
Morgan's tarot **257**
Morocco 20
Moser, Ditha 317
Moses 10, 11, 15
Mount Sinai 11, 15
Mountain Dream tarot 8, 9, 264, **265**
Muchery Astrological tarot **266**
Muchery, Georges 5, 266
Mulleague, Madilynne 176
Muller, H. F. 300
Municipal Library of Rouen 133
Municipality of Amsterdam 188
Murr, G. G. von 32
Musee du Louvre (see Louvre)
Museo, Biblioteca e Archivio di Bassana
  del Grappa 120
Museo Civico of Catania 108, 109
Museo Correr 120, 123
Museo Fournier 48, 99, 103, 106, 111,
  148, 154, 158, 159, 174
Museo Fournier Visconti-Sforza tarocchi
  cards 35, 63, 64, 99, 103, 106
Museum for Kunsthandwerk 132
Museum of Islamic Art 7
Musicha **38**, 39, 42
Muses 38, 39, 41, 42, 47
Muslim dervish 18
Mystical number seven 14

 N

N.P. 20
Nabuchodenasor 124
Nahipi 24
Nahui ollin 289
Na'ib 20, 53
Naib thani 53
Naibbe 24
Naibi 20, 24, 39, 53
Naipes 20
Napoleon I 14, 298, 320
Napoleon tarock **298**
Nara-simha 18
Natanabo 124
National Gallery of Art 43, 45, 46, 65,
  130, 131

National Museum of Warsaw 108, 109
Nature 261
Nawa Graha 20
Naypes 32, 53
Nec spe nec metu 104
Nefertiti 186
Nejedly, John 314
Nejedly tarock **314**
Nenbroto 124, **127**
Neptune 176, 266
Neptune's trident 164
Nerone 124, **126**
Nerva 29
Nessim, Barbara 180, **181**
Nettles, Bea 264, 265
Neubronner 24
Neuchatel 153
New (Hurley) tarot, The 8, 9, **267**
New Tarot for the Aquarian Age, The
  268
New Testament 11, 21
Nicolas Pepin (see Pepin)
Nike 170
Nile River 244
Nimbus 264
Nineteenth-century tarot decks 156-167
9th Dimension Tarot Game 232
Ninus 133
Nizah 180
Noah 11
Noah's Ark 11
Noonan, Julia 213
Nordic, Rolla K. 269
Nordic tarot **269**
Norman Conquest 21
Nostradamus, Casar 32
Novak, Gianni 172
Numerology 23, 140, 206, 208, 234, 237
Nuremberg 32, 34

 O

O.T.O. (see Order of the Temple of
  the Orient)
Ober 9
Octava spera 39, 46
Ode to tarot xv
Odell, Robert 206-208
Odell tarot 8, 206, **207**, 208
Oedipus Aegyptiacus 14
Old Man, The **51**, **52**, 54, **121**, **128**
Old Testament 11
Olinpia 124
Olivo 124, **127**
Ollgaard, Rita 208, **209**
Olympus 174
Omission of cards in literature 33
1JJ Swiss tarot 6, **8**, 9, **270**
Ono tarot 1
Opera and Operetta tarock **306**
Oral cultures 12
Orat 1
Order of the Band 31
Order of the Golden Dawn, The
  22, 23, 256, 272
Order of the Temple of the Orient 23
Oriental influence in cards 59, 299
Origins of tarocchi cards 12-23
Ormuzd 18
Orsini, Paolo 61
Ortega, Enrique **210**
Oscan & Samnite alphabet **15**
Osiris 137, 139, **190**, 191, 244

Osterreichische Nationalbibliothek 24, **25**
Ouspensky, P. D. 14
Oversize tarot cards 157, **162**
Ovid 33
Oysivete 31

P

Pachis 33
Pack of princely hunting cards 58, 59
Padua 20, 35, 178
Pagad 20, 295
Pagan idols 2
Pagan imagery 30
Pa-gat 298
Page 7, 8, 39, 40, 55, 57, 59, **75**, **78**, **81**, 84, **85**, 87, 94, **95**, 96, 97, 98, **99**, 100, **101**, **102**, 103, **104**, **105**, 108, 110, 111, **116-119**, 122, **127**, 134, **138**, **151**, **182**, 207, 208, 210, 214, 230, 231, 242, **252**, **268-270**, **273**, **274**
Page, female 87, 95
Painted Caravan, The 214
Painted Pasteboards 2
Palace of Minos 170
Palace of Plutus, The 137, **139**
Palamede 29
Palazzo Fibbia 33
Palazzo Pallavicini 33
Palazzo Sola 124
Palladini, David Mario 1, 200, 229
Pallas 7
Pan 174
Panch Pandava 20
Panfilio 124, **126**
Pano tarot 1
Papa **38**, **39**, **40**, 41, 47, 112
Papasse, La 49
Papus 15, 16, 18, 23, 162, 167, 211, 272, 282
Papus Tarot **211**
Paracu-rama 18
Paradise 15
Paris Scenic tarock **321**
Parisian tarot 134, **135**
Parke, Jessie Burns 23, 239
Parliament Rolls 26
Parravicino, Emiliano de 63
Party per pale 74, 75, 78, 85
Pastor, Edouard 212
Pastor tarot **212**
Pavia 60, 89, 106
Pavia, Prince of 106
Payen, Jean 146, **148**
Pazzo, Il 165
Peacock 132, **157**, 167, **270**
Peacock feathers 75, **95**, **98**, **101**, 229, 230
Peladan, Josephin 23
Pelerinaige de l'homme, le 31
Pelican heraldic device
 (see Bird heraldic device)
Pellerin 245
Penland School of Crafts 264
Pentagram 11, 176
Pentateuch 16
Pepin, Nicolas 20
Persephone 170
Perseus 256
Persia 217
Peterson, Diana 225
Petit Oracle des Dames, Le 157
Petrarch, Francesco 20, 21, 34, 61

Pfluger tarock 300, **301**
Phaeton 37, 45
Pharaoh, The **261**
Pharaohs 257, 260
Philosofia **38**, 39, 42, **47**
Philosophical Society 23
Philosophy 42, 47
Phoenician alphabet **15**
Phoenix tarot 176, **177**
Phote Mantenir 96
Phrygian king 133
Piatnik & Sohne, Ferd. 271, 307, 308, 313, 315, 317-319, 322, 324, 325
Piatnik/Pointner tarot **271**
Piazza universale di tutte le Professioni del Mondo 30
Picini, Andrea 176
Pictorial Key to the Tarot, The 23, 272
Picture cards 7
Piedmontese tarocchi **6**, **48**, 49, 157, **161**, 263
Pierpont Morgan-Bergamo tarocchi deck 1, 9, 35, 58, 60, 62-64, **65-86**, 87, 93, 94, 96, 98, 100, 102, 104, 106, 107, 124, **285**
Pierpont Morgan Library 1, 35, 63, 65-71
Pierre, Jean 153
Pietropaulo da San Chirico 28
Piggin, Julia Remine 213
Pignorius, Laurentius 14
Pinacoteca di Brera Collection 96-98
Pinchart, Alexandre 24
Pip cards 7, 8, 64, **75-77**, **79**, 80, 82, 83, 95, 98
Pipozzo di Sandro 31
Pisa 32
Pisces 181
Pitois, Jean Baptist 22
Planets 5, 14, 44
Platini, Baptista 26
Playing-Card Society, Journal of the 33
Playing Cards of Various Ages and Countries 151
Po River 22
Poesia **38**, 39, 42, **43**
Poesie leggende costumanze del medio evo 30
Poesie Pastorali 69
Poetry 43
Pointner, Rudolf 271
Polimnia **38**, 39, 42
Polisena 124
Polo sticks 53, 56
Pop/Rock Tarot Calendar **213**
Pope Clement, anti- 32
Pope John XXIII, anti- 61
Pope Pius VII 298
Pope, The xvi, 2-5, 15-19, 30, 33, 35, 36, **37**, 39, **40**, 47, **48**, 49, 53, **54**, 61, 64, 67, 69, 72, 82, 87, 100, **101**, **110**, 112, 113, **121**, **125**, 133-135, 137, **138**, **139**, 140, 148-150, 153, 155, 158-161, 163-166, 169, 170, 172, 178, 183, 185, 186, **187**, **188**, 189, **190**, 191, 192, **193**, 194, 196-199, 201-203, 205, 206, **207**, 208, **209**, 211-213, 216, 217, 219-221, 223, 224, 228, 229, 230, 231-233, 236-239, 240, 241, 242, 245-247, 248, 249, 250, **251**, 254, **255**-259, 260, 261-263, 264, **265**-269, 273, 275-278, **282**, **283**, **288**, 289, 290, **291**, **294**, 328
Popess, The xvi, 2-5, 15-17, 30, 33, 36,
48, 49, 53, 64, 66, 87, 91, **103**, 130, 134, **135**, **138**, **139**, 140, 145, 148-150, **153**-**161**, 163-166, 169, 172, 173, **175**, 176, **177**, **178**, 183-185, 188, 189, **190**, 192, 193, 194, 196-199, 201-205, 206, 207, 208, 209-212, 214, 215, 216, 219-221, 223, 224, 226, 228, 229, 230, 231-233, 236, 237-239, 240, 241, **242**, 245-247, 248, 249, 250, **251**, 253, 254, **255**, **258**, 259, 262, 263, 264, **265**, 267-270, 275-277, 279, 280, 282, **283**, 287, **288**, 290, 291, 292, 293, 294, 328
Porta, Guiseppe 28
Porter, David Lord 173
Posters **173**, 174
Postumio 124, **126**
Poupart, Charles 21, 24
Practical Astrology 189, 190
Praktische tarot 257, **258**
Prayer book 11
Pre-Columbian symbolism 19
Prehistoric man 12
Prevot of Paris 24
Priestess, The **269**, 287, **288**
Prima Causa 39, **43**, 46
Primo Mobile 39, 46, 47
Prince, The **219**, 244
Producciones y Ediciones Acuario S.A. 228
Prohibitions against playing cards 24
Prophetic Tarot, The 180
Provence 32, 110
Proverb tarock **311**
Prudence 47, 49, 51, **52**, 69, 137, **139**, 141-143, **146**
Prudencia **38**, 39, 44, 47, **144**
Pry, Charles 192, **193**
Ptolemaic system 44
Ptolemy 28
Published references to playing cards 24-33
Putto 72
Pythagoras 14

 Q

Quartes 24, 31
Queen 7, 9, 50, 54, 55, 58, 74, **75**, **78**, **81**, 84, 96, 97, 100, **101**, 108, **109**, **117**, **118**, **121**, **122**, **127**, 130, 137, **138**, **139**, **154**, **155**, **159**, 169, 176, **177**, **179**, 180, 208, **209**, 210, 214, 230, 231, 236, **237**, 242, 247, **250**, **251**, 253, 254, 260, 261, **262**, 264, **265**, 267-270, **273**, **274**, **282**, **291**, 292, 293
Queen of Sheba 11
Queen, The 186, **187**, 219
Quetzalcoatl 290
Quill (see Arrow)
Quince heraldic device 61, 107

R

Rachel 7
Rai, Ron 200
Rakoczi, Basil Ivan 214
Rakoczi tarot **214**, 215
Rama-chandra 18
Raman, Dio 258
Rano tarot 1
Raoul de Presle 32
Ravenswood Eastern tarot 8, 215, **216**, 217
Re 35, **38**, **39**, **40**, 41
Reaper, The 170, **171**, **219**, **236**

Reaping Skeleton, The **190,** 191
Rebetez, Rene 228
Red Book 24
Red Cross 318
Red suit values 28
Regardie, Francis Israel **256**
Rege et Regina game 33
Regnabo 69, 100
Regnavi 69, 100
Regno 69, 100
Remodini Collection 120
Renard le Contrefait 31
Renault 137
Rene of Anjou, King 26
Rep(-)u(-) 99
Resurrection of the Flesh, The 176, **177**
Rhetoric 47
Rhetorica **38,** 39, 42, 47
Rider and Company 23, 272
Rider-Waite tarot **8, 9,** 23, 197, 199, 215, 239, 247, 259, 264, 272, **273,** 294
Riminaldi, Mamma 30
Ringhieri, Innocentio 30
Rings heraldic device 61, **62,** 66, 79, 93, 107
Rip Van Winkle 206
Rivers, Larry 1, **178**
Ro 1
Robbins, Morgan 257
Rochias fils 146, **153**
Rodetzky, Field Marshall 313
Rog 1
Rolt-Wheeler, Francis 184
Roman alphabet **15**
Roman du Roi Meliadus de Leonnoys 31
Romance of King Meliadus 31
Romances in literature 34
Romanian Empress **173,** 174
Romany 21
Ronfa 30
Ros 1
Rosae Crucis, Ancient Order of 22
Rosenkreuze, Christian 22
Rosenthal Collection 59, 105
Rosenthal Visconti-Sforza tarocchi 35, 63, 64, 99, 106, 111
Rosenwald Collection 43, 45, 46, 65, 130, 131
Rosetta Stone 14
Rosicrucians 22
Rota 1, 224
Rota deck **181**
Rothschild, Edmond de 120-122, 128, 129
Rottgen, Herwarth 59
Royal Fez Moroccan tarot **8,** 272, **274, 275**
Royal Society of Arts, Journal of the 32
Royal Spanish Academy's Dictionary 20
Ruiz, Franco Mora 236
Ruler, The 287, **288**
Rupert III, Emperor 61, 74

♥ S ♣

Saba-Telli, Antonio 192, **193**
Sabino 124, **127**
Sacerdotal tarot **218**
Sacred Egyptian tarot **219**
Sacred Tarot, The 240
Sadhu, Mouni 176
Sage, The 137, **139, 219,** 240, **241**
St. Andrew's Cross 289
St. Anthony 26

St. Bernardin of Siena 26
St. Croix Inc. 232
St. George 122
Saint-Germain, Comte C. 189, 190
St. John 46
St. Luke 46
St. Mark 14, 46
St. Matthew 46
St. Peters 113
Salverte, Eusebe 22
Salviati 28
Samaritan alphabet **15**
Samothracian 170
Sample tarot card reading 343, 344
Samson 250
San fine (see Sine fine)
Sano tarot 1
Sanskrit 19, 33, 211, 282
Santambrogio, Marco 33
Saracen heraldic device 62, **95**
Saracens 19, 32
Sarafino 124
Satan 206
Sati 18
Satraps 49, **50,** 53
Saturn 234, 279
Saturno 39, **40, 46,** 112
Saturnus **27**
Satyr, The **173,** 174
Savoy 100
Savoy heraldic device 106
Scacchi 19
Schikowski tarot **220**
Schlossman, Sylvia **181**
Scholastic Book Services 213
Schreiber, Lady Charlotte 151
Schreiber, Wilhelm 31
Scimtars 53, 56
Scorpio 250
Scott, Sarah 192, **193, 220,** 221
Seasons 7
Secret Dakini Oracle 279
Seeker of the Truth, The 137, **139**
Senatus Venetus 124
Sepher Yesirah 4, 16, 180
Sephiroth 16, **17**
Sermones de Ludo Cumalis **xvi,** 2, 28
Serpent crest 106
Serpent heraldic device 60, 62, 99, 100, **101, 108, 110, 111**
Sesto 124, **126**
Seun-Ho 20
Seven 14
Seven wonders of the world 11
Sewera, W. 303
Sforza, Cardinal Ascanio Maria 33, 62, 100, 106, 107
Sforza, Francesco 33, 60-62, 67, 72, 89, 101, 106, 107
Sforza, Galeazzo Maria 62, 102
Sforza, Giangaleazzo 62
Sforza helmet 85
Sforza heraldic devices 61, 62
Sforza, Ludovico 62
Sforza, Muzio Attendolo (see Attendolo)
Sforzas 60
Shakespeare 202, 305
Shakti 279, 281
Sharp, Katherine **202**
Sharp, Rosalind 268
Shatranj 19
Sheets of uncut cards **52,** 65, 124, **125, 128-131,** 134

Shem 11
Sheridan, David 276
Sheridan/Douglas tarot 8, **276**
Sherman, Johanna 186, **187**
Ship, The 53, **55**
Shiva 217, 281
Shree Tatva Nidhi 20
Sicilian tarot packs 53, **55**
Sidjakov, Nicolas 200
Sigler, Dorothy **178, 179,** 180
Silver Age 14
Simon, J. M. 230, 237, 262
Sine fine 104
Singer, Samuel Weller 19, 28, 31
Sirius 137
Sironi, G. 163, **164**
Siva 18
Size of cards **9**
Skell, Sue 192, **193**
Skor-Mor Corp. 283
Slinger, Penny 279
Sloane Collection 47
Smith, Pamela Colman 1, 23, 272
Sociatas Rosicruciana in Anglia 22, 23
Sol 39, 45, 112
Sola Busca 124, **126, 127**
Solar system **142**
Soldaten tarock No. 217   318
Soldier's Almanack 11
Solis, Virgil 132
Solomon 11, 16
Solve 176
Sorcerer, The 287, **288**
Sorel, Agnes 7, 313
Sorti, Le 28
Sota, La 9
Spades 7, 8, **134**
Spanish conquest 19
Spanish tarot **8, 277**
Speranza 39, 44, 47
Sphinx, The **190,** 191, 222, 256
Sphinx Verlag Basel 292
Spreading the tarot deck 337-345
 Gypsy spread 342
 Horseshoe spread 339, 340
 Name spread 339
 Royal spread 341
 Seventh-card spread 341
 Ten-card spread with forty-two cards 339
 Ten-card spread with twenty-two Major Arcana cards 337
Stadthaus at Ulm 26
Staffs 53
Stahly, F. 182
Star, Ely 5, 23
Star of David 192
Star, The xvi, 3-5, 15-17, 30, 33, **48, 49, 52,** 53, **55,** 60, 64, 72, 87, 91, 99, 103, 104, 106, 117, 118, 128, 129, 131, **135, 136,** 139, 140, 146, 148-150, 154, 158-161, 164-166, 175, 183, 185, 188, 189, 190, 191, 196-198, 203, 205, 211, 213, 216, 217, 220, 223, 224, 232, 233, 236, 238, 239, 240, 241, 246, 247, 250, 251, 254, 255, 264, 265, 267, 269, 273, 276, 277, 282-285, 288, 290, 291, 331
Starter tarot 278
Statute of 1496   26
Staves 4, 5, 6, 7, 49, 56, 76, 78-80, 93, 96, 97, 99, 103, 105, 111, 117, 118-125, 133, 134, 138, 139, 154, **159,** 182, 206, 208, **209, 210,** 217, 218, 230,

231, 233, 242, 243, 244, **252, 253, 254, 259, 262, 267, 269, 270, 273, 275, 282, 291, 292, 293,** 333, 334
Steele, Robert 26, 32
Stephen de Vignoles 7
Stewart-Patterson, Cleveland 63, 64, 100, 102
Stone of Scone 281
Stonehenge 192
Strambo, F. 163, **165**
Strauss, Walter 47
Strength xvi, 3-5, 15-17, 30, 33, 36, 39, **40, 48,** 49, **50-52, 54, 55,** 64, 69, 70, 72, 106, 112, 114, 115, 130, **131, 135,** 137, **139,** 140, 141, 142, 144, **145,** 147-150, 153, 154, 156, 158-161, 163-166, 169, 170, 172, 175, 180, **181,** 183, **185,** 188, 189, 190, 191, **194,** 196-199, 201, **203,** 205, 206, **207,** 208, **209, 212, 213, 216, 217, 219-221, 223, 224, 228, 229,** 230, **232, 233, 236, 238, 239,** 240, **241, 245-247,** 248, **249,** 250, **251, 252, 259,** 260, **261, 263,** 264, **265, 267, 269, 271, 272, 275-277, 282, 283, 288,** 289, 290, **291, 294,** 330
Suit signs in United States and Europe **10**
Suits 5, 6, 7, 18, 49, 66
Sultan, The **134**
Sum sine regno 69, 100
Sun heraldic device **61,** 67, 71, 78, 79, 81, **82, 104, 105**
Sun, The xvi, 3-5, 15-17, 30, 33, 39, 49, **50, 52, 53, 54, 55,** 60, 64, 72, 73, 99, 110, 111, 112, **115, 117, 118,** 128-130, **135, 136, 137, 139,** 140, **143, 147, 148, 154,** 157-161, 163, 164, 166, 169, 170, 171, **176, 177,** 180, 181, 183, 185, **188,** 189, 190, 191, 192, **193, 196-198,** 203-205, 208, 209, 213, 216, 217, 220, **221, 223, 224, 225,** 232, 233, 234, **235, 236, 238, 239,** 240, **241, 242, 245-247,** 248, **249,** 253, 254, **255, 257, 258,** 260, **261, 264, 265, 267, 269-271, 272, 273, 276-278, 280, 281, 282-286, 288,** 290, **291,** 331, 332
Supreme being 176
Surch, Josef 308
Surgite ad judicium 90
Susio, Grambattista 30
Swords 4, 5, **6,** 7, 28, 49, 53, **74-76,** 92, 93, 99, 108, 110, 111, 117-120, 122-124, **125,** 131, 133, 134, 138, 139, 148, 149, 151, 153, 154, 159, 160, 169, 178, 183, 200, 206, 208, 209, 210, 214, 215, **229,** 230, 231, 233, 240, 242, 243, 244, 247, 253, 254, 262, 264, 265, **267,** 269, 270, 273-275, 282, 286, 292, 293, 332, 333
Swords upright or reversed **76**
Synod of Langres 26
Synod of Wurzburg 31

♥ T ♣

Table of Cebes 18
Tablet of Isis 14
Tack holes 63, 117, 118
Taj 18
Talia **27, 38,** 39, 42, 47
Tamed Lion, The 191
Tang, Professor 53

Tano tarot 1
Tantric tarot 8, 279, **280,** 281
Taor 1
Tar 1
Taro Adivinhatorio 8, **282**
Taro River 21
Taro Village 21, 22
Tarocchi 1, 28, 30, 47, 49, 53, 63-138
Tarocchi of Mantegna **26,** 27, 35, **37, 38,** 39, **40-47,** 112
Tarocchi of Venice **48,** 49
Tarocchini di Bologna 32, 49, **50,** 53
Tarocchini of Mitelli 53, **54**
Tarocco 1, 29
Tarocco Siciliano 53, **55**
Tarock decks 295-326
Tarock No. 4 **323**
Tarock No. 36a **325**
Tarok Tso Lake 22
Tarot 1
Tarot: A Key to the Wisdom of the Ages 23
Tarot anagrams 1
Tarot and cards as separate games 3, 26, 30
Tarot Cards For Fun and Fortune Telling 270
Tarot Cards Painted by Bonifacio Bembo, The 20, 22
Tarot Classic **8, 9, 242**
Tarot de Acuario **228**
Tarot der Eingeweihten 220
Tarot des Bohemians, Le 23
Tarot Divinhatoire, Le 162, 167, 211, **282**
Tarot, Le 184
Tarot of Marseilles **6, 9,** 23, 49, 119, 137, 138, 230, 242, **262, 278**
Tarot of the Witches 253
Tarot Revélé, Le 180
Tarot Sacerdotal, Le **218**
Tarot Shows the Path, The 269
Tarot, The 276
Tarotée 1, **8**
Tarotiers 1
Tarotrump **323**
Tas 18
Taurus 244, 256
Tavaglione, Giorgio 186, **187**
Taylor, Connie **222**
Tellurian tarot **223,** 224
Temperance xvi, 3-5, 15-17, 30, 33, 39, **40, 48,** 49, **50-52,** 53, **54, 55,** 60, 64, 69-71, 72, 91, 100, **102,** 106, 107, 110, 112, **115,** 117, 118, **131, 132, 135, 136, 137, 139,** 140, 141, **143,** 144, 147-152, **154,** 156-166, 169, 170, 171, 175, 176, 177, 183, **185,** 188, 189, 190, 191, 194-198, 203-205, 206, **207,** 208, **209,** 212, 213, 219-221, **223, 224, 226, 229,** 230, **232, 233, 236, 238, 239,** 240, **241, 246,** 248, **249,** 250, **251, 252,** 254, **255, 256, 258, 259,** 260, **261, 263,** 267-269, **275-277,** 282-285, **288,** 290, **291, 294,** 330
Temperancia 38, 39, 40, 44, 112
Templars 22
Temple of Solomon 22
Temple, The 180, **181**
Temptation 222
Ten Commandments 11
Teotihuacan 224
Terminology 1

Terpsicore 38, 39, 41
Terza et ultima parte dé Ragionamenti del divino Pietro Aretino, La 28
Terzo, Ottobuono 61
Tetragrammaton 14, 18, 22, 23, 224, 244
Thalia 35, 47
Theatrical tarock **310**
Theologia **38,** 39, 43
Theological virtues 44, 49, 87
Theology 42
Theosophical Society 23
Thimble-Rigger, The 137
Thirteen Tarot Cards from the Visconti-Sforza Set 100, 101
Thoth 12, 249, 257
Thunder-struck Tower, The **190,** 191
Tibet 22, 257
Tikal 19, 287, 289
Tikal Museum 287, 289, 290
Tilley, Roger 21
Time 21, 137
Timur Lenk 21
Titze and Schinkay 306
Toledo 32
Toltec 290
Tonal 287
Tonalamatl 19
Topkapi Sarayi Museum 53, 56
Tora 1, 224
Torah 14, 214, 215, 290
Torquemada 19
Torresino, Giacomo 33, 106
Tortona 63, 106
Tower, The xvi, 3-5, 15-18, 30, 33, **48, 49, 50-52, 53, 54, 55,** 64, 65, **71, 72,** 112, **115, 125,** 128, **129-132, 135, 136,** 137, **139,** 140, **142, 143,** 146, 148-150, **152,** 154, **156,** 159-162, 164-166, 169, 170, 172, 175, **179,** 180, **181,** 183, **185,** 189, 190, 191, 196-198, 201-203, 205, 213, 216, 217, 220, **223, 224, 226, 232, 233, 236, 238, 239,** 240, **241, 242, 245, 246,** 248, **249,** 250, **251,** 254, **255, 267,** 269, 270, 273, **276-278, 280,** 281, 282-286, **288,** 290, **291,** 331
Tozzi, Piero 35, 63, 64, 100, 101
Traitor 49, **50, 51, 54,** 141, 142
Transitional tarot **225**
Translation errors 31-33
Transylvania 174
Trappola 53, **57**
Trattato del governo della famiglia 31
Trease, Geoffroy 61
Treatise of Theology 26
Treatise on the Government of the Family 31
Tree of Knowledge 224
Tree of Life 15, **17,** 23, 170, 186, 234, 292 , 331
Trefoils 7
Trictrac 24, 31, 32, 33
Trinity 11, 46, 192, 206
Trionfi 1, 28
Trionpho della Fortuna 28
Triumphi 1
Triumphi poem 20, **21**
Troa 1
Trojan 29
Trojan warrior 7
Trotta, Diana 30
Trotta, Virginia 30
Troy, siege of 29

Trumps 1, 28, 30, 49, 243, 295, 296
Tuchim 32
Tulio 124, **126**
Turkish Costume tarock 300
Tutankhamen 257
Tutti i trionfi 30
Twelve Apostles 11
Twelve Tribes of Israel 11
20th Century tarot **283**
Twentieth-century tarot decks 168-294
Typhon 137, **139**, 191, 237, 248
Tzolkin 19

U

U. S. Games Systems, Inc. 70, 84, 234, 242, 253, 270, 272, 274, 285
Ulm 21, 24, 26
Umiliata Order 66
Underknaves 58
United States Playing Card Company, The xvi, 136, 146, 156, 297, 300
Universe, The 45, 176, **177**, 208, **209**, **257**, 295
University Press 272
Unter 9
Upper Burma 22
Upper Egypt 260
Uraeus 260
Urania **38**, 39, 41, 47
Uranus 234, 266
Urban VI 32

V

Vacchetta, Giovanni 166
Vacchetta tarot 163, **166**
Vajradhara 281
Vamana 18
Vandenborre tarot **6**, **145**, **152**, **284**
Varah 18
Varallo 165
Veiled Lamp, The **190**, 191
Velim Fundam Dari Miki 133
Venice, magistracy of 26
Venturio 124, **126**
Venus 28, 39, **40**, 45, **54**, 202, 224, 230, 243, 266, 279, 290
Verard 31
Vereinigte Stralsunder Spielkarten Fabriken 311
Versino, Giuseppe **161**
Vices and Virtues 248
Victoria **27**
Victoria and Albert Museum 35, 59, 63, 64, 99, **104**, 105
Victoria and Albert Visconti-Sforza tarocchi 63, 64, 103, **104**
Viking 256
Viper heraldic device 95
Virtues 4, 7, 30, 44, 49, 51, 69, 87, 137
Visconti, Bernabo 60

Visconti, Bianca Maria 33, 60-62, 67, 72, 89, 100, 101, 106, 107
Visconti, Filippo Maria 26, 60, 61, 87, 89, 96, 98, 106, 107
Visconti, Galeazzo 60
Visconti, Giangaleazzo 60, 100
Visconti, Giovanni Maria 60
Visconti heraldic devices 60-62, 186
Visconti-Savoy tarocchi 106
Visconti-Sforza tarocchi 12, 22, 32, 33, 35, **36**, 39, 60, 63-107, **285**
Viscontis 60, 63
Vishnu 7, 18, 163, **167**
Viterbo 32
Vives, Ludovico 28
Voile d'Isis, Le 23
Voisin, P. 146, **151**
Volaterranus 33
Von Bartsch 35, 62-64, **100-102**, 107, 111
Vulcan **173**, 174

W

Waite, Arthur Edward 15, 16, **23**, 192
Waldberg, Patrick 254
Waldenses 20
Waldner, Francesco **202**
Waldo, Peter 20
Wands (see staves)
Wang, Robert **256**
Warburg Institute 243
Wardrobe Rolls of Edward I 33
Warrior, The **288**, 289
Warriors on cards 124, 186
Water **51**, 279
Wayland, Virginia and Harold 105
Wedding tarock **297**
Wegmuller, Walter 292, 293
Weil, Susan L. **202**
Weiss, Elizabeth Sexton 170, **171**
Wenceslas and Jeanne 24
Wenceslas, Emperor 60, 61, 66, 76
Westcott, W. Wynn 14
Western Emperor, The 49, **51**, 53
Wheel of Fortune, The xvi, 3-5, 15-17, 30, 33, **36**, 37, 39, 48, 49, **50-52**, 53, **54**, **55**, 61, 64, 69, 96, 100, 107, 115, 116, 124, **125**, **128**, **130**, 134, **135**, 137, **139**, 140, 141, 143, 145, **147-150**, **153**, **154**, **156**, **158-166**, 169, **170**, 172, **173**, 175, 180, 181, **183**, **185**, 189, 190, 191, **194-199**, 201, 203, 205, 212, 213, 216, 217, **219-223**, 224, **225**, **228**, **229**, 230, **231-233**, 234, **235**, **236**, **238**, **239**, 240, 241, 242, 245-247, 248, **249**, 250, **251-253**, 254, **255-257**, 259, 260, **261**, **263**, 264, **265**, **267-269**, 271, **275-278**, **280**, 281, **282**, **283**, **288**, 289, **294**, 329, 330
Wheel of Life, The 180, **181**
White Goddess, The 192

White, Meryl 279
Willer tarock **320**
William de Guilleville 31
Williamson, Linda **173**, 174
Willshire, William Hughes 39
Winckelmann, Joachim 220
Winged Victory 170
Wirth, Oswald 5, 9, 15, 16, 23, 186, 272, **286**
Wirth tarot (see Oswald Wirth tarot)
Witz, Konrad 59
Wollenhaupt-Brenner tarot **226**
Woodblock printing 124
World, The xvi, 3-5, 15-17, 30, 33, 39, 45, 49, **50**, **52**, 53, **54**, **55**, 64, 72, 73, 92, 104, 106, 109, 110, 111, 112, **116**, **117**, **118**, 120, 121, **128**, **130**, 135, 137, **139**, 140, 141, 144, 148, **152**, **153**, **154**, **157-160**, 163, 164, **173**, 174, 176, **177**, **178**, **183**, **185**, 188, 189, **190**, 191, 192, **193**, **195**, 198, 201, 203, 204, 208, **209**, 211, **216**, 217, **218**, 220, **226**, **231**, **233**, **237**, **246**, 247, 252, 253, 254, **255-257**, **267-269**, 271, **273**, 278, **280**, 281, **282**, **284**, **285**, **288**, 290, **291**, 292, **293**, 295, 332
World War I 318
World's Tiniest Rider-Waite tarot 9
Wurzburg (see Synod of Wurzburg)

X

Xipe-Totec 290
Xultun tarot 8, 9, 287, **288**, 289, 290

Y

Yale University 63, 87, **88-95**, 117
Yang 189
Yaqui 290
Yeager, Marty 290
Yeager tarot of Meditation 290, **291**
Yeats, William Butler 23
Yetzirah 7
Yin 189
Yod-He-Vau-He 7, 18, 224
Yoga 279
Yogini 279
Yucatec dialect 287

Z

Zain, C. C. 23, 240
Zatrikion 19
Zeus 174
Zigeuner tarot 9, 292, **293**
Zingari 21
Zintilomo **38**, 39, 41
Zodiac 10, 49, 51, 53, 181, 186, 224, 240, 244, 248-250, 256
Zohar 16
Zolar's New Astrological tarot **294**